THE CONTEXT OF SCRIPTURE

VOLUME III

Archival Documents from the Biblical World

THE CONTEXT OF SCRIPTURE

Canonical Compositions, Monumental Inscriptions, and Archival Documents from the Biblical World

General Editor William W. Hallo

Associate Editor K. Lawson Younger, Jr.

The Context of Scripture

VOLUME III

Archival Documents from the Biblical World

Editor

William W. Hallo

Associate Editor

K. Lawson Younger, Jr.

Consultants

Harry A. Hoffner, Jr.
Robert K. Ritner

BRILL
LEIDEN · BOSTON
2003

This book is printed on acid-free paper.

Cover: An Ostracon found at Mesad Ḥashavyahu (so named after the find), south of Yaveneh Yam in Israel, dating to the 7th Century B.C.E. and pleading the case of a harvester whose garment has been wrongfully confiscated or distrained. See text on page 77.
Collection of Israel Antiquities Authority Exhibited & photo© Israel Museum.

Library of Congress Cataloging-in-Publication Data

The context of Scripture / editor, William W. Hallo ; associate editor, K. Lawson Younger.
p. cm.
Includes bibliographical references and index.
Contents: v. I. Canonical compositions from the biblical world.
ISBN 9004135693 (pbk.: v. 3)
1. Bible. O.T.—Extra-canonical parallels. 2. Middle Eastern literature—Relation to the Old Testament. 3. Bible. O.T.—History of contempory events—Sources. 4. Middle Eastern literature –-Translations into English. I. Hallo, William W. II. Younger. K. Lawson.
BS1180.C+ 2003
2003052060

ISBN 90 04 135693 (Vol. III)
ISBN 90 04 131051 (Set)

PRINTED IN THE NETHERLANDS

CONTENTS

AKKADIAN ARCHIVAL DOCUMENTS

SUMERIAN ARCHIVAL DOCUMENTS

PREFACE

The Context of Scripture has claimed the attention of publisher, editors, and contributors for a full decade from conception through execution (1991-2001). The original schedule proved too optimistic by half. According to his memorandum of agreement of December 20, 1991, the editor was "to deliver to the Publisher the final and complete material of Volume 1 not later than two years from the signing of this Agreement; Volume 2 not later than three years from the signing of this Agreement; and Volume 3 not later than four years from the signing of this Agreement."

Had this ambitious five-year schedule been maintained, the publication dates might have read 1994, 1995 and 1996 instead of 1997, 2000 and 2002, respectively. But short of "genius grants" to relieve them of all other duties in the interim, neither the editor nor his tireless associate editor could have delivered on such an undertaking.

In fact, however, those other duties continued unabated throughout the course of the undertaking. In the case of the associate editor, moreover, the project spanned his move from LeTourneau University in Texas to Trinity International University in Illinois; in the editor's case, its completion coincides with his retirement from formal teaching at Yale and the curatorship of its Babylonian Collection.

While thus falling short of "all deliberate speed," the more realistic pace at which the project actually proceeded entailed a number of compensatory benefits: the inclusion of some of the latest textual discoveries; the incorporation of constructive criticisms offered by the reviewers; the utilization of emerging technologies in communicating with contributors and in preparing the layout of their contributions, to mention only a few.

At the same time it would be disingenuous to claim that all the aims of the original undertaking have been met. According to the Preface to volume 1, these constituted "a test of some of my long-held and long-taught methodologies: not only the contextual approach, but also my taxonomy of ancient documentation, and my theories of translation" (*COS* 1:xi). Of these objects, the first two have been satisfied, but hardly the last.

The theories of translation in question were briefly set forth in the Introduction to volume 1, where their application "to ancient Near Eastern texts *apart* from the Bible" were adjudged as "theoretically ... possible — though difficult in practice" (*COS* 1:xxvi). In the event, theory has had to bow to practice. There has been no attempt to correlate with each other all translations from any one language, let alone from different languages.

Nevertheless, the basis for such correlations is laid by the extensive index furnished with this concluding volume. The basic index is the work of John G. Wright (Yale '01); it has been rendered more user-friendly by the identification of proper nouns in a manner first developed in the editor's *Origins* (Brill 1996). Others who have made the completion of the project possible include the contributors, the consultants, Lawson Younger the indefatigable associate editor, and the ever-helpful Mattie Kuiper of Brill. It is a pleasure to thank them all, however inadequately, for their devoted labors.

William W. Hallo
December 2, 2001

ABBREVIATIONS AND SYMBOLS

(* For abbreviations not listed here, please consult volumes 1 and 2)

AASF — Annales Academiae Scientiarum Fennicae. Helsinki: Suomalainen Tiedeakatemia.

AECT — F. M. Fales. *Aramaic Epigraphs on Clay Tablets of the Neo-Assyrian Period.* Studi Semitici 2. Materiali per il lessico aramaico 1. Rome: Università degli studi "la Sapienza," 1986.

AP — A. E. Cowley, *Aramaic Papyri of the Fifth Century B.C.* Oxford: The Clarendon Press, 1923.

ARWAW — Abhandlungen der Rheinisch-Westfälischen Akademie der Wissenschaften.

AUA — M. Lidzbarski. *Altaramäische Urkunden aus Assur.* Leipzig: J. C. Hinrichs'sche Buchhandlung, 1921.

AUCT — Andrews University Cuneiform Texts. Berrien Springs, MI: Andrews University Press.

BJPES — *Bulletin of the Jewish Palestine Exploration Society.*

CHANE — Culture and History of the Ancient Near East. Leiden: Brill.

FT — *Faith and Theology.*

GEA — T. Muraoka and B. Porten. *A Grammar of Egyptian Aramaic.* Leiden: Brill, 1998.

HBM — S. Alp, *Hethitische Briefe aus Maşat-Höyük, Atatürk Kültür, Dil ve Tarih Yüksek Kurumu, Türk Tarih Kurumu Yayınları, VI.* Dizi-Sa. 35. Ankara: Türk Tarih Kurumu Basımevı, 1991.

HH — E. Laroche, *Les hiéroglyphes hittites.* Paris: Éditions du Centre national de la recherche scientifique, 1960.

HKM — S. Alp, *Hethitische Keilschrifttafeln aus Maşat-Höyük Atatürk Kültür, Dil ve Tarih Yüksek Kurumu, Türk Tarih Kurumu Yayınları, VI.* Dizi-Sa. 34. Ankara: Türk Tarih Kurumu Basımevı, 1991.

HPBM 4 — Hieratic Papyri in the British Museum. 4th series.

HUS — W. G. E. Watson and N. Wyatt, Editors. *Handbook of Ugaritic Studies.* HdO, Erste Abteilung: Der Nahe und Mittlere Osten 39. Leiden: E. J. Brill, 1999.

ILR — *Israel Law Review.*

JJP — *Journal of Juristic Papyrology.*

MAIBL — *Mémoires présentés par divers savants à l'Académie des Inscriptions et Belles Lettres de l'Insitut de France.*

MEE — Materiali epigrafici di Ebla.

MHUC — Monographs of the Hebrew Union College.

NESE — R. Degen, W. W. Müller and W. Röllig, Editors. *Neue Ephemeris für semitische Epigraphik.* 3 Vols. Wiesbaden: Harrassowitz, 1972-78.

PEFQS — *Palestine Exploration Fund Quarterly Statement.*

PJB — *Palästinajahrbuch des deutschen evangelischen Instituts für Altertumswissenschaft des heiligen Landes zu Jerusalem.*

RAI 45/1 — T. Abusch, et al. Editors. *Historiography in the Cuneiform World.* Proceedings of the XLVe Rencontre Assyriologique Internationale, Part 1: Harvard University. Bethesda, MD: CDL Press, 2001.

REJ — *Revue des Études Juives.*

RES — Répertoire d'épigraphie sémitique.

RES — *Revue des études sémitiques.*

RgB — B. Janowski, K. Koch and G. Wilhelm, Editors. *Religionsgeschichtliche Beziehungen zwischen Kleinasien, Nordsyrien und dem Alten Testament. Internationales Symposion Hamburg 17.-21. März 1990.* OBO 129. Göttingen: Vandenhoeck & Ruprecht, 1993.

RSOu 1 — O. Callot. *Une maison à Ougarit. Étude d'architecture domestique.* RSOu 1. Paris: Éditions Recherche sur les Civilisations, 1983.

RSOu 5/1 — P. Bordreuil and D. Pardee. *La trouvaille épigraphique de l'Ougarit.* 1 *Concordance.* RSOu 5/1. Paris: Éditions Recherche sur les Civilisations, 1989.

RSOu 10 — O. Callot. *La tranchée « Ville Sud ». Études d'architecture domestique.* RSOu 10. Paris: Éditions Recherche sur les Civilisations, 1994.

SCCNH — Studies on the Civilization and Culture of Nuzi and the Hurrians.

SJLA — Studies in Judaism in Late Antiquity.

Studies Baumgartner — B. Hartmann, et al. Editors. *Hebräische Wortforschung. Festschrift zum 80. Geburtstag von Walter Baumgartner.* VTSup 16. Leiden: E. J. Brill, 1967.

Studies Bittel — R. M. Boehmer and H. Hauptmann, Editors. *Beiträge zur Altertumskunde Kleinasiens: Festschrift für Kurt Bittel.* Mainz-am-Rhein: Philipp von Zabern, 1983.

Studies Gordon 1998 — M. Lubetski, C. Gottlieb, and S. Keller, Editors. *Boundaries of the Ancient Near Eastern World. A Tribute to Cyrus H. Gordon.* JSOTSup 273. Sheffield: Sheffield Academic Press, 1998.

Studies Goulder — S. E. Porter, et al., Editors. *Crossing the Boundaries: Essays in Biblical Interpretation in Honour of Michael D. Goulder.* Leiden: Brill, 1994.

Studies Houwink ten Cate — T. P. J. van den Hout and J. de Roos, Editors. *Studio Historiae Ardens. Ancient Near Eastern Studies Presented to Philo H. J. Houwink ten Cate on the Occasion of his 65th Birthday.* Istanbul: Institut historique et archéologique néerlandais de Stamboul, 1995.

Studies Jacobsen 2 — T. Abusch, Editor. *Studies in the Ancient Near East in Memory of Thorkild Jacobsen.* Winona Lake, IN: Eisenbrauns, forthcoming.

Studies Koschaker — T. Folkers, J. Friedrich, J. G. Lautner and J. Miles, Editors. *Symbolae ad iura Orientis Antiqui pertinentes Paulo Koschaker dedicatae.* Leiden: Brill, 1939.

Studies Lipiński — K. van Lerberghe and A. Schoors, Editors. *Immigration and Emigration Within the Near East. Festschrift E. Lipiński.* OLA 65. Leuven: Peeters, 1995.

Studies Lohfink — G. Braulik, W. Gross and S. McEvenue. Editors. *Biblische Theologie und gesellschaftlicher Wandel: Für Norbert Lohfink SJ.* Freiburg/Basel/Wien: Herder 1993.

Studies Mendenhall — H. B. Huffmon, F. A. Spina, and A. R. W. Green, Editors. *The Quest for the Kingdom of God: Studies in Honor of George E. Mendenhall.* Winona Lake, IN: Eisenbrauns, 1983.

Studies Milgrom — D. P. Wright, D. N. Freedman and A. Hurvitz, Editors. *Pomegranates and Golden Bells: Studies in Biblical, Jewish, and Near Eastern Ritual, Law, and Literature in Honor of Jacob Milgrom.* Winona Lake, IN: Eisenbrauns, 1995.

Studies Moortgat — *Vorderasiatische Archäologie. Studien und Aufsätze. Anton Moortgat zum 65. Geburtstag gewidmet von Kollegen, Freunden und Schülern.* Berlin: Verlag Gebrüder Mann, 1964.

Studies Pintore — O. Carruba, M. Liverani, and C. Zaccagnini, Editors. *Studi orientalistici in ricordo di Franco Pintore.* Studia Mediterranea 4. Pavia: GJES Edizioni, 1983.

Studies Robert — *Mélanges bibliques, rédigés en l'honneur de André Robert.* Travaux de l'Institut catholique de Paris 4. Paris: Bloud & Gay, 1956.

Studies Römer — W. H. Ph. Römer, M. Dietrich, O. Loretz, and T. E. Balke, Editors. *Dubsar anta-men: Studien zur Altorientalistik: Festschrift für Willem H. Ph. Römer zur Vollendung seines 70. Lebensjahres, mith Beiträgen von Freunden, Schülern und Kollegen.* AOAT 253. Münster: Ugarit-Verlag, 1998.

Studies Sommer — H. Krahe, Editor. *Corolla linguistica: Festschrift Ferdinand Sommer zum 80. Geburtstag am 4 Mai 1955, dargebracht von Freunden, Schülern und Kollegen.* Wiesbaden: O. Harrassowitz, 1955.

Studies Wacholder — J. C. Reeves and J. Kampen, Editors. *Pursuing the Text: Studies in Honor of Ben Zion Wacholder*. JSOTSup 184. Sheffield: Sheffield Academic Press, 1994.

Studies Williams — J. K. Hoffmeier and E. S. Meltzer, Editors. *Egyptological Miscellanies: A Tribute to Professor Ronald J. Williams*. Ancient World 6. Chicago: Ares, 1983.

TFS — S. M. Dalley and J. N. Postgate. *The Tablets from Fort Shalmaneser*. CTN 3. Oxford: British School of Archaeology, 1984.

TH — J. Friedrich, et al. *Die Inschriften vom Tell Halaf. Keilschrifttexte und aramäische Urkunden aus einer assyrischen Provinzhauptstadt*. AfO Beiheft 6. Reprint 1967. Osnabrück: Biblio-Verlag, 1940.

ZAH — *Zeitschrift für Althebräistik*.

LIST OF CONTRIBUTORS

JAMES P. ALLEN
Metropolitan Musuem of Art

WALTER E. AUFRECHT
University of Lethbridge

WILLIAM W. HALLO
Yale University

MICHAEL HELTZER
University of Haifa

RICHARD S. HESS
Denver Seminary

JAMES K. HOFFMEIER
Trinity International University — Divinity School

HARRY A. HOFFNER, JR.
University of Chicago, *emeritus*

BARUCH A. LEVINE
New York University, *emeritus*

WILLIAM MORAN ‡
Harvard University, *emeritus*

DENNIS PARDEE
University of Chicago

BEZALEL PORTEN
The Hebrew University, Jerusalem

ROBERT K. RITNER
University of Chicago

NILI SHUPAK
University of Haifa

PIOTR STEINKELLER
Harvard University

MARIANNA VOGELZANG
University of Groningen

DAVID B. WEISBERG
Hebrew Union College–Jewish Institute of Religion

K. LAWSON YOUNGER, JR.
Trinity International University — Divinity School

‡ Deceased

INTRODUCTION

UNDERSTANDING HEBREW AND EGYPTIAN MILITARY TEXTS: A CONTEXTUAL APPROACH*

James K. Hoffmeier

The disciplines of Egyptology and Assyriology were born at approximately the same time (ca. 1800), with scholars in both fields having strong interests in the biblical world in general, and specifically because it was thought that archaeological discoveries in these two great riverine civilizations in some way would reflect positively in the Old Testament.[1] After all, the setting of the events of Genesis 1-11 is the Tigris-Euphrates valley, and it was Abraham's homeland prior to migrating to the land of Canaan (Gen 11). As for Egypt, the Joseph story is set there (Gen 39-50), as are the events in the book of Exodus (Exod 1-14). In subsequent biblical history, these two superpower neighbors continued to exert influence on Israel. So it is little wonder that the early pioneers of biblical archaeology thought that the new disciplines of Assyriology and Egyptology would be natural allies of Biblical Studies.

As the nineteenth century gave way to the twentieth, Egyptology had not produced any direct evidence for Joseph, Moses or the Hebrew sojourn, although the "Merneptah (Israel) Stela" had been discovered by Petrie in 1896. (More on this text later). Edouard Naville, the Swiss biblical scholar and archaeologist, thought he had discovered cities related to the exodus in the Wadi Tumilat, but was subsequently proven wrong, which earned him the wrath of Sir Alan Gardiner.[2] I believe that it was the Oxford don's tremendous stature among Egyptologists and his unusually harsh criticism of what might be called "biblical Egyptology" that caused generations of Egyptologists to avoid the study of Hebrew and Biblical Studies in general. This had the positive outcome of Egyptology becoming a discipline in its own right, but the negative result of Egyptology being isolated as a cognate field of Biblical Studies. Assyriology too gained its independence from Biblical Studies and from the excesses of the "Pan-Babylonian" approaches that had characterized the nineteenth and early twentieth centuries. However, inasmuch as Akkadian is cognate with Hebrew, many students of the Bible continued to study the cuneiform scripts, while Egyptian texts have been largely ignored by biblical scholars. This proclivity is surprising given the fact that Egypt and Canaan/Israel were next door neighbors, and Egypt is known to have exerted tremendous influence on the Levant especially during the Late Bronze Age, both through trade and through its military domination.[3] Babylon, on the other hand, is located approximately 900 miles from Jerusalem (following normal travel routes), and not until the Neo-Assyrian period was there much direct contact between the Tigris-Euphrates world and the Levant.

The late Ronald Williams offered the following explanation for the tendency of biblical scholars to give priority to Mesopotamian sources in the study of the Bible over those of Egypt:

> By the very nature of their training, Old Testament scholars are more likely to have acquired a first-hand knowledge of the Canaanite and cuneiform sources than they are to have mastered the hieroglyphic and hieratic materials of Egypt. For this reason they have had to depend to a greater degree on secondary sources for the latter. It is not surprising, then, that Israel's heritage from Western Asia in such areas as mythology, psalmody, theodicy, proverb collections, legal "codes" and practices, suzerainty treaties and royal annals has been more thoroughly investigated. Yet Egypt's legacy is by no means negligible ....[4]

A quarter century has passed since Williams penned these insightful words, and Egyptology's place in Biblical Studies, I believe, has improved somewhat. Certainly the number of Egyptian texts in *The Context of Scripture* (*COS*) indicates that the editors recognize the importance of Egyptian sources to the comparative or contextual approach to studying the Bible. Nearly a decade ago, this writer proposed to the Society of Biblical Literature program committee

* This essay and the three that follow reproduce, with some changes, the remarks delivered to the joint meeting of the Midwest Sections of the Society of Biblical Literature, the American Oriental Society, and the American Schools of Oriental Research, 2000, for a panel on "The Context of Scripture," chaired by William W. Hallo.

[1] P. R. S. Moorey, *A Century of Biblical Archaeology* (Louisville: Westminster/John Knox Press, 1992) 11-24.

[2] A. H. Gardiner, "The Geography of the Exodus," in *Recueil d'études Égyptologiques dédiées à la mémoire de Jean-François Champollion* (Paris: Bibliothèque de l'école des hautes études, 1922) = "The Geography of the Exodus, An Answer to Professor Naville and Others," *JEA* 10 (1924) 87-96; and E. Naville, *The Store-City of Pithom and the Route of the Exodus* (London, 1903); "The Geography of the Exodus," *JEA* 10 (1924) 18-39.

[3] For cultural influences, see R. Giveon, *The Impact of Egypt on Canaan* (OBO 20; Göttingen: Vandenhoeck & Ruprecht, 1978), and linguistic influences, see Y. Muchiki, *Egyptian Proper Names and Loanwords in North-West Semitic* (SBLDS 173; Atlanta: Scholars Press, 1999).

[4] "'A People Come Out of Egypt': An Egyptologist looks at the Old Testament," *VTSup* 28 (1975) 231-232.

the establishment of a Consultation on Egyptology and Ancient Israel, and it was warmly received. This was the first such consultation concentrated on investigating the relationship between Egyptology and the Hebrew Bible. It has since become a permanent "Section," and is thriving, having attracted the participation of many established scholars, as well as younger scholars, all of whom are engaged at some level of Egyptological and biblical research. These signs are encouraging and indicate that Egyptology may one day take its rightful place as a cognate field of Biblical Studies.

I share William W. Hallo's commitment to the contextual or comparative method that he has so compellingly advocated over the past several decades,[5] as well as his essay in *COS* (1:xxiii-xxviii). His identification of the two dimensions of the contextual approach is helpful. First, there is the "horizontal dimension" which examines "the geographical, historical, religious, political and literary setting in which it was created and disseminated" (*COS* 1:xxv). Secondly there is the "vertical axis" which examines the relationship "between the earlier texts that helped inspire it and the later texts that reacted to it" (*COS* 2:xxv-xxvi).

Under the heading "Monumental Inscriptions" in *COS* 2 are Egyptian texts that span the period from the Old Kingdom Pyramid Texts (ca. 2400 BCE), to the stela of Piankhy (or Piye) (ca. 734 BCE), and they represent a wide range of genres, viz., Royal, Biographical, Funerary, and Hymnic. Owing to the limits of space and time for this presentation, it will focus primarily upon some of the so-called "Royal Inscriptions" of the New Kingdom found in *COS* 2 (and a few not included) because they touch on the question of historiography which has been a major subject of discussion by biblical scholars in the last two decades of the twentieth century. It will be suggested that there are possible Egyptian influences upon the Hebrew scribal traditions. The texts in this category in *COS* 2 are: The Armant and Gebel Barkal stelae and the Annals of Thutmose III, and the Memphis-Karnak Stelae of Amenhotep II from the Eighteenth Dynasty. This writer was responsible for translating these, and thus has given considerable thought to this material. From the Nineteenth Dynasty come the various military Campaign Inscriptions of Seti I in Western Asia from Karnak, along with his two Beth Shean stelae, the Battle of Kadesh inscriptions of Ramesses II, translated by Kenneth Kitchen, and the hymnic portion of the Merneptah Stela which the writer translated.

The reason for examining these particular texts is because they are not usually considered by biblical scholars when engaged in comparative study. Nevertheless, it appears that upon careful study these texts are germane for comparison with the Bible. A notable exception to the tendency to ignore this corpus of literature is Lawson Younger's seminal study *Ancient Conquest Accounts* which appeared in 1990.[6] After a thoughtful and thorough comparative study of Assyrian, Hittite and Egyptian military reports with those in the book of Joshua, Younger concluded

> This study has shown that one encounters very similar things in both ancient Near Eastern and biblical history writing. While there are differences (e.g., the characteristics of the deities in the individual cultures), the Hebrew conquest account of Canaan in Joshua 9-12 is, by and large, typical of any ancient Near Eastern account. In other words, *there is a common denominator, a certain commonality between them*, so that it is possible for us to speak, for purposes of generalization, of a common transmission code that is an intermingling of the texts' figurative and ideological aspects.[7]

Independently, I arrived at conclusions similar to those of Younger.[8] Hence, it will be argued that there is still much light Egyptian royal inscriptions of the New Kingdom can shed on Hebrew military writing.

Owing to the supposed "aetiological" nature, the theological affirmations and ideological nature of the "conquest" narratives in Joshua, coupled with the hyperbolic claims of wiping out the population of certain parts of Canaan (particularly in chapter 10), many recent studies of the Joshua narratives have dismissed the biblical account of Israel's arrival in Canaan.[9] With the Hebrew writings confined to the sidelines, the Merneptah or Israel stela has been thrust onto center stage, and historical minimalists have become preoccupied with this text. Ironically, historical minimalists of the Bible, like Ahlström[10] and Lemche[11] became maximalists, accepting at face value an Egyptian

---

[5] "Biblical History in Its Near Eastern Setting: The Contextual Approach," in *SIC 1*, 1-26.

[6] K. L. Younger, Jr., *Ancient Conquest Accounts: A Study in Ancient Near Eastern and Biblical History Writing* (JSOTSup 98; Sheffield: Sheffield Academic Press, 1990).

[7] Ibid., 265 (emphasis mine).

[8] J. K. Hoffmeier, "The Problem of 'History' in Egyptian Royal Inscriptions," in *VI Congresso Internazionale De Egittologia Atti* (ed. by Silvio Curto; Turino: 1992) 291-299; "The Structure of Joshua 1-11 and the Annals of Thutmose III," in *FTH* 165-179; *Israel in Egypt* (New York/Oxford: Oxford University Press, 1997) Chaps. 1 & 2. The arguments on the Joshua narratives presented in this essay echo those found in these earlier works.

[9] Some examples include G. Ahlström, *Who Were the Israelites* (Winona Lake: Eisenbrauns, 1986) 1ff.; N. P. Lemche, *Ancient Israel: A New History of Israelite Society* (Sheffield: JSOT Press, 1988) chaps. 2-3; J. Van Seters, "Joshua's Campaign and Near Eastern Historiography," *SJOT* 2 (1990) 1-16; R. B. Coote, *Early Israel: A New Horizon* (Minneapolis: Fortress, 1990) 3.

[10] *Who Were the Israelites?* (Winona Lake, IN: Eisenbrauns, 1986) 37-43.

[11] Lemche, *Early Israel: Anthropological and Historical Studies on the Israelite Society before the Monarchy* (Leiden: Brill, 1985) 430-431.

document, despite the fact that it too is religious and ideological, replete with hyperbole and propaganda, whereas, when similar literary and rhetorical devices are found in Joshua, the historical value of those narratives is summarily dismissed. The methodological inconsistency is self-evident.

In recent years there has been some comparative analysis of the Joshua narratives alongside cognate Near Eastern military writings. Moshe Weinfeld in his study of the Deuteronomistic School offered parallels between Neo-Assyrian texts and Joshua to show the 7th century date of the latter.[12] However, he completely failed to consider earlier texts of the 2nd millennium as possible analogues. This omission led Jeffrey Niehaus to reexamine features which Joshua and Neo-Assyrian texts share in common (e.g. war oracles, the command-fulfillment chain, divine involvement in warfare) and to agree that "it is only fair to recognize that the literary phenomena in Joshua have first-millennium extrabiblical analogues."[13] However, he goes on to show that these very same features are well attested in Ugaritic and Middle Assyrian texts of the 2nd millennium, thus severely weakening the rationale for an exclusive connection between Deuteronomist and Neo-Assyrian parallels.

In contrast to Younger's comprehensive study, an essay published by John Van Seters in the same year drew parallels solely between Neo-Assyrian royal inscriptions and the Joshua narratives.[14] Parenthetically, it should be noted that Van Seters and other like-minded scholars have often criticized the comparative method when it is used to date biblical stories to the 2nd millennium BCE.[15] However, 1st millennium parallels are readily accepted, and often without any critical evaluation when arguing for the lateness of a biblical text. In so doing, Van Seters, Thomas Thompson,[16] and others are not in fact repudiating the comparative method or contextual approach. Rather, they are using it selectively, not comprehensively, with their conclusions predetermined. The contextual approach as advocated by Hallo and Kitchen considers all pertinent material from all periods before reaching conclusions about the biblical materials.[17]

I had the occasion to critique Van Seters' treatment of the Joshua narratives in a study published in 1994.[18] A summary of that analysis is offered here. Like Weinfeld, Van Seters was trying to demonstrate that the "Conquest" narratives of the DtrH originated at the time suggested by Neo-Assyrian parallels. All ten parallels (topoi) Van Seters drew between the Joshua and Neo-Assyrian royal inscriptions were treated by Younger who has identified comparable 2nd millennium analogues.[19]

Van Seters, for instance, believes that the motif of the Israelites crossing the Jordan during flood stage is borrowed from reports of Sargon II and Ashurbanipal's crossing the Tigris and Euphrates during "high water of the spring of the year."[20] Based on just these two texts, he concludes, "The special emphasis on the crossing (Josh 3-4) can only be explained as a topos taken from the Assyrian military accounts."[21] Van Seters' treatment of this matter fails on two points. First, the spring of the year was the traditional time for kings to go to war in Israel (cf. 2 Sam 11:2) as well as in Mesopotamia; as Robert Gordon has observed, "Spring was the time for launching military campaigns, when the winter rains had stopped and the male population was not yet involved in harvesting."[22] Spring is also when the rivers, the Jordan as well as the Tigris and Euphrates, are at their highest levels because of melting snow from the mountains to the north (cf. Josh 3:15). Secondly, the seemingly miraculous crossing of raging rivers by a king is well-attested in earlier Near Eastern sources. Hattušili I (ca. 1650 BCE) boasts of his accomplishments in this respect, likening them to those of Sargon the Great (ca. 2371-2316 BCE).[23] On one occasion, Tiglath-pileser I (1115-1077 BCE) records that this particular crossing of the Euphrates was his twenty-eighth, and it was "the second time in one year."[24] It is clear that when Sargon II (721-705 BCE) broadcasts his achievement, he is emulating his warrior

[12] Moshe Weinfeld, *Deuteronomy and the Deuteronomic School* (Oxford: Clarendon, 1972) 50.

[13] J. J. Niehaus, "Joshua and Ancient Near Eastern Warfare," *JETS* 31 (1988) 45-50.

[14] Van Seters, *SJOT* 2 (1990) 1-16.

[15] Van Seters, *Abraham in History and Tradition* (New Haven/London: Yale University Press, 1975).

[16] T. L. Thompson, *The Historicity of the Patriarchal Narratives: The Quest for the Historical Abraham* (BZAW 133; Tübingen: de Gruyter, 1974).

[17] Kitchen is especially emphatic about looking at texts for all periods, the early as well as the late, for pursuing serious comparative study. Kitchen praises Van Seters and Thompson for exposing sloppy and careless comparative work done by those eager to support the Bible, but goes on to affirm: "However, these same advocates themselves then fail to match up to this selfsame standard of reviewing the patriarchal data against *all* periods. Instead they neglect the 3rd millennium BC entirely, along with whole sections of relevant evidence from the early 2nd millennium, and give exaggerated attention to 1st millennium materials" (K. A. Kitchen, *The Bible in Its World* [Exeter: The Paternoster Press, 1977] 58).

[18] J. K. Hoffmeier, *FTH*, 165-179. In addition, some of the comments in this section were presented in a paper ("Recent Developments in Historiography: Implication for the Study of Egyptian 'Historical' and Old Testament Texts") at the Society of Biblical Literature annual meeting in November 1993 in Washington D.C.

[19] Younger, *Ancient Conquest Accounts*, chapters 5 and 6.

[20] Van Seters, *SJOT* 2 (1990) 6-7.

[21] Ibid., 7.

[22] R. P. Gordon, *1 & 2 Samuel: A Commentary* (Grand Rapids, MI.: Zondervan, 1986) 252.

[23] See Hoffmeier, *FTH*, 178 for references.

[24] *ARAB* §330.

predecessor rather than inventing a new motif.[25] Consequently, there is no basis for Van Seters' assertion.[26] The river crossing in Joshua 3 by Israel's forces accurately reflects the seasonal realities of military life in the Near East throughout the three millennia BCE.

Another literary borrowing the Deuteronomistic History (DtrH) made from Assyria, according to Van Seters, is the practice of describing only a few major battles in a report and giving only cursory accounts of others. However, this characteristic is well known in New Kingdom Egyptian military writings, especially in the Annals of Thutmose III. There, lengthy reports (e.g. the Battle of Megiddo) can be compared with those in Joshua (e.g. Jericho), and terse reports such as Thutmose III's sixth campaign are similar to Joshua 10:28-42. Not only are these general observations striking, but there are other points to consider, but before this is done, we need to consider the nature of the composition of the Annals of Thutmose III.

Pioneering studies by Martin Noth[27] and Hermann Grapow[28] have recently been updated and expanded by Anthony Spalinger[29] and Donald Redford. Spalinger thinks that there were several sources behind the Annals, the "day book" and the scribal war diary being the principal ones. He believes that the latter was compiled by military scribes who accompanied the king on his campaigns and reported on the personal involvement of the monarch.[30] Redford dismisses this proposal on the grounds that there is no evidence for a "daybook of the army."[31] Grapow had demonstrated that the "daybook style" (*Tagebuchstil*) can be traced back to the Thirteenth Dynasty in Pap. Bulaq 18 and as late as the end of the Nineteenth Dynasty in Pap. Anastasi III. The *Tagebuchstil* is characterized by the use of bare infinitives and lacked literary features. In fact, it reads more like the log of a ship than a flowing narrative. Redford documented sixteen surviving Daybooks, the earliest of which dated to the Twelfth Dynasty.[32] He too recognized the "rigid" format and the use of infinitives in Anastasi III. The same is found in the sixth campaign of Thutmose III's Annals which are divided into three parts:

1. Introduction:

> Regnal year 30. Now his majesty was in the foreign land of Retenu[33] on this 6th victorious campaign of his majesty.

2. Daybook Summary

> Arriving at the city of Kadesh, destroying it, cutting down its trees and plucking its barley. Proceeding from Shesryt, arriving at the City of Djamer, arriving at the city of Irtjet (*Irṯwt*). Doing likewise against it.

3. List of Tribute

> The list of the gifts[34] which were brought by the chieftain of Retenu because of the awe of his majesty ... male and female servants 181, horses 188, ...

A similarity between the elements of the *Tagebuchstil* witnessed here and in the military reports in Joshua 10:28-39 is striking indeed. Consider Joshua 10:29-30,

> Then Joshua passed on from Makkedah, and all Israel with him, to Libnah, and fought against Libnah; and the Lord gave it also and its king into the hand of Israel; and he smote it with the edge of the sword, and every person in it; he left none remaining in it.

The Libnah report, like the others in Joshua 10:28-42, contains terse, stereotyped formulas that are repeated frequently. The Hazor pericope (11:10-14) shares the same features, but like the year 30 report in the Annals concludes with a reference to the booty: "All the spoil of these cities and the cattle, the people of Israel took for their booty."

---

[25] That Sargon II deliberately borrowed from his 3rd millennium namesake has been long recognized by Assyriologists; cf. Sidney Smith, "Esarhaddon and Sennacherib," in *CAH* 3 (1973) 46.

[26] Van Seters, *SJOT* 2 (1990) 7.

[27] M. Noth, "Die Annalen Thutmose III. als Geschichtsquelle," *ZDPV* 66 (1943) 156-174.

[28] H. Grapow, *Studien zu den Annalen Thutmosis des Dritten und zu ihnen verwandten historischen Berichten des Neuen Reiches* (Abhandlungen der Deutschen Akademie der Wissenschaften zu Berlin. Jahrg. 1947. Phil.-hist. Kl. 2; Berlin: Akademie-Verlag, 1947).

[29] A. J. Spalinger, *Aspects of the Military Documents of the Ancient Egyptians* (YNER 9; New Haven and London: Yale University Press, 1982).

[30] Ibid., 120-121.

[31] D. B. Redford, *Pharaonic King-Lists, Annals and Day-Books: A Contribution to the Study of the Egyptian Sense of History* (Mississauga: Benben Publications, 1986) 122.

[32] Ibid., 103-121.

[33] Retenu is a general term that includes the area of Lebanon and Syria. Eg. scribes could distinguish between upper and lower Retenu, but the dividing line between the two regions is unclear (Gardiner, *AEO* 1:142*-149*).

[34] The word used here is *inw*, literally "that which is brought."

Van Seters thinks an Assyrian prototype lies behind Joshua's use of the fame and terror of Israel's army causing the enemies to submit. However, as I showed many years ago, such motifs are well known in second millennium Egyptian royal inscriptions.[35] A few examples will suffice to illustrate this point. Concerning Thutmose III it is said,

> He (Amun-Re) caused that all foreign lands (come) bowing because of the power of my majesty, my dread being in the midst of the Nine Bows, all lands being under my sandals.[36]

The poetical stela of Thutmose III contains the speech of Amun-Re who recalls that he placed his "bravery" (*nḫt*), "power" (*bꜣw*), "fear," (*snḏ*) and "dread" (*ḥryt*) in the king so that all lands would submit to him.[37] This type of language abounds during the New Kingdom. In Mesopotamia similar expressions are used, as Alan Millard has demonstrated, in Middle Assyrian texts from the end of the 2nd Millennium.[38]

The summary statement, a device used in Joshua 10:40-43, 11:16-20, and 12, is another feature Van Seters considers the DtrH to have borrowed from the Neo-Assyrian scribal tradition. Here too, earlier analogies from Middle Assyrian and 18th Dynasty Egypt are readily available.[39] The *sḥwy* (review or summary) of Egyptian texts is found in Thutmose III's annals as well as in the Armant stela of the same pharaoh.[40]

Van Seters also thinks that hyperbole that is so typical in Joshua derives from Neo-Assyrian practice. Once again, however, New Kingdom royal inscriptions are replete with examples of this type of exaggeration. Consider the lofty claims of Thutmose III in the Gebel Barkal Stela and Amenhotep II in the Memphis stela in *COS* 2:

> He is a king who fights alone, without a multitude to back him up. He is more effective than a myriad of numerous armies. An equal to him has not been, (he is) a warrior who extends his arm on the battlefield, no one can touch him. He is one who immediately overwhelms all foreign lands while at the head of his army, as he shoots between the two divisions of troops, like a star he crosses the sky, entering into the throng, [while a bl]ast of his flame is against them with fire, turning into nothing those who lie prostrate in their blood. It is his uraeus that overthrows them for him, his flaming serpent that subdues his enemies, with the result that numerous armies of Mitanni were overthrown in the space of an hour, annihilated completely like those who had not existed, ... great of might in the mêlée, who slaughters everyone, by himself alone, the king of Upper and Lower Egypt, Menkheperre, may he live forever (*COS* 2:14-15).
>
> Now at that time the ruler raged like a divine falcon, his chariots were shooting like a star in the sky. His majesty entered (the fray). Its chieftains, children and wives were carried off as prisoners-of-war, and all its inhabitants likewise, and all its property without end: its cattle, its chariots, and all the herds in front of him (*COS* 2:21).

Exaggerated numbers are also found in the Battle of Kadesh report in which boast is made of Ramesses II that he was "more valiant than hundred-thousands" (*COS* 2:33) and "Amun I found more help to me than millions of troops, than hundred-thousands of chariotry, than ten-thousands of men" (*COS* 2:35). The much quoted Merneptah stela also contains farfetched claims of devastating entire regions within the same section that makes reference to conquest of particular cities like Gezer and Ashkelon. It begins with the boast that none of the Nine Bows (Egypt's traditional enemies) could so much as lift a head after Pharaoh's onslaught, and then concludes by saying that "*all* lands are united" (under Merneptah) and "*all* who roamed have been subdued."[41] Thus we have in the same literary unit lofty assertions of universal conquest, side by side with sober statements about taking individual cities. This same combination is found in the Joshua narratives (compare Josh 10:40-11:1-5 with Josh 8:1-29).

Additionally, the Poetical Stela of Thutmose III contains an interesting comparison with Joshua 10:20:

> When Joshua and the men of Israel had finished slaying them with *a very great slaughter, until they were wiped out*, and *when the remnant which remained* of them had entered into the fortified cities, all the people returned safe to Joshua at the camp of Makkedah.[42]

The Stela boasts: "The heads of Asiatics are severed" ... "none escape (death)."[43] It goes on to claim that there were no survivors because of the swashbuckling king, but later in the same text, thousands of prisoners of war are reported

[35] Hoffmeier, "Some Egyptian Motifs Related to Enemies and Warfare and Their Old Testament Counterparts," In *Studies Williams* 53-70. It should be pointed out that Van Seters' *SJOT* study does not cite this work.

[36] Translation ibid., 66; text: *Urk*. IV 161.14-16.

[37] Text in *Urk*. IV. 612.7-9; the translation is my own.

[38] A. R. Millard, "The Old Testament and History: Some Considerations," *FT* 110 (1983) 46.

[39] Younger, *Ancient Conquest Accounts*, 231-232 and 251-253.

[40] See Hoffmeier, *FTH*, 175-176 for references and discussion. See the Armant Stela (COS 2.2C).

[41] Text in *KRI* IV, 19.3 & 8, the translation is my own.

[42] The italics are meant to show the apparently contradictory statements.

[43] *Urk*. IV. 614.1-2.

to have been taken.[44] Thus what appears to a western reader of this text to be a patent contradiction in Joshua, appears to be a well-known device in Egypt.

Hyperbole, as Younger has shown, was a regular feature of Near Eastern military reporting. The failure of J. Maxwell Miller,[45] William G. Dever,[46] Redford[47] and others to recognize the hyperbolic nature of such statements in Joshua is ironic because the charge is usually leveled at maximalist historians that they take the text too literally! As a consequence of this failure, these scholars have committed "the fallacy of misplaced literalism" which David Hackett Fischer defines as

> the misconstruction of a statement-in-evidence so that it carries a literal meaning when a symbolic or hyperbolic or figurative meaning was intended.[48]

The above quoted Egyptian statements must be understood to be hyperbolic in nature so as to perpetuate Egyptian royal ideology.[49] This does not mean, however, that the Levantine campaigns of Thutmose III and Amenhotep II, Ramesses' Battle of Kadesh, and Merneptah's invasion of Canaan did not take place. Egyptologists, while recognizing the propagandistic nature of the material, nevertheless ascribe some historical worth to the bombastic claims.[50] The critical reader of the texts needs to understand the rhetoric and the propagandistic nature of the material, but should not throw out the proverbial baby with the bath water by dismissing the more sober reports in the body of the same text. However, when similar hyperbole is found in the Bible, the account is often viewed *a priori* as unhistorical. This is true especially if there is a hint of divine intervention. And yet, divine involvement or intervention in military affairs is a regular feature of Near Eastern military writing.[51] The Merneptah stela provides an excellent illustration. In line 14, the capture of the Libyan chieftain is described as follows: "a great wonder (or miracle) happened" (*bi*ꜣ*t* ꜥꜣ*t* *ḫprt*).[52] Despite the claim of a miracle and use of hyperbole in this inscription, Egyptologists accept the historicity of the Libyan war of Merneptah.[53] A good example of Egyptologists embracing the historical worth of this miraculous story is J.F. Borghouts.[54] In his comprehensive study, "Divine Intervention in Ancient Egypt and Its Manifestation (*b*ꜣ*w*)," he acknowledges the "propagandistic statements" in the account of Merneptah's Libyan campaign, "but," he concludes, "that need not prevent them from being taken literally in regard to the purpose intended."[55]

Another type of divine intervention found in biblical and Egyptian sources is theophany before a battle. Joshua 5:13-15 reports that Joshua experienced a divine visitation on the eve of battle in order to assure him of victory against Jericho. Similarly, Amenhotep receives words of encouragement from Amun-Re in a dream while on campaign. The report on the Karnak-Memphis Stela states:

> A Pleasant thing which happened to his majesty: The majesty of this august god, Amun-Re, Lord of the Throne of the Two Lands came before his majesty during sleep, in order to encourage his son, Aakheperure. His father Amun-Re was the guardian of his body, while protecting the ruler (*COS* 2:21-22).

To summarize the foregoing discussion on the literary nature of the Joshua conquest narratives, it is maintained here that comparative study of the Hebrew material must include documents from the second millennium, and not just the first millennium. Van Seters is absolutely right when he concludes, "His (DtrH) historiographic method is to write

[44] *Urk.* IV. 612.14-16.

[45] J. M. Miller, "The Israelite Occupation of Canaan" in *Israelite and Judaean History* (Ed. by J. H. Hayes and J. M. Miller; Philadelphia/London: Westminster Press, 1977) 215.

[46] W. G. Dever, *Recent Archaeological Discoveries and Biblical Research* (Seattle: University of Washington Press, 1990) 57-59.

[47] D. B. Redford, *Egypt, Canaan, and Israel in Ancient Times* (Princeton: Princeton University Press, 1992) 264.

[48] *Historians' Fallacies: Toward a Logic of Historical Thought* (London: Routledge and Kegan Paul, 1971) 58.

[49] John Wilson, "The Royal Myth in Ancient Egypt," *PAPS* 100, no 5 (October 1956) 439-442; A. R. Schulman, "The Great Historical Inscription of Merneptah at Karnak: A Partial Reappraisal," *JARCE* 24 (1987) 22.

[50] For examples, see G. Posener, *Littérature et politique dans l'Égypte de la XXe dynastie* (Paris: 1956) 14-15; R. J. Williams, "Literature as a Medium of Political Propaganda in Ancient Egypt," *Studies Meek*, 14-30.

[51] For numerous examples, see Millard, *FT* 110 (1983) 34-53; Niehaus, *JETS* 31 (1988) 37-50; Younger, *Ancient Conquest Accounts*. I have also dealt with this issue in Eg. "historical texts"; see Hoffmeier, "The Problem of 'History,'" in *VI Congresso Internazionale De Egittologia Atti*, 296-297.

[52] Text: *KRI* IV, 19.4-5; the translation is my own.

[53] See for example R. O. Faulkner in *CAH* 2/2:232-235; Schulman, *JARCE* 24 (1987) 21-22. Even though Redford is somewhat skeptical about the historic worth of the Asian campaign, he nevertheless believes that there was a smaller scale campaign during Merneptah's tenure. He does not appear to question the Libyan invasion in which "the great miracle" took place; see Redford, "The Ashkelon Relief at Karnak and the Israel Stela," *IEJ* 36 (1986) 188-200. Robert Coote takes Redford's scaled down campaign and offers a further reduction saying, "While Merneptah might have sent soldiers to Palestine during the first year or two to display imperial muscle, the campaign implied by the stela inscription may never have occurred" (*Early Israel: A New Horizon*, 74).

[54] J. F. Borghouts, "Divine Intervention in Ancient Egypt and its Manifestation (*b*ꜣ*w*)," in *Gleanings from Deir el-Medîna* (ed. by R. J. Demarée and J. J. Janssen; Leiden: Netherlands Institute for Near Eastern Studies, 1982) 1-70.

[55] Ibid., 28.

past history in the form and style of contemporary historical texts."[56] The question is, what contemporary historical texts influenced the Hebrew scribal tradition? By restricting his parallels to Neo-Assyrian texts of the first millennium and ignoring those of the Late Bronze Age (as Weinfeld did earlier), Van Seters is able to finesse the results to his desired conclusion. However as Niehaus, Younger and this writer have shown, sources from the previous millennium cannot be ignored simply because the material invalidates one's presuppositions about the dating of the Joshua narratives and DtrH. The earlier parallels are just as valid, if not more compelling, and thus might suggest a date of composition centuries before the reforms of Josiah at the end of the 7th century BCE.

Another feature of Egyptian battle inscriptions that has a literary parallel in the Bible can be introduced. The Chronicler frequently includes the prayers of pious kings, especially in battle or crisis situations. Examples of this phenomenon are the prayer of Asa when facing Zerah's invasion in 2 Chronicles 14:11 and that of his son, Jehoshaphat, prior to taking on the invading coalition from Transjordan in 2 Chronicles 20:51-52. In the case of Jehoshaphat, he was vastly outnumbered and called upon the Lord, and was able to win the battle. In the Battle of Kadesh, when Ramesses II finds himself outnumbered by the Hittite chariotry and "hundred-thousands of men," he calls on Amun for help, and a lengthy prayer follows (*COS* 2:34-35). From distant Thebes Amun responded and Egypt was victorious.[57] Interestingly, his appeal, "What will people think, if (even) a minor mishap befalls him that depended on your counsel," sounds strikingly like Moses's appeal in Exodus 32:12 and Numbers 14:13ff. when he asks "What would the Egyptians say" if the Israelites were to die in the wilderness. In both biblical and Egyptian theological perspectives, there was a clear connection between one's military success and the power of a nation's deity, and that may be what is reflected here. Additionally, the Chronicler, with his penchant for drawing on earlier sources, may well have been familiar with this old Egyptian literary device of including the king's prayer in the crisis of battle, and employed it.

This essay has attempted to show that Egyptian monumental inscriptions, particularly royal ones, can shed light on the Hebrew scriptures, both on the literary and structural levels. Furthermore, the similarities in the two corpora of literature may even suggest that books like Joshua date earlier than the seventh century as is widely accepted or, minimally, that the Hebrew author(s) drew on earlier (Late Bronze Age) sources. Despite the brevity of this study, it is hoped that Biblical scholars will agree with Williams' thesis that Egypt's legacy is vital to the task of studying the Hebrew Scriptures, and that students and scholars alike will use these Egyptian sources because they are a part of the context of scripture.

---

[56] Van Seters, *SJOT* 2 (1990) 11-12.

[57] Comparing Ramesses II texts with those of the Chronicler in no way is meant to argue that the Chronicler is a pre-exilic work, but it does illustrate that he used earlier sources. Similarities in language and ideology between the thirteenth century Eg. texts and a ninth century Judaean monarch might be attributable to similar views of deity.

HITTITE-ISRAELITE CULTURAL PARALLELS

Harry A. Hoffner, Jr.

Although, it was biblical references that ultimately led to the rediscovery of the Hittites in the first decade of the twentieth century, very few Hittitologists today show a significant interest in the bearing of their materials on the interpretation of the Bible.[1] There are several reasons for this: (1) the secularization of ancient Near East scholarship during the past century, (2) the unfamiliarity of Hittitologists with biblical material, and (3) the geographical and cultural remoteness of the Hittites from Israel, which is often perceived by scholars in both disciplines as evidence for lack of significant influence.

For their part, most biblical scholars have reciprocated by showing little interest in Hittite sources. Like the Hittitologists (1) they are tempted to view the geographical and cultural remoteness of Hittites as evidence for little if any influence, (2) many assume that most if not all biblical texts originated much later than the fall of Hatti in 1190 BCE, and (3) they assume that too much time and effort would be necessary to learn the Hittite language and investigate its sources. I for one sympathize with the biblical scholars. For Hittitologists do nothing to assist non-specialists by finding and making known to biblical scholars potentially relevant material. Be that as it may, it is a fact that if graduate students in Biblical Studies learn any languages other than Greek, Hebrew and Aramaic, they are Ugaritic, Phoenician or Akkadian, not Hittite. As a language Hittite is too different from the Semitic languages that are the standard fare of Old Testament scholars. I can attest to that unhappy situation even at the University of Chicago. In my 26 years on its faculty, one Egyptology major, two or three Assyriology majors, and no West Semitics majors have enrolled in beginning Hittite. One faculty member in Assyriology took two years of Hittite.

Still, a few scholars in both fields have attempted to evaluate mutually relevant materials. And although very few comprehensive surveys have been attempted, quite a number of individual items in Hittite texts have been compared in print to biblical materials.

Obviously, volumes like *ANET* and the new *Context of Scripture* volumes — like their German counterparts (the older Bousset-Gressmann, and the newer *TUAT* — are making translations of important ancient Near Eastern texts available to a broader public. And the SBL series entitled *Writings from the Ancient World* (SBLWAW) has produced around ten volumes of translated documents from the ancient Near East, including two consisting entirely of Hittite texts (Beckman's *Hittite Diplomatic Texts* and my *Hittite Myths*, both now in revised second editions,[2] and a third, Martha T. Roth's *Law Collections*,[3] which contains my translation of the Hittite laws.[4]

There are not many studies which attempt to survey the subject comprehensively. Early surveys, when little was known from the Hittite texts themselves, focussed on how the Hittites described in the Old Testament could be related to the newly discovered materials from the Hittite capital in Turkey. But already they also tried to apply Anatolian Hittite evidence — both archaeological and textual — to the Bible's own contents. One of the earliest publications was a 1928 article by Archibald Henry Sayce, entitled "Hittite and Mittannian Elements in the Old Testament."[5] One of the pioneers of Hittitology, Emil Forrer, even saw in the ubiquitous references in Hittite cult texts to "drinking" various gods a forerunner of the Christian Eucharist.[6] Another early survey, which was largely confined to the question of how "Hittites" are described in the Bible, was the 1947 Tyndale Archaeology Lecture given by the New Testament scholar F. F. Bruce.[7]

Twenty-one years later, in 1969, I gave the annual Tyndale Archaeology Lecture on "Some Contributions of

[1] Symptomatic is the small number of Hittitologists (as opposed to the biblical scholars who contributed) represented in the volume B. Janowski, K. Koch and G. Wilhelm, eds. *Religionsgeschichtliche Beziehungen zwischen Kleinasien, Nordsyrien und dem Alten Testament. Internationales Symposion Hamburg 17.-21. März 1990* (OBO 129; Göttingen: Vandenhoeck & Ruprecht, 1993). Henceforth *RgB*.

[2] G. M. Beckman, *Hittite Diplomatic Texts* (2nd ed.; SBLWAW 7; Atlanta: Scholars Press, 1999); H. A. Hoffner, Jr., *Hittite Myths* (SBLWAW 2; 2nd Rev. Ed.; ed. by S. Parker; Atlanta: Scholars Press, 1998).

[3] M. T. Roth, *Law Collections from Mesopotamia and Asia Minor* (2nd Ed.; SBLWAW 6; Atlanta: Scholars Press, 1997).

[4] H. A. Hoffner, Jr., "The Hittite Laws," in *Law Collections from Mesopotamia and Asia Minor*, 211-247.

[5] A. H. Sayce, "Hittite and Mittannian Elements in the Old Testament," *JTS* 29 (1928) 401-406.

[6] E. Forrer, "Das Abendmahl im Ḫatti-Reiche," in *Actes du XXe Congrès Internationale des Orientalistes (Bruxelles 1938)* (Louvain, 1940) 124-128.

[7] F. F. Bruce, *The Hittites and the Old Testament. Tyndale Archaeology Lecture 1947* (London: Tyndale Press, 1947).

Hittitology to Old Testament Study,"[8] in which I sought to update the summary of both what was known about Hittites in Palestine and about Hittite materials which could elucidate the Old Testament. I concluded from the onomastics and customs of persons called "Hittites" in the pre-monarchic period that these were not of Anatolian Hittite origin. References to Hittites in the period of the monarchy I considered to pertain to the so-called "Neo-Hittite" kingdoms of Syria. Aharon Kempinski[9] and James Moyer[10] did not share my conviction that the pre-monarchic "Hittites" of the Bible were not true Anatolian Hittites, but cited archaeological evidence for Hittite or at least Anatolian influence in Bronze Age Palestine from Amarna texts and artefacts excavated in Israel. A similar point of view was held by Nahum Sarna in his JPS commentary on Genesis,[11] citing the non-Semitic names ÌR-Ḫepa (usually read with West Semitic ᶜ*Abdi*- rather than Akkadian *Warad*- or Hurrian *Purame*-) and Šuwardata identifying Amarna period rulers in Palestine alongside of Hittite pottery types and hieroglyphic Luwian seals found in Late Bronze sites in Israel. Since no finds of Hittite or Hurrian *texts* have been made in these regions, Sarna argued that these Hittites or Hurrians in Hebron and the Judean hill country were culturally "Hittite" but no longer linguistically so. Hence, in the Bible too they used the same Semitic language as the patriarchs.

Meanwhile, regardless of whether they believe that pre-monarchic "Hittites" in the Bible were really Anatolian Hittites, scholars have continued to mine Hittite texts for material to elucidate the Old Testament.

Fifteen years after my Tyndale Archaeology Lecture, James Moyer[12] reviewed many suggested parallels which I had already adduced in 1968, but also summarized and evaluated proposals made by others in the intervening years. Since Moyer's article, no other book or article that I am aware of has appeared which has attempted to review systematically all proposals of Hittite or Hurro-Hittite materials having a bearing on Old Testament interpretation. But an international symposium was held in March of 1990 in Hamburg which addressed the subject of "History of Religions Connections between Anatolia, North Syria and the Old Testament." Papers from the symposium were published in 1993, edited by Janowski, Koch and Wilhelm.[13] A paper delivered by Moshe Weinfeld at this symposium approximates the general coverage achieved by Moyer, but without its detailed evaluations.[14]

No reasonably complete bibliography of the subject has been published. A start was made by Moyer in 1983. A somewhat larger, but still only partial bibliography of publications through 1995 on this subject was published in 1996 by the late Vladimir Souček and his wife Jana Siegelová.[15]

The area that has drawn the most attention among biblical scholars is the question of the origin of the covenantal form or forms found in the Bible. It was George Mendenhall who in 1955 first posited a connection between the Israelite covenantal form and the international treaties of the late second millennium, represented almost exclusively by Hittite vassal treaties of the 14th and 13th centuries.[16] Since that time scholars have lined up — pro and con — on whether the Hittite material has significant relevance to the central biblical formulations of the Sinai covenant. In addition, central covenant vocabulary — such as the verbs "love" (ᵓ*āhab*) and "know" (*yāda*ᶜ)[17] — have been compared to the usage of Hittite treaty terminology. And passages from the Israelite prophets in which the people are indicted for blaming Yahweh's punishment of them upon the transgressions of their forebears have been interpreted in the light of statements in Hittite treaties.[18]

Although I participated with Grayson, Van Seters and others in a Symposium on Ancient Historiography held in the late 1970's at the University of Toronto, the papers of which were published separately rather than in a symposium volume,[19] the first somewhat systematic attempt to show an appreciable similarity between Israelite and Hittite histori-

[8] H. A. Hoffner, Jr., "Some Contributions of Hittitology to Old Testament Study. The Tyndale Archaeology Lecture, 1968," *TB* 20 (1969) 27-55.

[9] A. Kempinski, "Hittites in the Bible — What Does Archaeology Say?" *BAR* 5 (1979) 20-45.

[10] J. C. Moyer, "Hittite and Israelite Cultic Practices: A Selected Comparison, *SIC* 2 (1983) 19-38.

[11] N. M. Sarna, *Genesis* (Ed. by N. M. Sarna and C. Potok; The JPS Torah Commentary; Philadelphia, New York, and Jerusalem: Jewish Publication Society, 1989) 395-396.

[12] Moyer, *SIC* 2, 19-38.

[13] See note 1.

[14] M. Weinfeld, "Traces of Hittite Cult in Shiloh, Bethel and in Jerusalem," in *RgB*, 455-472.

[15] V. Souček and Jana Siegelová, *Systematische Bibliographie der Hethitologie 1915-1995. Teilband 1.* Praha: Národní Muzeum, 1996; *Systematische Bibliographie der Hethitologie 1915-1995. Teilband 2.* Praha: Národní Muzeum, 1996); *Systematische Bibliographie der Hethitologie 1915-1995. Teilband 3.* Praha: Národní Muzeum, 1996).

[16] G. E. Mendenhall, *Law and Covenant in Israel and the Ancient Near East* (Pittsburgh, PA: The Biblical Colloquium, 1955).

[17] W. L. Moran, "The Ancient Near Eastern Background of the Love of God in Deuteronomy," *CBQ* 25 (1963) 77-87; H. B. Huffmon, "The Treaty Background of Hebrew *yāda*ᶜ," *BASOR* 181 (1966) 31-37; H. B. Huffmon and S. B. Parker, "A Further Note on the Treaty Background of Hebrew *yāda*ᶜ," *BASOR* 184 (1966) 36-38.

[18] A. Malamat, "Doctrines of Causality in Hittite and Biblical Historiography: A Parallel," *VT* 5 (1955) 1-12; J. B. Geyer, "Ezekiel 18 and a Hittite Treaty of Mursilis II," *Journal of the Society for Old Testament* 12 (1979) 31-46.

[19] Grayson's and mine were published in the same issue of *Orientalia* 49. H. A. Hoffner, Jr., "Histories and Historians of the Ancient Near East: The Hittites," *Or* 49 (1980) 283-332.

ography was made in 1976 by Hubert Cancik.[20] Four years later in 1980 Kyle McCarter was able to build upon Hittite historical materials that were first compared to the stories of Saul and David by Herbert Wolf and me[21] in order to construct his own analysis of what he called "the Apology of David."[22]

A second area within Hittitology that has produced information of interest has been less widely discussed among biblical scholars. That is the legal formulations found in the Hittite "code." Although in 1953 Manfred Lehmann, somewhat unconvincingly, claimed that Hittite law (specifically laws §§46-47) explained the conditions of property transfer between Abraham and "Ephron the Hittite" (Gen 23),[23] more cogent examples of Hittite laws bearing a resemblance to laws in the Pentateuch have appeared in publications not usually consulted by biblical scholars.[24] Among the topics worthwhile exploring are: levirate marriage (§§192-193), the case of the unknown manslayer (§6 and §IV), laws about sexual relations with animals (§187, §199), and compensation for bodily injuries (§§7-16).[25] Many of the possible parallels between Hittite and Israelite laws are identified in the center column of *COS* 2:106ff.

Other areas of interest, many briefly surveyed by Moyer, are: (1) necromancy,[26] (2) rites of gender transformation,[27] (3) purity regulations concerning contact with unclean animals, (4) ritual elimination of impurity by scapegoats, (5) regulations regarding the duties and responsibilities of priests and temple officials, (6) rituals for the summoning of a departed deity, (7) drink ordeals to determine perjury, which cause the forswearing person to swell up, (8) the symbolism of cult gestures, (9) the occasional use of the contest of champions in warfare, and (10) the characteristics of texts employed to legitimize royal usurpers (the so-called "apologies").

In addition there is the interesting area of shared lexical items, words which need not have been loan words from Hittite to Hebrew or vice versa, but which appear to be common to both Hittite or Anatolian Hurrian and biblical Hebrew. Chaim Rabin surveyed this field almost 40 years ago,[28] but new evidence has accrued.

In his 1993 article entitled "Traces of Hittite Cult in Shiloh, Bethel and Jerusalem" delivered orally at the 1990 Hamburg symposium,[29] Moshe Weinfeld listed a large number of examples of Hittite influences in the biblical description of the Israelite cult. Some are more convincing than others. Several are simply based upon inaccurate recording or interpreting of the Hittite or biblical data.

1. He claims that "The quantity of festival offerings in the Bible equals the quantity of the offerings in the Hittite festival calendars" (455f.). But he has arbitrarily selected one Israelite festival to compare with one Hittite one, where the distribution of victims happens to be the same, without demonstrating the need to associate particularly these two. The correlation would not work if one selected a different Israelite or Hittite festival.

2. In rituals for the purification of a childbearing woman, a distinction is made between cases in which the child is male or female, but the offerings at the end of the purification period are identical in both cultures: one lamb and one bird (Lev 12:6, compared with a Hittite ritual).[30] This is a valid observation, but one wonders if in *all* Hittite or Hurrian birth rituals the same offerings were used. It was not uncommon in Hurrian-type rituals from Kizzuwatna — and not just purification or birth rituals — to offer a single lamb and a single bird. Usually the species of bird is not given, but occasionally it is a "large bird" (MUŠEN.GAL).

3. Weinfeld mentions the ceremonies for purification of a house which according to him employ two birds, cedar and crimson. Leviticus 14:49ff. is the biblical example he cites, which also involves hyssop. It is true that cedar and red wool are used together in some Hittite rituals of Kizzuwatnean origin (e.g., CTH 477.1, and CTH 483), but not

---

[20] H. Cancik, *Grundzüge der hethitischen und alttestamentlichen Geschichtsschreibung* (Wiesbaden: Harrassowitz, 1976).

[21] H. M. Wolf, *The Apology of Hattusilis Compared with Other Political Self-justifications of the Ancient Near East* (Ph.D., Brandeis University, 1967); H. A. Hoffner, Jr., "A Hittite Analogue to the David and Goliath Contest of Champions?" *CBQ* 30 (1968) 220-225.

[22] P. K. McCarter, Jr., "The Apology of David," *JBL* 99 (1980) 489-504.

[23] M. Lehmann, "Abraham's purchase of Machpelah and Hittite Law," *BASOR* 129 (1953) 15-18.

[24] E. Neufeld, *The Hittite Laws* (London: Luzac and Co. Ltd., 1951); H. A. Hoffner, Jr., *The Laws of the Hittites* (Ph.D. Dissertation, Brandeis University, 1963); "Incest, Sodomy and Bestiality in the Ancient Near East," in *Studies Gordon*, 81-90; Moyer, *SIC 2*, 19-38; R. Westbrook, *Studies in Biblical and Cuneiform Law* (Cahiers de la Revue Biblique 26; Paris: J. Gabalda et Cie, 1988); E. Otto, "Körperverletzung im hethitischen und israelitischen Recht," in *RgB*, 391-426; R. Haase, "Deuteronomium und hethitisches Recht. Über einige Ähnlichkeiten in rechtshistorischer Hinsicht," *WO* 25 (1994) 71-77; Hoffner, "On Homicide in Hittite Law," in *Studies Astour*, 293-314; "Agricultural Perspectives on Hittite Laws §§167-169," in *Acts of the IIIrd International Congress of Hittitology. Çorum, September 16-22, 1996* (ed. by S. Alp and A. Süel; Ankara: Grafik, Teknik Hazirlik Uyum Ajans) 319-330; and *The Laws of the Hittites. A Critical Edition* (Documenta et Monumenta Orientis Antiqui 23; Leiden: Brill, 1997).

[25] See the commentary in Hoffner, *The Laws of the Hittites*, 175-178.

[26] Esp. the use of the Israelite *ʾôb* and the Hurro-Hittite *âbi*; cf. H. A. Hoffner, Jr., "Second Millennium Antecedents to the Hebrew *ʾÔB*," *JBL* 86 (1967) 385-401.

[27] Cf. H. A. Hoffner, Jr., "Symbols for Masculinity and Femininity: Their Use in Ancient Near Eastern Sympathetic Magic Rituals," *JBL* 85 (1966) 326-334.

[28] C. Rabin, "Hittite Words in Hebrew," *Or* 32 (1963) 113-139.

[29] Weinfeld, "Traces of Hittite Cult in Shiloh, Bethel and in Jerusalem," in *RgB*, 455-472.

[30] G. M. Beckman, *Hittite Birth Rituals* (StBoT 29; Wiesbaden: Otto Harrassowitz, 1983) 206f. (i 10′-12′).

to my knowledge in the best known example of a ritual to purify a house (CTH 446).[31] Weinfeld refers to data in an earlier article,[32] which I have not checked yet.

4. The scapegoat ritual of Leviticus 16 according to Weinfeld is "very close to the substitution ritual among the Hittites." Here the fundamental studies were by van Brock, Kümmel, Gurney, Moyer, Wright, and Janowski and Wilhelm.[33] It should be noted that in the Hittite examples the animal carrier of the impurity is not always a domestic animal like a bull, sheep or goat. In one case it is a mouse.[34] Wright and Weinfeid claim that one difference between the Hittite and biblical examples is that in Hittite the scapegoat is intended both to appease an angry deity and to remove the impurity. But not all Hittite examples of its use entail appeasement of a deity. Nor in all examples is the animal a substitute for a person who has offended the gods. It has been noticed that the Hittite carrier is sent not into the desolate wilderness or desert, but to an enemy country. It would seem that the "scapegoat" in Hittite religion was not a unified concept. Some aspects of its employment concur with the Leviticus scapegoat and others do not. Scholars have so far only compared these Hittite scapegoat rituals with Leviticus 16. But equally relevant in this discussion is the account in 1 Samuel 5-6 of the sojourn of the ark of the covenant in Philistine territory. To be sure the ark, which is eventually sent back into Israel with gifts to pacify Yahweh, is not a scapegoat in the usual sense. But the occasion of the sending is a plague of tumors sent upon the Philistines by Yahweh. And the ark is sent back by allowing the oxen which draw the cart on which it sits to go where the god wishes them to. The "guilt offering" (Heb. *ʾāšām*) that is sent to Yahweh with the ark consists of gold images of the mice and tumors which ravaged the Philistine cities (1 Sam 6:5-17). The ark is sent to the enemy land which is the land of the offended deity, not to transfer the evils to that land, but to return the cult object to its owner. To be compared here is the Middle Hittite ritual of the city of Gamulla (CTH 480 KUB 29.7 + KBo21.41) translated by Goetze in *ANET* 346 and reproduced in part with discussion by Gurney (1977:51f.). The carrier in this case is inanimate, but capable of transporting propitiatory gifts: it is a boat. Into this boat they place little silver and gold representations of the oaths and curses which have oppressed them. Then the boat is floated downstream to a river and eventually by the river to the sea. The Philistine gold mice and tumors compare well with the gold and silver images of the curses. And since both are made of precious metals, they should not be thought of as impurities to be removed, but as propitiatory gifts in the shape of the calamities, sent to the deities who sent the calamities.

In the Leviticus 16 ritual a crux has always been the term *laʿᵃzāʾzēl* rendered in the Septuagint and Vulgate by "as a scapegoat" (followed by the English AV), but replaced in more recent English translations by "for Azazel," sometimes thought to denote a wilderness demon. Appealing to scapegoat rites in the Hurrian language from the Hittite archives, Janowski and Wilhelm would derive the biblical term from a Hurrian offering term, *azazḫiya*. This is particularly appealing to me. There were two goats used in the Leviticus 16 ritual. One is designated for Yahweh as a "sin offering" (Heb. *ḥaṭṭāʾt*, LXX *peri hamartias*) (16:9), and the other is "for Azazel," but is presented alive before Yahweh to make atonement, and is sent away into the wilderness "to/for Azazel." The contrast is twofold: (1) Yahweh versus Azazel, and (2) sin offering versus Azazel. If one adopts the first, Azazel seems to be a divine being or demon, who must be appeased. But if one adopts the second as primary, the word *ʿᵃzāʾzēl* represents the goal of the action. In the system of Hurrian offering terms to which Wilhelm's *azazḫiya* belongs, the terms represent either a benefit that is sought by the offering (e.g., *keldiya* "for wellbeing," cf. Heb. *šᵉlāmîm*), or the central element offered (e.g., *zurgiya* "blood"). If Janowski and Wilhelm's theory is correct, the Hebrew term would not denote a demon as recipient of the goat, but some benefit desired (e.g., removal of the sins and impurities) or the primary method of the offering (e.g. the banishment of the goat).

David Wright has also called attention to the similarity in the use of a hand placement gesture in Israelite (Heb. *sāmak yādô*) and Hittite ritual (*kiššaran dāi-*), noting that in each it has the same two possible implications: (1) conferring authorization on another to act (usually in a ceremony) on behalf of the gesturing person, and (2) to attribute the offering material to the one performing the hand placement.[35] The fact that both cultures preserve the same two significances is striking and important. But Weinfeld goes a step further, claiming that in both it is a two-

[31] See edition in H. Otten, "Eine Beschwörung der Unterirdischen aus Boğazköy," *ZA* 54 (1961) 114-157; translation and discussion in V. Haas, *Geschichte der hethitischen Religion* (HdO 1. Abteilung 15; Leiden: Brill, 1994) 283ff., and translation in *COS* 1:168ff.

[32] M. Weinfeld, "Social and Cultic Institutions in the Priestly Source against their Ancient Near Eastern Background," in *Eighth World Congress of Jewish Studies. Panel Sessions, Bible Studies and Hebrew Language* (Jerusalem, 1983) 95-129, esp. p. 101.

[33] N. van Brock, "Substitution rituelle," *RHA* 17/65 (1959) 117-146; H. M. Kümmel, "Ersatzkönig und Sündenbock," *ZAW* 80 (1968) 289-318; O. R. Gurney, *Some Aspects of Hittite Religion* (London: Oxford University Press, 1977); Moyer, *SIC 2*, 19-38; D. P. Wright, *The Disposal of Impurity: Elimination Rites in the Bible and in Hittite and Mesopotamian Literature* (SBLDS 101; Atlanta: Scholars Press, 1987); "The Gesture of Hand Placement in the Hebrew Bible and in Hittite Literature," *JAOS* 106 (1986) 433-446; B. Janowski and G. Wilhelm, "Der Bock, der die Sünden hinausträigt. Zur Religionsgeschichte des Azazel-Ritus Lev 16,10.21f.," in *RgB*, 109-170; Weinfeld, "Traces of Hittite Cult in Shiloh, Bethel and in Jerusalem," in *RgB*, 455-472.

[34] CTH 391.1 KUB 27.67 i 37ff.; cf. Gurney, *Some Aspects*, 50.

[35] Wright, *JAOS* 106 (1986) 433-446.

handed placement for the first significance and a one-handed one for the second. There is good evidence in the Bible for this distinction, but in Hittite texts there is no evidence for it: rather in both significances the texts read "he places the hand (singular!)." Other parallels cited by Weinfeld are too general to constitute anything specifically Anatolian and are sometimes garbled in their details.[36] For example, that ritual slaughter was accomplished by cutting the throat of the animal is extremely widespread. Weinfeld misunderstood Cord Kühne's key article on the Hittite practice.[37] He claims the Hittite slaughterer cut the "windpipe" of the victim, whereas Kühne's proposal for the difficult term *auli-* was "neck artery."[38] Nor is the provision prohibiting persons with physical disabilities from entering the sacred temple precincts something exclusively Hittite or Israelite.[39]

But there are a few new sources not mentioned by Moyer or Weinfeld. A fairly recently published source of great relevance to this question is the 15th century Hurro-Hittite bilingual literary text called the "Song of Release," the edition of which was published in 1996.[40] A substantial portion of this text contains parables or fables illustrating with stories involving animals or inanimate objects certain kinds of undesirable or foolish human behavior. One is about a coppersmith who makes a beautiful cup, only to have it curse him, so that he in turn pronounces a curse on the cup. The Hurro-Hittite text compares this behavior to that of an ungrateful son, who by his refusal to care for his weak and aged parent earns his father's curse. This is obviously an early source of the biblical *topos* about the potter and his clay creation, used both by the prophets Isaiah (29:16, 45:9) and Jeremiah (18:6) and by St. Paul (Rom 9:20-21). But the main part of the story concerns the demand by the god of the city of Ebla (Teššub) that its citizens free the men of the town Ikakali, who are currently their slaves. It is still unclear if they are also debt slaves. When the citizens resist this demand, the god threatens to destroy the city. Haas and Wegner have suggested that the intention of this composition was to explain the destruction of Ebla.[41] In similar manner the Judean chronicler attributed the destruction and exile of the kingdom of Judah to her failure to observe 70 of Yahweh's sabbatical years (2 Chr 36:17-21). The stated beneficiaries of the biblical sabbatical year are the poor, the wild animals and the soil (Exod 23:10-11). The principal objection to observing it would be the greed of the land owners. If there is a common thread running through all parts of the Song of Release — parables, feast in the netherworld palace of Allani, demand for debt release, threatened destruction of Ebla — it may be that in refusing to release their slaves the wealthy leaders of Ebla personify the foolish figures described in the fables, who despise their weak and elderly parents and are overweening in their ambition for wealth and advancement. And in the episode where the leaders refuse to obey Teššub's demand to release their slaves, they even defend themselves by pledging their willingness to relieve the god Teššub himself, if he should ever fall into poverty and need. One is reminded here of the scene of the Last Judgment in Matthew 25, where Jesus says to those granted admission to the Kingdom of Heaven: "I was hungry, and you fed me, naked, and you clothed me, in prison, and you visited me .... For if as you have done this to the least of my brothers, you have done it to me" (Matt 25:31-46). The promise of the leaders of Ebla to help Teššub is a hollow one, since his need is for them to release their own slaves, which they refuse to do.

A second important new source published in 1991 is the corpus of letters from the Hittite provincial capital of Tapikka, modern Maşat Höyük.[42] In several of the letters from this site (numbers 58 and 59), and reportedly from an unpublished letter from the Hittite center at Šapinuwa,[43] there is mention of the employment of blinded captives in the mill houses, just as was done to Samson by the Philistines. Furthermore, lists of captives to be used as hostages include the notations "blinded" or "sighted" and specify the proposed ransom price for each captive.[44] In these texts it appears that these blinded captives worked in groups in the mill houses. The incident involving Samson is in a Philistine context. He too has been captured and was blinded in order to make him less dangerous and to prevent his attempting to escape, precisely the same motivations assumed for the Tapikka and Šapinuwa prisoners. And since the Philistines' Anatolian connections are well known, and Hieroglyphic Luwian seals have been found

[36] Weinfeld, "Traces of Hittite Cult in Shiloh, Bethel and in Jerusalem," in *RgB*, 455-472.

[37] C. Kühne, "Hethitisch *auli-* und einige Aspekte altanatolischer Opferpraxis," *ZA* 76 (1986) 85-117.

[38] The Hittite word for "windpipe" or "trachea" is *ḫu(r)ḫurta-*, not *auli-*. See H. A. Hoffner, Jr., "An English-Hittite Glossary," *RHA* 25/80 (1967) 99; "From Head to Toe in Hittite," in *Studies Young*, 247-259.

[39] On the disabled in Hatti see H. A. Hoffner, Jr., "The Disabled and Infirm in Hittite Society," in *EI* 27 (2001) (Miriam and Hayim Tadmor Volume) (forthcoming).

[40] E. Neu, *Das hurritische Epos der Freilassung I: Untersuchungen zu einem hurritisch-hethitischen Textensemble aus Ḫattuša* (Wiesbaden: Harrassowitz, 1996); English translation in Hoffner, *Hittite Myths*, 65-80.

[41] V. Haas and I. Wegner, "Literarische und grammatikalische Betrachtungen zu einer hurritischen Dichtung," *OLZ* 92 (1997) 437-455.

[42] S. Alp, *Hethitische Briefe aus Maşat-Höyük, Atatürk Kültür, Dil ve Tarih Yüksek Kurumu, Türk Tarih Kurumu Yayınları, VI.* (Dizi-Sa. 35; Ankara: Türk Tarih Kurumu Basımevı, 1991); and *Hethitische Keilschrifttafeln aus Maşat-Höyük Atatürk Kültür, Dil ve Tarih Yüksek Kurumu, Türk Tarih Kurumu Yayınları, VI.* (Dizi-Sa. 34; Ankara: Türk Tarih Kurumu Basımevı, 1991). Below, *COS* 3.13-29.

[43] A. Süel, "Ortaköy'ün Hitit çağındaki adı," *Belleten* 59 (1995) 271-283.

[44] H. A. Hoffner, Jr., "The Treatment and Long-term Use of Persons Captured in Battle According to the Maşat Texts," in *Recent Developments in Hittite Archaeology and History* (ed. by H. G. Güterbock, H. A. Hoffner, Jr. and K. A. Yener; Winona Lake, IN: Eisenbrauns, 2002) 61-71.

at Philistine Aphek,[45] there is every reason to regard this detail in the Samson story as reflecting historical reality and to relate it to the information in the Maşat texts.

A final example of the new possibilities is that the term used in the Bible to designate pagan priests (*kōmer*) originated in Anatolia, where it is found in both Old Assyrian and Hittite documents. If my theory, propounded in 1996,[46] is correct, this Hittite word *kumra-* — like its Old Assyrian counterpart *kumrum* — alternates with the Sumerogram GUDU$_{12}$ and denotes one of the top two classes of male priestly personnel of the Hittite temple. If this Anatolian source for biblical *kᵉmārîm* correct, it suggests a conduit for Anatolian cult influences observable in Ugaritic and biblical Hebrew, namely the use in Syro-Palestine of a class of priest originating in Anatolia in the Second Millennium.

Even if some proposals have been unconvincing, there remain far too many points of similarity — especially in legal, ritual and cultic matters — between Hittite culture and the Bible for us to dismiss them as coincidental or accidental. Moreover, many cannot be attributed to a late first millennium intermediary. So we must take seriously the possibility of a channel of cultural influence in the late second and early first millennium that allowed influences from Anatolia to be felt in Palestine. In the past I have been reluctant to say that this was attributable to the "Hittites" and "sons of Heth" mentioned in the narratives of events antedating the reigns of Saul and David. I am still not quite ready to reverse myself on this point, since I believe the observable cultural influence could have been mediated by groups who were in contact with Hittite culture. But in the future scholars in both Hittitology and Biblical Studies must pay more attention to the developing evidence. Hittitologists can provide checks from their side, and biblical scholars controls from theirs. Neither group can safely address the issue in isolation.

[45] I. Singer, "A Hittite Hieroglyphic Seal Impression from Tel Aphek," *Tel Aviv* 4 (1977) 178-190; "Takuhlinu and Haya: Two Governors in the Ugarit Letter from Tel Aphek," *Tel Aviv* 10 (1983) 3-25; M. Kochavi, "Canaanite Aphek. Its Acropolis and Inscriptions," *Expedition* 20 (1978) 12-17. For Takuhlinu, see also below *COS* 3.94.

[46] H. A. Hoffner, Jr., "Hittite Equivalents of Old Assyrian *kumrum* and *epattum*," *WZKM* 86 (1996) 154-156.

THE "CONTEXTUAL METHOD": SOME WEST SEMITIC REFLECTIONS

K. Lawson Younger, Jr.

Let's go back for a moment 200 years — instead of 3000 years or more (i.e., about 1800 CE). Suppose biblical scholars gathered for an august conference like this and wanted to discuss the context out which the Hebrew Bible arose. What could they discuss? Not much. The earliest manuscripts of the Hebrew Bible are not even a millennium old at that point. The Old Greek or Septuagint offered a small window into a much earlier understanding, but this was more like a tiny porthole at the water-line at best. A few classical writers could be investigated, e.g. Herodotus or Josephus. But again these were only very tiny portholes at the water-line and ones with a large amount of seaweed stuffed in them! A recent article by Steven Holloway illustrates this. Investigating the various interpretations of the identification of "Pul" in 2 Kings 15:19-20, he documents that among biblical commentators and historians of the ancient world writing prior to 1850, Pul was universally recognized as the first Assyrian conqueror to trouble Israel, followed immediately by Tiglath-pileser (i.e., two separate kings).[1] Today, we know that Tiglath-pileser III was Pul, though there is still some discussion among Assyriologists concerning the etymology and use of the name Pul.[2] In 1800, there was not one single known extrabiblical Hebrew inscription. Egyptian hieroglyphics were known, but not yet deciphered. In fact, the Rosetta Stone was still in Egypt in French hands. Cuneiform inscriptions, for the most part, still lay in the ground in Mesopotamia.

Fortunately, all that situation of the early 1800's has dramatically changed. Today a number of persons or events of the Hebrew Bible are attested in extrabiblical materials; in fact, one may even be pictured (Jehu on the Black Obelisk — though some scholars believe it is only Jehu's emissary that is pictured).[3] In addition, we may have seals or seal impressions of some biblical characters like Baruch, the scribe of Jeremiah.[4] A newly published ostracon mentions a king ᵓAshyahu — Joash or Josiah.[5] The Ketef Hinnom Amulet scrolls provide the earliest attestation of a biblical text, recording a version of the Aaronic blessing at the end of Numbers 6.[6]

Discoveries in the last two decades in Syria alone have been impressive and insightful: Ebla and Emar are noteworthy; so too the number of Assyrian, Old Aramaic, Phoenician and hieroglyphic Luwian inscriptions; and more tablets from Mari, Ugarit and Alalaḫ have been discovered and/or published. And thankfully, we possess much better readings of some of the texts discovered earlier in the twentieth century due to the photographic efforts of B. Zuckerman, W. T. Pitard, T. J. Lewis, A. G. Vaughn, et al.

Yet in the same two decades of these discoveries in Syria, Biblical Studies has moved from author-oriented readings of the Hebrew Bible, to text-oriented readings, to reader-oriented readings. Today, different methodologies jockey for the pole position. Increasingly, biblical literary critics are turning their attention to the relationship between text and reader and to the social context of the reader's "production of meaning." At its most extreme, such literary criticism treats biblical literature in even greater isolation from its cultural environment, with the entire interpretive transaction taking place between the Bible and the modern reader. This approach, as Simon Parker has recently observed,[7] puts the reader rather one-sidedly in control of the literature, conforming it to the categories and interests of current criticism without regard to the categories and interests of ancient literature. Rather than seeking to let the literature of ancient Israel address us on its own terms — however remote from ours and however we may finally judge them — it too easily makes of biblical literature a reflection of our own concerns at the end of the twentieth century, whether secular or theological.[8]

---

[1] S. W. Holloway, "The Quest for Sargon, Pul, and Tiglath-Pileser in the 19th Century," in *Mesopotamia and the Bible: Comparative Explorations* (JSOTSup 341; ed. by M. W. Chavalas and K. L. Younger, Jr.; Sheffield: Sheffield Academic Press, 2002) 68-87. This essay demonstrates some of the dangers of "biblicizing" ancient texts by forcing on them features drawn from the Bible. For a discussion of this problem, see J. M. Sasson, "Two Recent Works on Mari," *AfO* 27 (1980) 127-135.

[2] That the names Tiglath-pileser (*Tukulti-apil-Ešarra*) and Pul (*Pūlu*) were used to designate a single ruler is no longer seriously called in question. For a further discussion, see *COS* 2:285, n. 21.

[3] For the text, see the Black Obelisk, Epigraph 2 (*COS* 2.113F). For the relief, see *ANEP* figs. 351-355.

[4] See *COS* 2.70A.

[5] See *COS* 2.50.

[6] See *COS* 2.83.

[7] S. B. Parker, *Stories in Scripture and Inscriptions. Comparative Studies on Narratives in Northwest Semitic Inscriptions and the Hebrew Bible* (New York/Oxford: Oxford University Press, 1997) 4.

[8] Ibid. In addition to these two factors, Parker points out a third factor, a religious factor. Since the Bible is a direct communication from God

But undoubtedly the response of ancient audiences to many of the features of the ancient documents must have been different from ours. Their rhetoric was designed to create a certain impression on the hearer or reader, and that impression is lessened or confused by a reader's ignorance of the ancient rhetorical devices and the presuppositions that these texts employ. Some apprehension of the ancient culture and social environment that their rhetoric presupposed and addressed — in which the composer made his or her choices — is essential for fulfilling the role of "implied reader."

Please don't misunderstand me. The different reading strategies employed today have provided many new and valuable insights — some to greater or lesser degrees. And I am not interested in this essay devolving into a discussion of philosophical hermeneutics.[9] But in most cases, these readings, especially the reader-oriented ones, are fundamentally ahistorical. Some even violate the integrity of the text.[10] Thus there is little interest in comparative analyses with ancient Near Eastern texts among many biblical scholars.

At the same time as the rise of reader-oriented readings, there has been a trend within biblical scholarship to date all biblical materials to the Persian or Hellenistic periods. This has had an obvious impact on how certain scholars view the relevance of much of the ancient Near Eastern data now at our disposal. Some scholars may question whether they should really purchase *The Context of Scripture*! Now if they are questioning that because of the price, well that's understandable. But if they are questioning whether it is important for Hebrew Bible scholars to bother reading any of these texts, that's another issue.

Unfortunately, some past comparative studies have indulged in great excesses in over-emphasizing the comparisons. This indiscriminate use of the comparative method has especially occurred when new discoveries are first published and such excesses undercut the importance of the comparative process.[11] Over-emphasis for agenda reasons also undermines legitimate comparisons. In this regard, Ugarit has perhaps been the most abused of all the ancient Near Eastern materials.[12] In a newly published book, Mark Smith has compiled a history of interpretation of the Ugaritic materials which demonstrates many of these abuses.[13] In a number of instances, scholars have been too quick in attempting to do comparative study without allowing time to fully establish the proper reading and understanding of the newly discovered text.

In spite of some of these trends and factors, it seems apparent — at least to me — that one of the best ways to improve one's literary competence in reading the Hebrew Bible is to read as much of the literature under consideration as possible within the Bible, but also and especially within the ancient Near East. Adequate understanding, explanation, and assessment of ancient texts require attention to all dimensions of the text — literary and historical, internal and external, intellectual and social.

Historians who recognize the literary character of the written narratives gain access to ancient Israel's intellectual and social world in a way denied to those who read them naively as direct representations of past events or who dismiss them altogether as historical sources because they do not provide documentary evidence. The former produce "histories" that simply retell the stories of the Bible, while the latter produce histories that ignore the richest material for reconstructing — to use Philip Davies' term with a little tongue and cheek — "historic" Israel.[14]

Over the last one hundred and fifty years, questions of how to handle the "parallels" between the biblical text and the ancient Near Eastern materials have received different answers. On the one hand, some scholars have been guilty

---

to us, many believe that "the Bible must be comprehensible on its own, without having to read the literature of cultures that Israel — indeed God — condemned. In addition, some feel an anxiety about discovering the Bible's human dimension or historical rootedness, which, in their view, might lessen the divine character of the message" (S. B. Parker, "The Ancient Near Eastern Literary Background of the Old Testament," in *The New Interpreter's Bible* [ed. by L. E. Keck; Nashville: Abingdon Press, 1994] 228-243, esp. p. 229.

[9] For some common sense remarks, see A. Berlin, "A Search for a New Biblical Hermeneutics: Preliminary Observations," in *The Study of the Ancient Near East in the Twenty-First Century* (ed. by J. S. Cooper and G. M. Schwartz; Winona Lake, IN: Eisenbrauns, 1996) 195-207.

[10] An example can be see in J. C. Exum, "Feminist Criticism: Whose Interests Are Being Served?" in *Judges and Method. New Approaches in Biblical Studies* (ed. by G. A. Yee; Minneapolis: Fortress Press, 1995) 65-90, esp. 83-88. Her interpretation ends up being the opposite of what the text actually says!

[11] The tendency has been to overemphasize the importance of new discoveries to the Old Testament, and then when the flaws become obvious, approach comparative data from the standpoint of skepticism, causing many to completely ignore comparative material altogether. See J. J. M. Roberts, "The Ancient Near Eastern Environment," in *The Hebrew Bible and its Modern Interpreters* (ed. by D. Knight and G. Tucker; Philadelphia: Fortress, 1985) 96.

[12] On the current status of Ugaritic studies, see W. G. E. Watson and N. Wyatt, editors, *Handbook of Ugaritic Studies* (HdO, Erste Abteilung: Der Nahe und Mittlere Osten 39; Leiden: E. J. Brill, 1999) = *HUS*; and its review by D. Pardee, "Ugaritic Studies at the End of the 20th Century," *BASOR* 320 (2000) 49-86.

[13] M. S. Smith, *Untold Stories: The Bible and Ugaritic Studies in the Twentieth Century* (Peabody, MA: Hendrickson, 2001); and "Ugaritic Studies and the Hebrew Bible, 1968-1998 (with an Excursus on Judean Monotheism and the Ugaritic Texts)," in *Congress Volume. Oslo 1998* (VTSup 80; ed. by A. Lemaire and M. Sæbø; Leiden: Brill, 2000) 327-355.

[14] According to Davies, "historic" Israel would be the Israel referred to in ancient Near Eastern inscriptions from its first occurrence in the Merenptah Stela down to the Assyrian sources of the first millennium. See P. R. Davies, *In Search of "Ancient Israel"* (JSOTSup 148; Sheffield: Sheffield Academic Press, 1992).

of overstressing the parallels, a type of "parallelomania,"[15] while others — often in reaction to the excesses of the former — have downplayed the parallels to the point of ignoring clear, informative correlations, producing a type of "parallelophobia."[16] One scholar has actually argued that Israel was so unique among the peoples of the ancient Near East that it is unnecessary to do any comparative study![17] Interesting, isn't it, that a comparative argument can be used to dismiss the need of doing comparative analyses![18]

The fact is that presuppositions often shape the comparative evaluation. Some scholars emphasize the Old Testament's similarity to and continuity with ancient Near Eastern literature. In this way they seek to demonstrate that the Old Testament is authentic or, on the other hand, that it is merely a product of its environment. Other scholars emphasize the Hebrew Bible's divergence from and contrast with its background. In this, they seek to demonstrate that it is absolutely different or, on the other hand, that each of the ancient Near Eastern literatures should be appreciated on its merits, not just in comparison with the others.[19]

In this light, the importance of William W. Hallo's work in proposing a balanced approach — a "contextual method"[20] — that seeks to observe both comparisons as well as contrasts in the literature of the ancient Near East and the Hebrew Bible is paramount. The best comparative studies recognize that the literature of the ancient Near East was produced not only out of a particular culture but also out of a larger literary tradition, and that comparison with other literature that is similar within that tradition — serving the same purpose, using the same structure, or referring to the same subject — reveals certain aspects of a text that might remain hidden.[21] Moreover, this can serve as a counterbalance to speculation derived from the analysis of one text in isolation. A contextual study may lessen the conjectural element in historical analysis, as well as lessen the subjective element in literary criticism by exposing what is traditional, conventional, or generic in a story. In other words, a contextual approach may produce the genre "expectations" necessary to read the biblical text competently. While excessive concentration on similarities or differences among texts distorts any conclusions about their relationship, giving due weight to both contributes to the understanding and explanation — both of the individual texts and of the features they share with others.

A Four-pronged Assessment Process

In the development of criteria for the evaluation of parallels, the keyword must be "caution." I believe that balance in the evaluation of the evidence is achieved through the assessment of propinquity along four lines: linguistic, geographic, chronological, and cultural (not necessarily in this order). A parallel that is closer to the biblical material in language, in geographic proximity, in time, and culture is a stronger parallel than one that is removed from the biblical material along one or more of these lines. That does not mean that a parallel further removed is not relevant evidence. There may be circumstances that strengthen its relevance. For instance, one mitigating factor along the chronological axis is that of a medium for the transmission of tradition. Thus, in the conservative ancient Near East, if there was a clear medium by which a more ancient tradition could accurately be transmitted to a later time period, then the relevance of that parallel may be increased in the evaluation process. This means, for example, that a Sumerian parallel may be more relevant along the chronological axis then it first appears.

By implementing such a four-pronged assessment process, caution signs may appear that slow down the tendency to over-state the evidence. For the problem with the traditional comparative approach, as Dennis Pardee has pointed out, is not that it compares or contrasts, but that it sometimes begins comparing with distant parallels rather than with the proximate ones, or that it does not nuance its use of comparisons with distant entities, or that it is selective, choosing only those comparisons which favor a certain thesis.[22]

I would like to illustrate this by looking at a curse formula that involves the "baking of bread in an oven" which parallels Leviticus 26:26. The texts are:

---

[15] E.g., see M. Dahood, *Psalms* (AB; Doubleday,). For the term parallelomania, see S. Sandmel, "Parallelomania," *JBL* 81 (1962) 1-13.

[16] R. Ratner and B. Zuckerman, "'A Kid in Milk?': New Photographs of *KTU* 1.23, Line 14," *HUCA* 57 (1986) 15-60, esp. p. 52.

[17] R. J. Thompson argues that because Israel was unique in the ancient Near East (Israel alone developed real historiography), the relevance of the comparative material is questionable (*Moses and the Law in a Century of Criticism Since Graf* [Leiden: E. J. Brill, 1972] 118-120).

[18] For further discussion, see K. L. Younger, Jr., *Ancient Conquest Accounts: A Study of Ancient Near Eastern and Biblical History Writing* (JSOTSup 98. Sheffield: Sheffield University Press, 1990) 52-53.

[19] Parker, *The New Interpreter's Bible*, 234.

[20] "Biblical History in its Near Eastern Setting: The Contextual Approach," in *SIC* 1:1-12; "Compare and Contrast: the Contextual Approach to Biblical Literature," in *SIC* 3:1-30; *The Book of the People* (Brown Judaic Studies 225; Atlanta: Scholars Press, 1991) chapter 2: "The Contextual Approach."

[21] Ibid. Parker states: "A just comparison gives due weight to both commonalities and differences and seeks to explain both — as respectively part of the common culture Israel shared with its neighbors and antecedents, or as part of the particular culture or sub-culture of the individual work — or indeed of the creativity of its author(s)."

[22] D. Pardee, "Review of *SIC* 2," *JNES* 44 (1985) 220-222, esp. p. 221. For some further methodological discussion, see S. Talmon, "The 'Comparative Method' in Biblical Interpretation — Principles and Problems," *VTSup* 29 (1977) 320-356; M. Malul, *The Comparative Method in Ancient Near Eastern and Biblical Legal Studies* (Neukirchen-Vluyn: Neukirchener Verlag, 1990) 13-78.

A. The Tel Fakhariyah Inscription (c. 850-825 BCE)[23]

Aramaic

(22)*wmʾh . nšwn . lʾpn . btnwr . lḥm .*
wʾl . ymlʾnh

(22) And may one hundred women[24] bake bread in an oven,
but may they not fill it.

Akkadian

(35) 1 ME *a-pi-a-te la-a ú-<šam>-la-a* (36)NINDU [var. possibly *la-a ú-<ma>-la-a*][25]

May one hundred women bakers not be able to fill an oven.

B. The Sefire Treaty (IA.24) (c. 760-740 BCE)[26]

Kaufman 1982

wšb^{c} bnth yʾpn b ˚ ˚ṭ lḥm
wʾl ymlʾn

And should his seven daughters bake bread in an oven(?),
but not fill (it).

Fitzmyer 1995; *COS* 2.82

wšb^{c} bkth yhkn bšṭ lḥm
wʾl yhrgn

and should seven hens(?) go looking for food,
may they not kill(?) (anything)!

C. The Bukān Inscription (c. 725-700 BCE)[27]

wsb(7)^{c} *. nšn . yʾpw . btnr . ḥd* [.]
wʾl . ymlʾ(8)*why .*

And may seven (7) women bake (bread) in one oven,
but may they not fill (8) it.

D. Leviticus 26:26

b^{e}šibrî lākem maṭṭēh leḥem
w^{e}ʾāpû ^{c}eśer nāšîm laḥm^{e}kem b^{e}tannûr ʾeḥād
w^{e}hēšîbû laḥm^{e}kem bammišqāl
waʾ^{a}kaltem
w^{e}lōʾ tiśbā^{c}û

When I break your staff of bread,
then ten women shall bake your bread in one oven,
and they shall dole out your bread by weight,
and you will eat,
but not be satisfied.

The ancient Near Eastern texts are arranged in chronological order. They all come from Old Aramaic texts — although the Tel Fakhariyah inscription is a bilingual and each text exhibits some dialectal traits. Thus on the

[23] *COS* 2.34. Since the curse under consideration comes from the second part of the inscription, it is unaffected by diachronic issues related to the inscription's sources. For discussion of these, see C. Leonhard, "Die literarische Struktur der Bilingue vom Tell Fakhariyeh," *WZKM* 85 (1995) 117-79; S. B. Parker, "The Composition and Sources of Some Northwest Semitic Royal Inscriptions," *SEL* 16 (1999) 49-62, esp. 50-82.

[24] On the unusual form *nšwn*, see S. A. Kaufman, "Reflections on the Assyrian-Aramaic Bilingual from Tell-Fakhariyeh," *Maarav* 3 (1982) 137-175, esp. p. 169; and J. W. Wesselius, "Review of Abou Assaf, Bordreuil and Millard 1982," *BiOr* 40 (1983) col. 182.

[25] Pardee and Biggs state: "Since most double consonants in this text are not written double, an emendation to *ú-<ma>-la-a* seems more likely. The line would then read 1 ME *a-pi-a-te* <NINDA> *la-a ú-<ma>-la-a* NINDU 'a hundred woman bakers will not be able to fill an oven with bread.'" See D. Pardee and R. D. Biggs, "Review of Abou Assaf, Bordreuil and Millard 1982," *JNES* 43 (1984) 253-257, esp. p. 257. The Bukān inscription makes the first emendation <NINDA> unnecessary since it leaves out *lḥm* (probably an ellipsis).

[26] *COS* 2.82; *KAI* 2:238-274, 342; *SSI* 2:18-5; S. A. Kaufman, "Reflections on the Assyrian-Aramaic Bilingual from Tell-Fakhariyeh," *Maarav* 3 (1982) 137-175; A. Lemaire and J.-M. Durand, *Les inscriptions araméennes de Sfiré et l'Assyrie de Shamshi-ilu* (Geneva/Paris: Librairie Droz, 1984); J. A. Fitzmyer, *The Aramaic Inscriptions of Sefire* (Biblica et Orientalia 19a; Rev. ed; Rome: Biblical Institute, 1995).

[27] *COS* 3.89.

linguistic axis they are more or less equal. While they all come from the general chronological range of c. 850-700 BCE, there is approximately one hundred and fifty years between the Tel Fakhariyah inscription and the Bukān inscription. Geographically, the Sefire text would be closest and the Bukān text the furtherest away (coming from the state of the Manneans in what is today modern Iran). However, there are difficulties with the reading of the Sefire text (note the differences between Kaufman and Fitzmyer — both scholars recognize the problems in the reading of this line). Thus this text is a significantly weaker parallel, if it is a parallel at all. Culturally, it is important to note that, as Biggs has pointed out, this curse formula appears to be West Semitic in origin. There do not appear to be any clear Akkadian parallels.[28] So on the cultural axis, there is basic equality. But in the contextual analysis, its differences must be noted too. In this regard, on closer inspection, none of the Old Aramaic texts is an exact parallel to the Leviticus passage. In fact, there are slight differences between all the texts. Therefore, it would be wrong, in my opinion, to argue for a direct borrowing on the part of the Hebrew Bible from any of these inscriptions. Moreover, it would be wrong to argue for a particular date for the passage in Leviticus based on this comparison. It appears that there were some stock West Semitic curse formulae that could be drawn from in the composition of curse passages and that these could be adapted to the particular needs of the ancient writers. In the case of the biblical writer, the apodosis of the curse is modified. In the Old Aramaic texts, the result is that the women baking bread in a single oven may not fill the oven (in spite of all their efforts to do so). This may, in turn, imply a resultant hunger. In the case of Leviticus 26:26, the apodosis does not emphasize the inability to fill the oven, but a resultant hunger in spite of baking and eating. By comparison and contrast, a deeper understanding and appreciation of the nuance of the biblical passage is obtained.

I do not intend to suggest by this example that the process of evaluating ancient Near Eastern parallels by means of propinquity will be an easy process. There will be immediate disagreement among biblical scholars regarding the date of the biblical texts that are being evaluated along the chronological axis (some arguing for early dates, others for late dates). Such a difficulty might be overcome by suggesting a range of dates for the biblical material, though this ultimately will not solve the problem. On the other hand, by evaluating the evidence along multiple axes, there is the possibility of "a preponderance of the evidence" which could help minimize some of the disagreement.

Generally the geographic axis and linguistic axis will not be difficult, though certain texts will vex scholarly consensus along linguistic lines (e.g. the Deir ᶜAlla texts).[29] But some difficulties in evaluation may arise along the cultural axis. An example is the relationship between the Ugaritic texts and Canaanite culture. The question whether the Ugaritic texts should be considered exemplars of Canaanite literature, i.e., literature from the same cultural milieu as found in the southern Levant, has been debated off and on for decades. It would appear to me that in this case a balanced view, such as expressed by Wayne Pitard[30] that stresses both the cultural continuity and individual distinctives of the southern Canaanite and Israelite contexts, is the best way forward.

Additional Considerations

Besides the assessment of the evidence along lines of propinquity, there are other items which need to be kept in mind. Some of the following items may seem to be issues of common sense. But unfortunately this has not always prevailed. The fact is that when people evaluate parallels, they act as mediators between the observed contexts. Thus since it relies on mediators, the shaping of comparisons will always be a subjective enterprise, and its goal will always seem apologetic.[31] If we want it to be more than just intuition, there must be certain reasonable controls implemented. Also, this is by no means intended as an exhaustive list — these are items which come most immediately to mind in terms of areas of abuse.

1. The evaluation of parallels should generally be based on parallel types or genres. Thus we should compare epistles with epistles and not epistles and epic poetry.[32] However, one must be cautious not to apply an overly strict view of genre, since modern categories may not reflect the ancient types. It would be very unfortunate to eliminate legitimate comparative data simply on the basis of modern literary assumptions. Furthermore, there may be instances where it is very beneficial to note comparisons and contrasts between two disparate genres. But as a general rule and cautionary control, generic considerations should be observed, and where there are differences these should be noted and weighed in the evaluation of the evidence.

---

[28] Pardee and Biggs, *JNES* 43 (1984) 255. For a discussion of the Old Aramaic curses in these inscriptions (except for the Bukān inscription), see K. J. Cathcart, "The Curses in Old Aramaic Inscriptions," in *Studies McNamara*, 140-152.

[29] See B. A. Levine, "The Deir ᶜAlla Plaster Inscriptions," *COS* 2.27.

[30] W. T. Pitard, "Voices from the Dust: the Tablets from Ugarit and the Bible," in *Mesopotamia and the Bible: Comparative Explorations* (JSOTSup 341; ed. by M. W. Chavalas and K. L. Younger, Jr.; Sheffield: Sheffield Academic Press, 2002) 250-274.

[31] J. M. Sasson, "About 'Mari and the Bible,'" *RA* 92 (1998) 91-123, esp. p. 91.

[32] In this regard, a recent statement by Dennis Pardee is very interesting. Concerning the nature of the Hebrew Bible and Ugaritic corpora, he states: "... the two corpora are, therefore almost mirror-images of each other: there is very little narrative poetry in the Hebrew Bible but much narrative prose, while in Ugaritic there is very little poetry that does not have a narrational structure and nothing comparable to most of the Pentateuch and Former Prophets in the Bible." See D. Pardee, "Review of Simon B. Parker, editor, *Ugaritic Narrative Poetry* (trans. by M. S.

2. It is very important that the ancient text actually contains the reading that we think it contains. A favorite explanation for Exod 23:19 (34:26; Deut 14:21) "you shall not boil a kid in the mother's milk" disappeared when collation and further study revealed that the Ugaritic text (*KTU* 1.23) did not contain the reading that many thought that it did.[33] In fact, nothing in the Ugaritic text gets "boiled." That's because the verb "to boil" or anything like it simply does not appear here. Instead the text reads something like:

   Over the fire, seven times the sweet-voiced youth (chants):
   coriander in milk,
   mint in butter ...[34]

   Those who read West Semitic inscriptions know that an unfortunate number of the texts are fragmentary and sometimes quite difficult. The Deir ᶜAlla plasters come immediately to mind. Another fragmentary text that comes to mind is the recently discovered Tel Dan inscription. Of course, making assessments for comparisons with biblical texts is not impossible with these texts; but caution must rule the day.

3. It is also very important that the interpretation of the ancient Near Eastern text is accurate. A particular interpretation of the Ugaritic text *KTU* 1.119, "Ugaritic Prayer for a City under Siege," is a case in point. A passage of that text was interpreted to mention child sacrifice as a means of relieving a city under siege. This, in turn, was used as a way of explaining the story of Mesha's sacrifice in 2 Kings 3.[35] This particular explanation for the 2 Kings 3 passage appeared recently in a new textbook on the history of Israel.[36] Laying aside the fact that the Hebrew text of 2 Kings 3 may be interpreted differently,[37] the point here is that the Ugaritic text's interpretation was wrong in the first place. It is extremely doubtful that child sacrifice is in view anywhere in the text — see Pardee's translation in *COS* 1.88 with appropriate notes (p. 285, n. 23).

   Somewhat in this same vein are the *Rāpīʾūma* texts from Ugarit. (Sorry, I seem to be picking on the Ugaritologists, but some of them, or perhaps more accurately some biblical scholars working with the Ugaritic materials, have provided the most infamous examples of abuses of comparative studies). Quite a number of scholars from almost the beginning of Ugaritic studies have made comparisons between the *rāpīʾūma* of the Ugaritic texts and the *rephāîm* of the biblical texts. The secondary literature on this topic is absolutely enormous. This comparison may not, of course, be altogether invalid, but the difficulties of the Ugaritic materials are legion. Wayne Pitard, in his recent discussion of these texts in the *Handbook of Ugaritic Studies* states:

   > [I]n the final analysis, no decisive conclusions about the identity of the *rpum* can yet be drawn ... Only further discoveries of texts relating to the *rpum* are likely to improve the present situation ... It is clear that these texts [i.e. *KTU* 1.20-22] are exceedingly ambiguous and that great caution should be used in drawing upon them to reconstruct aspects of Ugaritic or Syro-Palestinian culture. In many cases such caution has not been employed ... It is important not to place too much interpretational weight on ambiguous and problematic texts such as these. Before they can be used as sources for dealing with the wider issues of Canaanite religion and society, a clearer understanding of the texts themselves is necessary.[38]

4. Be aware of the limits of the comparison or contrast. Try not to conclude more than the evidence indicates. This is especially important in places where the evidence is silent. The motif of grasping the hem of the garment is attested in a number of ancient West Semitic contexts. It is found in texts from Alalaḫ,[39] Ugarit[40]

Smith, et al.; SBLWAW 9; Atlanta: Scholars Press, 1997)," *JNES* 60 (2001) 142-145, esp. p. 142, n. 1.

[33] See Ratner and Zuckerman, *HUCA* 57 (1986) 15-60.

[34] Following Pardee, *COS* 1.87 (pp. 278-279). I understand *ǵzrm* as a singular with enclitic *m* (following W. G. E. Watson, "Aspects of Style in KTU 1.23," *SEL* 11 [1994] 3-8, esp. pp. 5, 7). Pardee translates as a plural "youths (chant)" (p. 278). Cf. another recent translation:

"Seven times by fire, youthful voices
a *gd* in milk,
a *annḫ* in butter ..."

See T. J. Lewis, "The Birth of the Gracious Gods," in *Ugaritic Narrative Poetry* (ed. by S. B. Parker; SBLWAW 9; Atlanta: Scholars Press, 1997) 208. See also M. Dietrich and O. Loretz, "Mythen und Epen in ugaritischer Sprache," *TUAT* 3/6 (1997) 1089-1369.

[35] B. Margalit, "Why King Mesha of Moab Sacrificed His Oldest Son," *BAR* 12 (1986) 62-63, 76.

[36] W. C. Kaiser, *A History of Israel. From the Bronze Age Through the Jewish Wars* (Nashville, TN: Broadman & Holman, 1998) 334.

[37] For the most recent discussions, see J. M. Spinkle, "2 Kings 3: History or Historical Fiction," *BBR* 9 (1999) 247-270; W. W. Hallo, "A Ugaritic Cognate for Akkadian *ḫitpu*?" in *Studies Levine*, 43-50.

[38] W. T. Pitard, "The RPUM Texts," *Handbook of Ugaritic Studies* (ed. W. G. E. Watson and N. Wyatt; Leiden: E. J. Brill, 1999) 259-269, esp. pp. 268-269. Cf. also *COS* 1.105.

[39] See in particular the extensive use of the metaphor in the land grant of Abbael to Yarimlim. See *COS* 2.137, n. 4; and D. J. Wiseman, "Abban and Alalah," *JCS* 12 (1958) 124-129 (lines 47-49).

[40] *CTA* 6 2:9-11 and 30-31. See E. L. Greenstein, "'To Grasp the Hem' in Ugaritic Literature," *VT* 32 (1982) 217-218.

and in the Panamuwa[41] inscription from Zinçirli and, of course, in 1 Samuel 15:27. These ancient texts elucidate the custom of grasping the hem of the garment. Specifically, it was a gesture in which a suppliant beseeches, or indicates his submission to, his superior by grasping the hem of the superior's garment which explains what Saul was doing in grasping the hem of Samuel's garment. But the occurrence of this motif in these ancient Near Eastern texts cannot establish the date of the biblical text. In fact, the practice of dating a text on the basis of the occurrence of a particular motif — unfortunately a common practice among biblical scholars in the twentieth century — is, in my opinion, an impossible task. For without a *terminus a quo* and a *terminus ad quem* — i.e., a starting point and ending point — for the use of the motif, it is impossible to know when a motif may have been utilized in a corpus of literature and, perhaps most important, when it ceased being used in that literature.

5. Be careful in positing directions and amounts of influence. Do not say more than the evidence allows. In some cases the direction and amount of influence is very clear. For example, the Assyrian Aramaic contracts, in particular the grain loan dockets, demonstrate a very strong Akkadian influence, frequently calquing the Assyrian loan phraseology and, in the case of the grain loans, even taking on the triangular shape of the clay dockets.[42] But then this should be expected considering the locations where these Assyrian Aramaic documents are found. On the other hand, in the vast number of instances, it is quite difficult, if not impossible, to posit the direction and amount of influence.[43] In many cases we simply to do not possess enough information to make intelligent guesses. Far too often the term "borrow" has been used to indicate a literary dependence that cannot be proven and is often simply wrong in the light of later scholarly reflection.[44]

6. It is important to stay cognizant of the fact that all literary works may manipulate the evidence, consciously or not, for specific political and artistic purposes. Therefore, it is important to recognize the ideological and literary structures behind these documents.[45] This is manifest in the use of hyperbole. Two West Semitic examples will suffice. In line 7 of the Mesha inscription, Mesha claims: "and Israel has utterly perished forever" (*wyśrᵓl . ᵓbd . ᵓbd . ᶜlm*). In the Tel Dan inscription, the Aramean king appears to claim to have "killed [seve]nty kin[gs]."[46] As noted elsewhere, such hyperbole is used for emphasis and persuasion and reinforces the ideology of the text.[47]

7. We need to recognize the degree of uncertainty in the interpretive process. This may also require a willingness on our part to be prepared to change our historical reconstructions. Hazael's Booty inscription may be cited to illustrate this point.[48] The inscription reads: "That which Hadad gave to our lord Hazael from ᶜAmq in the year when our lord crossed the river." "The river" may be understood to be the Euphrates, as in biblical and cuneiform texts[49]; but in the context as it is mentioned in conjunction with ᶜAmq, the Orontes river may be the river that the inscription denotes.[50] An analogous situation may be seen in 2 Samuel 8:3-8 where we are

---

[41] See *COS* 2.37, esp. n. 24.

[42] See *COS* 3.56-58 (Aramaic) and *COS* 3.111-118 (Assyrian); and J. N. Postgate, "Middle Assyrian to Neo-Assyrian: the Nature of the Shift," in *RAI* 39 (1997) 159-168.

[43] For a discussion of the issue of "borrowing," see J. Tigay, "On Evaluating Claims of Literary Borrowing," in *Studies Hallo*, 250-255; and N. S. Fox, *In the Service of the King: Officialdom in Ancient Israel and Judah* (HUCM 23; Cincinnati: Hebrew Union College Press, 2000) 9-42, esp. pp. 9-14.

[44] An example of the problems inherent in positing literary "dependence" is seen in the problem of the relationship between the Egyptian wisdom work Amenemope (see *COS* 1.47) and the "words of the wise" in Proverbs 22:17-24:22. Some scholars have assumed that Proverbs 22:17-24:22 "borrowed" its material from Amenemope (e.g. M. Lichtheim, *AEL* 2:147; A. Erman, "Eine ägyptische Quelle der 'Sprüche Salomos,'" Sitzungsberichte der Preussischen Akademie der Wissenschaften [phil.-hist. Kl. 15; 1924] 86-92, taf. vi and vii). A few scholars have argued the opposite (e.g. G. L. Archer, *A Survey of Old Testament Introduction* [Chicago: Moody, 1974) 473-474). Both of these explanations concentrate on the similarities without adequately accounting for the differences. But other scholars have overemphasized the differences to the exclusion of some of the obvious similarities (e.g. R. N. Whybray, "The Structure and composition of Proverbs 22:17-24:22," in *Studies Goulder*, 83-96). Another proposal is seen in the work of I. Grumach, *Untersuchungen zur Lebenslehre des Amenope* (Münchner Ägyptologische Studien 23; Munich: Deutscher Kunstverlag, 1972). She argues that both Amenemope and Proverbs 22:17-24:22 are dependent on a common source. While theoretically possible, this can only remain an hypothesis without the discovery of such a source. A more adequate type of explanation is seen in J. Ruffle, "The Teaching of Amenemope and its Connection with the Book of Proverbs," *TynBul* 28 (1977) 29-68. He argues that the writer of Proverbs 22:17-24:22 *culled* a number of proverbs from Amenemope (in some cases directly, in other cases with slight modifications) and that this writer also added a significant amount of new material to this culled material. This is a more sophisicated model than the simple model of literary "borrowing" and thus seems to be a better explanation for both the similarities and differences between the two works. For the most recent discussion of the problem, see J. A. Emerton, "The Teaching of Amenemope and Proverbs XXII 17-XXIV 22: Further Reflections on a Long-Standing Problem," *VT* 51 (2001) 431-465.

[45] M. Liverani, "Memorandum on the Approach to Historiographic Texts," *Or* 42 (1973) 178-194.

[46] Parker, *Stories in Scripture and Inscriptions*, 58. Cf. *COS* 2.23; 2.39.

[47] Younger, *Ancient Conquest Accounts*, 227-228, 235.

[48] See *COS* 2.40.

[49] P.-E. Dion, *Les Araméens à l'âge du fer: histoire politique et structures sociales* (Études bibliques, nouvelle série 34. Paris: J. Gabalda, 1997) 201-202.

[50] A. R. Millard, "Eden, Bit Adini and Beth Eden," *EI* 24 (1993) 173*-177*.

told that "David beat Hadadezer of Rehob, king of Zobah, as he was going to set up his monument at the river." Again, is the Euphrates river in view or is it the Jordan or Jabbok as Parker has recently suggested.[51] Whatever our personal inclinations are in the identifications of the rivers in these texts, we must admit a degree of uncertainty due to the texts' lack of specificity (at least to the modern reader).

Conclusion

Thus, if these common sense admonitions are joined to assessments of ancient Near Eastern parallels along the lines of propinquity outlined above, I believe that very much can be gained in the understanding of the environment of the biblical texts. I hope that I have, at least in some small way, demonstrated the necessity of a contextual method for biblical interpretation via a few West Semitic examples. It may be noticed that I have restricted my remarks to texts, the epigraphic evidence. I, in no way, mean to imply that there are not additional points to be gained through the rich material cultural remains that archaeology has been providing the biblical interpreter for over a century and a half. But it is the written sources that provide the greatest gains in the interpretation of a written corpus like the Bible. Today, we no longer peer through a tiny porthole, but stand on the deck having the opportunity to take in a large part of the panoramic view of the vast sea of twenty-four books of the Hebrew Bible.

---

[51] Parker, *Stories in Scripture and Inscriptions*, 69.

THE IMPACT OF ASSYRIOLOGY ON BIBLICAL STUDIES*

David B. Weisberg

150, 100, or even 50 years ago if one had been asked to write on "The Impact of Assyriology on Biblical Studies," the task would have been much easier. But during recent decades, due to the flood of information from many sites (see below), that task has become highly complex, almost unmanageable. However, what makes one's work much simpler at this time is the comprehensive, up-to-date and authoritative series *COS*. For a review of the great syntheses of comparative texts beginning in 1872 with Eberhard Schrader and his *The Cuneiform Inscriptions and the Old Testament* and running to *Ancient Near Eastern Texts Relating to the Old Testament* edited by James B. Pritchard in 1954 see Hallo's introduction to *COS* 1.

It is noteworthy how deep and swift-moving is the stream of scholarly output in this area, as can be noticed by the large number of outstanding scholars lavishing their attention upon it. In addition, it is interesting to note how many references can be cited to publications of the past decade, and especially of the last few years. First, let us briefly review the history of the question of "Bible and ancient Mesopotamian civilization."[1]

H. W. F. Saggs drew a valuable contrast between Old Testament studies and Assyriology:

> The Old Testament has been studied continuously since the canon of Scripture took its final form. Assyriology, on the other hand, is a branch of investigation into the human past which has developed only within the last century and a half. Even now, this branch of learning is only on the fringe of the cultural awareness of a not inconsiderable number of educated people.[2]

Saggs reviewed the efforts of several scholars who worked at the dawn of the scientific study of Assyriology. He mentioned the memoirs of Claudius James Rich, who visited Babylon in the second decade of the 19th century, the work of Paul E. Botta "who began to dig at Assyrian sites in the neighborhood of Mosul" in 1842 and the efforts of Austin Henry Layard, author of *Nineveh and its Remains*.[3]

Saggs noted a fact of interest in the present connection, namely that "The impact made upon the British public by Layard's revelation of the Assyrians was due to the biblical relevance of the finds."[4] Referring explicitly to "those parts of Assyrian history which bore upon the history of the Bible,"[5] George Smith in 1866 subsequently discovered a part of the Akkadian version of the flood story. The discoveries of Smith illustrate what may be termed the "oscillations" in the relationship between the two fields. On the one hand there was a tendency to confirm, as it were, the teachings of the Bible, whereas in the reaction against this outlook one might see the inescapable swing of the pendulum to the opposite approach, one that came to be known as the "Pan-Babylonian Hypothesis."

The writings of Friedrich Delitzsch (1850-1922), whose "Pan-Babylonianism" was downplayed in Franz Weissbach's biographical note in *RlA*,[6] Hugo Winckler (1863-1913)[7] and Alfred Jeremias (1864-1935), whom D. O. Edzard called "einer der prominenten 'Panbabylonisten'"[8] are the foremost scholars representing the Pan-Babylonian position, which held that "Most of the major stories in the Old Testament, and some in the New, came to be explained in the light of Babylonian mythological motifs."[9]

Commenting upon the "vast quantity, and the enormous scope, of Assyriological epigraphic material," Saggs estimated it to be "of the order of at least twenty times the entire extent of the Old Testament."[10]

---

* It is a pleasure to thank Bill T. Arnold, William W. Hallo and K. Lawson Younger, Jr., for their valuable help.

[1] H. W. F. Saggs, "Assyriology and Biblical Studies," in *Dictionary of Biblical Interpretation* (ed. by J. Hayes; Nashville: Abingdon, 1999) 1:77-83, esp. p. 77.

[2] H. W. F. Saggs, *Assyriology and the Study of the Old Testament* (Cardiff: University of Wales Press, 1969) 4.

[3] Ibid., 8f.

[4] Ibid., 10.

[5] Ibid., 11.

[6] *RlA* 2 (1938) 198; cf. R. Lehmann, *Friedrich Delitzsch und der Babel-Bibel-Streit* (OBO 133; Freiburg: Universitätsverlag, Freiburg Schweiz; Göttingen: Vandenhoeck & Ruprecht, 1994). For the original, see F. Delitzsch, *Babel und Bibel. Ein Vortrag* (Leipzig: Hinrichs, 1902).

[7] Ibid., 38ff.

[8] "Jeremias, Alfred," *RlA* 5 (1976-80) 276.

[9] Saggs, *Assyriology and the Study of the Old Testament*, 12.

[10] Ibid., 13.

We now turn to more recent developments in the field. In his 1999 Presidential address to The Midwest Region of the Society of Biblical Literature, Mark Chavalas dealt with "Assyriology and Biblical Studies: a Century and a Half of Tension."[11] He "urged that the two disciplines continue to interact, as long as they retain their own methodology and autonomy."[12] He "traced some of the major developments of the relationship between the two fields since the discovery and subsequent decipherment of 'Babylonic' cuneiform in the mid-nineteenth century,"[13] outlining the results of recent finds from Ur, Nuzi, Ugarit, Mari, Alalakh, Ebla and Emar. With regard to Ur, Chavalas reviewed the question of the historicity of the biblical flood.

As for Nuzi, it has been "a source of documentation for the socio-economic practices in Mesopotamia."[14] A central theme in this area since the days of E. A. Speiser has been "The Wife-Sister Motif in the Patriarchal Narratives,"[15] though there have been re-evaluations since then.[16]

Material from Ugarit bearing upon biblical culture has largely been in Ugaritic — as opposed to Akkadian texts from Ugarit — and thus falls outside the purview of the present survey. As for Mari, it represents "one of the most important discoveries for Bible research," according to A. Malamat. He has sought to provide "a window on" and "view from Mari." He emphasized in the main "societal components - nomadic and sedentary modes of life" — as seen from the perspective of the tribal ambiance — and "aspects of West Semitic ritual" such as the institutions of prophecy and the ancestral cult.[17]

While evidence from Alalakh often does not relate directly to biblical materials, many have shown how it does shed some light thereon. For example, noting "Gifts of lands and towns" reported in both Alalakh Level VII as well as Joshua 13 (and Joshua 20 and 21), Richard Hess observed that "these gifts either are closely attached to or actually form part of treaty documents or divine covenants ...."[18] M. Tsevat wished to emphasize just such a comparison: Part II of his article on "Alalakhiana" ("The Alalakh Texts — The Language of Canaan — The Bible") was "written with the biblical scholar in mind. There I put down what I think is of interest in the Alalakh texts to Canaanite linguistic and Hebrew literary studies."[19]

Robert D. Biggs' "The Ebla Tablets. An Interim Perspective" helped clarify the relevance of the Ebla texts to biblical material with the following caveat: "Ebla has indeed opened up new vistas. I would stress again, however, that in my opinion, the Ebla tablets will have no *special* relevance for our understanding of the Old Testament."[20]

Daniel Fleming has noted that "Emar's rich collection of cuneiform tablets ... may offer a closer social comparison for biblical Israel than those of the Ugaritic city-state ... Emar ritual texts inform us about the community's calendrical practices, patterns of festival construction, anointing practices, and rites for the dead. For the study of ancient Israelite worship Emar now challenges Ugarit's preeminence."[21] Two recent dissertations on Emar, by Jan Gallagher and Tim Undheim respectively, are also worthy of note.[22]

The tablets from El Amarna play an important role in our understanding of the impact of Assyriology upon Biblical Studies. In a correspondence spanning "at most about thirty years, perhaps only fifteen or so,"[23] especially that of the Egyptian vassals, we glean priceless information about the history, language and politics of the ancient Near East in an age marked by international diplomacy. With regard to the language of these vassals, Anson Rainey has stated: "... the Amarna texts, especially those from Canaan, were a vital source for linguistic, social, historical and geographic information about the ancient inhabitants of the land of Canaan."[24]

---

[11] Meeting jointly with the Middle West Branch of the American Oriental Society and of the American Schools of Oriental Research. The address was delivered by Gordon D. Young.

[12] "Assyriology and Biblical Studies: a Century and a Half of Tension," (MS) 3. See now *Mesopotamia and the Bible: Comparative Explorations* (ed. by M. W. Chavalas and K. L. Younger, Jr.; JSOTSup 341; Sheffield: Sheffield Academic Press, 2002) 21-67, esp. p. 23.

[13] Ibid., 23f.

[14] Ibid., 53f., note 120.

[15] Reprinted in E. A. Speiser, *Oriental and Biblical Studies* (Philadelphia: University of Pennsylvania, 1967) 62-82.

[16] See, for example, S. Greengus, "The Wife-Sister Motif," *HUCA* 46 (1975) 5-31 and B. Eichler, "Nuzi and the Bible," in *Studies Sjöberg*, 107-119.

[17] A. Malamat, *Mari and the Early Israelite Experience* (Schweich Lectures 1984; Oxford: Oxford University Press, 1989); idem, *Mari and the Bible* (Leiden: Brill, 1998).

[18] *COS* 2.127-129, esp. p. 329.

[19] M. Tsevat, "Alalakhiana," *HUCA* 29 (1958) 109-134, esp. p. 110.

[20] *BA* 43/2 (1980) 76-87, esp. p. 85.

[21] Fleming, "More Help from Syria: Introducing Emar to Biblical Study," *BA* 58/3 (1995) 125, 139-147, esp. p. 125.

[22] J. Gallagher, *Emar: Study of a Crossroads City* (Ph.D. dissertation. Hebrew Union College - Jewish Institute of Religion; Cincinnati, 1998); Timothy Undheim, *The Last Wills and Testaments of the Late Bronze Age Middle Euphrates Compared With their Ancient Near Eastern Analogues* (Ph.D. dissertation. Hebrew Union College - Jewish Institute of Religion; Cincinnati, 2001).

[23] W. L. Moran, *The Amarna Letters* (Baltimore: The Johns Hopkins University Press, 1992) xxxiv.

[24] A. F. Rainey, *Canaanite in the Amarna Tablets. A Linguistic Analysis of the Mixed Dialect used by the Scribes from Canaan* (4 vols. HdO 25; Leiden: Brill, 1996) 1:xxiii.

As we move into the later periods of Near Eastern antiquity, the links with the Hebrew Bible become more explicit. Many important contributions have appeared in recent years on both sides of the equation.

For a convenient presentation of matters from the side of the biblical world in a field that is fast-moving and has a high volume of new literature each year, David Baker and Bill T. Arnold have produced a volume on "the present state of Old Testament scholarship." It provides up-to-date information as well as valuable bibliographies with many chapters worthwhile for those biblicists who wish to see the Hebrew Bible in its Ancient Near Eastern context.[25]

Hayim Tadmor, who has devoted himself primarily to Assyrian history and Ancient Near Eastern historiography, has edited several works in this area, including the *Encyclopaedia Biblica*,[26] whose entries often illustrate how Assyriological evidence helps to clarify biblical texts. The notes and comments to The Anchor Bible's *II Kings*, co-authored with Mordechai Cogan (1988), make it clear how problematic it is to understand historical sources such as Kings and Chronicles without benefit of Assyriological knowledge. Finally, *The Inscriptions of Tiglath-pileser III*, though demonstrating how difficult it is to arrange in order the Annals, Summary Inscriptions and miscellaneous texts, is nevertheless an indispensable tool for evaluating evidence from 2 Kings, Isaiah and Chronicles on the Assyrian ruler's campaigns.[27]

Nadav Naᵓaman has written extensively on the history of the Assyrian empire, its geography and relationship to events recorded in the biblical historical books.[28]

Recent works by K. Lawson Younger, Jr. addressed two central areas in which Assyriology has made an impact upon Biblical Studies: "The Fall of Samaria in Light of Recent Research,"[29] and "Israel and the Assyrian Exile: A Reassessment."[30] In the first article, Younger reviewed the evidence for the number of reconstructive theories: how many events surrounding the fall of Samaria are described in II Kings and how many claims can one find in the Babylonian Chronicle for the role of the conqueror? In the second article, Younger investigated "various filtering processes used by the Assyrians that determined deportee status, as well as the differences that the deportees' exile location made for their everyday lives." Younger also "examined the implication of these matters to ascertain the personal impact of these extraditions on the people of the northern kingdom" and "sought a more comprehensive understanding of the different levels of assimilation or acculturation to Assyria."

J. A. Brinkman's *Prelude to Empire* recognizes the impact of Assyriology upon biblical sources and vice versa, weighing them against Josephus' accounts of the relevant events.[31] D. J. Wiseman's contributions to our knowledge of the period of Nebuchadnezzar and the Chronicles of Chaldaean Kings have shed much light on the Neo-Babylonian period.[32]

When we turn from specific places and periods to the broader question of comparative institutions, it is well to keep in mind the strictures of William Hallo, who many years ago remarked to a student that in order to contrast or compare two things, one needed to know both sides of the equation. He therefore counseled his students that if they wanted to engage in this exercise they would have to know the two areas under consideration (in this case, Assyriology and Biblical Studies). In attempting to bring fairness and balance to this endeavor, Hallo addressed the issue of contrast as well as comparison of biblical with ancient Near Eastern institutions, beginning with the contrastive approach:

> ... a comparative approach that is truly objective must be broad enough to embrace the possibility of a negative comparison, i.e., a contrast. And contrast can be every bit as illuminating as (positive) comparison. It can silhouette the distinctiveness of a biblical institution or formulation against its Ancient Near Eastern matrix.[33]

---

[25] D. W. Baker and B. T. Arnold, *The Face of Old Testament Studies: a Survey of Contemporary Approaches* (Grand Rapids: Baker, 1999).

[26] 8 Volumes, completed in 1982 (Jerusalem: Bialik Institute).

[27] See, for example, H. Tadmor, "Tiglath-pileser's Campaigns against Israel 733-732 — The Textual Evidence," in *The Inscriptions of Tiglath-pileser III King of Assyria* (Jerusalem: Israel Academy of Sciences and Humanities, 1994) 279-282.

[28] E.g., N. Naᵓaman, "Historical and Chronological Notes on the Kingdoms of Israel and Judah in the Eighth Century B.C.," *VT* 36 (1986) 71-92. See also the Akkadian bibliographies of *COS* volumes 2 and 3.

[29] Younger, *CBQ* 61 (1999) 461-482.

[30] Paper delivered to the Middle West Branch of the American Oriental Society, Cincinnati 1999. See "'Give Us Our Daily Bread' — Everyday Life for the Israelite Deportees," in *Life and Culture in the Ancient Near East* (ed. by R. E. Averbeck, M. W. Chavalas and D. B. Weisberg; Bethesda, MD: CDL (forthcoming).

[31] J. A. Brinkman, *Prelude to Empire. Babylonian Society and Politics, 747-626 B.C.* (Occasional Publications of the Babylonian Fund 7; Philadelphia: University Museum, 1984) nn. 60, 242, 268, 580f.

[32] D. J. Wiseman, *Nebuchadrezzar and Babylon* (The Schweich Lectures 1983; Oxford: Oxford University Press, 1985); idem, *Chronicles of Chaldaean Kings (626-556 B.C.) in the British Museum* (London: British Museum, 1956).

[33] W. W. Hallo, "New Moons and Sabbaths: a Case-study in the Contrastive Approach," *HUCA* 48 (1977) 1-19, esp. p. 2.

Subsequently, he introduced the concept of the "contextual approach" to embrace both positive and negative comparison.[34] We turn then to five institutions illustrating the impact of Assyriology on Biblical Studies: law, the calendar, textual criticism, religion and satire.

(1) Law. In the field of comparative law, Martha Roth has collected and elucidated indispensable material bearing upon biblical topics such as for example, the *batultu*, *nu*ᵓ*artu*, the *nudunnû*, divorce and adultery, to mention but a few.[35] Her transcriptions, translations and comments relating to the legal material from Mesopotamia present the material in such a fashion as to invite comparatists to scrutinize it and its effect upon biblical law.[36]

Samuel Greengus addressed the issue of "The Wife-Sister Motif."[37] Some of the edifice built by the late Ephraim A. Speiser[38] has tumbled down to the ground but, by Greengus' estimate, perhaps some 50% still remains intact.

(2) The Calendar. In his chapter on "The Calendar," Hallo observed:

> In Mesopotamia, ... the month of twenty-nine or thirty days, based on the observation of the new moon, served as the basic unit of time. It was learned early on that a cycle of twelve or thirteen such months saw the recurrence of the same seasonal (solar) phenomena, giving rise to a year which was a compromise between lunar and solar considerations .... As eventually regularized, it provided for a thirteenth (intercalary) month in seven out of every nineteen years. This system, with minor adjustments, was subsequently taken over by the Jews together with the Babylonian month names and serves as the basis for the Jewish religious calendar to this day.[39]

Hallo went on to discuss the "The Hour," "The Week" and "The Era."

Adjustments made by the rabbis internally once the calendar was taken over from the Babylonians may have their bases in the earlier biblical period, especially when the Judean exiles began to absorb the culture of Mesopotamia after their exile in 587. Illustrative of these long-lasting links, B. Wacholder and the present author tried to show that:

(a) the system of sighting the moon in cuneiform literature was very close to that of rabbinic records.
(b) The standard 19-year-cycle emerged in Babylonia in 481 BCE after two distinct earlier stages had been passed through, beginning in about 747 BCE.
(c) The Talmud preserves the older system of observation of the lunar crescent, as it was practiced in Assyria and Babylonia.[40]

Michael Fishbane discussed the term "Sabbath" and its possible relationship to Akkadian *šapattu*. He argued that "the term and status of the day as one of special character were retained, but the astrological associations were truncated and given new religious significance within the week."[41] Saggs contended that "as an institution [Shabbat] neither derived from nor corresponded to the Babylonian *šapattu*."[42]

Writing in *The World of the Bible*, M. A. Beek stated:

> For the Seleucids themselves and also for the Jewish historiographers, a new era started with Seleucus I. The Seleucid calendar, also adopted by the writer of 2 Maccabees, begins in the fall of 312. For a long time this calendar has been determinative for the chronology, in some parts of the Middle East even until the modern age.[43]

Clearly without the benefit of the pioneering work of Assyriologists beginning at least as early as the 1890s, the thorough understanding of the ancient calendar characteristic of today's scholarship could not have been achieved.

(3) Textual criticism. As Alan Millard has observed,

> Although earlier copies of any part of the Bible are denied us, neighboring cultures can show how ancient scribes worked, and such knowledge can aid evaluation of the Hebrew text and its history.[44]

---

[34] W. W. Hallo, "Biblical History in its Near Eastern Setting: the Contextual Approach," 1-26, esp. p. 2.

[35] M. Roth, *Babylonian Marriage Agreements: 7th - 3rd Centuries B.C.* (AOAT 222; Neukirchen-Vluyn: Neukirchner Verlag, 1989) 3-9 et passim.

[36] M. Roth, *Law Collections from Mesopotamia and Asia Minor* (SBLWAW 6; 2nd Edition 1997; Atlanta: Scholars Press, 1995).

[37] Greengus, *HUCA* 46 (1975) 5-31.

[38] Speiser, *Oriental and Biblical Studies*, 62-82.

[39] Hallo, *Origins*, 120-143, esp. p. 121.

[40] B. Z. Wacholder and D. B. Weisberg, "Visibility of the New Moon in Cuneiform and Rabbinic Sources," *HUCA* 42 (1971) 227-242.

[41] M. Fishbane, *Biblical Interpretation in Ancient Israel* (Oxford: Clarendon, 1985) 149.

[42] Saggs, "*Assyriology and Biblical Studies*," 79.

[43] M. A. Beek, "The Seleucids: History of the Ancient Nea East from the Time of Alexander the Great to the Beginning of the Second Century A.D.," in *The World of the Bible* (ed. by A. S. van der Woude; Grand Rapids: Eerdmans, 1986) 332.

[44] A. R. Millard, "In Praise of Ancient Scribes," *BA* 45/3 (1982) 143-153, esp. p. 143.

He noted that "throughout the history of cuneiform writing there was a tradition of care in copying."[45] In this observation, Millard is carrying forward a theme broached by A. L. Oppenheim, who emphasized the element of conservatism characterizing Mesopotamian scribal activity:

> There is the large number of tablets that belong to what I will call the stream of tradition — that is, what can loosely be termed the corpus of literary texts maintained, controlled and carefully kept alive by a tradition served by successive generations of learned and well-trained scribes.[46]

In the spirit of the above remarks, i.e., with a desire to show how Assyriology — and especially an appreciation of Mesopotamian scribal practice — can illumine the textual study of the Bible, the present author offered the suggestion that a phenomenon preserved in the Masoretic Text of the Hebrew Bible entitled "Break in the Middle of a Verse" such as occurs in Genesis 4:8, 35:22 and elsewhere, might owe its origin to — or at least be clarified by — the Mesopotamian scribal practice of recording a "Break on a Tablet" by using words or expressions such as:

> *ḫīpu* "break";
> *ḫīpu 1 šumi* "break of one line";
> *ḫīpu labīru* "old break" and
> *ḫīpu eššu* "new break."[47]

This is only the tip of the iceberg. Thus, in order to make a sophisticated contribution to this area, one would have to have expert knowledge of Akkadian lexical texts and scribal tradition on the one hand, and a specialist's erudition in the study of the Masorah on the other. Either one by itself would be rare, both together would be rarer still. But the field holds enormous promise to anyone who would venture into it.

(4) Religion. Due to "the nature of the available evidence, and the problem of comprehension across the barriers of conceptual conditioning," Oppenheim put forth the proposition "Why a 'Mesopotamian Religion' should not be written."[48] Many scholars have had the suspicion that he was writing with tongue-in-cheek, since after stating this proposition, he proceeded to write a valuable chapter on Mesopotamian religion. He spoke about shrines and temples, statues of the gods, prayers and mythological and ritual texts.

Recent scholarship on ancient religious institutions has compared mythological elements — many of which have a Mesopotamian source — to some biblical traditions.[49] Other elements such as prophecy by various cult functionaries, especially at Mari, have been compared or contrasted with classical biblical prophecy.[50]

(5) Satire. One final issue concerns classics of the mythological tradition, such as the Babylonian Creation Epic. Does it represent "primitive" story or "elegant satire?" Oppenheim, always interested in the Babylonian Creation story, portrayed it thus:

> Shorter than the Epic of Gilgamesh, the Creation story ... has seven tablets ... [I]t tells the story of the theogony, the sequence of the generations of the primeval deities up to the birth of Marduk, who will assume the role of organizer of the universe ... *[T]he plot of the story is primitive*[51] .... When Ea, the wise god full of wiles and stratagems, fails, Marduk acts as savior and defeats the evil power in a battle against Tiamat, the monstrous personification of the primeval ocean .... The battle itself is decidedly not a heroic encounter but rather a contest of magic powers, in which Marduk, quite in style, wins by trickery.[52]

Benjamin Foster noted that "The poem is a work of great complexity and abounds with conceptual and philological problems."[53] Part of that complexity involves the dating of the text. Whereas Speiser had dated it to "the early part of the second millennium BC," W. G. Lambert held that "the traditions moved westwards during the Amarna period [fourteenth century BCE] and reached the Hebrews in oral form."[54] But part of the complexity involves the sophistication of the ancient author(s).

---

[45] Ibid., 146.

[46] A. L. Oppenheim, *Ancient Mesopotamia: Portrait of a Dead Civilization* (2nd edition; ed. by E. Reiner; Chicago: University of Chicago Press, 1977) 13.

[47] D. B. Weisberg, "'Break in the Middle of a Verse': Some Observations on a Massoretic Feature," in *Studies Wacholder*, 43ff. [For the "double accentuation" of Gen 35:22, cf. already Gesenius-Kautzsch-Cowley, *Hebrew Grammar* (Oxford: Clarendon, 1910) 63 §15p. WWH]

[48] *Ancient Mesopotamia*, 172.

[49] See e.g. Saggs, "Assyriology and Biblical Studies," 80: "Data bearing on foreign influences on Israelite religion."

[50] See Moran, "Divine Revelations," *ANET*[3] 623-626.

[51] Emphasis mine. DBW.

[52] Oppenheim, *Ancient Mesopotamia*, 264. For Gilgamesh, see *COS* 1.132.

[53] Foster, *BM* 1:352.

[54] W. G. Lambert, "A New Look at the Babylonian Background of Genesis," *JTS* 16/2 (1965) 287-300, esp. p. 300.

In a series of deft strokes, Herbert Brichto introduced readers to his technique of understanding stories dealing with the "Primeval History," including the creation story. Of special significance are "The Bearing of *Enuma elish* on Genesis I,"[55] and "Literalism and Metaphor in Genesis I and *Enuma elish*."[56]

In the latter, Brichto observed that we moderns would probably not fail to recognize the use of poetic language and diction were they used in the works of "a contemporary of ours. Yet in regard to the creation stories ... the overwhelming number of scholars assume that even the learned readership of these tales in antiquity would have accepted them on the literal end of the literal-figurative spectrum."[57] It is our contention that in *Enuma elish* too, the mythological material is to be taken figuratively and not literally.

In offering "A Poetic Reading of *Enuma elish*,"[58] in which the keynote of the reading is *Enuma elish as satire*, Brichto commented upon the "elegance of style" of the poem. He observed:

> When the choice diction and seductive rhythms of a resourceful stylist appear in a narrative, in elevated prose, or in epic verse, a critical alarm should sound for the reader if all this talent seems put to the service of nonsensical plot and idiotic personae. Is that author ... sending two different signals ...? for one audience made up of both dull-witted naifs and perspicacious sophisticates? ... the former would be reading the message as serious and straightforward ... the latter as tongue-in-cheek, perhaps bordering on comic; in short ... satire.[59]

They were lampooning the old gods and the old ways:

> ... the protean metaphors — of Tiamat as shapeless liquid mass, dragon-monster with two legs and gaping maw, human-like in maternal tenderness, black magician spewing incantations; of Apsu, also watery mass, cradling on his knees the childlike vizier Mummu, who embraces his neck, and ogre-father who would rather strangle his children than diaper them — are surely as meaningless as they are silly, an author's invention and not an inherited time-hallowed religious tradition....[60]

Why, one wonders, would the poet of *Enuma elish* resort to such bizarre and outlandish symbols to portray these supernatural beings? Brichto opines: "Could it be a playful and less than reverential attitude toward the gods that is responsible for the grotesquerie?"[61] Elsewhere he stated: "What we are suggesting is that perhaps a millennium earlier, in Babylon, a genius weaned himself from the outworn pagan creed in which had been suckled ...."[62]

Also of special interest here are "The Babylonian Flood Story as a Critique of Paganism,"[63] and "Noah's Deluge and Utnapishtim's: A Comparison."[64] An element of humor, a touch of the nonsensical, should hint at a point of view we would otherwise not glimpse: "A ship in the shape of a cube: this absurdity of nautical design is the clue to the larger design of our narrator."[65] The "comic-strip vividness"[66] shows us that some of this material was designed to be cartoon-like, yet we are treating it with a straight face.

Commenting upon the section containing the fifty names of Marduk, Brichto notes:

> The proclamation of his fifty names, ascribing to him the powers and attributes of the gods, comes across to us almost as a paradoxical paroxysm: polytheism straining for a monotheistic rebirth. In vesting all power and praise in Marduk, paganism comes close to abandoning polytheism altogether; like a number of hymns from ancient Egypt, it all but breaks through to a formulation of monotheism.[67]

As we continue to assess the Impact of Assyriology upon Biblical Studies, we cannot fail to note the sophistication of the pagan cultures surrounding Israel and their influence upon Israel. Nor should we fail to note the advanced nature of biblical society and its impact upon the surrounding peoples. Hopefully, we can do both these things while recognizing in these ancient cultures two features that are among the finest of our own: an open mind and a sense of humor.

---

[55] H. C. Brichto, *The Names of God* (New York: Oxford University Press, 1998) 37ff.
[56] Ibid., 50ff. For *Enuma elish*, see *COS* 1.111.
[57] Ibid., 50.
[58] Ibid., 53ff.
[59] Ibid., 53.
[60] Ibid., 55.
[61] Ibid., 56.
[62] Ibid., 126.
[63] Ibid., 125ff.
[64] Ibid., 161ff.
[65] Ibid., 117.
[66] Ibid., 120.
[67] Ibid., 400.

SUMER AND THE BIBLE: A MATTER OF PROPORTION[1]

William W. Hallo

The reviewers of the first two volumes of *The Context of Scripture* have been almost unanimously generous in their assessments of the project, its intentions, its scope, and its execution. But one point on which many of them have taken a more critical stance is the *title* of the work, and with it the notion that the (Hebrew) Bible should play so central a role in determining the selection of texts from five cultures that, in their own terms, existed quite independently of the culture that produced the Bible. The following is a sampling of the opinions on this score as expressed in the reviews.

> Herewith we have again come up against the sad topic of whether the texts offered really have anything to do with the biblical world, and whether they serve to illuminate it, if only *per viam negationis*.[2]
>
> ... I cannot help wondering whether this does not continue to betray the old philosophical presuppositions of *ANET* that the voluminous textual records of the ancient world are ultimately to be assessed according to their utility in elucidating the biblical text, that is, by a criterion outside their own purview.[3]
>
> Can we in good conscience regard the ancient Near East as primarily 'the context of Scripture'? ... it seems a little ethnocentric to describe the ancient Near East as primarily a context for a different book.[4]
>
> ... perhaps it is time to rethink one of the central criteria of selection ... — whether scriptural relevance is a necessary or altogether helpful criterion for inclusion into a volume of ancient Near Eastern and Egyptian texts.[5]

This chorus of courteous critiques calls for a response. It is reminiscent of the campaign to free Assyriology of its role as handmaiden of Biblical Studies and to recognize the *Eigenbegrifflichkeit* of ancient Mesopotamian culture. That campaign was launched 75 years ago, in 1926, by the late great Benno Landsberger. It insisted on studying the ancient cultures in their own terms. It was not enough to compile dictionaries of lexical equivalents to our modern languages, let alone cognates to other ancient (Semitic) languages. Rather, the very different semantic systems of the ancient languages had to be approached first of all through the discovery of a system of "autonomous grammatical concepts."[6] Only then could one move on to other manifestations of the ancient systems, such as their apprehension of space, or law and commerce. In the event, Landsberger practiced what he preached: he identified the basic grammatical categories of Akkadian and Sumerian which were then elaborated and justified by his students while he himself devoted the bulk of his own research to lexicography.

Landsberger laid out his programme in his inaugural lecture at the University of Leipzig, and then published it in a volume of the University's own new journal *Islamica*, in a special issue dedicated to the great Arabist August Fischer — all indications of the importance he attached to his remarks.[7] The term "Eigenbegrifflichkeit" was presumably his own coinage; one looks in vain for it in German dictionaries and despairs of translating it. I suggested "conceptual autonomy" in an article of 1973[8] and this was adopted by the team of translators when the original essay appeared in English in 1976.[9] The concept, if not the term, also informed his three seminal essays on the Sumerians

---

[1] Remarks delivered to the colloquium on "The Future of Biblical Archaeology: Reassessing Methods and Assumptions" held at the Divinity School of Trinity International University, Deerfield, IL, August 13, 2001.

[2] O. Loretz, *UF* 28 (1996) 792. (Translation mine.)

[3] N. Wyatt, *JSOT* 79 (1998) 168.

[4] R. S. Hendel, *Bible Review* 14/4 (August 1998) 16.

[5] G. N. Knoppers, *Review of Biblical Literature* 3 (2001) 88-91, esp. p. 91.

[6] Landsberger (below, n. 9) 63.

[7] "Die Eigenbegrifflichkeit der babylonischen Welt," *Islamica* 2 (1926) 355-372; reprinted as vol. 142* of the series *Libelli* (Darmstadt, Wissenschaftliche Buchgesellschaft, 1965) 1-18, together with a short "Nachwort" by the author (p. 19) and W. von Soden's "Leistung und Grenze sumerischer und babylonischer Wissenschaft" (pp. 21-133).

[8] W. W. Hallo, "Problems in Sumerian Hermeneutics," *Perspectives in Jewish Learning* 5 (1973) 1.

[9] "The Conceptual Autonomy of the Babylonian World," tr. by T. Jacobsen, B. Foster and H. von Siebenthal, *Monographs on the Ancient Near East* 1/4 (1976) 59-71.

which were published in Turkish and German during the thirteen years when he found refuge in Ankara (1935-1948).[10] In 1948, Landsberger received a call to the Oriental Institute of the University of Chicago where I had the personal privilege of studying under him for five years (1951-56). I learned to heed his strictures on the conceptual autonomy of each of the principal ancient Near Eastern cultures.[11] I even became the first of a line of assistants who aided him in his later years. But I chose to write my dissertation under another of my Chicago teachers. And I parted company with those who, in the name of his "Eigenbegrifflichkeit," went beyond merely ridding ancient Near Eastern studies of excessive or even exclusive preoccupation with their relevance for Biblical Studies and began to imply the irrelevance of the one for the other, throwing out the biblical baby with the Babylonian bath, so to speak.[12] My own career over the fifty years since I first entered Landsberger's classroom demonstrates that. This personal jubilee is then a golden opportunity to answer both the critics of *COS* and Landsberger and to make the case for "Sumer and the Bible."

Let me begin on the most obvious level, the case of literary borrowings or what in recent terminology is sometimes referred to as intertextuality. Here a case in point is the Preacher's saying "the three-ply cord is not easily cut" (Eccl 4:12). As first shown by Samuel Noah Kramer, the biblical use of this saying was anticipated by a passage in the Sumerian tale of Gilgamesh and Huwawa.[13] And lest it be said that the Sumerian text could not have been known to the biblical author, we can point to the subsequent discovery of the missing links, so to speak, in both space and time: the publication in 1959 of a fragment of the Akkadian counterpart of the story of Gilgamesh and Huwawa found at Megiddo, and in 1965 of a fragment of the Akkadian Gilgamesh Epic which includes the very same passage and relieves the translation of the earlier Sumerian version of any doubt that it is indeed talking about a cord as in the Hebrew and not a garment,[14] though I will admit that the latest translation of the Sumerian reverts to the garment.[15]

Moving upward on the literary scale, we can proceed from the isolated topos or (common)place to the level of whole compositions. Here, by way of illustration, we may cite another contribution by Kramer, the indefatigable recoverer and reconstructor of Sumerian literature. In 1955 he published a composition to which he gave the title "Man and his God," and the subtitle "a Sumerian version on the 'Job' motif."[16] And indeed it anticipates the biblical book of Job in content, raising as it does the perennial question of theodicy, the justice of God, and doing so by the example of the just sufferer or what, if that seems to beg the question of whether the suffering was or was not justified, can perhaps better be called the pious sufferer.[17] A number of Akkadian compositions take up the same theme; they are not simply translations or even adaptations of the Sumerian composition, but they fill the chronological interim, being attested for Old Babylonian, Middle Babylonian and Neo-Assyrian times.[18] Some of them, in addition, introduce the dialogue structure characteristic of the biblical treatment of the theme.

The next logical step in the literary progression is the genre, something to which the Sumerians were notably sensitive. Though they had no word for the concept as such, they did have a rich terminology of separate genres and were careful to indicate generic classification in the rubrics and colophons of individual compositions and in the literary catalogues which, often enough, grouped numbers of compositions by genre. I can again illustrate the point by appeal to proverbs, and will combine these here with the genre or sub-genre of riddles. Both proverbs and riddles are of course well-nigh universal genres, and often endure for millennia and across linguistic boundaries in either oral or written form. The Sumerian examples of both genres are the oldest known anywhere, and have a special connection to their biblical counterparts. I have already illustrated this for proverbs by an instance, not from the Book of Proverbs, but from Ecclesiastes. For riddles the Bible has of course only isolated examples, the most famous being the riddle posed by Samson to the Philistines. In his narrative, Samson even provides the name of the genre: *ḥîdā* (Judg 14:12-19). This is cognate with Akkadian *ḫittu*, and that in turn is the equivalent of Sumerian I.BI.LU.(DU$_{11}$.GA). The existence of the Sumerian genre-designation, and of examples of the genre so labelled, goes some way toward explaining the occurrence of a corresponding genre within biblical narrative.

A further example is provided by the letter-prayer. This genre, first recognized among Sumerian examples to be dated to the 20th and 19th centuries BCE, continues with bilingual (Sumero-Akkadian) examples from the latter second and early first millennia. It thus provides a possible precedent for the prayer of Hezekiah in Isaiah 38, there described as a "letter" (literally, a writing).[19]

---

[10] Translated by Maria deJ. Ellis as "Three Essays on the Sumerians," *Monographs on the Ancient Near East* 1 (1974) 23-40.

[11] Cf. Hallo, "New Moons and Sabbath: a Case-Study in the Contrastive Approach," *HUCA* 48 (1977) 1-18, esp. p. 2.

[12] Cf. e.g. A. L. Oppenheim, *Ancient Mesopotamia: Portrait of a Dead Civilization* (Chicago, University of Chicago Press, 1964) 21: "There are scholars who are inextricably entangled in attempts to relate Assyriological data to the Old Testament in some acceptable way, ..."

[13] S. N. Kramer, *JCS* 1 (1947) 40 *ad* line 107.

[14] A. Shaffer, "New Light on the 'Three-Ply Cord'," *EI* 9 (1969) 138f.

[15] D. O. Edzard, *ZA* 81 (1991) 202.

[16] See *COS* 1.179 for the latest translation and bibliography.

[17] G. L. Mattingly, "The Pious Sufferer: Mesopotamia's Traditional Theodicy and Job's Counselors," *SIC* 3:305-348.

[18] See *COS* 1.151-154.

[19] See *COS* 1.164f. and literature cited there.

We can go yet one step further in literary taxonomy and speak of coherent *groups* of genres. Here even our own terminology fails us and perhaps the term super-genre can be suggested — on the analogy of sub-genre — to cover the phenomenon. For when genres as diverse as myths, epics, and songs of praise are all labelled as "hymns" (ZÀ.MÍ) in Sumerian, we realize that such hymns are more than a simple genre. Or to take the more familiar case of the genres I have already delineated: proverbs, riddles, and "pious sufferer" compositions are readily recognized as forming a super-genre of "wisdom-literature." This term, borrowed from the language of biblical criticism where it has long been serviceable in linking the rather diverse genres represented by the books of Proverbs, Job and Ecclesiastes, reminds us that the relevance of Sumerian for Biblical Studies is a two-way street. Sumerian, however, adds other genres to the mix: fables, disputations, debates, and diatribes to mention only the most obvious.[20] And their rediscovery has led in turn to the recognition of comparable phenomena within the biblical corpus, albeit not in the form of discrete compositions, let alone whole books. I refer here to such pericopes as the fable of the trees and the thornbush (Judg 9:8-15) or of the thistle and the cedar of Lebanon (2 Kgs 14:9; 2 Chr 25:18). And long ago, it was pointed out that the Book of Job not only reflects the debate format in its poetic portions, but that its prose-frame too ends in the manner typical of some of the Sumerian literary debates: when the "friends of Job" acknowledge his rhetorical triumph, they do so by each presenting him with a gold ring and a *qᵉśîṭā* (Job 42:11) — and whether that is a coin or some other token gift can be debated, but it provides an interesting parallel to the gold and silver which Summer gives to Winter at the end of their disputation.[21]

The ultimate level of literary classification is the totality of sub-genres, genres and super-genres, or what I have long ventured to call the canon. That term had already been used by Landsberger at least as long ago as the "Eigenbegrifflichkeit" article of 1926, and at intervals thereafter.[22] In 1945 he spoke specifically of "the literary canon established in the Kassite period." The term was borrowed *not* from *biblical* criticism but from *general* literary criticism. In other words it was not a matter of investing the term with the overtones of the sacred and authoritative which adhere to the concept of the biblical canon, but of using it as literary critics do when they speak of e.g. the Chaucer canon to refer to all those compositions which careful study attributes to Chaucer.

Of course there are other differences between the biblical canon and the cuneiform canons. I summarized these a decade ago.[23] But despite these and other disclaimers,[24] the subtitle of volume I, "Canonical Compositions from the Biblical World," exercised the critics almost as often as the main title. Here again is a selection of their animadversions:

> Many students of the Bible (lay and professional), for whom the term 'canon' is associated with sacred texts that function as a permanent rule or standard for all, will be confused by this designation ....[25]
>
> ... the titles of the book are misleading. 'Scripture' and 'biblical' refer to the Old Testament alone, and 'canonical' is not used in the normal sense as when referring to the Bible.[26]
>
> Biblical scholars will have a different understanding of the term from that used by students of ancient Near Eastern texts more generally, and even there the term is not clearly defined.[27]

This cacophony of cavils notwithstanding, I maintain that there was a Sumerian canon or rather, over the millennia of the existence of the language, a succession of three Sumerian canons. I have identified these as the Old Sumerian, the Neo-Sumerian, and the post-Sumerian canon respectively.[28] Without repeating the details of their history, suffice it to say that each in turn formed the core of the curriculum of scribal schools wherever Sumerian was taught — often far from Sumer and ultimately long after the demise of Sumerian as a living language. The persistence of Sumerian compositions, sometimes with translations into Akkadian and other languages, at scribal schools in Syria — places like Emar on the Euphrates and Ugarit on the Mediterranean coast — to the very end of the Bronze Age in or about 1200 BCE (and beyond) provides the technical basis for at least their potential transmission into Canaan in the Iron Age and for the survival of Sumerian topoi, pericopes, compositions and genres in alphabetic scripts.[29]

---

[20] See *COS* 1.178, 180-186 for examples.

[21] Cf. *COS* 1.183:313.

[22] *Islamica* 2 (1926-27) 355 = p. 61 of the English version; *ZA* 41 (1933) 184; *MSL* 1 (1937) iii; "Die Sumerer" (1943) (above, n. 10) 99 = p. 27 of the English version; "Die geistigen Leistungen ..." (1945) (above, n. 10) 155 = p. 38 of the English version.

[23] Hallo, "The Concept of Canonicity in Cuneiform and Biblical Literature: a Comparative Appraisal," in *SIC* 4:1-19, esp. pp. 10-11.

[24] See now also my introduction to *COS* 2:xxi-xxii.

[25] D. I. Block, *Review and Expositor* 94 (1997) 607.

[26] W. G. Lambert, *JTS* 49 (1998) 210.

[27] D. W. Baker, *Ashland Theological Journal* 30 (1998) 106.

[28] Hallo, "Toward a History of Sumerian Literature," *Studies Jacobsen*, 181-203.

[29] Hallo, "The Syrian Contribution to Cuneiform Literature and Learning," in *New Horizons in the Study of Ancient Syria* (ed. by M. W. Chavalas and J. H. Hayes; BiMes 25; Malibu: Undena, 1992) 69-88.

But the contextual approach is not confined to the literary sphere. If it were, then *The Context of Scripture* could have ended with volume I. True, the soil of the Holy Land is singularly poor in monumental inscriptions from the biblical period; the possible reasons for this are discussed in the introduction to volume II. But there are ample biblical reflexes of the monumental category as defined in my taxonomy of documentation, i.e. inscriptions on stone, metal or other mediums designed to last into the future, or produced in multiple copies to the same end, or copied from such inscriptions. This definition, admittedly broad, makes room for such genres as law codes, known as inscribed on stone steles since the discovery of the Laws of Hammurapi on the great stele in Susa (along with fragments of two others) at the end of the nineteenth century CE. It also includes treaties, long familiar as carved on the walls of temples in Egypt but more recently seen to have been inscribed on bronze plaques deposited in temples among the Hittites. Both genres have reflexes in the Bible.

Specifically, the casuistic legislation of Exodus and Deuteronomy includes startling parallels with the laws of Hammurapi, sometimes explained as evidence that these laws, which survived to later periods as models of both Akkadian style and legal acumen, became known to the Israelites during the Babylonian captivity. But Hammurapi was preceded by and drew on earlier compilations, and these did not survive their immediate period of composition. When therefore we find closer parallels than with the Laws of Hammurapi between biblical legislation and the Laws of Eshnunna, as in the case of the goring ox, we can no longer content ourselves with the hypothesis of a sixth century date of transmission. Rather we may have to operate with the concept of an oral body of legal wisdom shared widely across the "fertile crescent" in the nineteenth century BCE — much as is Bedouin law in poetic form in the identical geographical parameters to this day.[30]

But the ultimate origins — or at least the first attested examples — of precedent law are, once more, to be sought in Sumer. While the Reforms of Uruinimgina (Urukagina) in the 24th century cannot claim to be casuistic or conditional in formulation, the laws attributed to Ur-Nammu (or Shulgi) in the 21st and Lipit-Ishtar in the 20th definitely can. It remains for future investigation to trace the chain of transmission by which Sumerian precedents passed via Akkadian, Amorite and Canaanite intermediaries to their Hebrew reformulation, but the connection is apparent.[31]

The chain is shorter for treaties. The "net-cylinders" of Enmetena (Entemena) have long been recognized as a sort of vassal treaty imposed by a victorious Lagash on its defeated neighbor state of Umma. More recently, the treaty of Ebla with a state variously read as A.BAR.SILA$_4$, Apishal, or even Assur has been found to represent the earliest known parity treaty. But neither of these 3rd millennium documents served as models for their respective genres known from the late second and early first millennia. It is the latter that influenced biblical formulations, for example in the introduction and conclusion to the "book of the covenant" in Exodus or the curse formulas of Deuteronomy.[32]

What then of archival documents, the titular topic of the last volume of *COS*? Long ago, there was recognition of "archival data in the Book of Kings" by Montgomery, and "the descriptive ritual texts in the Pentateuch" by Levine.[33] More importantly, however, Sumerian archival texts reveal *institutions* which have biblical echoes. Take the case of the "Sumerian amphictyony." Forty years ago, I used a Greek concept to characterize this Sumerian institution, leaving it to others to draw the logical implications for biblical history.[34] This was done most equitably, in my opinion, by Chambers in 1983.[35] Among Sumerologists, some like Maeda have generally supported the theory,[36] others like Tanret[37] have questioned aspects of it. The main challenge has come from Steinkeller and his student Sharlach, who have gone beyond the BALA of the provincial governors in particular to the BALA in general and have reinterpreted that as a redistribution system for agricultural products rather than as a specific means of channeling livestock to the sacrificial cult.[38] The basic link between the calendar and the provincial contribution known as BALA ("turn") remains unchallenged, however, and with it the potential link to Solomon's taxation system and its congeners.

Another example can be drawn from the sacrificial cult. Here the abundant Sumerian archival material helps to explain the comparable biblical institutions not so much by comparison as by contrast. Both cultures featured deities and temples, but while Israelite religion developed into monotheism with a single deity and, eventually, a single

---

30 See for now Hallo, *Origins*, 55, 245.

31 See *COS* 2.130-134, 153-154.

32 See *COS* 2.17-18, 127-129 and references there. For Apishal, see *COS* 3.90, n. 5.

33 J. A. Montgomery, *JBL* 53 (1934) 46-52; B. A. Levine, *JAOS* 85 (1965) 307-318.

34 Hallo, "A Sumerian Amphictyony," *JCS* 14 (1960) 88-114; cf. esp. p. 96, n. 72a.

35 H. E. Chambers, "Ancient Amphictyonies, Sic et Non," *SIC* 2:39-59.

36 T. Maeda, "Bal-ensi in the Drehem texts," *ASJ* 16 (1994) 115-164.

37 M. Tanret, "Nouvelles données à propos de l'amphictyonie néo-sumérienne," *Akkadica* 13 (1979) 28-45.

38 P. Steinkeller, "The Administrative and Economic Organization of the Ur III State: the Core and the Periphery," in *Centre and Periphery in the Ancient World* (ed. by M. Rowlands, et al.; Cambridge University Press, 1987) 19-41; T. M. Sharlach, *Bala: Economic Exchange between Center and Provinces in the Ur III State* (Ph.D. Dissertation, Harvard, 1999).

sanctuary, the polytheistic cults of Mesopotamia generated ever more deities and temples, 5580 of the former by one count[39] and 1439 of the latter by another.[40] The fundamental focus of the Sumerian cult was the cult statue of the deity, while the Israelite cult was fundamentally aniconic or even anti-iconic. The Mesopotamian cult involved first and foremost the "care and feeding of the gods" in the guise of their cult statues, as attested by thousands of archival account tablets best described as "descriptive rituals," i.e. after-the-fact accounts which describe in detail the expenditures incurred in cultic exercises against the possibility of future accounting to and auditing by higher authority. In the process they provide an invaluable objective account of what actually transpired as against the idealized and subjective instructions, not necessarily carried out, which characterize the canonical texts best described as "prescriptive ritual texts." We gain a better understanding of the distinctive procedures of the Israelite sacrificial cult in light of the archival texts from Sumer even where the canonical literature of both cultures assigns it somewhat comparable origins. In Mesopotamia, the sacrificial animal was first stripped of its entrails, including intestines, lungs, and especially the liver. All these were evidently considered unfit for consumption but instead became the basis for an elaborate system of divination by means of the *exta* (entrails) or "extispicy" and more especially by means of the liver ("hepatoscopy"). The rest of the meat offerings were offered in their entirety, ostensibly to the deity — but in actuality to the statue of the deity, which consumed nothing, leaving the meat thus sanctified to the priesthood and worshippers to enjoy. In Israel, the meat offering was divided in advance between deity, priest and worshipper, and the portion assigned to the deity was truly consumed entirely by fire, whose smoke went up to produce the "pleasant savor" for divine enjoyment; hence the meat sacrifice was called *ᶜōlāh* in Hebrew (something which *goes up*) and holocaust in the Greek translation (something wholly consumed, i.e. by fire).[41]

The foregoing has done no more than illustrate the proposition that, just as Sumer is relevant for the Bible, so too the biblical debt to, reaction against, or amplification of the themes struck by the Sumerian documentation help to illuminate the latter in crucial ways. "Conceptual autonomy" cannot, in other words, mean cultural isolation. The ancient Near East was a geographical unit; then as now, developments in one part spread rapidly and enduringly to other parts. The five linguistic cultures included in *The Context of Scripture* were inextricably linked with each other; the indices below help to make this clear. But they were also linked with biblical culture, which it is the special purpose of the middle column of each page to demonstrate. Cultural interdependence is not primarily a function of proximity, whether in space or time; it is rather a function of the degree to which the channels of communication are open across the frontiers of both space and time.

My personal response to Landsberger's "conceptual autonomy" is the "contextual approach," which I have defined in various venues as being made up in equal parts of comparison and contrast,[42] and of setting the biblical evidence both in its vertical dimension as the product of historical kinship with precedents, or intertextuality, and in its horizontal dimension as an expression of the geographical context in which it is set. But even this broad basis does not exhaust the possible analogies that can usefully be drawn from the evidence.

In his essay of 1926, Landsberger had used mathematical formulas to express the scope and limits of comparison. The English version of 1976 put it this way: "All understanding consists first of all in establishing some link between the alien world and our own. In the initial stage this is expressed by a number of simple equations, which are compiled in grammar and lexicon, e.g. ending *-um* [=] nominative singular, root *halak* [=] 'to go'; but such full equations are possible only to a limited extent, most often we have to content ourselves with partial equations of the type: part of Babylonian concept *x* corresponds with part of our concept *y*. All these equations are correct in so far as both *a* and *b* are beyond any doubt."[43]

Landsberger was talking about comparisons between Babylonian and modern (actually: German) concepts, but the same strictures would apply to comparisons with biblical evidence. A year later, though not necessarily with reference to Landsberger, I extended his resort to mathematical formulas to argue that if A is the biblical text or phenomenon and B the Babylonian one, their relationship can often be expressed mathematically as $A = B$, or $A \sim B$, or $A < B$ or $A > B$ or even $A \neq B$.[44] But even these more variegated equations do not exhaust the possibilities, limited as all of them are to two terms. Sometimes the analogy involves a relationship among four terms, e.g. between A and A_2 on the one hand and between B and B_2 on the other, or again between developments from A to A_2 in the one culture and from B to B_2 in the other. In such cases the analogy of the relationships or of the development can best be expressed by four terms in proportion: $A{:}A_2 = B{:}B_2$.

---

[39] Hallo, "Albright and the Gods of Mesopotamia," *BA* 56/1 (1993) 18-24, esp. p. 21.

[40] A. R. George, *House Most High: the Temples of Ancient* (Mesopotamian Civilizations 5; Winona Lake, IN: Eisenbrauns, 1993) 171.

[41] Hallo, *Origins*, 212-221.

[42] For the latter see above, n. 11.

[43] Landsberger 1976:62. The confusion between *x* and *y*, *a* and *b* is in the original.

[44] See above, n. 11.

A first example of this sort that I came up with was drawn from Akkadian rather than Sumerian evidence. It involved the relationship between the Laws of Hammurapi and the Edicts of his successors on the one hand, and between the biblical laws of the Sabbatical and the post-biblical institution of the *prosbol* on the other.[45]

Other examples could be cited to illustrate the inherent potential of this "proportionate technique." In terms of Sumerian, one can support the concept of a Sumerian amphictyony[46] by appeal to more recent history. Its calendaric basis is paralleled by the Greek institution, by the Solomonic administrative system of taxation (of the northern tribes), and by a contemporary Egyptian system. But beyond its purely fiscal aspect, the Solomonic system also pursued a political agenda. It served to break up the old tribal boundaries and therewith attempted to strike a blow at old tribal loyalties. It may have represented a clever attempt — ultimately unsuccessful — to centralize royal power in Jerusalem by using the outward form of a traditional intertribal cultic institution to mitigate the real threat to tribal identity implied in the abrogation of the old borders. I have always thought of it as an analogy to the French Revolution, which sought — more successfully — to destroy old provincial boundaries and loyalties by creating smaller and more numerous *départements* on a purely mechanical basis. Among the proposals put forward in the Constitutional Assembly of 1789-90, there was even one to subdivide France into "eighty rectangular departments, each with a half-diagonal of eleven to twelve leagues, (which) would permit travelers from any point to reach the administrative center in a day's journey."[47] We could thus set up a proportion:

> pre-monarchic tribal lands : Solomonic administrative districts =
> pre-revolutionary French provinces : French *départements*.

The proportion lends support to the older theories of a pre-monarchic tribal league, now not much in favor. But it does not stand or fall with these theories.

Moving beyond the Sumerian evidence, we can cite the debate on history and tradition. To my knowledge, this began with Redford's study of the Hyksos.[48] It was taken up with enthusiasm by Van Seters, whose dissertation dealt with the Hyksos, but who applied the concept more particularly to patriarchal traditions.[49] I resisted this approach, on the grounds and to the extent that Mesopotamian historiography seemed at the time exempt from it. That has since ceased to be the case, notably with respect to the traditions about Sargon of Akkad and the rest of the Old Akkadian period, an expansion of the concept to which I have taken exception more recently.[50] But whatever one's stand, it is possible to set up another proportion, according to which, arguably,

> Sargonic history : Sargonic tradition =
> patriarchal history : patriarchal tradition =
> Hyksos history : Hyksos tradition.

If the premises of the proportionate technique are granted, then it furnishes a further avenue for overcoming the problems of distance in time and space and for breathing new life into the contextual approach.

---

[45] Hallo, "Slave Release in the Biblical World in Light of a New Text," *Studies Greenfield*, 79-93, esp. pp. 92f.; cf. *COS* 2.134 and references there.

[46] Above, at nn. 34-38.

[47] T. W. Margadant, *Urban Rivalries in the French Revolution* (Princeton: Princeton University Press, 1992) 103.

[48] D. B. Redford, "The Hyksos Invasion in History and Tradition," *Or* 39 (1970) 1-51.

[49] J. van Seters, *Abraham in History and Tradition* (New Haven: Yale University Press, 1975).

[50] Hallo, "New Directions in Historiography (Mesopotamia and Israel)," in *Studies Römer*, 109-128; "Polymnia and Clio," in *Historiography in the Cuneiform World* (*RAI* 45/1; 2001) 195-209.

EGYPTIAN ARCHIVAL DOCUMENTS

A. LETTERS

1. MIDDLE KINGDOM LETTERS

THE HEQANAKHT LETTERS (3.1)

James P. Allen

The three letters translated here provide a unique glimpse into the life of a middle-class Egyptian family of the early Middle Kingdom. They were written by a ka-servant named Heqanakht, who served the mortuary cult of an official's tomb in Thebes, probably during the first decade of the reign of Senwosret I, second king of the 12th Dynasty (ca. 1971-1926 BCE). The letters, along with a number of Heqanakht's accounts and some scribal equipment, were stored in an adjacent, unused tomb. When the latter was used for a burial, apparently during Heqanakht's absence, the documents were sealed up behind a wall used to block access to the burial chamber. As a result, the letters were never sent and remained undisturbed until their discovery by an expedition of the Metropolitan Museum of Art in 1922. With the exception of one account, all the documents are now in the collection of the Metropolitan Museum.

The letters were intended for delivery to Heqanakht's home in the north, probably near Memphis or Herakleopolis, and were written within a few days of one another in response to news brought by one of his employees. At the time of writing, in May, the grain harvest in Heqanakht's fields had just ended, with a yield lower than normal as the result of a low inundation the previous year. Since grain, particularly barley, was the preferred medium of exchange, Heqanakht was faced with the need to stretch his resources over the year ahead until the next harvest, anticipating the possibility that another low inundation in the coming summer would produce an equally poor harvest. His letters concern the three options open to him: reducing his household's monthly salaries (paid in barley), collecting grain debts owed him, and renting more land to farm.

Each of the three letters is primarily concerned with one of these options. Letter I, written to one of Heqanakht's overseers, contains instructions for leasing additional fields for the coming agricultural season. In Letter II Heqanakht first addresses his household as a whole, detailing the salary reduction for each individual; he then speaks to two of his overseers, with instructions for the distribution of the salaries and an addendum on the leasing of farmland. Both letters also deal with domestic disputes, particularly the treatment of Heqanakht's wife, who was apparently an unwelcome newcomer to the family. Letter III is addressed to a high official in a village near Heqanakht's home, asking him to assist the two men who will negotiate for new land leases by facilitating their collection of grain debts owed Heqanakht. The debts themselves are further specified in one of Heqanakht's accounts.

The language of Letters I-II is probably close to the colloquial of Heqanakht's own dialect; epigraphic features indicate that they were written by Heqanakht himself. Letter III, more formal in tone, is couched in the standard literary dialect of the time and was written for Heqanakht by another scribe.

LETTER I (3.1A)

(vo. 18-19) From ka-servant Heqanakht to his household of Sidder Grove.[1]

(ro. 1) To be said by ka-servant[2] Heqanakht to Merisu.[3] As for every part of our land that is inundated,[4] you are the one who plows it — take heed — and all my people as well as you. Look, I hold you responsible. Be very diligent in plowing. Mind you that my seed-grain is watched over and that all my property is watched over. Look, I hold you responsible. Mind you about all my property.

(ro. 3) Arrange to have Heti's son Nakht and Sinebniut[5] sent down to Perhaa to plow a plot of land for us on lease.[6] They should take the cost of its lease from that cloth you have to be woven. If,

[1] Address written on the outside of the letter when folded for delivery.

[2] Priest responsible for the presentation of daily offerings and other services at a private tomb, as contracted by the tomb owner during life. Heqanakht acted as ka-servant in Thebes, probably for the tomb of an official of some rank, such as the vizier Ipi, in whose tomb-complex the letters were found. His letters were written from there to his home in the north.

[3] Probably Heqanakht's steward.

[4] Heqanakht is writing shortly before the beginning of the annual Nile flood in July, several months in advance of the planting season that began after the floodwaters receded.

[5] Two of Heqanakht's fieldhands. Letter II indicates that Heti's son Nakht was second in rank to Merisu, even though Letter III describes him as "the one who sees to all my property."

[6] Land leases of this kind were contracted in advance of use, for an annual payment of one-third the projected crop (see n. 10) or any com-

however, they will have collected the equivalent value of the emmer that is owed me in Perhaa, they should use it there as well. Should you have nothing but that cloth I said to weave, they should take it valued from Sidder Grove and lease land for its value. Now, if it is easy for you to plow 20 arouras[7] of land there, plow it. You should find land — 10 arouras in emmer, 10 arouras in full barley — in the good land of Khepshyt. Don't farm the land everyone else farms. You should ask from Hau Jr. If you don't find any from him, you will have to go before Herunefer.[8] He is the one who can put you on watered land of Khepshyt.

(ro. 9) Now look, before I came upstream here, you calculated for me the lease of 13 arouras of land in full barley alone.[9] Mind you do not short a sack of full barley from it, as if you were one dealing with his own full barley, because you have made the lease for it painful for me, being reckoned in full barley alone, not to mention its seed — although, when doing full barley, 65 sacks of full barley from 13 arouras of land, being 5 sacks of full barley from 1 aroura, is not a difficult rate, since 10 arouras of land will yield 100 sacks of full barley.[10] Mind you do not take liberties with its oipe.[11] Look, this is not the year for a man to be lax about his master, his father, or his brother.

(ro. 14) Now, as for everything for which Heti's son Nakht will act in Perhaa — look, I have not calculated more than a month's salary for him, consisting of a sack of full barley, with a second one of 0.5 sack of full barley for his depen-dents for the first day of the month. Look, if you violate this, I will make it on you as a shortage. As for that which I told you, however — "Give him a sack of full barley for the month" — you should give it to him as 0.8 sack of full barley for the month.[12] Mind you.

(vo. 1) Now, what is this, having Sihathor[13] come to me with old dried-up full barley that was in Djedsut, without giving me those 10 sacks of full barley in new good full barley? Don't you have it good, eating fresh full barley while I am *outcast*! Now, the barge is moored at your harbor,[14] and you act in all kinds of bad ways. If you will have had old full barley brought to me in order to stockpile that new full barley, what can I say? How good it is. But if you can't calculate a single measure of full barley for me in new full barley, I won't calculate it for you ever.

(vo. 5) Now, didn't I say "Snefru[15] is now an adult"? Mind you about him. Give him a salary. And greetings to Snefru as "Foremost of my body" a thousand times, a million times. Mind you, as I have written. Now, when my land is inundated, he and Anubis[16] should plow with you — you take heed — and Sihathor. Mind you about him. You should send him to me only after the plowing. Have him bring me 2 sacks of wheat along with whatever full barley you find, but only from the excess of your salaries until you reach Harvest.[17] Don't be neglectful about anything I have written you about. Look, this is the year when a man is to act for his master.

(vo. 9) Now, as for all the area of my irrigated land and all the area of my basin-land in Sinwi, I have done it in flax. Don't let anybody farm it. Moreover, as for anyone who will approach you (about farming it), you should go to Ip Jr.'s son Khentekhtai[18] about him. Now, you should do that basin-land in full barley. Don't do emmer there. But if it will be a high inundation, you should do it in emmer.[19]

(vo. 12) Mind you about Anubis and Snefru. You die with them as you live with them. Mind you, there is nothing more important than either of them

modity of equivalent value.

[7] About 13.6 acres.

[8] The official to whom Heqanakht writes in Letter III (*COS* 3.1C).

[9] About 8.9 acres. As opposed to other contracts, the lease arranged by Merisu apparently specified payment in barley alone (see note 6). This arrangement is "painful" both because of barley's greater value (see Letter III, n. 9 below) and because it negates Heqanakht's ability to negotiate for payment in some other commodity. "Full barley" is probably *Hordeum hexastichum*.

[10] This sentence reflects a rental fee of 5 sacks of grain (about 7.9 bushels) per aroura, one-third the projected yield of 15 sacks per aroura.

[11] The oipe was standard device for measuring grain, equivalent to 0.4 sacks (about 0.6 bushels).

[12] This payment is equivalent to the amount of the monthly salary listed for Heti's son Nakht and his dependents in Letter II, and apparently represents a reduction. The usual rate was 1 sack per month.

[13] Another of Heqanakht's men, and the family's scribe, who had evidently come from Heqanakht's home to Thebes with grain and messages for Heqanakht.

[14] Apparently a metaphor for responsibility.

[15] A junior member of the household. The greeting that follows suggests he was a son of Heqanakht. Cf. also 3.1B, n. 15.

[16] Another junior member of the household and perhaps another son of Heqanakht. He was probably older than Snefru, to judge from the order of their names in the salary list of Letter II.

[17] Barley harvest began in early February, some nine months in the future when this letter was written.

[18] Apparently a neighbor of Heqanakht. Letter II indicates that he had fields available for rent.

[19] Young barley plants do not do well in wet soil.

in that house with you. Don't be neglectful about it.

(vo. 13) Now, get that housemaid Senen out of my house — mind you — on the very day Sihathor reaches you (with this letter). Look, if she spends a single day in my house, take action! You are the one who lets her do bad to my wife.[20] Look, why should I make it distressful for you? What did she do against (any of) you, you who hate her?

(vo. 15) And greetings to my mother Ipi a thousand times, a million times. And greetings to Hetepet,[21] and the whole household, and Nefret.[22] Now, what is this, doing bad things to my wife? Have done with it. Do you have the same rights as me? How good it would be for you to stop.[23]

(vo. 17) And have a writing brought about what is collected from those (debts) of Perhaa. Mind you, don't be neglectful.

[20] The noun *ḥbswt* "wife" is used in this letter and Letter II with reference to Heqanakht's wife, rather than the normal *ḥjmt* "woman." It evidently denotes a second wife taken after the first had died or was divorced.

[21] Heqanakht's household had two women named Hetepet. The senior was probably an unmarried sister or aunt of Heqanakht; in the salary list of Letter II her name is second to Heqanakht's mother. The other Hetepet was Heqanakht's wife. The senior woman is probably meant here.

[22] The arrangement of names in the salary list of Letter II suggests that Nefret was a daughter of Heqanakht's wife, either by Heqanakht himself or a previous husband.

[23] The verb means lit. "be silent," indicating that the family's abuse of Heqanakht's wife was primarily verbal.

LETTER II (3.1B)

(vo. 5-6) From ka-servant Heqanakht to his household of Sidder Grove.[1]

(ro. 1) A son who speaks to his mother, ka-servant Heqanakht to his mother Ipi, and to Hetepet:[2] how is your life, soundness, and health? In the blessing of Montu, lord of Thebes.[3] To the whole household: how are you and how is your life, soundness, and health? Don't concern yourselves about me. Look, I am healthy and alive.

(ro. 3) Look, you are like the one who ate to his satisfaction when he was hungry to the white of his eyes.[4] Look, the whole land is dead and you have not hungered.[5] Look, before I came upstream here, I made your salary to perfection. Now, has the inundation been very high? Look, our salary has been made for us according to the state of the inundation, which one and all bear. Look, I have managed to keep you alive until now.

(ro. 7) Writing of the salary of the household:

Ipi and her maidservant	0.8 (sacks)
Hetepet and her maidservant	0.8
Heti's son Nakht, with his dependents	0.8
Merisu and his dependents	0.8
Sihathor	0.8
Sinebniut	0.7
Anubis	0.4
Snefru	0.4
Sitinut[6]	0.4
May's daughter Hetepet[7]	0.5
Nefret[8]	0.3½
Sitwerut[9]	0.2
Totalling to	7.9½ (sacks)[10]

(ro. 5b) When a salary is measured for Sinebniut in his full barley, it should be at his disposal for his departure to Perhaa.[11]

(ro. 24) Lest you get angry about this, look, the whole household is just like my children, and everything is mine to allocate. Half of life is better than total death. Look, one should only say hunger about real hunger. Look, they've started to eat people here.[a] Look, there are none to whom this salary is given anywhere. You should conduct yourselves with diligent heart until I have reached you. Look, I will spend Harvest here.[12]

[a] Isa 9:19; Mic 3:3

[1] Address written on the outside of the letter when folded for delivery.

[2] See Letter I, n. 21. The senior Hetepet is probably meant here.

[3] Heqanakht is writing from Thebes.

[4] The wording suggests that the reference is to a proverbial character.

[5] Heqanakht is writing some weeks after the annual harvest, which was evidently poor owing to a low inundation the previous year, causing widespread hunger. In Heqanakht's case the reduced crop has limited his barley reserves, occasioning the salary reductions detailed in this letter.

[6] A woman, perhaps a younger sister of Anubis and Snefru.

[7] Heqanakht's wife. The use of her father's name here distinguishes her from the other Hetepet.

[8] See Letter I, n. 22.

[9] Another female, perhaps a younger sister of Nefret. If so, the fact that she is not greeted in Letter I would suggest she was fairly young.

[10] The salary list originally totaled 7.9½ sacks (about 12.6 bushels). After the list was written Heqanakht emended it by reducing some of the salaries a total of 1 sack (Sinebniut from 0.8 to 0.7, Anubis from 0.5 to 0.4, Snefru from 0.8 to 0.4, Hetepet from 0.8¾ to 0.5, and Nefret from 0.3¾ to 0.2), but neglected to change the original total as well. The salary listed for Heti's son Nakht and his dependents here is approximately 80% of the normal 1 sack per month, suggesting that the other reductions were similar in scale.

[11] This provision was made for Sinebniut's salary for the mission ordered in Letter I. It was inserted here secondarily, after the salary list had been written, apparently because Heqanakht forgot to include it along with the salary specified for Nakht's part in the mission in Letter I.

[12] Letter II was written at the same time as Letter I, shortly before June (see Letter I, n. 4). The term "Harvest" is used both of a calendrical

(ro. 29) To be said by ka-servant Heqanakht to Merisu and to Heti's son Nakht subordinately. You should give this salary to my people only as long as they are working. Mind you, hoe all my land tilled by tilling. Hack with your nose in the work. Look, if they are diligent, you will be thanked and I will no longer have to make it distressful for you. Now, the salary I have written you about should start being given per month, on the first of the month, from the first of Khentekhtai-perti.[13] Don't be neglectful about those 14 arouras of land that are in pasturage, that Ip Jr.'s son Khentekhtai gave — about hoeing them.[14] Be very diligent. Look, you are eating my salary.

(ro. 34) Now, as for any possession of Anubis's that you (Merisu) owe him, give it to him. As for what is lost, replace it for him. Don't make me write you about it another time. Look, I have written you about it twice already.

(ro. 35) Now, if Mer-Snefru[15] will be wanting to be in charge of those cattle, you'll have to let him be in charge of them. For he didn't want to be with you plowing, going up and down, nor did he want to come here with me. Whatever else he might want, you should make him content about what he might want. But as for anyone who will reject this salary, woman or man, he should come to me, here with me, and live as I live.

(ro. 38) Now, before I came here, didn't I tell you "Don't keep a friend of Hetepet's from her, whether her hairdresser or her domestic"?[16] Mind you about her. If only you would be as firm in everything as you are in this. Now, since you apparently don't want her, you'll have to have Iutenhab[17] brought to me. As This Man lives for me,[18] I will speak out against the one who is discovered to have made any of my wife's business a matter of contention. He is against me and I am against him.[b] Look, that is my wife, and the way to behave to a man's wife is known. Look, as for anyone who will act for her, the same is done for me. Furthermore, will any of you bear having his woman denounced to him? Then I would bear it. How can I be in the same community with you? Not when you won't respect my wife!

(vo. 1) Now look, I have had 24 copper deben[19] for the lease of land brought to you by Sihathor. Now, have 20 arouras[20] of land plowed for us on lease in Perhaa beside Hau Jr., using copper, clothing, full barley, or anything else (to pay for it), but only when you have first collected the value of oil or of anything else owed me there. Mind you, be very diligent. Be watchful, now, and farm good watered land of Khepshyt.

b Gen 16:12

season and the natural period of harvest. The latter use is probably meant here. The calendrical season covered the months of August through November during this period (early Dynasty 12). In Letter I Heqanakht orders Snefru sent to him with a supply of grain "after the plowing." He is unlikely to have given this order if he had intended to return home at the end of the calendrical Harvest, since plowing would have begun in the following November, after the annual inundation had receded. Heqanakht is therefore referring to the natural harvest period, from the following February through April.

[13] Khentekhtai-perti is the name of the tenth lunar month. It began in mid-September.

[14] Heqanakht has apparently bought or rented pasture land from Khentekhtai, and has ordered it converted to crops, probably to compensate for the poor harvest just ended. The plot is approximately equivalent to 9.5 acres.

[15] Mer-Snefru is apparently the formal name of the individual otherwise called Snefru in these letters. Egyptians in the Middle Kingdom frequently had two names, one formal and the other more familiar.

[16] The context indicates that this is a reference to Heqanakht's wife, May's daughter Hetepet.

[17] Iutenhab is the formal name of Heqanakht's wife (see n. 15).

[18] This clause follows the format of Eg. oaths in the Middle Kingdom, which were sworn on the name of the king or a superior. "This Man" refers either to the king or to the tomb-owner whom Heqanakht served as ka-servant (see Letter I, n. 2).

[19] About 11½ oz. The exchange value at this period is unknown, but the instructions that follow suggest it was not sufficient to satisfy the entire rental fee.

[20] About 13.6 acres.

LETTER III (3.1C)

(vo. 3)To Delta-overseer Herunefer.[1]

(ro. 1) Funerary-estate worker, ka-servant Heqanakht, who speaks.[2] Your condition is like living, a million times. May Harsaphes, lord of Herakleopolis, and all the gods who are (in the sky and on earth) act for you. May Ptah South of His Wall sweeten your heart greatly with life and a (good) old age. May your final honor be with the life force of Harsaphes, lord of Herakleopolis.[3]

[1] Address written on the outside of the letter when folded for delivery. The title "Delta-overseer" denoted an official of the central bureaucracy who had responsibilities in Lower Egypt, but not necessarily one who lived or was stationed there.

[2] The designation "funerary-estate worker" reflects Heqanakht'e sphere of employment.

[3] These four sentences are a standard epistolary formula of the Middle Kingdom, used in formal letters such as this one. Their presence here is strictly pro-forma, as indicated by the fact that the scribe has omitted the ends of two of them (added in parentheses in the translation) at the ends of two columns of the text.

(ro. 3) Your humble servant[4] speaks that I might let Your Excellency[5] know that I have had Heti's son Nakht and Sinebniut come about that full barley and emmer that is owed me there. What Your Excellency should do is to have it collected, without letting any of it get mixed up, if you please.[6] And after collection it should be put in Your Excellency's house until it has been come for. Now look, I have had them bring the oipe[7] with which it should be measured: it is embellished with black hide.

(ro. 6) Now look, **15** (sacks of) **emmer**[8] are owed by Neneksu in Hathaa, and 13.5 of full barley by Ipi Jr. in Isle of the Sobeks. That which is in New District: owed by Nehri's son Ipi, **20** (sacks of) **emmer**; his brother Desher, **3**. Total: **38** (sacks of emmer) and 13.5 (sacks of full barley).

(ro. 8) Now, as for one who would give me the equivalent in oil, he shall give me 1 jar for 2 (sacks of) full barley or for **3 of emmer**.[9] (vo. 1) But look, I prefer to be given my property in full barley.

(vo. 1) And let there be no neglect about Nakht or about anything he comes to you about. Look, he is the one who sees to all my property.

[4] Lit., "the worker therein," referring to the designation of Heqanakht at the beginning of the letter (see n. 2).
[5] Lit., "Your Scribe, may he be alive, sound, and healthy," a respectful circumlocution for the second person.
[6] Lit., "like all your goodness, as you are alive and healthy."
[7] See Letter I, n. 11.
[8] The items in boldface are written in red in the original. Amounts of emmer were often distinguished from those of barley in accounts by the use of red ink.
[9] A sack of emmer was worth two-thirds that of barley. The capacity of the jar is unknown.

REFERENCES

Text, translations and studies: James 1962:1-50, pls. 1-8; Baer 1963; Goedicke 1984:1-85, pls. 1-8; Wente 1990:58-63; Parkinson 1991:101-107; Allen 2002:15-18, pls. 26-37.

2. NEW KINGDOM MODEL LETTERS

THE CRAFT OF THE SCRIBE (3.2)
(Papyrus Anastasi I)

James P. Allen

This extended model letter was probably composed during the early reign of Ramesses II (Dyn. 19, ca. 1279-1213 BCE). Its most complete copy occupies a single papyrus, now in the collection of the British Museum (EA 10247); 84 additional copies are known, all shorter or more fragmentary than Papyrus Anastasi I. The letter takes the form of one scribe's patronizing reply to his addressee's unwarranted claims of scribal learning and experience. Its purpose was both to expose young scribes to the harsh realities of military service and to educate them in the more advanced scribal arts, including practical calculations and foreign topography. Much of the letter deals with the scribe's military role as *mahir*, a Semitic term denoting an officer concerned with logistics and reconnaissance. In line with its instructional purpose, the letter is full of loanwords from Western Asiatic languages, which are transcribed in Egyptian by a semisyllabic orthography known as "group writing." The following translation reflects this feature by rendering the loanwords in the Egyptian vocalization indicated by their orthography; translations and cognates in the parent languages are given in the notes. The items in boldface are written in red in the original.

The letter is a literary composition, written in a form of the language that combines colloquial Late Egyptian with formal and grammatical features of classical Middle Egyptian. Its interest lies not only in its numerous Semitic placenames and loanwords but also in its vivid descriptions of contemporary Canaanite life and customs.

Salutation

(1.1) **The scribe of choice heart** and lasting counsel, whose phrases excite when they are heard, skilled in hieroglyphs and without ignorance,[1] ... Hori, son of Wenennefer, of the Abydene nome's Isle of Two Maats, born in the district of Bilbeis of Tawosret, chantress of Bastet in Field-of-the-God nome,[2] **greeting** his friend and accomplished

[1] A long series of laudatory epithets follows, omitted here.
[2] The writer's name, parentage, and provenance establish him as a mythological rather than real character. Hori is a diminutive of the name of the god Horus; Wenennefer ("continually young") is an epithet of the god Osiris, father of Horus, whose main cult center was in Abydos; Tawosret ("the powerful") is an alias of the goddess Isis, wife of Osiris and mother of Horus, who gave birth to Horus in the marshes of the Delta

brother, the royal command scribe of shock troops ...[3] scribe of recruits of the Lord of the Two Lands, Amenemope, son of the steward Mose, possessor of honor.

(2.7) **May you live, become sound and healthy**, accomplished **brother**, equipped and stable, with no "I wish" for you, having what you need of life in sustenance and nourishment, happiness and laughter joined in your path. ...[4]

Opening

(4.5) **Furthermore**: Your letter reached me in the hour of midday rest; your message found me reposing beside the horse that was in my care. I was excited and joyful and ready to meet it, and entered my horse-stall to read your letter, but found it had neither blessings nor rebukes. Your phrases are switched, this one with that; all your words are flipped and disconnected; your whole document is disjointed and unconnected; your very beginning [...; ...] mixed, applying the bad to the choice and the best to [...]. Your utterances are neither sweet nor bitter: all that has come from your mouth is emetic and honey, and you have taken pomegranate wine with vinegar.

(5.3) I wrote to you like a friend teaching one greater than him to be an accomplished scribe. Now as for me, since you have spoken I will respond, with cooler words than your utterance. You have treated me like one who is upset for fear of you, but I was never afraid of you, knowing your character. I thought you would answer on your own, but your supporters are standing behind you. You have collected many secret *ᶜadjiru*,[5] like those you would harness, with your face grim, and you stand cajoling backers, saying: "Come to me and give me a hand." You have set *birku*[6] before every man, and they have told you: "Steady your heart: we will overpower him." ...[7]

(6.8) Look, you are the army's command-scribe: what you say is listened to and not ignored. You are experienced in writing, without ignorance, but your letter is too much like that of an apprentice to command attention, and you have been misrepresented by your pointless papyrus. If you had known beforehand that it was not good you would not have sent it to speak so falsely of you. ...[8]

(7.4) **I will respond to you in like manner** in a letter, new from the first edge to the *qirr*,[9] full of the utterances of my lips, which I have created alone by myself, no other with me. As the life force of Thoth endures, I have acted by myself, without calling to a scribe for dictation. ...[10] My words will be sweet and pleasant in speech.[a] I will not do as you when you replied: you have begun against me with curses from the very beginning; you have not greeted me in the start of your letter. ...[11] I will make you a document like a diversion, and it shall become entertainment for everyone. ...[12]

a Ps 119:103; Pr 16:23

Response to Amenemope's claims

(10.9) **You have come** provided with great mysteries. You have told me a phrase of Hardjedef,[13] but you don't know whether it is good or bad. Which is the chapter before it and what is after it? You are a scribe at the front of his associates; the scrolls' teaching is engraved on your heart. Your tongue will glorify itself when you speak; one phrase will come out of your mouth worth more than 3 deben.[14] You threw a *ḫirfi*[15] at me to make me afraid. My eyes are clouded from what you have done; I am aghast, since you said "I am deeper in writing than the sky, than the earth, than the Duat, and I know mountains deben by *hin*."[16] But the library is concealed and unseeable, its Ennead hidden and far from [...]. Tell me what you know and I will respond, but beware lest your fingers approach the hieroglyphs. If an apprentice [...], being enraged like one who sits to play at Passing.[17]

(11.8) **You have said to me**: "You are not a scribe nor are you a soldier, and have made yourself the superior, but you are not on the list." Since you

(site of Bilbeis and Field-of-the-God nome).

[3] A short series of laudatory epithets follows, omitted here.

[4] A series of wishes for the addressee's well-being in life, death, and the afterlife follow, omitted here.

[5] *ᶜw-ḏ*ᵓ*j-rw*, plural of Semitic *ᶜzr/ᶜḏr* "helper": Hoch 1994 #108.

[6] *b*ᵓ*-jr-k*ᵓ*w*, plural of Semitic *brk* "gift": Hoch 1994 #129.

[7] A short section describing the addressee's "helpers" is omitted here.

[8] A short characterization of the addressee's letter is omitted here.

[9] *q*ᵓ*-[j]r*, probably Semitic *gly* "uninscribed edge": Hoch 1994 #427.

[10] A few sentences in the same vein as the preceding are omitted here.

[11] In a short section omitted here, the writer claims that he will not be affected by the addressee's taunts and curses.

[12] A long section omitted here describes seven despicable or ludicrous characters.

[13] A son of the 4th-dynasty pharaoh Khufu (Cheops), to whom a wisdom text of Middle Kingdom date was ascribed.

[14] The deben, a weight of copper (approximately 3.2 oz. Troy), was used as a standard measure of value.

[15] *ḫ*ᵓ*-nr-fj*, Semitic *ḥrp* "taunt": Hoch 1994 #340.

[16] Sky, earth, and Duat (the netherworld) represent the totality of the ancient Eg. world. For the term deben, see n. 14 above. The *hin* was a measure of capacity (slightly more than one pint). It was cognate with, but smaller than, the biblical *hīn*.

[17] "Passing" (or "Senet," Eg. *znt*) was a popular game. [See Hallo, *Origins* 115]. The lacuna makes the significance of its mention here unclear.

are a scribe of the king, who records the army, and all the [...] of the sky are unrolled before you, you should go to the place of the record-keepers, that they may let you see the box of name-lists, and once you have taken an offering to the *ḥarša*,[18] [b] he will open my report for you quickly. You will find my name on the list as a soldier of the great stable of Ramesses II, LPH, and you will learn of the command of the stable, with a bread-ration in writing in my name. Then I will be (seen to be) a soldier, then I will be (seen to be) a scribe, with no child of my generation to match me in distinction. Inquire about a man from his superior: go to my leaders, and they will tell you the report of me.

(12.6) **Again you have said against me**: "A high *harru*[19] is in front of you, for you have entered a wild *harru* without knowing it." If you had entered before me, I would have come after you. If only you had not approached it, you would not come near it. But if you find its interior when I have withdrawn, beware of giving your hand to take me out.

(13.1) **You have said to me**: "You are not a scribe, O empty, pointless name! You have taken the palette wrongly, without having been authorized." Am I a fool? Are you to teach me? Tell me the errors, you who know the explanation. You have harnessed yourself against me again another time. Your phrases are erroneous, and no one will hear them. Let your letters be taken before Onuris[20] and he will discern which of us is right, so that you may not be angry.

Problems in calculation

(13.4) **Another matter**. Look, you have come that you might fill me with your office.[c] I will let you learn your situation, since you said: "I am the command-scribe of the troops." But you were given a plot to excavate and you came to me to ask how to give rations to the people. You told me: "Reckon it," and abandoned your office, and teaching you how to do it has fallen on my neck. Come, that I may tell you more than what you have said. I will make you happy, and explain to you the command of your lord, LPH. You are his scribe and have been sent with responsibility for great monuments for Horus, the lord of the Two Lands.[21] Look, you are a learned scribe who is at the head of the troops.

(14.2) A ramp is to be made of 730 cubits, 55 cubits wide, of 120 *rigata*,[22] full of reeds and beams, of 60 cubits height at its head, its middle of 30 cubits, with a batter of 15 cubits, whose base is of 5 cubits. The bricks needed have been asked of the overseer of the workforce. The scribes are all assembled, without one who knows. They have all trusted in you, saying: "You are a learned scribe, my friend. Decide for us quickly. Look, your name has come forth. Let one be found inside the place to magnify the other thirty. Don't let it be said of you there is something you don't know. Answer us the bricks needed. Look, its site is before you, each one of its *rigata* of 30 cubits and 7 cubits wide." ...[23]

(17.2)[24] **You scribe**, sharp and elucidative, ignorant of nothing, who lights a torch in the darkness before the troops and makes light for them,[d] you have been sent on a mission to Djahi at the head of shock troops to trample those rebels called *naʿaruna*.[25] The archers that are before you make 1,900, with 520 Shirdana, 1,600 Qahaq, 100 Meshwesh, and 880 Nubians; **total** 5,000 in all, not counting their leaders. A *šarmata*[26] has been brought before you, of bread, sheep and goats, and wine, but the tally of people is too great for you and the things too few for them: 300 *kamaḥa*,[27] 1,800 *ipita*,[28] 120 various kinds of sheep and goats, and 30 wine. The army is many and the things underrated, as if you had stolen some of them. You have received them so that they are lying in the camp. The troops are ready and waiting. Partition them quickly, each man's share in his hand, for the Shasu are looking to steal them. O *tjupir yadiʿa*,[29] [e] midday has come, the camp is hot, and they are saying: "It is time to start." Don't make the commander angry. "Many marches are before us," they say. "Why are there no rations at all? Our cot is far off. What's with you, Who-Is-It,[30] [f] this punishing us, since you are a learned scribe? You

b 1 Chr 9:15; Ezra 2:52; Neh 7:54

c cf. Exod 28:11, etc.

d Ps 18:29

e Ps 45:2; 1 Chr 27:32

f Ruth 4:1

[18] *ḥw-jr-šʾ*, perhaps Heb. *ḥaraš* "cutter, artisan." The context suggests a term referring to someone entitled to open official documents: thus, perhaps, a scribe specialized in the fabrication and utilization of seals. Alternatively, a proper name (see note ***b***): Fischer-Elfert 1986:108 n. c.

[19] *hʾ-⌈rw⌉*, Semitic *hr* "mountain": Hoch 1994 #294. The term is used here as a metaphor for knowledge accessible only to learned scribes.

[20] A god, cited here as an authority for oracular judgment.

[21] A reference to the pharaoh.

[22] *r-gʾ-tjwt*, plural of Semitic *ryqt* "(hollow) compartment": Hoch 1994 #287.

[23] Two further problems, omitted here, deal with the erection of an obelisk and the labor needed to empty a storehouse of sand.

[24] For a discussion of the military rations in this section compared with 1 Sam 25, see Malamat 1956.

[25] *nʾ-ʿʾ-rw-nʾ*, Semitic plural *nʿrn* "special forces": Hoch 1994 #245.

[26] *šʾ-jr-mj-tj*, Semitic *šlmt* "delivery": Hoch 1994 #409.

[27] *kʾ-mj-ḥw*, Semitic *qmḥ* "wheat bread": Hoch 1994 #464.

[28] *jw-pʾ-tj*, Semitic *ʾpyt*/*ʾpʾt* "baked goods": Hoch 1994 #7.

[29] *ṯw-pʾ-jr y-dj-ʿʾ*, Semitic *spr ydʿ* "learned scribe": Hoch 1994 nos. 540 and 64. Cf. 1 Chr 27:32. The Eg. counterpart, *ẕhʾw sšʾw*, occurs later in this same section.

[30] I.e., "so-and-so," circumlocution for a specific proper name. Cf. Ruth 4:1: "... sit down here, So-and-so!" (JPSV)

should start to give us supplies, since the time of day has come, for the scribe of the Ruler, LPH, is absent. This getting you to punish us, it is not good, boy. He will hear and send word to destroy you."

The scribe as mahir

(18.3) **Your letter** is rife with cuts and loaded with big words. Look, I will reward you with what they deserve; a load is loaded on you greater than you wished. "I am a scribe and *mahir*,"[31] [g] you said again. If there is truth in what you said, come out that you may be examined. A horse has been harnessed for you, swift as a leopard, with red ear, like a gust of wind when he goes forth.[32] You should let loose of the reins and take the bow, so that we can see what your hand can do. I will explain to you the manner of a *mahir*, and let you see what he has done.

g Ps 45:2; Ezra 7:6

(18.7) You do not go to the land of Hatti; you do not see the land of Upi. Khadum's manner you do not know, nor Yagadiya either. What is it like, the Zimira of Ramesses II, LPH? The town of Aleppo is on which side of it? What is its river like? You do not campaign to Qadesh or Dubikh; you do not go to the region of Shasu with the archers. You do not tread the road to the Magara, where the sky is dark by day. It is overgrown with junipers and *alluna*[33] and cedars (that) have reached the sky, where lions are more numerous than leopards and bears, and surrounded with Shasu on every side. You do not climb the mountain of Shuwa; you do not plod with your hands on your legs, your chariot netted with ropes, your horses in tow.

(19.6) Hey, come that you may see Birata and make *ḥafidja*[34] from its ascent, having crossed its river. You will see what it's like to be a *mahir* when your *markabata*[35] is set on your shoulders because your aide is exhausted. When you finally unburden yourself in the evening, your whole body is crushed and battered, your limbs thrashed. You will lose yourself in sleep only to awake at reveille in the short night, alone at the harnessing, for no brother comes to (help) brother. The *naharuʾa*[36] have entered the camp, the horses are untied. The [...] has withdrawn in the night; your clothes have been stolen. Your *maruʾa*[37] has awakened in the night, learned what he did, and taken the rest. He has gone over to those who are bad; he has mingled with the Shasu tribes and made himself an Asiatic. The enemy has come to make *šadda*[38] in thievery and found you inert. You will awaken and find no trace of them; they have made off with your things. Now you know what it's like to be a *mahir*.

(20.7) **I will mention to you** another inaccessible town, the one named Byblos. What is it like? And its goddess? Once again, you do not set foot in it. Inform me, please, about Beirut, and about Sidon and Zarepta. Where is the river of Litani? What is Uzu like? They tell of another town on the *yumma*,[39] named Tyre of the Port. Water is taken to it in freighters; it is richer in fish than sand.

(21.2) **I will tell you** another subject. The passage of Zirʿam is difficult. You will say it burns more than a sting: how sick is the *mahir*! Come, put me on the road north to the region of Akko. Where does the way to Aksap start? At which town? Inform me, please, about the mountain of Wasir. What is its *rušaʾu*[40] like? Where does the mountain of Shechem start? Who can take it? Where does the *mahir* march to Hazor? What is its river like? Put me on the track to Hamat, Dagan, and Dagan-el, the parade-ground of every *mahir*. Inform me, please, about its road, and let me see Yaʿanu. When one is marching to Adamim, where is he facing? Don't withhold your teaching: let us know them.

(22.2) **Come**, that I may tell you other towns that are above them. You do not go to the land of Takhsi, Gur-Maruni, Tamintu, Qadesh, Dapur, Asya, or Hermon. You do not see Qiryat-ʿanabi and Beit-sopiri. You do not know Aduruna, or Zitti-padalla either. You do not know the name of Khalsa, which is in the land of Upi, a bull on its borders,[41] the place where the troops of every hero have been seen. Inform me, please, about the manner of Qiyana. Let me know Rehob, and explain Beit-sheʾan and Tirqa-el. The river of Jordan, how is it crossed? You should let me know the pass of Megiddo, which is above it.

(23.1) You are a *mahir* learned in the work of heroism. May a *mahir* like you be found to *sagga*[42]

[31] *mj-hʾ-jr*, Semitic *mhr* "logistics officer": Hoch 1994 #190. For the combination "scribe and *mahir*," cf. Ps 45:1, Ezra 7:6.

[32] A metaphor indicating that the addressee has gotten himself into a situation too difficult for him to handle.

[33] *jwn-rw-nʾ*, Semitic plural *ʾln* "oaks": Hoch 1994 #11.

[34] *ḥw-fj-ḏʾ*, Semitic *ḥpz/ḥfz* "flight in terror": Hoch 1994 #310.

[35] *mjr-kʾ-<bw>-tjt*, Semitic *mrkbt* "chariot": Hoch 1994 #189.

[36] *nhʾ-rw-jw*, perhaps a collective "refugees" from the Semitic root *nhr*: Hoch 1994 #255.

[37] *mj-rw-jʾ*, Semitic *mrʾ* "groom" or "squire": Hoch 1994 #173.

[38] *šʾ-dʾ*, Semitic *šdd* "assault": Hoch 1994 #418.

[39] *yw-mj*, Semitic *ymm* "sea": Hoch 1994 #52.

[40] *rw-šʾ-jw*, Semitic *rʾš* "head, peak": Hoch 1994 #285.

[41] Perhaps a metaphor for the scene of many battles: Fischer-Elfert 1986:187 n. e.

[42] *sʾ-gʾ*, Arabic *šaqqa* "trail-blazing": Hoch 1994 #382.

in front of the army. Oh *maryana*,[43] forward to shoot! Look, the face of the *murad*[44] is a *šadiluta* 2000 cubits deep,[45] full of scree and pebbles, so that you must make a *sawbib*.[46] You will take the bow and make a *pirtji*[47] on your left so that you might let the chiefs see. Their eye is good, and weakness is in your hand: "*abatta kama eri mahir naᶜimu*."[48] You will make the reputation of every *mahir* of Egypt who passes: your reputation will become like that of Qatsra-yadi, the king of Asuru, when the bear found him in the *bikaᵓi*.[49]

(23.7) The face of the pass is dangerous with Shasu, hidden under the bushes. Some of them are 4 or 5 cubits,[50] [h] nose to foot, with wild faces. Their thoughts are not pretty, they do not listen to cajoling, and you are alone, no *ᶜadjira*[51] with you, no *djabiᵓu*[52] behind you. You do not find the *irᵓir*[53] to make passage for you. The decision is made to go forward, but you don't know the way. Your face starts to *djanna*,[54] your head is *šalafi*,[55] your ba lies in your hand. Your path is full of scree and pebbles, with no toehold to pass, overgrown by *asbarru*[56] with dangerous *qadja*,[57] and wolfspaw. The *šadiluta*[58] is on your one side, the mountain stands on your other. You go in *hastakkata*,[59] with your chariot on its side, afraid to press your horse, lest he be thrown to the Duat. Your yoke has been thrown off and bare, your *kušana*[60] has fallen. You will unharness the team to renew the yoke in the middle of the pass, but you are not experienced in the manner of binding it, and do not know how to

h Num 13:32f; 1 Sam 17:4; 1 Chr 11:23

i Jon 1:3, etc.

j Exod 22:15f

refasten it. The *anqafqafa*[61] has been thrown from its place, too heavy for the team to bear. Your heart is disgusted; you will start to trot. When the sky is open (again), you think the enemy is behind you. You will start to tremble: if only you had a wall of shrubs, that you might put him on the other side. The team has been worn down by the time you find a cot; you will see the taste of sickness.

(24.2) You have entered Joppa[i] and will find the field verdant in its season. You will break through for food and find the little maiden who is guarding the garden, and she will fraternize with you as a companion and give you the color of her embrace. It will be perceived that you have given witness and you are judged with a *mahar*.[62] [j] Your cloak of fine linen, you will sell it.

(25.6) Tell me how you will lie down each evening, with a piece of *sagga*[63] over you. You will go to sleep exhausted and have stolen the bronze fitting of your bow, the knife of your belt, and the piece of your *aspata*.[64] Your reins have been cut in the dark and your team takes off, taking *maruᵓa*[65] on the *ḫirqata*,[66] the path stretched out before it. It will give your *markabata* a drubbing and make your *magasa*.[67] Your leather armor has fallen on the ground: it is buried in the sand and has become part of the barren land.

(26.2) Your boy will ask for the [...] of your mouth: "May you give a meal and water, for I have arrived sound." But they will play deaf and not listen,

---

[43] *mjr-ynᵓ*, Semitic *mryn* "knight" (from Hurrian *marijannu*): Hoch 1994 #175.

[44] *mwj-rd*, Heb. *morad* "slope": Fischer-Elfert 1986:196.

[45] *šᵓ-dj-rw-tjt*, evidently a feminine noun "ravine," perhaps related to Arabic *sadala* "hang down, lower" or Semitic *š.yrd* "lower": Hoch 1994 #419. The measurement is equivalent to 3,445 feet.

[46] *sᵓ-wᵓ-bᵓ-bᵓ*, Semitic *ṯwbb/šwbb* "drawing back": Hoch 1994 #360. In the context, perhaps "detour."

[47] *pᵓ-jr-ṯᵓ*, Semitic *prs/frs* "split": Hoch 1994 #155. The context suggests that this refers to the action of drawing the bow.

[48] *j-bᵓ-t kᵓ-mj jᵓ-jr mj-hᵓ-jr nᶜmw*. This sentence represents the Semitic utterance of the "chiefs" at the sight of the addressee's clumsiness in shooting. The Eg. writing leaves the translation of this sentence open to several interpretations (Hoch 1994 #6). In the context, the best is perhaps an ironic *ᵓbdt kmᵓ ᵓr(y) mhr nᶜmw* "You have gone astray like a ram, soft *mahir*."

[49] *bᵓ-kᵓ-jw*, Semitic *bkᵓ* "fruit tree": Hoch 1994 #141. The reference is evidently to a tragic or comical literary episode.

[50] Approximately 6.8-8.6 feet.

[51] See n. 5 above.

[52] *ḏᵓ-bᵓ-jw*, plural of Semitic *ṣbᵓ/ḍbᵓ* "troop": Hoch 1994 #573.

[53] *jw-r-jw-r*, evidently a word meaning "guide," perhaps from the Semitic root *ᵓwl* "first": Hoch 1994 #19.

[54] *ḏᵓ-n-nᵓ* "bristle" (of hair standing on end), perhaps related to Heb. *ṣeninim* "thorns" and *ṣenina* "prickly": Hoch 1994 #584.

[55] *šᵓ-nr-fj*, Semitic *šlp* "disheveled": Hoch 1994 #404.

[56] *js-bw-jr-rw*, probably metathesized from Semitic *brš/brṯ* "juniper": Hoch 1994 #29.

[57] *qᵓ-ḏᵓ*, Heb. *qoṣ/qoṣa* "thornbushes": Hoch 1994 #445.

[58] See n. 45 above.

[59] *hᵓ-st-kᵓ-tj*, metathesized from Semitic *htšggy* "careening": Hoch 1994 #302.

[60] *kᵓwj-šᵓ-nᵓ*, Akk. *gursanu/kušanu* "saddle pad, cushion": Hoch 1994 #453.

[61] *jwn-qfqft*, perhaps "chassis" (of a chariot), etymology uncertain: Hoch 1994 #15.

[62] *mj-hᵓ-jr*, Heb. *mohar* "bride price": Fischer-Elfert 1986:219-221. The passage evidently refers to a sexual dalliance that results in a "shotgun wedding," with the *mahir* forced to sell his linen cloak for the bride price: cf. Exod 22:15-16.

[63] *sᵓ-gᵓ*, Semitic *śq(q)* "sackcloth": Hoch 1994 #383.

[64] *js-pᵓ-tj*, Semitic *ᵓṯpt/ᵓšpt* "quiver": Hoch 1994 #34.

[65] *mᵓ-rw-jᵓ*, Semitic *mwrᵓ* "fright": Hoch 1994 #174.

[66] *ḫjr-qᵓ-{tj}tjt*, Semitic *ḫlqt* "slippery ground": Hoch 1994 #351.

[67] *mg-[sᵓ]*, Semitic (Heb.) *miqshah* "hammering": Hoch 1994 #229. This instance is not cited by Hoch, but the context and traces suit the other attested example of the word.

and don't heed your tales. You will be led instead inside the armory, where craftshops surround you and craftsmen and leathermen are in your path. They will do all you have wanted — they will take care of your *markabata* so that it stops being useless; your wood piece will be *garpa*[68] anew, and its sockets will be reset; they will give straps to your aft hand, seat your yoke, and set your chassis with metalwork to the *maḫita*;[69] they will put an *itjmaya*[70] on your *asbar*[71] and tie *matadjiᵓu*[72] on it — so that you may go forth quickly to fight on the battle-field, to do the work of heroism.

Conclusion

(26.9) **Who-Is-It**, you select scribe, *mahir* who knows his hand, leader of the *naᶜaruna*,[73] first of the *djabiᵓu*,[74] I have told you of the farthest lands of the land of the Canaan, but you do not answer me, good or bad; you do not report to me.

(27.2) Come, that I may tell you much of your [journey to] the fortress of the Ways of Horus. I will begin for you with the House of Ramesses II, LPH: you do not set foot in it at all, you do not eat the fish of its well, you do not wash inside it. What if I recall to you Husayin? Where is its fortress? So come to the Wadjet District of Ramesses II, LPH, its Stronghold of Ramesses II, LPH, Suba-el, and Abi-sagaba. I will tell you the manner of ᶜAynayna: you do not know its system; and Nakhasi to Haburta: you do not see it since your birth. Oh *mahir*, where is Raphia? What is its wall like? How many river-miles is it in going to Gaza? Answer quickly, give me a report, that I may call you *mahir* and boast to others of your name as a *maryana*.

(28.1) You will become angry with the speech I have made to you, but I am competent in every office. My father has taught me what he knew and testified to it millions of times, and I know how to take the reins much more than your expertise in action. There is no hero more distinguished than myself; I am experienced in the procession of Montu.[75]

(28.2) How damaged is all that comes forth on your tongue! How futile are your phrases! You have come to me *bindu*[76] in mixups and loaded with wrongs. You have split words in forging ahead, not caring whether you shatter them. Be strong and forward, make haste: you will not fall. What is he like who does not know what he has attained?

(28.4) And how will this end? I will back off now that I have arrived.[77] Submit, let your mind become weighty, your heart set. Don't get upset: let complaints wait. I have shorn for you the end of your letter and responded to what you have said.[78] Your reports are gathered on my tongue and stay on my lip, but are mixed up in hearing: there is no interpreter who will explain them. They are like the words of a Delta man with a man of Elephantine.[79]

k Gen 34:30

(28.6) But you are a scribe of the great double gate, who reports the needs of the lands, perfect and beautiful to the one who sees them, so that you cannot say "You have made my name stink"[k] to others and everyone. See, I have told you the manner of a *mahir*, gone around Retenu[80] for you, and assembled the foreign lands to you in one place, and the towns according to their systems. Would that you would see them for us calmly, that you might be able to relate them and become with us an esteemed official of the treasury.[81]

[68] *gᵓ-jr-pw*, Semitic *glb* "planed": Hoch 1994 #516.
[69] *mj-ḫj-tj*. The context suggests "undercarriage"; the etymology is uncertain: Hoch 1994 #197.
[70] *jw-ṯᵓ-mᵓy*, perhaps "ferrule"; etymology uncertain: Hoch 1994 #39.
[71] *js-bw-jr* "whip," perhaps from Semitic *prš/prṯ*: Hoch 1994 #28. [But note that Akk. *paruššu* is a loan-word from Sum.]
[72] *mj-tj-ḏᵓ-jw*, probably "lashes" (plural), perhaps from the root of Heb. *ṣirᶜah* "hornets": Hoch 1994 #233.
[73] See n. 25 above.
[74] See n. 52 above.
[75] Montu was the Eg. god of war.
[76] *bᵓ-⌈nd⌉w*, Semitic *bnṭ* "girded": Hoch 1994 #121.
[77] I.e., "I am finished expounding and have come to the end."
[78] I.e., "I could go on, but have curtailed my exposition."
[79] This sentence is evidence for dialectical distinctions in Eg. well before the attested dialects of Coptic.
[80] The Eg. designation for the Levant.
[81] Papyrus Anastasi I ends here. Another copy of the text continues with several more fragmentary lines.

REFERENCES

Text, translations and studies: British Museum 1842 pls. 35-62; Gardiner 1911:1*-34*, 2-81; *ANET* 475-479; Fischer-Elfert 1983; 1986; Wente 1990:98-110.

PRAISE OF PI-RAMESSU (3.3)
(Papyrus Anastasi III)

James P. Allen

The papyrus from which this letter is taken, now in the British Museum (EA 10246), is dated to the third regnal year of Merneptah, son and successor of Ramesses II (Dyn. 19, ca. 1213-1203 BCE). It contains several model letters and other scribal exercises, some of which appear in other contemporary papyri. The letter translated here celebrates the charms of the Ramesside capital Pi-Ramessu (House of Ramesses), the biblical Raamses.

(1.11) Scribe Pabes informing his lord, scribe Amenemope, in LPH. It is word sent to let my lord know. Another informing my lord that I have arrived at the House of Ramesses II, LPH. I have found it well very, very excellently. It is a perfect estate, without equal, with the layout of Thebes. Re himself is the one who founded it.

(2.1) The residence is sweet of life. Its field is full of everything good. It is in food and sustenance every day, its fish-ponds in fish, its pools in birds, its gardens flooded with vegetation, the plants of 1½ cubits,[1] the sweet melons like the taste of honey,[a] with fields of loam. Its granaries are full of barley and emmer: they reach to the sky. There are hills of onions and leeks,[a] groves of lettuce, pomegranates, apples, and olives, orchards of figs, sweet wine of Kankemet, surpassing honey. There are redfish of the canal of the Residence,[a] that live on lotuses, *bʾ-dj* fish of the riverway, various *bʾ-jr-y* fish and *bʾ-gʾ* fish, [...]-fish of the *pw-hʾ-jr-tj*,[2] mullet of the waterway [...] of Baal, *hʾ-wʾ-ṯʾ-nʾ* fish of the mouth of the waterway "Fig-tree" of "Great of Force."[3] The Lake of Horus[b] has salt, the Canal[4] has natron. Its ships set out and dock, and the food of sustenance is in it every day.

(2.10) Joy dwells within it and there is no one who says to it "I wish." The small are in it like the great. Come, let's celebrate for it its festivals of the sky and its season beginnings.

a Num 11:5

b Josh 13:3; Isa 23:3; Jer 2:18; 1 Chr 13:5

(2.11) To it come the papyrus-marshes with rushes and the Lake of Horus with reeds: shoots of the orchards, wreaths of the vineyards. To it comes the bird from the cataracts, that it might rest on it; [...] the sea with *bʾ-gʾ* fish and mullets. To it do their farthest regions direct offerings.

(3.2) The youths of "Great of Force" are in dress every day, sweet moringa-oil on their heads, with new coiffures, standing beside their doorways, their hands bent with foliage, with greenery for the House of Hathor, and flax of the Canal, on the entrance day of Ramesses II, LPH, Montu in the Two Lands, on the festival morning of Khoiakh,[5] every man like his fellow, saying their petitions.

(3.5) There is sweet mead of Great of Force. Its *dbyt*-drink is like *šʾʿw*,[6] its syrup like the taste of *jnw*,[7] surpassing honey. There is Qedy-beer of the docks, wine of the vineyards, sweet salve of Sapakayna, wreaths of the grove. There are sweet singers of Great of Force, from the school of Memphis.

(3.8) Dwell with sweet heart, promenade without straying from it — Usermaatre Setepenre, LPH, Montu in the Two Lands, Ramesses Meramun, LPH, the god.[8]

[1] Ca. 2.5 feet tall.

[2] A body of water, perhaps from Semitic *bhl* or *bhr*: Hoch 1994 #156.

[3] "Great of Force" (*ʿʾ-nḫtw*) was an epithet of Pi-Ramessu.

[4] *pʾ ḥw-jr* (Sem. *ḥarra*: Hoch 1994 #322). Name of a navigable, brackish body of water in the eastern Egyptian Delta, perhaps joining an arm of the Nile to the Lake of Horus.

[5] An Eg. festival, celebrated in the Ramesside Period in the latter half of the inundation season (autumn).

[6] *dbyt* was a beverage probably made from figs. *šʾʿw* is an unknown plant or fruit.

[7] An unknown plant or fruit.

[8] The pharaoh Ramesses II of Dyn. 19 (ca. 1279-1213 BCE), builder of Pi-Ramessu.

REFERENCES

Text, translations and studies: British Museum 1842 pls. 74-76 (1.11-3.9); Gardiner 1918:185-186; 1937:28-29; Caminos 1954:101-103; *ANET* 471.

A REPORT OF ESCAPED LABORERS (3.4)
(Papyrus Anastasi V)

James P. Allen

Like Papyrus Anastasi III, the papyrus from which this letter is taken, now in the British Museum (EA 10244), contains a number of model letters and other scribal compositions, some of which appear in other contemporary papyri. Since several of these, including the letter translated here, mention the pharaoh Seti II (Dyn. 19, ca. 1200-1194 BCE), the papyrus was probably written during his reign, but the mention of Regnal Year 33 elsewhere in the papyrus dates at least one of its compositions to the earlier reign of Ramesses II. The interest of this letter lies in its description of two laborers fleeing from Egypt through the northern Sinai. Although the fugitives are described only as "workers," their route suggests they were Asiatics rather than Egyptians, attempting to escape to Canaanite territory.

(19.2) Bowmen-chief Kakemwer of Tjeku[a] to bowmen-chief Any and bowmen chief Bakenptah in LPH, in the blessing of Amun-Re, King of the Gods, the life force of the King of Upper and Lower Egypt Weserkheperure-setepenre, LPH, our young lord, LPH.[1]

(19.4) I am saying to Preᶜ-Harakhti: "Make healthy Pharaoh, LPH, our young lord, LPH. Let him make millions of Sed Festivals,[2] with us in his blessing daily."

(19.6) Further: I was sent from the broad-halls of the king's house, LPH, on 3 Harvest 9,[3] at the time of evening, after those two workers.[b] When I reached the fortress of Tjeku, on 3 Harvest 10, they told me: "They are reporting from the south that they passed on 3 Harvest 10." When I reached the fort they told me: "The groom has come from the desert, saying: 'They have passed the wall of the Tower of Sety Merneptah,[4] LPH, beloved like Seth.'"

(20.3) When my letter reaches you, send word to me about the whole story with them. Who found them? Which squad found them? What people are after them? Send word to me about the whole story with them and how many people you had go after them. Farewell.

a Exod 12:37(?)
b Exod 14:8

[1] The pharaoh Seti II of Dyn. 19 (ca. 1200-1194 BCE).
[2] A royal festival of renewal, traditionally celebrated on the thirtieth anniversary of the king's accession and every three years thereafter.
[3] This date fell in mid-April during the reign of Seti II.
[4] The pharaoh Seti I of Dyn. 19 (ca. 1294-1279 BCE).

REFERENCES

Text, translations and studies: British Museum 1842 pls. 113-114 (19.2-20.6); Gardiner 1920:109; 1937:66-67; Caminos 1954:254-258; *ANET* 259.

A REPORT OF BEDOUIN (3.5)
(Papyrus Anastasi VI)

James P. Allen

This model letter is one of four unique scribal exercises compiled in a single papyrus, now in the British Museum (EA 10245). The opening protocol of the papyrus is dated to the reign of Seti II, but the regnal year mentioned in the letter translated here is probably that of his predecessor, Merneptah. The letter refers to the arrival of bedouin and their flocks from the northern Sinai desert at one of the Egyptian border fortresses erected during the Ramesside period. As such it reflects the careful control that Egypt exercised during this period on traffic in and out of the eastern Delta.

(4.11) Scribe Inena informing his lord, treasury scribe Kagab[1] [...] in LPH. It is word sent to let my lord know. Another information for my lord that I am doing every mission assigned me well and firm as brass. I am not being lax.

(4.13) Another information for my lord that we have just let the Shasu tribes of Edom[2] pass the

[1] Probably identical with the scribe of "The Two Brothers" (*COS* 1.40), written Kagab and Ennana there (see the colophon).
[2] See *COS* 2.4A, n. 1.

Fortress of Merneptah-hetephermaat,[3] LPH, of Tjeku, to the pool of Pithom[a] of Merneptah-hetephermaat,[b] of Tjeku,[c] in order to revive themselves and revive their flocks[d] from the great life force of Pharaoh, LPH, the perfect Sun of every land, in Regnal Year 8, third epagomenal day, the birth of Seth.[4]

a Exod 1:11

b Josh 15:9; 18:15(?)

c Exod 12:37 (?)

d Gen 47:4

(5.2) I have sent them in a copy of report to where my lord is, together with the other names of days on which the Fortress of Merneptah-hetephermaat, LPH, of Tjeku, was passed [...]. It is word sent to let my lord know.

[3] The pharaoh Merneptah of Dyn. 19 (ca. 1213-1203 BCE). Cf. *COS* 2.6.

[4] The beginning of the papyrus is dated to the reign of the pharaoh Seti II of Dyn. 19 (ca. 1200-1194 BCE). During his eighth regnal year (ca. 1193 BCE), the date in question fell around June 4th.

REFERENCES

Text, translations and studies: British Museum 1842 pls. 125-126 (4.11-5.5 = 51-61); Gardiner 1937:76-77; Caminos 1954:293-96; *ANET* 259.

B. CONTRACTS

1. SAÏTE DEMOTIC SELF-SALES INTO SLAVERY

PAPYRUS RYLANDS VI (3.6)

Robert K. Ritner

A cultivator Peftjauawykhonsu, attested in five papyri from El-Hîbeh in Middle Egypt, sells himself into slavery in return for payment and actions performed by the priest Nessematawy "in year 2 when I was dying."[1] Subsequent documents renew the initial contract and record temporary transfers of ownership. The self-sale documents are distinct from most slave contracts, in which the slave is treated as chattel rather than an active party in the transaction. In contrast, self-sales are perhaps best understood as voluntary debt-servitude, or as a means to ensure survival in difficult times. The wording closely parallels a Saïte "contract of sonship" in which the adopted party acknowledges receipt of payment and subservience to the buyer with regard to all children and property. In accordance with contemporary format, the initial contract of sale is followed by five copies written and signed by individual witnesses.

Regnal year 3, first month of inundation, of Pharaoh Ahmose,[2] LPH. There has said Peftjauawykhonsu son of Heribast, whose mother is Kausyenise, to the Comforter of the Father's Heart, Nessematawy son of Peteise, whose mother is Tasherentairna: "You have caused my heart to be satisfied with my silver-payment for acting for you as a slave. I am your slave forever. I shall not be able to act as a free man with respect to you ever again — up to and including all silver, all grain, and every manner of property on earth — together with my children who are born and those who will be born to us, and the clothes which are on our backs, and everything which is ours, and that which we shall acquire from regnal year 3, first month of inundation, onward to any year forever."

Written by the Comforter of the Father's Heart, Iahtefnakht son of Ienharou.

[1] P. Rylands V, l. 2.
[2] 567 BCE.

REFERENCES

Text: Griffith 1909:50-59, 213-15, and pls. xvii-xix.

---

2. DEMOTIC SELF-DEDICATION TEXTS

Robert K. Ritner

Attested from Memphis and the Faiyum during the Ptolemaic period, "self-dedication texts" date to the second century BCE. The texts show similarities both to the Saïte self-sales into slavery and to earlier oracular amuletic decrees issued by temples in the name of a protective deity. Amuletic decrees of the Third Intermediate Period (Dynasties 21-22) present the god as listing a long series of individual evils from which he would protect the supplicant. In the self-dedication texts, the supplicant offers perpetual servitude in exchange for similarly detailed guarantees. As a high percentage of dedicants are said to be fathered by "anonymous" (literally, "I do not know his name"), the documents have been considered evidence of temple prostitution. Deriving from the central temple archives of the Faiyumic town of Tebtunis, forty-four "self-dedications" are preserved in the British Museum on thirty-seven documents. Two representative examples of single dedications have been published by Herbert Thompson (1941), and these are translated below. A complete edition of the British Museum corpus is in preparation by W. J. Tait. Two further examples from Tebtunis with multiple dedications were published by Bresciani 1965. The more complete of these, P. Mil. Vogl. 6, is translated below. Additional examples have been identified in collections at Berlin, Copenhagen, Freiburg and Leipzig. For publication of the Freiburg and Berlin texts, see Daniel, Gronewald and Thissen 1986:80-87. For the amuletic decrees, see Edwards 1960. A further example from Cleveland will be published by Bryant Bohleke.

PAPYRUS BRITISH MUSEUM 10622 (3.7A)

Regnal year 33, second month of winter, day 23 of Pharaoh Ptolemy (VIII)[1] and Cleopatra the beneficent gods, descendants of Ptolemy (V) and Cleopatra the gods manifest, and of Queen Cleopatra his wife,[2] the beneficent goddess, and of the priest of Alexander, the savior gods,[3] the brotherly gods,[4] the beneficent gods,[5] the father-loving gods,[6] the gods manifest,[7] the god whose father is exalted,[8] the mother-loving god,[9] and the beneficent gods, who is in Alexandria, and of the bearer of the prize of valor before Bernice the beneficent goddess,[10] who is in Alexandria, and of the bearer of the golden basket before Arsinoë who loves her brother,[11] who is in Alexandria, and of the priestess of Arsinoë who loves her father,[12] who is in Alexandria.

There has said the female servant Tapanebteptem[13] daughter of Sobekmen, whose mother is Isetwery, before my master Sobek, Lord of Tebtunis, the great god: "I am your servant[14] together with my children and the children of my children. I shall not be able to act as a free person in your estate forever and ever. And you will protect me and you will save me and you will guard over me and you will cause that I be healthy and you will protect me from every male spirit, every female spirit, every sleeping man, every ghost, every magical practice,[15] every spoken spell,[16] every slaughtering demon,[17] every dead man, every man of the river,[18] every man of the desert-edge,[19] every demon, every red thing, every ill-fortune, and every pestilence on earth. And I shall give to you 1¼ kite — whose half is 5/6 kite — making 1¼ kite again, in copper at the rate of 24 to two silver kite as my servant-fee each and every month from regnal year 33 second month of winter until the completion of 99 years, making 1,204½ months, making 99 years again. And I shall give it to your priests each and every month without having caused the payment to be altered from one month to another among them. You and your agents are those who are entrusted regarding everything which has been said with me on account of everything which is above. And I shall do them at your bidding, compulsorily and without delay." Written by Pasy son of Marres.

[1] Ptolemy VIII Euergetes II; 137 BCE.
[2] Cleopatra III, daughter of the chief Queen Cleopatra II and secondary wife to her uncle Ptolemy VIII.
[3] Ptolemy I Soter and Bernice I.
[4] Ptolemy II and Arsinoë II Philadelphos.
[5] Ptolemy III and Bernice II Euergetes.
[6] Ptolemy IV and Arsinoë III Philopator.
[7] Ptolemy V and Cleopatra I Epiphanes.
[8] Ptolemy VII Eupator.
[9] Ptolemy VI Philometor.
[10] Princess Bernice, daughter of Ptolemy III and Bernice II Euergetes.
[11] Arsinoë II Philadelphos.
[12] Arsinoë III Philopator.
[13] "She of the Lord of Tebtunis."
[14] The addition of an "evil" determinative indicates that the nuance of "slave" is meant.
[15] Misread as "drowned man" by Thompson, the term is *heka*; see Ritner 1993:14-28.
[16] Lit., "craft of the mouth," see Ritner 1993:42-43.
[17] *ḫṯ*-demon; misread as *ḥms* "incubus(?)" by Thompson.
[18] I.e. "drowned man."
[19] I.e. "man of the cemetery."

PAPYRUS BRITISH MUSEUM 10624 (3.7B)

Regnal year 10, second month of winter, of Ptolemy (V),[20] son of Ptolemy (IV) and Arsinoë the father-loving gods, and of the priest of Alexander, the brotherly gods, the beneficent gods, the god manifest whose goodness is beautiful, and Pharaoh Ptolemy Eucharistos,[21] Zoilos son of Andron, while the lady athlophoros[22] Iamneia daughter of Hupermassas is the bearer of the prize of valor before Bernice the beneficent goddess, while the lady Purrha daughter of Philinos is the bearer of the golden basket before Arsinoë who loves her brother, and while Eirene daughter of Ptolemy is the

[20] 195 BCE.
[21] Redundant transcription of the Greek epithet for Ptolemy V, translated into Demotic in the preceding line as "whose goodness is beautiful."
[22] The transliterated Greek title redundantly translated as "bearer of the prize of valor."

priestess of Arsinoë who loves her father.

There has said the male youth, born of the staff,[23] I[mhotep(?)] son of anonymous, whose mother is Tasheramon, before Sobek, Lord of Tebtunis: "I am [your servant] together with my children and the children of my children and everything and all property [which is mine] and that which I shall acquire from today onward. And I shall give [2½] silver-kite as servant[-fee] before Sobek, Lord of Tebtunis, each and every month without my having caused the payment to be altered among them regarding me from one month to another. What is altered, I shall give [it together with its penalty of 1 at 1½] in the month that follows the said month, beyond the fee [that is above], without delay — while no demon, ill-fortune, destruction [...], sleeping man or man of the West will be able to exercise power over me and my [children and] the children of my children except you. I shall not be able [to act as a free person] with my children and the children of my children in your [estate forever."]

Written by Petethouty son of Petamon. Written by Sobek[... son of ...]

Written by Sobek[... son of ...] Written by [... son of ...]

Written by Pahapy son of [...] Written by [... son of ...]

[23] Reading *ḫ-pr*. Thompson read *ḫ-nmḥ* "born free."

PAPYRUS MILAN 6 (3.7C)

There has said the female servant born within the estate, Taamon daughter of anonymous, whose mother is Baket,[24] the one who says before Sobek, Lord of Tebtunis, the great god: "I am your servant together with the children of my children from today onward. And I shall give to you 2½ kite as servant-fee every month. No male or female spirit, sleeping man, ghost, drowned man, demon, ill-fortune or pestilence will be able to exercise power over me except you from today onward. I shall not be able to act as a free person in your estate forever."

There has said the female servant born in the house, Tasebek daughter of anonymous, whose mother is Baket, the one who says before Sobek, Lord of Tebtunis, the great god: "I am your servant together with my children and the children of[25] my children from today onward. And I shall give to you 2½ kite as servant-fee [every] month. [...]"

[24] "Servant."

[25] Mistakenly written "and."

REFERENCES

Text: Thompson 1941; Bresciani 1965:188-194; Daniel, Gronewald, and Thissen 1986:80-87; Edwards 1960.

C. COURTCASES

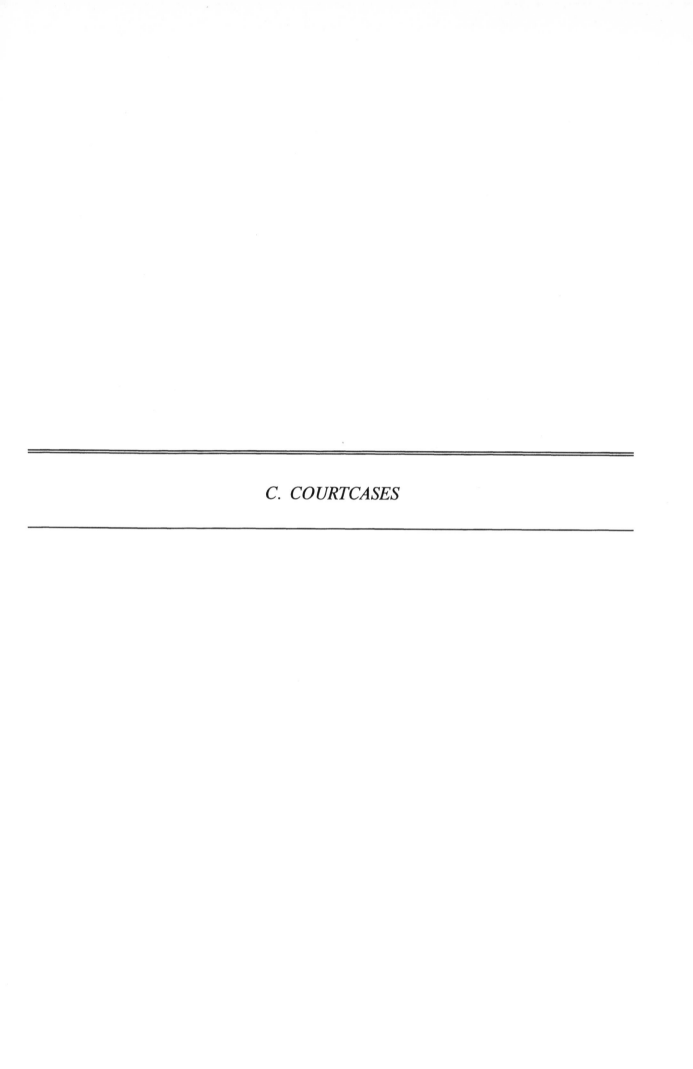

THE TURIN JUDICIAL PAPYRUS (3.8)
(The Harem Conspiracy against Ramses III)

Robert K. Ritner

At an undetermined point in the thirty-two year reign of Ramses III, a harem conspiracy led by a minor queen Tiye attempted to overthrow the king in favor of her son, prince Pentawere. The relative success of the plot is unclear. Pentawere was likely proclaimed ruler by this faction, since it is euphemistically noted that he was "called by that other name" (col. v.7). Ultimately the conspiracy failed, and those involved were investigated by a commission supposedly convened by Ramses III, who is however already deceased in the surviving records of the trials, being "among the righteous kings" dwelling with Amon-Re and Osiris (col. iii.3-4). Like the great Papyrus Harris, the posthumous proclamation of the trial records served to bolster the legitimacy of the dynastic victor, Ramses IV. Many of the guilty were executed, the more exalted being allowed to commit suicide. An unmummified body, seemingly buried alive in a wrapping of ritually impure sheepskin, was found among the cache of royal mummies at Deir el-Bahari and could well be the corpse of Pentawere.[1] During the course of the trials, three members of the investigating commission were seduced by women of the harem who turned the commissioners' office into a beer hall before the officers were themselves arrested and disgraced. Further documents from the trials describe the prominent use of magic in the conspiracy; see Papyri Rollin and Lee, *COS* 3.9 below.

[King Usermaare-Meriamon, LPH, son of Re, Ramses,] Ruler of Heliopolis, [LPH, said: "...] the land of [...] the land to [... thei]r cattle [...] to bring them to [...] all [...] in their presence [...] bring them while the [...] people, saying: [...] since (ii.1) they are the abomination of the land. And I commissioned the overseer of the treasury Montuemtawy, the overseer of the treasury Pefrowy, the fan-bearer Karo, the butler Paibes, the butler Qedendenna, the butler Baalmahar, the butler Peirsunu, the butler Djhutyrekhnefer, the royal herald Penrenenut, the scribes May and Preemhab of the archives, and the standard-bearer of the troops Hori, saying: 'As for the matters which the people — I do not know them — have said, go and examine them.' And they went and they examined them, and they caused to die those whom they caused to die by their very own hands, although I do not know them, and they inflicted punishment upon the others, although I do not know them either, whereas [I] had commanded [them strictly], saying: 'Be mindful and beware of causing someone to be punished wrongfully by an official who is not in charge of him.' So I said to them continually. (iii.1) As for all that which has been done, it is they who have done it. Let all that which they have done be on their heads, whereas I am exempted and protected forever, as I am among the righteous kings who are in the presence of Amon-Re, King of the Gods, and in the presence of Osiris, Ruler of Eternity."

(iv.1) PERSONS who were brought in concerning the great crimes which they had committed and put in the Place of Examination in the presence of the great officials of the Place of Examination in order to be examined by the overseer of the treasury Montuemtawy, the overseer of the treasury Pefrowy, the fan-bearer Karo, the butler Paibes, the scribe of the archives May, and the standard-bearer of the troops Hori.[2] And they examined them; they found them guilty; they caused that their punishment overtake[3] them; their crimes seized them.

The great criminal Paibakemon,[4] who used to be a chamberlain. HE WAS BROUGHT IN concerning the collusion that he had formed with Tiye and the women of the harem. He had made common cause[5] with them; he had begun to bring their words outside to their mothers and their brothers who were there, saying: "Gather people and incite enemies to make rebellion against their lord." He was put in the presence of the great officials of the Place of Examination; they examined his crimes; they found that he had committed them; his crimes

[1] See Andrews 1984:67-68. The corpse was the inspiration for the plot of the Boris Karloff film "The Mummy."

[2] Half of the commission is resident at the "Place of Examination," while the other half seem to have travelled to undertake investigations; see the end of the first list of the accused, below.

[3] Lit., "adhere to."

[4] As a *damnatio memoriae*, the names of the three major conspirators have been consciously deformed. Here, the name "The servant of Amon" has been recast as "The blind servant." For the phenomenon, see the bibliography in Ritner 1993:194.

[5] Lit., "made one with them."

laid hold on him; the officials who examined him caused that his punishment overtake him.

The great criminal Mesedsure,[6] who used to be a butler. HE WAS BROUGHT IN concerning the collusion that he had formed with Paibakemon, who used to be a chamberlain, and with the women to gather enemies to make rebellion against their lord. He was put in the presence of the great officials of the Place of Examination; they examined his crimes; they found him guilty; they caused that his punishment overtake him.

The great criminal Painik,[7] who used to be overseer of the royal harem of the travelling court harem. HE WAS BROUGHT IN concerning the common cause that he had made with Paibakemon and Mesedsure to make rebellion against their lord. He was put in the presence of the great officials of the Place of Examination; they examined his crimes; they found him guilty; they caused that his punishment overtake him.

The great criminal Pendua, who used to be scribe of the royal harem of the travelling court harem. HE WAS BROUGHT IN concerning the common cause that he had made with Paibakemon, Mesedsure and this other criminal[8] who used to be overseer of the royal harem, and the women of the harem to make a conspiracy with them to make rebellion against their lord. He was put in the presence of the great officials of the Place of Examination; they examined his crimes; they found him guilty; they caused that his punishment overtake him.

The great criminal Patjauemtiamon, who used to be an agent of the travelling court harem. HE WAS BROUGHT IN concerning his having heard the matters which the men had plotted together with the women of the harem and he did not go (to report) concerning them. He was put in the presence of the great officials of the Place of Examination; they examined his crimes; they found him guilty; they caused that his punishment overtake him.

The great criminal Karpes, who used to be an agent of the travelling court harem. HE WAS BROUGHT IN concerning the matters which he had heard and he had concealed them. He was put in the presence of the great officials of the Place of Examination; they found him guilty; they caused that his punishment overtake him.

The great criminal Khaemope, who used to be an agent of the travelling court harem. HE WAS BROUGHT IN concerning the matters which he had heard and he had concealed them. He was put in the presence of the great officials of the Place of Examination; they found him guilty; they caused that his punishment overtake him.

The great criminal Khaemaal, who used to be an agent of the travelling court harem. HE WAS BROUGHT IN concerning the matters which he had heard (and he had) concealed them. He was put in the presence of the great officials of the Place of Examination; they found him guilty; they caused that his punishment overtake him.

The great criminal Setiemperdjheuty, who used to be an agent of the travelling court harem. HE WAS BROUGHT IN concerning the matters which he had heard and he had concealed them. He was put in the presence of the great officials of the Place of Examination; they found him guilty; they caused that his punishment overtake him.

The great criminal Setiemperamon, who used to be an agent of the travelling court harem. HE WAS BROUGHT IN concerning the matters which he had heard and he had concealed them. He was put in the presence of the great officials of the Place of Examination; they found him guilty; they caused that his punishment overtake him.

The great criminal Waren, who used to be a butler. HE WAS BROUGHT IN concerning his having heard the matters from this chamberlain[9] with whom he had been close and he had concealed them; he had not reported them. He was put in the presence of the great officials of the Place of Examination; they found him guilty; they caused that his punishment overtake him.

The great criminal Ashahebsed, who used to be an assistant of Paibakemon. HE WAS BROUGHT IN concerning his having heard the matters from Paibakemon for whom he was plotting and he had not reported them. He was put in the presence of the great officials of the Place of Examination; they found him guilty; they caused that his punishment overtake him.

The great criminal Paluka,[10] who used to be a butler and scribe of the treasury. HE WAS BROUGHT IN concerning the collusion that he had formed with Paibakemon; he had heard the matters from him and he had not reported them. He was put in the presence of the great officials of the Place of Examination; they found him guilty; they caused that his punishment overtake him.

The great criminal, the Libyan Inini, who used to

[6] A deformed name: "Re hates him."
[7] A deformed name: "This snake."
[8] Painik.
[9] Paibakemon.
[10] "The Lycian."

be a butler. HE WAS BROUGHT IN concerning the collusion that he had formed with Paibakemon; he had heard the matters from him and he had not reported them. He was put in the presence of the great officials of the Place of Examination; they found him guilty; they caused that his punishment overtake him.

(v.1) The wives of the men of the gate of the harem, who were in league with the men who had plotted the matters, who were put in the presence of the great officials of the Place of Examination; they found them guilty; they caused that their punishment overtake them: Six women.

The great criminal Pairy son of Ruma, who used to be overseer of the treasury. HE WAS BROUGHT IN concerning the collusion that he had formed with the great criminal Penhuybin.[11] He had made common cause with him to incite enemies to make rebellion against their lord. He was put in the presence of the great officials of the Place of Examination; they found him guilty; they caused that his punishment overtake him.

The great criminal Binemwase,[12] who used to be archery commander of Cush. HE WAS BROUGHT IN concerning his having been written to by his sister who was in the travelling court harem, saying: "Gather people, make enemies, and come back to make rebellion against your lord." He was put in the presence of Qedendenna, Baalmahar, Peirsunu and Djhutyrekhnefer; they examined him; they found him guilty; they caused that his punishment overtake him.

Second List of Accused

PERSONS who were brought in concerning their crimes, concerning the collusion that they had formed with Paibakemon, Payis and Pentawere.[13] They were put in the presence of the great officials of the Place of Examination in order to examine them; they found them guilty; they left them in their own hands in the Place of Examination; they killed themselves without punishment having been inflicted upon them.

The great criminal Payis, who used to be commander of the army.
The great criminal Messui, who used to be a scribe of the House of Life.
The great criminal Prekamenef,[14] who used to be a chief lector priest ("magician").[15]
The great criminal Iyroy, who used to be an overseer of priests of Sakhmet.
The great criminal Nebdjefau, who used to be a butler.
The great criminal Shadmesdjer,[16] who used to be a scribe of the House of Life.
Total: six.

Third List of Accused

PERSONS who were brought in concerning their crimes to the Place of Examination in the presence of Qedendenna, Baalmahar, Peirsunu, Djhutyrekhnefer and Merutsiamon. They examined them concerning their crimes; they found them guilty; they left them in their places; they killed themselves.

Pentawere, the one who used to be called by that other name. HE WAS BROUGHT IN concerning the collusion that he had formed with Tiye his mother when she was plotting the matters with the women of the harem concerning making rebellion against his lord. He was put in the presence of the butlers in order to examine him; they found him guilty; they left him in his place; he killed himself.

The great criminal Henutenamon, who used to be a butler. HE WAS BROUGHT IN concerning the crimes of the women of the harem, among whom he had been, which he had heard and he had not reported them. He was put in the presence of the butlers in order to examine him; they found him guilty; they left him in his place; he killed himself.

The great criminal Amonkhau, who used to be a deputy of the travelling court harem. HE WAS BROUGHT IN concerning the crimes of the women of the harem, among whom he had been, which he had heard and he had not reported them. He was put in the presence of the butlers in order to examine him; they found him guilty; they left him in his place; he killed himself.

The great criminal Pairy, who used to be a scribe of the royal harem of the travelling court harem. HE WAS BROUGHT IN concerning the crimes of the women of the harem, among whom he had been, which he had heard and he had not reported them. He was put in the presence of the butlers in order to examine him; they found him guilty; they left him in his place; he killed himself.

Fourth List of Accused

(vi.1) PERSONS who were punished by cutting off their noses and their ears because of their having abandoned the good instructions which I[17] had said

[11] A deformed name: "He of evil Huy." Huy is a nickname for Amenhotep. See Papyrus Lee, col. i, *COS* 3.9 below.

[12] A deformed name: "The evil one of Thebes."

[13] These persons are the prominent conspirators of lists one, two and three.

[14] A deformed name: "Pre blinds him."

[15] Biblical *ḥarṭom*. For the role of magic in this conspiracy, see Papyri Rollin and Lee, *COS* 3.9 below.

[16] A deformed name: "His ear is cut off."

[17] Translators have consistently disregarded the royal first-person suffix pronoun, but the following list includes members of the investigating court who were instructed by the king personally (col. ii).

to them. The women went and reached them at the places where they were; they made a beer hall[18] with them and Payis; their crime seized them.

The great criminal Paibes, who used to be a butler.[19] This punishment was done to him; he was left alone; he killed himself.
The great criminal May, who used to be a scribe of the archives.[20]
The great criminal Taynakht, who used to be an officer of the troops.
The great criminal Nanay, who used to be a chief of police.

Fifth List of Accused
PERSON who was in league with them. He was rebuked sternly with harsh words; he was left alone; punishment was not inflicted upon him.

The great criminal Hori, who used to be a standard-bearer of the troops.[21]

[18] I.e. "caroused."
[19] The seduced Paibes was a member of the investigating commission (cols. ii.2 and iv.1).
[20] Like Paibes, May had been on the commission (cols. ii.3 and iv.1).
[21] Hori had also been a commission member (cols. ii.4 and iv.1).

REFERENCES

Text: Devéria 1866 pls. i-iv; Kitchen 1983 5:350-360. Translations and studies: de Buck 1937; *ANET* 214-216; Breasted 1906 4:208-19, §§416-453.

PAPYRI ROLLIN AND LEE (3.9)
(Magic in the Harem Conspiracy against Ramses III)

Robert K. Ritner

Although fragmentary, these trial records provide more detail regarding the techniques of the conspirators than the complementary summary, "The Judicial Papyrus of Turin" (see *COS* 3.8). The role of magic in the conspiracy is clearly evident, with the use of spells, potions and wax figures following procedures found in scrolls taken from the royal library of Ramses III. As the conspirators included a temple priest, two scribal archivists and a magician (*ḥry-tp* = Biblical *ḥarṭom*),[1] all of whom would have had access to standard execration rituals, the use of such respected techniques is not surprising. The papyri are often described inaccurately as records of a trial against sorcery, but as shown by the royal and sacerdotal origin of the procedures, such techniques of sorcery were hardly illegal in themselves. It is only the use of such accepted procedures against the state that constituted a "great crime worthy of death."[2]

PAPYRUS ROLLIN

[...] He began to make writings of magic for exorcizing and for disturbing, and he began to make some gods of wax and some potions for laming the limbs of people. They were placed in the hand of Paibakemon, whom Pre did not allow to be chamberlain,[3] and the other great enemies, saying: "Let them approach,"[4] and they let them approach. Now after he allowed the ones who did the evil to enter — which he did but which Pre did not allow him to be successful in[5] — he was examined, and truth was found in every crime and every evil which his heart had found fit to do, (namely) that truth was in them, and that he did them all with the other great enemies like him, and that they were great crimes worthy of death, the great abominations of the land,[a] which he had done. Now when he realized the great crimes worthy of death which he had done, he killed himself.

[a] Gen 43:32

[1] See The Judicial Papyrus of Turin (*COS* 3.8), col. v.5. For the term "magician," see Ritner 1993:220-221.
[2] For the legality of magic in Egypt, see Ritner 1995.
[3] The terminology, like the deformed name "The blind servant," represents an act of *damnatio memoriae* falsifying the actual state of affairs to deprive the victim of any underworldly benefits accruing from his earthly status. For the conspirator Paibakemon, see The Judicial Papyrus of Turin (*COS* 3.8), col. iv.2.
[4] I.e. "Smuggle them in!"
[5] A formulaic phrase for magical purposes; the relative success of the conspiracy is open to question.

PAPYRUS LEE

(column i) [... was made to swear an oath] of the Lord, LPH, of undertaking fealty, swearing at every [time ... saying, "I have not given] any [magical roll] of the place in which I am to anyone on earth." But when Penhuybin,[6] who was overseer of cattle said to him, "Give to me a roll for giving to me terror and respect," he gave to him a writing of the scrolls of Usermaare-Meriamon, LPH, the great god,[7] his lord, and he began to petition god for the derangement of the people, and he penetrated the side of the harem and this other great deep place. And he began to make inscribed people of wax in order to cause that they be taken inside by the hand of the agent I(d)rimi for the exorcizing of the one crew and the enchanting of the others, to take a few words inside and to bring the others out. Now when he was examined concerning them, truth was found in every crime and every evil which his heart had found fit to do, (namely) that truth was in them, and that he did them all with the other great enemies whom every god and goddess abominate like him. And there were done to him the great punishments of death which the gods said: "Do them to him."

(column ii) [...] ... [...] on the basket, and he went off [...] his hand lame. Now as for [every crime and every evil which he did, he was examined concerning] them, truth was found in every crime and every evil which his heart had found to do (namely) that truth was [in them, and that he did them all with the other] great enemies whom every god and goddess abominate like him, and that they were great crimes worthy of death, the great abominations of [the land, which he had done. Now when he realized the] great crimes worthy of death which he had done, he killed himself. Now when the officials who were in charge of him realized that he had killed himself [... abomination(?) of] Pre like him, which the hieroglyphic writings say: "Do it to him!"

[6] "He of evil Huy"; see The Judicial Papyrus of Turin (*COS* 3.8), col. v.2.

[7] Living kings are called "the great god," a further indication that Ramses III is deceased at the time of this investigation; see The Judicial Papyrus of Turin (*COS* 3.8), col. iii.3-4.

REFERENCES

Text: Devéria 1867 pls. v (Rollin) and vi-vii (Lee); Kitchen 1983 5:360-363. For translation, discussion and full bibliography, see Ritner 1993:192-214.

A LAWSUIT OVER A SYRIAN SLAVE (3.10)
(P. Cairo 65739)

Robert K. Ritner

Likely dating to the reign of Ramses II, this papyrus records the oral arguments before a Theban court regarding the ownership of a female Syrian slave and a second, male slave of unknown nationality. In the lost beginning of the transcript, the citizeness Irineferet was accused by a soldier Naky of purchasing these slaves with the property of another woman. The preserved portion of the text begins with the defendant's response. Evaluations are calculated in terms of weight in units of silver. The deben (about 91 grams or 3 oz. Troy) contained 10 kite, and the ratio of silver to copper was 100 to 1, calculated to the nearest fraction. At 4 deben and 1 kite, or 410 copper deben, the value of the female slave was quite high, costing more than three oxen in contemporary prices.

[...] STATEMENT OF the citizeness Irinefret: "[As for myself, I am the wife of the district superintendent Simut,] and I came to dwell in his house, and I worked in [weaving(?)], caring for my clothing. Now in regnal year 15, in the seventh year of my having entered into the house of the district superintendent Si[mut], the merchant Raia approached me with the Syrian slave Gemniherimentet,[1] while she was a [young] girl, [and he] (5) said to me: 'Buy this young girl and give to me her price' — so he said to me. And I took the young girl and I gave to him her [price]. Now look, I am saying the price which I gave for her in the presence of the authorities:

1 shroud of fine linen, amounting to 5 kite of silver
1 sheet of fine linen, amounting to 3⅓ kite of silver
1 robe of fine linen, amounting to 4 kite of silver

[1] "She whom I found in the west"; the Egyptian name given to the Syrian by her purchaser.

3 aprons of the best fine linen, amounting to 5 kite of silver
1 dress of the best fine linen, amounting to 5 kite of silver
Bought from the citizeness Kafi: 1 bronze bowl weighing 18 deben, amounting to 1⅔ kite of silver
Bought from the chief of the storehouse Pyiay: 1 bronze bowl weighing 14 deben, amounting to 1½ kite of silver
Bought from the priest Huy-Pa-(10)-nehsy: 10 deben of beaten copper, amounting to 1 kite of silver
Bought from the priest Ani: 1 copper bowl weighing 16 deben, amounting to 1½ kite of silver, and 1 pot of honey amounting to 1 *heqat* measure (4.5 liters), amounting to 5 kite of silver
Bought from the citizeness Tjuiay: 1 cauldron weighing 20 deben, amounting to 2 kite of silver
Bought from the steward Tutui of the estate of Amon: 1 bronze jar weighing 20 deben, amounting to 2 kite of silver, and 10 shirts of the best fine linen, amounting to 4 kite of silver.
TOTAL of the silver from everything: 4 deben and 1 kite.

And I gave them to the merchant Raia, without there being any property of the citizeness Bakemut among them, and he gave to me this little girl, and I called her Gemniherimentet by name."

STATEMENT OF the council of judges to the citizeness Irineferet: "Make an oath of the Lord, LPH, saying: 'Should witnesses be arraigned against me that there is anything belonging to the citizeness Bakemut among the silver which I gave for this servant and I concealed it, I shall be subject to 100 blows, being deprived of her.'"

OATH of the Lord, LPH, which the citizeness Irineferet said: "As Amon endures, and as the Ruler, LPH, endures, should witnesses be arraigned against me that there is anything belonging to the citizeness Bakemut among this silver which I gave for this servant and I concealed it, I shall be subject to 100 blows, being deprived of her."

STATEMENT OF the council of judges to the soldier Nakhy: (20) "Present to us the witnesses of whom you said: 'They know that this silver belonging to the citizeness Bakemut was given to buy this slave Gemniherimentet,' together with the witnesses of this tomb of which you said: 'It was the citizeness Bakemut who made it, but the citizeness Irineferet gave it to the merchant Nakht and he gave to her the slave Telptah in exchange for it.'"

QUANTITY OF witnesses whom the soldier Nakhy named in the presence of the council: the chief of police Mini[...]; the mayor Ramose of the west (of Thebes); the priest Huy-Panehsy, the elder brother of the district superintendent Simut; the citizeness Kafi; (25) the wife of the chief of police Pashed, who is deceased; the citizeness Weretneferet; the citizeness Hutia, the elder sister of the citizeness Bakemut — TOTAL: 3 men and 3 women — TOTAL: 6. And they stood in the presence of the council and they made an oath of the Lord, LPH, and likewise a divine oath, saying: "It is in truth that we speak. We shall not speak falsely. Should we speak falsely, let the servants be taken from us."

STATEMENT OF the council of judges to the priest Huy: "State for us the situation of the Syrian slave [Gemniherimentet ...]."

REFERENCES

Text and translation: Gardiner 1935; *ANET* 216-217. For discussion, Janssen 1975.

D. ACCOUNTS

SEMITIC SLAVES ON A MIDDLE KINGDOM ESTATE (3.11)
(P. Brooklyn 35.1446)

Robert K. Ritner

In active use for about 90 years, this Theban papyrus contains a series of administrative documents concerning servant laborers from the reign of Amenemhet III to that of Sebekhotep III. In the reign of the latter king, two insertions established the woman Senebtisy's right of ownership to ninety-five household workers, whose names, nicknames, occupations and totals are listed in four columns on the verso. Of the seventy-nine names preserved, thirty-three are Egyptians, while forty-five are designated as Asiatics and bear Semitic names in addition to their imposed Egyptian slave names. The Egyptian laborers assigned to fieldwork are probably criminals or descendants of such, but the Asiatic slaves are largely skilled workers perhaps taken as prisoners of war. One child (l. 8) was the son of an Egyptian father and an Egyptianized Semitic mother.

These are her people, being a gift of regnal year 2, month 2 of [...], day 8 [in] the reign of [the Majesty of the King of Upper and Lower Egyp]t, Sekhemre [Se]wadjtawy, the son of [Re, Sebek-hotep, living forever and ever ...] the servants [...] whom they transported:

The king's slave, Renesseneb's son Ankhu; called Hedjri; steward; 1 man.

The female slave, Aye's daughter Satgemeni; it is her name; hairdresser; a woman.

Her daughter Reniseneb; it is her name; a child.

The king's slave, Iusni's son Asha; it is his name; cultivator; 1 man.

(5) (ditto), Aye's son Ibu; it is his name; cultivator; 1 man.

The Asiatic Senebresiseneb; it is his name; cook; 1 man.

The female Asiatic Rehuy; called Kaipunebi; warper(?) of linen; a woman.

Her son, Nefu's son Resiseneb; called Renefresi; a child.

The Asiatic [^{c}A]pra-Rashpu;[1] [called ...]; brewer; 1 man.

(10) The female Asiatic Hay'immi;[2] called [...]n; weaver of fine linen; a woman.

The female Asiatic Munahhima;[3] (called) S[...]tenef; weaver of fine linen; a woman.

a 2 Chr 20:37

b Exod 1:15

The Asiatic Su[..]i; called Ankhuse[ne]b; cook; 1 man.

The female Asiatic Sakratu;[4] called Werditninub; weaver of fine linen; a woman.

(ditto) Immisukru;[5] (called) Seneb[sen]wosret; weaver of fine linen; a woman.

(15) (ditto) Aduttu;[6] (called) Nub[...]; weaver of fine linen; a woman

(ditto) [Sa]kratu;[7] (called) Sen[eb...]; weaver of linen; a woman.

The female Asiatic Ahāti-mil(katu?);[8] called Henutipuwadjet; warper(?) of fine linen; [a woman].

The Asiatic Dôdi-hu'atu;[9] [a] called Ankhuemhesut; steward; [1 man].

The Asiatic Qu'a[...]; called Resiseneb; steward; 1 man.

(20) The king's slave Iywy's son [...]; it is his name; steward; 1 man.

The female Asiatic Shiprah(?);[10] [b] called Senebhenutes; weaver of fine linen; [a woman].

The female Asiatic Sukrapati;[11] called Meritnebu; warper(?) of linen; a woman.

The female Asiatic Ashra(?);[12] called Werintef; weaver [...]; a woman.

Her daughter Senebtisy; it is her name; a child.

(25) The female Asiatic ^{c}An[at]'a(?);[13] called Nebuemmerqis; weaver of fine linen; a woman.

---

[1] "Fosterling of Reshep"; see Hayes 1955:94.
[2] "Where is (my) Mother?"; see Hayes 1955:94-95.
[3] "(Such and such a God) Shows Mercy"; see Hayes 1955:95.
[4] "The Favorite"; see Hayes 1955:95-96.
[5] "The Favorite (goddess) is my Mother"; see Hayes 1955:95-96.
[6] "Lady"; see Hayes 1955:96.
[7] See note 4, above.
[8] "My Sister is Queen"; see Hayes 1955:96.
[9] "My Beloved is He"; see Hayes 1955:96.
[10] "Beautiful"; see Hayes 1955:96.
[11] "The Favorite (goddess) is my Fair One"; see Hayes 1955:97.
[12] "Prosperous"; see Hayes 1955:97.
[13] "Anat ..."; see Hayes 1955:97.

The female Asiatic Shamashtu(?);[14] called Senebhenut[es]; warper(?) of fine linen; a woman.
The female Asiatic Iᶜsibtu;[15] called Amenem[...]; tutor; [a woman].
The female slave, Wewi's daughter Irit; it is her name; [...; a woman].
The female Asiatic [...]a'hu'atu;[16] called Menhesut; [...; a woman].
(30) Her daughter Ded[et]mut; [it is her name; a child].
Her son Ankhseneb; [called ...]; a child.
The female Asiatic ᶜAhā[ti...];[17] [called ...; ...] of fine linen; a woman.
The female Asiatic Aduna';[18] called Senebhe[nutes; ...]; a woman.
Her son Ankhu; called Hedjeru; a child.
(35) The female Asiatic Baᶜaltûya;[19] called Wahresiseneb; laborer(?); [a woman].
Her daughter Senebtisy; it is her name; a child.
The female Asiatic ᶜAqabaᶜ;[20] called Resiseneb-wah; warper(?) of fine linen; [a woman].
[The female slave], Senaaib's daughter Reniseneb; it is her name; gardener; a woman.
Her [daughter] Henutipu; it is her name; a child.
[(40) The female slave], Henutipu's daughter Sennut; it is her name; reciter(?); a woman.
[The king's slave, ...]'s son Ibiankh; it is his name; cultivator; 1 man.
[The king's slave, ...'s son [...]hesut; it is his name; cultivator; 1 man.
[The king's slave, ...]y's son Hetep(?); it is his name; and Reyet; it is her name; gardener; a woman.
[Her son ...]; it is his name; a child.
(45) [...]y; [called ...]; magazine employee; a woman.
The king's slave, [...]; sandalmaker; 1 man.
The female Asiatic [...]una; called Neferet; warper(?) of linen; a woman.
The female slave, Henutipu's daughter [...]esni; called Neferettjent[et]; [...; a woman].
Her son {...}; it is his name; [a child].
(50) The king's slave Resiseneb, called [...; 1 man].
The Asiatic ᶜAmu[...]; called Werni;[...; 1 man].
The female Asiatic R[...]; called Iunesi[...]; [...; a woman].
The king's slave, R[...]; it is his name; [...; 1 man].
The female slave [...]; it is her name;[...; a woman].
(55) The female Asiatic ᶜAk[...]; called [...]nefereten[...]; weaver of fine linen; [a woman].
The female Asiatic [...]; called Ahay; magazine employee; [a woman].
Her daughter Hu[...; ...].
Her son Ankhu; [called] Paamu ("The Asiatic"); a child.
The female Asiatic ᶜAnat[...;[21] called] Iunerton; warper(?) of linen; [a woman].
(60) The female slave Iyti; called Bebisherit's daughter Iyt(i); weaver [...; a woman].
The female Asiatic Rayenet; called Senebhe[nut]es; weaver of fine linen; [a woman].
The female Asiatic Ayya'abi-'ilu(?);[22] called Nehniemkhaset; magazine employee; [a woman].
Her son ᶜAbu[...]m;[23] called Senebnebef; [a child].
[The female Asiatic ....]-Baᶜal;[24] called Netjeremsa[i]; warper(?) of fine linen; a woman.
(65) [The female slave Wadjet(?)]hau; it is her name; warper(?) of linen; a woman.
Her son [Res]iseneb; it is his name; a child.
The female Asiatic Sakar;[25] called Nebuerdies; [...]; a woman.
The king's slave Resiseneb; it is his name; steward; 1 man.
The female Asiatic Tjenatisi;[26] called Petimenti; magazine employee; a woman.
(70) The female slave Hetepet; it is her name; warper(?) of linen; a woman.
Her son Ankhu; it is his name; [a child].
The king's slave Resisen[eb]; called Burekh[...]; cultivator; [1 man].
[...; called ...]ri; [...].
[...; called ..]y[..; ...].
(75) [The female slave] Henu[t]ip[u]; [...].
[...]
(80) The female Asiatic Hay'ôr[27] [...]
The king's slave Nefruhetep [...]
The female slave, Iuy's daughter Mer[...]

[14] "The sun god (is my Father?)"; see Hayes 1955:97.
[15] "Herbage"; see Hayes 1955:97.
[16] "[...] is He"; see Hayes 1955:97.
[17] "Sister [...]"; see Hayes 1955:97.
[18] "Lord"; see Hayes 1955:97.
[19] Compounded with the deity "Baal"; see Hayes 1955:97.
[20] See Hayes 1955:97.
[21] Compounded with the deity "Anat"; see Hayes 1955:97.
[22] "Where is (my) Father?"; see Hayes 1955:94-95.
[23] Compounded with *abu* "Father"; see Hayes 1955:97.
[24] Compounded with the deity "Baal"; see Hayes 1955:97.
[25] "The Favorite"; see Hayes 1955:95-96.
[26] Compounded with the deity Sin, the moon god?; see Hayes 1955:98.
[27] "The Living One Shines"; see Hayes 1955:98.

[...]
(85) [The king's slave I]bi [...]
[The king's slave] Nefuemantiu [...]
The female [As]iatic ʿAqabtu[28] [...]
[The female Asiatic] Tjenaterti[29] [...]
[...]

[28] See Hayes 1955:97.

[29] Compounded with the deity Sin, the moon god?; see Hayes 1955:98.

REFERENCES

Text, translation and study: Hayes 1955:87-109, 123-25, and pls. viii-xiii; Albright 1954; Schneider 1987; 1992.

SEMITIC FUNCTIONARIES IN EGYPT (3.12)
(*KRI* 4:104-106)

Robert K. Ritner

Following the Hyksos Period, occasional appearances of Semitic names on funerary stelae from the Nile valley attest to the Egyptianization of resident Asiatic servants and functionaries. From the Amarna Period, a Berlin stela (14122) depicts a Syrian soldier *Trwrʿ* drinking beer through a bent straw with the assistance of a servant in the company of his wife, "the housewife ʾIʾirbwrʿʾ." The high official Tutu of Amarna has been thought to represent the most prominent early example of such assimilation, with an Egyptianized form of the Asiatic name Dûdu.[1] This seems unlikely, however, as a native Egyptian name (and deity) Tutu ("Image") becomes increasingly common, even serving as the initial element of the name Tutankhamon. From Abydos during the reign of Merneptah, a Cairo stela (JdE Temporary Register 3/7/24/17) of the fanbearer and chief herald Ramsesemperra betrays the official's foreign origin by mention of his now "tertiary" Asiatic name and homeland. On the stela, Ramsesemperra adores his royal patron Merneptah, just as he adores Tuthmosis III, the long deceased conqueror of Asia, on a stela from Gurob now in Brussels (E. 5014).

Before Osiris "Lord of the Sacred Land" identified with the deified king "Lord of the Two Lands, Baenre-meriamon, Lord of Diadems, Merneptah-hetephermaat," adoration is offered "by the royal butler, whose hands are pure for the Lord of the Two Lands, the royal fanbearer on the right of the King, the first herald of His Majesty, the great royal butler of the offering chamber, Ramsesem-perra ('Ramses in the estate of Re'), the justified, called Meriunu ('Beloved of Heliopolis'), the justified."

Below the kneeling Ramsesemperra appear his Asiatic father *Yupʿʾ*, his unnamed mother, and a repetition of his titles. The main text consists of the traditional funerary prayer.

An offering which the King gives to Osiris, Foremost of the West, that he might give invocation offerings consisting of bread, beer, oxen, and fowl to the spirit of the royal butler, whose hands are pure for the Lord of the Two Lands, the royal fanbearer on the right of the King, the first herald of His Majesty, the great royal butler of the offering chamber of the palace, LPH, the great royal butler of the beer (chamber), Ramsesemperra, the justified, the man of Ramses-meriamon (Ramses II)[2] beloved like Re, called Ben-'ozen (*Bnʾiṯn*) of Ziribashani (*Ḏrbsn*).

[1] Cf. above *COS* 3.11, n. 9.

[2] The expression indicates that Ramses II was Ben-'ozen's original patron.

REFERENCES

Text and study: Kitchen 1982 4:104-106; Janssen 1951:50-62.

EGYPTIAN BIBLIOGRAPHY

ALBRIGHT, W. F.
1954 "Northwest-Semitic Names in a List of Egyptian Slaves from the Eighteenth Dynasty B.C." *JAOS* 74:222-233.

ALLEN, J. P.
2002 *The Heqanakhte Papyri*. Publications of the Metropolitan Museum of Art Egyptian Expedition 27. New York: The Metropolitan Museum of Art.

ANDREWS, C.
1984 *Egyptian Mummies*. London and Cambridge, MA: British Museum and Harvard.

BAER, K.
1963 "An Eleventh Dynasty Farmer's Letters to his Family." *JAOS* 83:1-19.

BREASTED, J.
1906 *Ancient Records of Egypt*. 5 Vols. Chicago, 1906-1907. Reprint New York, 1962.

BRESCIANI, E.
1965 *Papyri della Università degli Studi Milano*. Vol. III. Milan: Cisalpino, 1965.

BRITISH MUSEUM
1842 *Select Papyri in the Hieratic Character from the Collections of the British Museum*. London: W. Nicol.

DE BUCK, A.
1937 "The Judicial Papyrus of Turin." *JEA* 23:152-164.

CAMINOS, R.
1954 *Late-Egyptian Miscellanies*. Brown Egyptological Studies 1. Oxford: Oxford University Press.

DANIEL, R. W., M. GRONEWALD, and H. J. THISSEN.
1986 *Griechische und demotische Papyri der Universitätsbibliothek Freiburg*. Bonn: Rudolf Habelt, 1986.

DEVÉRIA, T.
1866 *JA* 6: pls. i-iv.
1867 *JA* 6: vol. 10. pls. v-vii.

EDWARDS, I. E. S.
1960 *Oracular Amuletic Decrees of the Late New Kingdom*. HPBM 4. London: British Museum, 1960.

FISCHER-ELFERT, H.-W.
1983 *Die satirische Streitschrift des Papyrus Anastasi I*. Kleine ägyptische Texte. Wiesbaden: Otto Harrassowitz.
1986 *Die satirische Streitschrift des Papyrus Anastasi I., Übersetzung und Kommentar*. Ägyptologische Abhandlungen 44. Wiesbaden: Otto Harrassowitz.

GARDINER, A. H.
1911 *Egyptian Hieratic Texts*. Series 1: *Literary Texts of the New Kingdom*. Part 1: *The Papyrus Anastasi I and the Papyrus Koller together with the Parallel Texts*. Leipzig: J. C. Hinrich.
1918 "The Delta Residence of the Ramessides." *JEA* 5:127-138, 179-200, 242-271.
1920 "The Ancient Military Road between Egypt and Palestine." *JEA* 6:99-116.
1935 "A Lawsuit arising from the Purchase of Two Slaves." *JEA* 21:140-146 and pls. xiii-xvi.
1937 *Late-Egyptian Miscellanies*. Bibliotheca Aegyptiaca 7. Brussels: Fondation Égyptologique Reine Élisabeth.

GOEDICKE, H.
1984 *Studies in the Hekanakhte Papers*. Baltimore: Halgo.

GRIFFITH, F. Ll.
1909 *Catalogue of the Demotic Papyri in the John Rylands Library Manchester*. Manchester: The University Press.

HAYES, W. C.
1955 *A Papyrus of the Late Middle Kingdom*. Reprinted 1972. Brooklyn: The Brooklyn Museum.

HOCH, J. E.
1994 *Semitic Words in Egyptian Texts of the New Kingdom and Third Intermediate Period*. Princeton: Princeton University Press.

JAMES, T. G. H.
1962 *The Ḥekanakhte Papers and Other Early Middle Kingdom Documents*. Publications of the Metropolitan Museum of Art Egyptian Expedition 19. New York: The Metropolitan Museum of Art.

JANSSEN, J. J.
1975 *Commodity Prices from the Ramesside Period*. Leiden: E. J. Brill.

JANSSEN, J. M. A.
1951 "Semitic Functionaries in Egypt." *CdÉ* 26:50-62.

KITCHEN, K. A.
1982 *KRI*.
1983 *KRI*.

MALAMAT, A.
1956 "Military Rationing in Papyrus Anastasi I and the Bible." Pp. 114-121 in *Studies Robert*.

PARKINSON, R. B.
1991 *Voices from Ancient Egypt, an Anthology of Middle Kingdom Writings*. Oklahoma Series in Classical Culture. Norman: University of Oklahoma Press.

RITNER, R. K.
1993 *The Mechanics of Ancient Egyptian Magical Practice*. SAOC 54. Chicago: The Oriental Institute.
1995 "The Religious, Social, and Legal Parameters of Traditional Egyptian Magic." Pp. 43-60 in *Ancient Magic and Ritual Power*. Ed. by M. Meyer and P. Mirecki. Leiden: E. J. Brill.

SCHNEIDER, Th.
1987 "Die semitischen und ägyptischen Namen der syrischen Sklaven des Papyrus Brooklyn 35.1446 verso." *UF* 19:255-282.
1992 *Asiatische Personennamen in ägyptischen Quellen des Neuen Reiches*. OBO 114. Freiburg: Universitätsverlag.

THOMPSON, H.
1941 "Two Demotic Self-Dedications." *JEA* 26:68-78 and pls. xii-xiii.
WENTE, E. F.
1990 *Letters from Ancient Egypt*. SBLWAW 1. Atlanta: Scholars Press.

HITTITE ARCHIVAL DOCUMENTS

A. LETTERS

1. MIDDLE HITTITE PERIOD (ca. 1450-1350 BCE)

Harry A. Hoffner, Jr.

Maşat was a provincial center situated some 30 miles due east of Ḫattuša. The letters found there date to the Middle Hittite Period (ca. 1450-1350 BCE). Their background is formed by the conflict between the Hittite rulers in Ḫattuša and the Kaška of northern Anatolia (3.13, note 2).

THE KING TO KAŠŠŪ IN TAPIKKA 1 (*HKM* 1) (3.13)

Thus speaks His Majesty: Say to Kaššū:
(4) Concerning the matter[1] of the enemy[2] about which you wrote to me, saying: "The enemy is holding the city Kašaša":
(8) Be advised that I have just dispatched chariotry. Be very much on guard against the enemy.[3]

[1] The sections beginning with the word "Concerning the matter of ..." (lines 4-7) confirm to the letter's recipient the sender's receipt of the letter which dealt with the referenced matter. In this case the letter received by the king from Kaššū was a report on enemy activities in his area, specifically the capture and occupation of the city Kašaša.

[2] The "enemy" referred to anonymously in these letters found at Maşat is thought to have been the non-sedentary tribal people called the Kaška. When the sender has no substantial comment to make on the matter about which his correspondent has just written him, he may simply refer to the subject matter and add "I have heard it." See 3.15, line 4, and 3.21, line 6 below.

[3] Lines 8-10 in Boley 2000.

REFERENCES

Text: *HKM* 1; *HBM* 120f., 302. Translations: *HBM* 121.

THE KING TO KAŠŠŪ IN TAPIKKA 2 (*HKM* 2) (3.14)

Thus speaks His Majesty: Say to Kaššū:
(4) Concerning the matter of chariotry[1] about which you wrote to me: Be advised that I have already dispatched chariotry. Wait for it.
(10) Concerning the matter of Ḫimuili's brother about which you wrote: I am dispatching him now.
[PS][2] (14) Say to Uzzū, my dear brother: Thus speaks Šuriḫili, your brother: With me all is well.
(17) May all be well also with you, dear brother.[3]
(19) May the gods, including Ea,[4] the King of Wisdom, keep you, the wife, and (your son?) Tazzukuli, well.
(l.e. 1) Here in your house all is well. So stop worrying, dear brother.[5]

[1] The term translated "chariotry" (line 4), lit. "horses," refers to mounted fighting men together with their steeds. Kaššū has requested additional troops in his district, specifying mounted ones. The king assures him that the contingent has been dispatched and is on its way.

[2] The portion of the tablet beginning in line 14 and noted in the translation as "[PS]" is not a true postscript by the primary author, in this case the king, but is what is called a "piggy-back letter," that is, a personal letter by the scribe. When the letters are sent to higher officials, the piggy-back letters accompanying them are usually to the recipient's scribe. Thus, Šuriḫili is the king's scribe in Ḫattuša, while Uzzū is the scribe of Kaššū in Maşat.

[3] Wishes (or prayers) that the gods may protect the correspondent are common in this correspondence.

[4] Here it should be noted that in addition to the general subject "the gods," the god "Ea, King of Wisdom" is added. This is because one scribe is addressing another. Ea was the patron deity of scribes. In Akkadian his epithet was "Lord of Wisdom," which the Hittite scribes modified to "King of Wisdom."

[5] Lines 4-13 in Boley 2000:78a.

REFERENCES

Text: *HKM* 2; *HBM* 120f-123, 302f. Translations: *HBM* 121, 123.

THE KING TO KAŠŠŪ IN TAPIKKA 3 (*HKM* 3) (3.15)

Thus speaks His Majesty: Say to Kaššū:
(3) Concerning the matter of the enemy about which you wrote me: I have heard it.
(5) Because I have already written you, Let the troops which are in his land not come out again.[1] Let them remain there. And let the land be very much on guard against the enemy.

[PS][2] (14) Say to Uzzū, my dear brother: Thus says Šuriḫili, your brother:
(17) May all be well with you, and may the gods, including Ea,[3] the King of Wisdom, keep you well.
(21) At present all is well in your house and with your wife. So stop worrying, my dear brother. Send me back your greeting, my dear brother.

[1] Lines 5-10 in Boley 2000:174a.
[2] From this PS we learn that Uzzū, the scribe in Tapikka-Maşat, had a house and perhaps family in the capital city. Šuruḫili reassures him of their safety and well-being.
[3] On Ea see 3.14, note 4 above.

REFERENCES

Text: *HKM* 3; *HBM* 122-125, 303f. Translations: *HBM* 123ff.

THE KING TO KAŠŠŪ IN TAPIKKA 4 (*HKM* 4) (3.16)

Thus speaks His Majesty: Say to Kaššū:
Write to me quickly concerning the condition of the vines, the cattle, and the sheep, in that land.[1]

[1] This letter reveals the direct concern of the king for viticulture and livestock in the provinces, a fact we would otherwise not have known. It is well known, however, that the material prosperity of the land, as often measured by these two criteria, depended upon the king's proper relationship with the gods who had entrusted the land and its governance to him.

REFERENCES

Text: *HKM* 4. Edition: *HBM* 124-127, 304.

THE KING TO KAŠŠŪ IN TAPIKKA 5 (*HKM* 5) (3.17)

Thus speaks His Majesty: Say to Kaššū:
(3) Concerning the fact that you took the cattle of the city of Kašipūra and distributed them in the district of EN-tarawa[1]:

(7) From now on you must not levy veteran troops and auxiliary troops[2] out of the district of EN-tarawa. Let him keep the aforementioned cattle. But let him not fail in his work.

[1] This letter reveals that Kaššū in his official capacity was authorized to move royal livestock from one administrative district under his oversight to another: in this case, from Kašipūra, whose governor's name is not give here, to the unnamed district governed by EN-tarawa.
[2] Kaššū was authorized to levy troops in the king's name. Two types are specified in lines 8 and 9: "veteran troops" (lit. "old" ones) and "auxiliary troops," which would have been less experienced ones to be used only when it was absolutely necessary to supplement the veteran "regulars."

REFERENCES

Text: *HKM* 5. Edition: *HBM* 126f.

THE KING TO KAŠŠŪ IN TAPIKKA 6 (*HKM* 6) (3.18)

Thus speaks His Majesty: Say to Kaššū:
(3) Concerning what you wrote me, saying: "The enemy has come. He pressed[1] the city of Ḫapara on that side of me and the city of Kašipūra on this side. But he himself passed through, and I don't know where he went."
(11) Was that "enemy" perhaps enchanted, that you did not recognize him?
(15) Now be very much on guard against the enemy.
(17) Concerning what you wrote me, saying: "I have just sent out scouts,[2] and they have scouted out the cities of Malazziya and Taggašta." I have heard it. Fine.
(24) Now get with it. Be very much on guard against the enemy.

[1] Once again Kaššū reports military matters to the king. He says that the enemy has "pressed" two cities, which probably means attacking them. If they were walled cities, which we do not know, it might mean he besieged them.

[2] This same letter reveals that Kaššū had "scouts" (line 19) at his disposal to track moving contingents, but failed to discover where the marauding enemy was headed next. This lapse angered the king, who then resorts to sarcasm, asking whether Kaššū thinks he was dealing with an enchanted foe (lines 11-12)!

REFERENCES

Text: *HKM* 6. Edition: *HBM* 126ff.

THE KING TO KAŠŠŪ IN TAPIKKA 7 (*HKM* 7) (3.19)

Thus speaks His Majesty: Say to Kaššū:
(3) Concerning what you wrote me, saying: "I have sent out scouts, and they have proceeded to scout out Takkašta and Ukuiduna.
(7) ......, and he has 'drawn down.'"
(9) Get involved with that matter.[1] Send forth scouts, and let them scout thoroughly, and ... And because I, My Majesty, have written you previously, draw out behind that road.
(16) ... I will come ... Troops already assembled [...]
(23) As I know you, Kaššū, send to the Kaška, and let them be protected beforehand.

[1] Cf. KUB 14.15 iv 48-49 (AM 74-75): "Mit den Leuten von Mira sollen sie sich nicht einlassen".

REFERENCES

Text: *HKM* 7. Edition: *HBM* 128ff.

THE KING TO KAŠŠŪ IN TAPIKKA 8 (*HKM* 8) (3.20)[1]

Thus speaks His Majesty: Say to Kaššū:
(3) Concerning the matters about which you wrote to me: how the enemy is damaging the crops, how in the city of Kappušiya he has attacked (the property) of the House of the Queen, how he has [seized] one team of oxen belonging to the House of the Queen, and how they have led away captive 30 oxen of the poor people, and 10 men — (all this) I have heard.
(12) Because the enemy marches into the land at a moment's notice, if you would determine his location, and if you would attack him, you must be very much on guard against the enemy.

[1] This letter gives a pretty good idea of the scope of most of the military operations of the Kaška enemy. They were razzias, raids on villages, rather than large scale pitched battles. One sees here too the typical size of the losses: 30 oxen and 10 men. What was most troublesome to the Hittite king and his officials was the frustrating situation that these enemies could appear at a moment's notice, do damage and then escape. The damage done to the crops was perhaps more serious than the small numbers of lost animals, because this attacked the future food supply not only of Tapikka itself, but the capital city, which may well have received supplies from towns like Tapikka in the Hittite "bread basket."

REFERENCES

Text: *HKM* 8. Edition: *HBM* 130ff.

THE KING TO KAŠŠŪ IN TAPIKKA 9 (*HKM* 9) (3.21)[1]

Thus speaks His Majesty: Say to Kaššū:
(3) Concerning the fact that you dispatched (to me) 13 (apprehended) fugitives: They have brought them.
(6) Concerning the matter of horse (troops?) about which you wrote to me: I have heard it.

[1] Here we see another of Kaššū's common duties: apprehending fugitives and sending them under guard to the capital. The fugitives are Hittites fleeing their masters. They are being returned to the king for him to decide how to return them to their masters. Although the text is cryptic, it is likely that the "horses" Kaššū has asked about are teams of chariot horses and their drivers.

REFERENCES

Text: *HKM* 9. Edition: *HBM* 132f.

THE KING TO KAŠŠŪ IN TAPIKKA 10 (*HKM* 10) (3.22)

Thus speaks His Majesty: Say to Kaššū:
(3) Concerning the matter of Piḫinakki about which you wrote to me: As Piḫinakki is settling the city of Lišipra, he has already settled 30 families.[1]
(7) Piḫinakki said to me: "I intend actually to transfer 300 families (to make up the community of) Lišipra which I am settling.[2] Then I will send the leading men (of the city) before Your Majesty. Eventually we will transfer the (entire) city." I have heard this. It is fine. Do that very thing.
(14) Concerning the matter of Piḫapzuppi and Kaškanu about which you wrote me: "They have already made peace (with us)," I have heard it.
(17) Concerning what you wrote me: "Kaškaean men are coming here in large numbers to make peace. How will Your majesty write to me?" Keep sending to My Majesty the Kaškaean men who are coming to make peace.
(23) Concerning what you wrote me: "Until Your Majesty writes me about this matter of the Kaškaean men coming to make peace, I will be waiting word in the land of Išḫupitta." Just because the gods already [......], you keep wearing me out with queries, and keep writing me the same things!
(33) Concerning what you wrote me: "When I arrived in the land of Išḫupitta, behind me the enemy attacked the city of Zikkatta, and led away 40 cattle and 100 sheep. I threw him back, and eliminated 16 men of the enemy, counting both captured and killed." I have heard it.

PS (42) Say to Ḫimuili, my dear brother: Thus speaks Ḫattušili, your brother: May all be well with you. May the gods keep you alive, and keep you in good circumstances.
(47) Concerning the matter of your live-in sons-in-law[3] about which you wrote me, I have it in mind, and will inform the palace of it. A person will go to them and conduct them to His Majesty.

[1] Lit., "30 houses".
[2] *HBM* 135 translates "I will carry off 300 families from Lišipra, which I am resettling," which makes good sense, but which violates the grammar of the text.
[3] Tentatively, we follow *HBM* in regarding the term in line 47, *andatiyattalla-*, as synonymous with *antiyant-* "live-in son-in-law." The latter is a technical term denoting a young man whose family is too poor to afford the usual bridal gift presented to the family of the bride. Consequently, the bride's family pays this gift to him, and in return he goes to live with them instead of the bride going to live with his family. See Hittite laws §36 (translated in Hoffner 1997:222; *COS* 2.19, p. 110). In the present letter more than one such person is involved, and both (or all) of them are to be brought before the king, perhaps to adjudicate a dispute between them. But it is also possible that the word in this letter is rather synonymous with *ḫantitiyattalla-* "accuser, plaintiff, opponent-at-law." In that case the persons referred to may be bringing charges or claims against Ḫimuili.

REFERENCES

Text: *HKM* 10. Edition: *HBM* 134ff.

THE KING TO KAŠŠŪ IN TAPIKKA 11 (*HKM* 12) (3.23)[1]

Thus speaks His Majesty: Say to Kaššū:
(4) Seize Tarḫumiya and [send] him before [My Majesty]. [......] (Reverse) [......] and [let them] conduct him immediately before [My Majesty].

[1] What remains of this short letter appears to be an arrest order.

REFERENCES

Text: *HKM* 12. Edition: *HBM* 136ff.

THE KING TO KAŠŠŪ IN TAPIKKA 12 (*HKM* 13) (3.24)

Thus speaks His Majesty: Say to Kaššū:
(3) Concerning the capitulation(?) of Maruwa, the ruler of the city of Ḫimmuwa, about which you wrote me: "I have dispatched him (to you)." On a tablet you wrote to me: "I have dispatched him (to you)," but as of now he has not come. Now put him in the charge of an officer, and have him conduct him quickly before My Majesty.
(13) Otherwise, you will become responsible for his failure.[1]

[1] In interpreting this brief letter much depends on what is meant by "his failure" (lit., "his sin") in lines 13-14. This "failure" of Maruwa is what is called his "capitulation(?)" (*ḫaliyatar*) in line 4. The action called *ḫaliya-* in military annals is the posture of a surrendering commander. Since he is called the "ruler (lit. 'man') of Ḫimmuwa," and the latter is a Hittite city, we must assume that his sin was surrendering to the Kaškaean enemy.

REFERENCES

Text: *HKM* 13. Edition: *HBM* 138f.

THE KING TO KAŠŠŪ IN TAPIKKA 13 (*HKM* 14) (3.25)

Thus speaks His Majesty: Say to Kaššū:
(3) As soon as this tablet reaches you, drive quickly before My Majesty, and bring with you Maruwa,[1] the ruler of the city of Kakattuwa. Otherwise they will proceed to blind[2] you in that place (where you are)!

[1] It is not clear whether this Maruwa, who is called "the ruler of the city of Kakattuwa," is the same man as the "ruler of the city of Ḫimmuwa" who was mentioned in 3.24 (*HKM* 13) above. Nor is it clear if he is to be brought to the king as a culprit or not. But the urgency of the matter is obvious, hence the threat of blinding Kaššū if he does not quickly comply with the king's command.

[2] Blinding was a punishment reserved for the most serious offences, usually treason. Deliberately disobeying a direct order of the king would certainly qualify as treason. See also Letters 3.27 (*HKM* 16) below and *HKM* 84 (not translated here). For discussion, see Hoffner 2001; 2002.

REFERENCES

Text: *HKM* 14. Edition: *HBM* 139f.

THE KING TO KAŠŠŪ AND ZULAPI IN TAPIKKA 1 (*HKM* 15) (3.26)

Thus speaks His Majesty: Say to Kaššū and Zilapi: (4) As soon as this tablet reaches you, quickly — within three days[1] — bring before My Majesty the assembled troops and the chariotry which is with them.

[1] Line 11 informs us that Tapikka lay within 3 days' march of Ḫattuša.

REFERENCES

Text: *HKM* 15. Edition: *HBM* 140f.

THE KING TO KAŠŠŪ AND ZULAPI IN TAPIKKA 2 (*HKM* 16) (3.27)

Thus speaks His Majesty: Say to Kaššū and Zilapi: (5) As soon as this tablet reaches you, drive quickly before My Majesty. (11) Otherwise, they will proceed to blind you[1] in that place (where you are).

[1] See comment above on 3.25 (*HKM* 14).

REFERENCES

Text: *HKM* 16:1-15. Edition: *HBM* 142f.

THE KING TO KAŠŠŪ, ḪULLA AND ZULAPI IN TAPIKKA (*HKM* 17) (3.28)[1]

Thus speaks His Majesty: Say to Ḫulla, Kaššū and Zilapi:
(4) Concerning what you wrote me: "While we were in Ḫattuša, the Kaškaean men heard, and they drove away cattle, and kept the roads under their control."
(9) When I sent you and Ḫulla out (last) winter, (the enemies) didn't hear you. But now, of all things, they did hear you?
(13) Concerning what you yourselves have now written: "Pizzumaki told us: 'The enemy is on his way to the city of Marešta. I [have] sent Pipitaḫi out to scout the area. And we will attack the sheepfolds[2] which are in the vicinity of the city of Marešta.'" Fine. Do as you have said. (22) And if the grain crop is ready, let the troops take it.
(24)[3] Concerning what you wrote me: "How [shall I] take the city?[4] Or shall we attack the city of Kapapaḫšuwa?"
(28) Since Kapapaḫšuwa is well protected, so that [the capture] of Kapapaḫšuwa is not likely to succeed for me, they will keep its territory pressed on this side, and lie in ambush against you. [......]
(33) From the direction of Taggašta you should attack whatever [... and] the cultivated land, [and] it will succeed. And you will make ... Because [of the ...] there is no one for him.

PS (37) Say to Ḫulla, Kaššū and Zilapi: Thus speaks Ḫašammili, your servant: May all be well with you, and may the gods protect you.
(41) [......] was already released. [......] already are dressed. [...] my dear brother, keep eating (*pl.*), and [...]

[Lines 45-53 are too broken for translation]

(Left edge) [Say] to Uzzū: [Thus speaks Ḫašammili,] your brother. [May] the gods [keep you alive and

[1] In this letter the king shows his concern for several matters. He is quite displeased that the movements of his officials are so successfully monitored by the enemy that they are able to strike in his officials' absence. As usual, in his rebuke he employs heavy sarcasm (lines 9-12). He approves of their plan to scout the area of Marešta and to attack the sheepfolds there (lines 13-21), but instructs them to harvest the crops before they can be damaged or stolen by the enemy.

[2] For other indications of how the enemy used sheepfolds see *HKM* 36.

[3] In lines 24 and following the king advises his commanders on military strategy in reply to their request. Among other matters he warns them against possible ambushes.

[4] The clause at the end of line 25 is unclear. *HBM* 144's reading, *ma-an-wa ma-ah-ha-an-d*[*a*], makes no sense. But the form of the next clause, *nu ...-ma,* points to an alternative question.

protect you in well-being.] Get busy with [the ...], and write me [how the ...] are [...]-ing. But don't take anything from him until [......] something. And you must ... it just as I instruct you in writing.

REFERENCES

Text: *HKM* 17. Edition: *HBM* 142ff.

THE KING TO KAŠŠŪ AND PULLI IN TAPIKKA (*HKM* 18) (3.29)

Thus speaks [His Majesty]: Say to [Kaššū and Pulli]:

[Lines 3-15 are too badly broken for translation]

(16) And send them before My Majesty.

(17) Concerning the matter of troops about which you wrote me: I have some troops of the Upper Land and of the land of Išḫupitta here with me. I will send them to you.

PS (21) Thus speaks Pišeni: Say to Kaššū and Pulli, my dear sons:

(23) The grain which the troops of Išḫupitta and *zaltayaš* have for cultivation, now His Majesty is very concerned(?) about that grain. Send .... And quickly now. Because grain has been sown/cultivated there for them (or: for you [*pl*.]), get busy: gather it in and store it in storage pits.[1] Then [write] to His Majesty.

[1] On these pits, termed ESAG$_2$ in the texts (Hoffner 1974:34-37), see Seeher 2000; Neef 2001.

REFERENCES

Text: *HKM* 18. Edition: *HBM* 146ff.

2. LATER NEW KINGDOM (ḪATTUŠILI III TO SUPPILULIUMA II) (ca. 1250-1180 BCE)

Harry A. Hoffner, Jr.

LETTER FROM QUEEN NAPTERA OF EGYPT TO QUEEN PUDUḪEPA OF ḪATTI (3.30)

§1 Thus says Naptera, Great Queen of Egypt: Say to Puduhepa, Great Queen of Hatti, my sister:

§2 It is well with me, your sister. It is also well with my land.

§3 May it be well with you, my sister. May it also be well with your land. I have learned that you, my sister, wrote inquiring about my health, and that you wrote inquiring about the state of the alliance between the Great King of Egypt and the Great King of Hatti, his brother.

§4 The Sungod (Rē) and the Stormgod (Teššub) will exalt you, and the Sungod will cause peace to prevail and will strengthen the alliance of brotherhood between the kings of Egypt and Hatti forever.

§5 I send you herewith a present as a "greeting-gift," my sister.

§6 May they inform you, my sister, about the present that I send you in the care of Pariḫnawa, the king's messenger:

§7 One colorful necklace of fine gold made up of twelve strands and weighing 88 shekels.

§8 One dyed linen cloak.

§9 One dyed linen tunic.

§10 Five dyed linen garments of good fine thread.

§11 Five dyed linen tunics of good fine thread.

§12 A total of twelve linen garments.

REFERENCES

Text: KBo 1.29 + KBo 9.43. Edition: Edel 1978:137-143; Edel 1994 1:40-41, 2:63-64. Translations: Beckman 1996:123.

LETTER FROM ḪATTUŠILI III OF ḪATTI TO KADAŠMAN-ENLIL II OF BABYLON (3.31)

§1 Thus says Ḫattušili, Great King, King of Hatti: Say to Kadašman-Enlil, Great King, King of Babylonia, my brother:

§2 It is well with me. It is also well with my household, my wife, my sons, my infantry, my horses, [...], and with all that is in my land.

§3 May it be well with you, with your household, your wives, your sons, your infantry, your horses, your chariots, and all that is in your land.

§4 When your father and I made peace and became "brothers," we did not do so for just a single day. Was it not for eternity that we became "brothers" and concluded peace?[a] We made a pact as follows: "Since we are mortal, the survivor shall protect the children of the one who dies first." Then when your father died, but the gods [let me live long,] I wept for him like a brother.[b] [After] I had completed [the period of mourning] for your father, I dried my tears and dispatched a messenger to the nobles of Babylonia, saying: "If you do not support the progeny of my brother as the rightful rulers, I will declare war on you. I will come and conquer Babylonia. But if (you support the progeny of my brother, and) an enemy arises against you, or some other trouble occurs, write to me, and I will come to your aid." But you, my brother, were only a child in those days, and they did not read my tablet in your presence. Are none of those scribes still alive? Are my tablets not accessible? Let them read those tablets to you now. I wrote those words to them with the best intentions, but Itti-Marduk-balatu — whom the gods have let live far too long, and whose hateful words are without end — disturbed me with his reply: "You don't write us like a brother. You order us around as if we were your subjects."

§5 ...

§6 In addition, my brother: Because you wrote to me: "I have discontinued sending messengers to you, because the Aḫlamu are hostile." But how can this be? Is your kingdom so weak, my brother? Or has my brother discontinued the messengers because Itti-Marduk-balatu has poisoned my brother's mind against me? In my brother's land horses are more numerous than straw. Did I have to send a thousand chariots to meet your envoy in Tuttul, so that the Aḫlamu would have kept their hands off? And if my brother should object: "The King of Assyria will not allow my messenger to pass through his land," the infantry and chariotry of the King of Assyria does not equal those of your land. ...

§10 Regarding what you wrote: "My merchants are being killed in the land of Amurru, the land of Ugarit, [and ...]" , in Hatti they do not kill [....,] they kill [...]. When the king hears of it, [they ...] that matter. They seize the murderer [and turn] him over to the relatives of the murdered man, [but they let] the murderer [live. The place] where the murder occurred is purified. If his relatives will not accept [the compensatory payment], they may take the murderer [as a slave]. If a man who has committed a crime against the king [flees] to another land, it is not permitted to put him to death. Just ask, my brother, and they will tell you. [...] So I ask you: Would people who do not kill murderers kill a merchant (of yours)? [But with regard to] the Subarians, how do I know if they are killing people? [Send] me the relatives of the murdered merchants so that I can investigate their claims.

§11 Concerning Bentešina, (King of Amurru,) of whom my brother wrote to me: "He continually curses my land": When I asked Bentešina, he replied to me as follows: "The Babylonians owe me three talents of silver." Right now a servant of Bentešina is coming to you, so that my brother can judge his case. And concerning the curses against the land of my brother, Bentešina swore by my gods in the presence of Adad-šar-ilani, your messenger. If my brother doesn't believe this, then let his servant, who claims to have heard Bentešina curse the land of my brother, come here and face him in court. And I will press Bentešina. For Bentešina is my servant. And if he has truly cursed my brother, has he not cursed me too?[c]

§12 Furthermore, [my brother,] concerning the physician whom my brother sent here: When they received the physician, he did many [good] things. When he became ill, I did all I could for him. I instituted many oracular inquiries about him.[d] But when when his time came [...], he died. My messenger will bring his servants to you, so that my brother can [interrogate] them, and they can tell my brother all that the physician did. ... [Let] my brother [take note of] the chariot, the solid-wheeled wagon, the horses, the fine silver, and the linen that I gave to the physician. I have

a 1 Kgs 9:13-14; 20:32

b 2 Sam 10:1-2

c 2 Sam 16:9-10; 1 Kgs 21:8-14; Eccl 10:20

d 1 Kgs 14:1-3

sent the tablet on which they are written down to my brother, so that my brother can hear it.

The physician died, when his time came. I certainly did not detain the physician.

REFERENCES

Text: KBo 1.10 + KUB 3.72. Edition: Hagenbuchner 1989:281-300. Translation: Beckman 1996:132-137.

LETTER FROM PIḪA-WALWI OF ḪATTI TO IBIRANU OF UGARIT (3.32)

§1 Thus says Prince Piha-Walwi: Say to my "son" (i.e., subordinate), Ibiranu:

§2 All is well at present with His Majesy.

§3 Why have you not come before His Majesty since you became king in the land of Ugarit? Why have you not sent your messengers? His Majesty is very angry about this matter. So send your messengers to His Majesty quickly and send presents to the king together with presents also for me.

REFERENCES

Text: RS 17.247. Edition: Nougayrol 1956:191. Translation: Beckman 1996:121.

B. COURTCASES

1. RECORDS OF TESTIMONY GIVEN IN THE TRIALS OF SUSPECTED THIEVES AND EMBEZZLERS OF ROYAL PROPERTY

Harry A. Hoffner, Jr.

These texts, called "Gerichtsprotokollen" in German and "Procès" and "documents de procédure" by Laroche in *CTH* pp. 45-46, go by the name "depositions" in the *CHD*. They appear to be written records of testimony given by persons capable of clarifying cases involving the misappropriation of royal property. We do not know whether all these persons were also suspects themselves or whether some were simply associates of the true suspects. It is difficult to suppose, as some scholars do, that these are minutes of the procedure, since they do not report statements by a judge, but are confined to statements by witnesses or suspects. After preliminary remarks about the genre in Güterbock 1939, Güterbock 1955 and Gurney 1990:77, a summary of the text type (Werner 1964-1969) and an edition of all known pieces appeared (Werner 1967). A significant study of the *modus operandi* of the depositions and of the peculiar language and structure of these texts (Tani 1999) appeared after Werner's edition. As Werner 1964-1969 noted, this type of text corresponds to what in Old Babylonian is called a *ṭuppi būrti(m)*, which the *CAD* B sub *būrtu* B translates as "tablet with a sworn statement, deposition."

The texts of this type date from the second half of the New Hittite period, the reign of Ḫattušili III and his successors. They were published in the volumes KUB XIII, XXIII, XXVI and XL, and KBo XVI. Many are fragmentary, and since duplicate copies of texts of this type were not kept in the archives, we have no way to restore the lost parts. This makes producing a connected translation of most of these texts very difficult. The official edition of most of these texts is Werner 1967. A German translation of excerpts of the Ura-Tarḫunta text, based on Werner 1967, is Haase 1984. There is a much fuller translation in Spanish in Bernabé and Álvarez-Pedrosa 2000:216-220. Since only a few small fragments of this type have been identified since the publication of Werner's edition we will give here only lengthy exerpts from the better preserved tablets in his edition.

THE CASE AGAINST URA-TARḪUNTA AND HIS FATHER UKKURA (3.33)

This tablet was found in the East magazine of the Great Temple in the Lower City (quadrant L/19). It was kept there, because since it contained statements supported by oaths taken in the temple of Lelwani, its proper repository was a temple. Not all such tablets, however, were kept in that location. Some were recovered in Buildings A, D, and E of the Acropolis and others in the so-called "House on the Slope" (cf. Cornil 1987 25f. for the documentation). The plaintiff in this case was Puduḫepa, the queen and consort of Ḫattušili III. The accused were Ura-Tarḫunta ("Great is the Stormgod Tarḫunta") (for this individual cf. van den Hout 1995:157ff.) and his father Ukkura, who held the office "Overseer of Ten." The primary explicit charge was Ura-Tarḫunta's failure to keep documentation of his activities in distributing items entrusted to him by the queen. Implied is a suspicion of misappropriation or embezzlement (German *widerrechtliche Aneignung oder Verwendung,* Italian *malversazione*, Spanish *malversación,* French *détournement*).

§1 With respect to the fact that [the queen] on several occasions turned over to Ura-Tarḫunta, the son of Ukkura, the Overseer of Ten, various items — namely, chariots, items made of bronze and copper, linen garments, bows, arrows, shields, maces (or perhaps 'weapons'), civilian captives, large and small cattle, horses and mules, (the charge is that) he regularly failed to indicate on a sealed tablet what was issued to whom. He also had no manifest(?) or receipt. The queen says: "Let the 'Golden Grooms,' the queen's *šalašḫā*-men, Ura-Tarḫunta and Ukkura proceed to make comprehensive statements under oath in the temple of Lelwani."

§2 So Ukkura, the Queen's Decurius, took an oath. He made the following declaration[1] under oath: "Regarding whatever items belonging to the Crown I had, I never acted in an untrustworthy manner, and I have not taken anything for myself. I never 'skimmed off' for myself anything of what the queen from time to time entrusted to me. For the horses and mules in my custody I had a wax-coated

[1] Cf. *anda peda-* in *CHD* P 351 (1 b 2′ b′).

wood-tablet (the equivalent of the above-mentioned 'manifest'?) and a sealed receipt. They sent me to Babylonia. And while I was going to Babylonia and returning, no one was ...-ing behind my back. Yet because of that matter I am now in trouble. But when I returned from Babylonia, they sent to me an inspector too.[2] But again afterwards the matter of ... went along with (it). It was certainly a case of careless incompetence, but by no means deliberate deceit. I [have] not been misrepresenting(?) the king's words. And it never entered my mind that I should make something vanish from the king and take it for myself.

§3 Nor do I do this kind of thing. What is this? I had already sworn (to keep faith with the king)! Would I afterwards(?) take something for myself? I was obligated to that matter too. I do not subsequently take something for myself. I had hitched up three mules belonging to the palace (for my personal use), and they died. Consequently, I have already given two mules as compensation. I still owe one mule.

§4 Ura-Tarḫunta made this additional statement in regard to himself: "I took for myself three high quality harnesses for horses for the Festival of the Year. I also took for myself two mules, which died while in my possession. One mule, however, I gave to Tarḫunta-nani, the eunuch.

§5 From time to time I have been taking for myself old materials (i.e., items no longer in use by the crown): halters, wheels, leather straps, large and small *NAMTULLU*-harnesses. And whenever they bring here new bits and snaffles, I have been accepting the new ones for the service of the crown, but of the old ones I have been taking for myself as many as I liked. I took one wagon pole with mud guards for myself. I took two large axes and a hatchet for myself. And whenever they install wall hangings, I receive the new hangings for the king's house, but I have been taking for myself as many of the old ones as I liked.

§6 Yet I have been (secretly) exchanging the mules[3] of those to whom the queen has charged me to give them, saying: 'Go, give (them) to them!' I either take my own (mules) or (those) of someone else and give them to him (i.e., the person for whom the queen intends them). Then I take the mules of the palace for myself. To the other person I give mules of compensation, but under no circumstances do I give the good ones to them.

§7 Of the civilian captives that they have been giving me from the palace I took for myself one man and one woman.

§8 Of the materials from the seal house of the city Partiya that they have been giving me I took for myself the following: — (the scribe apparently inserts the following additional note:) Ura-Tarḫunta sent to his father two bolts of Palaic linen and a copper vase[4] — I took for myself ten copper items, one spear, one wash bowl, one copper *NAMMANTU*-vessel, one copper sieve, one large axe, and one chariot with leather fittings, and I sent it to my mother.[5]

[§§9 and 10 too broken for useful translation]

§11 I took for myself three cows of the *šalašḫa*-man/men and drove them to my house, where they died.

§12[6] (ii.28-37) The gold-plated bows which the queen had taken stock of I found open[ed and] stripped. I did [not] take the gold for myself. Nor did I take bows from there for myself. Nor do I know who stripped them. When I discovered it, I was very frightened on account of it. So I took the gold of my mother[a] and plated them with that. And although I did not mention it at the time, it was because Pallā the goldsmith said: 'Do not denounce me,' that I kept silent.[7]

§13 (ii.38) I did not take for myself any offering-bowl (ornamented with) 'Babylonian stone.'[8]

§14 (ii.39-45) Of the asses which I had (charge of) I took for myself nothing. Five asses died, and I replaced them from (my own) house. Five asses died from abuse. They will drive back here five jackasses (as replacements). Admittedly they haven't yet driven them here. Mr. AMAR.MUŠEN the animal-driver worked them to death,[9] and he hasn't yet replaced them. But I took nothing for myself.

[a] Judg 17:1-6

[2] Cf. Tani 1999:185. For the Hittite use of wooden tablets coated with wax, see Güterbock 1939 and Bossert 1958.

[3] It is significant that the animals given by the queen are mules, for the mule (as a sterile, non-bred animal) was the most expensive of the domestic animals. Cf. Hoffner 1997:7 with Table 2, and *COS* 2.19, §180.

[4] Pala was located in later Paphlagonia, north-northwest of Ḫattuša.

[5] Cf. §12 for more references to Ura-Tarḫunta's mother. Although his father Ukkura is still alive, his mother seems to be financially independent.

[6] The events described here remind one of Judg 17, where the mother of the Ephraimite Micah took 200 shekels of silver, had it melted down, and used to cast or plate cult images for use in a domestic shrine.

[7] Cf. *CHD* L-N 49 s.v. *lawarr-*, and Gurney 1940:97.

[8] Or perhaps: "I did not take *the* offering-bowl (ornamented with) 'Babylonian-stone' (i.e., one that Ura-Tarḫunta was perhaps accused of taking)." For the minerology cf. Polvani 1988:145.

[9] On this line and the situation portrayed by it see Sommer 1932:27.

§15 (iii.1-2) They originally gave me 30 asses; now 13 remain.[10]

§16 (iii.3-4) Of the valuable items in the storehouse I received two linen (garments), two ingots of copper, six bows, one hundred arrows, two bronze bands (for reinforcing pillars?),[11] one veil (lit. 'eye-cloth'), and one copper *dammuri*.

§17 (iii.5-8) I became ill. But when I became well again, I found in checking that we now had three ingots of copper, ten valuable bronze items, ten bows, and fifty arrows. I saw no chest belonging to Ibri-šarruma, and I declared none.

§18 (iii.9-12) Maruwa stated (as follows): "(The queen) gave a pair of mules to Ḫellarizzi."[12] Ura-Tarḫunta replied: I took the mules from Ḫ. for cultivation work (i.e., plowing),[13] and gave him colts in return."

§19 (iii.13-14) Maruwa stated: (The queen) gave [x] mules to Piḫa-Tarḫunta, the eunuch." Ura-Tarḫunta replied: "They do [not] belong to the pen."

§20 (iii.15-17) Yarra-zalma, a "Golden Groom," stated: "Zuwappi sold a horse (belonging to the queen) and thereby gained for himself a talent of copper." Ura-Tarḫunta replied: "He told me it had died."

§21 (iii.18-19) "Yarra-zalma took one mule for himself, and Maruwa took one mule for himself (from the queen's stock). But (the mules) were 'milk-sisters'."

§22 (iii.20-29) This is what Tarḫu-mimma, Nanizi, Maruwa, Yarrazalma, Pallā, Yarra-ziti the son of Tuttu, Yarra-ziti the son of Laḫina-ziti declared (on oath) before the god: "(May the gods destroy us,)[14] if we have either sold or exchanged for profit the horses or mules of the queen.[b] We neither hitched them up for ourselves nor caused their death through abuse. Furthermore, we who are supervisors, if any one (of us) took for himself horses (or) mules, or [sold] it for profit, or exchanged it, or caused its death, [.........].

b Gen 14:23; Num 16:15; 1 Sam 12:3

[Followed by seven badly broken lines]

§23 (iii.38) Kukku, the *šalašḫa*-man, is absent (and therefore unable to give testimony).

§24 (iii.39-48, iv.1-19a) Ḫapa-ziti, Kaššā, Tarwiššiya, Pallū, Kaška-muwa, Kunni, Magallū, Apattiti, Ḫuḫa-armati, Zuwā, Mutarki, Alalimmi, Šawuška-ziti, Arma-piya, Zidā, Alamūwa the boy, Tarwaški, Zuwā, (and) Šalwini — twenty (men) in all — (swore): "Regarding the chariots (with spoked) wheels, carts/wagons (with) disk wheels,[15] silver, gold, (leather) shields, maces, bows, *parzašša*-arrows, bronze implements, large axes, hatchets, bronze swords, cloth, wall-hangings, (and) leather goods belonging to the queen which we have in custody: we have not taken anything for ourselves, we have not exchanged anything, nor have we hitched up a disk-wheeled chariot or a spoke-wheeled one. Rather, when we finish (using) it, we bring it back and replace it in the controlled stock. If we take garments (or) hangings, and exchange them, or leave them out, or if our superior has taken for himself spoke-wheeled chariots, disk-wheeled wagons, silver, gold, bronze items, maces, bows, arrows, garments, (or) hangings, or if he gives one of the king's 'wheels' (i.e., a spoke-wheeled chariot?) in good condition to someone and takes three broken-down ones in exchange, or if in the future our superior takes something for himself, while we say nothing about it, or if in the future we take something for ourselves, (may the gods destroy us)!" (The queen then addresses the royal servants:) "Whatever I have previously entrusted to you of 'old' items (i.e., those no longer in active use), whether utensils, or spoke-wheeled chariots, garments, hangings, let that no longer be covered (under this oath you have taken). But now in the future you shall not take what gleams(?) (i.e., valuables as typified but not limited to gold, silver, etc.)."[16]

§26 (iv.20-27) Thus says Arlawizzi: "In the presence of the deity I make the following statement of the facts. Whatever utensils Ibri-šarruma delivered to me I brought and delivered to Ura-Tarḫunta. But (may the gods strike me dead) if I broke open a box or broke a seal or took anything for myself or Ura-Tarḫunta took anything for himself and I said nothing about it."

§27 (iv.28-34) Thus says Ḫuzziya, the Wood-Tablet Scribe: "Whatever utensils they gave to me sealed, I transfered in good condition. I did

[10] The mathematics here is unclear, since a total of 15 asses are reported dead in §14 (ii.39-45), which should leave 15, not 13.

[11] Cf. Akk. *miserru* and *CAD* M/2:110-111. GURU$_x$ (=E.ÍB). ZABAR is mentioned in the list of *melqētu* in KBo 16.68 i.13.

[12] Perhaps what is meant here is that mules belonging to (Akk. *ana*) Ḫellarizzi were given to Ura-Tarḫunta, for this would make sense of the latter's defense statement.

[13] It is the view of Melchert 1999 that Hittite *tuk(kan)zi* means "cultivation, breeding."

[14] See also §§25, 26, 27. This mode of expressing an oath is common in ancient Israelite speech: see Gen 14:23; 42:15, Num 14:23; 2 Sam 11:11, etc. Cf. *BDB* s.v. *ʾim* 1 b (2).

[15] So, following *CAD* A/2:486 (*atartu* C). Others translate: "chariots, wheels, light two-wheeled chariots."

[16] The Luwian loanword used here, *mišti-*, shares both root **maiš-/miš-* and suffix (*-t-*) with its Hittite cousin *maišt-* "brilliance, luster, glory" and the derived adjective *mišriwant-* "brilliant, lustrous, illustrious" (cf. Rieken 1999:137f.), and shows the same vocalic stem extension vis-à-vis

not break a seal, and I did not break open a box. I brought them here and delivered them to Ura-Tarḫunta. (May the gods strike me dead,) if Ura-Tarḫunta took anything for himself, and I did not report him."

§28 (iv.35-47) Thus says Ukkura, the Queen's Decurius: "When they sent me to Babylonia, I sealed the *LE᾿U*-tablets that I had concerning the horses and mules. Also a receipt was not formalized. For that very reason I didn't pay close attention. As soon as the horses and mules arrive, I will seal them in the same way. It was presumptuous of me, but it was not a deliberate offence. I didn't just look the other way, saying: 'Some things get lost, others don't.' I didn't take a horse or mule for myself or give one to anyone else.

§29 (iv.48-51) The mules that they mention died. They released [......]. [Yarra]-zalma took one mule for himself, and Maruwa also took one mule for himself."

its Hittite cognate *maišt-*, as Luwian *akk(a)ti-* "hunting net" does to Hittite *ēkt-* (of the same meaning). Earlier interpretations, including those in *CHD* L-N, must now be abandoned.

REFERENCES

Text: KUB 13.35 + KUB 23.80 + KBo 16.62 (*CTH* 293). Edition: Werner 1967 3-20.

C. ACCOUNTS

1. CULT INVENTORIES

Harry A. Hoffner, Jr.

Cult Inventories are administrative texts which were designed to keep records for royal use of the temples (both in Hattuša and in the provincial cities), their staff, the cult images found there, and the offerings and festivals held in fall and spring. They exist in several sub-sets. The first set, exemplified by KBo 2.1 (*CTH* 509) and edited by Carter 1962, place their emphasis on the various cities where temples and other cult installations were found, detailing all aspects of the cult and its equipment, but in summary fashion. A second type, exemplified by KUB 38.2, translated below, focus on the deities worshiped, and describe the images or cult objects intended to represent the deities. These Cult Image Descriptions are usually referred to under the German term *Bildbeschreibungen*.

CITY INVENTORIES

KBo 2.1 (*CTH* 509) (3.34)

Šuruwa (ii.9-20)[1]
The former state (of the cult in the city Šuruwa): four deities in all —
one stela representing the Stormgod of Šuruwa,
one stela representing the Sungoddess,
one stela of Mt. Auwara,
one stela of the spring Šinaraši.
(The present state:) one iron bull-statue of one *šekan* in size (representing the Stormgod of Šuruwa),
one silver stela of the Sungoddess, on which rays are depicted in silver,
one club with a sun disk and a crescent as ornamentation and on which is one iron figure of a standing man one *šekan* in size (representing the Mountain-god Auwara),[2]
one iron statue of a seated woman the size of a fist (representing the female deified spring Šinaraši).
Four deities of the city Šuruwa which His Majesty commissioned to be made.
(Šuruwa has) ten festivals (each year): five in the fall and five in the spring. (The offerings for each festival are) 12 sheep, 6 *PARISU*-measures and two *SŪTU* of flour, [?] vessels of beer, 3 *PARISU* of wheat for the temple storage vessels.
(Šuruwa has) one temple built. Piyama-tarawa is in charge of the silver and gold.

Wattarwa (ii.21-31)
(The state of the cult in the city Wattarwa:) one stela representing the Stormgod of Wattarwa and one statue, plated with tin, one and a half *šekan* in size. This latter shows a standing man wearing a helmet, holding a club in his right hand and a copper *ḫenzu* in his left hand. This is the former state. His Majesty had an iron bull-statue of one *šekan* height made.
For the Stormgod of Wattarwa the daily offering is as follows: one handful of flour, one cup of beer.
(Wattarwa has) two festivals (each year): one in the fall and one in the spring.
His Majesty has instituted (as the offerings for each festival) one bull, 14 sheep, 5 *PARISU* and 4 *SŪTU* of flour, 4 vessels of low-grade beer, 10 vessels of regular beer, 1 *ḫuppar* vessel of beer, and 3 *SŪTU* of wheat for the temple storage vessels. The city shall give them.
(Wattarwa has) one temple built. The priest has fled.

Ḫuršalašši (ii.32-39)
The former state (of the cult in the city Ḫuršalašši): (the deities are presented by) 1 bronze *wakšur*-vessel, 1 stela (representing the female) deified spring Ḫapuriyata.
His Majesty has made 1 iron bull statue 1 *šekan* in size, 1 small iron statue of a seated woman representing the spring Ḫapuriyata.
(The city Ḫursalašši has) 3 festivals (each year): one in the fall and two in the spring.
(Offerings for each festival are:) 1 bull, 4 sheep, 4 *PARISU* and 1 *SŪTU* of flour, 1 vessel of low-grade beer, 11 vessels of regular beer. The city will give (these things).
(The town has) 1 temple built. The priest has fled.

Aššaratta (ii.40-45)
Stormgod of Aššaratta: one stela from earlier

[1] Translated by Güterbock 1983a:216.
[2] See the discussion of such TUKUL's in Güterbock 1983a:214f.

times.
His Majesty has made: 1 iron bull statue 1 *šekan* in size.
(The town has) 2 festivals (each year): one in the fall and one in the spring.
His Majesty has instituted (as offerings for each festival): 1 bull, 4 sheep, 3 *PARISU* of flour, 1 vessel of low-grade beer, 8 vessels of regular beer, and 3 *SŪTU* (of wheat) for the temple storage vessels.
(The town has) 1 temple built. Nattaura is in charge of the silver.

Šaruwalašši (iii.1-6)
The former state (of the cult in Šaruwalašši): The Stormgod of Šaruwalašši is represented by 1 stela.
His Majesty has made: one iron bull statue one *šekan* in size.
(The town has) 2 festivals (each year): one in the fall and one in the spring.
His Majesty has instituted (as offerings for each festival): one bull, 4 sheep, 2 *PARISU* of flour, 6 vessels of beer, and 3 *SŪTU* of wheat for the temple storage vessels.
(The town has) one temple built. But it has no priest yet.

Šanantiya (iv.1-16)
The former state (of the cult of) [the Stormgod] of Šanantiya: 3 sun disks of silver, of which one sun disk is of iron (i.e., 2 of silver, one of iron), [one] *wakšur* vessel of bronze, one "thunder horn."
His Majesty has had 2 (representations of) deities made: one iron bull standing on all fours, 2 *šekan* in size, whose eyes (i.e., face) is plated with gold, one silver statue of a seated woman, one *šekan* in size, under which are two iron mountain sheep, under which is an iron base, (and) ten gold rays, representing the Sungoddess of Šanantiya.
[The daily offering is] one handful of flour.
There are 8 festivals each year: 2 in the fall, [2] in the spring, one festival of the rain, one propitiation(?)-festival, one festival of the sickle, one 'mercy'-festival. And His Majesty has instituted in addition 2 more festivals: one festival of the entry of the new (priest), and one festival of [...].
(Yearly offerings:) 3 bulls, of which [His Majesty instituted] one bull, 93 sheep, 33 *PARISU* of wine for the temple storage vessels, of which His Majesty instituted 2 *SŪTU* [of wine for the temple storage vessels]. The city provides (these) for him (i.e., for the Stormgod).
The temple is not yet built. The king was able (to care) for the Stormgod of Šanantiya.

REFERENCES

Text: KBo 2.1. Edition: Carter 1962:51-73.

CULT IMAGE DESCRIPTIONS

The posture of the images and the objects they hold in their hands are illustrated by many cult figures depicted on reliefs and in particular by the great relief scene on the walls of Yazılıkaya (Laroche 1952; Beran 1962; Bittel, Naumann, and Otto 1967; Laroche 1969; Güterbock 1975; Masson 1981; Güterbock 1982). For a convenient line drawing of the procession in a popular book see Gurney 1990:118f. figure 8.

KUB 38.2 (Bildbeschr. Text 1) (3.35)

(i.7-20) *IŠTAR* (Šauška) [a cult-image ......] seated; from (her) shoulders [wings protrude;] in (her) right hand [she holds] a gold cup; [in her left hand] she holds a gold (hieroglyphic sign for) "Good(ness)."[1] [...] Below her is a silver-plated base. [Under] the base lies a silver-plated *awiti*-animal.[2] To the right [and left] of the *awiti*-animal's wings[a] stand Ninatta and Kulitta, their silver eyes plated with gold. And under the *awiti*-animal is a wooden base. Her daily offering is "thick bread" made from a handful of flour, and a clay cupful of wine. Her monthly festival includes Ninatta and Kulitta together. She has (at present) no priest. (Another of her images is) one gold

[a] Exod 25:20; 37:9; 1 Kgs 6:23-28; 8:6-7; Isa 6:1-2

[1] This is the sign that looks like a triangle (Laroche *HH* sign no. 370) with the new "Latinographic" transcriptional value BONUS_2.
[2] Most likely a lion-griffin (Güterbock 1975:190) or lion-sphynx (Güterbock 1983a:205, n. 15). For literature and summary of research, see also *HW*[2] A and *HED* A s.v.

vessel in the form of and ox's head and neck.
(i.21-27, ii.1-3) Šauška[3] of the Battle Cry[4]: a cult image made of gold, a standing man; from his/her shoulders wings protrude; in his/her right hand he/she holds a gold axe;[5] in his/her left hand he/she holds a gold (hieroglyphic sign for) "Good(ness)"; standing on his/her *awiti*-animal,[6] having a silver-plated tail[7] and a gold-plated chest; but [behind], to the right and left of its wings stand Ninatta and Kulitta. [......] /His/Her [two festivals] are in fall [and spring]. She has no monthly festival [......]
(ii.4-7) [Karmah]ili: a cult image (of) a seated man; [his eyes are] gold-plated; [in his right hand] he holds a club. Beneath him is a silver base. The small ruined cities celebrate his [two festivals] in fall and spring. His has no servant.
(ii.8-13)[8] The Stormgod of Heaven: cult image (of) a seated man, gold-plated; in his right hand he holds a club; in his left hand he holds a gold (hieroglyphic sign for) "Good(ness)." He stands[9] on two silver-plated mountains (represented as) men. Beneath him is a silver base. Two silver animal-shaped[10] vessels (are there). His two festivals are in fall and spring. [They give it] from the house [of the king.]
(ii.14-16) The Stormgod of the House: (His cult emblem is) a silver ox's head and neck including the front quarters kneeling. His two festivals are [in fall] and spring. [They] give (it) from the house of the king.
(ii.17-23) The Warrior-god "Zababa": a silver cult-image of a man, [standing]; in his right hand he holds a club; in his left [hand] he holds a shield. Beneath him there stands a lion figure, and under the lion a silver-plated base. The men of Kammama celebrate two festivals in fall and spring. One silver ZA.ḪUM-vessel. He has no servant.[11]
(ii.24-26, iii.1-4) The Tutelary Deity (^{d}LAMMA): a gold-plated cult image of a standing man with gold-plated eyes. In his right hand he holds a silver lance; in his left hand he holds a shield. He stands on a stag. Beneath him is a silver-plated base. The ruined cities of Dala celebrate his two festivals in fall and spring. He has no servant.
(iii.5-8) The Sungod of Heaven: silver cult image of a seated man. On his head is a silver ...[12]; beneath him is a wooden base. The men of Pada celebrate two festivals (for him) in fall and spring.
(iii.9-11) Stormgod of the (Royal) House: a silver (vessel in the shape of an) ox's head and neck with the front quarters in standing position. The men of the city celebrate his two festivals in fall and spring (with) one silver ZA.ḪUM vessel.
(iii.12-17) Ḫatepuna: cult image of a woman, veiled(?) [like] a ...,[13] her eyes plated with gold. She holds in her right hand a silver cup. Beneath her is a wooden base. The men of [......] celebrate her two festivals in fall and spring. She has a *šiwanzanni*-priestess.[14]
(iii.18-20) Mt. Išdaḫarunuwa:[15] a *ḫutuši*-vessel for wine silver-plated on the inside, one silver *ašzeri*-vessel. The men of Pada (celebrate his two festivals) in fall and spring.
(iii.21-24) *Ḫegur*-house of Temmuwa: likewise a *ḫutuši*-vessel for wine silver-plated on the inside. The men of Dala ce[lebrate] two festivals in fall and spring.

[The tablet breaks at this point]

[3] The tablet has the signs ^{d}LIŠ which indicate a female deity of the *IŠTAR* type. Von Brandenstein emended to ^{d}U (stormgod), because the cult image is of a man. But since *IŠTAR* is bisexual, and he/she is attended here by his/her handmaids Ninatta and Kulitta, it is preferable (with Laroche 1952:116f., 119) to leave the tablet unemended.

[4] So both Laroche 1952 and Güterbock 1983a:205 n. 11.

[5] Such an axe may be depicted on the Hattuša Warrior Gate; Bittel 1976 pls. 267-268.

[6] Depicted so on the Ashmolean Gold Ring (Hogarth 1920 seal no. 195).

[7] "Tail" (Güterbock 1975:190), not "teeth" (von Brandenstein 1943).

[8] Güterbock 1975:189.

[9] Or, less likely, IGI DU-*anteš* (with Otten, cited in Güterbock 1975:189) "(two) forward striding (mountains)."

[10] Perhaps bull-shaped (Güterbock 1975:189).

[11] The Sumerogram ^{d}ZA.BA$_{4}$.BA$_{4}$ can stand for various deities in Hittite texts. This description does not match any of the warrior-god types depicted at Yazılıkaya (Güterbock 1983a:205).

[12] One reading of the signs, adopted by von Brandenstein 1943:8, is KU$_{6}$.ḪI.A-*za* "fishes." If the reading is correct, one can only venture the guess that the scribe here misunderstood the winged sun-disk that often stands over this god's head as a fish symbol (Güterbock 1983a:206). This deity is depicted in Yaz. No. 34.

[13] If read $^{\langle MUNUS\rangle}$KAR.K[ID?] (without determinative!), lit. "prostitute." But see objections of Güterbock 1983a:206. So also in the last sentence of this paragraph.

[14] AMA.DINGIR, so read by L. Rost.

[15] In Hittite cosmology mountains are male deities and springs are female ones.

REFERENCES

Text: KUB 38.2. Edition: von Brandenstein 1943:4-11, with commentary on 23-45. See the tabular presentation of the data for each deity on his foldout tables 1 and 2. Discussions: Jakob-Rost 1963, 1963; Güterbock 1964; Orthmann 1964; Güterbock 1983a.

2. VOTIVE RECORDS

Harry A. Hoffner, Jr.

This category of texts records vows made by members of the royal family in order to secure favors from the gods and goddesses. The earliest example in the corpus dates to the reign of Muwatalli II. But the vast majority of preserved examples date from the reign of his second successor, Ḫattušili III. The most frequent person making these vows is Ḫattušili's famous consort, Queen Puduḫepa. The texts often indicate the god or goddess to whom the vow is made and the city in which it was made in the course of the royal couple's travels to preside at regional festivals. The items most frequently promised to the deity were items of precious metal (gold, silver, etc.), of which the weight is given as well, but not the dimensions. Many (but by no means all) such entries conclude with a notation as to whether or not the vowed items have been given yet. Outside of this text category we know of examples of dreams which gave rise to vows and how they were fulfilled. The best-known example is the dream in which Šawuška sent Prince Muwatalli to his father Muršili, promising that the seriously ill Prince Ḫattušili would recover and live to a ripe old age provided that Muršili would devote him to Šawuška's priesthood. This Muršili did, and Ḫattušili III in fact lived to an advanced age (cf. *COS* 1.77, §3). The complete corpus as it was known at the time was edited in the Dutch Ph.D. dissertation of de Roos 1984 (English summary on pp. 175-180), who notes in his comparative survey of the major cultures of the ancient Near East that the closest parallels to the Hittite vow texts are to be found in Ugarit and in ancient Israel (pp. 178f.). The following text illustrates the type. The votary gifts always match something in the request: bath house, ear, etc. The same procedure is seen in 1 Sam 6:4, where the Philistine lords bribe Yahweh to remove the plague of mice and tumors by giving him gold images of the same, and five in number because of the five Philistine cities affected.

KUB 15.1 (*CTH* 584.1) (3.36)

(i.1-11)[1] Ḫebat of the city Uda. Dream of the queen. When ......, the queen in the dream vowed to Ḫebat of Uda as follows: "If you, O goddess, my lady, will preserve the life of His Majesty, i.e., you will not allow him to come to harm, I will make for Ḫebat a gold statuette, and I will make for her a gold rosette, and they shall call it 'Ḫebat's rosette.' I will also make a gold toggle pin for your breast, and they shall call it 'the goddess's toggle pin.'"

(i.12-14) Dream of the queen. In my dream Ḫebat asked for a necklace with sun-disks and lapis lazuli. We inquired further by oracle, and it was determined that (this Ḫebat was) the Ḫebat of Uda.

(i.15-18) Dream.[2] In the dream the king said to me: "Ḫebat says, 'In the land of Ḫatti let them make *zizzaḫi* for me, but in the land of Mukiš let them make wine for me.'" Further investigation by oracle will be made.

[The rest of the column is too fragmentary for coherent translation.]

(ii.1-4) In a dream [the king] made the following vow to the king's deity ZA.BA₄.BA₄ (warrior god): If you, O god, my lord, will preserve my life, I will plate for you a stela and an altar.

(ii.5-10)[3] Šarruma of Urikina. Since in a dream some young men molested (lit. shut in) the queen behind the bath house in the city Iyamma, in the dream the queen vowed one silver (model of a) bath house to Šarruma of Urikina.

(ii.11-12) The queen vowed to Šarrumanni of Urikina one gold ZI-ornament of unspecified weight, and one silver ZI of 10 shekels weight.

(ii.13-24)[4] As these curses were determined by oracular investigation, now because it is impossible to undo them, while I look after that matter, and while I complete the offerings, if Šarruma? of Urikina(?), my lord, [will ......] to/for His Majesty, [......] ...... [......], I will make for Šarruma, my lord, one silver shield trimmed with gold of unspecified weight.

(ii.25-27) And if you, Šarruma, my lord, incline your ear to me in this matter, i.e., you hear me, I will give to Šarruma one gold ear of 10 shekels weight, and one silver ear of one mina weight.[5]

(ii.28-36)[6] And if you two Šarrumanni-deities and one Allanzunni-deity, who have emerged from the deity's knees,[7] if you hear this my plea, and relay it (favorably) to Šarruma, so that no evil matter shall befall His Majesty, then while he is undoing these curses (with offerings), I will make for each of the two Šarrumanni-deities and the one Allan-

[1] Discussed in Oppenheim 1956:254.

[2] A different logogram is used here: U₃.NUN instead of simple U₃.

[3] Discussed in Oppenheim 1956:227. See below in ii.37-44, where the queen had the same dream in the city of Layuna.

[4] Discussed in Güterbock 1957:359.

[5] In Hurrian-influenced rituals invoking the assistance of netherworld deities, models of ears in silver or gold were lowered into ritual pits for the gods (Hoffner 1967).

[6] Discussed in Beckman 1983:40.

[7] I.e., they are his offspring.

zunni-deity one gold ear and one silver ear of unspecified weight.
(ii.37-41) Šarruma of the city Layuna. As in a dream in the city of Layuna certain young men were molesting the queen behind the bath house, in the dream the queen vowed to Šarruma of Layuna one gold (model of a) bath house.
(ii.42-44) A dream of the queen. Šarruma spoke to me in a dream. But on top of the mountain(s) he will give food in 12 (cult) locations. Further investigation by oracle will be made.
(ii.45-52) In a dream the queen made the following plea to (the goddess named) the Queen of Tarḫuntašša for the days of the Festival of Torches: If His Majesty doesn't get any worse on my account, I will [sacrifice to] the Queen of Tarḫuntašša [......] ......

[Several paragraphs are too broken to translate here.]

(iii.7-16)[8] [Dream of the queen.] When the matter of the deity Kurwašu [......], as Kurwašu spoke to the queen in a dream: "That matter regarding your husband which you hold in your heart, he will live. I will give to him 100 years (of life)!" In the dream the queen made the following vow: "If you will do that for me, and my husband will live, I will give to the deity three large storage jars: one filled with oil, one with honey, and one with fruit.
(iii.17-21) His Majesty made the following vow to the goddess Kataḫḫa: "If the city of Ankuwa survives, i.e., it isn't totally burned, I will make for Kataḫḫa one silver (model of a) city[9] of unspecified weight, and I will give one ox and 8 sheep."
(iii.22-26) The queen made the following vow to the Stormgod of Heaven: "If the city of Ankuwa survives, i.e., it isn't totally burned, I will make for the Stormgod of Heaven one silver (model of a) city of unspecified weight, and I will give one ox and 8 sheep."
(iii.27-31) His Majesty made the following vow to the Stormgod of Zippalanda: "If the city of Ankuwa survives, i.e., it isn't totally burned, I will make for the Stormgod of Zippalanda one silver (model of a) city of unspecified weight, and I will give one ox and 8 sheep."
(iii.48-53) [The queen] made the following vow [on behalf of] the royal prince, the king of Išuwa: "If the prince recovers from this illness, I will [.........] and I will give to the deity on behalf of the prince, the king of Išuwa, a sword, a dagger(?), and one silver ZI-ornament of unspecified weight.

[Most of the rest of the text is too badly broken for translation.]

[8] Cf. Oppenheim 1956:254f. and Kammenhuber 1964:171.
[9] On the votive cities of silver and gold, see Hoffner 1969.

REFERENCES

Text: KUB 15.1. Edition: de Roos 1984:184-197, 324-336.

3. ARCHIVE SHELF LISTS

Harry A. Hoffner, Jr.

These texts, also called "catalogs," list the tablets in the state archives of Ḫattuša. They indicate the author and/or title/incipit of the work, how many tablets it comprised, the tablet's form (ordinary tablets called DUB, special tablets called IM.GÍD.DA "long tablet"), and whether or not all known tablets were found. All such tablets were found in Boğazköy itself; to date none has been reported in Maşat (Tapikka), Kuşakli (Šarišša), or Ortaköy (Šapinuwa). What is translated below is only a small selection to give an impression of these texts. They are identified by the find spot, if that information is available. A new and complete edition is being prepared by Paola Dardano for the series *Studien zu den Boğazköy Texten*.

FROM BÜYÜKKALE, BUILDING A, ROOMS 1-2 (3.37)

(i.18-20) One tablet, whose composition is not complete, entitled "[If/When ......] his ZI's are constantly ...-ing, this incantation is intended for him. The word of Ḫutupi, the physician." The second tablet (on which the composition would have been completed) is missing.
(i.21-22) Tablet Two of (the Ritual for) the Tutelary Deity of the Hunting Bag,[1] containing the completion (of the composition) — the Tablet One is missing — (with the incipit) "When the king himself worships the Tutelary Deity of the Hunting Bag."

[1] On this deity and his cult see McMahon 1991.

(i.23) Tablet Two of the city of Turmitta, with the composition finished, of the invocation of the fate-deities.[2]
(i.24) [Tablet] One of the invocation of the god Telipinu.
(i.25-26) [Tablet One], complete of "When in Arinna [......] seats [...]"

a 1 Sam 28:8-14

(i.27) [Tablet One,] complete of the invocation of the Sungod(dess). (i.28-29) [Tablet One,] complete of the invocation entitled "If/When a dead person is evoked for someone".[a]
(i.30-32) [Tablet One, complete:] "When in the fall the holy priest drives [......] to his house in order to unseal [the temple storage jars]."

[2] For these *gulses*-deities, see Bossert 1957; Otten and Siegelová 1970; Haas 1994:272-275, 779-781; Popko 1995:72, 81, 111, 124.

REFERENCES

Text: KUB 30.60 + KBo 14.70. Edition: Laroche 1971:153-193. Studies: Laroche 1949; Otten 1986; Güterbock 1991-92; Košak 1995.

FROM BÜYÜKKALE, BUILDING A, ROOMS 4-5 (3.38)

(B ii.3-4) [Tablet ?: "When] (they perform) for *IŠTAR* of Mt. Amana the festival of the doves, the festival of lamentation, and the festival of birth(?)"[1]
(B ii.5-7) [Tablet ?.] The ritual (lit. word) of Ammiḫatna, Mati and Tulpiya: "[If] they find some sacrilege in a holy temple, this is how they re-consecrate it."[2]
(B ii.8) [Tablet ?]: "If the Great King has a fit of anger in Ḫattuša".[a]
(A ii.8-10) [Tablet ?:] "If a person is not consecrated, [...] a mouse [in the ...] of the Stone House, or (if) he is consecrated, and someone [...-s] this to him [...]"
(A ii.11-13) Two tablets: "When they build a new temple, and pound [the *kupti*] in", and one tablet: "When [the ...] pounds the *kupti* in [...]"[3]
(A ii.14-17) Two tablets, the ritual (lit. word) of Eḫal-Teššub, the exorcist from Aleppo: "[If a man and woman] are not in harmony[4] [...] beforehand, or if [a man and a woman] are always quarreling, or if they keep having bad [dreams], then the exorcist [performs] this ritual." (Composition) [finished.][5]
(A ii.18) One tablet[6]: "If (the consequence of) serious perjury (or: 'a powerful oath') seizes a person," [finished].
(A ii.19-28) Three tablets. The ritual of Yarinu, the man from the city Ḫaršumna: "If [...,] or if he [...s] somehow into impurity, or] his years are 'troubled', or if he is designated (lit. 'spoken') [for ...], or if [he keeps seeing] bad [dreams], or if he has taken an oath (falsely?), or if [his] father and mother have cursed him before the gods,[7] [b] or if [...] a wife of second rank, or if some wife of second rank[8] [committed(?)] an impure act with him, ..."

a 1 Sam 16:14-23
b Judg 17:2

[1] Or: "and the festival of giving birth(?)."
[2] The text referred to is preserved as *CTH* 472. Cf. also KUB 30.42 iv.19-23.
[3] For the *kupti*-, see Puhvel 1997:259f. with lit. cited there.
[4] For *ḫandai*- with this meaning, see Güterbock 1983b.
[5] This ritual seems to concern itself with troubled marriages, much like the Maštigga Ritual (*CTH* 404, English translation in *ANET* 350f. "Ritual Against Domestic Quarrel").
[6] The duplicate adds: "The ritual of Arma-ziti, the exorcist".
[7] In the Hurrian-Hittite bilingual, see Hoffner 1998:70-72.
[8] An Akkadogram ^{MUNUS}*NAPTĀRTU*.

REFERENCES

Text: A = KUB 30.51 + 45 + HSM 3644; B = KUB 30.58 + 44 (+) KBo 7.74). Edition: Laroche 1971:159ff. Studies: Laroche 1949; Otten 1986; Güterbock 1991-92; Košak 1995.

FROM BÜYÜKKALE, BUILDING A (3.39)

(iv.3-5) Tablet Two: "When the king, queen and princes give substitutes to the Sungoddess of the Netherworld." (Composition) finished. We didn't find the first tablet.
(iv.6-7) Tablet One: The word of Annana, woman from Zigazḫur: "When I invoke the deity Miyatanzipa." (Composition) finished.
(iv.8-10) One "long tablet": "When the singer libates in the temple of the deity Inar, breaks thick loaves, and recites in Ḫattic as follows." (Composition) finished.
(iv.11-13) Tablet One of the *zintuḫi*-women. How they speak before the king in the temple of the Sungod(dess). (Composition) finished.
(iv.14) One "long tablet": The songs of the men of Ištanuwa. (Composition) finished.
(iv.15-18) Tablet One; a treaty. How Išputaḫšu, King of the land of Kizzuwatna, and Telepinu, King of the Land of Ḫatti, concluded a treaty. (Composition) finished.
(iv.19-24) One "long tablet": The word(s) of Ammihatna, Tulpiya, and Mati, the *purapši*-men of the Land of Kizzuwatna: "If they find any sacrilege in the temple, the holy place, this is its ritual;" (composition) finished.

REFERENCES

Text: KUB 30.42 rev. iv.2ff. Edition: Laroche 1971:163ff. Studies: Laroche 1949; Otten 1986; Güterbock 1991-92; Košak 1995.

FROM BÜYÜKKALE, BUILDING E (3.40)

(iii.2-3) "When they give [a festival(?)] in Šapinuwa to [the Stormgod(?)] in the third year."
(iii.4) "When [they draw] from the road the Mother goddesses of the (king's?) body."
(iii.5-6) "When they celebrate the Spring Festival in Kulella for the Stormgod of Kul[ella]."
(iii.7-9) The word of Kantuzzi[li, Chief of the] priests (and) Prince: "When they pour [......], and they call a little [......], how they put down [......] at his feet in the temple;" the ritual [...]
(iii.10-13) The word of Eḫal-Teššub, the exorcist from Aleppo: "When a person's male and female slaves are [not] in harmony, or a man and woman are not in harmony, or a man and woman are having bad dreams, how one [offers] to the deity the ritual of alienation from a evil person."
(iii.14) "When someone offers *ḫarnalianza* to the Goddess of the Night."
(iii.15) "Whenever they move the gods from their (usual) places."
(iii.16-17) "How from Ḫattuša one goes to renew the Tutelary Deity of Ḫalinzuwa and Tuḫuppiya."
(iii.18) "When someone [...-es] before the deity Alawayammi."
(iii.19-20) "When the king worships the Stormgod of the Army, the Overseer of the thousands of the Field and the dignitaries give cattle and sheep."
(iii.21-22) "When from Šamuḫa the *IŠTAR* of the Battlefield comes along with His Majesty, how the ritual material (*ḫazziwi*) comes on the return trip."

[Rest of the column fragmentary]

REFERENCES

Text: KUB 30.56 iii.2-22. Edition: Laroche 1971:163ff. Studies: Laroche 1949; Otten 1986; Güterbock 1991-92; Košak 1995.

HITTITE BIBLIOGRAPHY

BECKMAN, G. M.
1983 *Hittite Birth Rituals*. StBoT 29. Wiesbaden: Harrassowitz.
1996 *Hittite Diplomatic Texts*. SBLWAW 7. Atlanta: Scholars Press.

BERAN, T.
1962 "Das Felsheiligtum von Yazılıkaya. Deutung und Datierung." *Zeitschrift für Kulturaustausch. Institut für Auslandsbeziehungen Stuttgart* 12/2-3:146-152.

BERNABÉ, A., and J. A. ÁLVAREZ-PEDROSA.
2000 *Historia y Leyes de Los Hititas. Textos del Imperio Antiguo. El Código*. Madrid: Akal.

BITTEL, K.
1976 *Die Hethiter. Die Kunst Anatoliens vom Ende des 3. bis zum Anfang des 1. Jahrtausends vor Christus*. München: C. H. Beck.

BITTEL, K., R. NAUMANN, and H. OTTO.
1967 *Yazılıkaya: Architektur, Felsbilder, Inschriften und Kleinfunde*. Neudruck der Ausg. 1941. ed. WVDOG 61. Osnabrück: Zeller.

BOLEY, J.
2000 *Dynamics of Transformation in Hittite. The Hittite Particles -kan, -asta and -san*. IBS 97. Innsbruck: Institut für Sprachwissenschaft der Universität Innsbruck.

BOSSERT, H. T.
1957 "Die Schicksalsgöttinnen der Hethiter." *WO* 2:349-359.
1958 "Sie schrieben auf Holz." Pp. 67-79 in *Minoica. Festschrift zum 80 Geburtstag von Johannes Sundwall*. Ed. by E. Grumach. Deutsche Akademie der Wissenschaften zu Berlin. Schriften der Sektion für Altertumswissenschaft 12. Berlin: Akademie-Verlag.

CARTER, C. W.
1962 *Hittite Cult Inventories*. Ph.D. Dissertation, University of Chicago.

CORNIL, P.
1987 "Textes de Boghazköy. Liste des lieux de trouvaille." *Hethitica* 7:5-72.

DE ROOS, J.
1984 "Hettitische Geloften. Een teksteditie van Hettitische geloften met inleiding, vertaling en critische noten." Ph.D. dissertation, Universiteit van Amsterdam.

EDEL, E.
1978 *Der Brief des ägyptischen Wesirs Pašijara an den Hethiterkönig Hattušili und verwandte Keilschriftbriefe*. NAWG 1. Phil.-hist. Kl. Jahrgang 1978, Nr. 4. Göttingen: Vandenhoeck & Ruprecht.
1994 *Die ägyptisch-hethitische Korrespondenz aus Boghazköi in babylonischer und hethitischer Sprache*. ARWAW 77. Opladen: Westdeutscher Verlag.

GURNEY, O. R.
1940 "Hittite Prayers of Mursili II." *AAA* 27:3-163.
1990 *The Hittites*. Second edition with revisions. Baltimore: Penguin Books.

GÜTERBOCK, H. G.
1939 "Das Siegeln bei den Hethitern." Pp. 26-36 in *Studies Koschaker*.
1955 "Zu einigen hethitischen Komposita." Pp. 63-68 in *Studies Sommer*.
1957 "Review of J. Friedrich, *Hethitisches Wörterbuch* (Heidelberg 1952)." *Oriens* 10:350-362.
1964 "Religion und Kultus der Hethiter." Pp. 54-75 in *Neuere Hethiterforschung*. Ed. by G. Walser. Wiesbaden: Franz Steiner.
1975 "Die Inschriften." Pp. 167-187 in *Das hethitische Felsheiligtum Yazılıkaya*. Ed. by K. Bittel, J. Boessneck, B. Damm, H. G. Güterbock, H. Hauptmann, R. Naumann and W. Schirmer. Berlin: Gebr. Mann.
1982 *Les hiéroglyphes de Yazılıkaya: A propos d'un travail récent. Institut francais d'études anatoliennes*. Paris: Editions Recherche sur les Civilisations.
1983a "Hethitische Götterbilder und Kultobjekte." Pp. 203-217 in *Studies Bittel*.
1983b "A Hurro-Hittite Hymn to Ishtar." *JAOS* 103:155-164.
1991-92 "Bemerkungen über die im Gebäude A auf Büyükkale gefundenen Tontafeln." *AfO* 38-39:1-10.

HAAS, V.
1994 *Geschichte der hethitischen Religion*. HdO 1. Abteilung. 15. Band. Leiden: Brill.

HAASE, R.
1984 *Texte zum hethitischen Recht. Eine Auswahl*. Wiesbaden: Reichert.

HAGENBUCHNER, A.
1989 *Die Korrespondenz der Hethiter. 2. Teil*. THeth 16. Heidelberg: Carl Winter.

HOFFNER, H. A., Jr.
1967 "Second Millennium Antecedents to the Hebrew ᵓÔḆ." *JBL* 86:385-401.
1969 "The 'City of Gold' and the 'City of Silver.'" *IEJ* 19:178-180.
1974 *Alimenta Hethaeorum: Food Production in Hittite Asia Minor*. AOS 55. New Haven: American Oriental Society.
1997 "The Hittite Laws." Pp. 211-247 in *Law Collections from Mesopotamia and Asia Minor*. 2nd Ed. Ed. by M. T. Roth. Atlanta: Scholars Press.
1997 *The Laws of the Hittites. A Critical Edition*. Documenta et Monumenta Orientis Antiqui 23. Leiden: Brill.
1998 *Hittite Myths*. Ed. by S. Parker. 2nd revised ed. SBLWAW 2. Atlanta: Scholars Press.
2001 "The Disabled and Infirm in Hittite Society." Pp. in *EI* 27 (Miriam and Hayim Tadmor Volume). Ed. by A. Ben-Tor, I. Ephal and P. Machinist. Jerusalem: Israel Exploration Society.
2002 "The Treatment and Long-term Use of Persons Captured in Battle According to the Maşat Texts." Pp. 61-71 in *Recent Developments in Hittite Archaeology and History*. Ed. by H. G. Güterbock, H. A. Hoffner, Jr. and K. A. Yener. Winona Lake, IN: Eisenbrauns.

HOGARTH, D. G.
1920 *Hittite Seals*. Oxford.
HOUWINK TEN CATE, Ph. H. J.
1998 "The Scribes of the Maşat Letters and the GAL DUB.SAR(.MEŠ) of the Hittite Capital during the Fnal Phase of the Early Empire Period." Pp. 157-178 in *Studies Römer*.
JAKOB-ROST, L.
1963 "Zu den hethitischen Bildbeschreibungen, I." *MIO* 8:161-217.
1963 "Zu den hethitischen Bildbeschreibungen, II." *MIO* 9:175-239.
KAMMENHUBER, A.
1964 "Die hethitischen Vorstellungen von Seele und Leib, Herz und Leibesinnerem, Kopf und Person." *ZA* 56:150-222.
KOŠAK, S.
1995 "The Palace Library 'Building A' on Büyükkale." Pp. 173-180 in *Studies Houwink ten Cate*.
LAROCHE, E.
1949 "La bibliothèque de Hattusa." *ArOr* 17/2:7-23.
1952 "Le Panthéon de Yazılıkaya." *JCS* 6:114-123.
1969 "Les dieux de Yazılıkaya." *RHA* XXVII/84-85:61ff.
1971 *CTH* 75.
MASSON, E.
1981 *Le pantheon de Yazılıkaya: Nouvelles lectures*. Paris: Institut Français d'Études Anatoliennes.
MCMAHON, J. G.
1991 *The Hittite State Cult of the Tutelary Deities*. Ed. by T. A. Holland. AS 25. Chicago: The Oriental Institute of The University of Chicago.
MELCHERT, H. C.
1999 "Hittite tuk(kan)zi- 'cultivation, breeding'." *Ktema* 24:17-23.
NEEF, R.
2001 "Getreide im Silokomplex an der Poternenmauer (Boğazköy)—Erste Aussagen zur Landwirtschaft." *AA*.
NOUGAYROL, J.
1956 *PRU* IV.
OPPENHEIM, A. L.
1956 *The Interpretation of Dreams in the Ancient Near East*. TAPS NS 46.3. Philadelphia: American Philosophical Society.
ORTHMANN, W.
1964 "Hethitische Götterbilder." Pp. 221-229, plates 23-30 in *Studies Moortgat*.
OTTEN, H.
1986 "Archive und Bibliotheken in Hattuša." Pp. 184-190 in *Cuneiform Archives and Libraries*. *RAI* 30. Ed. by K. R. Veenhof. Leiden and Istanbul: Netherlands Institute for the Near East.
OTTEN, H., and J. SIEGELOVÁ.
1970 "Die hethitischen Gulš-Gottheiten und die Erschaffung der Menschen." *AfO* 23:32-38.
POLVANI, A. M.
1988 *La terminologia dei minerali nei testi ittiti. Parte prima*. Eothen 3. Firenze: Edizione Librarie Italiane Estere (ELITE). Edizioni librarie italiane estere.
POPKO, M.
1995 *Religions of Asia Minor*. Trans. by I. Zych. Warsaw: Academic Publications Dialog.
PUHVEL, J.
1997 *Hittite Etymological Dictionary*. Volume 4: *K*. Ed. by W. Winter and R. A. Rhodes. Trends in Linguistics. Documentation 5. Berlin and New York: Mouton de Gruyter.
RIEKEN, E.
1999 *Untersuchungen zur nominalen Stammbildung des Hethitischen*. StBoT 44. Wiesbaden: Harrassowitz.
SEEHER, J.
2000 "Getreidelagerung in unterirdischen Grosspeichern: Zur Methode und ihrer Anwendung im 2. Jahrtausend v. Chr. am Beispiel der Befunde in Ḫattuša." *SMEA* 42:261-301.
SOMMER, F.
1932 *Die Ahhijava-Urkunden*. ABAW Phil.-hist. Abt., NF 6. München: Verlag der Bayerischen Akkadamie der Wissenschaften.
TANI, N.
1999 "Osservazioni sui processi ittiti per malversazione." Pp. 167-192 in *Studi e Testi II*. Firenze: LoGisma editore.
VAN DEN HOUT, T. P. J.
1995 *Der Ulmitešub-Vertrag, Eine prosopographische Untersuchung*. StBoT 38. Wiesbaden: Harrassowitz.
VON BRANDENSTEIN, C.-G.
1943 *Hethitische Götter nach Bildbeschreibungen in Keilschrifttexten*. MVAG 46. Band, 2. Heft. Hethitische Texte. Heft 8. Leipzig: J. C. Hinrichs Verlag.
WERNER, R.
1964-69 "Gerichtsprotokolle, hettitische." *RlA* 3:209-211.
1967 *Hethitische Gerichtsprotokolle*. StBoT 4. Wiesbaden: Harrassowitz.

WEST SEMITIC ARCHIVAL DOCUMENTS

A. LETTERS

1. HEBREW LETTERS

THE MEṢAD ḤASHAVYAHU (YAVNEH YAM) OSTRACON (3.41)

Dennis Pardee

Two archaeological campaigns in 1960 at the site of Meṣad Ḥashavyahu, located about a mile south of Yavneh Yam, unearthed seven Hebrew inscriptions, the longest of which was a fifteen-line text written on an ostracon. In a Hebrew that is very close to standard Biblical Hebrew prose, a harvest worker pleads with his superior that a confiscated garment be returned. Apparently the worker was accused by an overseer of not having furnished his quota. He claims to have done so and requests the return of his garment, out of pity if for no other reason.

The plea is presented in direct speech and, by the definition for an epistolary document as "a written document effecting communication between two or more persons who cannot communicate orally" (Pardee et al. 1982:2), this text has been classed among the Hebrew letters (ibid., p. 23). It lacks the regular epistolary formulae, however, and the identification as a letter has been questioned (Smelik 1992). In any case, this document clearly belongs to a sub-category of texts consisting of a plea to a superior for the return of what the plaintiff considers to be wrongfully seized property (Westbrook 1988:30-35; Dobbs-Allsopp 1994). Because the definition of a letter cited above is functional, whereas the description just given is formal (cf. Dobbs-Allsopp 1994:54, n. 10), both classifications are applicable and it is somewhat artificial to reject one in favor of the other.

The editor hypothesized that the documents should be assigned to the time of Josiah and taken as evidence for a previously unrecorded Judaean control of the coastal area (Naveh 1960:139), and this opinion has become widespread in works on the history of the late seventh century BCE. Other proposals have been made, for example a Judaean occupation under Jehoiakim (Wenning 1989), or Judaean mercenaries serving in an Egyptian fortress (Naᵓaman 1991:44-47). If we assume that the plea was addressed to the official in the language of the ostracon itself, i.e., without the benefit of translation, that official was at the very least a Hebrew speaker.

The text does not provide enough details to allow a precise identification of the principal personages: Was the official ({šr} = /*śar*/) the local governor, or a lower military or administrative official? Was the harvest worker a servant, a slave, or a freeman completing a corvée responsibility? Was the one who seized the garment part of the official's administration or did he belong to another chain of command? The biblical requirement for the return of a confiscated garment (Exod 22:25-26; Deut 24:12-15, 17) is mentioned in the context of a pledge for a loan; because the circumstances of this case are different, it raises the question of how widely the moral requirement not to keep a distrained garment may have been construed (cf. Deut 24:17).

The plea for a hearing (lines 1-2)
May the official, my lord, hear[a] the plea[1] of his servant.[2]

Self-identification (lines 2-4)
Your servant is working in the harvest; your servant was at Ḥaṣar-Asam (when the following incident occurred).

The circumstances of the confiscation (lines 4-9)
Your servant did his reaping, finished,[b] and stored (the grain) a few days ago[3] before stopping (work). When your servant had finished (his) reaping and had stored it a few days ago, Hoshayahu ben Shabay came and took your servant's garment.[c] When I had finished my reaping, at that time, a few days ago, he took your servant's garment.

a 1 Sam 26:19
b Ruth 2:21
c Deut 24:17

[1] The word is *dābār* in Hebrew, "word," probably a collective noun meaning "speech, statement." The plea itself is stated neutrally, *yišmaᶜ ᵓet-dᵉbar ᶜabdōh*, with the simple notation of the definite direct object *ᵓet*, rather than with the prepositions *l* or *b*, which would imply greater involvement on the part of the official.

[2] *ᵓādōn*, "lord," and *ᶜebed*, "servant," are the standard means of expressing social superiority and inferiority in direct speech. Note the switch from third person address in the plea ("may [he] hear" ... "his servant") to second person address ("your servant") in the self-identification. Such person-switching is a common result of the use of the nouns "lord" and "servant" to express the social relationship. Below the speaker will again use third-person speech for his lord and will switch back and forth between third-person and first-person speech for himself.

[3] The expression *kymm*, lit. "like days," occurs twice (lines 5, 7) and *zh ymm*, lit., "thus, days" (*zh* has an adverbial function here), once (l. 9). *kymm* seems to be a pluralization of the expression *kayyôm*, "today," known from BH, with the meaning "a few days (back in time)" and *zh ymm* seems simply to be a back-reference to the previous occurrences of *ymm* (cf. *zeh yammîm rabbîm* in BH).

Possible witnesses cited (lines 10-12)
All my companions[d] will vouch for me, all who were reaping with me in the heat of the sun:[e] my companions will vouch for me (that) truly[4] I am guiltless of any in[fraction[f]].

The specific request (lines 12-15)[5]
[(So) please return[g]] my garment. If the official[6] does not consider it an obligation[h] to return [your servant's garment, then have] pity[i] upon him [and return] your servant's [garment] from that motivation. You must not remain silent[j] [when your servant is without his garment].

d Judg 9:26, 31, 41; 1 Sam 30:23; 2 Sam 1:26; 2 Kgs 9:2; Amos 1:9; Neh 4:17; 5:10, 14 *e* 1 Sam 11:9; Neh 7:3 *f* Gen 26:10; Jer 51:5; Ps 68:22; Prov 14:9 *g* Exod 22:25; Deut 24:13 *h* Mic 3:1 *i* Zech 7:9 *j* Jer 14:9

[4] The word is ʾ*mn* and it has been explained either as designating what the reapers will say, as I translated previously, or it may be the first word of the reaper's claim to innocence (see, with previous bibliography, Pardee 1978a:37, 51-52; Pardee et al. 1982:21, 22). The principal problems have been to explain why the phrase ʾ*hy y*ʿ*nw ly*, "my brothers will vouch for me," was repeated if the phrase stopped there, and, if ʾ*mn* belongs to the previous phrase, why the reaper's profession of innocence starts with the verb *nqty*, a very rare construction in this text (verb-initial phrases usually begin with *w*). It now appears plausible to explain the construction as owing to switch from direct to indirect speech and the consequent switch of persons: "they will vouch for me: truly he is guiltless" → "they will vouch for me (that) truly I am guiltless."

[5] The right corner of the ostracon has been broken and lost, except for a small fragment of lines 13-15, and the restorations are hypothetical, though plausible. The restorations suggested are those of Cross 1962:42-46 and Naveh 1964. For another proposal, see Dobbs-Alsopp 1994:53.

[6] Here the plaintiff refers to his superior by his official title (*śar*) rather than by the general title of superiority (ʾ*ādōn*).

REFERENCES

Text, translations and studies: Booij 1986; Cross 1962; Dobbs-Allsopp 1994; Lindenberger 1994; Naʾaman 1991; Naveh 1960; 1962; 1964; Pardee 1978a; Pardee, Sperling, Whitehead, Dion 1982; Parker 1997; Smelik 1992; Wenning 1989; Westbrook 1988.

LACHISH OSTRACA (3.42)

Dennis Pardee

Some thirty-six inscriptions have been discovered at Tell ed-Duwêr/Tel Lachish, including Proto-Canaanite inscriptions, inscribed seals and weights, several Egyptian inscriptions, and an Aramaic inscription on a Persian-period altar (for a recent overview with bibliography, see Pardee 1997c). The so-called "Lachish Letters," nineteen inscribed ostraca discovered in 1935 and 1938 and published rapidly by Torczyner (1938, 1940) are the best known of these texts, for several are relatively long and well preserved and of great interest from a variety of perspectives.

At least twelve of these nineteen texts are letters, of which the six best-preserved are translated here; one is a list of names; several are too poorly preserved for identification.[1] The letters are at least partially homogeneous, for five of the ostraca are sherds from the same vessel (L. Harding *apud* Torczyner 1938:184). Whether this means that the documents are drafts of letters written on the site and sent elsewhere (Yadin 1981) is open to debate (Rainey 1987; Parker 1994). They are generally dated to the period before the fall of Judah (586 BCE), perhaps in 589, and they provide glimpses of the workings of the royal administration, primarily military, in this period shortly before the Babylonian exile. Because they are letters, they also give precious insights into the personal aspects of these administrative workings.

From the perspective of the history of discovery, the Lachish inscriptions were the first cohesive body of original texts from the pre-exilic period in Hebrew and they were therefore very important in providing data on all aspects of the Hebrew of that period: palaeography, grammar, rhetoric, and, specifically, epistolary usages.

LACHISH 2: THANKS AND GOOD WISHES (3.42A)

Salutation (lines 1-2)
To my lord Yaush.[2] May Yahweh[3] give you good news[4] [a] at this very time.

a 1 Sam 2:24; 1 Kgs 10:7; 2 Kgs 19:7; Jer 51:46; Prov 15:30; 25:25

[1] To avoid confusion with previous publications, the letters translated here are referred to below by their original numbering as established by Torczyner 1938, 1940.

[2] Yaush (written {yʾwš}, apparently *plene* writing of a name pronounced /yaʾūš/), is the officer to whom several of these letters are addressed, either the recipient of the letters themselves at the site known today as Tell ed-Duwêr or the person to whom the letters were sent and who was located elsewhere, according to the hypothesis that identifies the surviving texts as copies (Yadin 1981). In this letter the writer does not identify himself; all the formulae are those from an inferior to a superior.

[3] There is no indication in any of these texts that the divine name (the "tetragrammaton") was not used currently nor that it was not pronounced as written, i.e., something along the lines of /yahwē/. In later periods, of course, this divine name was replaced in pronunciation by "ʾ*ᵃdōnāy*." Though the precise vocalization of the name is uncertain, it appears better to indicate a vocalization than to give the impression that it may have already been receiving some special treatment at this time.

[4] Lit. "cause you to hear a report of well-being," a standard formula, with several variations, in these texts.

Humble Thanks for Being Remembered (lines 3-5)
Who is your servant (but) a dog[5] [b] that my lord should remember[6] his servant? May Yahweh give my lord first knowledge[7] of anything you do not already know.

b 2 Kgs 8:13

[5] On the self-comparison with a dog as a self-abasement formula, see Coats 1970 and Pardee et al. 1982:81; on the pre-history of the Hebrew formula, see Galán 1993. Because the normal transition phrase between *praescriptio* and body (see note 9 below) is missing whenever this self-abasement formula is present, the latter serves in these texts both as a transitional formula and as the first phrase of the body. It is clear from Lachish 6 that it is not purely transitional, for there the entire body of the letter depends on this humble expression of thanks.

[6] The humble expression of thanks in the following letters always has to do with the addressee having forwarded correspondence to the writer. Perhaps the formula with *zkr*, "remember," refers to a letter that the addressee has addressed personally to the present writer.

[7] The reading of this verb has been uncertain, though a recent consensus has formed for {ybkr} rather than {yʿkr}, and there is no certain interpretation of either reading (Pardee et al. 1982:80).

LACHISH 3: COMPLAINTS AND INFORMATION (3.42B)

Salutation (lines 1-3)
Your servant Hoshayahu (hereby) reports[c] to my lord Yaush. May Yahweh give you the very best possible news.[8]

Complaint and Self-Defense (lines 4-13)
And now,[9] [d] please explain[e] to your servant the meaning of the letter[10] which you sent to your servant yesterday evening. For your servant has been sick at heart[11] [f] ever since you sent (that letter) to your servant. In it my lord said: "Don't you know how to read a letter?" As Yahweh lives, no one has ever tried to read *me* a letter! Moreover, whenever any letter comes to me and I have read it, I can repeat it down to the smallest detail.

Military Information (lines 13-18)
Now your servant has received the following information: General[g] Konyahu[12] son of Elnatan has moved south in order to enter Egypt.[h] He has sent (messengers) to fetch Hodavyahu son of Aḥiyahu and his men from here.

A Prophet's Letter (lines 19-21)
(Herewith) I am also sending[13] to my lord the letter of Ṭobyahu, servant of the king, which came to Shallum son of Yada from the prophet and which says "Beware."[14] [i]

c Gen 32:6; 2 Sam 11:22
d 2 Kgs 5:6; 10:2
e Cf. Isa 42:20
f Isa 1:5; Jer 8:18; Lam 1:22; 5:17
g 1 Sam 17:55; 1 Kgs 1:19
h Jer 26:22; 37:5-11; Ezek 17:15; 29:1-16; 30:20-26; 31:1-18; Lam 4:17
i 2 Kgs 6:9; Isa 7:4

[8] There seems to be a consensus now on reading *yšmʿ yhwh ʾt ʾdny šmʿt šlm w šmʿt ṭb*, lit. "May Yahweh cause my lord to hear a report of well-being and a report of goodness" (for bibliography, see Pardee 1990:89).

[9] A literal translation, for want of a better, of *wʿt*, the standard formula of transition from the *praescriptio* to the body of a letter; it corresponds formally and rhetorically to BH *wᵉʿattāh*, which is used to mark the transition from topic to comment in any discourse and is actually attested before the cited body of letters in BH narrative (Pardee et al. 1982:172-173). Corresponding formulae are also used as paragraph markers in Aram. letters. Cf. Pardee et al. 1982:149-150.

[10] Lit. "cause to be opened please the ear of your servant with regard to the letter" (*hpqḥ nʾ ʾt ʾzn ʿbdk l spr*; see Pardee 1990:89-91).

[11] Better parallels for the formula "be sick at heart" (here *lb ʿbdk dwh*) are now known from Ug. than were cited by Pardee et al. 1982:85: two letters from the 1994 campaign (RS 94.2284 and RS 94.2545+) contain the phrase *mrṣ lb*, identical to the Akkadian formula (*marāṣu* + *libbu*).

[12] Konyahu's title is *šr hṣbʾ*, "officer of (= over) the army." The personage is unknown from other sources, as are the others named in this report.

[13] This is one of the clearer cases of the "epistolary perfect" in these letters: the verb is perfective in form and refers to sending another document with the present letter. The perfective verb form expresses the perspective of the addressee when reading the letter (Pardee 1983).

[14] This sentence is enigmatic on several counts, from that of the syntax, which does not make clear who the author of the letter was, to that of the historical situation, since the prophet goes unnamed and none of the other personages is known (bibliography in Pardee 1990:93-94). In the interpretation proposed in the *Handbook*, the letter was written by the prophet and found in Ṭobyahu's possession; either Ṭobyahu had confiscated the letter or else he was part of the chain of transmission. In any case, it is not clear whether the addressee had ever seen it or not (Pardee et al. 1982:84-85). As regards Smelik's 1990 interpretation: (1) if one accepts, as does Smelik, that "Beware" is a quotation from the document, I conclude that it is highly likely that the document is a letter in at least the broad sense of the word, for the form in question is an imperative (that Lachish 3 would have referred to a literary text containing an embedded imperative is surely not a likely scenario); (2) though it is possible to accept that Ṭobyahu wrote the letter which would have been transmitted by the prophet to Shallum (Smelik's preferred interpretation — see further below), it is unlikely that the letter was *about* Ṭobyahu and only transmitted by the prophet (Smelik's second possible interpretation), for that would mean that Lachish 3 mentions three names, none of which would be the author of the letter. As regards Parker's 1994 interpretation, I do not see how the Hebrew phrase can be made to say that the letter was written by Ṭobyahu about a message from a prophet, because "from the prophet" follows the quasi-relative formulation *hbʾ*, "which came" (see Pardee 1990:93). If one accepts Parker's observation that *spr ṭbyhw* should mean "a letter written by Ṭobyahu," then the phrase would mean that the prophet had come into possession of a letter written by Ṭobyahu that he subsequently forwarded to Shallum. This would mean, it appears clear to me, that it was Ṭobyahu who had said "Beware," not the prophet, an interpretation that many biblical scholars would be loath to accept (but not Smelik, whose first translation is "the document written by ... Tobiah" [1990: 135]). I now find convincing the arguments against the genitive phrase *spr ṭbyhw* meaning only that Ṭobyahu was in secondary possession of the letter, and propose the following reconstruction of events (suggested to me by one of my students, John Walton). We know from the Jeremiah stories that the king's officials were not always totally opposed to his activities (Jer. 26:24; 36:19; 38:7-13). This fact allows for the possibility that Ṭobyahu, a member of the royal establishment (*ʿbd hmlk*), composed and sent a written message (*spr ṭbyhw*) to an unknown prophet telling him to "Watch out!" (i.e., warning him to refrain from subversive activities) and that the prophet passed the letter on to Shallum (*hbʾ ... mʾt hnbʾ*), who in turn passed it on to the author of this letter who is in turn sending it on to Yaush. In this scenario, if the prophet gave the letter to Shallum, it could only be because he assumed Shallum to be sympathetic to his cause; our knowledge

of the situation is too poor to allow us to determine whether Shallum's passing the letter on to Hoshayahu constituted a betrayal of the prophet's trust and, perhaps, in the long run a betrayal of Ṭobyahu. The grammatical advantage of this reconstruction of events is that it is not amenable to the criticisms that I once voiced against Hoftijzer's analysis, viz. that it did not properly reflect the layers of embedding of this complicated sentence (Pardee 1990:93). Finally, the identification of the prophet with Jeremiah which so sorely tempted many of the early commentators of this text is purely speculative, but the possible allusion to conflict between prophet and royal authority is reminiscent of Jeremiah's career, as would be the existence of an official who sided discreetly with the prophet.

LACHISH 4: MILITARY REPORTS (3.42C)

Salutation (lines 1)
May Yahweh give you good news at this time.

General Statement (lines 2-4)
And now, your servant has done everything my lord sent (me word to do). I have written down[j] everything you sent me (word to do).

Report on Bet-HRPD (lines 4-6)
As regards what my lord said about Bet-HRPD, there is no one there.

The Semakyahu Situation (lines 6-12)
As for Semakyahu, Shemayahu has seized him and taken him up[k] to the city.[15] Your servant cannot send the witness there [today]; rather, it is during the morning tour that [he will come (to you)]. Then it will be known[16] that we are watching the (fire)-signals[l] of Lachish according to the code which my lord gave us, for we cannot see Azeqah.[17] [m]

j Jer 36:23
k Josh 7:24; Judg 13:19; 1 Kgs 17:19; Jer 39:5
l Judg 20:38, 40; Jer 6:1
m Jer 34:7

[15] Though "the city" could refer to the writer's own city, it appears more likely that the verbal form used (the causative form of ʿ*lh* "to go up") would refer to taking someone to Jerusalem. If it could be determined that "there" in the next sentence refers to the same place, it would be quite certain that the city was not the writer's. Unfortunately, the adverb could conceivably mean "there where you are" = "to you."

[16] The readings at the end of lines 8 ("witness") and 9 ("will come") are uncertain, rendering uncertain the logical sequence from the seizure of Semakyahu (lines 6-7) to the beginning of line 10, where the verbal phrase *wydʿ* may either mean "and he will know," with the witness as subject, as I previously interpreted (Pardee et al. 1982:91-93) or "and one will know" (indefinite subject, the basis for the new translation offered above); yet another possibility is the analysis as a Hiphil ("and he will cause to know"), though one might expect the orthography {ywdʿ} for such a form — the inscriptional data are insufficient to determine this point. I suggest now that the opposition is between the witness not being able to make his report today and being able to do so tomorrow. The same interpretation holds if one restores "I will send (him)" at the end of line 9 (Cross 1956) instead of "he will come." I remain, in any case, dubious that the sequence *w ydʿ ky* means "and he will know (something) for," as Lemaire has proposed (1977:110), or "and may (my lord) know," as Cross has proposed (1956:25; interpretation accepted by Renz 1995 1:422): "my lord" is simply not in the text and the context does not require that that word be understood here, while the phrase *ydʿ ky*, "know that" is so common as to render implausible the analysis of *ydʿ* as an absolute usage ("he will know something") which is nonetheless followed by *ky*. If lines 6-12 constitute a single message unit, as the syntax seems to imply (lines 4-6 may also belong to this unit, but the uncertainty regarding Bet-HRPD requires leaving that question open), then Semakyahu has apparently accused the writer's military contingent of not being alert.

[17] The two places Lachish and Azeqah are the only well-known places mentioned in this collection of documents. On the controversy surrounding whether the naming of Lachish supports or weakens the identification of Tell ed-Duwêr with ancient Lachish, see Pardee et al. 1982:94; Lemaire 1986:153; Parker 1994:67-68.

LACHISH 5: THANKS AND REMARKS ON THE HARVEST (3.42D)

Salutation (lines 1-2)
May [Yahweh] give my lord the best possible [news at this very time].

Humble Thanks for Correspondence (lines 3-7)
Who is your servant (but) a dog that you should have sent to your servant these letters?[18] Your servant (herewith) returns the letters to my lord.

The Grain Harvest (lines 7-10)
May Yahweh allow my lord to witness a good harvest today. Is Ṭobyahu going to send royal grain to your servant?[19]

[18] Lit.: "the letters like this" ({ʾ[t] h⌈s⌉[prm k] zʾ[t]}). The use of the plural (*sprm* is intact in lines 6-7) seems to indicate that the reference is to a group of documents sent by the addressee to the writer for him to read, not simply to the addressee's own letter. Compare Lachish 6 below, where the origins of a group of letters are mentioned.

[19] The readings and resultant interpretation behind this translation are owing to Lemaire (1977:117-118).

LACHISH 6: REACTIONS TO FORWARDED CORRESPONDENCE (3.42E)

Salutation (line 1)
To my lord Yaush. May Yahweh make this time a good one for you.[20]

Letters that Weaken Resolve (lines 2-15)
Who is your servant (but) a dog that my lord should have sent (him) the king's letter and those

[20] Lit., "May Yahweh cause my lord to see this time (in) well-being" (*yrʾ yhwh ʾt ʾdny ʾt hʿt hzh šlm*).

of the officials asking me to read them? The [officials']²¹ statements are not good — (they are of a kind) to slacken your courage[22] *n* and to weaken that of the men[...]. Won't you write to [them] as follows: "[Why] are you acting thus?"? [...] As Yahweh your God lives, ever since your servant read the letters he has not had [a moment's peace].

n Jer 38:4

[21] Parker (1994:76-77) prefers the restoration {h[nbˀ]}, "the words of the [prophet]."

[22] Lit. "the words of the [officials] are not good; for the going slack of your hands (are they)" (*dbry h*[*šrm*] *lˀ ṭbm lrpt ydyk*). Lemaire (1986:-153) does not explain why "Chaldeans" in his proposed restoration ({ydy k[šdm]}, "the hands of the Chaldeans," in place of {ydyk [...]}, "your hands") would have been written without the -*y*- of the gentilic ending, elsewhere used consistently in pre-exilic epigraphic Hebrew, almost certainly because the plural ending was pronounced /iyyīm/ at the time (rather than /īm/, as occurs later). Thus it still appears preferable to see a break between *l ṭbm* ("not good") and *l rpt* ("to go slack"), rather than to take these words as a single unit ("the words are not proper to cause slackening"). See the detailed discussion in Pardee et al. 1982:101.

LACHISH 9: REQUESTS (3.42F)

Salutation (lines 1-2)
May Yahweh give my lord the [best] possible news.

Release to Bearer (lines 3-4)[23]
[And] now, give ten (loaves of) bread and two (*bat*-measures?)[24] of wine (to bearer).

Request for Information (lines 4-9)
Return word*o* [to] your servant by the intermediary of Shelemyahu regarding what we are to do tomorrow.

o 1 Sam 17:30; 2 Sam 3:11; 1 Kgs 12:6

[23] The "release-to-bearer" note is common in the Arad letters (3.43 below; see in particular Arad 3 [3.43C] and note 11 to the translation) and it is on the basis of these that Lemaire (1977:127-128) proposed the new readings and intepretations on which this translation is based. That the function of these documents is to authenticate that a given person is authorized to receive stores is clear from the fact that they can be addressed from inferior to superior, as here. It is uncertain whether the bearer of this note, unnamed, is identical with the the person by whose intermediary the writer requests a response in the next paragraph, or whether this person, referred to by name as Shelemyahu, is a member of the recipient's staff.

[24] When the liquid measure is not indicated, the reference seems to be to a standard-sized jar that held something over twenty liters; the measure was known in Hebrew as a *bat*. In the new excavations at Tell ed-Duwêr (Ussishkin 1978:85-88), a complete jar has been discovered with a capacity of about twenty-one liters and bearing the inscription *b*/, "one *b*(*at*-measure)" (regarding the abbreviation *b*/, see the Arad Ostraca (3.43A, note 4) below.

REFERENCES

Text, translations, and studies: Coats 1970; Cross 1956; Cross and Freedman 1952; Dion, Pardee, and Whitehead 1979; Diringer 1953; Dussaud 1938; Galán 1993; Hoftijzer 1986; Lemaire 1977; 1986; Lindenberger 1994; Pardee 1983; 1990; 1997c; Pardee, Sperling, Whitehead, and Dion 1982; Parker 1994; Rainey 1987; Renz 1995; Smelik 1990; Torczyner 1938; 1940; Ussishkin 1978; Yadin 1981.

ARAD OSTRACA (3.43)

Dennis Pardee

Over two hundred inscribed objects were discovered during excavations at the site of Tel Arad in the northern Negeb, one hundred and twelve in Hebrew, eighty-five in Aramaic, two in Greek, and five in Arabic; in addition there were thirteen inscribed seals, and nine *l mlk* seal impressions on jar handles (Aharoni et al. 1975/1981). Though some of the Hebrew inscriptions may date back as far as the late tenth century, the bulk of the readable ones are from strata VII and VI, dated to the end of the seventh/beginning of the sixth centuries; some of these texts may be dated a bit earlier than the Lachish ostraca. This comparative abundance of documentation — by far the largest group of pre-exilic Hebrew documents from a single Palestinian site — has provided a wealth of information on the history and economy of south Judah/north Negeb in the last years before the fall of Judah. Good summaries are available in Aharoni's edition, up-dated in the English translation (Aharoni et al. 1975/1981), by Lemaire (1977:145-235; and 1997a), and by Lawton (1992).

Of the Hebrew inscriptions, ninety-one were in ink on pottery, for the most part ostraca; the others were incised in clay bowls or on stone seals. Most were found during regular excavations that took place from 1962 to 1967, though the important text no. 88 was found on the surface in 1974 and some of the excavated inscriptions are dated palaeographically rather than stratigraphically (for an overview of the problems that exist in dating the archaeological strata and the inscriptions, see Manor and Herion 1992; for an attempt at typological dating of the texts from strata VIII, VII, and VI, see Drinkard 1988:432-437).

The texts on ostraca are principally administrative in origin, for the most part letters and name lists, with a few account texts. The epistolary documents either are letters of disbursal (like Lachish 9 above) or they deal with various personal and military affairs (Pardee et al. 1982:24-67).

ARAD 1: ORDER FOR ALLOTMENT OF SUPPLIES (3.43A)

To Elyashib.[1] And now,[2] give to the Kittim[3] three *b*(*at*-measures)[4] of wine and write down the date.[5] [a] From what is left of the first meal, have one *ḥomer*-measure (?) of flour loaded up so they can make bread for themselves.[6] [b] It is wine from the craters that you are to give (to them).[7]

a Ezek 24:2
b Josh 9:12

[1] The simple form of address, with no indication of the writer's name or rank, indicates that the writer was the addressee's superior. He was therefore the superior officer located in a military center, perhaps even Jerusalem. Elyashib's precise rank is unknown, but he was certainly in charge of the storehouse at Arad, for all letters that deal with distribution of supplies from Arad refer to him. We know from text 17 and from three seals (Arad 105-7) that Elyashib's father's name was Eshyahu, but nothing beyond that. Elyashib's name was in all probability pronounced /ʾelyāšīb/, meaning "El causes to return," for the spelling of the name with {y} *mater lectionis*, {ʾlyšyb}, is attested in a fourth-century Aram. text from Arad (Aram. text no. 7) and in the Hebrew Bible. In the Hebrew texts from Tel Arad, the name is always spelled without the *mater lectionis*. The defective spelling of /ī/ in three words in this short text ({ʾlyšb}, {ktym} = /kittiyyīm/, and {trkb} = /tarkīb/; perhaps {rʾšn} as well, if pronounced /rī(ʾ)šōn/ as in BH) obliges one to take with a grain of salt the assertion that "*yôd* for medial *î* is regular at Arad" (Lawton 1992:336).

[2] See note 9 to the Lachish Ostraca (3.42B).

[3] This ethnic entity (ethnicity indicated by the gentilic suffix *-y-*), meaning lit. "persons from Kition (a town on Cyprus)," is never defined in these texts, and it is uncertain whether it is used narrowly to designate inhabitants of Kition or broadly for the inhabitants of Cyprus in general, and whether these Kittim were primarily Phoenician-speakers or Greek-speakers, or, finally, whether the term might designate Greeks in general, whether or not from Cyprus (see overview in Dion 1992). Whatever their ethnic origin and linguistic orientation, the fact that they received supplies from the Arad storehouse has generally been interpreted as meaning that they were mercenaries in the service of the king of Judah. The large amount of supplies mentioned in this text, approximately four bushels of flour and over thirty liters of wine, indicates either that these Kittim were numerous or that they were a small group entrusted with delivering supplies elsewhere. The formula "to make bread for them(selves)" (see note 6 below) seems to indicate the first interpretation, as does the specific time designation in Arad 2.

[4] The interpretation of the graphic sequence "*b*/ \\\" here follows that of the editor (Aharoni 1966:2-3). The interpretation as "1 *bat*, 3 *hin*," i.e., 1½ *bat* (1 *hin* = 1/6 *bat*) proposed by Naveh (1992) does not take into account the writing "\\\ b/" in Arad 3:2 (cf. also 7:5 and 8:5). Nor does it take into account that the *bat*-measure corresponded to an actual vessel (see note 24 to the Lachish Ostraca [3.42F]) small enough to be the one in which the wine was both stored and shipped.

[5] The Hebrew expression for "the date" is *šem hayyōm*, "the name of the day."

[6] This sentence has several uncertainties: (1) what is meant by "first flour" (*hqmḥ hrʾšn*); (2) the measure of the flour is written as a symbol of which the meaning has not been firmly established; (3) why the specific verb *trkb*, "load up," is used instead of a verb of giving or handing over (others have interpreted *trkb* as meaning "to grind," but it seems strange to grind the *qmḥ*-flour into another form of flour); (4) the clause expressing the making of the bread is expressed infinitively and without a subject (*lʿšt lhm lḥm* "to make bread for them"). See discussion in Pardee et al. 1982:31-32.

[7] The form of the sentence, with the word "wine" fronted (*myyn hʾgnt ttn*), seems to indicate that this is a back-reference to the first order regarding wine, not a new quantity (as I first interpreted: Pardee 1978b:297, n. 46). What is meant by *myyn hʾgnt*, lit. "from (= some of) the wine of the craters," is uncertain. What is clear is that it was not wine stored in craters, for these vessels were large open vessels used for mixing wine prior to drinking, and could therefore not have been used for storage. On the other hand, the Hebrew formula is inappropriate to express the concept of "wine for mixing in craters" (Lemaire 1977:159; more explicitly Bron and Lemaire 1980:8: "vin destiné à être mélangé avec de l'eau dans des cratères"). Rather than "wine for mixing," the Hebrew expression could more plausibly be taken as meaning "mixed wine," i.e. "pre-mixed wine." If the Kittim were to be traveling in dry country, where water was scarce, perhaps their wine ration was in this instance to be issued already cut with water, whether or not mixed with honey and/or spices, according to the Greek preference. On the other hand, the bread was not pre-baked; according to these texts, the grain stored at Arad could be issued unprocessed or as flour, dough (Arad 3), or bread (Arad 2).

ARAD 2: ORDER FOR ALLOTMENT OF SUPPLIES (3.43B)

To Elyashib. And now, give to the Kittim two *b*(*at*-measures) of wine for the four days,[8] three hundred loaves of bread, and a(nother) full *ḥomer*-measure of wine.[9] Send them out on their rounds[10] [c] tomorrow; don't wait. If there is any vinegar[d] left, give (that) to them (also).

c 1 Sam 7:16; 2 Chr 17:9; 23:2
d Ruth 2:14

[8] The Hebrew expression is definite (*l ʾrbʿt hymm*), but the point of reference is unknown.

[9] The reason for the two distributions of wine is not indicated. The *ḥomer*-measure was some ten times larger than the *bat* (i.e., over 200 liters). It seems plausible to assume that the smaller amount was for the personal consumption of the Kittim, while the larger was for delivery to the smaller forts located in the vicinity of Arad. One must assume that the wine from the large *ḥomer*-vessel was transferred into smaller vessels or skins (cf. Josh 9:4, 13) for shipment and would, therefore, have to have been consumed within a relatively short period of time. The *ḥomer*-vessel would have been one of the large pithoi often found buried to the neck for cooler storage and to avoid breakage.

[10] Lit. "cause them to go around" (Hiphil of $\sqrt{sbb}$).

ARAD 3: ORDER FOR ALLOTMENT OF SUPPLIES (3.43C)

To Elyashib. And now, give three *b*(*at*-measures) of wine (to bearer).[11] Moreover, Ḥananyahu has given you orders[12] concerning Beersheba: you are yourself to load up and convey there two donkey loads[e] of dough.[13] Calculate the (amount of) wheat ([at Arad?]) and count the (loaves of) bread (already made).[14] Take [...][15]

e 2 Kgs 5:17

[11] When the indirect object is not indicated in the text, it must be assumed that the document entitled its bearer to receive the supplies.

[12] This formulation expresses a third layer of communication: in addition to the writer and the addressee, a third party, probably superior to both Elyashib and the writer, has issued orders that the writer only transmits.

[13] If the reading {bṣq} is correct, we have evidence for dough being transferred from the central storehouse to a fortress that could not be too far away. Lemaire (1977:165) has questioned the reading, but his interpretation ("harness them with a harness") is not particularly attractive (cf. Rainey in Aharoni et al. 1981:18, n. 3). The syntax of this entire sentence is, however, awkward and hence uncertain. A more literal translation would be: "And Ḥananyahu orders you upon Beersheba with a load of a pair of donkeys and you are to bind (upon) them dough ..."

[14] Lit.: "count the wheat and the bread" (*spr hḥṭm w hlḥm*).

[15] Traces of six lines of writing are visible on the *verso* of the ostracon, but they are too fragmentary to be translated.

ARAD 4: ORDER FOR ALLOTMENT OF SUPPLIES (3.43D)

To Elyashib. Give to the Kittim one (jar of) oil.[16] Seal (the jar) and send it. Also give them one *b*(*at*-measure) of wine.

[16] The text is "*šmn* /," where the oblique stroke indicates the number, but with no indication of the measure. Since the standard abbreviation for *bat*-measure is not used in these texts when oil is mentioned, it is quite possible that oil was circulated in containers of a different size.

ARAD 5: ORDER FOR ALLOTMENT OF SUPPLIES PLUS A POSSIBLE MENTION OF TITHE (3.43E)

To Elyashib. And now, send some of the flour which you have left from the [first (batch)], which [...] flour [to make] bread for the Kittim [...] [...] (someone) will [send] you the tithe in it, before the month passes.[17] And from the surplus of [...]

[17] This text of fifteen lines is poorly preserved, and the presence of the word for "tithe," only partially preserved ({hm^{c}[šr]}, appears plausible, though far from certain. "In it," of which the point of reference is uncertain, was previously read as the abbreviated form of *bat* plus the number "three"; however, the three strokes are not arranged one after the other, but one above the other, and the combination seems rather to form the sign {h}, interpreted as the pronominal suffix of the third person. The word for "month" is *ḥdš*, which may refer either to a full lunar month or to the festival of the new moon (cf. Amos 8:5); I retain the first interpretation here because the designation of the feast-day is clearly "1 *l ḥdš*," i.e., "the first (day) of the month," in text 7.

ARAD 7: ANOTHER ORDER FOR ALLOTMENT OF SUPPLIES (3.43F)

To Elyashib. And now, give to the Kittim for the (period from) the first (day) of the tenth (month) until the sixth (day) of (that) month three *b*(*at*-measures of wine?). [And] make a record (of this)[f] on the second (day) of the tenth month.[18] Also seal (a jar of) oil [and send it ...].[19]

f Josh 8:32; Isa 65:6; Mal 3:16; Est 2:23; 1 Chr 24:6

[18] This formulation seems to imply an urgent situation requiring a release of supplies on the feast-day of the new-moon, though the religious character of this day only permitted registering the transaction on the following day (cf. Pardee et al. 1982:41).

[19] The writing at the bottom of this ostracon is faded and only traces of the line translated in brackets are visible.

ARAD 16: A LETTER BETWEEN BROTHERS (3.43G)

Your brother Ḥananyahu (hereby) sends greetings to (you) Elyashib and to your household. I bless you to Yahweh.[20] And now, when I leave your house I will send the money,[21] eight shekels, to the

[20] Without patronyms, it is impossible to know whether this Ḥananyahu is the same person as the one bearing the same name who is mentioned in text 3, but the familiar tone of this letter, as compared with the official tone of the one in which Ḥananyahu is mentioned as a third party, indicates that the references may be to different individuals. Whether Elyashib and Ḥananyahu are blood brothers or only social equals is uncertain; if the former, they now occupy different households, since Ḥananyahu sends greetings to Elyashib's "house" (*l bytk*). On the sets of greetings used between social equals and family members, quite different from what we have seen up to this point, see Pardee et al. 1982:49-50. The transitive formula *brk l*, "pronounce a blessing (upon someone) to (a deity)," is not attested in the Bible, though the passive formulation is frequent

sons of Ge⸾alyahu [by] the intermediary of] Azar-yahu, as well as the [...][22]

(*bārūk l* ..., "blessed to"). Cf. also the inscriptions from Kuntillet ᶜAjrud, *COS* 2.47.

[21] The time frame involved here is uncertain, for the first verb ("when I leave") is formulated infinitively and the second is preceded by the conjunction *w*, which may or may not be "*wāw*-consecutive." Because we do not know which house Ḥananyahu is leaving (he both sends greetings to Elyahib's house and speaks of leaving it) nor when he is leaving it, it appears better to observe normal BH syntax here and interpret the *wāw* as "consecutive" (we previously took it as "conjunctive": Pardee et al. 1982:48).

[22] There are traces of six more lines, too fragmentary for interpretation.

ARAD 17: ANOTHER ORDER FOR ALLOTMENT OF SUPPLIES, WITH POSTSCRIPT (3.43H)

To Naḥum. [And] now, go to the house of Elyashib son of Eshyahu and get from there one (jar of) oil and send (it) to Ziph right away (after) affixing your seal to it.

Dated Postscript (lines 8-9)
On the twenty-fourth of the month Naḥum gave oil to the Kitti (for delivery) — one (jar).[23]

[23] Naḥum, whose function and identity are unknown and who may have been located anywhere other than in Elyashib's house (Pardee 1985:70), bore this ostracon to Elyashib's house as proof that he was entitled to receive a jar of oil. The postscript, written on the back of the ostracon, indicates that Naḥum in turn entrusted the oil to a single member of the Kittim (*ntn ... b yd hkty*, "put into the hand of the Kitti") for delivery to the fortress at Ziph. The reading of the place name is the editor's; today the ostracon is too faded to read in this spot (for another reading, see Lemaire 1977:176; 1983a:446). The sealing of the jar would have been accomplished by putting a lump of wet clay over the mouth of the container and impressing the seal into the clay. The function of the seal was the same as that of similar seals across the millennia: to ensure that the commodity arriving in Ziph was the same as that which had left Arad.

ARAD 18: A LETTER FROM ONE OF ELYASHIB'S SUBORDINATES (3.43I)

To my lord Elyashib. May Yahweh concern himself with your well-being.[24] And now, give Shemaryahu a *letek*-measure (?) (of flour ?) and to the Qerosite[g] give a *ḥomer*-measure (?) (of flour ?).[25]

A Confidential Matter (lines 7-10)
As regards the matter concerning which you gave me orders: everything is fine now: he is staying in the temple of Yahweh.[26] [h]

g Ezra 2:44; Neh 7:47
h Neh 13:4-9

[24] The idiom Š⸾L + ŠLM + personal name/pronoun, lit. "to ask (about) the well-being of someone," is common in the Levantine area from the Late Bronze Age on (see below on Ug. letter RS 17.434+, *COS* 3.45J, note 62).

[25] The first part of this letter leaves no doubt that persons of inferior rank to Elyashib could authorize release of supplies from the Arad storehouses. One can only determine the rank of the writer from the form of address. The two measures indicated for an unnamed commodity are written as symbols the interpretation of which is uncertain. For *letek*, cf. Hos 3:2. Regarding the sparse references to temple personnel and other matters in these texts, see list and bibliography in Pardee 1978b:317.

[26] The enigmatic form in which this confidential allusion is couched has left the modern interpreters dangling. Though interpreting this reference to a temple (i.e. "house," *byt* in Hebrew) as linked with the sanctuary excavated at Arad has been tempting, this is ruled out for archaeological reasons (Herzog et al. 1984), and the reference appears to be, therefore, to the temple in Jerusalem.

ARAD 21: A SON'S LETTER (3.43J)

Your son Yehukal (hereby) sends greetings to (you) Gedalyahu [son of] Elyair and to your household. I bless you to Yahweh. And now, if my lord had done [...] may Yahweh reward[i] my lord [...].[27]

i 1 Sam 24:20; Prov 13:21; 25:22

[27] This letter was originally ten lines long, but only the *praescriptio* and the beginning of the body are reasonably well preserved.

ARAD 24: MILITARY MOVEMENTS (3.43K)

[...][28] from Arad five[29] and from Qinah [...] and send them to Ramat-negeb under[j] Malkiyahu son of Qerabur. He is to hand them over to[k] Elisha son of Yirmeyahu at Ramat-negeb[30] lest anything happen[l]

j 2 Sam 18:2
k Jer 40:7
l Gen 42:4

[28] There was a text of eleven lines on the *recto* of this ostracon, but only a few traces are preserved: Elyashib's name occurs, but only in line 2, so this letter, like text 17, was apparently addressed to a third party.

[29] The number is indicated by the Egyptian hieratic symbol, but it is uncertain whether it is the symbol for "five" or for "fifty," though the former now appears more likely.

[30] The towns mentioned in this text are known from the Bible, though the exact localization of the last two, especially that of Ramat-Negeb, is debated (cf. Aharoni 1970:21-25; Lemaire 1977:191-192; Pardee et al. 1982:29; Beit-Arieh and Cresson 1991:128).

to the city. This is an order from the king — a life-and-death matter for you. I send (this message) to warn you now:*m* The(se) men (must be) with*n* Elisha[31] lest (the) Edom(ites) (should) enter there.[32]

m Deut 8:19; 32:46
n 1Sam22:6; 2 Sam 1:11; 17:12; Jer 41:2, 7

[31] The absence of a verb in this sentence renders its interpretation problematic, but assuming the elision of the verb "to be" seems the best solution. The phrase *šlḥty ... hᵓnšm ᵓt ᵓlyšᶜ* alone cannot mean "I have sent Elisha's men" (Lemaire 1977:188; 1986:153) because the preposition *ᵓt* does not denote simple belonging and the sentence thus would include a double ellipsis, both of the notion of belonging to Elisha and of going to him (the Hebrew sentence corresponding to Lemaire's interpretation might be something like *šlḥty ... hᵓnšm [ᵓšr l ᵓlyšᶜ lhywtm] ᵓth*, "I have sent Elisha's men so that they might be with him" — this expresses better the double ellipsis than was done by Pardee et al. 1982:61). Nor is it likely that *ᵓt* here means "to" (Rainey in Aharoni et al. 1981:49; see Dion 1983:471). Finally, *hᵓnšm* should, in any case, be the subject of a new clause, not the object of the verb ŠLḤ, for a direct object complement of that verb is regularly preceded by the definite direct object marker *ᵓt* in these texts (Arad 5:11 [verb reconstructed]; 16:4; 40:14; the particle is plausibly restored in 13:2).

[32] This is the clearest passage in these texts referring to the Edomite menace, though text 40 as reconstructed by the editor (see next text) also refers to hostile Edomites (cf. Beit-Arieh and Cresson 1991:134). The verb "enter" is feminine in form, as with "Edom" in Mal 1:4.

ARAD 40: THE EDOMITE PROBLEM (3.43L)[33]

Your son Gemar[yahu], as well as Neḥemyahu, (hereby) send [greetings to] (you) Malkiyahu.[34] I bless [you to Yahweh]. And now, your servant has applied himself*o* to what you ordered.[35] [I (hereby) write] to my lord [everything that the man] wanted. [Eshyahu has come] from you but [he has not given] them any men. You know [the reports from] Edom. I sent them to [my] lord [before] evening. Eshyahu is staying [in my house.] He tried to obtain the report [but I would not give (it to him).] The king of Judah should know [that] we are unable to send the [X. This is] the evil which (the) Edom(ites) [have done].

o 1 Kgs 8:58

[33] The right side of this ostracon has mostly disappeared; I give the editor's restorations (Aharoni et al. 1975/1981:72-76/70-74) though they are speculative. This is the only text from Stratum VIII translated here. The end of this stratum is dated to 701, the date of Sennacherib's invasion of Judah (regarding the chronology of the strata at Arad, see the works cited in the introduction). If the general tenor of the message is correctly represented by the restorations, this text provides evidence for Edomite hostility at this time. Rainey (in Aharoni et al. 1981:74) suggests that the evil of Edom was to capitulate to the Assyrians without supporting the resistance of Judah.

[34] The letter is from two persons addressed formally to two (or more) persons: *bnkm* = "the son of you [plural)," but subsequent references to both writer and addressee are in the singular and Gemaryahu is, therefore, in fact writing to his father; the plural pronoun on the first word probably constitues, therefore, an allusive reference to both parents. As in Ug. letters, *ᵓadn*, "lord" is apparently here used for the genetic father, rather than as term of respect for a social superior (see *COS* 3.45I, n. 52 and *COS* 3.45S, n. 119). "Lord" and "servant" are appropriate terms to express the subserviency of the father-son relationship.

[35] Lit.: "your servant has stretched out his heart to what you said" ({hṭ⌜h⌝ [ᶜ]bdk [l]bh ᵓl ᵓšr ᵓm[rt]}).

ARAD 88: A FRAGMENT OF A COPY OF A ROYAL PROCLAMATION (3.43M)[36]

I have become king in [...][37]
STRENGTHEN[38] the arm*p* and [...]
the King of Egypt [...]

p Prov 31:17; cf. Ps 89:22

[36] This text as preserved has no epistolary features, and its literary genre remains in doubt (Pardee 1978b:290, n. 3) as do its date and historical significance (cf. Aharoni 1975/1981:103-104, 151/103-4, 150; Yadin 1976; Malamat 1988:120-122). Only the beginnings of three lines are preserved, and it is not clear whether the first line preserved was the first line of the text: there is a large space between this line and the upper edge of the ostracon, but the space between the preserved lines is also rather large. Because of the absence of epistolary features, it appears difficult to see this as a letter from the new king to his officers; moreover the humble medium (ostracon) makes it unlikely that this is the primary proclamation of a new king of Judah. It may, however, be — among other possibilities — a reproduction of such a proclamation that was circulated to the various military outposts, or a quotation from such a proclamation embedded in a longer document (conceivably epistolary if the first preserved line was not the first line of the original text), or even a scribal exercise.

[37] The first sign after the preposition "in" appears to be {k}, and the word *kl*, "all," is usually restored.

[38] In capitals because without the preceding context it is difficult to know precisely what form of the verb is used (imperative or perfect?).

REFERENCES

Texts, translations and studies: Aharoni 1966; 1970; Aharoni and Naveh 1975; Aharoni, Naveh, Rainey, Aharoni, Lifshitz, Sharon, and Gofer 1981; Beit-Arieh and Cresson 1991; Bron and Lemaire 1980; Dion 1983; 1992; Dion, Pardee, and Whitehead 1979; Drinkard 1988; Herzog, Aharoni, Rainey, and Moshkovitz 1984; Lawton 1992; Lemaire 1977; 1983a; 1986; 1997a; Lindenberger 1994; Malamat 1988; Manor and Herion 1992; Naveh 1992; Pardee 1978b; 1983; 1985; Pardee, Sperling, Whitehead, and Dion 1982; Yadin 1976.

THE WIDOW'S PLEA (3.44)

Dennis Pardee

This text did not come from regular excavations and the question of authenticity arises here as in other such cases. Because there are no irregularities in script or language, I continue to believe (see Bordreuil, Israel, and Pardee 1996 and 1998) that the text is authentic. To believe the opposite requires the hypothesis that the forger was a master epigrapher, a master grammarian (only an extremely skilled Hebraist could have produced a text that so perfectly reflects the intricacies of Biblical Hebrew morpho-syntax), a master of biblical law, and a master chemist (capable of producing ancient ink and an ancient patina [Rollston *apud* Bordreuil, Israel, and Pardee 1998:8-9]). The forger would also, however, have had to be cunning enough to produce some unexpected forms, such as {whyh ydk ^{c}my} (line 3), which, given the writer's clear mastery of morpho-syntax elsewhere in the text, must have been either deliberate or a simple scribal error. Eph^{c}al and Naveh 1998 have argued from certain similarities with phraseology in Biblical Hebrew and epigraphic Hebrew that the text may be a forgery. But such arguments are two-edged: unless inaccuracies are present, such arguments are equally valid in favor of authenticity, i.e., the features singled out are like pre-exilic Hebrew because that is how speakers of pre-exilic Hebrew spoke! In addition, the same authors point out a small number of epigraphic features that are distinctive — but that sort of argument is also two-edged, for a modern forger would have to be not only a master epigrapher but a very devious one to produce previously unattested forms consistently throughout two different texts.[1] Finally, Eph^{c}al and Naveh turn the tables and refute another argument against authenticity, viz., that certain expressions are characteristic of post-biblical Hebrew (Berlejung and Schüle 1998), by showing that other inscriptions about the authenticity of which there can be no doubt contain such expressions.[2]

Though very different in its forms of expression and in its particular theme (inheritance), the widow's plea provides in its genre a parallel to the Meṣad Ḥashavyahu text (*COS* 3.41). In both cases, someone addresses a plea to an official for redress of a situation that the plaintiff finds detrimental, describing the situation as he/she sees it and stating precisely the action desired of the official.

The two pleas show two primary literary differences. (1) The blessing formula at the beginning of the widow's plea is similar, though not identical, to known epistolary blessing formulae. In addition, the formula *w ^{c}t*, lit., "and now," separates the blessing from the plea itself. That phrase frequently marks the transition from the *praescriptio* to the body of a letter (see note 9 to *COS* 3.42B). These two features strengthen the case for these written pleas having been a sub-form of the epistolary genre (see introduction to *COS* 3.41). (2) The circumstances are recited here much more briefly than in the other plea, indeed are confined to just a few words {mt $^{\supset}$yšy l$^{\supset}$ bnm}, lit., "My husband is dead, no sons."

The Blessing (line 1)
May YHWH bless you[a] in peace.[b]

The Plea for a Hearing (lines 1-2)
And now, may my lord the official listen to your maidservant.

The Circumstances (lines 2-3)
My husband has died (leaving) no sons.[c]

The Specific Request (lines 3-6)
(I request politely that the following) happen: (let) your hand (be) with me[3] and entrust to your maid-servant[4] the inheritance about which you spoke to ^{c}Amasyahu.[5]

Reminder of One Action Already Taken (lines 6-8)
As for the wheat field that is in Naamah,[d] you have (already) given (it) to his brother.

a Num 6:24
b Ps 29:11
c Num 27:8-11; Deut 25:5-10; 2 Sam 14:5; 2 Kgs 4:1; 1 Chr 2:30, 32
d Josh 15:41

[1] This and another text were published together by Bordreuil, Israel, and Pardee 1996 and 1998, and they show an identical hand.

[2] Lemaire (1999) successfully refutes several other claims for aberrant usage made by Berlejung and Schüle; on the other hand, nothing speaks in favor of Lemaire's own hypothesis that the two texts would have been scribal exercises.

[3] The words {w hyh . ydk | ^{c}my} in lines 3-4 present the only significant problem for the superficial interpretation of the text: (1) is *hyh* used absolutely, as I have translated, (2) is its subject *ydk*, a feminine noun, and the verb is masculine because it precedes its subject, or (3) is this a scribal error (for {w hyt(h)}, as in 1 Chr 4:10)?

[4] *$^{\supset}$amh* functions as the female equivalent of *^{c}bd* as an expression of subservience in the mouth of an inferior writing to a superior (the same is true in Ug.: *COS* 3.45HH). "Entrust to" here translates NTN *byd*, "to give/put into the hand of," distinct from NTN *l*, "to give to," used below to express the transfer to the deceased's brother. This distinction allows the conclusion that the widow was not asking to become the legal owner of the land but only to have its use as a source of income to allow her to live.

[5] We hypothesize in the *editio princeps* that ^{c}Amasyahu was the name of the deceased husband. The use of the verb "to speak" here and the absence of reference to a written document appear to indicate that the official's promise to allow ^{c}Amasyahu's wife to continue living from the usufruct of his property was purely oral.

REFERENCES

Text, translations and studies: Berlejung and Schüle 1998; Bordreuil, Israel, and Pardee 1996; 1998; Eph^cal and Naveh 1998; Lemaire 1999; Younger 1998b.

2. UGARITIC LETTERS*

Dennis Pardee

Excavations began at the site of Ras Shamra in the spring of 1929 and have continued with some regularity to the present. Over four thousand inscribed objects have been discovered, including many texts in Ugaritic and Akkadian inscribed on clay tablets (overviews in Yon 1997 and Pardee 1997a,b). The Ugaritic poetic corpus has attracted the greatest attention (see introductions to the Ugaritic myths in *COS* 1), but the vast majority of texts are prosaic reflections of every-day life.

To date well over one hundred letters, often fragmentary, are known in Ugaritic and some one hundred and fifty in Akkadian (recent discoveries will more than double that number: Bordreuil and Malbran-Labat 1995:445). Roughly a third of the former, those well enough preserved to make an English translation of interest, are translated here. Less well-preserved texts are included only when they present a special interest (e.g., drafts of letters going out to other courts or the letter from the son of ʾUrtēnu that allowed the identification of that archive [RS 92.2005, 3.45JJ below]).

Letters written in Ugaritic tend to reflect correspondence within the kingdom of Ugarit, notably between Ugaritians, in particular members of the royal family, while Akkadian, the *lingua franca* of the time, was used much more frequently than Ugaritic for international correspondence. It is uncertain whether Ugaritic texts from foreign courts (e.g., here below the texts in part II) represent translations of texts originally written in Akkadian or whether Ugaritic scribes resided at foreign courts where the message may have been translated immediately from the local language into Ugaritic. It is in any case now certain that Ugaritic scribes did reside abroad,[1] but their precise role in the foreign court is still unknown. For overviews of the epistolographic traditions at Ugarit, see Kaiser 1970; Ahl 1973; Kristensen 1977; Cunchillos 1989.

The texts are organized here according to the following life situations:

I. Correspondence between members of the royal family (texts 1-7);
II. Correspondence from other courts (texts 8-12);
III. Correspondence to other courts (texts 13-16);
IV. Correspondence between king or queen and a non-royal personage (texts 17-27);
V. Correspondence between non-royal correspondents (texts 28-40);
VI. Correspondence exercises (texts 41-42).

Note to translations. Words are in all capital letters when the Ug. vocalization is unknown (e.g., SYR in RS 18.040, *COS* 3.45T below) and in the translation of words in broken contexts of which the basic meaning is clear but not the specific form or the subject (e.g., SEND indicates that the identification of the root as *lʾk* may be ascertained but not its precise function in the sentence).

* Acknowledgments. All textual notes here are based on personal collation, made possible by my membership in the Mission de Ras Shamra and funded by that Mission, by the University of Chicago, and by the Fulbright Fellowships. Some of the research behind the interpretations presented here was made possible by a grant from the National Endowment for the Humanities and another from the Gugenheim Foundation. The readings and interpretations of texts discovered since 1971 were achieved in collaboration with Pierre Bordreuil and of texts since 1994 with Robert Hawley. The manuscript was read by my students, in particular Blane Conklin and Robert Hawley, who enabled me to remove many errors. Responsibility for the translations presented here and for any remaining errors must, nevertheless, be ascribed to me.

[1] See Bordreuil and Malbran-Labat 1995:445 for the case of a Ug. scribe resident at the court of the king of Alashia (Cyprus).

The following is a concordance between the translations and the editions:

Edition Number		Number in COS Translation
RS 4.475	=	28 (3.45BB)
RS 8.315	=	3 (3.45C)
RS 9.479A	=	2 (3.45B)
RS 11.872	=	5 (3.45E)
RS 15.007	=	29 (3.45CC)
RS 15.008	=	1 (3.45A)
RS 16.078	=	15 (3.45O)
RS 16.264	=	17 (3.45Q)
RS 16.265	=	41 (3.45OO)
RS 16.379	=	6 (3.45F)
RS 16.402	=	24 (3.45X)
RS 17.063	=	30 (3.45DD)
RS 17.117	=	31 (3.45EE)
RS 17.434+	=	10 (3.45J)
RS 18.031	=	8 (3.45H)
RS 18.038	=	9 (3.45I)
RS 18.040	=	20 (3.45T)
RS 18.075	=	12 (3.45L)
RS 18.113A+B	=	21 (3.45U)
RS 18.147	=	11 (3.45K)
RS 19.011	=	32 (3.45FF)
RS 19.102	=	33 (3.45GG)
RS 20.199	=	25 (3.45Y)
RS 29.093	=	34 (3.45HH)
RS 29.095	=	35 (3.45II)
RS 34.124	=	4 (3.45D)
RS 34.148	=	23 (3.45W)
RS 34.356	=	14 (3.45N)
RS 92.2005	=	36 (3.45JJ)
RS 92.2010	=	37 (3.45KK)
RS 94.2406	=	18 (3.45R)
RS 94.2273	=	42 (3.45PP)
RS 94.2284	=	38 (3.45LL)
RS 94.2383	=	39 (3.45MM)
RS 94.2391	=	22 (3.45V)
RS 94.2479	=	26 (3.45Z)
RS 94.2592	=	27 (3.45AA)
RS 94.2619	=	39 (3.45MM)
RS 94.5015	=	16 (3.45P)
RS 96.2039	=	19 (3.45S)
RS [varia 4]	=	40 (3.45NN)
RIH 78.3+30	=	13 (3.45M)
RIH 78.12	=	7 (3.45G)

Number in COS Translation		Edition Number
1 (3.45A)	=	RS 15.008
2 (3.45B)	=	RS 9.479A
3 (3.45C)	=	RS 8.315
4 (3.45D)	=	RS 34.124
5 (3.45E)	=	RS 11.872
6 (3.45F)	=	RS 16.379
7 (3.45G)	=	RIH 78.12
8 (3.45H)	=	RS 18.031
9 (3.45I)	=	RS 18.038
10 (3.45J)	=	RS 17.434+
11 (3.45K)	=	RS 18.147
12 (3.45L)	=	RS 18.075
13 (3.45M)	=	RIH 78.3+30
14 (3.45N)	=	RS 34.356
15 (3.45O)	=	RS 16.078
16 (3.45P)	=	RS 94.5015
17 (3.45Q)	=	RS 16.264
18 (3.45R)	=	RS 94.2406
19 (3.45S)	=	RS 96.2039
20 (3.45T)	=	RS 18.040
21 (3.45U)	=	RS 18.113A+B
22 (3.45V)	=	RS 94.2391
23 (3.45W)	=	RS 34.148
24 (3.45X)	=	RS 16.402
25 (3.45Y)	=	RS 20.199
26 (3.45Z)	=	RS 94.2479
27 (3.45AA)	=	RS 94.2592
28 (3.45BB)	=	RS 4.475
29 (3.45CC)	=	RS 15.007
30 (3.45DD)	=	RS 17.063
31 (3.45EE)	=	RS 17.117
32 (3.45FF)	=	RS 19.011
33 (3.45GG)	=	RS 19.102
34 (3.45HH)	=	RS 29.093
35 (3.45II)	=	RS 29.095
36 (3.45JJ)	=	RS 92.2005
37 (3.45KK)	=	RS 92.2010
38 (3.45LL)	=	RS 94.2284
39 (3.45MM)	=	RS 94.2383
		RS 94.2619
40 (3.45NN)	=	RS [varia 4]
41 (3.45OO)	=	RS 16.265
42 (3.45PP)	=	RS 94.2273

I. CORRESPONDENCE BETWEEN MEMBERS OF THE ROYAL FAMILY

Dennis Pardee

(1) TALMIYĀNU TO HIS MOTHER ṮARRIYELLI (RS 15.008) (3.45A)[2]

Address (lines 1-3)
Message of Talmiyānu: To Ṯarriyelli, my mother, say:[3a]

Greetings (lines 4-6)
May it be well with you. May the gods of Ugarit guard you,[b] may they keep you well.[4c]

The Message: Talmiyānu Has Had an Audience with the King of Hatti (lines 6-13)
My mother, you must know[5d] that I have entered before the Sun[6e] and (that) the face of the Sun has shone upon me brightly.[f] So may my mother cause Maʾabu[7] to rejoice;[g] may she not be discouraged, (for) I am the guardian of the army.[8]

Report of Well-being and Request for Return of News (lines 14-20)
With me everything is well. Whatever is well with my mother, may she send word (of that) back to me.[9h]

a 2 Kgs 19:10 *b* Num 6:24, 26; Ps 40:12; Isa 42:6, etc. *c* Job 8:6 *d* Ezra 4:12, 13; 5:8; cf. Dan 3:18 *e* 1 Kgs 2:19 *f* Num 6:25; Pss 31:17; 67:2; 119:135 Dan 9:17; cf. Mal 3:20 *g* Deut 24:5; Prov 10:1 *h* Gen 43:27-28; 2 Kgs 4:26

[2] Text published in Virolleaud 1957:30-31, no. 15. Talmiyānu is the author of a letter addressed to the queen (2) and wrote another letter, jointly with a woman named ʾAḫātumilki, to his mother, unnamed in the address (3). Because in the present text the mother is identified as Ṯarriyelli, who is known to have been a queen of Ugarit, while no known king bore the name Talmiyānu, it may be conjectured that the author of these letters was the younger brother of a king. Ṯarriyelli was still living when the last known king took the throne (Bordreuil and Pardee 1982:128, 1991:162), and it is thus plausible to identify Talmiyānu's royal brother as Niqmaddu III (cf. van Soldt 1991:15-18, esp. n. 116), the next-to-the-last king of Ugarit, who died towards the end of the thirteenth century BCE.

[3] The address formulae in Ug. letters reflect in various ways the form of expression appropriate for dictating the letter to the messenger who would have borne the tablet and given the message orally, plausibly sometimes including more details than were present in the brief message inscribed in clay. The order of mention of writer and addressee are important, for they usually reflect the social status of each, the more important being mentioned first. The expression of social status may reflect either a familial situation ("mother," "father," "son" ...) or one of the other strata of society ("lord," "lady," "servant"); it may reflect equality ("brother"); and it may be mixed (as apparently here: in the family situation, the parent is superior, but Talmiyānu's social situation, which allows him to have an audience with the Hittite king, has permitted him to address himself to his mother as he would to an inferior).

[4] The most typical greetings included the verbs *šlm* (*yšlm lk*, "may it be well with you," and *ʾilm tšlmk*, "may the gods keep you well" [D-stem factitive]) and *nǵr* (≈ Hebr. *nṣr*, also with "gods" as subject, "may they guard you"). Only here in the Ug. correspondence are the gods qualified as those of Ugarit.

[5] An injunction that the addressee must "know" (√*ydʿ*) something may function either as an introduction to something that the author is about to say, as here, emphasizing the importance of what is about to be stated; or it may come at the end of a letter and function as an appeal to the addressee to take careful notice of what has been said. The latter appears to be the more strongly marked and to express both the gravity of the situation in which the author finds himself and anxiety on the author's part that his report may be overlooked.

[6] *špš*, the word that designates both the celestial orb and the solar deity, is used in Ug. letters to designate both the king of Hatti (see below [9] and [10]) and the king of Egypt (see below [13]). Because there are in the two texts translated below specific references to the king of Ugarit paying his respects to the Hittite court, it is assumed that this text reflects such a visit.

[7] The identity of the person referred to here by name only is unknown, but Talmiyānu wishes Ṯarriyelli to transmit to that person the news of his successful audience with the Hittite king. Because the gender of Maʾabu is unknown, it is not possible to determine whether the following verb, which is grammatically feminine, refers to Ṯarriyelli or to Maʾabu; in either case, the person is meant to be encouraged by the writer's assurances that the Ug. army is still in good hands. It is likely that this document is somehow related to the upheavals during the first years of the 12th century which eventually led to the destruction and abandonment of the city of Ugarit (see Astour 1965; Yon 1992; Liverani 1995).

[8] It has become clear in recent years that *ḫrd* is the Ug. term for "army" and that it is cognate with Akk. *ḫurādu*. See bibliography in Pardee 1987a:387 and more recently Vita 1995.

[9] This is the standard formula for saying in essence "I'm fine, how are things with you?" Both the writer's report and the request for news use the root *šlm*, "be well," revealing the psychology of the times as accentuating the positive (even, apparently, when things were not going well: see below, [9]). The formula may be double, as here, or may express only the writer's state (typically in letters from superior to inferior) or may only ask about the addressee's state (typically in letters from inferior to superior). Similar formulae are attested in the Akk. letters from Ugarit and from Emar (Tell Meskene), but not in the Amarna letters (see the exhaustive tabulation of the published examples from Ugarit in Pardee forthcoming c, d). Here the formula is placed after the body of the letter and thus functions as a closing formula, but in most cases (see here below [4] and [8], and the expanded form in [37] it occurs between the greetings and the body; the request for return of news appears at the end in (2), but that letter is entirely formulaic. Often the geographical distance between the correspondents is emphasized by the deictic adverbs *hnny/hlny*, "behold, here" and *ṯmny*, "there" (for example, in [3]), but they are omitted here.

(2) TALMIYĀNU KEEPS IN TOUCH WITH THE QUEEN (RS 9.479A) (3.45B)[10]

Address (lines 1-5)
To the queen, my lady, say: Message of Talmiyānu, your servant:

[10] Text published by Virolleaud 1938:127-31; re-edited *CTA* 141-42, no. 52. This letter presents all the earmarks of a letter from inferior to

Prostration Formula (lines 6-11)	*i* Gen 33:3	*Request for Return of News* (lines 12-15)
At the feet of my lady seven times and seven times (from) afar do I fall.[11i]		With my lady, whatever is well, may she send word (of that) back to her servant.

superior: the addressee is mentioned first, the only form of greeting is the prostration formula, and the author does not mention his own well-being but only asks for news from the addressee. Esp. given the absence of address to the writer's "mother," the addressee can hardly have been the same person as in (1). It appears likely, if the author is the same — which cannot be judged certain, since the name Talmiyānu was, with variants, fairly popular — the queen in question was not the queen-mother Ṯarriyelli but the reigning queen of Ugarit, perhaps Talmiyānu's sister-in-law (see note 2; on the position of the queen-mother, see below, note 15).

[11] The hollow root *ql*, "to fall, to prostrate oneself," is used to express as an epistolary fiction the physical act of obeisance that would be expected of inferiors when entering the presence of social superiors (on the force of the formula, see Pardee and Whiting 1987). When used, as in (4), to express polite obeisance by a king to his mother, the formula is doubly fictional, for it may be doubted that the king of Ugarit fell at his mother's feet every time he entered her presence. The noun *mrḥq(t)m* is sometimes added to the obeisance formula; it is used adverbially, meaning lit. "(at) a far-away place." It expresses the distance that separates an underling from his superior when he enters his presence, not the distance separating the two correspondents in an epistolary situation (Loewenstamm 1967:42). The equivalent phrase to *mrḥq(t)m* in Akk., *ištu rūqiš*, is common in letters discovered at Ras Shamra and Tell Meskene (ancient Emar), but not in the Amarna letters. That the act of obeisance would indeed be effected at a distance is reflected in different formulae in one of the Baᶜlu texts (see *COS* 1.86, n. 199) and in the Heb. Bible (Gen 33:3-4; Exod 24:1-2). From the Amarna letters we learn that the ideal prostration involved falling first on belly, then on back (e.g., *kabattuma ṣēruma, CAD K*, p. 14); according to the expression of this letter, that would occur seven times each way, for a total of fourteen prostrations. For a graphic depiction of foreigners prostrating themselves in these two positions in obeisance to the Eg. pharaoh, as well as in positions of rising and falling, see *ANEP*, pl. 5 (p. 2). Corresponding formulae in Anatolian literature show more variety (cf. the Song of Ullikummi, with its reference to thrice repeated prostrations [Hoffner 1998:63]). Do such variant formulae in Akk. texts discovered at Ugarit also reflect Anatolian views (e.g., "three times, nine times" in RS 25.138:5 [Lackenbacher 1989:318-19])? In the Ug. letters, the formula expressing the number of prostrations effected is never used when the addressee is a member of the writer's family, only when a writer of inferior social status addresses a superior.

(3) TALMIYĀNU AND ᵓAḪĀTUMILKI KEEP IN TOUCH WITH AN UNNAMED LADY (RS 8.315) (3.45C)[12]

Address (lines 1-4)		*Situation Report* (lines 10-14)[14]
To my mother, our lady, say: Message of Talmiyānu and ᵓAḫātumilki, your servants:[13]		Here with the two of us everything is very fine. And I, for my part, have got some rest.
Prostration and Greeting Formulae (lines 5-9)		*Request for Return of News* (lines 14-18)
At the feet of our lady (from) afar we fall. May the gods guard you, may they keep you well.		There with our lady, whatever is well, return word of that to your servants.

[12] Text published by Dhorme 1938:142-46; re-edited in *CTA* 140-41, no. 51. Here one of the authors identifies himself by name and refers to the addressee as "mother"; the presumption must be, though certainty is impossible, that these two are the same as the correspondents in (1). The entire structure of the letter differentiates these two from the second author, who is not the daughter of the addressee. A reasonable guess is that she is the wife of Talmiyānu. One thing that appears virtually certain today is that this ᵓAḫātumilki is not to be identified with the wife of Niqmêpaᶜ and mother of ᶜAmmiṯtamru II who bore the same name but who would have been born a century earlier (on this correction, see Freu 1999:27).

[13] The pronominal suffixes of ᵓ*umy* and ᵓ*adtny* distinguish explicitly between the two authors, for the first is 1st person singular while the second is 1st person dual, lit., "my mother, the lady of the two of us" (this suffix *-ny* peculiar to Ug. and preserved also in Eg., is present again below as the subject indicator attached to the verb "to fall" {qlny}). The last word, ᶜ*bdk*, is almost certainly in the dual, /ᶜabdêki/, lit., "the two servants of you." A similar situation is encountered below, (34).

[14] The writer's situation report is here separated from the request for return of news by a non-formulaic element of the situation report wherein the son reassures his mother to the effect that he is not working too much. These four words, *w* ᵓ*ap* ᵓ*ank nḫt*, though enclosed within a formula, constitute by their non-formulaic nature the body of the letter. They reveal clearly that the Ug. scribes were capable of modifying the standard epistolary formulae to fit a particular situation.

(4) THE KING TO THE QUEEN-MOTHER[15] IN THE MATTER OF THE AMURRITE PRINCESS (RS 34.124) (3.45D)[16]

Address (lines 1-3)		
[To the queen, my mother, say: Message of the]		k[ing, your son.]

[15] The restoration of *mlkt*, "queen," in line 1 is virtually certain, based on the occurrence of the word in the three following texts, (5), (6), and (7). The importance of the queen mother in Ug. society is seen most clearly in this text: it is she who decides what bodyguards to send to the king when he is absent from the city (lines 10-16) and, in his absence, it is she who presents his case in the matter of the Amurrite princess to

Prostration and Greeting Formulae (line 4-6)
At my mother's feet [I fall].[j] With my mother <may> it be well! [May the gods] guard you, may they keep [you] well.

Report of Well-being and Request for Return of News (lines 7-9)
Here with me [everythi]ng is well. There with you, whatever is well, sen<d> word (of that) back to me.

The King Complains Concerning the Royal Guard (lines 10-16)
Why do you send this *ḫuptu*(-soldier?) and not the royal guard?[17] If BN QL⌈-⌉, BN ᵓALYY,[18] and the royal guard go (elsewhere), inform me, and you will disappoint me severely.[19k]

The Affair of the Amurrite Princess (lines 17-?)[20]
Concerning your up-coming presentation to the city(-council)[21l] of the correspondence relative to the daughter of the king of Amurru:[22] if the city remains undecided, then why have I sent letters (to them) on the topic of the daughter of the king of Amurru?[m] Now Yabnīnu[23] has left for the court of Amurru and he has taken with him one hundred (shekels of) gold[n] and *mardatu*-cloth[24] for the king of Amurru. He has also taken oil in a horn and poured it on the head[o] of the daughter of the king of Amurru. Whatever si[n? ...] because my mother [...].

Conclusion (lines 42′-45′)
[...] is left and moreover [...] brought to an end by expiating[25] [...] your (male) ally/allies.[26] And I, for my part, [...] your (female) enemy.[p]

j 1 Kgs 2:19
k Ps 51:19; 147:3
l Cf. Deut 19:12, etc.
m 1 Kgs 11:1-3
n 1 Kgs 10:2, 10
o 1 Sam 10:1; 16:1, 13; 1 Kgs 1:39; 2 Kgs 9:1-3, 6; Pss 23:5; 133:2
p Exod 20:5-6, etc.

---

the representatives of the city of Ugarit (lines 17-24). It is virtually certain that the queen-mother retained the title of "queen" (*mlkt*) after her husband's death; but there is as yet no direct proof whether the new king's first wife also was honored with that title while the queen-mother lived or only received it on her death (cf. van Soldt 1985-86; Pardee forthcoming d on [3]). Apparent allusions to the wife of ᶜAmmurāpiᵓ as "queen" while the queen-mother Ṯarriyelli still lived make it likely, however, that both women bore the title.

[16] This letter was one of the texts rescued from the "tas de déblais" in 1973 (see description of the find in Bordreuil 1991); there was a preliminary edition by Caquot (1975:430-32), and a full edition by Bordreuil and Pardee (1991:142-50). Subsequent excavations have shown that the 1973 texts came from a large house in which one of the major officials active near the end of the kingdom of Ugarit lived. His name was ᵓUrtēnu and he was plausibly a member of the queen's administrative apparatus (see Yon 1995; Bordreuil and Malbran-Labat 1995; Malbran-Labat 1995a). This house is only second to the royal palace itself in the number of epistolary documents yielded that were written in Ug., a total of twenty-seven through the 1996 excavations. Others, from the 1992, 1994, and 1996 campaigns, are translated below.

[17] New textual discoveries have underscored the subservient nature of the *ḫupṯu* in Ug. society (see below, [19] and [27]). It may be expected that a single *ḫupṯu* (unless the term was used as a collective here) would not have been of much comfort compared with several members of the king's personal guard.

[18] Two proper names of the "son-of-X" type; the persons in question are unknown from other texts.

[19] In the Ug., the words are *ṯṯbrn lby*, lit., "you will break my heart," though the force of the Ug. idiom probably emphasizes disappointment over despondency (Bordreuil and Pardee 1991:146).

[20] In the break at the end of the *verso* (the upper edge of the tablet when viewed from the front) about seven full lines have disappeared. The same break has removed the beginning of each line of the text written on the left edge of the tablet (lines 42′-45′). These lacunae make it impossible to determine whether the end of the text as preserved continues the topic of the daughter of the king of Amurru, or whether the subject changed in the text that has disappeared. In the early days of the study of this text, three primary interpretations of the passage before the break were proposed: (1) the king is speaking of preparations for an up-coming marriage to an Amurrite princess (Caquot 1975:431-432); (2) the topic is an attempted reconciliation between the king of Ugarit, who would be ᶜAmmiṯtamru II (who reigned ca. 1260-1215 BCE), and his Amurrite wife after she had committed a "great sin" (Pardee 1977; with less conviction Bordreuil and Pardee 1991:150); (3) Yabnīnu's task is to bring about the death of the Amurrite queen of Ugarit after the same "great sin" (Brooke 1979:83-87). Each of these interpretations has weaknesses: the first does not explain the presence of the root *ḥṭ*[ᵓ], "sin," nor, if that topic continued through the break to lines 42′-45′, does it explain *kpr*, "to expiate," and the references to the queen-mother's allies and enemies; the second posits an attempted reconciliation to which no reference is made elsewhere in the various documents concerning the affair of the "great sin" and, if there be no link between the topic treated in lines 17-34 and that treated in lines 42′-45′, it relies entirely on the presence of the root *ḥṭ*[ᵓ]; the third is rendered precarious by the reference to oil poured on the head of the woman in question, for anointing is hitherto unattested in such circumstances (see Pardee 1977:14-19; Bordreuil and Pardee 1991:150). It appears more likely, therefore, that this texts deals with a marriage between a later Ug. king, plausibly ᶜAmmurāpiᵓ, the last king of Ugarit, and an Amurrite princess concerning which no Akk. textual data have yet appeared (Freu 1999:27-28).

[21] The role of the city (*qrt*) is twice mentioned in this text, here and in the second part of this sentence. We have very few data regarding the part that the non-royal segment of the city took in decisions regarding matters of primarily royal concern, such as foreign marriages or dissolutions thereof. This text, however, depicts the queen-mother as presenting the case at hand to the city and it implies that the city had a role in deciding policy, for it is depicted as, translating more lit., "remaining in a state of anguish" (*yṯbt b mṣqt*) over the messages that the king has sent regarding the affair.

[22] The reference is to the neighboring kingdom of Amurru, located to the south of the kingdom of Ugarit, in the region to the north of modern Tripoli (see Singer 1991; Klengel 1992:160-74).

[23] Yabnīnu is one of a relatively small number of important personages who were deeply involved in the distribution of resources in the city-state and who worked both within the royal administration and in a capitalistic fashion on their own. On Yabnīnu himself, see Courtois 1990; and on the role of these individuals and the "firms" they ran, the brief presentation in Malbran-Labat 1995a:105-6, 110-11. The identification of this Yabnīnu with the personage deeply involved in royal affairs at the end of the thirteenth century is the primary explicit basis for Freu's dating of this text to the time of ᶜAmmurāpiᵓ (see above, note 20).

[24] The word *mardatu* occurs in both Akk. and Ug. texts designating a textile produced in the west, a "fabric woven with several colors in a special technique" (*CAD* M 1:277). It is attested as a gift between western kings, as here, and from western kings to kings in Mesopotamia (Mari).

[25] The presence of the signs {kpr} is certain, but as the verb "to expiate" is otherwise unattested in Ug., other interpretations of the signs have been proposed (Brooke 1979:79).

[26] The translations "(male) ally/allies" and "(female) enemy" render the signs {[...]hbk} and {[...]nʾitk} and assume the restoration of basically nominal forms (plausibly participles, as in Heb.) of the roots *ʾhb*, "to love," and *šnʾ* (= *śnʾ*), "to hate." If the forms are indeed participles, it is impossible to determine whether the suffixed form in the case of the male allies is singular or plural.

(5) THE KING OF UGARIT TO THE QUEEN-MOTHER IN THE MATTER OF HIS MEETING WITH THE HITTITE SOVEREIGNS (RS 11.872) (3.45E)[27]

Address (lines 1-4)
To the queen, my mother, say: Message of the king, your son.

Prostration and Greeting Formulae (line 5-8)
At my mother's feet I fall. With my mother may it be well! May the gods guard you, may they keep [you] well.

Report of Well-being and Request for Return of News (lines 9-13)
Here with me everything is well. There with my mother, whatever is well, send word (of that) back to me.

Meeting with the Royal Hittite Sovereigns (lines 14-18)
From the tribute they have vowed a gift[28] to the queen. My words she did indeed accept[29] and the face of the king shone upon us.

[27] Text published by Virolleaud 1940:250-53; re-edited in *CTA* 139-40, no. 50.

[28] Various new explanations of the difficult sequence {ṯyndr | ʾiṯt . ʿmn . mlkt} in lines 14-16 (cf. the similar expression in lines 12-14 of the following text) have appeared in recent years, none of which is convincing. One of these takes {ʾiṯt} as a verb meaning "I am" and {ṯyndr} as a place name (Cunchillos 1988:46-47; 1989:289, n. 9), but there exists yet no proof that the particle *ʾiṯ* was inflected for person and the GN is as yet unattested as such. Subsequently, Dietrich and Loretz (1994:69-70) took up an old proposal by Hoftijzer (1967:131-32, n. 2) to see in the *mlk* of line 18 the king of Ugarit and in the author of the letter a royal scion named *mlk*; the former is not possible because it is the face of the "Sun," i.e., the Hittite king, that "shines" (see [1]), while the identification of *mlk* as a person by that name borders on the frivolous, as the personage is unknown and proper names are not used by members of the royal family in the address formula when writing to each other. The interpretation of {ṯyndr} offered here, "they have vowed a gift," is weakened by the absence of a word divider here and in the parallel text; I maintain the interpretation because seeing here an unattested GN makes little sense of the text.

[29] Because to date a better solution has not presented itself (cf. Pardee 1984:224), I translate according to the emended text {l | lq<ḥ>t} in lines 16-17.

(6) THE KING OF UGARIT TO THE QUEEN-MOTHER IN THE MATTER OF HIS MEETING WITH THE HITTITE SOVEREIGN (RS 16.379) (3.45F)[30]

Address (lines 1-3)
To the queen, my mo[ther], say: Message of the king, your son.

Prostration and Greeting Formulae (line 4-7)
At my mother's feet I fall. With my mo[ther] may it be well. May the god[s] guard you, may they keep [you] well.

Report of Well-being and Request for Return of News (lines 9-13)
Here with me it is [w]ell. There with my mother, whatever is we[ll, send] word (of that) back to me.

Meeting with the Hittite Sovereign (lines 14-18)
Here to the king from the tribute they have vowed a gift and [h]e (as a result has agreed to) augment his "vow?."[31]

Assurances (lines 16-24)
Now if the Hittite (forces) go up,[q] I will send you a message; and if they do not go up, I will certainly send one.[32] Now you, my mother, do not be agitated and do not allow yourself to be distressed

q Num 13:31; Judg 1:1, etc.

[30] Text published by Virolleaud 1957:28-29, no. 13. Though the difficult paragraph of the preceding text re-appears here (ll. 12-14) in a very similar form, only the king is present on this occasion and the author goes into more detail regarding the situation in which he finds himself. Because the last paragraph of the text fits the historical context of a time of military movements, it is plausible, though not certain, that both this text and the preceding date from the troubled times shortly before the fall of Ugarit (cf. [20], [24]).

[31] The text is damaged here (ll. 14-15) and there is an unsure sign: {w ht | [-]sny . ʾu!?ḏrh}. My translation assumes (1) the restoration {[y]sny}, root *sny*, "to increase" (de Moor 1965:358); (2) that the proto-Ug. root *nḏr* is spelled with {d} as a verb (see note 28) but with {ḏ} in the noun {ʾuḏr}; (3) that the noun "vow" refers to the Hittite king's reaction to the gift he had received, either abstract (he would make vows to the gods of Hatti and Ugarit) or concrete (reciprocal gifts to Ugarit in return for their military aid). The same word seems to appear again in (24):20 (see below).

[32] The spelling {ʿl} for the 3rd m.s.pf. of the root *ʿly*, "ascend," is anomalous (see Sivan 1984:290-91; Tropper 2000:664-65 [§75.534]), but no better interpretation has yet been offered (*ʿwl*, "do evil" [de Moor 1965:358], does not, I believe, work in this context). The reference may be to the mountainous territory north of the kingdom of Ugarit (see [20]).

in any way.[33]

[33] Lit., "and, moreover, do not place anything in your heart" (*w ʾap mhkm b lbk ʾal tšt*).

(7) A ROYAL SON TO HIS MOTHER AS REGARDS WARFARE (RIH 78.12) (3.45G)[34]

Address (lines 1-2)
To the queen, my mother, my lady:

Prostration Formula (lines 2-3)
At your feet I fall.

Report on ʿAbdimilki (lines 3-7)
When you sent ʿAkayu, (thereby) ʿAbdimilki the *šʿtq*[35] was saved. He (now) will uplift the heart of your son and (take away) your pain as well.

The Son's Efforts (lines 8-22)
Now as for me, for six days I have been fighting continuously. If ʿAbdimilki is not saved a[live?], then the heart [of your son? ...].[36] However that may be, ʿAbdimilki is (still) alive. If he should die, I will go on fighting on my own.

[34] Text published by Bordreuil and Caquot 1980:359-60; cf. Pardee's preliminary re-edition based on collation (1984:221-23). I have nothing new to offer here on the interpretation of the individual terms of this text and refer the reader to that study. The formulae are abbreviated (note absence of the messenger formula "say" and the abbreviated prostration formula, "at your feet," rather than "at the feet of my mother, my lady"), as well as the omission of any form of greeting, revealing plausibly the agitation of the military situation (for the absence of greeting, see below, (20), from a similar situation). The omission of the self-identification in the address was probably owing to the same factors, but it has deprived us of knowing whether the "son" was the reigning king or not. The presumption must be that the son was not king, for, in other letters containing that self-identification of the writer, the queen-mother is not addressed as "lady," but only as "mother." One can, however, easily imagine a young ʿAmmurāpiʾ off to his first battle so addressing Ṯarriyelli (on ʿAmmurāpi's youth at taking the throne, see below on [9]).

[35] A female *šʿtqt* is attested in the Kirta story as the effective means of removing his illness (*COS* 1.102, p. 342). Here the context is insufficient to allow us to determine ʿAbdimilku's precise role, though it was clearly in the sphere of removing pain (see next sentence).

[36] Plausibly, "the heart of your son will be downcast," the opposite of "being uplifted." After this lacuna, four more lines are too damaged for a coherent translation.

II. INCOMING CORRESPONDENCE FROM OTHER COURTS[37]

Dennis Pardee

(8) THE KING OF TYRE TO THE KING OF UGARIT IN THE MATTER OF STORM-DAMAGED SHIPS (RS 18.031) (3.45H)[38]

Address (lines 1-3)
To the king of Ugarit, my brother, say: Message of the king of Tyre, your brother.[39] *r*

r 2 Sam 5:11; 1 Kgs 5:15-25; 9:10-14

Greetings (lines 4-5)
May it be well with you. May the gods guard you, may they keep you well.

[37] It is generally assumed that all such documents are translations into Ug. from an Akk. original. Because Akk. was the *lingua franca* of the time and because of the hundreds of Akk. letters that have been discovered at Ras Shamra, this hypothesis must be judged likely. On the other hand, because there is not to date a single case where the original has been preserved as well as the translation, two other possibilities must be considered: (1) the Ug. text represents the writing down at Ugarit of a message that would have been delivered orally; (2) a Ug. scribe would have been present at the foreign court and it is he who would have done the translation of the original message into Ug.

[38] Text published by Virolleaud 1965:81-83, no. 59. New archaeological investigations have corrected the original excavator's identification of the locus where this and a large number of other tablets and fragments were found as an oven for baking tablets (references in Pardee 2000b:55). As is generally the case at Ras Shamra, the tablets found in "Cour V" and surrounding rooms had for the most part fallen from the upper story when the structure collapsed. No given text may certainly be dated, therefore, to the period immediately preceding the fall of the city, though most would belong to archives in current use and thus be of relatively recent date.

[39] There is no reason to suspect that the kings of Ugarit and Tyre were related, and the word "brother" here reflects a common usage, that of expressing equal social status among kings. Because neither king is named in this text, there is no precise element for dating it. The apparently free contacts with Egypt indicate, however, a time after the treaty that established peace between Egypt and Hatti during the reigns of Rameses II and Ḫattušili III, for Ugarit had been within the Hittite sphere during the period of open hostilities between the two great powers (Liverani 1979:1304-1312; Klengel 1992:100-180). Because this text deals with a shipment of grain, in all probability from Egypt northwards, recent scholarship on this text dates it to one of the periods of food shortage in the Hittite empire that occurred during the last four decades of its life, ca. 1225-1185 (Freu 1999; Singer 1999). As there is no obvious reason to prefer an earlier date over a later, the presumption must be that this text dates to the last few years of the kingdom of Ugarit.

Report of Well-being and Request for Return of News (lines 6-9)
Here with me it is well. There with you, whatever is well, send word (of that) back (to me).

The Storm at Sea (lines 10-27)
Your ships[40] [s] that you dispatched to Egypt[41] were wrecked[42] near Tyre when they found themselves caught in[43] a bad storm.[t] The salvage master,[44] however, was able to remove the ent[ire] (cargo of) grain[u] in their possession. (Then) I took over from the salvage master the entire (cargo of) grain, as well as all the people[v] and their food, and I returned (all these things) to them.[45] Now your boats have been able to moor[46] at Acco,[w] stripped (of their rigging).[47] So my brother should not worry.[48] [x]

s 1 Kgs 9:26-27; 10:11, 22 *t* 1 Kgs 18:45; Ezek 13:11, 13; Jon 1:4 *u* Deut 22:9 *v* Gen 12:5, etc. *w* Judg 1:31 *x* 2 Sam 13:33; cf. 2 Sam 19:20; Isa 42:25, etc.

[40] The word is ʾ*anykn*, consisting of ʾ*any*, plausibly a collective noun as in Heb. (Cunchillos 1989:351-52, n. 9), plus the 2nd m.s. suffix *-k-*, plus the enclitic particle *-n*, of uncertain function here. The noun ʾ*any* is of feminine gender, as is shown by the verbal forms in lines 13 (*mtt*), 24 (*ṯt*), and 25 (ʿ*ryt*). If the word is indeed collective and not singular, the precise number of boats was not stated by the king of Tyre because all that the Ugaritian king had sent were rescued; he was expected to know the number.

[41] The GN is regularly written *mṣrm* in Ug., a dual form as in the later Northwest Semitic languages, reflecting the Eg. perception of their land as consisting of two major segments, Upper and Lower Egypt.

[42] Lit. "died" (*mtt*, √*mt*, 3rd fem. sing.). It is clear from what follows that "died" did not imply sinking, only the stripping away of the rigging of the boats, leaving them at the mercy of the storm. It is also clear from what follows that the boats never foundered, for the local salvage master was able to remove everything of value in them and get them to port in Acco. One may surmise that the storm was violent but brief, that the event took place far enough south of Tyre to preclude attempting to bring the damaged boats back against the wind to Tyre, and that Acco was the next major port to the south able to take them in.

[43] Lit. "they found themselves in." The verb is *nškḥ*, N-stem perf. of *škḥ*; the 3rd masc. pl. form refers to the crews running the ships, not to the vessels themselves (of which the antecedent would be feminine singular, as we have seen). This form explains the recurring 3rd masc. pl. suffix *-hm* below (*bdnhm*, "in their hands" [l. 18], *ḏr*ʿ*hm*, "their grain" [l. 19], ʾ*aklhm*, "their food" [l. 21], *lhm*, "to them" [l. 23]).

[44] The meaning of *rb tmtt*, lit. "master of death," as denoting the local official in charge of wrecks is elucidated by the verb expressing the wrecking of the ships, i.e., *mt*, "to die" (Hoftijzer 1979:386). The appointment of a governmental official to be in charge of salvage (cf. English "receiver of wreck") thus has at least a conceptual precedent, if not a precise legal one, in the Late Bronze Age. From the statement below that the king took the salvaged items from the salvage master (the verb is *lqḥ*, the same as was used for the salvage master "removing" the grain from the boats), one may infer that the position was by royal appointment and that the official normally disposed of and therefore profited from the salvage. It may further be surmised that the king of Ugarit would subsequently have been responsible for remunerating the salvage master for his efforts, but that would of course have depended on the custom of the time (it is possible that the local king had the authority to dispose of the salvage as he wished, at least on occasion).

[45] The item mentioned first, in the preceding sentence, was the cargo of grain. Here the three principal components of the salvage are defined as the cargo of grain, the human beings (*kl npš*), and the supplies for feeding the crews during the voyage (ʾ*aklhm*). Whether *kl npš* may be understood as including passengers as well as crew, there is no way of knowing.

[46] Ug. had an originally biconsonantal verb, *ṯw* or *ṯy*, related to the Arabic verb *ṯwy* that denotes either the act of a person stopping somewhere or the hospitality extended to that person. The Ug. semantic field appears similar to the Arabic, for here the verb is used to express the finding of refuge in Acco, but in another Ug. letter ([31] [see below]) to express the act of furnishing bread and wine to a lodger. Here it is spelled {ṯt} and is a 3rd fem. sing. pf., apparently pronounced /ṯit/, from /*ṯiyat/ or /*ṯiwat/. The verb occurs three times in the imperf. spelled {ṯt} in (31); the form {yṯ}, "he will furnish (food)," may occur in (9):30 (see following text). The root was identified by Virolleaud in his ed. of (8) (1965:83). Attempts to identify {ṯt} as a form of the number "2" must be rejected (Pardee, forthcoming d).

[47] Lit. "stripped naked": ʿ*ryt* is an adjective, perhaps a G-stem verbal adjective from √ʿ*rw/y* (cf. Arabic ʿ*ariya*, "be naked"; the Heb. noun meaning "nakedness" shows III-*w*, viz., ʿ*erwāh*, a form of the root perhaps attested in RS 2.[003]+ i 7 [*KTU* 1.14]). The antonym is √*lbš*, "to clothe," attested once for the act of rigging a ship (RS 18.025:16 [Virolleaud 1965:129-30, text 106]; cf. Pardee 1975:616).

[48] The "not to worry" formula is expressed in the third person ("my brother" = "you") and consists of the injunction not "to take it to heart": *w* ʾ*aḫy mhk b lbh* ʾ*al yšt*, "may my brother not put anything in his heart." See above on (6):22-24.

(9) THE KING OF HATTI TO THE KING OF UGARIT (RS 18.038) (3.45I)[49]

Address (lines 1-2)
Message of the Sun: To ʿAmmurāpiʾ[50] say:

[49] Text published in Virolleaud 1965:84-86, no. 60. This letter, found with the same group of tablets as the previous text (see note 38), is frustrating, for most of the long paragraph that apparently deals with famine (lines 17-30) has been lost, the third and fourth paragraphs (lines 5-16) are also damaged, though plausible restorations based on the repetitiveness of the two paragraphs are here possible, and the final paragraph (lines 31-35) is both damaged and of uncertain interpretation. This text is included here, however, because it is the best preserved of several Ug. letters from the Hittite king to the king of Ugarit. See also the next text, from the Hittite queen to the king of Ugarit. (Many more letters written in Akk., both from the Hittite king himself and from his representative in Syria, the ruler of Carchemish, have been discovered at Ras Shamra.)

[50] ʿAmmurapiʾ is the last known king of Ugarit, who took the throne near the beginning of the 12th century BCE and, as far as we know, was on the throne at the time of the destruction of the city in the second decade of that century. The Hittite king, though here unnamed, may by synchrony be identified with Šuppiluliuma II (Klengel 1992:148); his father would have been Arnuwanda while ʿAmmurāpi's father would have been Niqmaddu III (cf. Freu 1999:37; Singer 1999: chart after p. 732). It is now known that ʿAmmurāpiʾ's father died young and that the son took the throne while too young to be considered a man: in RS 34.129:5-7 (Malbran-Labat 1991:38-39, text 12), the Hittite king writes to the

Report of Well-being (lines 3-4)
With the Sun everything is very well.[51]

The Hittite Sovereign's View of the Previous Reign (lines 5-10)
Bef[ore] the Sun's [fat]her [your] fath[er],[52] his servant, did indeed dwell submissively;[y] for a se[rvant] indeed (and) his possession[z] was he[53] and [his] l[ord] he did indeed guard. My father never lacked g[rain], (but) you, for your part, have not recognized (that this was how things were).[54] [aa]

ᶜAmmurāpi's Duty (lines 11-16)
Now you also belong to the Sun your master; a serv[ant] indeed, his possession are you. But [yo]u, for your part, you have not at all recognized (your responsibility toward) the Sun, your master. To me, the Sun, your master, from year to year,[55] why do you not come?

The Food Matter (lines 17-30)
Now concerning the fact that you have sent a (message)-tablet to the Sun, your master, regarding food, to the effect that there is no food in your land:[bb] the Sun himself is perishing.[56] [Now] if I go? [...] a gift[57] [...] the Sun [...] food he will furnish [...].[58]

The Enigmatic Conclusion (lines 31-35)
(In the month of) ʾIbᶜaltu [...][59] but I [have] no scribe. Our scribes are (normally) "pure." (Such) a man search out, wherever he may be, and have him sent to me.[60]

y Ps 23:6
z Exod 19:5, etc.
aa Exod 2:25, etc.
bb Gen 12:10; 26:1; 41:48-57

governor of Ugarit because of the youth of the king ("the king your master is little (*ṣe-ḫe-er*), he doesn't know anything"). The general content of (9) indicates that he had matured enough to have been expected to visit Hatti on a regular basis. Texts such as (5) and (6) reflect encounters between the two kings and plausibly date, therefore, after this one.

[51] As is generally the case in letters from the Hittite king to the king of Ugarit, both those in Ug. and those in Akk., the address is very brief and in it the sender is always mentioned before the addressee. Greetings are also brief or even omitted, as here, and the formula reporting on the sender's well-being is never accompanied by the request for return of news from the addressee (on the double formula see above note 9 and the other examples cited there). These are all characteristics of letters from superiors to inferiors when the social separation is great. If line 21 is correctly interpreted as "the Sun is perishing," the purely formulaic character of the report of well-being becomes clear.

[52] Two considerations permit a new interpretation of this text (as compared with Pardee 1981): (1) in Ug. prose, *ʾadn* normally designates the "(biological) father," not the "(political) father"; (2) restoring {ʾad[nk]} rather than {ʾad[nh]} in line 6 (suggested to me by A. Sumakai-Fink) permits this entire paragraph to be interpreted as the Hittite sovereign's view of how things were in the time of Niqmaddu III, rather than as the quotation of a previous letter from ᶜAmmurāpiʾ, as I had previously understood.

[53] The Ug. here is *k* ᶜ[*bd*(*m*)] *sglth hw*. The word translated "possession" is *sglt*, cognate to Heb. *sᵉgullāh*. See the detailed comparison with the Heb. data by Hoftijzer (1982:380-82).

[54] Here and in line 14, the verb is *ydᶜ*, used, as occasionally in BH, to express recognition of a state and its associated responsibilities (Huffmon and Parker 1966). Here the lack of recognition in the Ug. king is represented as not following his father's example in recognizing his responsibility as a vassal to provide his master with supplies of food in years of poor crops in Hatti. In the following paragraph, to this responsibility is added that of rendering regular visits to the overlord.

[55] Liverani has recently argued convincingly (1997), in fact taking up a point made several decades earlier (1964b:199-202), that the second word of the formula *šnt šntm* is not dual, as most scholars have thought, but singular with enclitic *-m*.

[56] Before the colon in my translation the Hittite king is quoting a previous letter from ᶜAmmurāpiʾ, wherein he claimed not to have any grain to send to his sovereign. The Hittite king then claims that he will perish without an influx of food supplies.

[57] At the beginning of line 23 the word *ytnt* is preserved, which could be either the noun "gift" or a perfective form of the verb *ytn*, "to give." Because the Ug. word *špš*, "sun," is feminine in gender, the scribe of this document used in line 21 a feminine verbal form with that noun when referring to the Hittite king (*špšn tʾubd* = "Sun" + "*nun* of apodosis" + "she perishes" [3rd fem. sing. impf.]) and the same could be true of *ytnt*. Because of the damaged text, it is not possible to decide the matter. It is in any case not clear, if the form is verbal, why it is perfective in line 23, as compared with the imperfectives in lines 21 (*tʾubd*) and 22 (*ʾalk*), though the perfective could be a part of the apodosis of the conditional sentence begun in line 22 (in Ug., as in Heb., the use of perfective and imperfective forms in conditional sentences reflects the aspectual nature of the verbal system). Nor would it be clear why the writer would refer to himself in the first person in line 22, sandwiched in between the self-references in the third person in lines 21 and 23. Whatever the correct analysis of the morphology and syntax of the form may be, we may surmise that the Hittite king is making reference to previous "gifts" in connection with providing him with food supplies, either his to the kings of Ugarit or theirs to him (i.e., the food itself).

[58] Only a few signs at the beginning of each of the lines 23-30 are preserved, insufficient to understand even the gist of the Hittite king's further description of his situation. That he continued to speak of food throughout is clear, however, from the repetition of the word *ʾakl*, "food," at the beginning of the last line of the paragraph, followed by {yṯ[...]}, here taken as a complete word (see above note 46 on *ṯṯ* in [8]), though the two signs could be only remnants of a longer word.

[59] The last sign before the break is {ʾa}, which may plausibly be interpreted as the beginning of a 1st com. sing. impf. verbal form, "I will/would [X]."

[60] The month of ʾIbᶜaltu probably fell in December-January, beginning with the winter solstice. See Pardee 2000a:156-58, 669-70 for the proposal to set back by one month the series of Ug. months in the solar year proposed by de Jong and van Soldt 1987-88:71 (for these authors ʾIbᶜaltu would correspond to January-February). Thus the Hittite king is referring to a situation that will occur in winter. One might think that the reference should be to the effects of a shortage of grain already visible when the letter was written, at the least several weeks before the winter solstice, but the rest of the paragraph only refers to the need for a scribe and to the matter of "pure" documents (*sprn ṭhrm*), whatever they may be. Under what circumstances would the king of Hatti have required a scribe to be supplied from Ugarit? Dijkstra (1976:438-39) believes that a specific scribe was being requested, but my collation of the tablet (Pardee 1981:155-56) has shown that the readings on which this interpretation were based are to be rejected. The only modification of my previous understanding of this text is that I now see the Hittite king referring to how things should be ("normally" our scribes are pure); the purity may refer to social status (cf. *ellu* in Akk.). The fact remains that he was in this letter apparently requesting that a single scribe be sent, plausibly a multi-lingual scribe, capable of understanding Hittite and Ug. (and other languages of the region) and of writing at least Akk. and perhaps Ug. as well.

(10) PUDUḪEPA, QUEEN OF HATTI, TO THE KING OF UGARIT (RS 17.434+) (3.45J)[61]

Address (lines 1-2)
[Messa]ge of Puduḫepa, [great] quee[n, que]en [of Hatti:] [To] Niqmaddu say:

Report of Well-being (lines 2-4)
He[re with] the Su[n and] with the queen, everything [is well]; now the well-being of your land and [of] the house of the king [...].[62]

First Matter: Tribute (lines 5-13)
Concerning the fact that you have sent to the royal palace your message (as follows): "Now [the g]old of my tribute[cc] [to] the Sun [I ?] hereby remit, [and,] as for you, the ⌜M⌝[R]⌜Ṯ⌝ that you stipulated in the tre[aty, certainly] you will receive it," I went to ʾUD and o[ur] king [stayed?] [in] the (capital-)city. We were to return with you by the midst of [...]. [...] But to me you have not come [... and] your messenger-party[63] you have not sent to me. [Now ?] according as you set (something) aside for me — a quantity of gold[...], [you, for your part,] have [not ?] remitted it to me; (only) to the Sun have [you] remitted [gold ...].[64]

cc 2 Sam 8:6; 1 Kgs 5:1, etc.

Second Matter: Problems with Caravans (lines 14-22, 23′-28′)[65]
[Sec]ondly (?): Concerning the fact that you sent word to the royal palace (as follows): "[X-e]d[66] are the caravans of Egypt and they have stopped; (indeed) th[e] ca[ra]vans of Egypt through the land of Ugarit [have been X-ed] and through the land of Nuḫašše they (now) must pass [...]."[67] [...] shall pass through the land of [X and through the land of] Qadesh[68] and through the land of [X ...]; and the land of [X] shall not harm (them) (or: shall not be harmed) [...].

[61] Text published by Caquot (1978a:121-34). It consists of nine fragments, of which three joined to form a single large fragment, all discovered in Room 56, locus 901, in the east section of the royal palace during the 1953 campaign at Ras Shamra. The larger fragments were numbered 17.434 through 17.438; to the four smaller fragments associated two each with RS 17.434 and RS 17.438 were added the letters A and B for purposes of identification (Bordreuil-Pardee 1989:148). Because of similarity of script and ware, it is likely that all these fragments belonged originally to a single letter, though it cannot be determined whether the letter was written on a single tablet or on two. (All the fragments could physically fit into the plausible outline of an original single tablet, but several are too small to permit reconstruction of a continuous text.) On the identification of writing on the back of the principal fragment, proving that that tablet was entirely inscribed, see Dijkstra 1994:125 (observation confirmed by my collation in June of 1996). The Puduḫepa who addressed the letter to a king of Ugarit named Niqmaddu was either the wife of Ḫattušili II who became queen in ca. 1285 BCE or another queen by the same name, currently unknown from other sources. The Niqmaddu in question is either the king conventionally known as the third by that name (which would imply great longevity for Puduḫepa since Niqmaddu III only came to the throne in ca. 1225 BCE), or the second by that name (which would imply that the Puduḫepa of this text was not the known queen since Niqmaddu II lived in the fourteenth century), or an as yet unknown king bearing that name (brief summary in Pardee 1983-84:326; many more details in Cunchillos 1989:363-86). With the new lines identified by Dijkstra, the text is now known to have been over sixty lines long. Only the beginning is translated here because of the fragmentary state of the rest of the text.

[62] Because the Hittite sovereigns generally do not inquire after the health of their correspondents of inferior status (see preceding text), and because no example of the formula expressing the inquiry after the health of the addressee begins like this one, it is impossible to restore the end of this version. The first words, partially preserved, are probably to be read {⌜w⌝ [. d] ⌜. bt⌝ [.] ⌜ml⌝k [...]} "and of the house of the king," but after these traces the end of the line has entirely disappeared. If the lacuna once contained a verb, it may have been *šʾl*, "to inquire after," for that idiom appears to be attested in Ug. in (31):2 (see below) and in Akk. texts of the period (Pardee 1982:46). The idiom is attested in Heb. letters in Arad 18 (see above, *COS* 3.43I).

[63] *mlʾaktk*, a feminine *mem*-preformative noun from the root *lʾk*, "to send," used in Ug. to designate the "embassy" sent with messages. The root is visible in Heb. in the masculine *mem*-preformative noun *malʾāk*, "messenger, angel."

[64] Because of the breaks in the text, it is difficult to determine who is doing what to whom here and at the beginning of this paragraph. I have interpreted the passage as referring to the king of Ugarit sending tribute to the reigning Hittite king but not to Puduḫepa. According to the treaty fixed between Niqmaddu II and Šuppiluliuma I in the fourteenth century, attested in both Akk. and a badly broken Ug. version (RS 11.772+ [*CTA* no. 64]), the Hittite queen was entitled to tribute (see the detailed comparison between the Akk. and Ug. versions in Dietrich and Loretz 1964-66). Whatever the precise historical circumstances here, one may surmise that the author was complaining about not receiving her quota, that all was going to the reigning king.

[65] Lines 14-22 are preserved on the principal fragment (RS 17.435 + RS 17.436 + RS 17.437, lines 14-22). The topic of passing through various lands continues on the next large fragment (RS 17.434, first six lines, numbered conventionally 23′-28′) but the break between the two makes it impossible to determine whether the text as preserved represents a single paragraph in the original or two paragraphs or more. And because the word "caravan" (*ntbt*, lit. "path") is not repeated in lines 23′-28′, it cannot be judged certain that the subject of the verb *tʿtq* (√*ʿtq*, "to pass on, through, by") in line 26′ was that noun and not another.

[66] The verb or adjective indicating the reason for the cessation of caravan activity along the coast has disappeared both here and in the following sentence.

[67] Assuming that the reference is to caravans traveling between Egypt and Hatti, the passage through Ugarit would mean, from the perspective of the northern journey, taking a coastal route as far as Ugarit, then heading inland past Aleppo and probably Carchemish before continuing north. The passage through Nuḫašše would imply an inland route turning in from the coast no further north than the Tripoli region, perhaps further south. The northernmost option would involve entering the valley of the Orontes through the Homs Gap, moving east, then leaving Qadesh (mentioned in the passage preserved on [RS 17.434] [see note 65]) on the right and continuing past modern Apamea, in which region the confederation of kingdoms known as Nuḫašše was located (cf. Klengel 1992:151-56). Cf. Judg 5:6.

[68] On the city-state of Qadesh, located on the Orontes south of modern Homs, see Klengel 1992:157-60.

Third Matter: Problems with Royal Purple (lines 29'-?)[69]
Now concerning the (message)-tablet that [you] sent [to the roy]al [palace] regarding royal purple[dd] [...:] "Here, why have the men of [my ?] master [X-ed red-dyed] cloth [...] when there is no red-dyed cloth in my house?" [...].[70]

[dd] Exod 25:4, etc.

[69] The treaty between Šuppiluliuma and Niqmaddu II mentioned above (note 64) explicitly lists various amounts of *ˀiqnˀu*, a word meaning basically "blue (the color of lapis-lazuli)" which is used to describe "royal purple of a darker hue," and *pḥm*, a word meaning basically "red (of hot coals)" which is used to designate "royal purple of a redder/browner hue." The Hittite king was to receive five hundred units of *pḥm* and five hundred of *ˀiqnˀu*, while the queen was to receive one hundred units each. The same smaller amount was also stipulated for the crown prince and for several high officials in the Hittite court. The word used in the first line of this paragraph of the letter is *qnˀim*, plausibly interpreted as a plural or by-form of *ˀiqnˀu* and used as a generic term including the two principal varieties of royal purple. As this paragraph is preserved, *pḥm* is attested below, but not *ˀiqnˀu*. On the other hand, we find attested in line 39', beyond the part of the paragraph translated here, for the first time the Ug. term used to designate those who produce royal purple, *qnˀuym*. On this most exclusive of Levantine products, exclusive because the authentic dye was produced from mollusks drawn from the Mediterranean and a great number of mollusks was required to produce a small amount of dye, see Jidejian 1969:142-59.

[70] The king of Ugarit seems to be saying that he has no stocks of royal purple with which to satisfy the Hittite king's tribute collectors.

(11) PGN TO THE KING OF UGARIT (RS 18.147) (3.45K)[71]

Address (lines 1-3)
Message of PGN, your father: To the king of Ugarit, [my son], say:

Greetings (lines 4-5)
May it be well with you. May the gods guard you, may they keep you well.

Report of Well-being and Request for Return of News (lines 6-8)
Here with me, it is well. There wi[th] my son, whatever is [w]ell, return word (of that) [to me].

Reference to Previous Correspondence Regarding a Famine (lines 9-?)
Concerning the fact that my son has sent a (message)-tablet regarding food (in which you said): "(Here) with me, plenty (has become) famine," let my son assign this: sea-faring boats. Let him [...] and food [...].[72]

[71] Text published by Virolleaud 1965:87-88, no. 61. The *recto* is reasonably well preserved, but the text on the back of the tablet has almost entirely disappeared. The text is included here because of the interest provided by the address: someone by the name of PGN describes himself as "father" (the word is *ˀab*, which designates the political "father," not the biological one — see above, note 52) to the king of Ugarit, his "son." The use of the terms *ˀab/bn* and the warmth of the greetings indicate an entirely different relationship between these two as compared with the hauteur that characterizes the Hittite sovereign's formulae, or lack thereof, when addressing the king of Ugarit. Because Akk. letters from a king of Alashia (Cyprus) named Kušmešuša show similar warmth (Malbran-Labat *apud* Bordreuil and Malbran-Labat 1995:445), the identification of PGN as another king of Alashia is probable. Malbran-Labat (ibid.) also describes, however, the king of Amurru as addressing himself to the Ugaritian king as his "father," and that identification must remain a possibility. The identification with a Hittite official named Pukana (Klengel 1974:169; 1992:149; Singer 1999:718) does not fit the pattern established by the epistolary formulae attested for letters from the Hittite sovereign and his officials, but one may perhaps surmise that a warmer relationship existed between a certain official of the Hittite empire and the king of Ugarit. Nevertheless, more than one person may have borne the name spelled {pgn} in Ug., and limiting the identification to the Hittite official because of the similarity of the names must be judged unlikely. The use of ships to transport the needed food (see following note) requires an identification with a sea-faring nation, and appears to eliminate Hatti, which was a receiver of food at this period, not a provider (see [9]).

[72] Instead of the generally accepted reading {mˀidy . w ǵbny} in line 11, where the meaning of the second word is unclear (it is usually taken to mean "fullness," from a basic meaning "thickness"), the tablet appears to read {mˀidy . ⌜r⌝ǵbny}, and the entirety of the Ug. king's previous message is therefore summed up in the three words {ˁmy | mˀidy . rǵbny}, a nominal phrase of which {rǵbny} is the predicate. If that is the entire message, as the use of *bny*, "my son," in line 12 appears clearly to indicate, then lines 12-14 contain the beginning of the author's reply: if the "son" needs food, he must send ships to pick it up.

(12) MUTUAL ASSISTANCE (RS 18.075) (3.45L)[73]

[...]

Greetings (lines 1'-2')
May it be w[ell with you.] May [the gods] gua[rd

[73] Text published by Virolleaud 1965:93, no. 65. Because the address is lost, it is impossible to determine whether this letter is incoming or one of the rare examples of a draft for an outgoing letter. It is included in this section because the former outnumber the latter. The use of the term *ˀḫ*, "brother," in lines 19', 21' and 23' shows that the correspondents were equals, either familial or social; the reference to a "servant" (line 15') and the topics of "desire" {ˀrš} and of "need" {ḫsr}, attested in Akk. letters of which the king of Ugarit is one of the correspondents (the closest set of parallels is in RS 17.116 [Nougayrol 1956:132-34], probably from Šaušgamuwa, king of Amurru, to the king of Ugarit), make it at least plausible that the correspondents of the present text were also royal.

you, may they keep] you [well].

[...][74]

I'll Scratch Your Back, You Scratch Mine (lines 15′-23′)

Now as for your servant, let him be empowered to speak (for you) to me! Whatever your desire may be (concerning something) that you lack, I will have it delivered to my brother. And I, for my part, whatever my lack (may be), may my brother have it loaded up there.[75] May my [br]other not leave me to perish![76]

[74] Lines lines 3′-14′ are too damaged to translate.

[75] The writer promises to "have delivered" what he sends ({ᵓaštn}, "I will cause to give"), whereas he uses the verb ᶜ*ms*, "to load" to express what he wishes his correspondent to do. The latter usage apparently reflects the servant's role as intermediary between the writer and the correspondent.

[76] {ᵓal ybᶜrn}, lit., "may he not destroy me," viz., by allowing him to perish rather than sending him what he needs. This is a strong expression and, unless it be pure hyperbole, indicates a situation where famine threatens.

III. OUTGOING CORRESPONDENCE TO OTHER COURTS[77]

Dennis Pardee

(13) ᶜAMMIṮTAMRU, KING OF UGARIT, TO THE KING OF EGYPT (RIH 78.3+30) (3.45M)[78]

Address and Prostration Formulae (lines 1-6)

[To the Sun],[79] the great king, the king of Egypt, the [goo]d [king], the just king,[ee] the [king of k]ings,[80] [ff] master of all lands, [...],[81] say: Message of [ᶜAmmiṯtam]ru,[82] your servant. At my [master's] feet I fa[ll].

[ee] Isa 11:4-5; Ps 23:3; 45:5
[ff] Ezek 26:7; Dan 2:37; Ezra 7:12

[77] Certain examples of what are apparently drafts for letters that would have gone out in Akk. have been discovered in the cases of three letters addressed to the Eg. king and of one to the Hittite emperor. The Eg. identification is certain for the first two texts because the addresses are preserved, probable in the third case because of the mention of Eg. gods. Though the address of the fourth text is lost, the Hittite identification appears certain on the basis of typical phrases used in the body of the letter. Because of the many letters from Canaanite cities discovered at el-Amarna and the letter from Ugarit discovered at Tel Aphek (below, *COS* 3.94) that were in Akk., it is generally assumed that the document actually sent would in each case have been in Akk. Because the situation is the opposite of that of incoming letters (see above, note 37), the documents translated in this section are perforce drafts of some kind, whether for translation, for a final Ug. text, for a letter that was in fact never sent, or for an archival copy.

[78] Text edited by Bordreuil and Caquot (1980:356-58 and fig. 9, p. 371). What remains of the original tablet is unfortunately only a corner fragment containing the ends of thirty lines, plausibly about half the number of lines in the original document (the original width can be estimated from the likely restorations at the beginning of lines 1-11; this permits, on the basis of an average height:width ratio of 3:2 in Ug. epistolary texts, the reconstruction of the original height as approximately twice that preserved). The letter clearly begins with the line that the editors numbered as line 1, and the lines that wrap around the right edge from the *verso* on to the *recto* appear to constitute exploitation of available space rather than to furnish arguments for reversing the *recto/verso* orientation proposed by the editors; it remains somewhat of a mystery, however, why the scribe left so much space at the end of lines 2, 4, 8, and 9. Because the continuation of a text on the *verso* was written on the left edge of any given tablet, we may hypothesize that the text on the *verso* of this tablet, apparently incomplete (*mlk ṣdq*, "just king" in line 30′ should be followed by *mlk mlkm*, "king of kings"), was once completed on the left edge, now destroyed.

[79] Because the phrase *špš mlk rb* is attested in the body of the letter (line 15′) and because the restoration {l špš} fills the space perfectly, we may surmise that the address began with this title, though one may consider the possibility that the Pharaoh's name, if it could be represented in Ug. by only three or four signs, was once here.

[80] The title *mlk mlkm* that appears also in (14) appears to be in imitation of the semantically equivalent title used in Egypt, particularly during the 18th Dynasty. At least until intervening attestations of the formula are found in WS inscriptions, the rare appearance of the cognate formula in later books of the Heb. Bible, once in Heb. and twice in Aram. (see note *ff*), must be seen as reflecting the later Mesopotamian use of such a formula, rather than the New Kingdom Eg. usage imitated in these Ug. letters (see brief discussion and bibliography in Milano 1983:157).

[81] The restoration at the beginning of line 4 is uncertain. In (14) lines 9-10, according to the restorations in Bordreuil's edition (1982:10-11), one finds the repetition of *mlk mlkm* and in the second position is found the sequence "master of all lands, king of kings" (*bᶜl kl ḫwt mlk mlkm*). That restoration appears difficult here, however, for it would require placing six signs ({[mlk . mlk]m}) in a lacuna that in every other instance in lines 1-10 is filled by four or five signs. The restoration of simply {[mṣr]m}, which had been my first idea (cf. *KTU*[2] vi, 196), and which could be interpreted as representing a part of the preceding formula ("master of all the land of Egypt"), appears too short, while that of {[mlk . mṣr]m}, "king of Egypt" (de Moor 1996:230, n. 34), is as long as {[mlk . mlk]m}, is equally repetitious, and, unlike *mlk mlkm*, does not appear to be repeated in a single sequence of formulae in (14).

[82] Though only the last part of the last sign is preserved, that sign must be {k} or {r}, and the only Ug. royal name to end with one or the other of those two signs in the period in which the Ug. script was used was {ᶜmṯtmr}, that is, ᶜAmmiṯtamru II, who was on the throne for some three decades in the middle of the thirteenth century (ca. 1260-1230 BCE). Because he wishes this document to date to a period later than that of ᶜAmmiṯtamru, de Moor (1996:230) has proposed reconstructing {[ᶜmrpᵓi . š]r ᶜbdk}, " ᶜAmmurāpiᵓ, the vassal-ruler, your servant." The restoration must be judged highly dubious, however, for the same reason of space as was adduced in the previous note (six letters in a space elsewhere occupied by four or five letters) and because the word *šr*, which would be cognate with Heb. *śar* and Akk. *šarru*, is not yet with certainty attested in Ug. (see note 13 to *COS* 1.87), and in any case not in prose.

Greetings (lines 6-?)[83]
With my master may it be well. [With your house], with your people, with your land, [with] your [horses], with your chariots, [with your troops], with all that belongs [to[gg] the Sun, the] great [k]ing, the king of Egyp[t], [the good king], the just king, [... may it be well].

gg Exod 20:17

Body
[...][84]

[83] The tablet breaks off after line 11 and the end of the list of entities for whom well-being is wished has disappeared. Judging from parallels to these flowery formulae in Akk. letters written at Ugarit (e.g., RS 15.178 [Nougayrol 1955:8]), the verb *yšlm*, "may it be well," which is extant in line 6 for the greeting to the king, would have been repeated at the end of the list. Similar lengthy "household greetings" are found in the Amarna letters, addressed to the king of Egypt, and in the Akk. letters from Ugarit, addressed to the king of Carchemish (as in the example just cited), to the king of Hatti (RS 20.243 [Nougayrol 1968:104, text 32]), and to the king of Alashia (RS 20.168 [Nougayrol 1968:80-82, text 21]).

[84] Approximately the bottom half of the tablet is lost and with it approximately thirty lines (see note 78). The text on the *recto* after line 11 would have contained the end of the greeting formulae and the beginning of the body. Three ruled paragraphs are partially preserved on the *verso* and upper edge, the beginning of all lines missing: the last two lines of the first paragraph (lines 12′-13′), the entirety of the second (lines 14′-22′), and the beginning of the third (lines 23′-30′). As indicated in note 78, the end of the text was in all probability inscribed on the left edge of the tablet. Only in the case of the royal titles is it possible to restore the broken text. Lines 14′-22′ dealt with a shipment or shipments of grain (*d̲rᶜ*, the same word as was used in [8], above), though it is uncertain who was in need of the grain, for no one statement regarding the grain is preserved completely that would reveal the identity of the party in need. In the following paragraph a matter of payment is treated (*ksp*, "silver," and *šsᶜn*, "he has paid it" are preserved) but here the word *d̲rᶜ* is not extant, so the topic may have changed. The presence in line 24′ of *mzn̲h*, "his/her food" (new reading as compared with the *editio princeps*), indicates, however, a similarity in the general topics of the two paragraphs.

(14) ᶜAMMURĀPIᵓ TO THE KING OF EGYPT (RS 34.356) (3.45N)[85]

First Address (lines 1-2)
[To the Sun, the] great [king], king of kin[gs], [my master], say: Message of ᶜAmmurāpiᵓ, [your servant].

First Body (lines 3-8)
[...] NMY, [your] messenger, has arrived [...] [the Sun], the great king, my master, to [me ...]. Then I, your servant, greatly re[joiced? ...] my good master [...] the Sun, my master, has sent [...] the [Su]n, the great king, my master[...].

Second Address (lines 9-11)
[To the] great [kin]g, the king of king[s, master of all l]ands, king of king[s, my master, sa]y: Message of ᶜAmmurāp[i your servant].

Second Body (lines 12-?)
[...][86]

[85] Text published by Bordreuil 1982:10-12. The upper right part of this tablet is preserved and the original width may be projected on the basis of line 4, where it appears that only {špš} is to be restored. The tablet clearly bears two sets of address formulae, both from ᶜAmmurāpiᵓ to the king of Egypt, and this document appears rather clearly, therefore, to contain either summaries of two letters or else two projects for a single letter. The brevity of the two addresses, as compared with the lengthy opening formulae of (13), is perhaps a further indication that these are only drafts.

[86] A few signs are preserved of line 12 as are a few signs of the last three lines of the text, located at the bottom of the *verso*. The tablet was thus entirely inscribed, but the remains that have been preserved are insufficient to give us any idea of what the structure of the rest of the text was or what topics were treated.

(15) PART OF A LETTER ADDRESSED TO THE KING OF EGYPT (RS 16.078) (3.45O)[87]

Reference to a Previous Communication from the Addressee (lines 1-8)
And according to the word of the Sun, the great king, my master, to ᶜT̲T, the [X] of the messengers of his servant:[88] "[...] your master that he must ḪP(N) my messengers (when they are) with him," so [will] your servant [do] when the messenger-party of the Sun, the great king, my master, arrives (here) with [me ...].[89]

[87] Text published by Virolleaud 1957:34, no. 18. This text begins *in medias res* and is, therefore, either the second tablet of a longer letter or else the draft of a letter for which the opening formulae were considered unnecessary. The fact that the first word of this text is the conjunction *w*, which does not normally appear as the first word of the body of a letter, makes the first option preferable.

[88] Typically polite form of self-reference: *ᶜt̲t* is the [chief, or whatever] of the messengers of the writer, who is servant to the Sun.

[89] The key word in this paragraph as preserved is {yḫpn} in line 4, for it tells what it is that the king of Egypt had asked the king of Ugarit to do for his messengers when(ever?) they arrived in Ugarit. Unfortunately, the meaning of the verb is unknown. It may have been something so simple as "to protest," but that is not certain. In any case, the king of Ugarit assures his correspondent that he will do as requested.

Protestations of Loyalty and Concern (lines 9-24)
I recognize [the X of the Sun], the great [kin]g, [my] master [...].[90] And I[, for my part ...], address requests[for the X ... of] the gre[at] king, my [master]; moreover, [I add]ress requests for [his] lif[e] to Baᶜ[lu] Ṣapunu, my master, and (address requests) that my master's days might be long[hh] before Amon and all the gods of Egypt, that they might protect the life of the Sun, the great king, my master.

hh Exod 20:12

Another Topic (lines 25-40)
[...][91]

[90] Lines 11-14 too damaged to translate.

[91] Though traces of all but one of these lines are preserved, none are sufficient to give any idea of what topic was treated here.

(16) [FROM THE KING OF UGARIT?] TO THE HITTITE EMPEROR (RS 94.5015) (3.45P)[92]

The Writer Refers to his Sovereign's Promises (lines 1-12)
[...] SAY [...] twice [...] GO [...] to ᵓAnzaḫu, I, even I, your servant. I will give donkeys, I will give troops (to be) with him."[93] Moreover, the Sun, the great king, my master, said: "I will cause (him) to return and he will ML."[94] Then, (because of) this, there was no war in the land of your servant. Also (my master said:) "I will surely give (you) the troops that are with him."

The Writer's Past Efforts to Get Action (lines 13-17, 18′-21′)[95]
To the Sun, the great king, my master, twice, three times[ii] [I wrote/requested], but you sent (no message) regarding troo[ps ...] GUARD ᵓAru and [...]. SENT [...] to your servant [...] troops and donk[eys ...] GO to ᵓAnzaḫu.

ii Amos 1:3, etc.; Prov. 30:18, etc.; Ps 62:12

Warning (lines 22′-37′)
Now the Sun, the great king, my master, must know that ᵓAri-Tēšub has assembled ᶜApirūma[96] with him and he is going to devastate your servant's country. I, for my part, your servant, all the royal personnel [...] in the country of your servant [...] I disposed them [...].[97] And a letter [...] troops to ᵓATḎN [...]. And the Sun, [the grea]t [king], my master, must know [...] and below, for there is [...] your servant and I ask [...] Amurru, GUARD the country[...].[98]

[92] Text to be published by Bordreuil and Pardee (in preparation). Only the upper part of the tablet has been preserved. Unfortunately, the upper left corner is damaged, leaving it uncertain whether the tablet ever bore the epistolary *praescriptio*. The words *rgm*, "speak/word," and *t̲nᵓid*, "twice," could belong to the address and the prostration formula, respectively, but these would have to have been much abbreviated from what the sovereign would normally expect to hear. This appears, therefore, to be — as expected — a draft in which the *praescriptio* was either omitted or abbreviated. Nothing specific allows the writer to be identified, but since the letter was found at Ugarit, it was either written there or intercepted there and the author was, therefore, most plausibly the king of Ugarit.

[93] The writer appears to be quoting what he himself has said on an earlier occasion, but the state of the tablet makes it impossible to know where the direct speech began or even whether he is in fact quoting someone else, perhaps even the great king.

[94] {w . ml}, an unknown expression in Ug. Perhaps a G-stem form of √*mll*, "languish, fade, disappear."

[95] Between lines 17 and 18′ an unknown number of lines has disappeared with the loss of the bottom portion of the tablet. It is thus uncertain whether the two portions of text belong together.

[96] This is the first reference in Ug. to bellicose ᶜApirūma (i.e., Habiru).

[97] The "royal personnel" are the *bnšm*, among whom are included various military categories. In spite of the lacunae, the king appears to be claiming here that he has mobilized absolutely all the royal personnel (*klm bnšm* /kulluma bunušīma/) and has disposed them (*štthm* /šātātuhumu/) appropriately.

[98] The signs {ᵓamr} are clear, but they do not necessarily mean "Amurru"; if they do, it is uncertain what the relationship is between Amurru and the need to protect the country. Is the claim that the king of Hatti should require Amurru to defend Ugarit, or is it that Amurru is somehow sponsoring ᵓAri-Tēšub?

IV. BETWEEN KING OR QUEEN AND A NON-ROYAL PERSONAGE

Dennis Pardee

(17) THE KING TO ḤAYYAᵓIL REGARDING AN ALLOTMENT OF LOGS (RS 16.264) (3.45Q)[99]

Address (lines 1-3)
Message (that) the king spoke: To Ḥayyaᵓil:[100]

[99] Text published by Virolleaud 1957:23-24, no. 10. On the possibility that the recipient of this letter is identical with a certain {ḫa-PI-il} known from an Akk. text discovered at Ras Shamra (RS 8.146:32 [Thureau-Dangin 1937:247, 253; not "RS 8.213," cf. Bordreuil and Pardee 1989:45]),

Reference to a Previous Letter from Ḥayyaʾil (lines 4-6)
Why do you keep sending me (the following message): "How am I to furnish[101] the timbers[102] *jj* for the temple of Damal?"?[103]

The King's Decision (lines 7-21)[104]
I will myself furnish you with the timbers (as follows): four logs (to be supplied) by (the town of) ʾAru, three by (the town of) ʾUburʿaya, two by (the town of) Mulukku, and one by (the town of) ʾAtalligu.[105] You are to provide an account*kk* of these logs. Do not burden Nūrānu; pay for them yourself, (a total of) sixty (shekels of) silver.[106]

jj Gen 6:14; Exod 25:5; 1 Kgs 5:20, 22, 24; 9:11

kk Ps 22:18

see Dietrich and Loretz 1974:454. The Ḥayyaʾil of the Akk. text is identified as a *kartappu*, a Sumerian loan-word into Akk. of which the original meaning was "groom" but that came to function in this period as a designation of a court official (*CAD* K 225-26). The identification is thus plausible though purely hypothetical.

[100] The address formulae are among the briefest attested in Ug. and the use of the verb *rgm* in the perf., expressing the utterance of the sender, instead of in the imperative, addressed conventionally to the messenger (see above, note 3), is unparalleled in the Ug. epistolary corpus. There is also a horizontal dividing line between the reference to the royal dictation and the person to whom the message was addressed (*tḥm mlk | l hyʾil*), a usage of the paragraph marker unparalleled in this epistolary formula. Below, one finds a horizontal line between three out of the four indications of the villages required to furnish the logs and the preceding paragraph (between lines 8-9, 12-13 and 14-15). This extensive use of the horizontal line is closer to that of the administrative texts, where sections marked off on the tablet often do not constitute complete sentences. The document may therefore be classified as being more narrowly administrative than is the usual Ug. letter and as constituting something closer to a memorandum than to a formal letter. Cf. letter-orders in Akk. and Sum.; below *COS* 3.132.

[101] This translation is based on the assumption that the horizontal dividing line between lines 5 and 6 ({ʾiky ʾaškn | ʿṣm l bt dml}) is anomalous. All attempts to interpret the passage by considering this divider as corresponding to regular usage have failed (including that of Cunchillos 1989:317, who claims to have solved the problem but in whose interpretation one finds that the transitive verb is construed as not having a direct object and that the nominal phrase after this verb is taken as an incomplete sentence: "... je fais les préparatifs. Des grumes pour le temple de Dml."). From a purely syntactic perspective, however, the use of the dividing line between the following sections is identical to this one: a dividing line is placed between the verb "I will give" in line 7 and its direct object "four logs" in line 9, and another between lines 12 and 13, and again between 14 and 15, that is between the verb and each of its direct objects with the exception of the second ("and three" in line 11). An identical structure is also found in one of the Ug. contracts: in RS 15.125:12′-13′ (Virolleaud 1957:17-18, text 5) {w mnkm . l yqḥ | ⸢s⸣pr . mlk . hnd}, "and no one shall take | this royal document."

[102] The word translated "timbers/logs" is *ʿṣm*, i.e., the plural of the noun *ʿṣ* meaning "wood." A distinct word for "planks," i.e., sawn-up logs, is not yet attested in the administrative texts, though one of the terms for ʾIlu's dwelling in the mythological texts may go back to such a word, viz. *qrš* (see note 29 to *COS* 1.86). In any case, the small number of pieces, a total of ten, and the relatively high price (six shekels each, whereas planks usually go for a fraction of a shekel), indicate that the pieces in question here are whole logs. Because the precise use of this wood in the temple is unstated, it is unknown whether the logs were intended to be used more or less whole as roof joists or to be sawn up and used as shorter beams, boards, or paneling. On construction techniques at Ugarit, including the various uses of wood and stone, see Callot's study of a typical house (1983) and his detailed treatment of an urban quarter (1994).

[103] Damal is a very poorly known deity (cf. Virolleaud 1957:24), but the correctness of the text is assured by a second attestation of the divine name in a ritual text (RS 15.130:20 = Virolleaud 1957:13-14, text 4; the structure and meaning of that text are, however, uncertain; cf. the new ed. in Pardee 2000a:439-45, where the *recto/verso* orientation proposed in the *editio princeps* is reversed). There is a possible third attestation in RS 15.115:34 (Virolleaud 1957:137-41, text 106), where one finds {[...]⸢-⸣t . l . dml[...]}.

[104] The king's response to his own rhetorical question begins with the conjunction *p* (cf. Arabic *fa*), used to mark more strongly than *w* a sequential relationship between two utterances. The quotation from the previous letter and the king's rhetorical question are thus in the Ug. expression strongly linked to the king's decision.

[105] The formulation of the requirements is as nominal phrases, lit., "four logs on/upon (= to the account of) ʾAru," etc. The four towns named are all located on the coast south of Ugarit in the Jeblé plain (cf. Bordreuil 1984:3-8). This means either that the logs in question were from trees of the type that would readily grow in the area, i.e., poplar-types, or that these towns controlled the distribution of logs that were floated down from the mountainous areas where conifers grow best. Because the conifers of the Syrian mountains were prized for temple and palace building throughout the ANE (mentioned in texts from Sumer to Judah to Egypt), and because of the relatively high price of these logs, the second solution appears preferable. The towns in question are located south of the principal river (the Raḥbānu, modern Nahr el-Kabir) that flows through Ug. territory and empties into the Mediterranean south of the Latakia promontory, and they could thus serve as staging points for logs floated down that river and assembled into rafts near the mouth of the river. The necessity of staging areas on the coast would arise from the fact that the floating of logs and log-rafts could only take place in spring when the seasonal flow of the tributary streams is sufficient to carry the logs. This same flow in the Raḥbānu could, however, carry the logs out to sea, whence they would have to be recovered. The details provided below on proper payment for the logs indicate that the logging business was not a royal monopoly.

[106] One of the long-standing difficulties of the Ug. letters is the sequence *nrn ʾal tʾud ʾad ʾat lhm* in lines 19-20. The presence of /ʾ/ and /d/ in the forms *tʾud* and *ʾad* has generally been interpreted as implying identity of root, but there is no single root in Ug. or in the cognate languages that allows for the different vocalizations reflected in the writing of the two forms nor for the difference in meaning required by the context. It thus appears necessary to identify the two forms as reflecting different roots. Heb. and Arabic have a hollow root, *ʾ(w)d*, that from a basic meaning of "bend" has in both languages developed the notion of "burden" (the word "distress" in Heb. betrays the development); Arabic has a root *ʾdy* that in the D-stem means "to pay." Thus the phrases are to be vocalized /nūrāna ʾal taʾud ʾaddi ʾatta lêhumu/ and translated as above. The formulation appears thus to be approaching a play on words, plausibly a bit of ancient royal irony. The king's decision thus included the stipulations that Ḥayyaʾil was to provide the proper "paper-work" for the logs (*w l ʿṣm tspr*, which does not mean "count the logs," but "provide an account for the logs") and to pay each town for the logs furnished, the payment not exceeding a total of sixty shekels of silver, i.e., six shekels per log (approximately sixty grams of silver per log). We may assume that Ḥayyaʾil was either to disburse the funds from the royal purse (if he had access to it) or that he was to be reimbursed later from royal funds. The name Nūrānu was popular at Ugarit and without the patronym it is impossible to identify this personage. Judging from the wording of the king's decision, one may hypothesize that he was an official of lesser rank than Ḥayyaʾil upon whom the latter might be tempted to shift the responsibility for correctly accounting for the logs and for properly paying for them. Nūrānu was perhaps, if the temple of Damal was located outside the capital city, the local representative of the palace in a district or in a particular village.

(18) DOUBLE LETTER: FROM THE QUEEN TO ʾURTĒNU AND FROM ʾILĪMILKU TO THE SAME (RS 94.2406) (3.45R)[107]

First Address (lines 1-2)
Message of the queen: To ʾUrtēnu say:

The Queen's Itinerary (lines 3-10)
I was on the sea when I gave this document (to be delivered) to you. Today I lodged at MLWM,[108] tomorrow (it will be) at ʾAdaniya,[109] the third (day) at SNǴR, and the fourth at ʾUNǴ. You are now informed.[110]

Instructions Regarding ʾUrtēnu's Property (lines 11-15)
As for you, all that belongs to you [...] establish for your name [...] and FINISH SERVANT [...] for (some) disaster has arrived[111] and [...] his/her request [...].

Instructions Regarding a House (lines 16-20)
Now a house [...] that ʾADR [...] those who cleanse BH[...].[112]

Instructions to Keep Quiet (lines 21-25)
As for you, not a word must escape your mouth until [X] arrives. Then I will send a message to Ugarit [...]. Should I hear that [she] has not agreed to guarantee you,[113] then I'll send a(nother) message.

Preparations (lines 26-30)
Now a *sp*-vessal (or: two *sp*-vessals) of M⸢-⸣P, two ʾIŠPR, and two GP are ready. (If) she does not guarantee you, does not (agree to) come to me,[114] she will send a message to the king and you can kiss your head good-bye.[115]

Second Address and Greeting (lines 31-33)
Message of ʾIlīmilku: To ʾUrtēnu, my brother, say: May it be well with you.

Reference to a Preceding Letter from ʾUrtēnu and ʾIlīmilku's Response (lines 33-40)
Concerning the fact that you sent me the message "Send me a message quickly," now I have spo-<ke>n (this) message in the presence of the queen. What you must do is to seize the house for

[107] Text to be published by Bordreuil and Pardee (in preparation). One will remark the extreme brevity of the first address and the fact that the second, from someone who is almost certainly himself not a member of the royal family because he addresses ʾUrtēnu as "brother," is not much longer (only *yšlm lk* is added). Whether the author of the second letter was the same ʾIlīmilku who inscribed the mythological texts signed by someone of the same name it is impossible to say, but the possibility is real (see note 3 to *COS* 1.86). That ʾUrtēnu was himself an important personage in the Ug. court is clear from the fact that the queen has communicated to him her itinerary. ʾUrtēnu is entrusted with some delicate tasks but told in no uncertain terms to keep his mouth shut about what is going on. From the queen's itinerary, it is clear that she is headed for Cilicia, but no circumstances or further indications of her long-term itinerary are indicated. It is not implausible that the queen in question is the daughter of the king of Hatti whom ʿAmmurāpiʾ married and later divorced (Freu 1999:27-28; Singer 1999:701-4, 706-7, prefers to identify Niqmaddu III as the husband of the Hittite princess Eḫli-Nikkalu). The lower right corner of the tablet has disappeared, and the precise content of the various instructions given to ʾUrtēnu is for that reason uncertain. Both messages speak of a house; the queen refers first to ʾUrtēnu's possessions (*klklk*, l. 11), and twice refers to a female who will guarantee ʾUrtēnu in some respect. Because one of the principal themes of both messages is property at Ugarit, in particular a house that ʾUrtēnu is instructed to seize (line 37, cf. line 16), it appears more plausible to see this letter as having to do with the departure of the divorced queen and some hasty scrambling to re-position her assets and her servants (in particular, it appears, these servants) than as reflecting a final desperate flight of another queen of Ugarit shortly before the fall of the city. Some aspect of the proceedings is problematic, however, for, if the female personage of lines 21-30 informs the king of them, ʾUrtēnu will lose his head.

[108] The verb is {btt}, either a perfective or a participle of the verb *bt*, "to lodge." If a perfective, the reference is to the preceding night, an indication that the "day" began at sunset, rather than at sunrise. The analysis as a participle, though formally possible, appears contextually unlikely, for one would expect an imperfective to be used to express what the queen would do when the present day's journey was complete. One may expect, therefore that it was at the port giving access to ʾAdaniya that the messenger who bore this letter began his journey back to Ugarit, perhaps on the same boat that the queen had taken.

[109] ʾAdaniya is the famous city of the Cilician plain mentioned in the Karatepe Phoen.-Luwian bilingual (*KAI* 26 A i 4 *et passim*; *COS* 2.31). None of the other towns is identifiable, but MLWM must have been a port between Ugarit and the port of disembarkation for ʾAdaniya, whereas the other two towns mentioned should be further inland. The word for "tomorrow" here is ʿ*lm*, lit. "hereupon/thereupon," used in the ritual texts, like here, in the sense of "on the next day" (Pardee 2000a:168-69). Assuming that the "day" began at sunset, the queen, during the second day of her voyage ("today" in the terms of the letter), dictated the present letter while still on the boat and foresaw spending the second night (the beginning of the third day since her departure, the second since the writing of the letter) at ʾAdaniya.

[110] Lit., "and know!"

[111] Neither internal nor comparative data have been cited that convincingly explain the meaning of *ṯh*, which appears again in (24):25, 29, and 37. It is in both texts translated from context. The word has also appeared now in RS 94.2457:10′ (too fragmentary for translation here).

[112] Perhaps {mrḥṣm bh[tm]}, "those who cleanse/purify houses," though the phrase is previously unknown in Ug.

[113] The feminine form of the verb ʿ*rb*, "to guarantee," is restored here because that is the form in which it appears in the next paragraph. We must assume that the person in question was identified in the badly damaged previous paragraph.

[114] Lit., "does not enter for you (= guarantee you), does not enter with me" (*l* ʿ*rbt bk l* ʿ*rbt* ʿ*my*). ʿ*rb b*, "to guarantee someone," is well attested, but ʿ*rb* ʿ*m* is not. It is either a new idiom, expressing a third party in a guarantee, or it means "enter with (someone)," here "come home with me." The latter solution appears linguistically more plausible and leads to the conclusion that the woman in question was part of the queen's entourage and now has the choice of remaining in Ugarit, and buying favor with the king by revealing the underhanded dealings of the former queen's ministers, or of joining her queen in her return to her home country.

[115] It is clear from (38) (see below) that the items mentioned at the beginning of this paragraph could be sent from one place to another.

me. Moreover, you must recognize that the queen also has left. But you must keep absolutely quiet (about all of this) at Ugarit.[116]

Only the meaning of *sp* is relatively clear, however: at Ugarit it denotes a container in contexts having to do with rations and the cognate term in Akk. and Heb. is associated particularly with wine (perhaps {m⌈-⌉p} should be restored as {m⌈ṣ⌉p} and seen as a variant of *mṣb*, attested as a type of wine in administrative texts). A word {gpt} is attested among food-stuffs in RS 94.2580:23, where its measure is the *kt*-vessel, of unknown quantity. It would seem that the items mentioned here have been prepared for the person who is expected to guarantee ᵓUrtēnu, apparently as a bribe, at the very least as travel provisions (see preceding note). If she refuses to cooperate and informs the king of what is going on, ᵓUrtēnu will suffer the consequences (l. 30: *w rᵓišk ẖlq*, "your head is dead").

[116] The word "also" (*ᵓap* in line 38) seems to imply that ᵓIlīmilku's trip was announced in advance to serve as a cover for the queen's departure; she would have left the palace and entered the boat at the last minute. One may surmise that her residence was in the palace on Ras Ibn Hani (Bounni, Lagarce, and Lagarce 1998), for that relatively remote location would make a secret departure more feasible than would have been one from the main palace at Ugarit. Apparently the queen's departure was to be kept secret until the property arrangement to which both she and ᵓIlīmilku refer could be completed.

(19) THE QUEEN TO YARMÎHADDU (RS 96.2039) (3.45S)[117]

Address (lines 1-3)

[Me]ssage of the queen: To Yarmîhaddu, my brother, say:

Reference to a Preceding Letter in Reference to a Servant Who Had Fled (lines 4-17)

(As for) the (message)-tablet (in which I said) "Your servant whom I took [...]; and I, for my part, gave his wife to you;[ll] and that servant worked on my farm;[118] [mm] but that servant returned to his wife at your house; and you are the 'father' Ḫ⌈-(?)⌉;[119] so this servant must be seized, and deliver him over to my messenger-party":[120]

The New Demand (lines 18-24)

Now, seeing that he has not moved, and (that) I have not sent a message to the king, but to you have I sent (this message),[121] so now, you must deliver him over to my messenger-party.

ll Exod 21:1-6
mm Judg 6:11

[117] Text to be published by Bordreuil and Pardee (in preparation). The queen refers to the addressee here as her brother, but the precise nature of the relationship so described is uncertain. One will note in particular that, in spite of the equality that that term expresses on one level, the *praescriptio* includes no greetings, very unusual among letters between equals. The tablet is virtually complete, but its surface is badly worn and small chips have occasionally removed all trace of the original writing; as a result, decipherment has been difficult. We believe that we have succeeded in the main, but two lacunae have to date defied attempts at reconstruction, one at the end of line 5 and the other at the beginning of line 14. Though several of the features of the language are novel, the general structure of the text is clear: the first paragraph of the body of the letter resumes a previous letter in which the queen has required Yarmîhaddu to return the servant who fled, while the second points out that nothing has been done and insists on action. Thus in form the entire letter after the *praescriptio* consists of a single long sentence consisting of a protasis (the quotation of the previous letter) followed by an apodosis (the present demand). The previous letter, however, consisted of a series of short sentences linked by conjunctions. In an attempt to represent the structure of both documents, I separate the quoted sentences by semi-colons. The word translated "servant" throughout is *bnš*, the standard word in Ug. administrative texts for members of the royal work force, from the humblest farm worker (here) to elite leaders of the military. This letter shows clearly that (at least some of) the *bnšm* were in fact chattel slaves.

[118] *w ht hn bnš hw b gty ḫbṯ*, lit., "and behold, that servant on my *gt*-farm did work." Specialists in Ug. grammar will remark the use of *hn* here before a noun that is further modified by the demonstrative adjective *hw*, a function that must have been paralleled in proto-Hebrew and led to the adoption of the particle *hn* there as a true definite article. One wonders if this peculiar usage does not betray the queen's foreign origin — could it be the second wife of ᶜAmmurāpiᵓ who Freu (1999:27-28) has suggested might have come from the kingdom of Amurru? Specialists in the Ug. economy will note the reference to the queen's farm (*gt* as an administrative sub-division below the village level and considered the property of the crown, of an official, or, perhaps, of a village) on which the *bnš* served as a *ḫupšu*. In these new texts (see below [27]) the spelling {ḫbṯ} is used when there is a vowel between the /b/ and the {ṯ} (e.g., this form would be /ḫabaṯa/), /ḫpṯ/ when there is not through progressive assimilation by the /b/ of the unvoicedness of the /ṯ/ (e.g., {ḫpṯ} would have been /ḫupṯu/). From this and the following text, it is clear that the *ḫupšu* did not do only military service, but manual labor as well.

[119] Line 13 reads {w ᵓadn . ᵓat}, "and father are you," but this is followed by the undeciphered first word of line 14, and the precise meaning of *ᵓadn* here is unclear. It may express a literal paternity, a figurative one, or the meaning "lord, master." In the last case, it may reflect another peculiarity of the queen's language, since *ᵓadn* normally designates the biological father in Ug. prose (see above, note 52 to [9]).

[120] Here and below, line 24, the demand is to hand the servant immediately over to the messenger who bore the tablet bearing each message. In order to force a slave to return to his owner, the messenger's escort must have been important.

[121] Lines 19-21 consist of the assertion that the author has not sent a letter to the king followed by another pointing out that, instead of writing to the king, she has written again to the addressee — all this a scarcely veiled threat to get the king involved in the case if Yarmîhaddu does not send the servant back immediately.

(20) T̲IPṬIBAᶜLU (SHIBTI-BAᶜLU) TO THE KING (RS 18.040) (3.45T)[122]

Address (lines 1-4)
To the king, my master, say: Message of T̲ipṭibaᶜlu, your [se]rvant:

Prostration Formula (lines 5-8)
[At] the feet of my master, [seve]n times, seven times, (from) a[f]ar do I fall.

nn 2 Sam 6:13; 1 Kgs 1:9, 19, 25, etc.

The (Military) Situation in Lawasanda (lines 9-19)
As for your servant, in Lawasanda I am keeping an eye (on the situation) along with the king. Now the king has just left in haste to SYR, where he is sacrificing*nn* MLǴ⌜ǴM⌝.[123]
The king, my master, must know (this).[124]

---

[122] Text published by Virolleaud 1965:90, no. 63. Though the surface of this tablet has suffered rather extensive damage, only easily restorable signs have totally disappeared, and the message it bore, a brief one, is thus complete. The absence of a greeting formula, of any kind, on the part of someone writing to the king probably reflects the agitation of the moment (as I surmised above with regard to [7]). The author is usually identified with the official and business man T̲ipṭibaᶜlu, who was also the king's son-in-law (see Vita and Galán 1997; Singer 1999:671, 690-91, 697). "The king, my lord" is, of course, the king of Ugarit, while "the king" below in the body of the letter is in all likelihood the king of Hatti, though it could be the king of Carchemish.

[123] The reading of the first sign of line 11 has long been in dispute. Collation shows it to be {ᵓa}, and the line consists, therefore, of a single word, the verb {⌜ᵓa⌝bṣr}, lit. "I do observe." On the meaning of *bṣr* in Ug., see *COS* 1.91, note 13, and *COS* 1.103, note 73. The consensus identification of {lwsnd} with the Cilician town of Lawazantiya (Astour 1965:257) means that this trusted official of the king of Ugarit is functioning as the latter's eyes and ears in Cilicia, in company with the king of Hatti. The use of *bṣr* implies a military situation and the Hittite king's hasty departure ({ns}, "to flee," in Heb.) to a place called SYR (perhaps the holy mountain {se-e-ra}, located in the same general region [my thanks to T. van den Hout for pointing out to me the existence of this name]) to offer sacrifices shows the situation to have been tenuous enough that special divine intervention was thought necessary.

[124] On the "take notice" formula at the end of a letter, see above note 5.

(21) FROM AN OFFICIAL IN ALASHIA TO THE KING (RS 18.113A+B) (3.45U)[125]

Address (lines 1-3)
To the king, [my] l[ord], s[ay]: Message of the Chief of Maᵓ[ḫadu, your servant].

Prostration Formula (lines 4-6)
At the feet of my master [(from) afar], seven times and seven times [do I fall.]

Greetings (lines 6-9)
I do pronounce to Baᶜlu-Ṣapuni, to Eternal Sun, to ᶜAt̲tartu, to ᶜAnatu, to all the gods of Alashi[a] (prayers for) the splendor of (your) eternal kingship.[126]

Beginning of Message (lines 10-13)
The king, my master, LAND [...] will cause to be late and with LO[RD ...] ten times SENT [...]. And my master, WHAT[...][127]

Paying for Ships (lines 31′-39′)[128]
And he said: "Don't give them the money until I send a message to the king." This (is) the message that [he] sends [to] the king. Now the king should instigate an inquiry into the[se (matters) ...] them. And as for the boats, if you/they [X ...] this merchant, I, for my part, will say [...] "The king is looking for ships." And I will g[ive? the money? ...] I will make the purchase. O king, send me [...].

---

[125] Text published by Virolleaud 1965:14-15, no. 8; preliminary re-edition by Pardee 1987b:204-10. The precise identification of the author is uncertain; he appears to have identified himself by title only, but the end of the second element has disappeared: {rb . mᵓi[--]}. It is usually restored as {mᵓi[ḫd]}, generally considered to be the principal port of Ugarit, modern Minet el-Beida, where remains of the Ug. civilization were first discovered. On this town of Maᵓḫadu, see the textual data assembled by Van Soldt 1996:675-76; 1998:743; for a correlation of the textual and archeological data, Saadé 1995. The person in question would have been the king's official in charge of running the port. Because this letter appears to have come from Alashia (on the basis of the blessing below by the gods of Alashia), it appears this port official also had responsibilities for the procurement of sea-going vessels (see below). Cf. also Hallo, *Origins* 3 and n. 15.

[126] It was long thought that *nmry* in line 9 was a reference to the Eg. pharaoh Amenophis III, one of whose names was pronounced Nimmuria by Semites (Astour 1981:15-16) and who reigned at the end of the fifteenth century (ca. 1415-1380). Because, however, this Ug. text shows no signs of such antiquity, it is either a recent copy/translation of such an old document or else the word has another meaning. Because *nmrt*, "(divine) splendor," is one of the virtues that the Rephaim are said to procure for the Ug. king (RS 24.252:23′, 25′ [Virolleaud 1968, text 2]), it may be considered plausible that *nmry* is a variant of that word (Liverani 1962:28, n. 6, already expressed doubt about the identification with Amenophis III; Rainey 1974:188 proposed the identification with *nmrt*, an idea followed by Van Soldt 1983:693 and 1990:345, n. 164; the explanation by √*mrr* proposed by Rainey cannot, however, be accepted — see Pardee 1988:115). Though the phrase *mlk ᶜlm* /mulku ᶜālami/, lit. "kingship of eternity," is new in Ug., it is worth observing that *mlk ᶜlm*, /malku ᶜālami/, "king of eternity," is a title that was, according to RS 24.252:1, ascribed to the head of the Rephaim, i.e., the member of the underworld chiefly responsible for transmitting to the king his divine splendor.

[127] Except for the small fragment RS 18.113B, which bears traces of six lines of writing, the entire message inscribed on the bottom of the tablet (lower *recto*, lower edge, upper *verso*) has disappeared.

[128] Damage subsequent to the editor's copy has caused the disappearance of several signs from the last line of text on the *verso* and from all

three lines on the upper edge (numbered 31′-34′ in the new ed. that I am preparing; they were given as 20′-23′ in my preliminary ed. [1987b:206], 19-22 in *KTU*² 181). The signs as indicated by the editor are translated here.

(22) ᶜUZZĪNU TO THE KING (RS 94.2391) (3.45V)[129]

Address (lines 1-3)
To the king, my master, say: Message of ᶜUzzīnu, your servant.

Prostration Formula and Greeting (lines 4-7)
At the feet of my master two times seven times (from) afar I fall. With my master may it be well. [...]

Taking Care of Someone (lines 10′-15′)
[...] pr[ie]sts before him. So nourish his well-being. And you should order for me that he go [somewhere]. (If) that happens, his well-being will be there.[130]

ᶜUzzīnu's Travels (lines 16′-21′)
I, for my part, have arrived in Qadesh and ˀUrīyānu has left for Upi (Damascus).[131] I will be "pure";[132] to [...] he will arrive [...].

[129] Text to be published by Bordreuil and Pardee (in preparation). The name ᶜUzzīnu, with several variant pronunciations, was common at Ugarit, and, without a patronym, it is impossible to identify with certainty any given bearer of the name with any other. That said, however, it is plausible that this ᶜUzzīnu was the person of that name who was governor (*skn*) of Ugarit (cf. Singer 1999:667), for not everyone could deal directly with the king on international matters. The bottom of the tablet has disappeared so that only the end of the body of the letter is preserved.

[130] This text contains a new form of the root *šlm*, viz., *šlmt*, apparently with a meaning similar to *šlm*, "well-being." The verb "nourish" in line 12′ is *zn*, and seems to be addressed to the king as an imperative; because the preceding text is damaged, however, it could be a 3rd masc. sing. pf., referring to a fourth party.

[131] This is the first attestation in Ug. of {ˀup}, the name used in the Amarna letters for the land in which Damascus was located.

[132] The precise nuance of {⌈ˀa⌉qy}, if indeed from *nqy*, "to be pure," is unclear in this damaged context.

(23) UNKNOWN TO THE KING (RS 34.148) (3.45W)[133]

Address (lines 1-4)
To the k[ing, my master], sa[y]: Message of [X], your servant.

Greetings (lines 4-6)
May it be well with the king, my master. May the gods guard you, keep you well.

Situation Report and Promise of Another (lines 7-8)
Now for the two of us, the border with the ki<ng>dom of Carchemish is holding solid.[134] I will send ˀAnaniˀ with a(nother) messenger-party to you.[135]

The Take-Notice Formula (line 12)
My master [must] know (this)!

[133] Text published by Bordreuil and Pardee 1991:163-64, no. 91. The upper right part of the tablet has disappeared and with it the most of the address.

[134] Line 7 reads {wlnyknpˀa⌈t⌉}, with no word dividers. Not knowing to whom the dual form *lny* would be referring, Bordreuil and Pardee 1991 divided *w ln ykn pˀat*, taking *ykn* as an imperfective not marked for gender agreement with *pˀat* (a feminine noun) because the verb precedes its subject. I wonder now if the correct division is not *lny kn*, and the dual reference is to the writer and the king, i.e., "for the benefit of both of us, the border with Carchemish" is (still in place)." The word translated "ki<ng>dom" is {mlt}, an apparent error for {mlk} or {mlkt}.

[135] The verb "to send" is imperfective ({ˀilˀak}). Since Ug. normally uses the perfective to express acts associated with the current letter, this reference must, therefore, be to a message yet to be sent. The formulation is not explicit as to whether ˀAnaniˀ is the messenger or someone being sent with the messenger-party for protection.

(24) MESSAGE OF ˀIRIRIṮARUMA TO THE QUEEN (RS 16.402) (3.45X)[136]

Address (lines 1-2)
[To the queen], my lady, [say: Mes]sage of ˀIririṯaruma, your servant.

Prostration Formula and Greeting (lines 3-4)
[At] my [l]ady's [feet] (from) afar [do I fall]. [W]ith my lady may it be well.

[136] Text published in Virolleaud 1957:25-28, text 12. The identity of the author, whose name is Hurrian, is unknown but, as he was capable of furnishing two thousand horses (see the "second matter" below), he must have been an official of some importance. The epistolary formulae, those used by an inferior addressing a superior, show him to be politically inferior to and dependent upon the king of Ugarit, whose demands

First Matter: A Royal Campaign (lines 5-21)[137]
[...] our king is strong [...] the enemy which in Mukiš [...] when the king will lodge [...] Mount Amanus[138] [...]. [And] may my lady know (this). Moreover, as for the king (and) his vow,[139] he must know that I am rejoicing on that account.

Second Matter: The King's Demand for Two Thousand Horses (lines 22-39)
Now (as for) the king, my master, why has he assigned this (responsibility) to his servant: (viz., that of furnishing) 2000 horses?[oo] You have (thus) declared peril against me.[140] Why has the king imposed this (duty) upon me?[141] The enemy has been pressing[pp] me and I should put my wives (and) children in peril before the enemy?! Now if the king, my master, declares: "Those 2000 horses must arrive here," then may the king, my master, send an intermediary[142] (back) to me with this messenger-party of mine. But the situation they encounter will be a perilous one. The 2000 horses [...] and RETURN.[143]

oo 2 Kgs 18:23

pp Deut 28:5-3, 55, 57; Isa 29:2, 7; 51:13

he may query but must ultimately meet. For lack of more complete data, it is not possible to determine the period and the situation reflected by this letter. It is often dated (cf. Klengel 1992:140-41) to the time of extreme Assyrian pressure on the Hittite empire under Tudhalia IV (ca. 1260-1220 BCE), though a dating nearer the end of the kingdom of Ugarit appears more plausible (cf. Astour 1965:257-58; Singer 1999:713, 723-25).

[137] This paragraph is too badly damaged to permit an overall interpretation, but the mention of enemies in Mukiš (the state to the north of Ugarit; cf. Astour 1969:386-87 and, in general, Klengel 1992), of Mount Amanus, and of the king "lodging" (*ybt*) somewhere, seem to indicate that the king is either planning a campaign to the north or has already embarked on it, and that ʾIririṯaruma has received a summons to furnish 2000 horses for that campaign (next paragraph). It is not clear why the letter is addressed to the queen, rather than to the king who has issued the disputed order. The letter assumes, in any case, that the king and the queen are in communication, for the queen is assumed to be able to transmit the writer's concerns to him. Either, therefore, the queen has accompanied the king at least part of the way to Mukiš or else the king is still in the region of Ugarit.

[138] There has been controversy over whether *ʾamn* designates the Amanus or another mountain in the same general area (see the discussion in Xella 1991:161-64). For the detailed argument in favor of the identification with the Amanus, see my commentary in forthcoming d.

[139] The word written {ʾuḏrh} is of uncertain meaning and the *-h* may be either pronominal ("his/her *ʾuḏr*") or locative ("in *ʾuḏr*"). I have interpreted it along the same lines as what is apparently the same word in (6) line 15 (see above).

[140] This phrase seems to be addressed to the queen (certainly not to the king, who is mentioned in this text only in the third person). On *ṯh*, see above, note 111 to (18).

[141] Lit., "placed them (i.e., the horses) upon me."

[142] The meaning of the phrase *bnš bnny* is uncertain. The interpretation reflected in the translation (which goes back to Albright 1958:38) sees *bnny* as the morphological equivalent of Medieval Heb. *bēnōnī*, "what is between, i.e. average," and the phrase as the rough equivalent of BH *ʾīš habbēnayim*, "the man of the double between," in context the "champion" who fights in single combat between two opposing armies (1 Sam 17:4, 23). The phrase so interpreted would have been used by ʾIririṯaruma in order to indicate that he wants the king to send someone of more importance than a simple messenger.

[143] Traces of five signs are visible at the beginning of the last line and about two more have completely disappeared. That *ṯb*, "return," was the last word of the paragraph is certain from the horizontal line below this line of text. Whether another paragraph may have been written on the left edge, now destroyed, it is impossible to say.

(25) ʾURǴITĒṮUB (URḪI-TEŠUB) TO THE QUEEN (RS 20.199) (3.45Y)[144]

To the queen, my lady, say: [Me]ssage of ʾUrǵitēṯub, your servant. At the feet of my lady (from) afar seven times and seven times do I fall. With my lady may it be well. May the [go]ds guard you, [may they keep] you well. [Her]e [with me], everything is [ver]y well. There with my lady, whatever is well, send word (of that) back to your servant.

[144] Text published so far only in transliteration (*KTU* 164, no. 2.68; cf. my preliminary study in 1984:213-15). It is, in my estimation, highly unlikely that the author of this letter is to be identified with the Hittite king of the same name who was dethroned and exiled in ca. 1270 BCE (Helck 1963; Cunchillos 1989:360-61, n. 3; 1999:368), for the text shows no signs of dating so early and I have trouble believing that a former Hittite king would address himself so servilely to the queen of Ugarit. On the other hand, it is possible that this personage would be identical to another Urḫiteššub who wrote from Carchemish to certain important personages at Ugarit (Malbran-Labat 1995b:39; Singer 1999:729). The author of this letter (RS 88.2009, as yet unpublished) identifies himself only by name, places himself hierarchically above his addressees by naming himself first, but uses no relational terms. He reports on movements of the king of Carchemish and proclaims solidarity with his correspondents. It is plausible, therefore, that an envoy of the court would address the leaders of the city with a superior attitude while addressing the queen as his own superior. Unfortunately, the present text is a "keeping-in-touch" letter, with no details of any kind on the writer's situation.

(26) THE GOVERNOR TO THE QUEEN (RS 94.2479) (3.45Z)[145]

Address (lines 1-2)
To the queen, my lady, say: Message of the governor, your servant.

Prostration and Greeting Formulae (lines 3-4)
[A]t the feet of my lady I fall. With my lady may it be well.

Report of Well-being and Request for Return of News (lines 5-10)
Here in the king's palace, everything is fine. There with my lady, whatever (is fine), may she return word (of that) to her servant.[146]

The Shipping Report (lines 11-21)
(From) here twenty [*dū*]*du*-measures of barley and five *dūdu*-measures of GDL and five *dūdu*-measures of N^c^R,[147] (one) *kaddu*-measure of oil (perfumed with) myrrh, (one) *kaddu*-measure of lamp-oil, (one) *kaddu*-measure of vinegar, (one) *kaddu*-measure of olives$^?$, (from) my lady's food provisions, all (of this) I herewith cause to be delivered (to you).

[145] Text to be published by Bordreuil and Pardee (in preparation). The tablet is very well preserved and entirely reconstructable. The text is a business letter, in fact a sort of cargo list, for the tablet would in all probability have accompanied the shipment to the queen from the governor of the items listed.

[146] This example of the double formula described above (note 9) contains one novelty (the specification that things are going well in "the house of the king" rather than with the writer) and one aberration (the absence of *šlm*, "well-being" in the second part of the formula). The first is certainly intended (the person of inferior status usually does not describe his own state of well-being, so here it is the palace that is mentioned), the second may be an error (this is the only example in Ug. and in the corresponding formula in Akk. where *mnm*, "whatever" is not followed by a complement).

[147] The conjunction *w* is used only before the second and third items of this list and may be interpreted as indicating that those items belong to a single category. Unfortunately, the *n^{c}r* and the *gdl* are still unidentified, but, in view of their association with barley in other texts, are probably either types of grains or types of flours. It is tempting to identify them etymologically as "small" and "big" or "young" and "old," but these apparently obvious etymologies do not tell us exactly what commodities we are dealing with and it is not impossible that they are in fact red herrings. Tropper once translates *n^{c}r* by « Röstmehl », but without giving his reasons (2000:411, § 69.223.21). The structure of the present text allows for these three entries either to express types of grain or one type of grain and two types of flour, coarsely ground and finely ground, for example. Because cereal names are usually in the pl. in Ug. (*š^{c}rm*, "barley," *ksmm*, "emmer-wheat," and *ḫṭm*, "wheat" are attested to date), as in the other Northwest-Semitic languages, the preference for the interpretation of *n^{c}r* and *gdl* must be as types of flours (Pardee forthcoming a). The amounts of grain and flour mentioned here are serious, for the *dūdu* probably measured in the neighborhood of fifty liters, a weight of about forty kilograms.

(27) UNKNOWN, PERHAPS THE QUEEN, TO UNKNOWN (RS 94.2592) (3.45AA)[148]

The Request for Particulars on the bnšm-*Personnel* (lines 3′-14′)
And I, for my part, I do not know who all the servants are who work there. So you, put (the names of) all the servants who work there in a document and have it delivered to me.[qq] I know what I will do with regard to these (servants). So, as for (every) worker, whoever he may be, put him (i.e., his name) on the document.[149]

[qq] Ezra 5:4, 10

[148] Text to be published by Bordreuil and Pardee (in preparation). The top of this tablet has disappeared and with it the address formulae. It is included with royal documents because the ᵓUrtēnu archive contained various texts dealing directly with the royal holdings and because text 19 shows the queen's involvement in *bnšm*-affairs. The author can hardly have been other than a member of the royal family or a very high official. If the form *yd^{c}t* following *ᵓinny* in lines 3′-4′ is a participle, the author is feminine and probably the queen.

[149] As in text 19, *bnš* is "servant" and the verb spelled {ḫbṯ} is translated "work"; here the noun spelled {ḫpṯ} is translated "worker."

V. BETWEEN NON-ROYAL CORRESPONDENTS

Dennis Pardee

(28) A MILITARY SITUATION (RS 4.475) (3.45BB)[150]

Address and Greeting (lines 1-3)
Message of ᵓEwariḏarri: To Pilsiya say: May it be well with you.

[150] Text published by Dhorme 1933:235-37. The tablet is perfectly preserved and the controversies regarding this text have revolved around

Hearsay and Request for Confirmation (lines 5-11)
Regarding Tarǵudassi and Kalbiya, I have heard that they have suffered defeat.[151] Now if such is not the case, send me a message (to that effect).

ᵓEwaridarri's Situation (lines 11-13)
Pestilence is (at work) here,[rr] for death is very strong.[152]

rr Exod 9:3

A Second Request for News (lines 14-19)
If they have been overcome, your reply and whatever (else) you may hear there put in a letter to me.[153]

interpretation. For a more literal translation than the one offered here and a defense of this interpretation, see Pardee 1987c.

[151] The author appears to be referring to the troops under Tarǵudassi and Kalbiya, for the verb form is marked for the plural, rather than for the dual.

[152] The nominal phrase translated by pestilence is *yd ᵓilm*. Because the {-m} may be enclitic rather than marking the plural, it may be translated "the hand of the god," "the hand of the gods," or even "the hand of ᵓIlu." The last interpretation is the least likely since ᵓIlu is not known for spreading pestilence.

[153] This is an example of the non-formulaic request for return of news (contrast the formula described in note 9).

(29) REQUEST FOR A FREE HAND (RS 15.007) (3.45CC)[154]

Address (lines 1-2)
Ganariyānu to Milkiyatanu:

Two Introductory Matters (lines 3-4)
Please put in a good word for me[ss] to the king.[155] [tt] (Whatever) you propose, I will provide.[156]

ss Ps 4:2, etc.; cf. Ps 109:12

tt Est 2:17; 8:5

The Meat of the Message (lines 5-10)
Please, my friend, send me (written?) authorization in regard to Šamunu, wherever he may be, so that I may seize him, (I) Ganariyānu. If Milkiyatanu (so says), I will accuse him (viz., Šamunu) of treason and I will seize (him).[157]

[154] Text published by Virolleaud 1957:40-41, text 20. This tablet is also well preserved but poses even more severe difficulties of interpretation than (28). This is, first, because the scribe used no word dividers, and all divisions into words of the strings of signs in each line are, therefore, the work of the modern interpreter; second, either because the author did not observe the standard conventions for use of the three *alif*-signs or else because the author and/or the scribe had a somewhat "Phoenicianizing" pronunciation of Ug. ("I will give" is written {ᵓitn}, rather than the expected {ᵓatn}, and "I will seize," {ᵓiḫd}, rather than {ᵓaḫd}; on the other hand, the writing of {ᵓiṯr} for Ug. /ᵓaṯra/, "place," does not correspond to the pronunciation of the word in any of the Canaanite languages). The address is atypically brief, perhaps another indication that the scribe was not trained in the epistolary conventions of the metropolis (see also [30]). Because the correspondents cannot be identified, it is impossible to do more than speculate about why such a letter ended up in the East Archives of the palace of Ugarit. The mention of "the king" in line 3 — assuming that the king in question is the king of Ugarit — shows nevertheless that the addressee was close enough to the throne to be able to speak to the king and that the sender was known to the king.

[155] Lit., "make me find favor before the king" (*ḥnny l pn mlk*).

[156] Lit., "your proposal I will give" (*šᵓink ᵓitn*), either in reference to a preceding request on the part of the recipient of this letter or an open offer on the part of the writer to help out the addressee. In either case, the implication seems to be that their aid should be mutual.

[157] The distribution of the personal names and pronouns in this section is complicated. The author mentions his own name after "I may seize him," apparently stating thereby that he will take full responsibility for the operation. Then the addressee is mentioned by name and the verb is in the 3rd person ({hm mlkytn yrgm}, "if Milkiyatanu says"), as in line 5 ({rᶜ yšṣᵓa ᵓidn ly}, lit. "May my friend cause an authorization to come out to me"). The verb in line 9 bears a pronominal suffix, of which the antecedent is clear only from the sense of the expression ({ᵓaḫnnn}, "I will accuse him of treason"), while the last one does not ({ᵓiḫd}, "I will seize").

(30) BROTHER TO SISTER (RS 17.063) (3.45DD)[158]

Address, Situation Report, and Third-Party Greetings (lines 1-3)
ᶜUzzīnu son of Bayaya to his sister ᶜUṯtaya: I am alive and well. Say to my mother: "Your 'master' is well."[159]

Dispatch (lines 4-6)
I (herewith) send to you [an X-measure of Y?] as well as a piece of linen, entrusted to ḤŠ.[160]

[158] Text published by Caquot 1978b:389-92; preliminary re-edition based on collation by Pardee 1982. This letter and the following show two primary non-standard characteristics: (1) a *ductus* attested only in these two texts; (2) epistolary formulae unattested elsewhere in Ug. As stated in Pardee 1982, these characteristics are not of the sort to permit identification of these texts as scribal exercises (*KTU* 403-4; *KTU*² 492-93). If a student scribe created these documents, he did not pass the course — and for good reason — for we have nothing else from his hand. For an authentic scribal exercise, see (41).

[159] It is uncertain whether this "master" ({bᶜlkm}) is the mother's husband, in which case probably not the father of this son, or a master in the social sphere.

[160] {ḥš} is either a proper name or else a participle of the verb *ḥš*, "go rapidly," hence, "entrusted to a rapid (messenger)."

Request (lines 7-9)
Have (him bring) me ten *lg*-measures of (olive)-oil[uu] and three *lg*-measures of perfumed (olive-)oil. Have one TZN sent to me.[161]

uu Lev 14:10, etc.

[161] The quantities of oil are not large, assuming that the Ug. *lg*-measure was identical to the Palestinian one (less than half a liter). The *tzn* is unidentified, but the existence of what is apparently a feminine form of the same word (RS 16.001:16 [Virolleaud 1957, text 130]; RS 23.028:6 [*KTU* 4.721]) shows it to be a real Ug. word.

(31) ᶜUZZĪNU AND ANOTHER AUTHOR TO MASTER AND FATHER (RS 17.117) (3.45EE)[162]

Address and Greeting (lines 1-2)
ᶜUzzīnu son of Bayaya a[nd ...]. May Baᶜlu inquire after your well-being.[163]

The Son's Message (lines 3-10)
As for me, your son, I am alive (and well thanks) to the Sun's proclamation.[164] [vv] I am living in the house of TRTN. (His) wife is furnishing my bread and, moreover, she is furnishing my wine (for) three (shekels of) silver.[165] She is working for (my) father [...].

ᶜUzzīnu's Message (lines 11′-23′)[166]
[...] And he asked your sister that she should not give (me) any *asa foetida*. If she does not furnish it sufficiently according to your order, would you give it to me?[167]
O my master, please give me also two *ḫipānu*-garments.[168] I beg of you, what you are going to give me, send [me a message (concerning that)] in a letter. What you give, entrust it to someone with a faithful heart.[ww] [...].[169]

vv Deut 8:3
ww Cf. Ps 51:12

[162] Text published by Caquot 1978b:392-98; preliminary re-edition based on collation by Pardee 1982. On the physical and epistolary characteristics of this letter, see note 158. This letter appears to have been addressed by ᶜUzzīnu and another person whose name is lost at the end of line 1 to someone who was the master of ᶜUzzīnu and the father of the other person. The servant appears to have been in charge of the son's mission, for he proclaims his importance by placing his name in first position. The son's personal message is, however, placed before the servant's (ll. 3-10 and 11′-23′, respectively).

[163] The upper right corner of the tablet has disappeared and there is, therefore, no way of knowing whether the addressee's name was indicated, as it was in the preceding text. The name was probably written on the destroyed right edge and *verso* of the tablet, i.e., on the original the entire address was inscribed in one long line that wrapped around the edge and ended on what would have been the lower right corner of the tablet viewed from the *verso*. The greeting formula that consists of wishing that a deity should "ask" (*šʾl*) after the well-being of the recipient is not attested elsewhere in Ug., though it is attested in first-millennium epistolary traditions (Pardee *et al.* 1982:56, 148).

[164] {ḥytn l p špš}, lit., "I live by the mouth of the Sun." Nothing in either text permits a decision as to whether the "Sun" is the Eg. or the Hittite king.

[165] The verb translated "to furnish" here and below in ᶜUzzīnu's message is {ṯṯ} (see above, note 46). For TRTN, cf. possibly Wilhelm 1970.

[166] Here the tablet breaks off after line 10, and a significant number of lines is lost before the text resumes again on the *verso*. It only becomes clear that the servant is speaking in line 16′, where the speaker refers to the addressee as "my master" ({bᶜly}). I make the preceding paragraph also part of the servant's message because the reference to the addressee's sister in line 12′ appears more easily understood in the mouth of the servant than coming from his son.

[167] The Ug. word for *asa foetida*, "fetid gum," is *tyt*. Given that the possibility of sending the commodity across a considerable distance is entertained here, the reference is almost certainly to the medicinal gum, not to the plant itself whence the gum is drawn (see Pardee, forthcoming b, commentary on RS 18.024:26).

[168] The precise type of garment or cloak represented by the word *ḫpn* is unknown (cf. Van Soldt 1990:328, 335 for attestations and previous literature).

[169] The final two lines of the message were written on the left edge of the tablet and are too poorly preserved for translation.

(32) EMERGENCY REPORT FROM A CITY-COMMANDER (RS 19.011) (3.45FF)[170]

Address (lines 1-2)
To ǴRDN,[171] my master, say:

The Report (lines 3-11)
BN ḪRNK has come (here), he has defeated the

[170] Text published by Virolleaud 1965:137, text 114. The historical circumstances are unknown, for the writer does not identify himself, the addressee is otherwise unknown, and it is uncertain whether the identification of the perpetrator of the attack (*bn ḫrnk*) is a name or a title. Because the object of the attack is a *qrt*, a "town" or "city," it may be assumed that the addressee exercised an official function at some level in the royal administration of the kingdom.

[171] Though originally read {ḏrdn}, the first sign is almost certainly {ǵ}. The name is previously unattested but appears to be Hurrian, consisting of the elements {ǵr} (= /ḫar/ or /ḫur/ in syllabic writing) and {dn} (= /danu/, /tanu/, /tenu/ in syllabic script).

(local) troops,[172] he has pillaged[xx] the town, he has even burned[173] our grain[174] [yy] on the threshing-floors[zz] and destroyed the vineyards.[aaa]

The Urgency of the Situation (lines 12-13)
Our town is destroyed[bbb] and you must know it.[175]

xx Isa 10:6, etc.
yy Exod 22:5
zz 1 Sam 23:1
aaa Cf. Judg 6:4; Mal 3:11 *bbb* Gen 13:10; 18:28; 19:13-14; 2 Kgs 19:12; Lam 2:8, etc.

[172] *hbṭ hw ḫrd* (on *hbṭ*, see note 11 to *COS* 1.91; on *ḫrd*, note 23 to *COS* 1.90, and now Vita 1995).
[173] "Burn" is here *bᶜr*, lit. "destroy (by fire)." The verb is used in the broader sense of "destroy" in RS 24.247+:41′, 56′, 58′ (*COS* 1.90), and here in (12) (see above, note 76) and RS 92.2010:23 (37) below.
[174] *ᵓakln*, lit. "our food."
[175] The "take notice" formula is here expressed as two asyndetic imperatives: *dᶜ dᶜ*, "Know! Know!"

(33) A DOUBLE LETTER TO YABNĪNU
(RS 19.102) (3.45GG)[176]

First Address (lines 1-5)
To Yabnīnu, my father, say: Message of Ta[lmi-y]ānu, your son.

Prostration Formula (lines 6-7)
At the fee[t of my father I] fa[ll]. [...]

Second Address (lines 13-16)
To Yabnī[nu], my master, s[ay]: Message of ᶜAbd[...], your servant:

Prostration Formula and Request for Return of News (lines 17-24)
At the feet of my master twice seven times from afar I fall. Whatever is well with my master, [retu]rn word (of that) [to] your servant.

[176] Text published by Virolleaud 1965:138, text 115. The primary interest of this text is that it consists of two letters, both addressed to the same person, one from a son, the other from a servant. Only five lines have disappeared from the bottom of the tablet (lines 8-12), and it is not unlikely that both letters were entirely formulaic, i.e., that the function of both letters was that of "keeping in touch." In spite of the fact that both the father's and the son's names are known, we cannot be sure whether the addressee of this letter was the famous Yabnīnu who was entrusted with the mission to Amurru which is one of the topics of (4) (see above).

(34) TWO SERVANTS TO THEIR MASTER
(RS 29.093) (3.45HH)[177]

Address (lines 1-5)
To Yadurma, our master, say: Message of Pinḥaṯu and Yarmîhaddu, your servants.[178]

Greetings and Prostration Formula (lines 5-10)
May it be well with our master. May the gods guard you, may they keep you well. At the feet of our master twice seven times (from) afar we fall.[179]

The Problem with Binu-ᶜAyāna (lines 11-19)
Here Binu-ᶜAyāna keeps making demands[ccc] on your maidservant.[180] So send him a message[181] and put a stop to this.[182] Here is what I have done: I hired a workman and had this house[183] repaired.[ddd]

ccc Cf. 1 Sam 20:6; Neh 13:6
ddd Neh 3:34; 1 Chr 11:8

[177] Discovered in 1966 in the so-called *Quartier Residentiel* to the east of the palace and published by Herdner 1978, this letter provides a well-preserved and reasonably well-understood example of a letter between persons of non-royal status, in this case two "servants" writing to their master. The servants, at least the one who states her case in the second paragraph, were persons with authority in their master's household. The master was someone who was wealthy enough to control at least two servants and to be absent from the estate where the two servants were employed. He may thus have been involved in one of the Ug. "firms" that are gradually becoming known, have possessed other land holdings elsewhere, been a member of the royal administration, or any combination of these possibilities. On the dual forms, see above, (3). Here, as in the above text, certain forms and expressions allowed one of the authors to distinguish him/herself from the other.
[178] The names Yadurma and Yarmîhaddu (or Yarimhaddu) are West-Semitic, while Pinḥaṯu is Eg. (corresponding to biblical Pinḥas). We learn in the second paragraph (lines 11-19) that one of the two writers was female; unfortunately, she does not indicate her name at that point. The reasons for believing that it was Yarimhaddu are provided in Pardee 1979-80:25-27.
[179] The formula expressing the number of prostrations here is *ṯnᵓid šbᶜd*, "two times seven times (equals fourteen times)" (see above, note 11).
[180] I use the rather archaic "maidservant" to express the switch from the dual masculine form *ᶜbdk*, used in line 5 to designate the two writers, to the feminine singular form *ᵓamtk*, used in this paragraph for the female servant who here expresses her particular problem. The object of Binu-ᶜAyāna's demands is not stated here; from what follows it appears to have something to do with the repairs mentioned there.
[181] {lᵓak} must be an imperative. It cannot be a 3rd masc. sing. pf. (Dietrich and Loretz 1984:66), which is {lᵓik} in Ug. Seeing here an infinitive functioning as 3rd masc. sing. pf. (ibid.) is unacceptable because there is no noun in the vicinity to serve as subject.
[182] Lit. "and refuse him" (*w kḥdnn*), a meaning of *kḥd* attested in Medieval Heb. and Aram., in Syriac, and in Arabic (Pardee 1979-80:28).
[183] The form translated "this house" is *hbt*, analyzed as the presentative particle *hn* + *bt*, "house," with the {n} assimilated (as in the later Heb. definite article). Liverani (1964a:181-82) has pointed out the peculiar usage of *hn* before several nouns in (24) (translated above); seeing a similar usage here compounded by assimilation appears more plausible than seeing here a case of "*w/b* interchange" ({hbt} = *hwt*, "word": Dietrich and Loretz 1984:66). A similar usage of the particle *h(n)-* may be attested in (35) line 14 {hmhkm} (see below, note 190).

So why did Binu-ᶜAyāna come back[184] and take two shekels of silver from your maidservant?

Food for the Servants, a Garment for the Master (lines 20-29)
Now as for your two servants, there with you is all (one could need), so you must give food to them. Moreover, that is what the (members of the) household of your two servants keep requesting.[185] And when your servant[186] comes to tender to you his formal greetings,[187] he will be sure to have a *ḫipānu*-garment made for my master, of whatever (is required) from your servant's own goods.

[184] Dietrich's and Loretz' intuition to read here *lm ṯb*, "why did he return?" (1984:66) had been pre-confirmed by the reading of a word-divider between the two words (Pardee 1981-82:260, n. 9; 1986:454).

[185] The same verb is used as in the case of Binu-ᶜAyāna's demands (*šᵓl*), but here in the G-stem (*tšᵓal*), rather than in the tD-stem (with metathesis), as above (*yštᵓal*). The two servants were apparently responsible for one of the master's households and are complaining that the master has not enabled them to provide for the needs of the other members of the household by giving them adequate foodstuffs (*tn ᵓakl lhm*, "give food to them," in line 22, refers to the two servants, i.e., the writers).

[186] It is clear from the form *bᶜly*, "my master," in line 28 that *ᶜbdk* in lines 26 and 29 is singular (/ᶜabduka/), rather than dual, as in lines 5 and 20 (/ᶜabdêka/ᶜabdāka/), and that the second part of this last paragraph represents the words of the male servant, Pinḫaṯu. The emendation of {bᶜly} to {bᶜl<n>y} (*KTU*² 191) has no objective basis and may not be admitted.

[187] The formula here used is unattested elsewhere: *ymġy ᶜbdk l šlm ᶜmk*, lit., "your servant arrives to ascertain what is well with you." The principal epistolary formulae incorporating *šlm* and a prep. are *šlm ᶜm*, "it is well with X" (see note 9) and *yšlm l*, "may it be well with (lit. 'for') X" (see note 4). The present phrase may either represent a variation of the former, expressing the writer's proposed presence with the addressee when ascertaining the latter's welfare, or a totally different usage, i.e., the D-stem with the notion of "render accounts" or the like (cf. Dietrich and Loretz 1984:67). In either case, this formula is unrelated to the final line of the letter, which does not represent the well-being formula used for the addressee (Pardee 1987b:210-11).

(35) A PROBLEM WITH RATIONS
(RS 29.095) (3.45II)[188]

Address (lines 1-2)
Message of Talmiyānu: To Pizziya say:

Greetings and Double Return of News Formula (lines 3-8)
May it be well with you. May the gods keep you well, may they guard you. Here with me it is w[el]l. There with you <whatever well-being there may be>, return word (of that) to me.[189]

What to Do about Rations (lines 9-19)
Now listen well: As ᶜDN has been continually requesting of you, he may take a *bīku*-jar (of wine) by permission of ᶜPR. Don't you w<or>ry about a thing! Until I arrive in ᶜRM, the rations of ᶜDN, (in the amount) of a *dūdu*-measure of the left-over grain, give to him.[190]

[188] Though a transliteration of this text was provided in *KTU* 2.71 (cf. *KTU*²), a copy or photograph has not yet appeared. One may reject out of hand the hesitant suggestion by *KTU*² that the text might be a scribal exercise, for difficulty of interpretation is not a criterion for ascription as a school text and this text shows no other sign of scholastic origin.

[189] The second part of the formula described above in note 9 reads {ṯmny ᶜmk rgm ṯṯb ly}, i.e., without the expected *mnm šlm*. Whether this was considered an acceptable abbr. or not is difficult to say, but I would guess not, as the use of the prep. *ᶜm* supposes *šlm* (the "well-being" is "with" the correspondent). Though the author of this letter is clearly superior to the addressee, for he names himself first and gives orders, the number of formulae in lines 3-8, in particular the two *šlm*-formulae and the request for return of news, betray an unusually warm relationship between the two. On that basis, we should probably assume that the hierarchical separation of the two correspondents was not great.

[190] This interpretation is far from certain. The biggest problem is line 12, which reads in context {pm yqḥ (13) bk . pᶜpr} and which may, at least in theory, be interpreted in several ways. Because the idiom *lqḥ b(y)d*, "take from the hand/possession of" is well attested, whereas *lqḥ b*, "take from," is not, I avoid translating "he may take *pᶜpr* from you." A word *pᶜpr* is, in any case, unknown, and I have divided it, therefore, as *p ᶜpr*, "(according to) the mouth of *ᶜpr* (personal name)." As suggested long ago (Dijkstra, de Moor, and Spronk 1981:379), {blk} in line 15 is to be emended to {b l<b>k} and the phrase *dbr hmhkm b l<b>k ᵓal tšt*, "any word/matter at all do not place in your heart," to be understood as an idiom for not worrying. If *ᶜrm* in line 17 refers to the town by that name, the whereabouts of the correspondents when sending and receiving this letter, which was, of course, discovered at Ugarit, are unknown, for that town appears to be located far to the north (Van Soldt 1998:728-30, 742). As a *dūdu* probably measured about fifty liters, the amount assigned here to *ᶜdn* would either be enough to last a single person for quite a long time or a household or an officer and his troops for an indeterminable period of time, because we have no way of knowing the number of persons in either group. I avoid translating *ᶜdn* as the noun that means "group, troop," however, because all the forms that refer to that word appear to be singular. It is not impossible, nevertheless, that that is the meaning of the term, treated throughout as a collective. As above in (32), the word here translated "grain" is *ᵓakl*, "food."

(36) DOUBLE LETTER, FROM ʿAZZĪʾILTU TO HIS PARENTS, FROM SAME TO HIS SISTER (RS 92.2005) (3.45JJ)[191]

First Address (lines 1-5)
[To ʾU]rtēnu, my [fa]ther, say, and to BḎ⌜-⌝R, my mother, say: Message of ʿAzzīʾiltu your son.

Greetings and Double Return of News Formula (lines 6-13)
May it be well with you. May the gods guard your well-being, may they keep you well.[192] Here with me it is well.[193] Whatever is well there, return word (of that) to me.

Body [...][194]

Second Address (lines 23-25)
Message of ʿAzzīʾiltu: To ʾAbīya, my sister, say:

Greetings and Double Return of News Formula (lines 26-32)
May it be well with you. [May] the gods keep (you) well, may they guard you, may they [keep] you [wh]ole.[195] [Here] with me [it is well. Whatever is we]ll [th]ere , return [word] (of that to me).

Body [...][196]

[191] Text to be published by Bordreuil and Pardee (in press). This badly damaged tablet is included here because, by its very nature and joined with other texts, esp. RS 92.2014 (*COS* 1.100), it indicates that the archives to which it belonged were those of ʾUrtēnu (see above, note 16).

[192] This letter contains the first attestation in Ug. of the phrase *l šlm*, "for well-being," inserted in the blessing formula, which reads {ʾilm l šlm tǵrkm tšlmkm}, lit., "the gods, for well being, may they guard you two, may they keep the two of you well." The phrase corresponds to *ana šulmāni* in the Akk. letters from Ras Shamra.

[193] This formula, and probably the corresponding formula in the second letter, also contains a novelty: instead of just {hnny} or {hlny} (see above, note 9), it reads {⌜h⌝ln . ⌜hn⌝ . ʿmn ⌜š⌝lm}, "Here, behold with me it is well." The facts (1) that *hln* here precedes *hn* and (2) that it can introduce the body of a letter while *hnny* does not, seem to indicate that *hln*(*y*) expressed the notion of "here" a bit more strongly than *hnny*.

[194] The body of this letter consisted of 9 lines, but they are too badly damaged to be translated. The presence of the word *ḥršy*, "my artisans," in line 20 may indicate that the message dealt with having something built or constructed (*ḥrš* is used for building houses, for making chariots, and for furniture making).

[195] In addition to the absence of a suffix on {tšlm}, attested elsewhere and probably a sylistic variant rather than an error, a blessing unattested elsewhere is partially preserved in line 28, {[--]⌜-⌝mmk}, plausibly restored as {[w t]⌜t⌝mmk}.

[196] The body of the letter to ʾAbīya was five lines long but is even more poorly preserved than that of the first letter on this tablet.

(37) ʾANANTĒNU TO HIS MASTER ḪIḎMIRATU (RS 92.2010) (3.45KK)[197]

Address (lines 1-4)
To Ḫiḏmiratu, my master, say: Message of ʾAnantēnu your servant.

Greeting and Prostration Formula (lines 4-9)
May the gods guard you, may they keep you well. At the feet of my master seven times and seven times (from) afar do I fall.

Expanded Return-of-News Formulae (lines 9-20)[198]
Here with your servant it is very well. As for my master, (news of) his well-being, (of) the well being of Nikkaliya, (of) the well-being of his household,[199] (of) the well-being of those who hear your good word(s),[200] [eee] you, (O master,) you must send back to your servant.

eee 1 Kgs 22:13; Ps 45:2

[197] Text to be published by Bordreuil and Pardee (in press). Like (34), the present text illustrates the servant-master relationship. None of the persons mentioned may be identified with well-known personages. Both servant and master here bear Hurrian names, while the third person mentioned, Nikkaliya, bears a name used locally that was based on the Mesopotamian divine name Nikkal (< Ningal). This goddess was the wife of the lunar deity Nanna/Sin and the mother of the solar deity Utu/Šamaš. That Nikkal was assimilated into Ug. culture is well illustrated by the myth of her marriage to the Ug. lunar deity Yariḫu (*CTA* no. 24) and by her appearance in ritual texts from Ugarit, both Hurrian and Ug. (see Pardee 2000a:183, 982, 1185).

[198] The basic forms of this epistolary formula are described above, note 9. The first part of the formula, expressing the writer's well-being, is brief. The second has been expanded beyond the normal reference to the addressee only and includes four other persons or groups of persons. The long sentence in which this formula is couched is impossible to translate smoothly for it starts out addressing the master in the third person (*w bʿly šlmh*, lit. "and my master, his well-being") then, after referring to news about the other persons, switches to the second person in the fourth well-being phrase (*rgmk*, "your word") and in the verbal phrase (*ʾat ṯṯb*, lit. "you, you must cause to return"), which has the repeated noun *šlm* of the preceding phrases as its accusative complements.

[199] Because it is between the reference to Nikkaliya and the shift to the second person when referring to the addressee, the antecedent of the pronoun in this formula is uncertain, either "my master" in line 12 or "Nikkaliya" in the immediately preceding phrase. Household greetings may be expressed either to the addressee (as here above, [13]) or in the third person with reference to a third party, and it is thus possible that the "return of news" formula could also refer to the well-being of a third party's household, in this case Nikkaliya's.

[200] The text is *w šlm šmʿ rgmk nʿm*, lit. "and the well-being of the hearer(s) of your word, the good one." If, because of the singular form of the attributive adjective, we can be sure that *rgm* in this phrase is singular, there is no way of determining the number of the hearers (either /šāmiʿi rigmika/, "the hearer of your word," or /šāmiʿī rigmika/, "the hearers of your word"). That *šmʿ rgm* was a title expressing some sort of function is clear from its appearance in administrative texts (Virolleaud 1957:127, text 100:3; Virolleaud 1965:18-20, text 11:10; 109, text 84:12). It also

A Plea for Clemency (lines 21-24)
Now may my master not destroy his servant's house(hold) by his (own) hand.[201]

appears clear that one official could have more than one *šm*ᶜ *rgm*, for in Virolleaud 1965:18, text 11:10-11, two individuals are identified, the first as *šm*ᶜ *rgm skn qrt*, the second as *šm*ᶜ *skn qrt*, where the latter formula appears to be an abbr. of the former (or an error). A comparison of the attested forms of the title (esp. the form in this text, "the hearer(s) of your word"), and the one in Virolleaud 1965:18 (*šm*ᶜ *rgm skn qrt*, "the hearer of the word of the governor of the city") shows that the basic function consisted of the inferior listening to the word(s) of the superior. Precisely what that act entailed and what evolution the basic function may have undergone cannot, however, presently be ascertained.

[201] Lit. "And my master, the house of his servant, may he not destroy (it) in his hand" (*w b*ᶜ*ly bt* ᶜ*bdh* ᵓ*al yb*ᶜ*r b ydh*). On *b*ᶜ*r*, see here above (32) line 9 and note 173. The ambiguity of the suffix on "hand," which could refer either to the servant or the master, leaves the basic meaning of the sentence unclear: is the author worried that Ḫidmiratu may come to destroy the house "by his (own) hand," i.e., that he will personally take charge of the destruction, or that Ḫidmiratu will destroy the house that is "in his (ᵓAnantēnu's) hand," i.e., a house that the author is managing (as seems to be the case of the house mentioned in (34), translated above)? The formulation of the letter and the circumstances that it implies seem to rule out the possibility that the house in question belonged to Ḫidmiratu and was managed by ᵓAnantēnu, for one may doubt that Ḫidmiratu would have contemplated destroying one of his own houses. It appears necessary to conclude, therefore, either that the house belonged to ᵓAnantēnu and that one could be a "servant" and a proprietor at the same time, or that the house was managed by ᵓAnantēnu for a third party, whom Ḫidmiratu would attack through ᵓAnantēnu. Only the proximity of the verb and the prepositional phrase indicate that the former solution may be preferable. Nothing is said in the letter about the circumstances that would have provoked the harsh action feared by ᵓAnantēnu.

(38) ᵓABNIYA ISN'T HAPPY (RS 94.2284) (3.45LL)[202]

Address (lines 1-3)
Message of ᵓAbniya: To ᵓUrtētub, ᵓUrtēnu, my brother, say: Here ...[203]

Objects Sent with the Letter (lines 4-6)
With <Ba>naᵓilu I (herewith) send (you) two ᵓIŠPR and three ᶜRMLHḤT and four jars (of wine).[204]

ᵓAbniya's Problem (lines 7-17)
Now, the heart of your sister is sick[fff] because they have treated me ill and I was never consulted. In the month of Ḫiyyāru — when nobody consulted me — a fattened bull[ggg] was slaughtered and nobody gave me (any). As you live, and as do [I],[hhh] (I swear that)[205] nobody gave [me (any)] and my heart is very sick. [...].[206]

Response to a Previous Letter (lines 18-23)
Now as concerns the letter (regarding) a *ḫipānu*-garment and a pair of leggings (that you sent me): Some remain (made) partially (of) purple wool. If I KǴ any purple wool, I will certainly put (some of those) with them. When Banaᶜilu is sent off, he will take your reply (i.e., my reply to your letter).[207]

Request for Return of News and Further Complaining (lines 24-34)
Whatever is said (there), send (me) back a report through![208] Banaᵓilu — he/it is/will be (in?) ᶜKD.[209] Now, you know how sick the heart of your sister will be if there is any (more) enmity. I'll give two ne<w>? *ḫipānu*-garments[210] (for?) the wine from the provisions that were not given to me. [...].[211] As for the money that you granted me, send it (to me) so I may cause (you) to sleep where your "soul" is going.[212] Why do you delay sending your messenger to me? Don't you know that my heart is

fff Prov 13:12
ggg 2 Sam 6:13; Isa 11:6; Amos 5:22
hhh 1 Sam 1:26; 17:55; 20:3; 25:26; 2 Sam 11:11; 14:19; 2 Kgs 2:2, 4, 6; 4:30

[202] Text to be published by Bordreuil and Pardee (in preparation). The writer's name is previously unattested at Ugarit, and the vocalization is thus uncertain. Because all forms of reference to the addressee in the rest of the letter are singular, it is clear that the names ᵓUrtētub and ᵓUrtēnu refer to a single person. The element /tēnu/ seems to be substitutable for /tētub/, the name of the Hurrian weather deity (Gröndahl 1967:260), and this text attests to one person bearing a name which may take either form. Comparison of this letter with the exercise (42) (see below), indicates that the writer may actually have been residing in ᵓUrtēnu's house and writing to him elsewhere.

[203] Immediately after *rgm*, "say," in line 3 is the word *hlny*, "here," followed by two small wedges and with a horizontal line between lines 3 and 4. It is uncertain whether *hlny* is considered the abbr. of the "return-of-news" formula or the first word of the body of the letter. Against the first explanation is the fact that other formulae usually intervene between the address and the "return-of-news" formula (I know of only one exception, RIH 77/21A, a fragment of a letter from superior to inferior); in favor of the second, the fact that *hlny* serves fairly often to introduce the body of a letter when the writer wishes to emphasize that the reference is to his/her location (cf. notes 9 and 193).

[204] On ᵓ*išpr* and the *sp*-vessel, see above (18) and note 115. {ᶜrmlḥt} is almost certainly a compound phrase, but the proper division is unknown.

[205] Attested for the first time in Ug. and written both times as a single word, (ḥnpšk . w ḥn[pšy]} is the oath formula corresponding to Heb. *ḥay/ḥê napšᵉkā* ...

[206] The last three lines of ᵓAbnīya's complaint are damaged, but the word {dbḥ[...]} "sacrifice" appears in line 17, indicating perhaps a cultic context for the sacrifice (the verb *ṭbḫ* was used above to express the slaughter of the bull).

[207] Aside from some clear individual terms, the sense of this paragraph is rather murky. One of the major problems is {ᵓak⌜ǵ⌝} in line 20, for which no meaning is clear. Also problematic is the use of *grš* for Banaᵓilu's departure; elsewhere in Ug. and in Heb., the verb has a strong negative polarity ("drive out, expel").

[208] Correct {bb} to {bd}, lit. "in the hand(s) of."

[209] The phrase translated after the dash is {hl ᶜkd}. Is ᵓAbniya asking for a reply in Akk.? [Would have to be ᵓkd. Ed.]

[210] The last word of {tn ḫpnm . ḥdm} is perhaps a mistake for {ḥdṯm}.

[211] For line 30, which reads {w ks . pᵓa . ᵓamḫt . ᵓakydnt}, I have found no plausible solution.

[212] {ᵓašhkr . l d hlkt . npšk}, a reference to preparing a tomb?

sick?

(39) PROVISIONS ARE RUNNING OUT
(RS 94.2383 + RS 94.2619) (3.45MM)[213]

Address and Greeting (lines 1-5)
To ʾUrtēnu, my brother, say: Message of ʿUṯtaya, your sister. May the gods keep you well, may they guard you.

The Problem (lines 6-13)
(It has been) three days now that there is no food in your house and for [... someone] struck and provisions CARRY (to) the house of the king. Twice now (someone) has taken (provisions?) and keeps asking [...] CARRY the (message)-tablet. Now oil [...] perfume [...] and wood [...] for him/her/it.[214]

[213] Text to be published by Bordreuil and Pardee (in preparation). The form of the tablet is fully preserved but surface damage has rendered its reading very difficult. The text was complete with line 13, inscribed on the lower edge, for the entire *verso* of the tablet was left uninscribed. I included this text because of who the correspondents were. An ʿUṯtaya was the recipient of (30) and addressed there as the sister of ʿUzzīnu. Judging from the reference there to the writer's mother, ʿUṯtaya may have been his true sister. Because of the absence of other such family references in the present text, it is difficult to determine whether the relationship between ʾUrtēnu and ʿUṯtaya was familial or purely social.

[214] The text is unfortunately too badly damaged to allow any certainty as to whether envoys of the king have been taking food from individual houses for the palace or whether people are seeking to receive provisions from the palace.

(40) GETTING ONE'S NAME BEFORE THE KING
(RS [Varia 4]) (3.45NN)[215]

Address and Greeting (lines 1-5)
Message of ʾIwariḏarri: To ʾIwaripuzini, my son, my brother,[216] say: May the gods guard you, may they keep you well.

A Letter Previously Sent to Ṯarriyelli (lines 6-9)
How is it with the (message)-tablet[217] *iii* that I sent to Ṯarriyelli? What has she said (about it)?

iii Cf. Isa 30:8

iij Cf. 1 Kgs 2:16-18

ʾIwaripuzini's Intervention Requested (lines 10-14)
Now may my brother, my son, inquire of Ṯarriyelli and may she in turn mention[218] my name to the king*iij* and to ʾIyyatalmi.

Report Requested (lines 15-19)
Now may my brother, my son, make this inquiry of Ṯarriyelli and return word to your brother, your father.

[215] This text first appeared, in transcription only, in Gordon 1947:168 (text no. 138), but the full *editio princeps* was not presented for decades thereafter (Bordreuil 1982:5-9 and pl. I). Gordon had received the transcription from de Vaux, who had announced that he would publish the text soon (1946:458, n. 3) but who never did so. The tablet was almost certainly removed from the site of Ras Shamra illegally, either during the final excavations before World War II or else while the site was abandoned during the war. The only well-known personage mentioned in the letter is Ṯarriyelli, the queen or the queen-mother (see above, note 2). All the names mentioned in the text are of Hurrian type. This letter makes reference to a previous letter and asks that the concerns expressed there be pursued by checking with the addressee of that letter (Ṯarriyelli) who is in turn to take the matter before the king. Nowhere, however, is the content of these concerns expressed. The mention of the otherwise poorly attested ʾIyyatalmi in the same breath with the king indicates that the writer's project somehow falls within the sphere of ʾIyyatalmi's activities. All we know about those is that ʾIyyatalmi was involved in real estate operations (Bordreuil 1982:9).

[216] Below the addressee is called "my brother, my son" (lines 10-11 and 15-16) while the writer's self-description is "your brother, your father." This double designation of each of the correspondents is unknown elsewhere. The word *ʾadn*, "lord/father," usually reserved for the paternal parent (*bʿl* is used for a social superior — see above, notes 52 and 119), implies a family relationship. In the first case, ʾIwariḏarri might be thought to be an older brother of ʾIwaripuzini, perhaps even one who had raised him like a son; in the second, the writer may be a senior member of one of the commercial enterprises that flourished at Ugarit and whose members referred to each other as "brothers" when of roughly equal age and status but with terms of inequality when of disparate age (cf. the Akk. text RS 34.171, second letter, addressed to two persons, one of whom is EN, "lord," the other ŠEŠ DUG$_{10}$.GA, "good brother," while the writer calls himself "the brother" of both (Malbran-Labat 1991:52-53).

[217] The expression *lḥt spr*, "tablet(s) of message," is attested only here, though similar but more precise phrases are well attested, e.g. *lḥt ʾakl* (9), line 17), translated above "a (message)-tablet... regarding food," or *lḥt qnʾim* (10) line 29′), translated above "(message)-tablet... regarding royal purple."

[218] The expression is *p rgm l mlk šmy*, "and SAY to the king my name," with the conjunction that emphasizes the sequentiality of two phrases (see above, note 104), and a verbal form not marked for feminine gender. *rgm* is, therefore, if Ṯarriyelli is the subject, the infinitive used absolutely. It could also be the masc. sing. impv., addressed to ʾIwaripuzini, but if the latter enjoyed immediate access to the king one wonders why the inquiry addressed to Ṯarriyelli and the addressee's intercession with the king would be mentioned in the same breath. If the two acts mentioned in this paragraph are indeed related, as the logic of the situation and the laconic formulation may be thought to indicate, then the "saying" of the writer's name may be thought to involve more than a mere mention, i.e. a presentation of his concerns, whatever they may have been.

VI. SCRIBAL EXERCISES

Dennis Pardee

(41) A SCRIBE SHOWS OFF
(RS 16.265) (3.45OO)[219]

Address and Greetings (lines 1-6)
[Me]ssage of ʾIṯtēlu to MNN: May the gods guard you, may they keep you well, may they strengthen you, for a thousand days and ten thousand years, through the endless reaches of time.[220] *kkk*

kkk Pss 111:8; 148:6

The Request (lines 7-16)
A request I would make of my brother, my friend, and may he ʾgrant it to his brother, his friend, (his) friend forever: May you give, and give!, and may you indeed give, and will you not certainly give?, give (me) a cup of wine that I might drink![221]

[219] Text published by Virolleaud 1957:39-40, no. 19. Except for the upper left corner, this tablet is well preserved, leaving no doubt about the "structure" of the text: lines 1-16, written on the *recto* and the lower edge with the rectangular tablet held in the vertical position, contain a practice letter, in which the scribe shows off his command both of epistolary formulae and of verbal conjugation; lines 17-28, written partially in cols. on the *verso* with the tablet held in the horizontal position, contain individual words; lines 29-31, written on the right edge, the upper edge, and the left edge, contain three partial alphabets (the two that are fully preserved both run from {ʾa} to {y}, i.e., the first eleven letters). Cf. *COS* 1.107. As lines 17-31 bear no real message, only the letter is translated here. The signs in the first two parts are cleanly and consistently executed, with very few forms that show any deviation from the more or less standard palace hands, and must have been inscribed by a student well along in his studies or by a young professional. In contrast, the signs of the partial alphabets are much more awkwardly formed and were surely done by a student fairly near the beginning of the curriculum. Because there is no reason to have kept such a tablet in the palace archives, one must conclude that it dates from the very last days of the kingdom of Ugarit. ʾIṯtēlu, the author of the letter, is unknown as a scribe. The addressee is {mnn}, which may be either an authentic personal name, attested elsewhere, or an expanded indefinite pronoun, meaning "Anyone."

[220] "May they strengthen you" (tʿzzk} is attested once in a genuine letter (RS 1.018:6 {tʿzz[k]}), but the temporal phrases are not yet attested elsewhere.

[221] The scribe runs through the four principal volitive forms, the jussive, the imperative, the imperfective with asseverative *l*, and the imperfective with emphatic ʾ*al* (translated here as a rhetorical negative, though this ʾ*al* may have been a particle separate from the negative volitive particle), then repeats the simple imperative before the direct object (*ttn w tn w l ttn w* ʾ*al ttn tn ks yn w* ʾ*ištn*).

(42) THE GREETINGS THAT ʾABNIYA MIGHT HAVE SENT (RS 94.2273) (3.45PP)[222]

Address and Greetings (lines 1-7)
[Mess]age of ʾAbniya to ʾUrtēṯub: [I] fall at the feet of my brother. Here from afar I fall; seven times, eight times, I fall. May the gods guard you, may they ke[ep you well].[223]

[222] Text to be published by Bordreuil and Pardee (in preparation). This is a small rectangular tablet inscribed as held horizontally with all seven lines of writing on the *recto*. Visible are many remnants of previous writing that have been incompletely erased. The tablet is too small, too poorly prepared, and these seven lines take up too much space to allow us even to contemplate that it may have been intended as the beginning of the letter that has come to us as (38), though it certainly contains some scribe's ideas as to how one of ʾAbniya's letters to her brother, perhaps in happier circumstances, may have begun. It is intriguing that both were found in the House of ʾUrtēnu when one would expect only (38) to have been sent — does this mean that ʾAbniya was at the time resident in her brother's house and he was away from home, i.e., that (38) was never actually dispatched? Because it is difficult to imagine that a rough partial draft like the present text would have been kept in anyone's archives, it appears necessary to conclude that the events of (38) occurred shortly before the fall of the city of Ugarit.

[223] Though not as flowery as (41), there are three unique features to this set of formulae: (1) the three-fold repetition of the verb "fall," with the first actual occurrence apparently added secondarily (it is written in a smaller script at the end of line 1, just above the phrase *l pʿn*, "at the feet of," in line 2); (2) the presence of an adverb {hllm}, "here/behold," previously unattested in this form and in this position in the formula, at the beginning of the second prostration formula; (3) the hyperbolic expression of number of prostrations as "seven times, eight times" rather than the expected "seven times, seven times" (see above, note 11).

REFERENCES

Text, translations and studies: Ahl 1973; Albright 1958; Astour 1965; 1969; 1981; Bordreuil 1982; 1984; 1991; Bordreuil and Caquot 1980; Bordreuil and Malbran-Labat 1995; Bordreuil and Pardee 1982; 1989; 1991; in press; in preparation; Bounni, Lagarce and Lagarce 1998; Brooke 1979; Callot 1983; 1984; Caquot 1975; 1978a; 1978b; Courtois 1990; Cunchillos 1988; 1989; 1999; Dhorme 1933; 1938; Dietrich and Loretz 1964-66; 1974; 1984; 1994; *KTU*; *KTU*²; Dijkstra 1976; 1994; Dijkstra, de Moor and Spronk 1981; Freu 1999; Gordon 1947; Gröndahl 1967; Helck 1963; *CTA*; Herdner 1978; Hoffner 1998; Hoftijzer 1967; 1979; 1982; Huffmon and Parker 1966; Jidejian 1969; de Jong and van Soldt 1987-88; Kaiser 1970; Klengel 1974; 1992; Kristensen 1977; Lackenbacher 1989; Liverani 1962; 1964a; 1964b; 1979; 1995; 1997; Loewenstamm 1967; Malbran-Labat 1991; 1995a; 1995b; Milano 1983; de Moor 1965; 1996; Nougayrol 1955; 1956; 1968; Owen 1981; Pardee 1975; 1977; 1979-80; 1981; 1981-82; 1983-84; 1984; 1986; 1987a; 1987b; 1987c; 1988; 1997a; 1997b; 2000a; 2000b; forthcoming a; forthcoming b; forthcoming c forthcoming d; Pardee, Sperling, Whitehead and Dion 1982; Pardee and Whiting 1987; Rainey 1974; Saadé 1995; Singer 1991; 1999; Sivan 1984; van Soldt 1983; 1985-86; 1990; 1991; 1996; 1998; Thureau-Dangin 1937; Tropper 2000; de Vaux 1946; Virolleaud 1938; 1940; 1957; 1965;

1968; Vita 1995; Vita and Galán 1997; Watson and Wyatt 1999; Xella 1991; Yon 1992; 1995; 1997.

3. ARAMAIC LETTERS

THE JEDANIAH ARCHIVE FROM ELEPHANTINE
(419/18 to after 407 BCE)

Bezalel Porten

The first identifiably Elephantine Aramaic papyrus was acquired in 1898/99 on the antiquities market by the Egyptologist Wilhelm Spiegelberg for the (now-named) Bibliothèque Nationale et Universitaire of Strasbourg and published by Julius Euting in 1903 (*COS* 3.50). While fragmentary, it reported the nefarious acts of the Khnum priests and foreshadowed the tale of the destruction of the Jewish temple. This was detailed in some ten documents uncovered by Otto Rubensohn and Friedrich Zucker in 1907-1908 and published by Eduard Sachau in 1911 (*TAD* A4.1-10). They have been brought together because they were addressed to the Jewish leader Jedaniah son of Gemariah (*COS* 3.46-48), were written by/for him (*COS* 3.51 and 3.53), or concern events in which he was involved (*COS* 3.49-50 and 3.52). Historically, this composite archive is of inestimable significance. It opened in 419 BCE with a fragmentary letter from an unknown Hananiah reporting a (missing) directive of Darius II to Arsames and instructing Jedaniah "and his colleagues the Jewish troop" on the proper observance of the Passover (3.46). It closed some dozen years later with a memorandum of a recommendation for Arsames, issued jointly by Bagavahya of Judah and Delaiah son of Sanballat, governor of Samaria, that the destroyed Temple be rebuilt on its site and (only) incense and meal-offering be made there (3.52); and an abridged draft letter of Jedaniah and his four named colleagues, probably to the same Arsames, offering a handsome bribe and accepting certain restrictions if the reconstruction of their Temple be authorized (3.53). The center piece is an elegantly written and rhetorically stylized draft petition, in two copies, the second revised, addressed to the Persian-named, but probably Jewish, governor of Judah, seeking his written intercession with the Persian authorities for the Temple's reconstruction (3.51 [only the first draft is presented here]). Hananiah's festal letter combined known provisions from the written Torah with innovations from a developing oral Torah. Whoever he may have been, whether a representative of Jerusalem or a delegate from the Persian court, his arrival in Egypt stirred up the Khnum priests on the island of Elephantine against the Jewish Temple. In a letter of recommendation on behalf of two Egyptians who had extricated the scribe Mauziah son of Nathan from a tight situation in Abydos, the latter wrote to Jedaniah, "To you it is known that Khnum is against us since Hananiah has been in Egypt until now" (3.48). Other letters intimated that both sides presented their claims before the Persian authorities in Thebes and Memphis — the Egyptians "act thievishly" (3.47) — and reported how the Jews took things into their own hands and pillaged Egyptian homes, for which they were imprisoned and forced to pay heavy reparations (3.49). All the intact letters open with a form of the standard salutation, "May the gods/God of Heaven seek after the welfare-of-my-lords/brothers/your welfare at all times" (3.46-49, 3.51).[1] Eight of the ten letters are presented here; today they are divided between the museums in Berlin (3.46, half of 3.49, 3.51-52) and Cairo (3.47-48, half of 3.49, 3.53) and the library in Strasbourg (3.50).

THE PASSOVER LETTER (3.46)
(419/18 BCE)

Bezalel Porten

Significant as this letter (*P. Berlin* 13464 [*TAD* A4.1]) is, its full intent eludes us because of our ignorance as to the identity of Hananiah and the loss of the command from Darius to Arsames (*Instructions I*). Hananiah arrived from outside of Egypt, either upon the initiative of the Jewish authorities in Jerusalem or of the Persian court or in response to a petition of the Elephantine Jews. If the latter, we may imagine that their observance of the dual Festivals of Passover and Unleavened Bread was being obstructed by the Egyptian priests. Hananiah succeeded in gaining the king's confirmation of their traditional rights and on his own initiative stated three or four biblical requirements (*Instructions II*), such as eating unleavened bread during the seven day festival, followed by an interlacing of biblical requirements, such as abstaining from work on the first and last days, and interpretative innovations concerning purity, fermented drink, and the storage of leaven (*Instructions III*). These latter may have been recent rulings in Jerusalem. Obscure is the manner in which the first night and day of the Festival of Passover was to be observed. A home sacrifice? A temple sacrifice? As a festal letter, this missive is reminiscent of the letters of King Hezekiah

[1] For the jussive form of the verb, see *GEA* 198.

about Passover, of Esther and Mordecai about Purim, and of the Jerusalem authorities about Hanukkah (2 Chr 30:1-9; Esth 9:2032; 2 Macc 1:1-2:18). The letter is heavily smeared and may have been a palimpsest.

Internal Address

(Recto)(1)[To my brothers[2] [a] Je]daniah[3] and his colleagues[4] [b] the Jewish T[roop],[5] your brother Hanan[i]ah.[6]

Salutation

The welfare of my brothers may the gods[7] [seek after (2)at all times]?[8]

Instructions I

And now,[9] this year, year 5 of Darius the king,[10] [c] from[11] the king it has been sent[12] to Arsa[mes ...].[13]

Instructions II

(3)[...] ... Now,[14] you,[15] thus[16] count[d] four[teen[17] (4)days of Nisan[18] *and on the 14th at twilight*[19] *the Passover* ma]ke[20] and from day 15 until day 21 of [Nisan *the Festival* (5)*of Unleavened Bread observe. Seven days unleavened bread eat.*[21]

Instructions III

Now], be pure[22] [e] and take heed.[23] [f] Work [do] n[ot do (6)*on day 15 and on day 21 of Nisan.*[24] *Any fermented drink*] do not drink.[25] And anything of leaven[26] do not [eat[27] (Verso) (7)*and do not let it be seen*[28] *in your houses* from day 14 of Nisan at] sunset until day 21 of Nisa[n at sun(8)set. *And any leaven which you have in your houses* b]ring into your chambers and seal[g] (them) up during [these] days.[29] (9)[...] ....

External Address

(10)[To] (*sealing*) my brothers Jedaniah and his colleagues the Jewish Troop, your brother Hananiah s[on of PN].

a 1 Kgs 20:32
b Ezra 4:7, 9, 17, 23, 5:3, 6, 6:6, 13
c Neh 12:22
d Lev 23:15-16; Deut 16:9
e Num 9:1-14; Ezra 6:20; 2 Chr 30:17
f Judg 13:4, 13; 1 Sam 21:5
g Dan 6:18

2 A designation used between peers.

3 Internal addresses rarely gave the patronymic of either correspondent. This was Jedaniah son of Gemariah, leader of the Jewish community at the end of the century, probably a cousin of Jedaniah and Mahseiah sons of Mibtahiah daughter of Mahseiah son of Jedaniah, and *possibly* a priest (reconstructed text in *TAD* A4.8:1; see *GEA* 252).

4 Collegiality in this period was the usual practice in correspondence and other bureaucratic procedures; e.g. 3.47:2 11, 3.51:1, 4; *TAD* A6.1:1, 2:11. Here Jedaniah's colleagues were the whole Jewish community; in his petition to Bagavahya they were just the priests (3.51:1; *TAD* A4.8:1).

5 The garrison at Elephantine was primarily Jewish and was defined ethnically (*TAD* C3.15.1). The one at Syene was more diverse and was known as "the Syenian troop" (*TAD* C3.14:32); Porten 1968:33-34.

6 Unfortunately, his patronymic was lost in the *External Address*. Though there were several Hanan's at Elephantine (3.68:16; *TAD* C13:2, 53, 55; 4.6:5), no one there bore the name Hananiah. He arrived from outside Egypt and his presence and actions stirred up the animosity of the Khnum priesthood (3.48:7).

7 The form is plural (*ʾlhyʾ*) and it is not clear, here and in other letters by Jews, whether it was understood as a majestic singular, whether a pagan formula was used unthinkingly, or whether a pagan scribe actually wrote the letter (see 3.49:1, 9).

8 This pagan *Salutation* was common in Jewish and non-Jewish private letters; see *TAD* A3.5:1, 3.9:1, 3.10:1 and is also restored in 3.47:1.

9 The body of virtually every letter began with some form of this transition word; see *EPE* 90, n. 9.

10 It is strange that no month and day date were given. Since the New Year began in Nisan, we may imagine that the rescript was issued at the end of year 5 (before April 15, 418 BCE), with an eye to the Passover of year 6.

11 The word order "from"-"to" was standard for a message from a superior to a subordinate; see *EPE* 115, n. 2.

12 The verb is impersonal, passive (*šlyḥ*), meaning "word has been sent."

13 This unique ten-word message does not lend itself to confident reconstruction.

14 Pursuant to Darius' message to the satrap, Hananiah issued some ten instructions on the proper observance of the festival. These may be restored on the basis of close parallels with Exod 12:6, 15-20, 13:7. Some instructions have no biblical parallels. See Porten 1979:91-92.

15 The 2mp independent personal pronoun regularly preceded an imperative for emphasis in epistolary instructions and commands; see 3.48:5, 8; *GEA* 298 and *EPE* 121, n. 72.

16 With cataphoric meaning —"as follows;" *GEA* 312.

17 For the form *ʾrb*[*ʿt ʿśr*], see *GEA* 90, n. 415.

18 The commandment to count in the Bible occurs only in relation to the festival of Shavuoth.

19 Restoration according to Exod 12:6 where the paschal lamb was to be sacrificed at twilight on the fourteenth of Nisan.

20 *ʿbd psḥ* = Heb. *ʿśh psḥ*, which occurs some 30 times in the Bible in eight different contexts. It is immaterial whether we translate these passages neutrally, with the RSV, "keep the Passover" or explicitly (with NJPS) as "perform the paschal sacrifice." The essence of observing this festival is performing the paschal sacrifce, as all the biblical sources make clear, explicating the expression with the verbs *hqryb*, "offer up" (Num 9:7, 13), *zbḥ* "sacrifice" (Deut 16:2, 4-6), and *šḥṭ*, "slaughter" (2 Chr 35:1, 6, 11).

21 Restoration according to Exod 12; 1 Sam 18; cf. Lev 23:6; Num 28:17.

22 Does this provision refer to the biblical requirement of purity for offering up the paschal sacrifice or to a recently instituted injunction of purity during the seven day festival (cf. Rosh Hashanah 16b; Porten 1979:92)?

23 Not to become impure; for the form see *GEA* 17, 116, 192.

24 Restoration on the basis of Exod 12:16; cf. Lev 23:7-8; Num 18:18, 25.

25 A postbiblical injunction (cf. Pesaḥ. 3:1 with its inclusion of Eg. *zythos* among the list of prohibited fermented drinks).

26 For the construction with *kl mndʿn*, see *GEA* 172, 246.

27 On the basis of Exod 12:20.

28 On the basis of Exod 13:7 ("no leaven shall be seen") which may logically conflict with Exod 12:19 ("no leaven shall be found"). The contradiction was resolved by putting it out of sight under seal (line 8).

29 This permission to store leaven out of sight was disallowed by normative Jewish law (cf. Pesaḥ. 5b, 28b).

REFERENCES

Text, translations, and studies: *EPE; GEA;* Porten 1968; Porten 1979; *TAD* A4.1.

REPORT OF CONFLICT AND REQUEST FOR ASSISTANCE (3.47)
(Late 5th Century BCE)

Bezalel Porten

Written on a three-ply protocol (first sheet) of a scroll (Cairo J. 43471 [*TAD* A4.2]), this letter defies proper understanding because of the loss of its left half and the use of numerous words and phrases that occur only here. An unknown subordinate, using the standard pagan *Salutation* formula, informed the leaders Jedaniah, Mauziah, and Uriah of proceedings at the court of Arsames in Memphis where he and his colleagues were bested by the Egyptians who proffered bribes and acted "thievishly" (lines 3-5). Timely appearance before Arsames would have altered the situation, but a counter-offer of goods should help to assuage anger (lines 8-11). The final paragraph is a Report on several discrete matters, including the arrival of Pasou from Elephantine, the detention of Ḥori, and the "damage" suffered by Arsames (lines 11-15).

Internal Address

(Recto)(1)To my lords Jedaniah,[1] Mauziah,[2] Uriah,[3] and the Troop,[4] [yo]ur servant[5] [a] [PN.

Salutations

The welfare of my lords may the gods, all (of them)[6]], (2)seek after at all times.[7] It is well for us here.[8]

Complaint

Now,[9] every day that[10] [...] (3)he complained[11] to the investigators.[12] One Jivaka,[13] he complained to an investigator ... [...] (4)we have[14] since the Egyptians give to them a bribe.[15] And from (the time) that [...] (5)of the Egyptians before Arsames, but act thievishly.[16]

Report I

Moreover,[17] [b] [...][18] (6)the province of Thebes[19] and thus say:[20] [c] It is Mazdayazna/a Mazdean who is an official[21] of the province[22] [...] (7)we are afraid[23] because we are fewer by two.[24]

Report II and Instructions

Now, behold,[25] they favored[26] [...]. (8)Had we re-

a Ezra 4:11, 7:12

b Ezra 5:10, 14, 6:5

c Gen 32:4

---

[1] See on 3.46:1.

[2] This was the scribe and leader Mauziah son of Nathan; see *EPE* 194, n. 40.

[3] Of unknown patronymic, Uriah may have been a priest; see on 3.48:1, 12.

[4] For the coordination in the address see *GEA* 317, 319.

[5] The sequence "lord"-"servant" was standard in Aram. letters, here and in the Bible, both private and official, to/from a superior from/to an inferior; see 3.48:1, 3.51:1; *GEA* 251.

[6] Alternately translate as adverb "unanimously;" *GEA* 248.

[7] For the blessing formula see on 3.46:1-2.

[8] See on *EPE* 93, n. 5.

[9] See on 3.46:2 ("And now").

[10] It was common for a letter to begin with a temporal reference or allusion, followed by a verb of motion or some other action; see 3.48:3, 3.51:4-5 and *EPE* 107, n. 6.

[11] Several of the letters in the Arsames correspondence opened with the announcement of a complaint (*TAD* A6.3:1, 6.8:1-3, 6.14:1; cf. 6.15:5, 11); see *EPE* 159, n. 13.

[12] Aram. *ptyprsn, ptyprsʾ, ptyprs* = Old Persian **patifrāsa-*, "provost" (Hinz 1975:186); see Porten 1968:53-54.

[13] An Iranian name (Komfeld 1978:106).

[14] *DAE* 388-389 restored [*lʾ*] *ʾyty ln*, "we do [not] have," implying that their approach was blocked because of Eg. bribes.

[15] The word *šḥd* occurs only here in all our texts. Bribery was not unusual in ancient Egypt; see *EPE* 47-48, 51, 311-312; Porten 1968:282-283. Unfortunately, the broken context does not allow for full reconstruction of the circumstances in our situation.

[16] The adverbial form *gnybt* occurred only here (*GEA* 93, 180, 275). The term is in line with the proffering of bribes, but again the precise meaning eludes us.

[17] The particle "moreover" (*ʾp*) introduces matters both unrelated to the previous topic (3.51:29-30) and matters continuing the previous topic (3.51:9, 17, 19, 21). Broken context does not allow determination of whether here a new matter is being introduced or not.

[18] *DAE* 389 restored "they arrived from," that is, Jews reported from Thebes.

[19] A subsequent letter reported the seizure and imprisonment "at the gate in Thebes" of five of the communal leaders and six unrelated women (3.49:4-7).

[20] "PN thus (*kn*) says" was a common formula in Imperial Aram. documents of all sorts — letters (*TAD* A4.7:4; 6.2:2, 6.3:6; etc.), a court record (*TAD* B8.7:3), and the Bisitun inscription (*TAD* C2.1:8, etc.); see *EPE* 116, n. 6. Heb. had a different word order — "Thus (*kh*) said PN" (e.g. Gen 32:4).

[21] This bland title (*pqyd*, "appointed one") designated the steward of Arsames and other Persian dignitaries who cared for their estates in Egypt and elsewhere. According to their names, they were Egyptians, Babylonians or Arameans, and Persians (*TAD* A6.4, 8-15); see Lindenberger 1994:72-73.

[22] The relationship between the province of Thebes and the province of Tshetres is not clear (see on 3.50:9; Porten 1968:42-43; *EPE* 311-312). For this cleft sentence construction see *GEA* 294-295.

[23] For imperfect *ndḥl* as present see *GEA* 197.

[24] Most enigmatic. Had two of their colleagues died, disappeared, been detained? For predicate-subject (*zʿyrn ʿnḥnh*) word order, see *GEA* 285-286.

[25] This double introduction appears also in 3.48:5, where, like here, it preceded an urgent request; see further *GEA* 329.

[26] Aram. *sbrw* occurs only here in our collection and once more the meaning eludes us.

revealed our presence[27] to Arsames prior to this, this(!) wou[ld] not [*have been done to us* ...] (9)he[28] will report our affairs before Arsames. Paisana pacifies us[29] [.... *So whatever*] (10)you will find[30] — honey, castor oil, string, rope, leather skins, *boards* [... — *send us since*] (Verso) (11)they are full of anger[31] [d] at you.

d Ezek 16:30

Report III

Pasou son of Mannuki[32] came to Memphis[33] and ... [...] (12)and the investigator. And he gave me silver, 12 staters[34] and happy with it [*am I*[35] ...] (13)Ḥori gave me when they detained[36] him because of the pitcher. Tiri... said: "[...] (14)at the order[37] of the king and they detain them. And the damage[38] [e] of Arsames and the compensation[39] of Djeḥ[o...] (15)and Ḥori[40] whom they detained."

e Esth 7:4; Ezra 4:22

Date

On day 6 of Phaophi the letters arrived [...][41] (16)we will do (the) thing.

External Address

(17)To (*sealing*) my lords Jaadaniah,[42] Mauziah, y[our] se[rvant PN].

---

[27] A unique expression (*gly ʾnp*); see *DNWSI* 223. A timely appearance at the satrapal court would have avoided their present difficulties. For the construction see *GEA* 327.

[28] Who?

[29] Another unknown idiom (*hšdk ʾnp*); the Persian Paisana served as conciliator (see Num 17:20 for the parallel Heb. word [*škk* = Targ. Jonathan *šdk*] in comparable context). He was mentioned in two other letters (*TAD* A3.8:2).

[30] The following six plus items were apparently meant as counter-bribe to assuage the anger of the unknown "they." Honey, string, and rope occurs only here in our collection. Honey was valued as food, used in medicine, and part of temple ritual, while the most common material for making ropes was fiber from the date palm, prominent in the cataract region (Porten 1968:36). Castor oil and skins from the cataract region were objects frequently sought after by travelers away from home (*TAD* A2.1:7, 2.2:13, 2.4:7-8, 12, 2.5:5). The *šp*-board was used in ship repair at Elephantine (*TAD* A6.2:11, 19).

[31] The expression *mly lbh*, "to be full of someone's wrath" = "to be full of wrath against someone" contains the Akk. loanword *libbātu*, "wrath" and occurs frequently in letters (*KAI* 2.233:19-20; *TAD* A2.3:6, 3.3:10, 3.5:4).

[32] This man with Eg. praenomen and Akk. patronym appeared in a list of ethnically mixed names (*TAD* C4.8:9).

[33] For verb-subject word order, see *GEA* 296.

[34] The Ionian stater appeared only at the end of the century, as the equivalent of two shekels (3.80:5-6; *TAD* 4.5:3, 4.6:7).

[35] The restoration of *ʾnh*, however, is problematic; see *GEA* 240, 292-293.

[36] The verb *kly* was quite malleable — "detain" a suspected party (as here), "withhold" salary (*TAD* A3.3:6), and "restrain" a builder (3.59:6-7, 9-10). For the verb form, see *GEA* 28, 127-128, 139, 153, 264.

[37] The word *ṣwt* occurs only here in our collection; see *GEA* 219. For Eg. and Akk. cognates, see Dion 1982:556.

[38] Because of the broken context, the syntax of *nzq*, "damage" is uncertain; see *DNWSI* 724 who appear to follow Cowley. It may be understood as an objective genitive on the basis of biblical analogies ("the damage caused to the king[s]").

[39] The word *kpr* should be understood in the same syntactical mode as the preceding *nzq*, that is as an objective genitive, "the compensation due Djeḥo"; differently *DNWSI* 531.

[40] Are these two the same as Djeḥo and Ḥor, the servants of Anani (3.48:4)?

[41] Only here is the arrival date of incoming letters recorded; see *GEA* 221-222 for the date formula. The date at the end of the document is usually that of dispatch (see *EPE* 109, n. 31). For the verb form, see *GEA* 101, 279.

[42] Only here is the common name *ydnyh* spelled with an *aleph* (*yʾdnyh*) leading to the explanation that it is an Aramaization of *yʾznyh*, "May YH hear"; *GEA* 4, 34.

REFERENCES

Text, translations and studies: *DAE*; Dion 1982; *EPE*; *GEA*; Hinz; *KAI*; Kornfeld; Lindenberger 1994; Porten 1968; *TAD* A4.2.

RECOMMENDATION TO AID TWO BENEFACTORS (3.48)

(Late 5th Century BCE)

Bezalel Porten

This bipartite letter of recommendation (Cairo J. 43472 [*TAD* A4.3]) set forth in the first half the benefit that Djeḥo and Ḥor had bestowed upon the writer, the scribe and leader Mauziah (lines 3-5), and in the second half recommended that upon their arrival at Elephantine they be handsomely reimbursed (lines 5-11). The Troop Commander of Elephantine arrested Mauziah in Abydos, either for complicity or negligence regarding the theft of a precious stone. Through the strenuous intercession of two Egyptian servants of Anani, and with divine assistance, his release was secured. As the servants headed for Elephantine, Mauziah wrote to Jedaniah and his colleagues that they should be well taken care of. He assured the leaders that the expenditure should not be viewed as a loss since it would ultimately be covered by the House of Anani. The letter revealed the antagonism that the arrival of Hananiah had aroused among the Khnum priesthood. Though himself among the community's leaders, Mauziah deferentially addressed them as "my lords" and penned a double *Salutation* (lines 1-3).

Internal Address

(Recto) (1)To my lords Jedaniah,[1] Uriah[2] and the priests[3] of YHW the God, Mattan son of Jashobiah[4] (and) Berechiah[5] son of [...]; (2)your servant Mauziah.

Salutations

The welfare of [my] lords [may the God of Heaven[a] seek after abundantly at all times and] in favor may you be before (3)the God of Heaven.[6]

Report

And now,[7] when Vidranga the Troop Commander[8] arrived[9] at Abydos[10] he imprisoned me on account of[11] a[12] dyer's stone[13] which (4)they found stolen[14] in the hand of the merchants.[15] Finally, Djeḥo and Ḥor,[16] servants of Anani,[17] intervened[18] with Vidranga (5)and Ḥarnufe,[19] with the protection of the God of Heaven,[20] until they rescued me.[21]

Instructions

Now, behold,[22] they are coming[23] there to you. You,[24] look after[25] [b] them. (6)Whatever desire[26] [c] and thing[27] that Djeḥo (and) Ḥor shall seek from you — you,[28] stand before[29] [d] them so that[30] a bad thing (7)they shall not find about you.[31] To you it is known[32] [e] that Khnum[33] is against us since Hananiah has been in Egypt until now.[34] (8)And whatever

a Ezra 1:2, 5:11-12, 6:9-10, 7:12, 21, 23; Neh 1:4-5, 2:4, 20; 2 Chr 36:23; see also Dan 2:18-19, 37, 44
b 2 Kgs 5:6
c 1 Kgs 5:22-23
d Num 16:9; Deut 10:8; 2 Chr 29:11
e Ezra 4.12-13, 5:8; Dan 3:18

[1] See on 3.46:1 and *GEA* 252.

[2] He was among the addressees of 3.47 and his prepositioning to the priests suggests that he was one himself; but see *GEA* 319.

[3] The term *khn* (as distinct from *kmr*) was used to designate a Jewish priest, as in 3.51:1, 18; for the construction see *GEA* 221, also 317.

[4] Designated "Aramean, Syenian," this Jew was party to a fragmentary document of withdrawal (*TAD* B5.2:2).

[5] Of unknown patronymic, he was one of those reported to have been imprisoned in Elephantine (3.49:3).

[6] The Jewish scribe Mauziah (see *EPE* 194, n. 40) employed a Jewish version of the epistolary salutation as did his colleague Jedaniah (3.51:2, 27); contrast Hananiah in 3.46:1-2. The title "God of Heaven," occurring thrice here, was common at this time in Judah; for the form see *GEA* 222. A variant of the second blessing ("in favor be" [*lrḥmn hww*]; *GEA* 291) was also employed by Jedaniah writing to Bagavahya; here favor is to be before the God of Heaven, there before Darius and the princes. This twofold blessing (welfare and favor) is found only here and in the great petition, where it was augmented by two more blessings (3.51:2-3).

[7] See on *TAD* A2.1:4.

[8] Vidranga had been Troop Commander at least between 420 and 416 BCE, when he bore the additional title, Guardian of the Seventh (3.66:4-5, 3.67:2-3, 3.77:2). Apparently his father, Nafaina, held the position ca. 434/33 BCE (*TAD* A5.2:7). Sometime before 410 BCE Vidranga was promoted to Chief (see *EPE* 192, n. 11) and the position of Troop Commander passed on to his son, also named Nafaina (3.50:4, 3.51:5, 7). For the form, see *GEA* 220.

[9] For the construction "temporal reference + verb of motion," see 3.47:2 and 3.51:4-5. For the subject-verb word order following *kzy*, see *GEA* 300.

[10] Located about 370 km traveling distance from Elephantine, Abydos saw many visitors, including Arameans, who scrawled their names and prayers on the walls of the Osiris Temple (Lidzbarski 1915:93-116). For verb of motion plus complement of place, see *GEA* 269.

[11] *ᶜldbr*, written as one word; *GEA* 40.

[12] Aram. *ḥd*, "one" = indefinite article; see 3.50:5-6, 3.51:19; *EPE* 153, n. 8; *GEA* 177.

[13] For the literature on this term, written as one word (*ᵓbnṣrp*), see *DNWSI* 976; *GEA* 81, 218.

[14] For the construction with object complement, see *GEA* 271; for *gnyb*, ibid., 119.

[15] Was Mauziah guarding a caravan and accused of connivance in the theft or malfeasance in the performance of his duties? This is the only place in our documents to mention merchants (*rklyᵓ*), though a witness to a grain delivery contract, apparently drawn up at Tahpanhes, bore the trade name Rochel (son of Abihu) (*TAD* B4.4:20).

[16] Were these the same as Djeḥo and Ḥori involved in the previous letter (3.47:14-15)?

[17] Was this fellow, so well known that his patronym need not be given, the Scribe and Chancellor who issued the order in Arsames' name to repair a boat (*TAD* A6.2:23)?

[18] For the verb *ᶜštdrw*, see *GEA* 26, 118, 189.

[19] Djeḥo, Ḥor, and Ḥarnufe are Eg. names.

[20] In his famous Bisitun Inscription, Darius I attributed each of his victories to the help and "protection" (*ṭll*) of Ahuramazda (*TAD* C2.1:10, 16, 42). For the form *bṭll*, see *GEA* 87.

[21] For the clause with *ᶜd* see *GEA* 333; for shafel *šzbwny*, see ibid., 116.

[22] Here, as in 3.47:7, a double introduction leads into an urgent request. See *GEA* 329.

[23] A similar construction ("PN is coming to you; take care of him") is found in a letter by Arsames (*TAD* A6.9:2) and in the biblical letter of the King of Aram to the King of Israel.

[24] For the pronoun before the imperative see on 3.46:3; also line 6 and 8 below.

[25] The expression "look after" (*ḥzy ᶜl*) occurs esp. with children as object (see *EPE* 98, n. 32).

[26] Aram. *ṣbw* = Heb. *ḥpṣ*; cf. the correspondence between Solomon and Hiram.

[27] Aram. *mlh* = Heb. *dbr*, "word," attenuated to "thing;" *GEA* 174.

[28] See note 24 above.

[29] To "stand before" is to serve. For a New Testament-Peshitta parallel, see Dion 1982:567.

[30] An imperative verb followed by the particles "so that" (*kn kzy*), in the sense of "lest something bad happen," is a standard epistolary construction (*TAD* A6.10:2, 6, 6.15:11); further, *GEA* 197, 312, 332.

[31] "Not to find something bad/damaging" is a positive statement; see 3.50:2. For the object-verb word order in categorical negations, see *GEA* 302-303.

[32] Usually found in the form "be it known to you," this statement always introduces a warning or a negative report (*TAD* A6.10:8-10). In one of the Arsames letters the warning follows upon the command to carry out the "desire" concerning his estate (*TAD* A6.8).

[33] Depicted as the ram god, Khnum along with Sati (3.65:5) and Anukis constituted the local divine triad. He was known as "Khnum, (the) great, lord of Elephantine" (*EPE* 374) and his priests and functionaries figured prominently in the demotic documents (*EPE* 277-338). See further 3.50:3, 3.51:5, where the name is written "Khnub."

[34] In some unknown fashion, Hananiah, presumably the one who arrived with the Passover Letter (3.46), aroused the ire of the Khnum priests, who ultimately brought about the destruction of the Jewish Temple (3.51); see discussion in Porten 1968:128-133, 279-282.

you will do[35] for Ḥor, for your [... [36] y]ou are doing. Ḥor is a servant of Hananiah.[37] You, lavish[38] from our houses (Verso) [(9)]goods. As much as[39] your hand finds[40] give him. It is not a loss for you.[41] For that (reason) I send (word) to you.[42] He [(10)]said to me, "Send a letter ahead of me." [...] If there is much loss, there is backing for it[43] in the house of Anani. Whatever you do [(11)] for him shall not be hidden[f] from Anani.[44]

f Gen 18:17

External Address

[(12)]To (*sealing*) my lords Jedaniah, Uriah and the priests, and the Jews;[45] your ser[vant] (*cord*) Mauziah son of Nathan.

[35] For object *mh zy* preceding imperfect verb, see *GEA* 172, 196, 303, 334.

[36] Lindenberger 1994:59-60 restored *lb*[*ᵓš*]*km*, "for your h[urt]." While graphically possible, this restoration and interpretation are highly improbable. If Ḥor had gone to great lengths to rescue Mauziah from prison, why would he be a threat to the Elephantine Jews?! Some positive word must have filled the gap.

[37] Thc relationships become confused; above (line 4) Ḥor, along with Djeḥo, was described as a "servant of Anani." Perhaps Hananiah worked out of the office of Anani. For the construction, see *GEA* 291.

[38] For the various interpretations of this difficult verb (*zwlw*), see *DNWSI* 307.

[39] For the compound preposition + conjunction *lqbl zy*, see *GEA* 87, 94, 332.

[40] I.e. as much as you are able to expend. This idiom (*ydkm mhškḥh* = Heb. *tmṣᵓ yd* [Lev 12:8]) occurs only here. The other idiom in these letters is *tmṭᵓ yd*, "(your) hand reaches." Like the idiom here, so the one in the Makkibanit letters is juxtaposed with the determination to "do" something for someone (*TAD* A2.4:4).

[41] The pronoun *hw* is of indefinite antecedent; see *GEA* 155. For the position of *lkm*, see ibid., 286 and for the negation ibid., 323.

[42] For the word order, see *GEA* 292.

[43] For the various suggestions on the meaning of this unique construction (*śymᵓ śym ᵓḥrwhy*), see *DNWSI* 1129. The idea seems to be that Anani will reimburse you.

[44] A significant "deed" by one of two related parties will not/should not be hidden from the other party. For the sentence construction, see *GEA* 169, 304, 316; for the verb *ytkswn*, ibid., 118, 142.

[45] The *External Address* was often more expansive than the *Internal* one. Here the Jews were also addressed because they were expected to give of their property for the benefit of Ḥor. For the construction, see *GEA* 319.

REFERENCES

Text, translations and studies: Dion 1982; *EPE*; *GEA*; Kornfeld 1978; Lidzbarski 1915; Lindenberger 1994; Porten 1968; *TAD*.

REPORT OF IMPRISONMENT OF JEWISH LEADERS (3.49)
(Last Decade of 5th Century BCE)

Bezalel Porten

Opening and closing with a pagan *Salutation*, a private letter (P. Berlin 13456 + Cairo J. 43476 [*TAD* A4.4]) from the otherwise unknown Islaḥ, son of Nathan, to an unknown son of Gaddul reported the fateful incarceration of several men in Elephantine and the seizure and imprisonment of six Jewish women and five Jewish leaders at the gate in Thebes. The men were apparently implicated in an invasion of private property and theft therefrom. They were forced to evacuate the property, return the goods, and pay a hefty fine of 1200 shekels. Hopefully, there would be no further repercussions (lines 7-9) but there was no word on their release from prison. Was this act on the part of the Jews part of their ongoing conflict with the Khnum priesthood (see 3.48:7) which eventuated in the destruction of the Jewish Temple at their instigation (3.51:5-6)? Perhaps the priests exploited the imprisonment of the whole Jewish leadership in Thebes to consummate their plot.

Internal Address

(Recto) [(1)][To my brother PN, your brother Islaḥ.[1]

Salutations

It is well for me here].[2] May the gods[3] seek after your welfare at all times.

Report I

And now,[4] [... [(2)] ...] PN son of PN went[5] to Syene and did/made ... [... [(3)] ...

Report II

Behold, these are the names[6] of the men wh]o were

[1] The writer's full name is preserved in the *External Address* but only the patronym remains of the recipient. It was not scribal practice to give the full name in the *Internal Address*.

[2] To fill in the missing space this *Salutation* has been restored here (see *EPE* 93, n. 5).

[3] For the form *ᵓlhyᵓ*, see above 3.46, note 7.

[4] See on 3.46:2.

[5] For verbs of motion at the beginning of a letter see 3.47:2, 3.48:3, 3.51:5 and *EPE* 107, n. 6.

[6] Letters often include lists of names, each usually followed by the notation *šmh*, lit. "his name" = "by name," and the numeral stroke, and concluding with a numerical total (3.53:1-5; *TAD* A4.6:13-15; 6.3:3-5, 6.7:3-5).

imprisoned in [Ele]phantine: Berechia,[7] Hose[a, ... (4) ...], Pakhnum.[8]

Report III

Behold,[9] this is[10] the names of the women[11] who were f[ound at the gate (5)in Thebes[12] and seized[13] as p]risoners:[14]

Rami, wife of Hodo,
Esereshut, wife of Hosea,
Pallul, wife of Islaḥ,
Reia, [wife/daughter of PN],
(6)Tubla, daughter of Meshullam (and) Kavla her sister.[15]

Report IV

Behold the names of the men who were found at the gate in Thebes and were seized[16] [as prisoners]:

(7)Jedania, son of Gemariah,[17]
Hosea, son of Jathom,[18]
Hosea, son of Nattum,[19]
Haggai, his brother,[20]
Ahio, son of Micai[ah.[21]

They left][22] (8)the houses into which they had broken in[23] at Elephantine and the goods which they took they surely[24] returned[25] to their owners.[26] However, they mentioned[27] to [their] owners [silver], (9)120 *karsh*.[28] May another decree no more be (delivered) to them here.[29]

Greetings

Greetings, your house and your children until the gods[30] let [me] behold[31] [your face in peace].[32]

External Address

(Verso) (10)[To (*sealing*) my brother PN son of] Gaddul,[33] your broth[er] Islah son of Nathan.[34]

---

[7] Probably the same person as in 3.48:1.

[8] Was he Jewish, despite his Eg. name, like all the other arrested parties? A name list of this time records one Ḥanan, son of Pakhnum (*TAD* C4.6:5).

[9] This word (*hʾ*) is regularly used in contracts to introduce the list of house neighbors, both with (as here) and without (line 6) a following demonstrative pronoun (see *EPE* 160, n. 21; *GEA* 289, 329).

[10] I.e. these are. The non-congruence of number in the title of lists is common (see *EPE* 160, n. 21; *GEA* 167, 284, 287-288).

[11] For the mismatch between form (*šm*; *ʾnth*) and grammatical gender (*šmht*; *nšyʾ*), see *GEA* 72-73, 75.

[12] See 3.47:6.

[13] For the verbal combination *ʾsr-ʾḥd*, see also *TAD* A4.6:16.

[14] Lindenberger 1994:70 observed, "The word 'gate' may refer to a law court. If so, we may translate, '... who were tried at the court in Thebes, and were put in prison.'" *Interpret* perhaps, but hardly *translate*.

[15] Of the six female names, three were Heb. (Rami, Pallul, Kavla [< Kaviliah, "Hope in YH"]), one or two were Aram. (Reia [*TAD* A2.3:1, 2.4:3] and perhaps Tubla [< *Tubliah, "Return to YH"]), and one was Eg. (Esereshut). Only the name Reia appears among the forty or so female names in the contemporary Collection Account (*TAD* C3.15:89). For the construction, see *GEA* 249.

[16] For the verb form, see *GEA* 16, 117-118, 124.

[17] He was the head of the Jewish community and the main correspondent in these letters; see above, note 3 on 3.46:1. For the abnormal spelling of his name with final *aleph* instead of *he*, see *GEA* 20.

[18] Appearing here second, he was listed fourth among five in the subsequent petition (3.53:4). Written Osea, he appeared as third in a list from ca. 420 BCE along with Haggai, son of Nattun, there first and in our letter fourth (*TAD* C4.3:1, 3). As Hoshaiah, son of Jathom, he appeared twice as a witness, in 434 BCE (3.73:24) and 404 BCE (3.78:23-24).

[19] Here third, he was fifth in the petition (3.53:5) and one of the contributors in the Collection Account (*TAD* C3.15:50). The scribe misspelled his patronym under the influence of the preceding name Jathom, writing Nattum instead of Nattun.

[20] Haggai, son of Nattun, appears in a contemporary name list (*TAD* C4.4:1).

[21] A Micaiah, son of Ahio, was witness in 451 BCE (3.70:12) and 427 BCE (3.74:17).

[22] If they returned the goods they had taken, then we may assume that they withdrew from the houses they had occupied and some such word as *šbq*, "leave, abandon" is needed to restore the gap.

[23] The expression *ʿll b-* (as distinct from *ʿl l-*, "enter into") has the meaning "break into" (3.51:9; *TAD* B7.2:4, 8 and perhaps *TAD* A6.7:7).

[24] For the particle *ʾm*, see *GEA* 338.

[25] For the afʿel form of the verb *ʾtbw*, see *GEA* 114-115, 131; for the word order, ibid., 302.

[26] One of the "Arsames" letters reported a complaint entered against a steward for misappropriation of property and the threat of monetary penalty if the property not be returned (verb *htb* as here [*TAD* A6.15:8-12]). For variation in the word for "owners," see *GEA* 24.

[27] For the spelling *dkrw*, see *GEA* 5.

[28] This may refer to a promise of reparations. One hundred and twenty karsh was the equivalent of twenty dowries, worth sixty shekels each.

[29] The meaning of this sentence is not quite certain. It seems to express the hope that the worst is over. The translation of Lindenberger 1994:61 ("There is no need for any further orders to be given here concerning them.") is off the mark.

[30] See above 3.46, note 7.

[31] For the form with the energic *nun*, see *GEA* 107, 146.

[32] This concluding *Greeting* forms an inclusion with the opening *Salutation* and employed a term (*ḥzh*, "to behold") frequently used therein (see *EPE* 90, n. 6 and the restoration of *TAD* 3.5:8).

[33] Two persons have Gaddul as father at the end of the century — the well attested Islaḥ (3.67:19; 3.76:44; *TAD* 4.5:2) and Menahem (3.66:17).

[34] He appears only here.

REFERENCES

Text, translations and studies: *EPE*; *GEA*; Lindenberger 1994; *TAD*.

PETITION FOR RECONSTRUCTION OF TEMPLE(?) (DRAFT) (3.50)

(Last Decade of 5th Century BCE)

Bezalel Porten

This letter (Strasbourg Aram. 2 [*TAD* A4.5]) was written not in a single vertical column, like the other letters, but in two parallel horizontal columns on the recto and a single vertical column on the verso. An estimated three lines are missing at the top and bottom of each column. Writing to an unknown official, the Jews protested their loyalty at the time of the (recent or earlier?) Egyptian rebellion (lines 2-4). In the summer of 410 BCE, when Arsames left to visit the king, the Khnum priests bribed Vidranga to allow partial destruction of a royal storehouse to make way for a wall (lines 4-5), apparently the ceremonial way leading to the shrine of the god, as reported in the contracts of Anani (3.78:8-9; 3.79:4). Furthermore, the priests stopped up a well that served the forces during mobilization (lines 6-8). Inquiry undertaken by the judges, police, and intelligence officials would confirm the facts as herein reported (lines 8-10). The very fragmentary column on the verso referred to Temple sacrifices and included a three-fold petition, apparently for protection and the Temple's reconstruction (lines 11-24).

The subject-object-verb word order (lines 1, 8), a pattern typical of Akkadian, was standard in the official petitions (see 3.51:6-7, 15; 3.53:12) and in the Arsames correspondence.[1]

(Recto)(Column 1)

[approximately three lines missing]

Loyalty

(1)... *we grew/increased*, detachments[2] [a] of the Egyptians rebelled.[3] We,[4] our posts did not leave (2)(erasure: and anything of) damage[5] [b] was not found in us.

Plot[6]

In year 14 of Darius the [ki]ng,[7] when our lord Arsames (3)had gone to the king,[8] this is the evil act[9] which the priests[10] [c] of Khnub the god[10] [di]d[12] in Elephantine the fortress[13] (4)in agreement[14] with Vidranga who was Chief[15] here: Silver and goods they gave him?[16]

Demolition and Construction

There is part (5)of the *barley-house*[17] of the king which is in Elephantine the fortress[18] — they demolished[19] [d] (it) and a[20] wall [they] built[21] [in] the midst[22] of the fortress of Elephantine ....

[at least three lines missing]

a Num 2:2-3, 10, 17-18, 25, 31, 34
b Ezra 4:22
c 2 Kgs 23:5; Hos 10:5; Zeph 1:4
d Exod 34:13; Deut 7:5; 12:3; Judg 2:2; 6:28; 30-32; 2 Kgs 10:27; 11:18; 23:7, 15; 17; 2 Chr 33:3; 34:7

---

[1] See Folmer 1995:525, 533-534; *GEA* 307-308.

[2] The word *dgl* was the standard term to refer to a military detachment, whether of Jews, Arameans, or Egyptians (see further *EPE* 152, n. 5), whether in Elephantine or Saqqarah (*TAD* B8.6:8-9). For the genitive construction, see *GEA* 222-223, 231; for word order *GEA* 301.

[3] It is not clear whether or not these were locally stationed troops. The Arsames correspondence makes frequent reference to "troubles," "unrest," and "rebelling" (*TAD* A6.7:6, 6.10:1, 4, 6.11:2) and we do not know whether the account in our letter refers to the same events and whether these were recent or went back to the period after the death of Artaxerxes I in 424 BCE; Porten 1968:279. For the subject-verb word order, see *GEA* 299-300.

[4] The disjunctive personal pronoun is used for contrast; *GEA* 157.

[5] For the possible nuances of this word, see *EPE* 108, n. 21; for the construction, see *GEA* 172.

[6] The same tale, in slightly different words, is repeated in the community's Petition to Bagavahya of Jerusalem (3.51:4-5). There the focus is exclusively on the destruction of the Temple; here it is on the partial destruction of the royal storehouse (line 5), the stopping up of a well (lines 6-8), and possibly the destruction of the Temple (lines 11-24).

[7] This was prior to the summer of 410 BCE (see 3.51:4). For the date formula, see *GEA* 91; for the title, *GEA* 250.

[8] No reason is given; perhaps to deliver a periodic report; also in 3.51:4.

[9] Aram. *dwškrtᵓ* < Old Persian **duškrta-* (Hinz 1975:90); for the sentence construction, see *GEA* 287-288.

[10] The term for priest is *kmr*, reserved in Heb. and our texts for pagan functionaries (3.51:5), as distinct from *khn*, the Jewish priest (3.48:1, 3.51:1, 18). Note the spelling Khnub for Khnum here and in 3.51:5.

[11] See 3.48:7, 3.51:5.

[12] For the subordinate clause introduced by *zy*, see *GEA* 300.

[13] For the word order, see *GEA* 249.

[14] Aram. *hmwnyt* < Old Persian **ham-au-nīta-* (Shaul Shaked); also 3.51:5.

[15] For title see on 3.48:3 and *EPE* 192, n. 9; for construction of the clause, see *GEA* 169, 178, 291.

[16] For the construction of this sentence, see *GEA* 264-265, 302.

[17] Aram. *ywdnᵓ* is an Old Persian loanword, probably **yau-dāna-* (Shaul Shaked). It is likely that this was part of the building known alternately as "house of the king" and "treasury of the king" (see 3.81:4, 6). Elsewhere, these two units appear to be distinct (*TAD* B4.3:13, 15-16, 4.4:12, 14). Perhaps one was a subdivision of the other (see *EPE* 258, n. 13). The "treasury of the king" lay on the eastern boundary of Anani's house (3.72:9, 3.75:6, 3.79:3-4). For the genitive construction see *GEA* 220.

[18] For construction of this clause with double *zy*, see *GEA* 245.

[19] The same word (*ndš*) is used for the destruction of the Elephantine Temple, which was razed to the ground (3.51:8-10; 3.52:6). It occurs in Aram. only in these texts (*DNWSI* 720) and is akin to Heb. *ntṣ* a standard word for the destruction of sacred sites.

[20] For the indefinite article, see 3.48:3.

[21] This was probably the "protecting (wall)" which the Egyptians built on Anani's eastern boundary to give access to the "house of the shrine of the god" which they had built earlier on his northern boundary (see on 3.78:8-9, 3.79:3-5).

[22] The word *bmnṣyᶜt* has been designated a "pseudo-preposition"; *GEA* 87.

(Column 2)

Report of Damage

(6)And now, that wall (stands) built in the midst of the fortress.[23] There is a[24] well[25] which is built[26] (7)with[in] the f[or]tress and water it does not lack to give the troop drink[27] so that whenever[28] they would be *garrisoned*[29] (there), (8)in[30] [th]at well the water[31] they would drink.[32] Those priests of Khnub,[33] that well they stopped up.[34]

Confirmation

If (9)it be made (8)known[35] (9)from[36] the judges,[37] overseers[38] and hearers[39] who are appointed[40] in the province of Tshetres,[41] (10)it will be [*known*] to our lord[42] in accordance with this[43] which we say.[44]

Moreover, separated are we[45] ...

e Lev 2:8; Isa 1:13; Jer 17:26

f Esth 5:4, 8; 8:5; Ezra 5:17

g Dan 3:29; 4:3; 6:27; Ezra 4:19; 5:17; 6:8, 11; 7:13, 21

[approximately three lines missing]

(Verso)

Spoliation

(11)[...]*d/rḥpny*ᵓ which are in Elephantine [the] fo[rtress ... (12) ...] we grew/increased [... (13) ...] was not found[46] in [... (14) ...] to bring[47] meal-offer[ing[48] *e* ... (15)...] to make there for YHW [the] G[od[49] ... (16) ...] *herein* ... [... (17) ...] but a *brazier*[50] [... (16) ...] the *fittings*[51] they took (and) [made (them) their] own[52] [...].

Threefold Petition

(19)[I]f to our lord it is abundantly good ... [..., (20) ...] we from/of the troop [...] (21)[If to] our lord it is good,[53] *f* may [an order] be issued[54] *g* [... (22)...] we. If to [our] l[ord it is good, ... (23) ...]

[23] Thematically, this sentence ("wall built") appears to adjoin directly the one in line 5 before the papyrus break. Papyrologically, however, as evidenced by the broken right margin on the verso, several lines intervened.

[24] For the indefinite article see note 20 above. The feminine adjective reveals the gender of the noun; *GEA* 72-73.

[25] Spelled here historically with medial *aleph* (*b*ᵓ*r*), it is twice written without *aleph* just below (*br*ᵓ [line 8]); *GEA* 22.

[26] The passive participle (*bnyh*) is used to indicate a state; *GEA* 139, 201. For discussion of the relative clause, see *GEA* 169.

[27] For the haphᶜel infinitive *lhšqy*ᵓ see *GEA* 109, 142; for syntax of the clause, see *GEA* 208-209, 308, 323.

[28] For the resultative *kzy* clause, see *GEA* 332-333.

[29] Appearing here and elsewhere (*TAD* A6.7:6) in a military context, *hnd(y)z* is an Old Persian loanword (**handiza*-); Hinz 1975:116. It is used not only of the troop as a whole but also of an individual (3.64:4).

[30] I.e. from that well.

[31] For the sequence *myn*, "water—*my*ᵓ (line 7), "the water," see *GEA* 180.

[32] For the object-verb word order, see *GEA* 302.

[33] For the syntactical structure of this phrase (a + b + [c]), see *GEA* 237, n. 980, 238.

[34] There is no indication whether this act was required by the building process of the Khnum priests or whether it was antagonistic against the Persian garrison.

[35] For this Old Persian loan word (ᵓ*zd*ᵓ < *azda*-, pass. part. "known"), see Hinz 1975:52; *DNWSI* 25; *GEA* 33, 370.

[36] I.e "by." The preposition *mn* here introduces the agent, not the object, of the inquiry; cf. the expression *mny yhyb*, "given from me" and see *GEA* 202 ("officialese"); *DNWSI* 25 (differently, 652) and the examples cited under No. 6 on p. 654; Lindenberger 1994:63 translates differently.

[37] "Judge" appears regularly in the contracts as one of the three parties before whom a complainant might bring a suit or register a complaint, the other two being lord and prefect (3.61:13, 24; etc.). In a case involving an inheritance they are called "judges of the king" (*TAD* B5.1:3) and in a petition seeking redress of grievances they are "judges of the province" (*TAD* A5.2:4, 7). When named, they are always Persian — Paisana (*TAD* A3.8:2); Bagadana (*TAD* A6.1:5-6), Damidata (3.60:6), Bagafarna and Nafaina (*TAD* B5.2:6) — and once Babylonian — Mannuki (*TAD* B5.2:6). They are here called upon to investigate not a private matter but one tantamount to civil disorder.

[38] Aram. *typty*ᵓ is an Old Persian loanword < **tipati*-; Hinz 1975:236; Porten, 1968:50; *GEA* 34, n. 165, 64, 373. They were seventh and last in a list of officials that began with the satraps (Dan 3:2-3).

[39] Aram. *gwšky*ᵓ is an Old Persian loanword < **gaušaka*-; Hinz 1975:105-106; Porten 1968:50-51. Known in classical sources as the "king's ears," they were intelligence agents.

[40] For this passive verb, see *GEA* 120.

[41] Aram. *tštrs* < Eg. *t*ᵓ*-št-rsy*, "the southern district," abbreviating *T*ᵓ*-št*ᵓ*-rsy-Niw.t*, "The district south of Thebes," i.e. the Thebaid (Malinine 1953: ##9:6, 18:5; Porten, 1968:42-43). The Persian and Ptolemaic demotic documents call the Chief of the province "He of Tshetres" (*EPE* 311, n. 1, 375, n. 10).

[42] The unknown recipient of the letter.

[43] For use of the masculine pronoun (*znh*), see *GEA* 177.

[44] Or "have said"; *GEA* 293.

[45] For the participle-pronoun word order, see *GEA* 292.

[46] For metathesis in the verb form ᵓ*štkḥ*, see *GEA* 25-26.

[47] For the haphᶜel verb *lhytyh*, see *GEA* 109, 123, 142.

[48] This extremely fragmentary section employs words that applied to the Jewish Temple or recurred in the correspondence for its reconstruction; for meal-offering, see 3.51:21, 25; 3.52:9; 3.53:11. The Heb. word for "bring" (*hby*ᵓ) is used in conjunction with meal-offering.

[49] In the subsequent correspondence, the word "make" (ᶜ*bd*) is used for the sacrifices (3.51:21-22).

[50] Aram. ᶜ*trwdn* is an Old Persian loanword whose first element is *ātr*, but whose second element is in dispute; see Hinz 1975:49; *GEA* 370. *DAE* saw it as the fire spot for burning all the flammable items, including the *fittings* (line 18), torn away during the Temple's destruction (cf. 3.51:10-12). But our fragmentary context implies that the *fittings* were taken as spoil.

[51] For this Old Persian loanword (ᵓ*šrn*ᵓ), see *EPE* 117, n. 6.

[52] To "take and make one's own" was a recurrent idiom for appropriating stolen goods (3.51:12-13; *TAD* B7.2:6).

[53] "If to PN it is good" is a standard Heb. and Aram. formula introducing a petition (3.51:23; *TAD* A5.2:9; 6.3:5, 6.7:8, 6.13:2). It is striking that it occurs here three times in rapid succession. For the grammatical construction, see *GEA* 289 (where incorrectly cited as A4.5:7).

[54] For this phrase, see *EPE* 114, n. 8; for the verb form *ytśym*, see *GEA* 118, 132.

they [*pro*]tect the things[55] which[56] [... (24) ...] the [*Temp*]le of ours which they demolished to [*build* ...].[57]

[55] For the indefinite pronoun *mnd*ᶜ*m*, see *GEA* 59-60, 172-174.
[56] If correctly restored, this would be a plea for "police protection."
[57] The restoration is conjectural and is based on the text in the subsequent Petition (3.51:23-25).

REFERENCES

Text, translations and studies: *DAE*; *DNWSI*; *EPE*; Folmer 1995; *GEA*; Hinz 1975; Lindenberger 1994; Malinine 1953; Porten 1968; *TAD*.

REQUEST FOR LETTER OF RECOMMENDATION (FIRST DRAFT) (3.51)
(25 November, 407 BCE)

Bezalel Porten

Historically, this is the most significant of all the Elephantine Aramaic texts (P. Berlin 13495 [*TAD* A4.7]). It is a well-balanced, carefully constructed bipartite petition (*Report* and *Petition*) addressed by Jedaniah, the priests, and all the Jews of Elephantine to Bagavahya, governor of Judah. It opens with a *Fourfold Salutation* (welfare, favor, longevity, happiness and strength) and concludes with a *Threefold Blessing* (sacrifice, prayer, merit). The *Report* has three parts: *Demolition* (lines 4-13), *Precedents* (lines 13-14), *Aftermath* (lines 15-22). The *Demolition* delineates the plot hatched between the Egyptian Khnum priests and the local Persian authorities, the Chief Vidranga and his son the Troop Commander Nafaina.[1] The *Precedents* were twofold: Egyptian Pharaohs authorized the Temple's construction and the Persian conqueror approved of its existence. The *Aftermath* relates the situation following the destruction: punishment of the perpetrators in response to prayer and fasting; silence of all Jerusalem authorities in the face of earlier petition; continued communal mourning; cessation of cult. The *Petition* sets forth the *Threefold Request* (take thought, regard, write) which, if successful, would lead, as indicated, to a *Threefold Blessing*. The letter concludes with a twofold *Addendum* and *Date*. The scribe was well-skilled in Aram. rhetorical style and cognizant of all the appropriate rhetorical formulae. His single-line message is that the perpetrator was "wicked" while the Jews were "men of goodness." Curiously, the first eleven lines were written by one scribe (Scribe A) while a second scribe (Scribe B) began writing in line 12 in the middle of a sentence and continued until the end of the letter. He also wrote the second draft (*TAD* A4.8), which was a distinct effort to polish the style and perfect the orthography.[2] The two versions were stored together and only the third dispatched to Jerusalem. A semiological analysis seeks to trace the "script" back to Neo-Assyrian complaints and petitions.[3] Linguistically, the document displays features typical of Akkadian, such as subject-object-verb word order (lines 6-7, 14, 15) and its language has been designated "Official Aramaic of the Eastern type."[4] Bare traces of the Temple itself may have been uncovered in recent excavations.[5]

Internal Address
(Recto)(1)To our lord[6] Bagavahya[7] governor of Judah,[8] [a] your servants Jedaniah[9] and his colleagues the priests[10] who are in Elephantine the fortress.[11]

a Hag 1:1, 14; 2:2, 21; Ezra 5:14

Fourfold Salutation
The welfare (2)of our lord may the God of Heaven seek after abundantly[12] at all times,[13] and favor may He grant you[14] before Darius the king[15] (3)and the

[1] For an attempt to explain the point of view of Vidranga, see Briant 1996.
[2] Porten 1998
[3] Fales 1987:463-469.
[4] Kutscher 1977:105-106; Folmer 1995:533; *GEA* 307-308.
[5] von Pilgrim 1999:142-145.
[6] For the sequence "lord"-"servant" see on 3.47:1.
[7] The name is Old Persian, but the person, proximate or subsequent successor to Nehemiah, may have been Jewish and thus not identical with Bagoas, strategos of Artaxerxes II, who imposed a seven-year fine on the sacrificial cult after the high priest Johanan murdered his brother Jeshua (Jesus) in the Temple (Josephus, *Ant.* XI.7.1, 297-301).
[8] One of 127 provinces in the Persian empire (Esth 1:1; Ezra 5:8).
[9] See on 3.46:1.
[10] For the term *khn* see 3.48:1. In the Passover Letter, Jedaniah was accompanied by "his colleagues the Jewish Troop" (3.46:1).
[11] A prepositional phrase which indicates location is often introduced by *zy*, "who, which"; *GEA* 244.
[12] The addition of this adverb of quantity (*GEA* 241,276) occurred only occasionally in the Jewish letters (*TAD* A3.5:1, 3.9:1; 3.48:1), modifying *š*ᵓ*l*, but regularly in the Arsham correspondence, where it modified *hwšr* (*TAD* A6.3-7, 16).
[13] For the word order object-subject-verb, see *GEA* 307.
[14] The verb form (*yšymnk*) is indicative (imperfect with energic nun) even though the meaning is jussive; see *GEA* 145, 198-200.
[15] For this double blessing, see on 3.48:2-3.

princes[16] [b] more than now[17] a thousand times,[18] [c] and long life[19] [d] may He give you,[20] and happy and strong[21] may you be[22] at all times.[23]

Report

(4)Now,[24] your servant Jedaniah and his colleagues thus say:[25] [e]

Plot In the month of Tammuz, year 14 of Darius[26] the king,[f] when Arsames (5)left[27] and went to the king,[28] the priests[29] of Khnub the god[30] who (are) in Elephantine the fortress,[31] in agreement[32] with Vidranga[33] who (6)was (5)Chief here,[34] (said),[35] (6)saying:[36]

"The Temple[37] of YHW the God which is in Elephantine the fortress[38] [g] let them remove[39] from there."

Order Afterwards,[40] that[41] Vidranga, (7)the wicked,[42] [h] a letter sent[43] to Nafaina his son, who was Troop Commander[44] in Syene the fortress,[45] saying: "The Temple which is in Elephantine (8)the fortress let them demolish."[46]

Demolition

Afterwards, Nafaina led the Egyptians with the other troops.[47] They came to the fortress of Elephantine with their implements,[48] [i] (9)broke into[49] that Temple, demolished it[50] to the ground,[51] [j] and the pillars of stone[52] which were there — they

b Ezra 6:10; 7:23
c Deut 1:11; Dan 3:19
d 1 Kgs 3:14
e Gen 32:4
f Neh 12:22
g Ezra 4:24; 5:2, 17; 6:12, 7:16-17
h Esth 7:6
i Gen 27:3
j Isa 21:9; Amos 3:14; Ps 74:7

[16] Monarch and princes were often associated in letters.

[17] For this comparative statement, see *GEA* 187.

[18] An idiomatic expression where *ḥd* serves as a multiplicative; *GEA* 240-241

[19] The absolute state of this noun is always spelled with a single *yod* — *hyn*; *GEA* 37.

[20] Longevity was a standard blessing for royalty; for the Eg. Aram. corpus see *TAD* A1.1:2-3 (Adon Letter) (*COS* 3.54 below); C2.1:72 (Bisitun). According to rule, the indirect object (*lh*) follows the verb; here the direct object precedes it; *GEA* 308.309.

[21] This combination of happiness and strength appeared in other official letters (*TAD* A5.1:4, 5.3:2). Both adjectives are in the absolute state; *GEA* 178, 207.

[22] The first three verbs in this salutation are jussive ("may DN seek after, grant, give"), while the fourth is imperative (*hwy*, "be"), addressed directly to the recipient and following the predicate; *GEA* 199, 291.

[23] Not uncommon in Eg. letters (see EPE 57-58), such a fourfold *Salutation* in the Aram. letters was indicative of the writers' deep-felt needs.

[24] See on 3.46, note 9 ("And now").

[25] For this formula, see on 3.47:6; *GEA* 204, 293, 308.

[26] This would have been July 14-August 12, 410, when the weather at Elephantine was very hot.

[27] For the construction "temporal reference + verb of motion," see 3.47:2; 3.48:3. In a subordinate clause introduced by temporal *kzy* the word order is regularly subject-verb; *GEA* 299-300.

[28] See 3.50, note 10.

[29] For the term *kmr* see 3.50, note 8. It is they, and not Khnub/Khnum, who is in Elephantine. The construction is the same as that in line 6; *GEA* 245-246.

[30] The word *ᵓlhᵓ*, "the god," was added supralinearly; for the word order, see *GEA* 249, n. 1018. For the spelling Khnub, cf. 3.50:3.

[31] For Khnum and his priests see 3.48, note 33; for construction of the clause, see *GEA* 245-246.

[32] See 3.50, note 14.

[33] For Vidranga see on 3.48, note 8.

[34] See 3.48, note 8; *GEA* 178, 182, 291.

[35] The infelicitous formulation, omitting the verb, was corrected in the revised draft (*TAD* A4.8:5).

[36] For discussion of the particle *lm* as a marker of direct speech, see *GEA* 339.

[37] Aram. *ᵓgwrᵓ* < Akk. *ekurru* < Sum. É.KUR (Porten 1968:109-110).

[38] "The Temple ... fortress" was the full title; cf. "The Temple of God which is in Jerusalem." This parallel and the abridged clause in line 7 eliminate the ambiguity which might take YHW and not the Temple as being in Elephantine; *GEA* 245-246.

[39] Aram. *hᶜdy* = Heb. *hsyr*, used for the destruction of the high places in Judah (2 Kgs 18:4). The form is jussive; *GEA* 141.

[40] For this adverb, see *EPE* 174, n. 18.

[41] A demonstrative pronoun (usually *zk*) is regularly added to a common or proper noun upon its repetition; *GEA* 166.

[42] This pejorative epithet is reminiscent of that applied to the Jewish foe Haman. For alternate translations, see *GEA* 237.

[43] The written order, terse as it was, gave the act official sanction. For the construction, see *GEA* 270.

[44] Written as one word (*rbḥyl*), as often occurs when the two words "form a close grammatical or logical whole"; for full discussion, see *GEA* 40-42, 230.

[45] Father and son shared the civil and military rule over Aswan and its environs. Following the practice of papponymy, Vidranga gave his son the name of the latter's grandfather (*TAD* A5.2:7; 3.67:2); see Porten 1968:235-237. The construction of this clause is the same as that identifying Vidranga in line 6; in both cases the title is in the absolute state; *GEA* 178, 182, n. 816, 291.

[46] For the verb *ndš*, see 3.50, note 19.

[47] Were these the Arameans, Caspians, and Khwarezmians who were also stationed in the forts of Aswan? For a different translation and interpretation, see *GEA* 181, 272, 281 n. 1112, 284, 300 ("N. led the Egyptians [= Khnum priests] with the troop [under his command], others [as reinforcements]").

[48] Aram. *tly* appears also in an ostracon (*TAD* D7.7:6) and some would translate the word, "ax, pickax," as if it were a tool of destruction and not a weapon to gain forced entry and stand guard during the demolition process; *DNWSI* 1216. The revised version of our document substituted an unambiguous term for weapon (*zyn* [*TAD* A4.8:8]).

[49] For the nuance *ᶜll b-* with the meaning of "forced entry," see *GEA* 270.

[50] The asyndesis of four verbs (led, came, broke into, demolished) highlights the speed of a military operation; *GEA* 258. Contrast the syndetic construction in lines 9-13.

[51] Destruction "to the ground" of sancta, and other buildings, was a familiar biblical image.

[52] For the grammatical construction, see *GEA* 182, 223, 231.

smashed them.[53] Moreover,[54] it happened (that the) (10)five (9)gateways (10)of stone,[55] built of hewn stone,[56] [k] which were in that Temple, they demolished.[57] And their standing doors,[58] and the pivots[59] (11)of those doors, (of) bronze, and the roof[60] of wood of cedar[61] [m] — all (of these) which, with the rest[62] of the *fittings*[63] [n] and other (things),[64] which (12)were (11)there — (12)all (of these) with fire[65] they burned.[66] [o] But the basins of gold and silver[67] [p] and the (other) things[68] which were in that Temple — all (of these) they took (13)and made their own.[69]

k 1 Kgs 5:31; 1 Chr 22:2
m 1 Kgs 5:22; 6:15-17, 18, 20, 36
n Ezra 5:3, 9
o 2 Kgs 25:9
p Num 7:13-85; 1 Kgs 7:48-50; 2 Kgs 25:15; Ezra 1:7-11, 5:14-15, 6:5; Neh 7:69; Dan 5

Precedents

And from[70] the days of the king(s) of Egypt our fathers[71] had built[72] that Temple[73] in Elephantine the fortress[74] and when Cambyses entered[75] Egypt — (14)that Temple, built he found it.[76] And the temples of the gods of Egypt,[77] all (of them),[78] they overthrew,[79] but anything in that Temple one did not damage.[80]

Aftermath

Mourning I (15)And when (the) like(s of) this[81] had

[53] For the grammatical construction, see *GEA* 267.

[54] For this particle, see 3.47, note 17. It recurs a half-dozen times in this letter (lines 9, 17, 19, 21, 29, 30).

[55] These five gateways, outfitted with wooden doors, probably stood in an enclosure wall; see Porten 1968:110; for the grammatical construction, see *GEA* 182.

[56] Hewn stone was used in building the Jerusalem Temple. That the gateways alone were distinguished as being built of hewn stone may mean that the rest of the structure was of brick. For the grammatical construction, see *GEA* 223, 231, 272.

[57] For a derivation of √*ndš* from Arab. *nadasa*, "to throw down, bring to the ground," see *GEA* 7, n. 24.

[58] The gateways were fitted with wooden doors, as was the inner sanctum and hall of Solomon's Temple (1 Kgs. 6:31, 34-35). For an alternate translation ("gateways they demolished while their doors were still standing"), see *GEA* 294, 322. For the elision of a shin in *dšyhm*, see *GEA* 38.

[59] Usually rendered "hinges," this word (*ṣyryhm*) is best understood, with Lindenberger 1994:67, as pivots, cf. Akk. *ṣerru* (Kaufman 1974:96) and see Prov 26:14; Kelim 11:2; Yoma 39b ("pivots of the Temple doors"); Pesaḥim 36b where the term for "gatekeepers" is "pivot keepers" (reference of Sh. Safral). A communication of Cornelius Von Pilgrim (3 November, 2000), Director of the Swiss Mission at Elephantine, reads "In fact, in Egypt doorwings were never mounted with hinges. All doors known to me have sockets and pivots." For the grammatical construction (prolepsis), see *GEA* 233 with n. 963. My attention was first drawn to this problem by Dov Zlotnick.

[60] For retention of the third radical in *mṭll*, see *GEA* 134, n. 623.

[61] Cedar was an expensive wood imported from Lebanon (see *TAD* C3.7Gr2:10 et al.) and was the dominant wood in the Jerusalem sanctuary. Does the expanded form ʾ*qhn* (as against ʾ*qn* [*TAD* C 1.1:88]) imply a wood of quality (Joüon 1934:53-54)? For the scribal correction, see *GEA* 225, n. 941.

[62] The word "rest" implies that the doors, pivots and roof were all considered *fittings*. For the spelling of *šyryt* with *yod* rather than *aleph*, see *GEA* 24, 69.

[63] Aram. ʾ*šrn*ʾ < Old Persian **āčarna*- was a generalized term referring to all the materials required to finish a boat (*TAD* A6.2:5), a house (3.72:23), or a temple. Perhaps it referred here to the internal wainscoting (cf. 1 Kgs 6:15-30).

[64] Such as the altar.

[65] The infelicitous absolute ʾ*šh* was corrected in *TAD* A4.8:11 to the determinate *b*ʾ*št*ʾ (*GEA* 182).

[66] All flammable material was burned. Nebuchadnezzar put the Jerusalem Temple to the torch.

[67] By singling out for special mention the spoliation of gold and silver basins — common bronze vessels were not even mentioned — the petitioners hoped to strike a responsive chord in the hearts of the Jerusalem officials. Such vessels played a prominent role in Israel's cultic history, in the desert tabernacle, in the construction, destruction, and particularly the restoration of the Jerusalem Temple, and in popular lore.

[68] For the indefinite pronoun *mndʿm* in the determinate state ("something" > "thing") and the syntax of the clause, see *GEA* 59-60, 101, 168, 173, n. 782, 174.

[69] For this recurrent idiom, see 3.50:18. The syndetic structure (demolished and burned but took and made [lines 9-13]) serves to heighten the petitioners' outrage; *GEA* 258.

[70] I.e. during.

[71] For the form ʾ*bhyn*, see *GEA* 74.

[72] English past perfect is simply *bnw* in Aram.; *GEA* 193.

[73] If construction of the Jewish Temple was allowed by the native Eg. Saïte rulers before the Persian conquest of 525 BCE what right did the local Eg. priests have to destroy it?

[74] For clarification of the construction, see *GEA* 245, n. 1006.

[75] The language of the *Petition* was structured to declare that the Egyptians, who connived with the Persian Vidranga, "entered" the Jewish Temple forcefully (ʿ*ll b*- [line 9]) whereas the Persian conqueror Cambyses "entered" Egypt peacefully, as it were (ʿ*ll l*- [see *GEA* 270]). In fact, Cambyses had conquered Egypt after a hard-fought battle at Pelusium and a siege of Memphis (Hdt. III.10-13).

[76] For the grammatical construction, see *GEA* 271,314.

[77] For this phrase, see *GEA* 228 n. 950.

[78] An alternate rendering as adverb, "altogether" (*GEA* 248, 276) is less likley since this *kl* is one of four in this draft (also line 17, 22, 27) that is corrected to *kl*ʾ in the revised *TAD* A4.8:13, 16, 22, 26 (Porten 1998:234).

[79] Herodotus reported that Cambyses allegedly inflicted a mortal wound on the sacred Apis bull in Memphis after suffering military setbacks in Nubia and the oasis of Ammon (III.27-29). Modern scholars consider these atrocity tales either lies or gross exaggerations (Porten 1968:19-20). Such views, however, gained currency and evolved into the desecration reported here. For the grammatical construction, see *GEA* 302.

[80] If the Persian conqueror sanctioned the Jewish Temple, what right did the local Persian governor have to authorize its destruction? For the grammatical construction, see *GEA* 173, 266, n. 1068, 303.

[81] Aram. *kznh*; see *GEA* 166-167, 201 ("such"), 276, n. 1097 (alternately "thus"), 312-313.

been done (to us), we,[82] with our wives and our children, were wearing[83] sackcloth and fasting and praying[84] [q] to YHW, the Lord of Heaven,[85] [r] (16)who let us gloat over[86] [s] that Vidranga, the cur.[87] They removed the fetter[88] from his feet[89] and all goods which he had acquired[90] were lost.

Punishment And all persons (17)who sought evil[91] for that Temple, all (of them),[92] were killed and we gazed upon them?[93]

Appeal Moreover, before this, at the time that[94] this evil[95] (Verso) (18)was done[96] to us, a letter we sent (to) our lord,[97] and to Jehohanan[98] [t] the High Priest and his colleagues the priests[99] [u] who are in Jerusalem, and to Avastana the brother (19)of Anani[100] [v] and the nobles of the Jews.[101] [w] A[102] letter they did not send us.

Mourning II Moreover, from the month of Tammuz, year 14 of Darius the king (20)and until this day,[103] we have been wearing sackcloth and have been fasting;[104] [x] the wives of ours[105] like a widow have been made[106] [y]; (with) oil (we) have not anointed (ourselves), (21)and wine have not drunk.[107] [z]

Cessation of Cult Moreover, from that (time)[108] and until (this) day, year 17 of Darius the king, meal-offering and ince[n]se and burnt-offering[109] (22)they did not make in that Temple.

Petition
Now, your servants Jedaniah and his colleagues

q Jon 3:5-9; Neh 9:1-2
r Dan 5:23; Tobit 10:12
s Ezek 28:17; Mic 7:10; Pss 22:18; 59:11; 112:8; 118:7
t Neh 12:22
u Neh 3:1
v 1 Chr 3:24
w Neh 4:8, 13; 5:7; 6:17; 7:5; 13:17
x Exod 34:28; Dan 10:3
y cf. Lam 5:3
z 2 Sam 12:20; 14:2; Dan 10:3

[82] The pronoun is a mark of self-assertiveness; *GEA* 157-158, 301, 308.

[83] Over a continuous period of time until their prayers were answered; see *GEA* 207, 318 (participle + auxiliary *hwyn*). There is no mention in biblical sources of children wearing sackcloth.

[84] Donning sackcloth, fasting, and praying were a threefold rite designed to lead the way from disaster, anticipated or experienced, to restoration.

[85] Occurring only here in the papyri, this epithet is rare elsewhere; for grammatical construction, see *GEA* 222.

[86] Aram. *ḥzy/ḥwy b-* (here and in line 13) = Heb. and Moabite *rʾh b-* is a frequently used idiom, particularly in poetic passages, to express gratification for divine assistance in bringing about the downfall of an enemy (Mesha 4, 7). The haphʿel form here (*hḥwyn*) is altered to the paʿel in the parallel text (*ḥwynʾ* [*TAD* A4.8:15; *GEA* 190, also 261]). The sentence construction has been called a "non-restrictive relative clause;" *GEA* 171-172.

[87] For this difficult word (*klbyʾ*), see *DNWSI* 510; *GEA* 237. Some would take it with the next word, translating, "The dogs removed the fetter" or "The auxiliaries (Akk. *kallāb/pu*) took away the anklet" (Fales 1987:408-409).

[88] For this difficult word (*kblyʾ*), see *DNWSI* 485. Some would render it "anklet." An imaginative but unsupported translation yields "May the dogs tear his guts out from between his legs" (Lindenberger 2001). Whatever the precise meaning, no doubt a pun was intended between *klbyʾ* and *kblyʾ*. See, further, *GEA* 195.

[89] Though Vidranga's goods were confiscated, his ultimate fate remains hidden behind the author's scathing pun.

[90] For *qnh* as past perfect, see *GEA* 193.

[91] Masculine adjective *bʾyš* used as noun in a generic sense, like Heb. *rʿ* (*GEA* 187), in contrast to the specific evil done to them, expressed by the feminine noun *bʾyštʾ* at the end of the line; *GEA* 177.

[92] For *kl* and the revised *klʾ* in *TAD* A4.8, see *GEA* 247-248.

[93] Their prayers were answered. Lindenberger's attempt (2001:144-154) to see this whole section as an actual prayer founders on the past tense of the verbs.

[94] For this construction, see *GEA* 227.

[95] The word order *zʾ bʾyštʾ* may be due to the emotionally charged nature of the document; see *GEA* 235-236. An identical word order is found below in *znh ywmʾ* (line 20).

[96] For the disagreement between the feminine subject *bʾyštʾ* and masculine verb *ʿbyd*, see *GEA* 279.

[97] That is, to the present addressee, Bagavahya.

[98] Known in the Bible as Johanan, he was grandson of Nehemiah's contemporary, Eliashib.

[99] The comparable Heb. title was "the High Priest and his brothers the priests."

[100] If this Anani was the last Davidic descendant biblically recorded, his relative ("brother") bore a Persian name, perhaps because of his quasi-official position vis-a-vis the Persian authorities.

[101] They played a prominent role in Judah during the time of Nehemiah. The more proper title was "nobles of Judah" (Jer 27:20; Neh 6:17, 13:17) and was so written in the revised draft (*TAD* A4.8:18). As Jehohanan stood over the priests, so Avastana, or Anani, stood over the nobles; see *GEA* 318.

[102] For "one" as the indefinite article, see on 3.48, note 12. Here an emphatic was intended — "not a single letter did they send us"; *GEA* 240.

[103] Though the perpetrators of the destruction had been punished, the mourning had not ceased. The pathos finds syntactic expression in the irregular word order *znh ywmʾ*; see *GEA* 13, 40, 236, 238.

[104] Moses had abstained from eating and drinking for forty days on Mt. Sinai and Daniel abstained from food, drink, and anointing for three weeks. A fast of forty-one months was probably carried out only from dawn to dusk. These three words (*śqqn lbšn wṣymyn*) repeat the statement in line 15, omitting the auxiliary *hwyn*; these two and the following participles have the force of the present perfect tense; *GEA* 62, 107, 203.

[105] Perhaps to emphasize the personal humiliation, the scribe opted for the *zyl-* construction "wives of ours" (*nšyʾ zyln*) in contrast to "our wives" in line 15; *GEA* 164.

[106] Was this a poetic image or indication that husbands refrained from sexual intercourse with their wives? The passive participle (*ʿbydyn*) is in the masculine gender (*GEA* 73, n. 362, 119, 279, 294) and indicates a present perfect; *GEA* 201. For omission of the conjunctive *waw* before this and the followinmg verb, see *GEA* 318-319. For the singular "widow," instead of the expected "widows," see *GEA* 280.

[107] Abstinence from drink and anointing were part of the fasting and mourning procedure; for the negator *lʾ* with the participle, see *GEA* 322.

[108] *mn zky*, an unusual elliptical construction, revised in *TAD* A4.8:20 to [*m*]*n zk ʿ*[*d*]*nʾ*, "[fr]om that t[im]e" (*GEA* 167, n. 762), another example of the irregular word order demonstrative + noun; see n. 95 above. See also *GEA* 58, 166-167.

[109] These probably referred to the daily regular offerings, such as were made in the desert Tabernacle and designed to maintain YHWH's presence; Porten 1968:113.

and the Jews,[110] all (of them) citizens of Elephantine,[111] [aa] thus say:

Threefold Request (23)If to our lord it is good,[112] [bb] take thought[113] [cc] of that Temple to (re)build[114] (it) since[115] they[116] do not let us (re)build it.[117] Regard[118] (24)your (23)ob(24)ligees[119] [dd] and your friends[ee] who are here in Egypt. May a letter from you be sent[120] to them about the Temple of YHW the God (25)to (re)build it[121] in Elephantine the fortress just as it had been built formerly.[122]

Threefold Blessing And the meal-offering and the incense and the burnt-offering they[123] will offer[124] (26)on the altar of YHW the God in your name[125] and we shall pray for you at all times[126] [ff] — we and our wives and our children and the Jews,[127] (27)all (of them) who are here. If thus they did[128] until[129] that Temple be (re)built, a merit[130] [gg] it will be for you before YHW the God of (28)Heaven (more) than[131] a person who will offer[132] him burnt-offering and sacrifices[133] [hh] (whose) worth is as the worth of silver, 1 thousand talents,[134] and about gold.[135] About this (29)we have sent (and) informed (you).[135] [ii]

Addendum 1

Moreover, all the(se) things in a letter[137] we sent in

aa Josh 24:11; Judg 9; 20:5; 1 Sam 23:11; 2 Sam 21:12 *bb* Esth 5:4, 8, 8:5; Ezra 5:17 *cc* Jon 1:6 *dd* Prov 3:27 *ee* 1 Kgs 5:15; Lam 1:2; Esth 5:10, 14, 6:13 *ff* Eccl 9:8; Esth 5:13 *gg* Gen 15:6; Deut 6:24-25, 24:10-13; Ps 106:31; cf. Ps 24:5 *hh* Exod 10:25, 18:12; 2 Kgs 5:17 *ii* Ezra 4:14

[110] Not just the leadership but the whole community was writing the letter.

[111] The term *bᶜl* in construct plural occurs in Heb., Aram., and Phoen. in the expression "citizens of GN," e.g. Jericho, Shechem, Gibeah, Keilah, Jabesh-Gilead, Arpad and *Ktk* (Sefire 1A4 = *KAI* #222 = *COS* 2.82), and Sidon (*KAI* #60:6). For other collocations of *bᶜl* in the Eg. Aram. texts, see *GEA* 230. For the expression with *kl*, see *GEA* 247-248.

[112] See 3.50, note 53.

[113] For this term (*ʾtᶜšt*), see 3.74:3-4 and 3.78:2. Rhetorically, the imperative is used to invoke a favorable stance (*ʾtᶜšt, ḥzy*) while the specific request is phrased in the jussive (*yštlḥ* [line 24]); *GEA* 198, 210-211, 257. This is the only conditional sentence in our documents where the protasis is a nominal clause and the apodosis an imperative (*GEA* 326).

[114] The verb *bnh* in peᶜal here has the meaning not of "build" but "rebuild;" *GEA* 120, n. 555. The grammatical construction leaves the subject of the infinitive undetermined; *GEA* 209, 260.

[115] This preposition + *zy* (*bzy*) construction introducing a clause is quite common in our documents; *GEA* 332.

[116] In this 3rd person masculine plural form, the referent is deliberately unclear (*GEA* 289, 316): the Egyptians or the Persians?

[117] For infinitive with suffix, see *GEA* 148; as complement, *GEA* 208.

[118] A common epistolary command (*ḥzy/ḥzw*) to call attention to a particular item (e.g. *TAD* A3.10:2).

[119] The precise nuance of this construct phrase (*bᶜly ṭbtk*) eludes us. The sense assumed here is that the "owner of goodness" is the beneficiary who is obligated to the benefactor. Others would render "well-wishers, allies, loyal clients" (e.g. Lindenberger 1994 #34:23-24). As a technical term, "friend" (*rḥm* = Heb. *ʾwhb*) may refer either to a peer, as Hiram to David, an ally, or to a subordinate, as Haman's cronies. See, also, *GEA* 225.

[120] The passive construction with *mn*, "from," indicating the intended subject was characteristic of epistolary officialese; *GEA* 202; but see *GEA* 315-316. Here the jussive served as a polite substitute for the imperative. For the discord in gender between feminine subject (*ʾgrh*) and masculine verb (*ystlh*), see *GEA* 278.

[121] Since the governor of Judah had no authority over the satrap of Egypt, the requested letter would not be an order but a strong recommendation from the Jewish center on behalf of one of its Diaspora communities.

[122] Restoration of the status quo figured prominently in Persian thought and deed (Ezra 5:11 [Jerusalem Temple]; *TAD* C2.1 III.1 = Akk. Bisitun 25 [royal line]). This consideration will recur in the subsequent correspondence (3.52:8, 10; 3.53.9).

[123] The Elephantine Jewish priests.

[124] The *he* of a haphᶜel form was erased to yield a paᶜel — *yqrbwn*; *GEA* 190, n. 852.

[125] Either as your representative (see 3.60:2) or on your behalf.

[126] This promise has its counterpart in the standard epistolary blessing/salutation, "The welfare of PN may DN seek after abundantly *at all times*" (see line 2). As its Heb. counterpart, the expression is in the singular, *bkl ᶜdn*.

[127] In addition to the sometime sacrifices offered by the priests, daily prayer would be offered by the whole community, men, women, and children.

[128] A scribal error for "you did," corrected in the revised draft to "you will do" (*TAD* A4.8:26). For discussion of the tense of the protasis, whether perfect or imperfect, see *GEA* 324-325.

[129] For the compound conjunction *ᶜd zy* with the added nuance of "in order that", see *GEA* 333, n. 1270.

[130] The performance of a meritorious deed established the doer's merit in the eyes of the deity; *GEA* 278. The conjunction *waw* preceding *ṣdqh* has apodictic force, "then;" *GEA* 94, n. 439, 327.

[131] The comparative is expressed simply by the preposition *mn*; *GEA* 187, 331.

[132] For construction of the relative clause, see *GEA* 169.

[133] *dbḥ* = Heb. *zbḥ* was the sacrifice of well-being, divided between altar, priest, and worshipper. It was regularly paired with the burnt-offering (*ᶜlwh* = Heb. *ᶜwlh*) in biblical texts, particularly when referring to offerings by pagans.

[134] Only in this hyperbolic statement does the *knkr* = Heb. *kkr* occur in Eg. Aram. texts (*GEA* 13, 35, 62, 221). It was the equivalent of either 3,000,000 or 3,600,000 shekels; see *EPE* 120, n. 62.

[135] These dangling words are puzzling. Perhaps "about" is a scribal error, anticipation of this word in the next sentence. The sense would then be "worth silver, 1000 talents, and gold."

[136] This may have been a formulaic ending.

[137] Aram. *ḥdh*, lit. "one" = indefinite article and here perhaps also serves as contrast to preceding plural *kl*, "all"; *GEA* 240, n. 992, 248.

our name to Delaiah and Shelemiah[138] sons of Sanballat[jj] governor of Samaria.[139]

Addendum II

(30)Moreover, about this which was done to us, all of it, Arsames did not know.[140]

Date

On the 20th of Marcheshvan, year 17 of Darius the king.[141]

jj Neh 2:19-20; 3:33-4:2; 6:1-9; 13:28

[138] These otherwise unknown Hebrew-named sons of Sanballat (here written Sinuballit) indicate that the official, enigmatically/derogatorily called the "Horonite," was a worshipper of YHWH.

[139] Though he had every appearance of being the governor of Samaria, Nehemiah never accorded him the same title which he, himself, held. While the aged father still bore the official title, the sons acted in his name.

[140] As a non-conspirator out of the country, Arsames bore no responsibility for the destruction and so did not have to reverse his own decision to authorize its reconstruction. The sentence is a striking example of object-subject-verb word order; *GEA* 307.

[141] For location of the date at the end, see *EPE* 109, n. 31. It is not apparent why this renewed request was drawn up just at this time. Perhaps the perpetrators had just been punished and so the Jews emerged free of blame. The absence of an external address indicates that the letter was a draft.

REFERENCES

Text, translations and studies: Briant 1996; *EPE*; Fales 1987; Joüon 1934; *KAI*; Kaufman 1974; Kutscher 1977; Lindenberger 1994; 2001; Porten 1968; Porten 1998; *TAD*; von Pilgrim 1999.

RECOMMENDATION FOR RECONSTRUCTION OF TEMPLE (3.52)
(After 407 BCE)

Bezalel Porten

If a written reply to the petition was sent, as requested, it has not been found. Preserved herein (P. Berlin 13497 [*TAD* A4.9]) is a concise and precise verbal message dictated jointly by the authorities in Jerusalem and Samaria. Written on a torn piece of papyrus by the same scribe as the second draft of the petition (*TAD* A4.8), it was much amended. Its close adherence to the petition indicates an essential endorsement of Jedaniah's claim. Yet the plot by the Egyptian priests of Khnum was ignored. Only the Persians were involved — the Jews are to assert before Arsames that the Jewish Temple at Elephantine which existed before *Cambyses* and was destroyed in the fourteenth year of *Darius* by that wicked *Vidranga* was to be restored. Jedaniah's argument from precedent carried great weight; the Temple which existed *formerly* (*mn qdmn*) was to be restored as *formerly* (*lqdmn*) and meal-offering and incense were to be offered up as *formerly* (*lqdmyn*). This authorization was a clear echo of the claim of Darius I in his Bisitun inscription that he reestablished his dynasty in its place as formerly (*TAD* C2.1III.3-4 = Akk. line 25) — "I made it just as (it was) before me" (Akk. line 29). The Aramaic version of this inscription had only recently been recopied and may have been counted among Jedaniah's treasures.[1] But the endorsement was not without serious reservation; the requested burnt-offering was passed over in silence, implying that such offerings were limited to Jerusalem.

The clear dependence of the memorandum on the petition allows us to surmise that the Hebrew proclamation of Cyrus (Ezra 1:2-4) was formulated on the basis of a Hebrew petition from the Jews.

Title

(Recto)(1)Memorandum.[2] [a] What Bagavahya and Delaiah said (2)to me.[3]

Subject of Petition

Memorandum. Saying,[4] "Let it be for you[5] in Egypt to say[6] (Erasure: bef)[7] (3)(Erasure: to me about)[8]

a Ezra 6:2-5

[1] *TAD* C, p. 59; Sachau 1911:186.

[2] The term *zkrn* indicates literally an item to be remembered. It occurred frequently as a caption in lists (*TAD* C3.8IIIB:16, 28, 34, 3.13:1, 10, 24, 34, 37, 44, 46, 48, 50, 55). Most relevant to our text is the Aram. *dkrnh* written on a papyrus scroll containing the authorization by Cyrus of the reconstruction of the Jerusalem Temple and restoration of its looted vessels.

[3] This must have been the messenger who delivered the petitions (3.51) to Bagavahya and Delaiah. It is tempting to surmise that this was Jedaniah himself.

[4] For the particle *lm* introducting direct speech, see *GEA* 339.

[5] If this "you" was the same person as the "me" at the beginning of the line, then the scribe was no doubt Jedaniah. If the parties were different, then Jedaniah wrote neither this nor the petition.

[6] Spelled only here with elision of the glottal stop, *lmmr* rather than the historically correct *lmᵓmr* (*TAD* C 1.1:163; D7.39:10); *GEA* 22, 108, 124.

[7] Proofing his text, the scribe realized that the words of Bagavahya and Delaiah were not being said directly to Arsames but were to be recited "before" him by the Jewish leaders. He thus added a whole line between line 1 and what is now line 3. Failing to write more than the first letter of the word *qdm*, "before," he erased it and added it in the margin at the beginning of new line 3.

[8] The scribe's original text read "What B and D said to me about." The words "to me about" were then erased and the text continued so as to read "... said (to) Arsames about ..." (see previous notes).

before Arsames about the Altar-house[9] [b] of the God of (Erasure: Heav)[10] (4)Heaven[11] [c] which in Elephantine the fortress built (5)it was[12] formerly before Cambyses[13] (and) (6)which Vidranga, that wicked (man),[14] demolished[15] (7)in year 14 of Darius the king:

b 2 Chr 7:12
c Ezra 6:3-5
d Ezra 5:15; 6:17
e Mal 1:11

Decision
'(8)to (re)build it on its site[16] [d] as it was formerly (9)and the meal-offering and the incense[17] [e] they shall offer upon (10)that altar just as formerly (11)was done.'"[18]

[9] The response avoided the Akk. loanword ᵓ*gwr*ᵓ and employed an expression unattested in Aram. (*byt mdbḥ*ᵓ) but found in Syriac and Mandaic; see Hurvitz 1995:178; *GEA* 230. Solomon's Temple was called a "House of sacrifice (*byt zbḥ*)" by the Chronicler.

[10] Only able to get three (*šmy*) of the four letters (*šmy*ᵓ) on the line, the scribe erased them and wrote the full word on the next line.

[11] The personal name of deity (YHW) was omitted as it was in the Memorandum of Cyrus.

[12] For the construction *bnh hwh*, with internal passive participle preceding the auxiliary, see *GEA* 206-207, 291.

[13] Repeating the reference to Cambyses (3.51:13) emphasizes the Temple's legitimacy in the eyes of the Persians.

[14] Alternately translate, "that wicked Vidranga" (*GEA* 237). Repeating the derogatory epithet of the petition (3.51:7) emphasizes the sacrilege involved.

[15] The subject-verb word order is common in subordinate clauses introduced by *zy*; *GEA* 300.

[16] This specification was included in the Memorandum of Cyrus and was certainly appropriate to counter any attempt to move the Temple elsewhere, say away from the nearby shrine of Khnum. Surprisingly, the word is not to be found in the first draft of the petition (3.51) nor can it readily be restored in the second (*TAD* A4.8). Perhaps it reflects the oral discussion between the messenger and the two governors.

[17] As the prophet Malachi said, "My name is great among the nations, and everywhere incense and (meal-offering) are presented to My name." The deliberate omission of reference to the burnt-offering, the third sacrificial component in the petition (3.51:21, 25), apparently indicated that such was limited to the Jerusalem Temple. Less likely is the view that it was intended to pacify either the Egyptian or the Persian authorities; see Porten 1968:291-93.

[18] This periphrastic tense, with external passive and verbal sequence reversed (*hwh mt*ᶜ*bd*), indicates iteration or habit — "what used to be done;" *GEA* 205, 207.

REFERENCES

Text, translations and studies: Hurvitz 1995; Porten 1968; Sachau 1911; *TAD* A4.9.

OFFER OF PAYMENT FOR RECONSTRUCTION OF TEMPLE (DRAFT) (3.53)
(After 407 BCE)

Bezalel Porten

The lower, left half of the text is lost and holes affect the reading of several other crucial words. As a draft (Cairo J. 43467 [*TAD* A4.10]), the letter omitted the *praescriptio* but listed in column form the names of the five leaders presenting the petition. Headed by Jedaniah, they were not priests or "Jews, citizens of Elephantine" (3.51:1, 22) but "Syenians, hereditary property-holders in Elephantine" (line 6). This designation was doubtless designed to impress the recipient, identified only as "our lord," that they were indeed capable of paying the promised silver and thousand ardabs of barley if their request to rebuild the Temple were approved. In their proposal they also committed themselves not to offer animal sacrifices but only incense and meal-offering. Inference that the Temple was indeed rebuilt may be derived from the final contract in Anani's archive (3.80:18-19; see *EPE* 249, n. 37). It has also been argued by von Pilgrim, who has been excavating on Elephantine.[1]

Introductory Formula
(Recto)(1)Your servants[2] —
Jedaniah, son of Gem[ariah],[3] by name,[4] [a] 1
(2)Mauzi, son of Nathan,[5] by name, [1]

a Ezra 5:14

(3)Shemaiah, son of Haggai,[6] by name, 1
(4)Hosea, son of Jathom,[7] by name, 1
(5)Hosea, son of Nattun,[8] by name, 1:

[1] von Pilgrim 1999:142-145.

[2] The usual *External Address* and *Salutation* were omitted in this draft and the scribe began with the body of the letter which opened with the oral messenger formula, "Your servants thus say;" cf. 3.51:4, omitting the introductory/transitional "(And) now." Unlike the petition, the names of five leaders were given and we may assume that they stood at the head of the community. Jedaniah and the two Hoseas were among the prisoners in 3.49:7.

[3] See 3.46:1.

[4] This tag was regularly attached to the name of a slave or a royal servant. Only here does it appear with names of communal leaders. See *EPE* 200, n. 12.

[5] He was a professional scribe; see 3.47:1, 17; 3.48:2, 12; and *EPE* 194, n. 40.

[6] Perhaps identical with Shammua son of Haggai in a list of ca. 420 BCE (*TAD* C4.4:5), this Shemaiah was apparently the son of the professional scribe Haggai son of Shemaiah who was active 446-400 BCE (see *EPE* 187, n. 41). Both he and the following Hosea son of Jathom, the latter as Osea, appeared in a list of ca. 420 BCE (*TAD* A4.3:3, 5)

[7] See on 3.49, note 18. Given the name Jathom, "Orphan," the baby's father must have died before he was born.

[8] See on 3.49, note 19.

all (told) 5 persons,[9] (6)Syenians,[10] *b* who in Elephantine the fortress are heredi[tary-property-hold]ers[11] — (7)thus say:

Offer of Payment
If our lord[12] [...][13] (8)and the Temple-of-YHW-the-God of ours[14] be (re)built (9)in Elephantine the fortress as former[ly] it was [bu]ilt[15] — (10)and sheep,[16] ox, (and) goat[17] *c* (as) burnt-offering[18] are [n]ot made there[19] (11)but (only) incense (and) meal-offering[20] *d* [*they offer there*] — (12)and should our lord a statement[21] mak[e[22] *about this, afterwards*] (13)we shall give[23] to the house of our lord[24] si[*lver* ... and] (14)barley, a thousa[nd] ardabs.[25]

b 1QIsa[a] 49:12
c Lev 7:23; 17:3; 22:27; Num 18:17
d Jer 17:26; 41:5

[9] Such tallying is standard practice in documents of all sorts — letters, lists, contracts — when more than one person is mentioned; *GEA* 247.
[10] From "Jews, citizens of Elephantine" in the petition (3.51:22) the writers have now become "Syenians, hereditary property-holders in Elephantine." "Syenian" was a rare designation in the Aram. papyri and usually applied to "Arameans" (*TAD* B5.2:2; C3.14:32). Yet the prophet Deutero-Isaiah knew that Jews were settled in the "land of the Syenians."
[11] Offering to make substantial payments to "our lord," the leaders indicated here that they were freeholders, burghers, reliable men of means; see *EPE* 164, n. 5 and Szubin and Porten 1982:8.
[12] Probably Arsames himself, who was free of any taint in bringing about the destruction (3.51:30).
[13] The text is too damaged to restore this word with any confidence.
[14] For the grammatical construction, see *GEA* 226 and n. 943a.
[15] Repeating the theme of the petition (3.51:24-25) and the recommendation of Bagavahya and Delaiah (3.52:8), while reversing the word order (*bnh hwh* [*mn*] *qdm*[*y*]*n* — > *qdmn bnh hwh*), the Jews sought restoration of the status quo.
[16] For elision of the glottal stop in *qn*, see *GEA* 22.
[17] This is a well-known sacrificial triad, albeit in the order "ox, sheep, and goat." For omission of the coordinating conjunction, see *GEA* 318.
[18] Aram. *mqlw* < Akk. *maqlūtu*, occurred only here and displaced the normal Aram. *ᶜlwh*, "burnt-offering," which was used in the petition (3.51:21, 25).
[19] The implicit exclusion of animal sacrifices in the recommendation of Bagavahya and Delaiah (see 3.52, n. 17) was here spelled out explicitly; see Porten 1968:291-93.
[20] Regularly "meal-offering and incense" (3.51:21, 25 and 3.52:12), the traditional word pair was here reversed, as were the animals in the above triad.
[21] Aram. *ᵓwdys* < Old Persian **avadaisa* (Hinz 1975:1).
[22] The subject-object-verb word order is typical of Akk.; *GEA* 307-308.
[23] With assimilation of radical *nun* in *ntn*; *GEA* 10, 125.
[24] Payment was not to be made to the royal treasury but to the private estate of the recipient.
[25] A thousand ardabs of barley would provide a month's rations for ca. 540 men according to the scale of 100 ardabs for 54 men (*TAD* C3.14:26-31).

REFERENCES

Text, translations and studies: *EPE*; Hinz 1975; Porten 1968; Szubin and Porten 1982; *TAD*; von Pilgrim 1999.

APPEAL OF ADON KING OF EKRON TO PHARAOH (3.54)
(ca. 604 BCE)

Bezalel Porten

Discovered in a clay jar at Saqqarah in 1942, along with Egyptian and Greek papyri, by Zaki Saad Effendi, this light-colored papyrus fragment (7.7/8.5 cm wide x 9.6/9.8 cm tall) rests now in the Cairo Egyptian Museum (J. 86984 = papyrus number 3483). It contains the right half of a nine-line Aramaic letter, addressed to "Lord of Kings Pharaoh" from "your servant Adon King of [...]" (line 1), appealing for help against the King of Babylon whose forces had reached Aphek (lines 4, 7). The identity of Adon had long been a mystery, until Porten discovered in 1978 a demotic filing notation on the letter's verso that points to its origin in Ekron. A double salutation blesses Pharaoh in the name of Heaven and Earth and Beelshemayin and wishes him longevity like the "days of (the) heavens and (the) waters" (lines 2-3). Adon based his plea for help on his having observed his treaty obligations (*tbth*) to the King of Egypt (line 8). The appeal (lines 6-7) is couched in the third person throughout ("Pharaoh knows," "your servant," "let him not abandon [me]," "your servant," "his good relations"). The last line (9) contains obscure references to a "governor" and a "letter" of a certain Sindur. The destruction of Ekron Stratum IB is dated by its excavator and others to 604 BCE, just after the failed appeal of our letter (Gitin 1998:276, n. 2; Fantalkin 2001:131-132, 144).

Internal Address

(recto)(1)To the Lord of Kings[1] [a] Pharaoh,[2] your servant Adon[3] King of E[kron].

Salutation

(2)May (1)the gods of] (2)Heaven and Earth[4] and Beelshemayin,[5] [the great] god[6] [seek after (1)the welfare of my lord, Lord of Kings Pharaoh, (2)abundantly at all times,[7]and may they lengthen the days of] (3)Pharaoh[8] like the days of (the) heavens[9] [b] and (the) waters.[10]

Report

[... the force][11] (4)of the King of Babylon[12] [c] has come (and) reached Aphek[13] and ...[...] (5)... they have seized and brought [...] in all [...]

Appeal

(6)For the Lord of Kings Pharaoh knows that your servant [...] (7)to send a force[14] [d] to rescue me.[15] Let him not abandon [me,[16] for your servant did not violate the treaty of the Lord of Kings][17] (8)and your servant preserved his good relations.[18]

Addendum I

And (as for) this commander [...] (9)a governor[e] in the land.[19]

Addendum II

And (as for) the letter of Sindur[20] ... [...].

Recipient's Notation

(verso [demotic])(10)What the Great One of Ekron gave to ...[...].[21]

a Dan 2:47
b Deut 11:21; Ps 89:30
c 2 Kgs 24:1, 7, 11-12, etc.
d Jer 37:5, 7, 11, 46:2
e Hag 1:1, 14,; 2:2, 21; Mal 1:8; Ezra 5:14; 6:7; Neh 2:7, 9; 5:14, 18

---

[1] The Aram. *mrʾ mlkn* is a translation of Akk. *bēl šarrāni*, an epithet which occurs in almost forty letters, primarily in the addresses and blessings, of the Assyrian monarchs Esarhaddon and Ashurbanipal, who at the height of the Assyrian Empire called up "22 kings of Hatti, the seashore, and the islands" for corvée labor and military campaigns (*ANET* 291, 294). The king of Egypt took on the title when he displaced Assyria in the Transeuphrates (Fitzmyer 1979:233-235; Porten 1981:39).

[2] Necho II.

[3] Adon is a hypocoristicon of a Northwest Semitic nominal sentence name. Almost all of the more than the dozen known names of the Philistine rulers, from Abimelech in patriarchal times through Abimilki and Mitinti in 667, were Northwest Semitic (Fitzmyer 1979:235, Porten 1981:39).

[4] Equivalent to Akk. *ilāni ša šamê u erṣeti* (*DDD* [1st ed.] col. 743). The combination "heaven and earth" occurs frequently in the Bible, e.g. referring to the deity as "creator of heaven and earth" (Gen. 14:19, 22), "maker of (making) heaven and earth" (2 Kgs 19:15; Isa 37:16; Jer 32:17; Pss 115:15; 121:2; 124:8; 134:3; 146:6), "filling heaven and earth" (Jer 23:24), and "shaking heaven and earth" (Hag 2:6, 21); "heaven and earth" praising the deity (Ps 69:35) or called by the deity to witness (Deut 4:26; 30:19; 31:28).

[5] A leading deity attested in Phoen., Aram., and Akk. inscriptions: Yaḥimilk of Byblos (*COS* 2.29); Azatiwada of Karatepe (*COS* 2.31, iii.18); Zakkur of Hamath (*COS* 2.35, line 2); and in the Baal-Esarhaddon treaty (Borger 1956:§69); *DDD* cols. 283-288.

[6] See Fitzmyer 1979:237. In Eg. Aram. texts the epithet was applied to Eg. Ptaḥ (*TAD* C 3.12:26) and Baby./Aram. Shamash (*TAD* D 22.49:2-3).

[7] The conjectural restoration of the blessing is based upon the fifth century BCE Elephantine Aram. letters (*TAD* A3.5:1, *COS* 3.511-2).

[8] The restoration of a blessing of longevity for a monarch is based upon *COS* 3.51:3.

[9] The heavens are a symbol of eternity.

[10] This image is otherwise unknown to me. Gen 1:2 depicts the existence of waters as present before God's creative acts. I had earlier read this word *rmyn*, "exalted" (Porten 1981:36). Were this reading to hold up it would give us the productive compound, "high/exalted heavens" (cf. *KAI* #15), reflected in Sanchuniathon's Samemroumos (Baumgarten 1981:159-163). Among Anath's epithets is *bʿlt šmm rmm*, "Lady of the High Heavens" (*DDD* [1st ed.] col. 1687). Unfortunately, close palaeographical analysis does not support this reading. Moreover, the *yod* is rarely represented in Aram. plurals at this time (Porten 1998:233).

[11] Restoring *ḥylʾ*, a collective which would take a plural verb (cf. the following asyndetic pair *ʾtw mṭʾw*), as in *TAD* C2.1:16, 33, 37-38, 44 [Bisitun]. For the phrase "force of the King of Babylon" see Jer 32:2; 34:21; 38:3; "force of the Chaldeans" (2 Kgs 25:5, 10; Jer 35:11; 37:10; 39:5; 52:8, 14). Also suggested was *ʿbdyʾ*, "the servants" (Fitzmyer 1979:237).

[12] Nebuchadnezzar marched about in Ḫatti-land in the years 605/4, 604, 602, 601/600, 599/98, 598/97, 597/96, 595/94, and 594/93 (Wiseman 1956:69-75).

[13] Tell Rosh ha-ʿAyin (Ras el-ʿAin), later Antipatris, stood at a major crossroads, where the several branches of the Via Maris in the Sharon plain came together (Fitzmyer 1979:238; Porten 1981:45).

[14] *GEA* 177.

[15] Fitzmyer 1979:239; *GEA* 148, 274 (where read *lhṣltny*).

[16] Third person jussive was the appropriate tone in the appeal of a vassal to his overlord (Fitzmyer 1979:239).

[17] The terminology of this restoration derives from the Sefire treaty (IB:27f, 37f, IIB:14, III:7, 9, 19f, 27; Porten 1981:39). See *COS* 2.82.

[18] Aram. *ṭbh nṣr* = Akk. *ṭābta naṣāru*, a technical expression for preserving treaty relations with a suzerain (Fitzmyer 1979:239-240). Assyrian possessions in the Levant were taken over by Egypt, apparently in exchange for Eg. support of Assyria against Babylon.

[19] Fitzmyer (1979:240-241) would see a direct link between these two half sentences — a commander of the Babylonian forces has begun the process of reorganization by setting up a "governor" in the conquered territory (cf. 1 Kgs 20:24). The title *pḥh* is borne by the rulers of Judah (Yehud) and Samaria in the Persian period (3.51:1, 29).

[20] *Sndwr*, an Akk. name, common to Assyria and Babylonia, meaning "Sin is (my) Fortress." Cf. biblical Shenazzar (1 Chr 3:18). Also possible is the Anatolian name Sanduarri and some scholars have equated the name here with the person who was king of Kundu and Sizu in Anatolia and rebelled against Assyria in the 670's. They would thus antedate the papyrus some seventy or a hundred years and weave an entirely different narrative (Krahmalkov 1981:197-198; Shea 1985:408-413). In either case the reference to a "letter" (*spr*) remains obscure.

[21] The demotic line was first interpreted by George R. Hughes, and then by Karl-Theodor Zauzich (Porten 1981:43-45) with an alternate reading which did not favor "Ekron." I had subsequently met together with Hughes and Zauzich and discussed the line with both of them at length. Zauzich conceded that "Ekron" was indeed a possible reading. It was also accepted as such by Richard Parker and since then by other Demotists with whom I have discussed the matter, namely, Cary Martin, John Ray, and Günter Vittmann. For an earlier inscription from Ekron, see the Ekron Inscription of Akhayus (*COS* 2.42).

REFERENCES

Text: Dupont-Sommer 1948b; Fitzmyer 1965; *SSI* 2: #21; *KAI* #266; Porten 1981; *TAD* A1.1. Translations and studies: Baumgarten 1981; Borger 1956; *DDD*; Dion 1982a; 1982b; *DOTT* 251-252; Fantalkin 2001; Fitzmyer 1965; 1979; Gibson 1975; Ginsberg 1940; 1948; Gitin 1998; Horn 1968; Hug 1993:15-16; *KAI* 2:36-52; Krahmalkov 1981; Lindenberger 1994:20-22; Porten 1981; 1998; Shea 1985; *TUAT* 1:634; Wiseman 1956; Yurco 1991:41-42.

B. CONTRACTS

1. PHOENICIAN

CEBEL IRES DAĞI (3.55)

K. Lawson Younger, Jr.

This inscription, written in good standard (Tyro-Sidonian) Phoenician and dating approximately to 625-600 BCE, was incised on a coarse, dark limestone in the rough shape of a prism with three sides (measuring .545 m maximum in length along its base, .175 m in height and .315 m maximum in depth). The three sides (designated A, B, and C) follow an interlocking order with a colophon in C3. The inscription was found at the site of an ancient city located mid-way up the slope of a prominent mountain known as Cebel Ires Daği (now Cebelireis Daği; see Lebrun 1992), about 15 km east of the city of Alanya (in southern Turkey). It is now housed in the Alanya Museum.

The inscription is a record of real estate transferrals. It is chiefly concerned with an individual named Masanazamis.[1] The first part of the inscription records a number of real estate transferrals. It begins with an initial land-allotment to Masanazamis by a governor named Asulaparna. It then records a real estate transferral by this same governor to two individuals named Mutas and Kulas. Next, the text records a personal real estate transferral made by Mutas to Kulas. This apparently included the giving of Mutas' daughter MSD to Kulas.[2] This personal transaction is certified and notarized by both the installation of a deity (Baᶜal of the "furnace") and the utterance of a curse against anyone who might misappropriate this personal real estate given by Mutas to Kulas.

At this point, the inscription relates an incident occurring under another governor (Aziwasis) in which Masanazamis was exiled (apparently by Kulas). But a royal reinstatement of Masanazamis by King Awariku (see note 25) is registered which entitles Masanazamis to all of Kulas' real estate. Finally, a royal codicil reports the transferral of Kulas' wife (the daughter of Mutas, i.e. MSD) to Masanazamis.

Gubernatorial transfer of real estate by Asulaparna to Masanazamis (1a-3a1)
Asulaparna,[3] the governor of YLBŠ,[4] gave[5] a land-allotment[6 a] to Masanazamis,[7] his servant, in TMRS.[8] He (Masanazamis) planted plants in the field of the First-born[9] during the term of office (lit. "days") of Asulaparna. He (Asulaparna) gave him another vineyard in Adrassus[10] as well as a vineyard in KW.[11]

a Num 26:52-56; 33:54; Isa 17:14; Nahum 3:10

[1] All the vocalizations are tentative. However, vocalizations are utilized where reasonable guesses are possible in order to make the text easier for the reader to follow.

[2] Cf. the Levantine example of such land/wife linkage which is described in Josh 15:13-19 ‖ Judg 1:10-15, 20. See also 1 Sam 18:20-27; 25:44; 2 Sam 3:12-16; Jer 6:12. Cf. the pledge of wive in *COS* 3.116.

[3] ᵓ*šlprn* is clearly a non-Semitic name, apparently composed of two elements *aššul* "goodness, kindness, favor" and *parna* "house." See Lemaire (1989:124) who vocalizes "Asulaparna." Note that Mosca and Russell (1987:6, n. 16) find the *aššul* element in the Aram. name ᵓ*šwlkrty* from a Persian period inscription, and also (n. 17) the name ᵓ*šlthy* on a Phoen. seal.

[4] Uncertain place name.

[5] In such a legal context *ntn* may connote the idea of "transfer." See Westbrook 1991a:25, 28.

[6] *grl* "an allotment of land." The word was previously unattested in Phoen., but is clearly cognate with Heb. *gôrāl*. In ancient Israel, casting lots was a common method of distributing the spoils of war, whether booty or conquered territory (cf. Num 26:52-56; 33:54; Isa 17:14; Nah 3:10) (Kitz 2000). Perhaps this allotment to Masanazamis is a reward for some successful military venture. See Mosca and Russell 1987:8; Greenfield 1990:157.

[7] *msn(*ᵓ*)zmš* is clearly Anatolian (Mosca and Russell 1987:8). There is good reason to assume an equation of *msnzmš* (lines 1b, 7b) and *msn*ᵓ*zmš* (lines 8b, c2). See Lemaire (1989:124) who vocalizes the name as Mas(s)anazêmis. Compare the Hieroglyphic Luwian name of a scribe in Karatepe 4 §2: ᴵDEUS-*na*-(OCULUS)*á-za-mi-sá-há* "Masanazamis" (Hawkins *CHLI* 1/1:69). See also Laroche 1966:115 (#773), 284, 318. On the Luwian element *massani-*, see Laroche 1966:284, 318. On *zmš*, see Zgusta 1964b:160 (§22) *zēmis*.

[8] Uncertain place name.

[9] For the phrase *šd bkr*, see Mosca and Russell (1987:9) who point out the parallel with the phrase *šd zbl* "the field of the Prince" (line 4b). Long and Pardee (1989:213) translate "in the *bkr*-field." See also *DNWSI* 164 s.v. *bkr* "first-born."

[10] For the possible identification of this place name (ᵓDRWZ) with Adrassus, see Mosca and Russell 1987:11; Lebrun 1992.

[11] Perhaps "a later, var. spelling of Que, the Neo-Hittite territory in the Cilician Plain?" (Mosca and Russell 1987:11 and n. 42; see also Lebrun 1992). A Hieroglyphic Luwian city named *ka-wa/i-za-na*(URBS) "the city Kawa" (= Que?) occurs in an inscription from Carchemish (Karkamiš A11b, §7, dated to the 10th or early 9th century; see Hawkins *CHLI* 1/1:103, discussion: p. 105). If Kawa equals Que, then the variant spelling does not necessarily need to be regarded as late. All spellings in Neo-Assyrian begin with either the QA sign or the QU sign (see Parpola 1970:288-289). But the Neo-Babylonian spelling is *Ḫu-me-e* (Ḫumē). See Zadok 1985:166 and Hawkins 1972-75.

Gubernatorial transfer of real estate by Asulaparna to Mutas and Kulas (3a1-3b)

And furthermore, he (Asulaparna) gave WLWY[12] in WRYKLY[13] to Mutas[14] and Kulas.[15]

Personal real estate transferral by Mutas to Kulas (4a-7a)

The transferral (4a-5a)

And furthermore, Mutas gave to Kulas the field of the Prince[16] and the vineyards within the field of the Prince below the town as well as the vineyards below ML.[17]

The installation of the deity (5b1)

And furthermore, he (Mutas) settled Ba^cal Kura[18] in it,

The curse (5b2-7a1)

and Mutas pronounced a mighty curse[19] [b] so that no one should illegitimately seize[20] it — field or vineyard — from the possession of the family[21] of Kulas among everything which Mutas had given to him.

The exile of Masanazamis (7a2-7b)

But when he (Kulas) exiled[22] Masanazamis[23] during the term of office (lit. "days") of Aziwasis,[24]

Royal reinstatement of Masanazamis (8a-8b)

then King Awariku[25] handed over[26] [c] to Masanazamis all these fields (of Kulas).

Witnesses (9a-c1a)

And present[d] before him were: Pihalas,[27] the

b Num 22-24

c 1 Chr 10:14; 12:24

d 1 Chr 29:17; 2 Chr 5:11; etc.

[12] This term might be understood as either a place name or a personal name with the former being the more probable understanding.

[13] A place name perhaps linked to *wryk* in line 8? i.e. *wryk* + *ly*?

[14] Clearly Anatolian. The name *mtš* is perhaps comparable to Mita/Μιδας, perhaps Mutta. See Mosca and Russell 1987:12.

[15] The name *klš* is perhaps comparable to Kula/Κουλας. See Mosca and Russell 1987:12. Cf. the *kula-* element in the name Kulamuwa (see *COS* 2.30, note 1). Cf. also Hiero. Luwian Kulis (*ku-li-ia*), Kululu Lead Strip 1, §3, 8; §9, 52; Lead Strip 2, §1, 6 (Hawkins *CHLI* 1/2:506-510).

[16] The phrase *šd zbl* "the field of the Prince" parallels *šd bkr* (note 9). *Zbl* is used as a divine title or epithet (Mosca and Russell 1987:13) and thus may be used in this way here, possibly of Baal or his Anatolian counterpart. Krahmalkov (2000:456, s.v. *šd*$_1$) sees *zbl* as the name of a city.

[17] Place name. Possibly a mountain. See Mosca and Russell 1987:14.

[18] The deity *B*^{c}*l kr* is found on a small four-sided gray marble bowl or mortar from Sidon (formerly in Berlin, VA 569, now lost). It measured 15 cm high, carved with bull-head handles, from whose mouths rings hang. The depression in the center of the top is encircled by a snake in relief. On the sides (their starting point is uncertain) are incised ritual scenes each in a rectangular panel, with other details below. See Barnett 1969 and Elayi 1990:63-64 (drawing p. 298). Three different interpretations have been proposed for the term *kr*: (1) some scholars understand *kr* as "pasturage" deriving the term from a root *krr* (Barnett 1969; Tomback 1978:149 s.v. *kr*$_2$); (2) other scholars connect the term to Heb. *kûr* "furnace" (Lipiński 1970:43; Mosca and Russell 1987:14; *DNWSI* 534 s.v. *kr*$_4$; Elayi 1990:64), hence Ba^{c}al of the "furnace" — one scene on the bowl appears to depict a large seething cauldron, and another a figure (representing Melqart?) bathed in flames. Elayi also notes the form of the bowl and its apparent intent for use in an oven or furnace (1990:64; see also Bonnet 1992; 1988:78-80); (3) some scholars connect *kr* with a West Semitic deity Kura, a deity attested at Ebla (Pettinato 1979:106; Mander 1990:235b; Pomponio and Xella 1997:223-248) as well as in first millennium contexts (Lipiński 1995:239-240; Dalley and Postgate 1984:100). There was a temple of the god ^{d}*Kur-a* in the Neo-Assyrian period (ADD 1252:13) (see Postgate 1976:117 (no. 19:13). Kura is also attested in personal names (e.g. Abdi-Kurra, see *PNA* 1/1:6; Amat-Kurra, see *PNA* 1/1:99). Ba^{c}al Kura may have been a deity of agriculture and harvest (Lipiński 1995:240) which nicely fits this context here of field and vineyards.

[19] Clear attestation of verb and noun from the root *qbb*. Greenfield (1990:157) argues that all the sure examples of *qbb* in BH are from the Balaam pericope (Num 22-24). But see *COS* 2.27 note *t*. The mention of Mutas' oath underscores his full surrender of any claim to the property in question and that it is fully and solely in Kulas's possession. This also paves the way for the transfer of ownership to Masanazamis (see below).

[20] *gzly* is a Qal inf. const. of *gzl* "to seize by force, acquire illegitimately" (*DNWSI* 219 s.v. *gzl*$_1$) + 3ms suf. The meaning of *gzl* here is clear— "to illegitimately seize and take as one's own," fitting the use in Heb. (Greenfield 1990:156). The use of the suffix is not as clear. Mosca and Russell (1987:15) argue that the suffix -*y* is a prospective object suffix to be resumed by *šd* ᵓ*m krm*. They translate: "so that no one might illegitimately seize it — field or vineyard ..." (see also Greenfield 1990:156). Long and Pardee (1989:213, n. 31) argue that the suffix -*y* is a proleptic 3ms possessive pronoun representing the subject, i.e., -*y* is proleptic to ᵓ*dm*. They translate: "so that no person should seize a field or vineyard ..." The difference is simply a matter of emphasis: does the emphasis fall on the subject or on the object.

[21] *špḥ* "clan, family" (*DNWSI* 1181 s.v. *špḥ*).

[22] Lemaire (1989:125-127) has suggested that the verbal form *ygl* is from the root *g*ᵓ*l* and is hence connected to the *g*ᵓ*l* "kinsman-redeemer" in the book of Ruth. Long (1991) has convincingly argued that the verb is derived from *gly* "(drive into) exile."

[23] This is the crux of the inscription. The sentence (*wkm* ᵓ*š ygl* ᵓ*yt msnzmš bymt* ᵓ*zwšš*) was translated by Mosca and Russell (1987:17-18) "And when MSNᵓZMŠ drove him (i.e. KLŠ) into exile in the days of ᵓZWŠŠ." Thus *msn(*ᵓ*)zmš* is the subject of the verb *ygl* and ᵓ*yt* is an independent object pronoun (a usage unattested in Phoen. proper for ᵓ*yt*). However, Long and Pardee (1989) suggest an interpretation that is more consistent with the grammar of the sentence. Surveying the *nota accusativi* (ᵓ*yt*) in Phoen., they demonstrate that Masanazamis must be the object of the *nota accusativi*, and not the subject, and that the most likely subject of the verb *ygl* within the context of the inscription is Kulas. As Long and Pardee comment: "It seems that this sentence describes the action of one who deposed MSN(ᵓ)ZMŠ from his rightful land but that a certain King WRYK intervened by giving to MSN(ᵓ)ZMŠ all the aforementioned fields — an action that, on the one hand, righted an injustice and, on the other, served as punishment for the initial deposer" (1989:210). This understanding best explains the award of fields to Masanazamis upon his royal reinstatement by Awariku and the punishment of Kulas both in terms of the real estate and his wife, since both are transferred to Masanazamis.

[24] For ᵓ*zwšš* see Lemaire (1989:124, 128, n. 8). Mosca and Russell (1987:19) note: ᵓ*z* = *aza-*; *asi(ya)* "to love" + *wšš* = *wasu-* "good."

[25] The name written in Phoen. *wryk* (Awariku in the Luwian source [*COS* 2.21, n. 11]; Urikki in the Assyrian sources, [*COS* 2.117A, n. 4) is attested at Karatepe and Hassan-Beyli where the references are to a king of the Danunians (Que). For Karatepe, see *COS* 2.21 and 31; Younger 1998a and Röllig 1999. For Hassan-Beyli, see Lemaire 1983b. While this is the same name in the Cebel Ires Daği inscription, it is not the same person (based on the dates of the inscriptions).

[26] *ysb* is a yiphil perf. 3ms of *sbb*. See *DNWSI* 773 s.v. *sbb* and Greenfield 1990:157. Mosca and Russell (1987:19) define as "transfer, hand over (the ownership of something)." This legal dimension is well documented for the Heb. verb in epigraphic, biblical and post-biblical texts. Cf. 1 Chr 10:14; 12:24 (transferring the kingdom). See also Sasson 1982. The use of the verb *ysb* in this inscription verbalizes Masanazamis' claim to have received the lands of Kulas by royal decree rather than by brute force (*gzl*). Therefore Masanazamis is not under the curse of Mutas with regard to the fields that Mutas had given to Kulas.

[27] The name *phlš* is clearly Anatolian. For the element *piḫa-* "glanzen, blitzen" in Luwian names, see Starke 1990:314-316.

envoy, and Logbasis(?),[28] the brother of Las[29] and Nanimutas.[30]

Royal codicil (c1a-c2)
And furthermore, Mutas had given MSD,[e] his daughter, to Kulas; but during the term of office (lit. "days") of Aziwasis, he (Awariku) handed her over to Masanazamis.[31] [e]

Colophon (c3)
Pihalas, the scribe, set down this inscription.

e Josh 15:13-19 ≈ Judg 1:10-15, 20; 1 Sam 18:20-27; 25:44; 2 Sam 3:12-16; Jer 6:12

[28] Based on the names λογβασις, λωγβασις, Ιδαλωγβασις. See Mosca and Russell 1987:22.

[29] The name Las (*la-sá*/la-ia) occurs in a number of Hiero. Luwian texts (Cekke Inscription 2, §17h [Hawkins *CHLI* 1/1:146]; Kürtül Inscription §1 [Hawkins *CHLI* 1/1:272]; Topada Inscription, §39 [Hawkins *CHLI* 1/2:454]; Kullulu Lead Strip 1, §4, 18 and 21 §9, 59 [Hawkins *CHLI* 1/2:506-509]). Mosca and Russell (1987:22) note the names λας, λαας.

[30] Clearly Anatolian with the elements *nani/a* "brother" + *mutas*. See Mosca and Russell 1987:22.

[31] It is likely that the giving of MSD to Kulas by Mutas was linked with the transferral of real estate from Mutas to Kulas. Compare the giving of Achsah to Othniel by Caleb (Josh 15:13-19 ≈ Judg 1:10-15, 20). The giving of a daughter to one husband and then to another is paralleled by Saul giving Michal to David, but then, because of David's treason (in Saul's eyes), to Palti. After the death of Saul, David recovers Michal (1 Sam 18:20-27; 25:44; 2 Sam 3:12-16). Jer 6:12 is a general parallel. It speaks of the transfer of wives as one consequence of exile: "Their houses shall be turned over (*wᵉnāsabbû*) to others, their fields (*śādôt*) and wives (*nāšîm*) together" (NRSV). Mosca and Russell (1987:23, n. 113) point out "In the bicolon from Jeremiah, the 'fields' and 'wives' of the B-line form a sort of merismus when placed in explanatory parallelism with the 'houses' of the A-line; i.e., houses = fields (and other property) + wives (and other family members). In our inscription, the 'fields' have already been dealt with in detail, and the sense of 'house' would thus be quite different."

REFERENCES

Text, translations and studies: Mosca and Russell 1983; 1987; Lemaire 1989; Long and Pardee 1989; Long 1991; Greenfield 1990.

2. ASSYRIAN ARAMAIC

A BARLEY LOAN FROM ASSUR (3.56)
(VA 7499; *AECT* 47)

K. Lawson Younger, Jr.

Discovered in excavations at Assur, this Assyrian Aramaic inscription recording a loan of barley is written on a triangular clay docket. It dates to the mid-7th century BCE based on its archival context.[1]

(Five fingernail marks on the top of the tablet)

(lines 1-reverse 1)
Barley belonging to Aššur-šallim-aḫḫē,[2]
(debited) against Akkadayu.[3]
3 (*emāru* "homers"), 3 (*sūtu* "seahs");
one harvester (as interest).[4] [a]

(lines reverse 2-left edge 1)
Witnesses:
Bēl-iddina[5]
Bēl-šar-uṣur[6]
Mannu-kī-Aššur[7]
Taqquni
Dādi-ibni[8]
Mannu-kī-Aššur.[7]

a Exod 22:24; Lev 25:36-37; Deut 15:2; 23:20-21

[1] Pedersén's analysis indicates that the Aram. tablets from Assur all come from archives comprising Assyrian dated tablets of the 7th century, and mainly from the post-648 period (Pedersén 1986:104-107, 119-120).

[2] Fales (1986:227-228) states: "The writing of the name in Obv. 2, *srslmḥ*, is at variance with nos. 46 and 48 for the same individual: such a writing may be quoted as a case of elision of the initial *aleph*, but reservations on the present case as an actual linguistic marker have been expressed." Kaufman (1977:121) states: "The first letter is rather severely abraded, and shows traces of a diagonal that can only belong to an *aleph*. One suspects an error, or even one letter inscribed upon another." See *PNA* 1/1:216-217, #11; Pedersén 1986:119f; Hug 1993:21ff.

[3] For the name *ʾkdy*, see *PNA* 1/1:95, #2.

[4] The so-called "harvester clauses" are known from Assyrian contracts; see Postgate 1976:44-45 who states: "the debtor should provide a given number of harvesters to assist at the harvest of the creditor's field." See also Lipiński 1975a:90-91. Regarding interest in the Israelite context, see Frymer-Kensky 2001.

[5] *PNA* 1/2:311-313, #23.

[6] For the Aram. spellings, see Lipiński 1975a:90. For this individual, see *PNA* 1/2:328-330, #15.

[7] See *PNA* 2/2:688-690, #23.

[8] See Kaufman 1977:121 contra Lipiński 1975a:89; *PNA* 1/2:363, #6.

REFERENCES

Text, translations and studies: Lidzbarski 1921 #2; *KAI* #234; Vattioni 1979 #144; Lipiński 1975a:90-91; Fales 1986:226-228, #47; Hug 1993:22-23.

A LOAN OF SILVER FROM ASSUR (3.57)
(VA 5831; *AECT* 50)

K. Lawson Younger, Jr.

Discovered in excavations at Assur, this Assyrian Aramaic inscription recording a loan of silver is written on a triangular clay docket. While the text contains no date, it can be dated on the basis of its archival context to the reign of Assurbanipal or later.[1]

(Five fingernail marks on the top of the tablet)

(lines 1-5a)
8 shekels of silver belonging to Balasî[2]
(debited) against Bēl-zērī.[3]
It will increase by a quarter.[4] [a]
The eighth month.[5] [b]

a Exod 22:24; Lev 25:36-37; Deut 15:2; 23:20-21
b 1 Kgs 6:38; 12:32, 33; Zech 1:1; 1 Chr 27:11

(lines 5b-r.4)
Witnesses:[6]
and Aplu-iddina[7]
and Apladad-erība(?)[8]
and Yadīc-il[9]
and Sagīb.[10]

[1] See *COS* 3.56, note 1 above.
[2] *PNA* 1/2:254-256, #9. See Pedersén 1986:106: N 17 (13).
[3] Radner (*PNA* 1/2:288, #3) vocalizes *blzr* as "Bēl-azūri," envisioned by the apheresis of two *ayins* from the name *b*c*lz*c*r*. See Pedersén 1986:106, N 17 (13). However, it seems more likely that *blzr* is the vocalization of the name "Bēl-zērī" (Fales 1986:234; Lipiński 1975a:104; Hug 1993:24; *PNA* 1/2:339-340).
[4] Lit. "it will increase by its quarter." For the reading, see Kaufman 1989:100. Thus the interest rate was 25% for a one year period (Lipiński 1975a:103). The formula *brb*c*h yrbh* is "a loan-translation of Neo-Assyrian (*kaspu*) *ana rabutti/u-šu irabbi*" (Fales 1986:234). See also Postgate 1976:40-41.
[5] Fales states: "As for *yrḥ*ᵓ *smnh*, it is of course not the month Simānu, but indicates, with Lipiński, the month VIII; and, while it is true that no 'Neo-Assyrian pronunciation' is attested for the eighth month of the calendar, ITIAPIN, it may be surmised that what we have here is nothing other than a rendering of Neo-Assyrian **šamaniu* 'eighth' — whether this was in fact the month name or simply used as an ordinal number" (Fales 1986:234-235).
[6] In the list of witnesses there is a multiple use of *w*'s, as in Fales 1986 #313, but here the *w* even precedes the first name.
[7] *PNA* 1/1:120, #2.
[8] *PNA* 1/1:113. The reading, however, is not certain. For Apladad as DN, cf. *COS* 2.115B, n. 5, and 2.125, n. 3.
[9] *PNA* 2/1:486-487, #9.
[10] This name is attested in roughly contemporaneous documents from Guzāna.

REFERENCES

Text, translations and studies: Lidzbarski 1921 #5; Lipiński 1975a:103-108; Vattioni 1979 #147; Fales 1986:233-235, #50; Hug 1993:24.

A BARLEY LOAN FROM GUZĀNA (3.58)
(*TH* 2; *AECT* 54)

K. Lawson Younger, Jr.

This triangular barley loan docket was discovered in excavations at Guzāna (Tell Halaf) (biblical Gozan). It dates to the period after the reign of Assurbanipal. The tablet contains a stamp seal impression which possibly features an incense stand.

(Stamp seal on top of tablet)

(lines 1-4)
Barley belonging to Il-manāni,[1]

a Ezek 18:8, 13, 17; 22:12; Prov 28:8

(debited) against Mattî.[2]
The in⌈tere⌉st[3] is: 2 (*emāru* "homers") into 4 (*emāru* "homers")[4] [a] in the seventh month.[5]

[1] *PNA* 2/1:521-522. This individual is attested as the lender in a number of Assyrian and Aram. contracts from Tell Halaf. See Lipiński 1975a:125-132.
[2] For this name, see Lipiński 1975a:126-129; *PNA* 2/2:746, #2.
[3] The reading of *ḥ*⌈*bl*⌉*n* follows Fales 1986:244-245. This would be the earliest attestation of the loanword from Akk. *ḫubullu* to Aram. *ḥbwl*ᵓ "interest, obligation." For this loanword, see Kaufman 1974:56. Here the plural may refer back to the Neo-Assyrian rendering of the word, *ḫabullu*, which is often given in the plural form (Fales 1986:245). Friedrich (1940:74) suggested a reading of *ḥ*⌈*ṣd*⌉ "reaper, harvester." See also Lipiński 1975a:129 and *DNWSI* 398, s.v. *ḥṣd*. Hence the translation would be "harvesters, 2 into 4 in the seventh month."
[4] Lipiński (1975a:125) states: "The interest here appears unconditional and amounts to 100%, a rate which is very high indeed, but which might be justified by the historical circumstances of unrest and war."
[5] See Fales 1986:245.

(lines reverse 1-4) Witness: Padî[6] Witness: [ ]DLR?N[7]		Witnesses:[8] Mate^{c}-<S>ē[9] and ⌜Ad⌝da-ḫāri.[10]

[6] A well-attested West Semitic name (Lipiński 1975a:129-131; Renz 1995 2/1:80-81; and *AHI* 469-470). The name *pdy* is attested in two recently discovered inscriptions from Tel Miqnê/Ekron (see *COS* 2.42 and n. 3). It also occurs in the inscriptions of Sennacherib (*COS* 2.119B), as well as in a docket for some silver from Nineveh (presumably attached as a label to the silver) (see Fales and Postgate 1995:42, #50).

[7] See Lipiński 1975a:129-131; Kaufman 1989:101.

[8] The last two witnesses are unified under the heading *šhdn* PN_1 *w* PN_2, since they were the witnesses on Il-manāni's side (Fales 1986:246). On the other hand, Lipiński (1975a:126) argues that this was a matter of space considerations on the triangular tablet (i.e. this was the only way to list the names, since there was not enough space to include the word *šhd* "witness" before each personal name).

[9] Following Fales' suggested emendation. Mate^{c}-Sē occurs as a witness in *all* of Il-manāni's contracts in cuneiform. For a discussion of this name, esp. with regard to the theophoric element, see Lipiński 1994:175, nn. 30-31; *PNA* 2/2:754, #3; Lemaire 2001:132 (line 7).

[10] While Hug 1993:26 reads *ʾd*^{c}*d* (following Friedrich 1940:74-75), the reading *ʾd*^{c}*r* seems more probable (Fales 1986:244; Kaufman 1989:101). He is very likely the same person from the Guzāna area attested in cuneiform documents from Tell Halaf as ^{m}10-*ḫa-ri* and who serves numerous times as a witness for Il-manani. See *PNA* 1/1:45, #5.

REFERENCES

Text, translations and studies: Fales 1986:244-246; Friedrich 1940:74-75, taf. 30, #2; Degen 1:53-54, Taf. v (Abb. 11-14); Vattioni 1979 #150; Lipiński 1975a:125-132; Hug 1993:25-26.

---

3. EGYPTIAN ARAMAIC

THE MIBTAHIAH ARCHIVE (471-410 BCE)

Bezalel Porten

In 1904, eleven Aramaic papyri were acquired from a dealer in Aswan by the British benefactors Lady William Cecil (*COS* 3.60, 3.64, 3.68, and half of 3.63) and Mr. (later Sir) Robert Mond (3.61-62, 3.65-67, and half of 3.63) and by the Bodleian Library in Oxford (3.59). The Cecil-Mond papyri are housed in the Egyptian Museum in Cairo and all were published in large format in 1906 by Archibald Henry Sayce and Arthur Ernest Cowley.[1] Believed at the time to have been discovered at Assuan, they actually came from the island of Elephantine and constituted ten contracts from the Mibtahiah family archive. Prosopographical study suggests that Mib/ptahiah daughter of Mahseiah son of Jedaniah was the aunt of the Jewish leader Jedaniah (see his archive in 3.46-53). Her archive of eleven documents (including one discovered in the Rubensohn excavations [*TAD* B2.5]) spans a period of just over sixty years and covers three generations. Opening in 471 BCE, it closed just months before the destruction of the Jewish Temple in 410. Mibtahiah was a woman of means, receiving property from her father and passing it on to her children, who bore the names of her father and grandfather, respectively. Her father held a piece of undeveloped property, whose neighbors included an Egyptian cataract boatman, one Khwarezmian and two Jewish soldiers. In 471 Mahseiah granted building rights on an outer wall to the Jew Konaiah (3.59), warded off by a family oath challenge to the property in 464 by Dargamana (3.60), and in a bequest of 459 bestowed the house upon Mibtahiah (3.61) with rights of usufruct for her husband, Jezaniah, the other neighbor, whose house lay opposite the Jewish Temple (3.62). Jezaniah soon disappeared, his house fell into Mibtahiah's possession, and in 449 she married the Egyptian Esḥor son of Djeḥo (3.63), who later became known as Nathan. Shortly thereafter (446 BCE), her father gave her a second house, also across from the Jewish Temple, in exchange for fifty shekels worth of goods she had given him earlier (3.64), and in 440 she emerged victorious in litigation with the Egyptian Peu about an array of goods, including a marriage contract (3.65). By 420 Esḥor was dead and his children were sued for goods allegedly deposited with their father but never returned (3.66). After their mother passed away, they came into possession, in 416 BCE, of the house that belonged to her first husband Jezaniah son of Uriah (3.67). Finally, in February 410, barely six months before the destruction of the Jewish Temple, the brothers Jedaniah and Mahseiah divided between them two Egyptian slaves of their mother, retaining two others in joint possession (3.68). Mibtahiah had had two or three husbands, three houses, and four slaves. The initial publication of her archive created a sensation in the scholarly world.

[1] A. H. Sayce and A. E. Cowley, *Aramaic Papyri Discovered at Assuan* (London: A. Moring, 1906).

GRANT OF A BUILT WALL (3.59)
(12 September, 471 BCE)

Bezalel Porten

Mahseiah had a run-down house plot (3.61:3; 3.62:3-5) in the midst of well-established neighbors, who inherited their property from their fathers and passed it on to their children (the Egyptian Peftuauneit to his son Espmet [line 13; 3.61:7] and the brothers Jezaniah and Hosea from their father Uriah [3.61:6-7; 3.67:5]). He was apparently saving it for his daughter on the occasion of her marriage, some twelve years away (3.63; 3.66). Meanwhile, the house became involved in two legal transactions. The first resulted in a "document of a built wall." This contract is unique, but most of its formulae are familiar. Konaiah approached Mahseiah in the manner of a groom imploring the father of the bride or a borrower beseeching a creditor, and was given access to Mahseiah's gateway to build there a wall which would continue all along the common wall between their two properties (lines 3-4). As Mahseiah's property was unimproved, Konaiah may have needed the double wall thickness provided by the new construction to improve his own property with a roof or second story. The point of the document was to assert that the wall was the property of Mahseiah (lines 4-5) and neither Konaiah nor his heirs could subsequently restrain Mahseiah from building on that wall or deny him free access through the gateway. To do so would incur a penalty of five *karsh*, many times the value of the wall (lines 6-14). Eight witnesses, and not merely four, were present because the transaction was probably considered tantamount to a bequest where there was no consideration. Only three of the witnesses were Jews; the others reflect a mixed onomasticon (Persian, Caspian, Babylonian, and Egyptian) that illustrates the cosmopolitan nature of the Elephantine community (lines 16-19). Practically, bringing in witnesses from the non-Semitic settlers would ultimately strengthen Mahseiah's claim to a piece of property whose one problematic border was a house to be occupied by a Khwarezmian (3.60:2, 8).

Date

(Recto)(1)On the 18th of Elul, that is day 28 of Pachons, year 15 of Xerxes the king,[1]

Parties

said (2)Konaiah[2] son of Zadak, an Aramean of Syene[3] of the detachment of Varyazata,[4] (2)to Mahseiah son of Jenadiah,[5] an Aramean of Syene (3)of the detachment of Varyazata, saying:

Building rights

I came to you[6] and you gave me the gateway of the house of yours to build (4)a[7] wall there.

Investiture

That wall is yours[8] — (the wall) which adjoins[9] the house of mine at its corner which is above.[10] (5)That wall shall adjoin the side of my house from the ground upwards, from the corner of my house which is above to the house of Zechariah.[11]

[1] Virtually every contract bore a double date, the first usually being the Babyl. date and the second the Eg. one. Only occasionally, as here (also 3.67; 3.73; 3.74; 3.79), do the two correspond exactly. Often the Babyl. date was one day ahead of the Eg. one, indicating that the document was written at night. For full discussion, see Porten 1990; *TAD* B 185-187.

[2] The tense of the verb in this theophorous name, "Yah Creates" (ptc. plus DN), is unusual. Verbs in names are usually in the perf. or imperf. tense.

[3] Though Jews with property in Elephantine, both Konaiah and Mahseiah were here designated "Aramean of Syene." This was a common designation applied originally to ethnic Arameans settled on the mainland (cf., e.g. 3.81:2) in contrast to "Jew of Elephantine" (3.60:3; 3.62:2) applied to the migrants from Judah who settled on the island. But more often than not the former designation was applied to Jews (3.64:2; 3.65:2-3; 3.66:3; 3.69:2; 3.71:2; 3.77:2-3; *TAD* 4.5:2; 7.1:2, 7.2:2, simply "Aramean") and one and the same person (Mahseiah) might be called either "Aramean of Syene" (as here and in 3.64:2; 3.65:2), "Jew of Elephantine" (3.60:3; 3.62:2), or "Jew, hereditary property holder in Elephantine" (3.61:2). Often the formula was expanded to "Jew of Elephantine the fortress," "Jew who is in Elephantine the fortress," or altered to "Aramean of Elephantine the fortress." Also found was the designation "Caspian of Elephantine the fortress" (3.73:4). Women were similarly designated — "Aramean of Syene" (3.66:3), "lady of Elephantine the fortress" (3.69:2), and possibly "*Jewess* of Elephantine the fortress" (*TAD* B5.5:1-2).

[4] Detachment commanders were Iranian, as here, or Babylonian, never Jewish or Aramean; four such Iranian commanders were attested for the years of Mahseiah's activity: Varyazata (also 3.64-66), Artabanu and Atrofarnah (3.60), and Haumadata (3.61-62). Six and one-half years later Konaiah would be in the detachment of Atrofarnah (3.60:8-9). See Porten 1968:30-31.

[5] A scribal error for Jedaniah. Mahseiah son of Jedaniah first appeared in our documents as a witness ca. 487 BCE (*TAD* B4.2:14).

[6] This expression, in variant forms ("I came to your house" or "I came to you in your house"), occurs regularly in documents of wifehood (3.64:3; 3.71:3; 3.76:3; *TAD* 6.1:3) and in a loan contract (3.81:2). It is followed by a verb of "giving" (with the second party as subject), whether a wife, grain, or, as here, a gateway.

[7] Aram. "one," written as a word (*ḥd*) or, as here, as the cipher "1," was often used for the indefinite article (e.g. 3.61:3, 23; 3.62:3).

[8] "It is yours (*zylk hw*)" was one of the two standard expressions recurring in the *Investiture* clause (3.61:19; 3.68:8; 3.73:4; 3.78:11) and repeated in the *Reaffirmation* (of *Investiture*) clause (line 11; 3.60:15; 3.68:16; 3.69:12; 3.73:16; 3.80:30; *TAD* 5.1:7). The other was *šlyt*, "empowered, have right to" (see 3.61, n. 28). The former formula would bestow full title while the latter might only convey right of possession; Porten and Szubin 1987a:185-86; *EPE* 153, n. 9.

[9] On the mound at Elephantine it is possible to discern house walls built one against the other.

[10] Aram. *lʿlyh*, meaning either "south," i.e. the direction of Upper Egypt, or more likely "north." The directional terms "above" and "below" occur regularly in our documents to indicate, respectively "north" and "south;" see 3.60, n. 25.

[11] Line 5 was a subsequent supralinear addition to explicate and elaborate on the location of the wall, which ran all along the western side of Mahseiah's house until it reached the house of Zechariah, who was son of Nathan (see 3.61:7) and father of Hazzul, heir to the house (3.68:5).

Restraint waiver I

(6)Tomorrow or the next day,[12] I shall not be able[13] [a] to restrain[14] you from building upon that wall of yours.

Penalty I

(7)If I restrain you, I shall give you silver, 5 *karsh*[15] by the stone(-weight)s of the king,[16] [b] pure silver,[17]

Reaffirmation I

and that wall (8)is likewise[18] (yours).[19]

Restraint waiver II

And if Konaiah dies[20] tomorrow or the next day, son or daughter, brother or sister,[21] (9)near or far,[22] member of a detachment or town[23] (8)shall not be able (9)to restrain Mahsah[24] or a son of his from building upon (10)that wall of his.

Penalty II

Whoever of them[25] shall restrain, shall give him the silver which is written above,[26]

Reaffirmation II

and the wall (11)is yours likewise and you have the right to[27] build upon it upwards.

Restraint waiver III

And I, Konaiah, shall not be able (12)to say[28] to Mahsah,[29] saying:

"(ERASURE: Not) That gateway is not yours and you shall not go out into the street which is (13)between us and between the house of Peftuau-

a Exod 32:20; Deut 12:17; 16:5; 17:15; 21:16; 22:3, 19, 29; 24:4

b 2 Sam 14:26

As neighbor, he would later witness the bequest of the house to Mahseiah's daughter (3.61:29) with rights of usufruct to her husband, Jezaniah (3.62:17).

12 This was a frequent formula in the *Waiver* clauses in conveyances (3.61:18, 20, 26; 3.62:8, 13; *TAD* 5.1:4) and appeared regularly in the *Death* and *Repudiation* clauses in the wifehood documents (3.64:17, 20, 22, 26; 3.71:7, 9, 10, 12, 13; 3.76:21) with the meaning "any time in the future"; for detailed discussion and references, see Fitzmyer 1979:261.

13 The verbs *khl* (line 11; 3.60:12; 6.61:15; 3.66:7; 3.67:10-11; 3.68:9-10; 3.69:7; 3.70:4; 3.71:13; 3.72:13, 17; 3.73:12-13; 3.75:14-15; 3.76:36-37, 39, 41; 3.77:4, 6; 3.78:18, 21; 3.79:9, 12; 3.80:25-27; *TAD* 5.5:4-5, 8; 6.4:5-6) and the less frequently attested *ykl* (3.64:31, 35; 3.65:8, 11; 3.69:11-12, 18; 3.72:12; 3.79:15; *TAD* 4.1:1, 3; 5.1:5; 5.4:2-4) bear the legal connotation of "entitled to" and their negative formulation regularly introduces the *Waiver* clause. Heb. *ykl* often bore the same judicial meaning.

14 This act is mentioned only here. Was it by physical force or legal action?

15 Penalties in the contracts were multiples of five, with most penalties being ten *karsh*: "five" (3.66:10; 3.70:8; 3.71:14; 3.73:15; *TAD* 5.1:7); "ten" (3.61:14, 21; 3.62:15; 3.64:11; 3.66:15; 3.67:15; 3.68:10-11; 3.73:21; 3.75:17); "twenty" (3.60:14; 3.64:30-31, 34, 36; 3.72:15, 18; 3.73:16; 3.76:31-32; 3.80:30); "thirty" (3.78:20; 3.79:10); and "fifty" (3.74:8, 15). A loan contract laid down a one *karsh* penalty (3.81:6) and a quitclaim a two *karsh* penalty (*TAD* B5.5:6). Usually they were many times the value of the object and were meant to be prohibitive.

16 Silver was weighed, not paid out in coin. In a single, early document (ca. 487 BCE), the standard was "the stones of Ptah" (*TAD* B4.2:2), comparable to the "treasury of Ptah" in Demotic documents beginning in the Persian period (*P. Wien* D 10150.5 [*EPE* C28]; *P. Wien* D 10151.4 [*EPE* C29]). All other Aram. documents weighed silver according to the "stones of the king" whereas the "weight of Syene" was employed in Byzantine Greek documents (*P. Münch.* 1.53 [*EPE* D29], et al.). See Porten 1968:62-69, though correcting the date of Cowley 11 according to B4.2; Kletter 1998:128-131 and passim.

17 Aside from this one early occurrence, reference to pure silver (*ksp ṣryp*) in the monetary notations occurred only at the end of the century, and always in the contracts of Haggai son of Shemaiah (3.74:15; 3.78:20; 3.79:11; 3.80:30; also 3.69:1; 3.81:6). For the usual expression, see on 3.60, n. 37.

18 The word *ʾpm* was the main component in the *Reaffirmation* clause (3.60:15; 3.61:15, 22; 3.67:15; 3.68:16; 3.73:16, 22; 3.77:8; 3.81:22; *TAD* B5.5:6; see also 3.81:2) and alternated with the less frequent *ʾm* (3.65:11; 3.72:16, 19; 3.78:21; 3.79:11, 14). Its nuance may be grasped from two non-legal passages in the papyri: "PN of the detachment of so-and-so to PN of that detachment *ʾpm*" (3.81:2) and, "If you find silver, come down immediately and if you do not find *ʾpm* come down immediately" (*TAD* A3.8:7-8). In the first passage it has the sense of "also, likewise," in the second, of "still, nevertheless." Though the precise translation in the legal context eludes us, the thrust of the term is that despite the penalty the claimant would fail in his goal and the challenged property would remain in the possession of the alienee and new owner.

19 The scribe omitted the word *zylk* in error, probably because of its similarity to the preceding *zk*.

20 This specification was found only here in the contracts but it applied generally — heirs would sue only after the death of the alienor; see Porten and Szubin 1987b:51-52, also for the following notes. With apparent aversion to a direct statement of death ("And if I, Konaiah, die") the scribe switched to the third person; see further on 3.73, n. 32 (*EPE* B38).

21 The order of persons in the *Waiver* clauses usually adhered to a descending order of inheritance.

22 This was a locus designation referring to the relatives and occurred in documents between 495 and 420 BCE (3.60:13; 3.65:10; 3.67:10 [truncated]; 3.70:9; 3.74:5; *TAD* B5.1:5-6); see also next note.

23 This was a status designation referring to the relatives and occurred between 471 and 420 BCE, though less frequently than the preceding phrase (3.65:10; 3.67:10 [truncated]; *TAD* B6.3:7). In this and other early documents between 495 and 440 the potential litigants covered in the warranty clauses were limited to blood relatives (3.60; 3.66; 3.70; *TAD* B5.1).

24 Mention of Konaiah by name at the beginning of the sentence led to the corresponding reference to Mahseiah, here and below in lines 12 and 20 abbreviated by omitting the theophorous element at the end.

25 I.e. whichever one of the heirs mentioned in the preceding clause.

26 This was a standard expression referring to previously mentioned fines (line 13; 3.63:1; 3.81:7), boundaries (3.68:8; 3.72:17-18; 3.79:11, 15; 3.80:29), or other items (*TAD* A4.6:15; 3.69:8; 3.81:5, 8-12; *TAD* B4.3:20, 4.4:11; 5.5:10). Often the word "above" was omitted (3.73:12; 3.76:23, 28; 3.78:12, 16; 3.79:15; 3.80:22; *TAD* B6.4:7). Some scribes preferred the expression "written in this document."

27 The expression *šlyṭ l-* was one of empowerment or entitlement to specific rights; see on 3.61, n. 28.

28 This self-denial ("I shall not be able to say") was a frequent mode of expression in the contracts (3.64:31; 3.69:11; 3.79:9; *TAD* B4.1:2; 5.4:3).

29 It was common practice to add the name of either party to first and second person affirmations (3.61:18; 3.62:5; 3.66:9, 18; 3.67:9; 3.68:8-9, 12; 3.69:3, 6, 8-9; etc.). If the name were also added to the second part of the sentence, the proper form would have required the addition of the conjunctive personal pronoun, thus "And I, Konaiah ... to you, Mahsah" (see 3.73, n. 9). But as here, the scribe usually omitted the pronoun (3.66:9-10; 3.78:5-6, 8).

neit the boatman."[30]

Penalty III
If I restrain you, I shall give you the silver which is written above

Reaffirmation III
(14)and you have the right to open that gateway and to go out into the street which is between us (and Peftuauneit).

Scribe[31]
(15)Pelatiah son of Ahio[32] wrote this document at the instruction of[33] Konaiah.

Witnesses
The witnesses herein[34]:

(16)(2nd hand) witness Mahsah son of Isaiah[35];
(3rd hand) witness Shatibarzana son of ᵓ*trly*[36];
(17)(4th hand) witness Shemaiah son of Hosea[37];
(5th hand) witness Phrathanjana son of Artakarana[38];
(6th hand) (18)witness Bagadata son of Nabukudurri[39];
(7th hand) *Ynbwly* son of Darga[40];
(8th hand) (19)witness Baniteresh son of Waḥpre[41];
(9th hand) witness Shillem son of Hoshaiah.[42]

Endorsement
(Verso)(20)Document[43] (*sealing*) of the wall which is built[44] which Konaiah wrote for Mahsah.

[30] He was a special cataract boatman, a job also followed by his son (see 3.60:10-11).

[31] Most Jewish scribes omitted the site of composition. The only ones to include it regularly, but not consistently, were Haggai son of Shemaiah (3.74:15-16; 3.78:22-23; 3.79:17; 3.80:32) and the Aramean scribes who drew up their documents in Syene (see 3.60, n. 41). Mauziah once recorded it when he wrote a document in Syene (*TAD* B7.1:8-9).

[32] This was the only document written by Pelatiah. The professional script, however, suggests that he came from a scribal family and was the brother of the scribe (*TAD* B4.2:1, 16) and witness (3.60:18) Gemariah son of Ahio and the father of the witness Ahio son of Pelatiah (3.69:22; [456 BCE]); Porten 2001:337. Both Aram. and Demotic contracts position the verb before the subject in this slot.

[33] Aram. *kpm* = Heb. *kpy*, lit., "according to the mouth of," is not the term for dictation, which, on the basis of Heb. analogy (cf. Jer 36:4, 17-18, 32), would be *mn pm*. Konaiah did not "dictate" the text to Pelatiah since he was presumably not familiar with all the technical terminology, but he did instruct him in what he wanted to say. Two early documents have the term ᵓ*l pm*, "upon the instruction of" (*TAD* B4.2:16, 4.4:18).

[34] Aram. *bgw*, lit. "within," is the standard expression in almost every witness formula and has been taken to mean that the witness signed on the "inside" (*recto*) of the document and not on the "outside" (*verso*), as they did in the Demotic documents (*P. Berlin* 13614.4-10 [*EPE* C27]; *P. Wien* D 10150.8-15 [*EPE* C28]; D 10151.9-24 [*EPE* C29]; *P. Berlin* 13554.13-28 [*EPE* C31], 13593.10-25 [*EPE* C33]; Porten 1968:198. The witnesses here signed in orderly fashion, two on each line. In three documents, Mahseiah called in several non-Jewish witnesses (lines 16-19; 3.60:19-21; 3.61:18-19). The number of witnesses was usually a multiple of four (3.63; 3.65-66; 3.68-69; 3.72-74; 3.80-81; *TAD* B4.2, 4.6;.5.5; 6.4), with eight witnesses present at deeds of withdrawal from realty (3.60; 3.68; 3.70), at certain bequests (3.78-79), and at a deed of adoption (3.77). Extraordinarily, there would be twelve witnesses (3.61-62). In an early Byzantine document from Syene the alienor stated at the beginning of the contract that he was providing the witnesses (*P. Lond.* V 1722.5-6 [*EPE* D22]).

[35] He witnessed two more documents for Mahseiah in 459 BCE (3.61:33; 3.62:21) and had one (now fragmentary) drawn up himself (*TAD* B5.3:6).

[36] A different son of ᵓ*trly* appeared as witness to another contract of Mahseiah and was there designated "Caspian" (3.65:18) as was a third son, *Ḥyḥ/Ḥyrw* (3.72:23).

[37] Appears only here.

[38] Both names are Iranian.

[39] Iranian son of a Babylonian.

[40] He was the only one not to preface his name with the word "witness." A *Ynbwly* son of Misday(a) was called "Caspian"; his abandoned house, sold by his neighbor Shatibara's son-in-law Bagazushta to Ananiah son of Azariah, lay on the other side of the Jewish Temple (3.72:9-10; 3.80:4). In the next document a neighbor of Mahseiah, Dargamana son of Khvarshaina, a Khwarezmian, withdrew his claim to Mahseiah's property (3.60:2). One of the witnesses to a third document of Mahseiah was Barbari son of Dargi(ya), a Caspian (3.65:19).

[41] The praenomen is Akk. and the patronym is Eg. For the divine name Banītu, see *COS* 2.60, n. 3.

[42] Appears only here.

[43] A space was left after the word "document" to allow for the cord and bulla sealing the document; see Kraeling 1953 pl. xxi.

[44] The endorsement usually contained a single noun which described the object conveyed, e.g. "house" (3.61:35-36; 3.65:21; 3.73:25; 3.79:21), or action undertaken, e.g. "withdrawal" (3.60:22; 3.66:14; 3.67:19; 3.68:20; 3.74:18). Occasionally it included an additional word or phrase (3.67:20; 3.68:17; 3.69:23; 3.72:25) or a title (3.72:25; 3.78:27). The operative verb was usually "wrote" but deeds of sale had "sold" (3.72:25; 3.80:35).

REFERENCES

Text, translations and studies: *TAD* B2.1; *EPE* B23; *EPE*; Kletter 1998; Kraeling 1953; Porten 1968; 1990; 2001; Porten and Szubin 1987a; 1987b; *TAD*.

WITHDRAWAL FROM LAND (3.60)
(2 January, 464 BCE)

Bezalel Porten

Six and one-half years after Mahseiah had allowed Konaiah to add a wall to his house (3.59), the Khwarezmian Dargamana showed up on Mahseiah's eastern border and complained that Mahseiah had taken his property. It was in evident disrepair and apparently neither party could produce a document of title. The court, headed by the Persian Damidata, settled the dispute by imposing an oath on Mahseiah, who with his wife and son swore by YHW, perhaps in the Elephantine Jewish Temple, that the plot did not belong to Dargamana (lines 4-7). The claimant was satisfied by the oath (lines 11-12) and drew up the present document of withdrawal, imposing a stiff twenty *karsh* penalty should he or any child or sibling in his name dispute the decision (lines 12-16). The scribe was Aramean, known only here, and so the document was drawn up in Syene. Only five of the eight witnesses were Jews; the others were Babylonian and Persian (lines 19, 21).

Date

(Recto)[(1)]On the 18th of Kislev, that is d[ay 13[1]+]4 (= 17) of Thoth, year 21 (of Xerxes the king), the beginning of the reign when [(2)]Artaxerxes the king sat on his throne,[2]

Parties

said Dargamana son of Khvarshaina, a Khwarezmian[3] whose place [(3)]is made[4] in Elephantine the fortress of the detachment of Artabanu, [(3)]to Mahseiah son of Jedaniah, a Jew who is in the fortress of Elephantine[5] [(4)]of the detachment of Varyazata,[6] saying:

Complaint

You swore to me by YHW the God in Elephantine the fortress,[7] you and your wife [(5)]and your son,[8] all (told) 3,[9] about the land[10] of mine which I complained[11] against you on account of it[12] before [(6)]Damidata and his colleagues[13] the judges,[14]

Oath I

and they imposed upon you for me the oath[15] to swear[16] by YHW on account of [(7)]that [(6)]land,

[1] The gap allows the restoration of the cipher for "10" and three unit strokes. The document was written at night; see Porten 1990:21.

[2] Reported cuneiform evidence for the death of Xerxes points to August 4-8, 465 BCE. The earliest dated Akk. tablet for Artaxerxes I was sometime after June 11, 464 (Parker and Dubberstein 1956:17). The Babylonians, and after them the Persians, followed a post-dating system whereby the first regnal year was counted from 1 Nisan following the accession.

[3] Dargamana is the only person in our documents with this ethnicon. The name is Iranian and appears abbreviated as Darga (3.59:18) and Dargi(ya), father of Barbari, a Caspian (3.65:19).

[4] I.e. whose station was fixed. This and similar designations ("of the place [...]" [3.65:19]) were attached only to soldiers of distant origin, such as Bactrians (Barznarava son of Artabarzana [*TAD* D2.12]), Caspians (Barbari son of Dargi(ya)), and Khwarezmians. A. D. H. Bivar (orally) suggested that they were recently assigned to the garrison after Xerxes' unsuccessful Greek campaign. But the Bactrian is still so designated at the end of the century.

[5] The formulation here was unique. For the usual formulation, see 3.59, note 3.

[6] The same detachment to which Mahseiah belonged in 471 BCE (3.59:3).

[7] The locus might refer either to the deity or to Mahseiah but the numerous references to the title of Anani son of Azariah argue for assigning it to deity, i.e. "YHW the God who is in Elephantine" (see 3.70, n. 5).

[8] Did wife and son swear as oath supporters or as parties with rights to the property?

[9] It was standard practice in Aram. documents, whenever mentioning more than one person, to total up the number with the word *kl*, "all (told)," e.g. "all (told) 2" (3.66:2, 3, 16, 19, 20; 3.67:8, 21; 3.68:2; 3.72:3, 10; 3.80:3, 11, 33; *TAD* B4.3:2).

[10] In the previous document this property was called "house" (3.59:3-5). It was evidently a plot with a run-down house on it. See 3.62, nn. 11, 12.

[11] Aram. *qbl* was the standard word for registering a complaint before prefect, lord or judge (3.61:13; 3.69:12, 18; 3.70:5-6; 3.78:19-20; 3.79:12; 3.80:28; *TAD* B5.4:2) in a judicial matter, or a complaint in a criminal case (*TAD* B7.2:4). The same term applied to registering complaints with the satrap or other government officials in matters of salary, property, and administration (*TAD* A2.2:10; 3.3:3-4; 4.2:3, 6.3:1, 6.14:1). On the model of a complaint in a loan contract ("You took from me a security" [3.69:13]), we may suppose that Dargamana's complaint was "You took from me my land." The complaint was basically different from "suit or process" but occasionally the scribe seemed to blend the two (see 3.70:4-6).

[12] The compound preposition *ʿldbr*. lit., "in the matter of" is used regularly in judicial contexts to designate an item in dispute, e.g. land, as here (also lines 6, 8, 16), a room given in bequest (3.73:13), a slave (3.69:8, 10, 11; *TAD* 5.6:6), and fish (*TAD* B7.1:3).

[13] Aram. **knt*, a loanword from Akk. *kinattu*, designates colleague(s) who accompanied officials at all levels, among the Jews (*TAD* A4.1:1, 10; *COS* 3.51:1, 4, 18, 22) as well as among the Persians (*TAD* A6.1:1, 5-7, 6.2:8; B8.5:16; cf. also A5.4:2). See Porten 1968:46-49.

[14] "Judge" appears regularly in the contracts as one of the three parties before whom a complainant might bring suit or register a complaint, the other two being lord and prefect (3.61:13, 24; 3.69:13, 19; 3.70:6; 3.80:28; *TAD* B4.6:14; 7.1:3). In a case involving an inheritance they are called "judges of the king" (*TAD* B5.1:3) and in a petition seeking redress of grievances they are "judges of the province" [*TAD* A5.2:4, 7). When named, they were always Persian — Paisana (*TAD* A3.8:2); Bagadana (*TAD* A6.1:5-6); Bagafarna and Nafaina (*TAD* A5.2:6); and, as here, Damidata — and once Babylonian — Mannuki (*TAD* A5.2:6).

[15] Aram. *mwmʾh* is the definite form of the noun *mwmʾ/mwmh* (3.61:4, 24; 3.66:4, 9; *TAD* 7.1:4, 5 [where restore *mwmʾh*], 7.3:1; 8.9:5); *GEA* 72-73 and n. 360.

[16] Since Mahseiah held possession of a piece of disputed, perhaps abandoned, property for which he could not produce any documentary evidence supporting title, the Persian judges decided that he should support his claim by judicial oath taken in the name of the deity.

(7)that it was not land of Dargamana, mine, behold I.[17]

Boundaries[18]

Moreover, behold the boundaries[19] of that land (8)which you swore to me on account of it[20]:

my house, Dargamana, I, is to the east[21] of it;

and the house of Konaiah son of Zadak, (9)a Jew of the detachment of Atrofarnah,[22] is to the west[23] of it;

and the house of [Jeza]niah son of Uriah,[24] (10)a Jew of the detachment of Varyazata, is below[25] it;

and the house of Espmet son of Peftuauneit,[26] (11)a boatman of the rough waters,[27] is above it.

Oath II

You swore to me by YHW

Satisfaction

and satisfied (12)my heart[28] about that land.

Waiver of suit

I shall not be able[29] to institute against you suit or process[30] [a] — I, or son of mine[31] or daughter (13)of mine about that land, brother or sister of mine, near or far[32] — (against) you, or son of yours or daughter of yours, brother or sister of yours, near or far.[33]

Penalty

(14)Whoever shall institute against you (suit) in my name[34] about that land shall give you silver, 20,[35] that is twenty,[36] *karsh* by the stone(-weight)s of (15)the king, silver 2 q(uarters) to the ten,[37]

Affirmation of investiture

and that land is likewise[38] yours and you are withdrawn[39] from (16)any suit (in) which they shall

a Prov 15:18; 28:25; 29:22

[17] Dargamana had claimed ownership, title and all (Szubin and Porten 1983b:282-83). The oath did not state that the land belonged to Mahseiah but merely denied the claim of Dargamana. Double emphasis of a name in a claim or in an affirmation of possession, as here and again in line 8 (with "I" added supralinearly), was not unusual, though the word order and the addition of the interjection "behold," are unique; cf. such expressions as "yours, you, Jedaniah and Mahseiah ..., in my name, I, Jedaniah" (3.67:8, 12), "to you ... you, Jedaniah ... to me ... I, Mahseiah" (3.68:3, 5), "the portion of mine, I, Anani ..." "my other portion, I, Anani" (3.73:9, 19).

[18] There was no fixed order for the boundary description. It ordinarily began with the adjoining property of a party to the transaction or of one related to or associated with that party; see note ad loc. in *EPE* B24.

[19] See note ad loc. in *EPE* B24.

[20] The *Boundaries* caption was often the opportunity for the scribe to repeat the operative verb(s) of the transaction — "which you swore" (here), "which I gave" (3.73:8; 3.78:8), which we sold (3.72:7), "which we sold and gave" (3.80:9, 17).

[21] Aram. *mwᶜ šmš*, lit., "going out of the sun" was the regular term for "east," usually written *mwᶜh šmš* (3.67:6, etc.; see note ad loc. in *EPE* B24). Only in this document did the boundary notations follow the house and not precede it.

[22] Six years earlier he was, with Mahseiah, in the detachment of Varyazata (3.59:2). It was unusual to add the affiliation of *all* the neighbors in the boundary description (as here and in lines 9-11); see further note ad loc. in *EPE* B24.

[23] Aram. *mᶜrb šmš*, lit. "going in of the sun" was the regular term for west (3.64:15; 3.67:7; etc).; see further note ad loc. in *EPE* B24.

[24] Five years later he will become Mahseiah's son-in-law (3.62:2-4).

[25] "Below" and "above" were the normal terms for the longitudinal directions, written *tḥtyh/tḥtyʾ/tht* and *ᶜlyh/ᶜlyh/ᶜly*, respectively (3.59:4-5; 3.61:4-5; 3.65:13; 3.67:5, etc.; see further note ad loc in *EPE* B24). Topographical arguments weigh in favor of the equation "above" = "north" and "below" = south; see Porten 1968:308-310; *TAD* B:177-182; von Pilgrim 1998:486-487.

[26] Six years earlier the house had belonged to the father (3.59:13). Had he since died?

[27] This was the title of the skilled pilots who navigated the rapids of the first Nile cataract and it corresponded to Eg. "boatman of the bad water" (*P. Berlin* 13614.1 [*EPE* C27]).

[28] *ṭyb lbb*, "(my/your/our) heart is good" (see 3.63, n. 14) were the regular terms of satisfaction recited by the party drawing up the contract after he had received goods, payment, or some other consideration (in our case an oath). In suits it was usually followed by a statement of withdrawal (see 3.66, n. 26), missing here.

[29] For this expression see 3.59, n. 13.

[30] The phrase *grh dyn wdbb* was one of the two standard expressions for taking legal action against someone (3.64:10; 3.65:7-8; 3.77:10, etc; see further note ad loc. in *EPE* B24). The more frequently used expression was *ršh dyn wdbb*, rendered freely "bring suit or process" (see 3.61, n. 35). On the model of Mahseiah's potential suit ("I did not give [the land] to you" [3.61:20; 3.62:14]), the suit would presumably have stated, "You did not swear to me."

[31] For discussion of the potential litigants, see 3.59, nn. 21-23.

[32] The words "brother ... far" were added supralinearly.

[33] The protected parties correspond exactly to the potential litigants — children and siblings, at home or away; see 3.59, n. 23.

[34] The scribe originally wrote "in the name of that land," the regular expression for designating an object in suit (3.61:12; 3.64:9; 3.65:8; 3.66:12; 3.70:5; 3.72:13, 17; 3.73:14; 3.80:25; *TAD* B5.4:7, 5.5:4, 10) and one familiar from Demotic legal texts (e.g. *P. Berlin* 13554.4 [*EPE* C31]), but then corrected it to read "in my name about that land" (see 3.67:12-13). The correction made explicit what was everywhere else implicit, namely that the *Penalty* clauses applied only to someone suing in the name of the alienor, i.e. the person issuing the warranty, in this case Dargamana (Porten and Szubin 1987b:50).

[35] This was a high penalty, found only in deeds of sale (3.72:15, 18; 3.80:30) and in one bequest (3.73:16); see further 3.59, n. 15.

[36] Repetition of numerical notations was frequent, both word repeating cipher, as here (3.61:14, etc.), and cipher repeating word (3.67:15, etc.).

[37] This monetary notation (also 3.61:14, 21; 3.62:15; 3.75:17) occurred in many variations — see further note ad loc. in *EPE* B24. It probably meant that a half shekel (= a zuz) had to be added to every Persian *karsh* (= 10 shekels) to bring its weight of 83.33 grams up to the weight of 87.6 grams (= 10 x 8.76 grams, the weight of the Eg. shekel); Porten 1968:305-307.

[38] See 3.59, n. 18.

[39] The promise to be removed from any further suit is reinforcement of the "likewise" (*ʾpm*) clause and occurs elsewhere in combination with that clause ("and he is likewise withdrawn from these goods" [3.66:15]) or in place of it. The failed claimant is removed from the object (3.66:15), from further suit (3.65:11), or from the other party and from further suit (3.68:11). The Aram. term *rḥq*, "be far, removed, with-

complain[40] against you on account of that land.

Scribe and place

Itu son of Abah wrote [(17)]this [(16)]document [(17)]in Syene[41] [b] the fortress at the instruction of Dargamana.

Witnesses[42]

(2nd hand) Witness Hosea son of Peṭekhnum[43];
(3rd hand) witness [(18)]Gaddul son of Igdal[44];
(4th hand) witness Gemariah son of Ahio[45];
(5th hand) Meshullam son of Hosea[46];
(6th hand) [(19)]Sinkishir son of Nabusumiskun[47];
(7th hand) witness Hadadnuri the Babylonian[48];
(8th hand) [(20)]witness Gedaliah son of Ananiah[49];
(9th hand) [(21)]witness Aryaicha son of Arvastahmara.[50]

Endorsement

(Verso)[(22)]Document (*sealing*) of withdrawal[51] which [Dargama]na son of Khvarshaina wrote for Mahseiah.

b Ezek 29:10; 30:6; Isa 49:12 in 1QIsa[a]

drawn" had its Demotic equivalent *wy* (*P. Berlin* 13554.3 [*EPE* C31]).

[40] The scribe has blended his legal terms; "suit" (*dyn*) was always associated with the verbs *grh* and *ršh*, never with "complain" (*qbl*); see above on lines 5 and 12.

[41] Aram. scribes, such as Itu son of Abah, normally drew up their documents in their place of residence, Syene, even when the transaction, as here, involved property in Elephantine. See *EPE* 162, n. 43.

[42] The scribe omitted the usual caption "The witnesses herein." For the number, see 3.59, n. 34.

[43] With an Eg. name, was the father of Hosea a native Eg. married to a Jewess (as Esḥor to Mibtahiah [3.63 below]) or a Jew who was given an Eg. name? Unlike the Arameans of Syene, as attested by the Makkibanit letters (*TAD* A2.1-7), the Jews rarely gave their children Eg. names. This witness appears only here.

[44] A certain playfulness was at work in the giving of the praenomen since it derived from the same root as the patronym (*gdl* "be great"). The witness appears only here.

[45] He drew up his own loan contract ca. 487 BCE (*TAD* B4.2) and appears in an ostracon found along with that document (*COS* 3.87I:2).

[46] Both Meshullam and the following witness, who appeared only here, failed to preface their signatures with the word "witness."

[47] Both names are Babyl.

[48] Though he bears an Aram. name, this witness, lacking patronymic, was called "the Babylonian." At the end of the century a person with the same name was father of Jathom ("Orphan") and grandfather of Malchiah (*TAD* C3.15:23). Chronologically, he could have been the same person as our witness.

[49] Appears only here.

[50] Both names are Iranian.

[51] The title of a document drawn up in settlement of a dispute (3.66:14; 3.67:19), in a case of probate (3.67:20), or for emancipation (3.74:18).

REFERENCES

Text and translation: *TAD* B2.2; *EPE* B24. *EPE*; GEA; Kraeling 1953; Parker and Dubberstein 1956; Porten 1968; 1990; Szubin and Porten 1983; *TAD*; von Pilgrim 1998.

BEQUEST OF HOUSE TO DAUGHTER (3.61)
(1 December, 459 BCE)

Bezalel Porten

On the occasion of Mibtahiah's marriage in 459 BCE to Jezaniah, one of Mahseiah's neighbors, her father gave her the plot which in 464 had been disputed by another neighbor Dargamana (3.60). In 471 he had allowed a third neighbor, Konaiah, to build a wall along the property (3.59). The fourth neighbor was an Egyptian boatman Peftuauneit who lived across the street (3.59:13) and had since passed his house on to his son Espmet (line 7). Mahseiah's bequest was a gift in contemplation of death with possession (line 9) and title (line 19) granted already *inter vivos* (line 3). It was to be treated as an estate perpetuated within the family or among designated heirs (lines 9-10), without any right to sell being granted. The guarantees were arranged in descending order of concern — challenge to the bequest: (1) from other beneficiaries claiming prior rights supported by a document (lines 9-18); (2) from Mahseiah himself (lines 18-22); (3) and from Dargamana (lines 23-27). In each case, it was a "document," the present one and the one written for Mahseiah by Dargamana (3.60), which was expected to turn back the challenge, while the standard ten *karsh* penalty was imposed on any suit by Mahseiah, his heirs, and beneficiaries (lines 11-14, 20-22). There was no penalty for attempted reclamation by Mahseiah (lines 18-19). The elaborate guarantees made this the longest bequest known (34+2 lines) with the largest number of witnesses (twelve). The normal eight were, topped off by two sons, a brother, and a neighbor (see notes to lines 29-31). Unlike Mahseiah's two earlier documents, all the witnesses were Jewish, though the scribe was Aramean and the document was drawn up in Syene (lines 27-28).

A contemporary Demotic conveyance (15 January-13 February, 460 BCE [P. *Wien* D 10151; *EPE* C29]) bears many structural and verbal parallels to this document.

Scribal note
(Recto)(0)Length, 13 and a handbreadth.[1]

Date
(1)On the 21st of Kislev, that is day ⌜20+⌝1 (= 21)[2] of Mesore, year 6 of Artaxerxes the king,[3]

Parties
said Mahseiah (2)son of Jedaniah, a Jew,[4] hereditary-property-holder[5] in Elephantine the fortress of the detachment of Haumadata,[6] to lady[7] Mibtahiah (3)his daughter,[8] saying:

Transfer I[9]
I gave[10] you in my lifetime and at my death[11]

Object
a[12] house, land,[13] of mine.

Measurements
(4)Its measurements (3)was:[14]
(4)its length from below to above, 13 cubits and 1 handbreadth;[15] (its) width from east[16] (5)to west, 11 cubits[17] by the measuring rod.[18]

Boundaries
Its boundaries:[19]
above it the house of Dargamana son of Khvarshaina (6)adjoins;[20] below it is the house of Konaiah son of Zadak;[21] east[22] of it is the house of Jezan[23] son of (7)Uriah your husband[24] and the house of Zechariah son of Nathan;[25] west of it is the house of Espmet[26] son of Peftuauneit, (8)a boatman of the rough waters.

Transfer II
That[27] house, land — I gave it to you in my lifetime and at my death.

Investiture I
(9)You have the right[28] to it from this day and for-

[1] This is a scribal note, written at the very top of the document, to serve as a memory aid for the length of the house recorded in line 4.
[2] The "20" mark is partially hidden in the papyrus crease.
[3] The two dates are a month off. For reconciliation see *EPE* 164, n. 3.
[4] Elsewhere he was called "Aramean"; see 3.59, n. 3.
[5] This technical term (*mhḥsn*) occurs four times in the contracts, once again, as here, with the intention of bolstering the status of someone whose title to a piece of property could not be established by written document (3.80:4-5); and once with the intent to bolster the reputation of a person accused of forced entry, theft and assault (*TAD* B7.2:2). The fourth text is fragmentary (*TAD* D2.12). For full discussion, see Szubin and Porten 1982:3-9; 1983a:40; *EPE* 164, n. 5.
[6] A Persian mentioned only here and in the companion document (3.62:2). In 471 and 464 BCE, Mahseiah had been in the detachment of Varyazata (3.59:3 [see note there]; 3.60:4) and would be there again in 449 and 446 (3.63:2-3; 3.64:2).
[7] The term *nšn* is often used to designate a female party to a contract, whether free, as here, slave or emancipated; *EPE* 164, n. 8.
[8] Here and again in the grant of 3.64:3, Mibtahiah was merely designated as Mahseiah's daughter. When she appeared opposite Peu son of Paḥe/Pakhoi, she was given a full affiliation — "of the detachment of Varyazata" (3.65:2-3).
[9] The *Transfer* clauses formed a symmetric inclusion (gave — lifetime/death — house/land: house/land — gave — lifetime/death) around the *Measurements* and *Boundaries* clauses (lines 3-8).
[10] This was the common term of conveyance, whether gift (as here), sale, or exchange; *EPE* 164, n. 11.
[11] Szubin and Porten 1983a:39.
[12] For the cipher "1" as indefinite article see 3.59, n. 7.
[13] The property which was called "house" in 471 (3.59:3-5) and "land" in 464 (3.60:5-8, 12-16) was now in 459 called, in apposition, "house, land" (lines 3, 8), or "land, house" (3.62:3), and then alternately "land" (lines 11-12, 16, 19, 24; 3.62:5, 8, 14) and "house" (lines 15, 22, 27, 35; 3.62:4, 6, 11), as interchangeable synonyms or as appropriate to the context (thus in 3.62). The plot had a gateway in 471 (3.59:3), but was run-down, as the advice to daughter and son-in-law "to renovate" clearly indicated (line 19; 3.62:5, 8, 12, 14).
[14] Sing. instead of plural verb; *EPE* 165, n. 15.
[15] The royal cubit measured 52.5 cm and the handbreadth 7.5 cm (Vleeming 1985:208, 214-215). The length was thus 6.9 m.
[16] For the term, see 3.60, n. 21.
[17] This would equal 5.78 m. The house would thus measure 39.88 sq m. Presumably, these were the external measurements.
[18] As silver was weighed by the stones of the king so property was always measured by the "measuring-rod" (ʿšt) (3.62:5; etc.)
[19] This terse, one-word caption (*tḥwmwhy*) is unique. For the fuller formulae, see *EPE* 160, n. 21. The location of the neighbors had been shifted 90°. In the previous document we found Dargamana-Konaiah-Jezaniah-Espmet in the order east-west-below-above (3.60:8-11); here they were above-below-east-west. True location must have been midpoint: above-east, below-west, east-below, west-above (NE, SW, SE, NW). See *TAD* B:177 and fig. 2.
[20] The houses of Dargamana and Mahseiah had a common wall.
[21] He was earlier given permission to build a wall on Mahseiah's property (3.59).
[22] For the spelling, see on *EPE* 160, n. 24.
[23] Abbreviated form of his name (Jezaniah), by which he was known also in later years (3.67:17 [416 BCE]). In the endorsement (line 35) the scribe would also abbreviate the name of his wife (Mibtah < Mibtahiah) and of his father-in-law, (Mahsah < Mahseiah). Jezaniah must have inherited the property from his father Uriah since "above" it in the year 416 lay the house of his brother Hosea (3.67:5).
[24] Apparently the couple had just been married and the plot was given to Mibtahiah, with rights of usufruct for Jezaniah (3.62), at the time of the wedding.
[25] As stated earlier, the new wall of Konaiah extended to the house of Zechariah (3.59:5), which later passed to his son Hazzul (3.67:5).
[26] He inherited the house and continued the occupation of his father (3.59:13; 3.60:10-11).
[27] This form of the demonstrative (*znk*) occurs only here and in the companion document (3.62:6).
[28] This term of empowerment (*šlyṭ*) was one of the two standard expressions, recurring in the *Investiture* clause — be it for realty (line 11), chattel (3.68:6), or goods (3.63:18) — and repeated in the *Reaffirmation* (of *Investiture*) clause (3.59:11, 14, etc.). It alternated in the conveyance documents with the expression "it is yours." In contrast to the latter expression which granted full title, this one may only have granted right of possession (see 3.59, n. 8). Full title, however, was granted in our document in a second *Investiture* clause (line 19); *EPE* 166, n. 30.

ever[29] [a] and (so do) your children after you.[30] [b] To whomever (10)you love[31] you may give (it). I have no other[32] son or daughter, brother or sister, or woman (11)or other man[33] (who) has right to that land but you and your children forever.

Penalty I

Whoever[34] (12)shall bring against you suit or process,[35] (against) you, or son or daughter of yours, or man of yours,[36] in the name of[37] (13)that (12)land (13)which I gave you or shall complain[38] against you (to) prefect or judge shall give you or your children (14)silver, 10, that is ten,[39] *karsh* by the stone(-weight)s of the king, silver 2 q(uarters) to the ten, without suit and without process,[40]

a Isa 9:5-6; Mic 4:7; Pss 113:2; 115:17, 18; 121:8; 125:2; 131:3

b Gen 17:8; cf. Gen 35:12

c Gen 31:9; Hos 2:11

Reaffirmation I

(15)and the house is your house likewise and your children's after you.[41]

Document validity I

And they shall not be able to take out[42] against you (16)a new or old document in my name[43] about that land to give (it) to another man. That document (17)which they shall take out against you will be false.[44] I did not write it[45] and it shall not be taken[46] in suit[47] (18)while this document is in your hand.[48]

Waiver of reclamation

And moreover, I, Mahseiah, tomorrow or the next day,[49] shall not reclaim (it)[50] [c] (19)from you to give

[29] This phrase occurs commonly in the *Investiture* clause in conveyances and manumissions (3.61:9; 3.68:7; 3.72:11; 3.73:4-5; 3.79:8; 3.80:23), in the *Withdrawal* clause in settlements (3.65:6-7; 3.66:9-10), in the satisfaction statement (3.66:9), and in the *Marriage* clause in documents of wifehood (3.63:4; 3.76:4; *TAD* B6.1:4). An abbreviated form (simply "forever") appears in two documents (3.64:16; 3.67:9, 16; also here, line 11). It is generally understood to indicate that the newly established legal relationship was not *a priori* limited in time (see Yaron 1958:4), but it must have been limited to the donor's lifetime since it was regularly followed by the phrase "and your children after you" (see next note). This temporal meaning is evident in the lines of Ps 115:17-18, "The dead cannot praise the Lord ..., but we will praise the Lord from now and forever."

[30] The addition "after you" (i.e. as your natural heirs) was regularly appended to the word "children" in the *Investiture* clause (3.64:8; 3.67:9; 3.68:7; 3.72:12; cf. 3.62:8; 3.73:5; 3.79:9; 3.80:23), in its *Reaffirmation* (line 15; 3.67:16; 3.68:12; 3.72:16, 19; cf. 3.78:21), and in the *Waiver* clause (3.78:19). It indicated that the conveyance was not limited to the lifetime of the recipient. See Szubin and Porten 1988:38; see also for next note.

[31] Mahseiah intended the bequest to be treated as an estate in fee tail, perpetuated within the family, and so gave Mibtahiah right to transfer it to a preferred, designated heir; for this meaning with parallels, see Szubin and Porten 1988:37-38; *EPE* 166, n. 33.

[32] The denial of any other heirs or beneficiaries occurred only here in our Aram. documents but is well paralleled in the Demotic contracts (*P. Wien* D 10150.2-3 [*EPE* C28]); *EPE* 166, n. 34.

[33] The addition of "another man (line 16), "another person" (3.65:9, 11, etc.), or "another whirlwind" (3.77:5) expanded the list of potential claimants beyond the circle of blood relatives. As is clear from the language of the clause, he was not an outsider but a possible beneficiary. "Another man" is next in line, one who comes "after" the natural heirs or in their stead if so designated by the testator. By including "woman" the scribe of our document preserved the male-female balance of the clause.

[34] Of the above heirs and beneficiaries in my name (see 3.59, nn. 21-23; 3.60:14). The scribe has deftly assimilated the *Penalty* clause (which was regularly preceded by a *Waiver* clause) to the *Investiture* clause.

[35] The phrase *ršh dyn wdbb* was the most frequently used expression for taking legal action against someone (line 20; 3.62:13; 3.64:9; 3.66:11; 3.78:18-19; 3.79:12; 3.80:25; *TAD* B5.5:4). It may be abbreviated to *ršh dyn* (3.66:14; 3.67:15; 3.68:9; 3.73:13; 3.80:27) or simply to *ršh* (lines 24, 26; 3.66:7, 11, 13-14, 16; 3.67:10, 12, 14, 17; 3.68:8-9; 3.78:19; 3.80:26-27).

[36] As the list of potential claimants was expanded to include beneficiaries, so the list of protected parties was expanded to include representatives.

[37] I.e. regarding; see 3.60, n. 34.

[38] The sequence of verbs in this sentence indicates that "sue" (represented by the verbs *ršh* and *grh* and their complements) and "complain" (*qbl*) are distinct and not synonymous legal acts; see further on line 20; *EPE* 167, n. 37.

[39] This was the most frequently imposed penalty (see 3.59, n. 15); for the numerical repetition, see 3.60:14.

[40] Aram. *wlʾ dyn wlʾ dbb*. This expression (lines 21-22; 3.62:15; 3.63:26 [mistakenly written *ydyn*], 29, 3.65:10, etc.) or the abbreviated "without suit" (3.67:17; 3.68:12, 14; 3.73:15; 3.76:32; 3.81:8) occurs regularly after the penalty or dowry sums to indicate that the affected party did not have to undertake any further legal action to realize payment; *EPE* 167, n. 42.

[41] For the *clausula salvatoria*, see 3.59, n. 18.

[42] I.e. to produce.

[43] Wills and testamentary bequests were customarily amended and periodically rewritten. The "new or old document" expression has its Demotic parallel at Elephantine (*P. Wien* D10151.7 [*EPE* C29]) and elsewhere, whence it is clear that "new" means recent and not future (Malinine 1953 #18:13-14). The clause also occurs in 3.65:12 and elsewhere, but only here did the scribe add explicitly "in my name," which was implicit from the continuation of the document, namely "I did not write it" (line 17).

[44] So too in 3.79:16; for parallels, see Szubin and Porten 1983a:40.

[45] This declarative statement was a known defense (3.64:12).

[46] I.e. shall not be accepted.

[47] I.e. admissible as evidence. The phrase *wlʾ ytlqḥ bdyn* occurs only here in our Aram. documents; *EPE* 168, n. 49.

[48] The two declarative statements are followed by an advisory one — hold on to this document! Here and elsewhere "this document in your hand" was designed to ward off future claims (line 22 [cf. line 27]; 3.69:12-13, 19-20).

[49] See 3.59, n. 12.

[50] The danger of reclamation (*hnṣl*) loomed large in bequests made "in love, affection" (*brḥmn* [3.67:11, 14; 3.73:4, 12; 3.76:41; 3.78:5, 12, 17; 3.79:9) *inter familium*, whether of realty, as here (3.62:10; 3.73:20; 3.75:15; 3.79:10), or of dowry (3.76:42), or of related chattel (3.71:13-14), and specific renunciation of such intentions was common (3.62:10 [wife from husband]; 3.71:13-14 [master of handmaiden bride from groom]; 3.73:20 [other heirs from daughter]; 3.75:15; 3.79:10 [father from daughter]; 3.76:42 ["brother" from sister]; *TAD* 6.4:8 [mother from daughter]). Monetary penalty was imposed only when ultimate ownership and unabridged dominion were granted (3.73:20-22; 3.79:9-11). In the present case, Mibtahiah's rights were limited by the parallel grant of a life estate of usufruct to her husband (3.62). See Szubin and Porten

to others.[51]

Investiture II

That land of yours[52] build up[53] and/or give (it) to whomever you love.

Penalty II

(20)If tomorrow or the next day I bring against you suit or process and say:[54]

"I did not give (it) to you,"[55]

(21)I shall give you silver, 10 *karsh* by the stone(-weight)s of the king, silver 2 q(uarters) to the ten, without suit (22)and without process,

Reaffirmation II

and the house is your house likewise.

Document validity II

And should I go into a suit,[56] I shall not prevail[57] while this document is in your hand.[58]

Document transfer

(23)Moreover, there is a[59] document of withdrawal[60] which Dargamana son of Khvarshaina, the Khwarezmian, wrote for me about (24)that land when he brought (suit)[61] about it before the judges and an oath[62] was imposed (upon me) for him and I swore to him (25)that it was mine,[63] and he wrote a document of withdrawal and gave (it) to me. That document — I gave it to you.[64] (26)You, hold-it-as-heir.[65] If tomorrow or the next day Dargamana or son of his bring (suit) (27)about that house, that document take out and in accordance with it make suit[66] with him.

Scribe and place

Attarshuri (28)son of Nabuzeribni[67] wrote (28)this document in Syene[68] the fortress at the instruction of Mahseiah.

Witnesses

The witnesses herein:[69]

(29)(2nd hand) witness Gemariah son of Mahseiah[70];

(3rd hand) witness Zechariah son of Nathan[71];

(30)(4th hand) witness Hosea son of Pelaliah[72];

(5th hand) witness Zechariah son of Meshullam[73];

(6th hand) witness Maaziah son of (31)Malchiah[74];

(7th hand) witness Shemaiah son of Jedaniah[75];

1988:38-39; *EPE* 168 n. 52.

[51] I.e., other heirs or beneficiaries.

[52] The Aram. form (*zylyky*) is emphatic; cf. a comparable form in 1QGenAp 19:20. For a different rendition, see *GEA* 55-56, 214-215.

[53] Is the form of the verb *peal* (as in 3.73:8 [scribe unknown]) or *pael*, as in *mbny*, "renovated, restored, improved," in three documents written by Haggai (3.78:12; 3.79:2-3; 3.80:12-13)?

[54] Here too, the second *Penalty* clause followed directly on the second *Investiture* clause without any intervening *Waiver* clause.

[55] Only rarely (3.62:14; *TAD* B5.1:5) was the nature of such a suit regarding a conveyance spelled out, but we may assume that this was the normal claim, namely, that the defendant possessed neither title nor ownership. Loss of suit would mean that loss of property was retroactive. See Porten and Szubin 1987c:237.

[56] I.e. take legal action.

[57] This whole clause ("go to suit ... not prevail") recurs twice elsewhere (3.69:19; 3.79:15).

[58] This document shall prevail against my suit as well as against that of my heirs and beneficiaries (lines 15-18).

[59] For the numeral "1" as indication of the indefinite article, see 3.59, n. 7.

[60] This was 3.60.

[61] Strictly speaking, Dargamana did not bring suit but complained (3.60:5).

[62] See on 3.60:6.

[63] In fact, Mahseiah only swore that the plot was not Dargamana's (3.60:7).

[64] It was standard procedure in sales and other conveyances in Egypt to transfer to the alienee previous documents attesting the right of the alienor to the property. See 3.80:31-32 and *P. Wien* D 10151.7 (*EPE* C29); Porten and Szubin 1982a:124-126.

[65] Make it part of your ancestral estate. The advisory statement (*hḥsnhy*) harked back to Mahseiah's designation as a "hereditary-property-holder" at the beginning of the document (line 2). The verb also occurs with the meaning "to take hereditary possession" in a document apportioning slaves between two heirs (3.68:14).

[66] The expression *ᶜbd dyn* with the meaning to "engage in a suit" occurs once more (3.65:3); for its other meanings see the documents of wifehood (3.63:31, etc.). The terms *grh* and *ršh* had the meaning of "initiating a suit" (see 3.60:12 and line 12 above) whereas the present phrase is used to describe the response to such initiation or the conduct of a suit.

[67] The praenomen is Aramean and the patronym, Babylonian.

[68] The Aram. scribe drew up the document at the site of his residence (see 3.60:16-17).

[69] There was not room on the *recto* for all twelve witness to sign their names and the last five had to sign on the *verso*, a rare occurrence (see *TAD* B4.4:19-21 where all the witness signed on the *verso*). Only four of the twelve Jewish witnesses are known elsewhere (Gemariah, Zechariah son of Nathan [line 29], Nathan [line 32], and Mahsah [line 33]).

[70] Probably Mahseiah's son whose signature gave added weight to Mahseiah's renunciation of all other heirs' rights to the property (lines 10-11). He also witnessed two documents in the Anani archive (3.71:15; 3.73:23) and his daughter, Meshullemeth, was the first contributor on the Collection Account recorded by the communal leader Jedaniah son of Gemariah, probably her brother (*TAD* C3.15:2); Porten 2001:334-335. In a Demotic bequest to a daughter, her male siblings and perhaps nephew signed as witnesses (*P. Wien* 10150.8-11 [*EPE* C28]).

[71] Mahseiah's eastern neighbor (line 7) acknowledged the new owner.

[72] Only here and in the companion document (3.62:17), where he signed first.

[73] Only here and in the companion document (3.62:18).

[74] Only here and in the companion document (3.62:19). Is this a unique defective spelling for Mauziah or a true variant (cf. Neh 10:9; 1 Chr 24:18)?

[75] Probably the brother of Mahseiah son of Jedaniah rather than the son of Jedaniah, the following witness, he appears only here and in the companion document (3.62:19); Porten 2001:334-335.

(8th hand) witness Jedaniah son of Mahseiah[76];
(Verso) (32)(9th hand) witness Nathan son of Ananiah[77];
(10th hand) Zaccur son of Zephaniah[78];
(33)(11th hand) witness Hosea son of Deuiah/Reuiah[79];
(12th hand) witness Mahsah son of Isaiah[80];
(34)(13th hand) witness Hosea son of Igdal.[81]

Endorsement
(35)Document (*sealing*) of a house [which] Mahsah son of Jedaniah wrote (36)for Mibtah[82] daughter of Mahsah.[83]

[76] Son of Mahseiah named after his grandfather (see on line 29), he appears only here and in the companion document (3.62:20). The Mahseiah son of Jedaniah who appears as a witness forty-three years later was probably his son (3.67:18); Porten 2001:334-335.

[77] Professional scribe who wrote two and perhaps three more documents for the Mahseiah archive (3.63:37; 3.64:17 and probably *TAD* B2.5), two documents for the Anani archive (3.69:20; 3.71:14), and two more (*TAD* B5.4; D2.22:1-2).

[78] Appears only here and in the companion document (3.62:20). He alone failed to preface his name with the designation "witness."

[79] Appears only here and in the companion document (3.62:21). The father's name would mean either "Know Yah" or "Yah is Friend." The letters *daleth* and *resh* are indistinguishable in this script.

[80] The first witness for Mahseiah in 471 BCE (3.59:16).

[81] Appears only here and in the companion document (3.62:22).

[82] In the endorsement the scribe abbreviated both Mahseiah (> Mahsah) and Mibtahiah (> Mibtah).

[83] Three documents contains two-line endorsements. The second line always begins with the name of the party for whom the document was written, preceded by the preposition "for" (3.66:19-20; 3.67:20-21).

REFERENCES

Text and translation: *TAD* B2.3; *EPE* B25. *EPE*; Malinine 1953; Porten 2001; Porten and Szubin 1982; 1987c; Szubin and Porten 1982; 1983a; *TAD*; Vleeming 1985.

GRANT OF USUFRUCT TO SON-IN-LAW (3.62)
(1 December, 459 BCE)

Bezalel Porten

At the same time that he gave Mibtahiah a bequest of a house plot, Mahseiah extended to her husband lifetime usufruct in that house. Typologically this document is unique among our texts. It was intentionally written on both sides of papyrus sheets cut from the same scroll as the previous document. The date is damaged and the endorsement is missing. Instead of an *Investiture* clause it presented a *Restriction on alienation*. Granted rights to renovate the house and advised to live there with his wife, Jezaniah was denied the right to sell or bequeath it to anyone other than his children from Mibtahiah (lines 3-7). Should Mibtahiah repudiate and leave Jezaniah after he had improved the house, she could not remove it from him to give to others. Should she wish to reclaim it, half would remain with Jezaniah as reward for his labor. In any case, the document thrice emphasized, it was only their joint children who had right to the house after their parents' death (lines 6-13). Attempted suit by Mahseiah, denying ever having granted building rights, would result in the standard ten *karsh* penalty (lines 13-16). The document treated the property as an estate to be passed on in perpetuity within a limited family circle. Scribe, witnesses, and site of redaction were identical with those in the previous document (3.61).

Date
(Recto)(1)On the 20[+1] (= 21st) of [Kis]le[v, that is da]y [20+]1 (= 21) of [Mes]ore, year 6 of Artaxerxes the king,[1]

Parties
said Mahseiah (2)son of Jedaniah, a Je[w o]f Elephantine of the detachment of Haumadata, (2)to Jezaniah son of Uriah in the same detachment,[2] (3)saying:

Object
There is[3] land of a[4] house of mine,[5] west of the

[1] This document was drawn up the same day as the previous one; unfortunately the date formula is damaged. See on 3.61:1.

[2] The expression occurs also in 3.67:4.

[3] Documents regularly begin with some action — "I came" (3.59:3; 5:3; 13:3; 18:3; 23:3); "I gave" (3.61:3; 3.64:2; 3.73:2; 3.75:3; 3.78:2; 3.79:2); "I sued" (*TAD* B5.2:3); "You swore" (3.60:2); "We sued" (3.66:4); "We withdrew" (3.67:4); "... we divided" (3.68:3); etc. The opening here resembles that in the official bipartite letter which begins with a statement of the situation introduced by the stative *ʾyty*, and then proceeded with the instruction introduced by *kʿn*, "Now" (line 5; *TAD* A6.7:2, 8, see also 5.5:11; 6.3:5; 6.10:5). Elsewhere in the contracts the stative appears at the beginning of a quotation of a suit (3.66:5). For another irregular beginning see 3.65:3-4. See *EPE* 173, n. 3.

[4] The cipher "1" was written for the indefinite article; see 3.59, n. 7.

[5] I.e., a house-plot.

house of yours,[6] which I gave to Mibtahiah (4)my daughter, your wife, and a document I wrote for her concerning it.[7]

Measurements

The measurements of that house:[8]

13 cubits and a handbreadth (5)by 11 by the measuring rod.[9]

Building rights

Now,[10] I, Mahseiah, said to you: That land build (up)[11] and ENRICH IT (or: PREPARE IN IT HER HOUSE)[12] (6)and dwell[13] [a] herein with your wife.

Restriction on alienation

But that house — you do not have right to[14] sell it[15] or to give (it) (7)lovingly to others[16] but it is your children from Mibtahiah my daughter (who) have right to it (8)after you (both).[17]

Repudiation

If tomorrow or the next day you build that land (up and) afterwards[18] my daughter hate you[19] (9)and go out from you, she does not have the right to take it and give it to others[20] but it (10)is (9)your children from (10)Mibtahiah (who) have the right to it in exchange for the work which you did.[21]

Reclamation

If she shall reclaim[22] (11)from you, half the house [s]h[al]l be hers to take but the other half — you have the right to it in exchange for (Verso) (12)the building (improvement)s which you have built into that house. And furthermore, that half — (13)it is (12)your children from Mibtahiah (13)(who) have the right to it after you.[23]

Penalty

If tomorrow or the next day I bring against you suit or process[24] (14)and say:

"I did not give you that land to build (up) and I did not write for you this document,"[25]

I (15)shall give you silver, 10 *karsh* by the stone(-weight)s of the king, silver 2 q(uarters) to the ten, without suit and without process.[26]

Scribe and place

(16)Attarshuri son of Nabuzeribni[27] wrote this document in Syene[28] the fortress at the instruction of Mahseiah.

Witnesses

The witnesses (17)herein:[29]

(2nd hand) witness Hosea son of Pelaliah;[30]

(3rd hand) witness Zechariah son of Nathan;

(18)(4th hand) witness Gemariah son of Mahseiah[31];

(5th hand) witness Zechariah son of Meshullam;

(19)(6th hand) witness Maaziah son of Malchiah;

[a] Jer 29:5

[6] See on 3.61:6-7.

[7] That was 3.61. The current document was cut from the same scroll. The peculiar preposition *ʾḥrwhy* in this clause (see also 3.64:7) alternates with the more regular *ʿlʾ* (3.64:3, 10, etc.).

[8] For the formula, see 3.61:4.

[9] The usual indications of "length" and "width" were omitted. The house measured 9 x 5.78 m = 39.88 sq. m. See 3.61, n. 15.

[10] This word (*kʿn*) is otherwise absent from the contracts; for its use here see n. 3.

[11] The run-down house given to Mibtahiah was meant to be the residence of the newly-married couple and needed to be built up and made inhabitable. See 3.61:19 and following notes.

[12] The reading and meaning elude us. Because of the *daleth-resh* similarity the word may be read either *ʿtr*, "wealth, enrich" or *ʿtd*, "prepare." The following vocable (*bhmyth*) runs into the end of the line and may be two words, but no separation yields a clear meaning; see Porten 1968:242, n. 14. One suggestion would view *myth* as scribal error for *byth*, "her house" (Stephen A. Kaufman).

[13] The double command to "build and dwell" was uttered by the prophet Jeremiah to the first Babylonian exiles.

[14] For this term see 3.61, n. 28.

[15] Right of sale was omitted from the deed for Mibtahiah (3.61) and is here explicitly denied.

[16] Nor may Jezaniah assign it to any one of his children from another marriage or to a beneficiary.

[17] The document is thus akin to the establishment of a trust for the benefit of Mahseiah's grandchildren.

[18] Frequent in narrative (*TAD* C1.1:8, et al; 1.2:2), historical inscriptions (*TAD* C2.1:12, et al) and letters (COS 3.51:6, 8; *TAD* A4.8:6 [added supralinearly], 7; 6.7:6), this adverb (*ʾḥr*) rarely occurs in contracts because these provided little occasion to describe events in sequence. While it usually begins an independent sentence (3.64:5; 3.66:8; 3.81:3), it is used by two Aramean scribes to introduce the subordinate penalty clauses (3.68:10; 3.81:6-8, 10 [repeatedly]).

[19] I.e., repudiate you. See Porten and Szubin 1995:54-57.

[20] I.e., children from another marriage or other beneficiaries.

[21] Jezaniah had only right of usufruct in the house but the work he would put into it would guarantee that it went to his children from Mibtahiah.

[22] For this act see 3.61, n. 50. The house, after all, belonged to Mibtahiah but Mahseiah denied her the right to reclaim more than half should her husband put in improvements.

[23] Even the half he was entitled to hold onto after Mibtahiah's act of reclamation was to go only to their joint children.

[24] For this phrase see 3.61, n. 35.

[25] A similar statement was posited for the potential suit of Mahseiah against Mibtahiah — "I did not give you" (3.61:20).

[26] The same penalty as in the potential suit against Mibtahiah (3.61:21-22), except that here there is no following *clausula salvatoria* (for which see 3.59, n. 18).

[27] He is the same scribe who drew up the document for Mibtahiah (3.61:27-28).

[28] See 3.60, n. 41.

[29] Except for the first and third witnesses, who exchanged slots, all the others signed in the same order here as in the previous document (3.61:29-34).

[30] He was the third witness in the companion document (3.61:30).

[31] He was the first witness in the previous document (3.61:29).

(7th hand) witness Shemaiah son of Jedaniah;
(20)(8th hand) witness Jedaniah son of Mahseiah;
(9th hand) witness Nathan son of Ananiah;
(10th hand) witness Zaccur son of Zephaniah[32];

(21)(11th hand) witness Hosea so[n of] Deuiah/Re-uiah;
(12th hand) witness Mahsah son of Isaiah;
(22)(13th hand) witness Hose[a son of I]gdal.

[32] The signature ran to the very end of the line and the final *he* was written supralinearly.

REFERENCES

Text and translation: *TAD* B2.4; *EPE* B26. Porten 1968; Porten and Szubin 1995; *TAD*.

DOCUMENT OF WIFEHOOD (3.63)
(14 October, 449 BCE)

Bezalel Porten

Although widowed, Mibtahiah may not be courted directly but only through her father. As a suppliant for a loan or for building rights approached his prospective lender or neighbor, the Egyptian royal builder Esḥor approached the father of his desired bride. Granted his request in exchange for a ten-shekel *mohar*, he invested her in her new status (lines 3-6), again like a petitioner, but with a statement echoing a biblical formula (see notes). The thrust of this and similar wifehood documents was the guarantee of the bride's pecuniary rights during the marriage and in case of repudiation by, or the death of, her spouse. Much space was devoted to detailed enumeration of the items of her dowry (totaling 65.5 shekels, including the *mohar*) and several supralinear additions and corrections suggest last minute changes (lines 6, 8, 16). All these personal items, garments, vessels, and toiletries, reverted to her in case of repudiation (lines 6-16, 24-25, 27-28). But the repudiating party lost the *mohar* and was obliged to pay a 7½ shekel compensation. Like Mibtahiah, Esḥor was probably married before and special clauses were required to guarantee Mibtahiah's rights and status. He could not alienate his property without her consent, could not bequeath it to a previous wife or children, and no one could evict her from his house after his death (a provision also in Jehoishma's contract [3.76:31-32) — all subject to twenty *karsh* penalty for violation (lines 29-36). The major clauses (*Repudiation* and *Death*), the ones recurring in the other wifehood documents, were reciprocally formulated, guaranteeing the rights of the husband as well as the wife (lines 17-29).

Date
(Recto)(1)On the 24th [of] Tishri, [that is day] 6 of the month of Epeiph, [y]ear [16 of Artaxerx]es [the] king,[1]

Parties
(2)said Esḥor son of Dje[ḥo],[2] a builder of the king[3] to Mah[seiah,[4] an A]ramean of Syene of the detachment of (3)Varyazata,[5] saying:

Marriage[6]
I [c]ame to your house (and asked you) to give me[7] your daughter Mipta(h)iah[8] for wifehood.[9]

[1] This date has been much scrutinized. Repeated examination of the papyrus revealed that we must read 24 Tishri = 6 Epeiph which will synchronize in 16 Artaxerxes I, yielding October 14, 449 BCE. See Porten 1990:21-22.

[2] His name and occupation indicate that he was Eg. but later documents for his sons designated them "sons of Nathan" (see 3.67, n. 6). Had he "converted?"

[3] An unpublished wooden tag found in the Aramean house M room 1, associated with Dayamana, adjacent to Mibtahiah (von Pilgrim 1995:491, Abb. 3 and oral communication). It reads *lʾsḥwr br ṣḥʾ ʾrdyklʾ* "[Belonging) to Esḥor son of Djeho, the builder." It is now in the Elephantine Museum. See further 3.65, n. 3.

[4] Quite uniquely, Mahseiah son of Jedaniah was recorded here without patronymic.

[5] This was the same designation he bore in 471 BCE (3.59:2-3).

[6] As at Elephantine, so in most Neo-Babylonian documents and in the early Eg. documents down through the end of the 26th Dynasty, the groom did not approach the bride but someone responsible for her. The statements in the *Marriage* clause were a narrative introduction and not "creative" of the matrimonial "relationship." They were declarative and not constitutive. See Porten and Szubin 1995:48-49.

[7] For this "supplicant" terminology see 3.59, n. 6.

[8] For the spelling of her name see 3.64, n. 3.

[9] The expression "give for wifehood" (*ntn lʾntw*) has its Akk. forerunner in *nadānu ana aššūti*. See Kraeling 1953:146.

Affirmation of status

(4)She is my wife and I am her husband[10] [a] from this day and forever,[11]

Mohar

I gave you (as) *mohar*[12] [b] for (5)your daughter Miptahiah:

5.0 shekels [silver], 5 shekels[13] by the stone(-weight)s of [the] king.

Satisfaction I

It came into you and your heart was satisfied[14] [c] (6)herein.

Dowry

[Your daughter] Miptahiah brought in to me in

12.0 shekels (ERASURE: your) her hand: silver money[15] 1 *karsh*, 2 shekels by the stone(-weight)s of the king, (7)silver 2 q(uarters) to the 10.[16]

She brought in to me in her hand:[17]

28.0 shekels 1 new garment of wool,[18] striped (8)with dye doubly-well[19] it was[20] (in) length 8 cubits by 5 (in width),[21] worth (in) silver 2 *karsh* 8 shekels (9)by the stone(-weight)s of the king;[22]

8.0 shekels 1 new SHAWL;[23] it was (in) length 8 cubits by 5 (in width), worth (10)(in) silver 8 shekels by the stone(-weight)s of the king;

7.0 shekels another garment of wool, FINELY-WOVEN;[24] it was (11)(in) length 6 cubits by 4 (in width),[25] worth (in) silver 7 shekels;

1.5 shekels 1 mirror of bronze,[26] worth (12)(in) silver 1 shekel, 2 q(uarters);

1.5 shekels 1 bowl of bronze, worth (in) silver 1 shekel, 2 q(uarters)[27];

a Hos 2:4

b Gen 34:12; Exod 22:15-16; 1 Sam 18:25

c Ruth 3:7

---

[10] This affirmative formula (also in 3.63:4; 3.76:4; *TAD* B6.1:3-4) echoes the negative biblical formulation, "She is not my wife and I am not her husband." As an oral formula at Elephantine it may have constituted the *verba solemnia* pronounced in contemplation of marriage, but in our documents it functioned as an *Investiture* clause affirming status. Such sequence appears in a building grant — "I came to you and you gave me the gateway of your house to build a wall there. That wall is yours" (3.59:3-4). Its main thrust was to introduce the events that precipitated the contractual obligations of the respective parties. See Porten and Szubin 1995:44-45; Szubin and Porten forthcoming. Similar declarations were to be found in cuneiform texts throughout the ages; Hugenberger 1994:216-239.

[11] The phrase occurred commonly in the *Investiture* clause in conveyances and manumissions (see 3.61, n. 29) and in documents of wifehood (3.76:4; *TAD* B6.1:4), where its legal thrust was of limited, though unspecified duration, hence ultimately finite. Precluding voluntary dissolution, the matrimonial status was binding only "until death do them part."

[12] Biblical law had a stock phrase "*mohar* of the virgins/maidens" (Exod 22:15-16). It was a gift (Gen 34:12) by the groom to the father of the bride, effecting betrothal (2 Sam 3:14). It might be paid in labor (Gen 29:18) or in kind (1 Sam 18:25) and it(s value) was normally returned to the young couple — witness the righteous indignation of Jacob's wives that their father Laban "sold us and indeed consumed our money" (Gen 31:15). Similar payments and practice of return were found throughout the ancient Near East — Akk. *terḫatum* (CH §§138-139, 159-161, 163-164, 166) Eg. *šp n s-ḥm.t* (*P. Berlin* 13593.3 [*EPE* C33]), and Arab. *ṣadāq* (*P. Or. Inst.* 10552r.3 [*EPE* F2]); Hugenberger 1994:240-247. For its disposition, see notes 17, 28, and 53.

[13] The *mohar* for the unwed maiden Jehoishma was 1 *karsh* (= 10 shekels), but none was paid for the handmaiden Tamet (3.76:4-5; 3.71.3).

[14] This term of satisfaction was used to receipt a *mohar* and dowry, as here and in line 15 (also 3.76:5; *TAD* B 6.1:5), the purchase price for a house (3.72:6; 3.80:6, 14, 26), payment (3.70:4) or oath (3.65:5) in settlement of a suit, or any sort of payment or transfer of goods (*TAD* B4 4:9; 5.5:7). Once it is preceded by the statement "you have satisfied our heart" (3.66:9).

[15] This was cash and Jehoishma had almost twice as much — 22.125 shekels (3.76:5-6). We find a similar payment in the Elephantine Demotic contract — "money as money, 1 (deben)" (*P. Berlin* 13593.5 [*EPE* C33]). After much haggling, Tamet secured 15 shekels cash and the amount was recorded in a separate statement on the *verso* of her contract after it had been all but tied and sealed. The language was similar to that here — "Tamet brought in to Anani in her hand silver, 1 *karsh*, 5 shekels" (3.71:16).

[16] The two shekels were added supralinearly, as an addition made after the document had already been completed (see note 29).

[17] See also 3.71:4. A var. formula was "Jehoishma your sister brought in to me in(to) my house" (3.76:5). Aram., unlike Demotic, had no single term for "dowry." The Demotic contract read "Here is the inventory of the woman's possessions (*nkt.w n s-ḥm.t*) which you brought to my house with you" (*P. Berlin* 13593.4 [*EPE* C33]). Marriage normally entailed *in domum deductio*. The *mohar* was not included in the following list though it was factored into the total (lines 13-15). Strictly speaking, it was not "brought in" by Mibtahiah, but probably given directly by Mahseiah.

[18] For discussion of these garments, see Porten 1968:88-89. The objects were listed in descending order of value.

[19] Alternately, two-toned.

[20] This singular verb (*hwh*) is repeated for the next two items and occurs elsewhere in the measurement formula for houses (3.61:2-3; 3.73:5-6; 3.75:4). Here it seems to be elliptical for "its measurements was (= were)."

[21] The 8 x 5 cubit size was apparently standard. Jehoishma's large new woolen garment measured just slightly less — 7 x 4 (3.76:6-7). The garments in the Eg. contract bore no measurements.

[22] Reaching the end of the line the scribe wrote six numerical strokes supralinearly. He later increased the amount by adding two more (see note 29 below).

[23] The same garment is found in Tshenese's dowry, but the precise meaning is no more certain there than here (*P. Berlin* 13593.5 [*EPE* C33]). It also appears in a fragmentary Aram. contract, where it measured 7 x 4 cubits and was valued at 4½ shekels (*TAD* B6.2:5-6), a little over half Mibtahiah's SHAWL worth 8 shekels.

[24] For inconclusive discussion of this *niphal* loanword (*nšḥt*), as well as the following bronze items (lines 11-13), see Fitzmyer 1979:257-258.

[25] The 6 x 4 cubit size was standard for the smaller garment. Jehoishma had five such small garments, both woolen and linen, with these, or approximately these, measurements (3.76:7-12; also fragment *TAD* B6.2:4-5).

[26] This and the following are literal translations of what concise English would designate "bronze mirror," "reed bed," "palm-leaf box." Jehoishma had the same five bronze vessels (mirror, bowl, 2 cups, and jug) and the values varied but slightly (3.76:13-15). In her contract, however, they were separately captioned and tallied, much as the copper objects in Tshenese's contract were grouped together (see note 28 below).

[27] The letter looks much more like a *kaph*, abbreviating *kp*, "hand" (= ⅓) than a *resh*, abbreviating *rb*^{c}, "quarter." See 3.73, n. 13 [*EPE* B38]).

2.0 shekels — 2 cups of bronze, (13)worth (in) silver 2 shekels;

.5 shekels — 1 jug of bronze, worth (in) silver 2 q(uarters).

Total — All the silver (14)and the value of the goods:[28]

65.5 shekels — (in) silver 6 *karsh*, 5 shekel[29] 20 hallurs by the stone(-weight)s of the (15)king, silver 2 q(uarters) to the 10.

Satisfaction II

It came into me and my heart was satisfied herein.[30]

6 Unpriced items — 1 bed of papyrus-reed on which are (16)4 (15)INLAYS[31] (16)of stone;[32]

1 TRAY of *slq*;

2 ladles;

1 new BOX of palm-leaf;

5 handfuls of castor oil;[33]

1 PAIR of sandals.[34]

Death of husband

(17)Tomorrow or (the) n[ex]t day,[35] should Esḥor die not (18)having (17)a child, male or female, (18)from Mipta[h]iah his wife, it is Miptahiah (who) has right to the house[36] (19)of Esḥor and [hi]s goods and his property and all that he has on the face of the earth,[37] (20)all of it.[38]

Death of wife

Tomorrow or (the next) day, should Miptahiah die not (21)having (20)a child, male or female, (21)from Esḥor her husband, it is Esḥor (who) shall inherit[39] from her her goods (22)and her property.

Repudiation by wife[40]

Tomorrow o[r] (the) next day, should Miptahiah stand up in an assembly[41] *d* (23)and say:

"I hated[42] Esḥor my husband,"[43]

d Gen 26:27; 29:31, 33; Deut 21:15-17; 22:13, 16; Judg 11:7; 15:2; Isa 60:15; Jer 12:7-8; Hos 9:15; Mal 1:3; 2:16; Prov 5:14; 30:23

---

[28] Jehoishma's contract specified the items — garments, bronze vessels, money, and *mohar*. Mibtahiah had a *mohar*, three woolen garments of considerable value, and five vessels of small value. Jehoishma likewise had a *mohar* and the same five bronze vessels but a larger wardrobe, including four woolen and four linen garments (3.76:5-15). The Eg. Tshenese had a woman's gift, five or six garments of considerable value, and at least four vessels of nominal value (*P. Berlin* 13593.5 [*EPE* C3). In all cases these were precisely appraised because they were to be returned in case of divorce. The Jewish woman had additional, unappraised items made of organic, non-metallic material — Mibtahiah, six such (lines 15-16) and Jehoishma, almost treble that amount (3.76:17-21). The Eg. woman, on the other hand, also had several pieces of gold jewelry and copper objects measured by weight, each group being evaluated separately (*P. Berlin* 13593.4-7 [*EPE* C33]). None of the documents included realty or chattel.

[29] The scribe had originally written "1 shekel" in the singular, added two strokes on either side of the single numerical stroke after he made the double 2-shekel additions in lines 6 and 8, but failed to emend the singular "shekel" to plural "shekels."

[30] The Demotic contract read "I received them from you; they are complete without any remainder; my heart is satisfied with them" (*P. Berlin* 13593.7 [*EPE* C33]); see further 3.80, n. 15 (*EPE* B45). There was no similar statement of receipt and satisfaction in the documents of Tamet (3.71:6-7) and her daughter Jehoishma (3.76:15-17).

[31] A second elusive *niphal* loanword (*nᶜbṣn*) in this document.

[32] The six items of toilette listed below carried no caption, evaluation, or summation and must have been of known, standard value. Jehoishma had eleven such items; in addition to the six listed here there were jugs, a wooden chest, and three different kinds of oil and some of the items were held in greater quantity or enhanced value, viz, 2 TRAYS, 5 ladles, and *Persian* sandals (3.76:17-21). See Porten 1968:90-94. The precise meaning of several of the words still eludes us. For discussion, see Fitzmyer 1979:257-259.

[33] A standard item in each of the dowries, this oil was frequently requested by relatives of Elephantine-Syene residents away from home; see on *TAD* A2.1:7 (*EPE* B1).

[34] The last two items were added supralinearly.

[35] See 3.59, n. 12.

[36] There was a double imbalance in these reciprocal clauses, one in favor of the surviving wife and one in favor of the surviving husband. Mibtahiah was granted rights to her deceased husband's house while no stipulation provided for the rights of Esḥor, should he survive, to Mibtahiah's house, even though she owned one (3.61). The same situation existed for Jehoishma vis-à-vis her husband, Anani (3.76:28-30, 34-36). On the other hand, Mibtahiah only "controlled" i.e. she had "right to" (*šlyṭ b-*) the "house, goods and property" of Esḥor while he "inherited" (*yrt*) her "goods and property" (line 21). Similarly, Jehoishma could only [HOL]D ON TO IT ([ʾ]*ḥdth*, namely, his property, but Anani like Esḥor "inherited" her (3.76:29, 35). In an early Greek will the surviving spouse "controls" the deceased's property but does not inherit it (*P. Eleph.* 2.3-4 [*EPE* D3]).

[37] This unique expansion was probably due to Esḥor's presumed prior marital status and conceivable encumbrances therefrom. The phrase emphasized that nothing whatsoever was to be excluded from Mibtahiah's possession.

[38] Theoretically, the Aram. word "all of it" (*klh*) could refer to the property or the earth. But the Demotic parallel (*nt nb* [*n nk.w*] *n pꜣ tꜣ* [*dr.f*], lit. "every which [of property] in the world [to its limit]" = "every kind of property in the whole world") argues for interpreting our phrase as "on the face of the whole earth." See Porten 1992:260.

[39] See note 36 above.

[40] Like the *Death* clauses so the *Repudiation* clauses were reciprocal and affected both parties. The opening statement was identical with chiastic reversal of the parties and titles — "Esḥor my husband" but "my wife Miptahiah." Similar chiastic reversal occurs in Tamet's contract, also written by the scribe Nathan — "Tamet my wife" vis-à-vis "my husband Anani" (3.71:7, 9).

[41] Demotion of matrimonial status required public notice, e.g. formal declaration in an assembly (*bᶜdh* [apparently a Heb. loanword]).

[42] Pronounced by both the husband and the wife, this word (*śnʾ*) has been taken as a technical term for divorce. But neither the biblical homonym, nor the Akk. synonym *zêru* and the Eg. synonym *mst*, both of which occur in marriage contexts, means "divorce." All three terms signify repudiation or rejection, the effect of which is a breach of contract and demotion in status. The presence in the Bible of the "hated wife" (e.g. Leah vis-à-vis Rachel [Gen 29:31-33]) and the law concerning the rights of the first-born by such a wife (Deut 21:15-17) are decisive for our understanding that in a polygamous society one wife would be primary, "beloved," and the other secondary, "hated." To "hate" a wife was to demote her to the status of a secondary wife, "a hated wife." To "hate" a husband meant negating her own status as primary wife and may have entailed denial of conjugal rights (cf. CH §142 and commentaries thereto). See Porten and Szubin 1995:55-56; Szubin and Porten forthcoming.

[43] Occurring also in Tamet's contract, this terse statement was expanded and varied in Jehoishma's document — "I hated my wife Jehoishma; she shall not be my wife" and "I hated you; I will not be your wife" (3.76:21-22, 25).

[44] The pecuniary consequence of demotion was the imposition of a fixed monetary compensation (7½ shekels [see also 3.71:8, 10; 3.76:22,

silver of hatred[44] is on her head.[45] She shall PLACE UPON[46] (24)the balance-scale and weigh out to Esḥor silver, 6[+1] (= 7) shekels, 2 q(uarters), and all that she brought in[47] (25)in her hand she shall take out,[48] from straw to string,[49] and go away wherever she desires,[50] without (26)suit[51] and without process.[52]

Repudiation by husband
Tomorrow or (the) next day, should Esḥor stand up in an assembly (27)and say:

"I hated my [wif]e Miptahiah,"

her *mohar* [will be] lost[53] and all that she brought in (28)in her hand she shall take out, from straw to string, on one day in one stroke,[54] and go (29)away wherever she desires, without suit and without process.

Expulsion + Penalty I[55]
And [who]ever shall stand up against[56] Miptahiah (30)to expel her[57] from the house of Esḥor and his goods and his property, shall give her (31)silver, 20 *karsh*,[58]

Reaffirmation of rights
and do to her the law of this document.[59]

Exclusion of other heirs
And I shall not be able to say:
(32)"I have another wife besides Mipta(h)iah and other children besides the children whom (33)Miptahiah shall bear to me.[60]

Penalty II
If I say: "I have other chi[ldren] and wife besides (34)Miptahiah and her children," I shall give to Miptahiah silver, 20 *karsh* by the stone(-weight)s of (35)the king.

Non-removal of property
And I shall not be able to RE[LEASE][61] my goods and my property from Miptahiah.

Penalty III
And should I remove[62] them (36)from her (ERASURE: in accordance with [this] document but), I shall give to Miptahiah [silve]r, 20 *karsh* by the stone(-weight)s of the king.[63]

Scribe
(37)Nathan son of Ananiah[64] wrote [this document at the instruction of Esḥor].

25]) paid to the repudiated spouse whose status was diminished. It was not a fine or a penalty imposed on a party bearing the blame, but a contractually imposed compensation regardless of fault.

[45] An idiom denoting responsibility; see Fitzmyer 1979:263-264.

[46] This requirement, stipulated also for Jehoishma (3.76:26), was not laid down for the handmaiden Tamet (3.71:10). The meaning of the word is uncertain and has caused scholars much consternation; for a different translation ("sit by the scale"), see Fitzmyer 1979:264, *GEA* 85-86, n. 397, 121.

[47] This provision makes it clear why the dowry items were enumerated and evaluated. Since strictly speaking *she* did not "bring in" the *mohar* (see n. 17 above), she would not take it out in case of repudiation by her just as she lost it in case of repudiation by him (line 27) and just as Jehoishma lost it if she repudiated Anani (3.76:24-25).

[48] The formula in Jehoishma's contract varied noticeably — "All that she brought in in(to) his house he shall give her," adding the amount to be paid (3.76:22-23).

[49] "An alliterative phrase, expressing figuratively a totality by the use of extremely small samples" (Fitzmyer 1979:264).

[50] The other option, offered Jehoishma, was to "go to her father's house" (3.76:28). No option was offered the handmaiden Tamet (3.71:10).

[51] The scribe mistakenly wrote *ydyn* for *dyn*.

[52] See 3.61, n. 40.

[53] I.e. forfeit. Was this payment in lieu of the "silver of hatred" or had the scribe omitted that payment by oversight or as an ellipsis? Jehoishma's contract specified loss of *mohar*, as well as payment of silver of hatred, in case of repudiation by the wife, not, as here, by the husband. But its loss was implicit in case of repudiation by the husband because the contract recorded the amount she was entitled to receive, and this included the *mohar* (3.76:23, 25).

[54] The property was not to be returned in installments nor the severance phased in time, thereby punctuating sharply the change of status. Presumably the same procedure followed in case of repudiation by the wife, as it did in the contract of Jehoishma (3.76:28). The clause was not included in Tamet's contract since she hardly had any property to begin with (3.71:9-10). The Demotic contract had the phrase "compulsorily, without delay" (*P. Berlin* 13593.7 [*EPE* C33]).

[55] In Jehoishma's contract this clause followed directly upon the *Death of husband* clause (see 3.76:28-32) and so here, too, it must have pertained to expulsion from Esḥor's house after his death. But the scribe placed the clause at the end because he wished to group together three clauses protecting Mibtahiah's pecuniary rights, each under a twenty *karsh* penalty (lines 29-36). The "expel" and "remove" prohibitions, here separated (see line 35), were combined in Tshenese's Demotic contract (*P. Berlin* 13593.7-8 [*EPE* C33]).

[56] See 3.74, n. 17 (*EPE* B39).

[57] See 3.75, n. 30 (*EPE* B40).

[58] The same penalty for eviction was levied in Jehoishma's contract (3.76:32); see on 3.59:7.

[59] The clause stipulated specific performance, i.e. guarantee of her right to Esḥor's property which the document stipulated (lines 17-20); similarly in 3.76:32. Identical language was employed in the Demotic contract of Tshenese against someone "throwing her out" of her husband's house or "removing" his possessions from her (see below lines 35-36 [*P. Berlin* 13593.7-8 [*EPE* C33}]).

[60] This provision asserts that there was no wife or children from a previous marriage who might lay claim to Esḥor's estate; Porten 1968:253-254. The early Greek marriage document stated, "Let it not be permitted to Herakleides to bring in another woman as an outrage to Demetria, nor to have children by another woman ..." (*P. Eleph.* 1.8-9 [*EPE* D2]).

[61] For restoration of the word [ʾ*hn*]*tr*, see Fitzmyer 1979:267.

[62] See on lines 29-30 and 3.79:31 (*EPE* B44).

[63] Alienation of his property without Mibtahiah's consent would cost Esḥor heavily.

[64] See 3.61, n. 77.

Witnesses And the witnesses herein:[65] (38)(1st hand) Penuliah son of Jezaniah;[66] (2nd hand) [...]iah[67] son of Ahio;	(3rd hand) Menahem son of [Za]ccur[68]; (39)(4th hand) witness: *Wyzblw*[69] [[bottom middle band and endorsement missing]

[65] One or two more witnesses may have signed in the missing band, possibly bringing the number up to six, a multiple of three, as in Tamet's contract (3.71:15). Six witness were present in Jehoishma's contract but the last band was lost and there may have been two more (3.76:43-44). Only four witnesses signed the fragmentary document of Abihi (*TAD* B6.4:9-10).

[66] Appears only here; probably the father of the witness Jezaniah son of Penuliah in 416 BCE (3.67:19); Porten 2001:348.

[67] Among the candidates for this name are the scribes Gemariah son of Ahio (3.60:18 [464]; *TAD* 4.2:16 [ca. 487]), who would be quite senior in 449, and (his brother?) Pelatiah son of Ahio (3.59:15 [471]; Porten 2001:337), but comparison of the handwriting is inconclusive due to the fragmentary nature of the signature here.

[68] He also witnessed the wifehood document of Tamet drawn up by the same scribe two months earlier (3.71:15).

[69] The name, or a var. thereof, appears twice again and each time is difficult to decipher. Once, as witness to another document of Mahseiah, it is partly restored, with the final *waw* uncertain, as son of ᵓ*trly*, (3.64:18) and the second time it is prefaced by the word "house" (3.72:24). In both cases the party is designated "Caspian."

REFERENCES

Text and translation: *TAD* B2.6; *EPE* B28. *EPE;* Fitzmyer 1979; *GEA;* Hugenberger 1994; Kraeling 1953; Porten 1968; Porten 1992; Porten 2001; Porten and Szubin 1995; *TAD*.

GRANT OF HOUSE TO DAUGHTER (3.64)
(17 November, 446 BCE)

Bezalel Porten

Much as this document is compositionally rife with spelling errors and inconsistencies, it is nonetheless aesthetically structured. The *Transfer* clauses (lines 2-7) are chiastically arranged with the key word "gave" (*yhb*) recurring seven times:

a I gave you the house which Meshullam son of Zaccur son of Ater, Aramean of Syene, gave me

  b and a document he wrote for me about it.

    c And I gave it to Miptahiah in exchange for her goods which she gave me.

      d I consumed them but did not find silver or goods to repay you.

    c I gave you this house in exchange for your goods worth 5 *karsh*.

  b And I gave you the old document which that Meshullam wrote for me.

a This house — I gave it to you and withdrew from it.

Wanting to maintain this tight structure intact, the professional scribe Nathan shifted the *Boundaries* clause to the end of the document (lines 13-15). This shift also gave him the opportunity to duplicate the *Investiture* clauses, granting Miptahiah limited rights of alienation the first time (line 7) and unlimited rights the second time (line 16). Any suit by Mahseiah or his related parties would be penalized by the standard ten *karsh* penalty (lines 8-11). He transferred to her Meshullam's deed of sale and affirmed that no alleged prior document by him would invalidate the present one (lines 6-7, 11-12). Uniquely, he signed his name as a witness; two of the remaining five were Caspians and one was Iranian (lines 17-20).

Date (Recto)(1)On the 2nd of Kislev, that is day 10 of the month of Mesore, year 19 of Artaxerxes the king,[1]	*Parties* said Mahseiah son of (2)Jedaniah, an Aramean of Syene of the detachment of Varyazata,[2] to

[1] In 19 Artaxerxes I (= 446 BCE), 2 Kislev = November 19 while 10 Mesore = November 17. Even if this document were written at night, the scribe Nathan son of Anani ran ahead of himself by one day, as he did in other contracts (3.69 [four day gap], 3.71); see Porten 1990:22-23, 25 and Figure 8 in *TAD* B.

[2] The same designation he had in 471 and 449 (3.59:2; 3.63:2-3). In 464 he was called a "Jew of Elephantine" but still with the detachment of Varyazata (3.60:3-4). Only in 459 was he uniquely designated "Jew, hereditary-property-holder in Elephantine of the detachment of Haumadata" (3.61:2).

Miptahiah[3] his daughter,[4] saying:

Transfer I
I gave[5] you

Object
the house

Pedigree[6]
(3)which Meshullam son of Zaccur son of Ater,[7] an Aramean of Syene,[8] gave me for its value[9] and a document he wrote for me about it.[10]

Transfer II
(4)And I gave it[11] to Miptahiah[12] my daughter

Consideration I
in exchange for her goods which she gave me. When I was GARRISONED[13] in (the) fortress, I consumed (5)them[14] but did not find silver or goods to (re)pay you.

Transfer III
Afterwards,[15] I gave you this house

Consideration II
(6)in exchange for those, your goods valued in silver (at) 5 *karsh*.

Document transfer
And I gave you the old document which (7)that Meshullam (6)wrote (7)for me concerning it.[16]

Transfer IV
This house — I gave it to you

Withdrawal I
and withdrew[17] from it.

Investiture I
Yours it is and your children's (8)after you and to whomever you love[18] you may give it.

Waiver of suit
I shall not be able[19] — I, or my children, or seed[20] of mine, or (9)another (8)person[21] — (9)to bring against you suit or process in the name of[22] that house which I gave you and (10)about which (9)the document I wrote for you.

Penalty
(10)Whoever shall institute against you suit or (pro)cess — I, or brother or sister, near or far, member of a detachment or member of a town[23] — (11)shall give you silver, 10 *karsh*,[24]

---

[3] In a /b/ > /p/ phonetic shift the name Mibtahiah ("Yah is Trust") often appeared as Miptahiah (lines 4, 21; 3.63 throughout, both drawn up by Nathan son of Anani; 3.65:14 [in alternation with Mibtahiah [line 2]]; *TAD* B5.5:3, 11, 13).

[4] See 3.61, n. 8.

[5] For the term, see on 3.61, n. 10.

[6] It was standard procedure in a bona fide conveyance to include a pedigree (see 3.73:3-4; *P. Wien* D 10150.2 [C28]; *P. Paris* 17.6-7 [*EPE* D14]; *P. Münch* 16.10-15 [*EPE* D21]; *P. Lond.* V 1722.14-17 [*EPE* D22]; *P. Münch* 8.15-20 [*EPE* D23]; et al.; and Eg. documents cited in Porten and Szubin 1982a:124-126).

[7] A prominent figure in the Aram. papyri, Meshullam appeared as creditor (3.69:2-3) and slave-owner, who gave away his Eg. handmaiden in marriage (3.71) and before his death emancipated and adopted her and her daughter (3.74). He was variously designated "Jew of Elephantine the fortress" (3.69:3 [456 BCE]), "Aramean of Syene of the detachment of Varyazata (3.71:2-3 [449 BCE]), "Aramean of Syene" (here [446 BCE]), and "Jew of Elephantine the fortress of the detachment of Iddinnabu (3.74:2 [427 BCE]) and was the link between the Mibtahiah and Anani family archives. It was npt unusual for a party or a witness to display a three- or four-generation genealogy (witnesses [3.66:18; 3.67:18]; mother of alienee [3.79:8; 3.80:2]). In two cases the identity of the grandfather was pertinent to the transaction (3.66:2, 18-19; 3.67:2).

[8] See previous note.

[9] Mahseiah deliberately omitted the price, perhaps to avoid invidious comparison between the high value of the goods received earlier in exchange (fifty shekels) and the assuredly lower value of the house. A much larger piece of property, albeit abandoned and run-down, cost Anani fourteen shekels (3.72:6) and many years later part of that, rebuilt and refurbished, went for thirteen shekels (3.80:5).

[10] This preposition (also line 10) alternates here with "concerning" (line 7); see 3.62, n. 7.

[11] But it did not turn up in our archive.

[12] The alternation between direct speech and third person address by name occurs not infrequently in the contracts (3.65:10; 3.75:16; 3.78:5-6, 8, 15-18; 3.79:10; *TAD* B2.5:0-3).

[13] For the Old Persian loanword *hndyz/hndz*, see on *TAD* A4.5:7 (*EPE* B 17).

[14] The goods were unspecified perishables.

[15] For this term, see 3.62, n. 18.

[16] Previous documents were the best evidence of pedigree and it was standard procedure to pass them on to the new owner; 3.80:31-32; *P. Wien* D 10151 4-6 (*EPE* C29); *P. Moscow* 135.4 (*EPE* C30); *P. Münch.* 16.13-14 (*EPE* D21); *P. Lond.* V 1722.26-28 (*EPE* D22); *P. Münch.* 4.18-19 (*EPE* D34); *P. Münch.* 9.61 (*EPE* D40).

[17] The technical term *rḥq* indicates that the alienor had relinquished all rights to the object. Withdrawal regularly followed upon conveyance, whether motivated (line 16; cf. 3.72:11, 13; *TAD* 5.5:4, 8) or not (3.67:4); or upon a loss of suit (3.65:6; 3.66:9; 3.70:7). In the latter instance, it was preceded by a statement of satisfaction. Occasionally the scribe added "from this day and forever" (3.65:6; 3.66:9; 3.72:11; *TAD* B5.5:4). Withdrawal was either from the alienee (3.65:6; 3.66:9; 3.70:7; *TAD* B5.5:4), from the object, as here (line 16; 3.72:11, 13), or from both (3.67:4; *TAD* B5 5:8).

[18] This clause would seem to limit further alienation to heirs and beneficiaries (see 3.61, n. 31), but was expanded in line 16.

[19] I.e. I am not entitled.

[20] The reference to grandchildren occurs only here in our documents.

[21] A beneficiary (see 3.61, n. 33).

[22] I.e. "regarding." See 3.60, n. 34.

[23] These three pairs are familiar from the first document in our archive (3.59:8-10). Here they supplement and do not repeat the three parties listed singly in the *Waiver* clause; thus the penalty would also cover "another person."

[24] This was the usual penalty; see 3.59, n. 15.

Reaffirmation
and (the) house is likewise yours.[25]

Document validity
Moreover, another person shall not be able to take out against you (12)a new or old (11)document (12)but (only) this document which I wrote and gave you. Whoever shall take out against you a docu(ment), I did not wri[te it].[26]

Boundaries
(13)Moreover, behold these are the boundaries of that house:[27] above it is the house of Jaush son of Penuliah;[28] below it (14)is the Temple[29] of YHH[30] (the) God; east of it is the house of Gaddul son of Osea[31] and the street is between them; (15)west of it is the house of Ḥarwodj son of Palṭu, priest of Ḥ•[•]• the god.[32]

Transfer V
That house — (16)I gave it to you

Withdrawal II
and withdrew from it.

Investiture II
Yours it is forever[33] and to whomever you desire,[34] give it.

Scribe
(17)Nathan son of Ananiah[35] wrote (17)this document at the instruction of Mahseiah.

Witnesses
And the witnesses herein:[36]
(2nd hand) Mahseiah wrote with (18)his own (17)hands[37];
(18)(3rd hand) Mithrasarah son of Mithrasarah[38];
(4th hand) *Wyzb[l(w)]* son of ᵓ*trly*, a Caspian[39];
(19)(5th hand) witness Barbari son of Dargi(ya), a Caspian of the place ...[40];
(6th hand) *Haggai* son of Shemaiah[41];
(20)(7th hand) Zaccur son of Shillem.[42]

Endorsement
(Verso)(21)Document (*sealing*) of a house [which Ma]hseiah son of Jedaniah [wrote for Miptahia]h his daughter.[43]

---

[25] See 3.59, n. 18.
[26] This is a common clause in house transfers; for a fuller version, see 3.61:15-18 and notes there.
[27] This section usually comes toward the beginning of the document (3.60:7-11; 3.61:5-8; 3.67:4-8; 3.72:7-10; 3.73:8-11; 3.75:5; 3.78:8-11; 3.79:3-6; 3.80:8-9a, 16-21). Putting it at the end provided the opportunity to reconfirm the *Transfer* and *Withdrawal* clauses and expand the *Investiture* clause to include parties beyond the circle of blood relatives and beneficiaries. For the boundaries formula, see 3.60, n. 18. For the orientation of the building, see plan in *TAD* B, Figure 3.
[28] Appears only here in our documents.
[29] For the term, see on *COS* 3.51, n. 37 (*EPE* B19).
[30] This earlier spelling of the name YHW occurs only in 3.71:2, by the same scribe as here, and regularly in the ostraca *COS* 3.87C:3; 3.87J:3; *TAD* D7.16:3, 7, 35:1); see Porten 1968:105-106.
[31] Appears only here.
[32] The Egyptian-West Semitic name combination is reminiscent of the names in the Makkibanit correspondence, e.g. Psami son of Nabunathan (*TAD* A2.3:14) and in the Saqqarah funerary inscriptions (*TAD* D18.4-6, 9-10, 13-14, 19.4-6). The Aramean soldiers had temples in Syene to Banit, Bethel, Nabu, and the Queen of Heaven, but the name of the deity here is unrecoverable. Less likely, the praenomen might be West Semitic, the same name as in 2 Kgs 21:19 (Haruz = "Diligent, Sharp").
[33] This abridged formula appears also in 3.67:9, 16; for the full formula, see 3.61, n. 30.
[34] Though occurring in the *Investiture* clause in the same construction as *rḥm*, "love," this word (*ṣby*) had a more expansive meaning and authorized alienation of the house as an estate in fee simple even to one outside the family circle of "loved ones;" see Szubin and Porten 1983a:38; 1988:38.
[35] Appearing as witness for Mahseiah in 459 BCE (3.61:32; 3.62:20), Nathan was a professional scribe who drew up one or two more documents for his family (3.63:37 [449 BCE]; *TAD* B2.5[?]), two more found in the Anani archive (3.69:20 [456 BCE]; 3.71:14 [449 BCE]) and perhaps another two more (*TAD* B5.4; D2.22).
[36] Here and perhaps in 3.76:43-44 there were only six witnesses, not the expected four or eight (see 3.59, n. 34). Was there also a system based on a multiple of three (as in 3.71:15), extending to nine (*TAD* B4.3:22-24, 4.4:19-21)?
[37] Only in one other case did a party to the contract (Mica son of Ahio) possibly sign as (third) witness (Micaiah son of Ahio [3.70:2, 10, 12]); see Demotic *P. Wien* D 10150.7 (*EPE* C28), *P. Wien* 10151.8 (*EPE* C29). The practice occurs regularly in contracts from the Judean desert (*DJD* 18:9; 19:26; 21:21; 23:827:6; 28:11-12; 33:4; et al.).
[38] The Persian son bore the same name as his father. Present in one of the Ptolemaic Greek documents from Elephantine (Neoptolemos son of Neoptolemos [*BGU* VI 1247.3 (*EPE* D8)]), the practice was otherwise unknown in the documents of the Achaemenid period. Was this witness the same as Mithrasarah the Magian who witnessed a contract of Anani in 434 BCE (3.73:24)?
[39] So far both names defy persuasive explanation. In 3.72:24, we have the strange witness signature "house of *Wyzbl*, a Caspian."
[40] See on 3.59:18; 3.60:7. He is the only one here to preface his name with the designation "witness."
[41] The praenomen is almost completely restored but the signature resembles the script of the professional scribe who was known to have written five or six contracts between 437 and 400 BCE (3.72:23; 3.74:15; 3.78:22; 3.79:17; 3.80:32; and probably *TAD* B4.6:18) and to have signed as the first witness to a seventh (3.76:43 [427 BCE]) and possibly, without patronymic, as the second witness to an eighth (3.81:13).
[42] With the same large, elementary script he was the second witness in a contract drawn up by the preceding witness Haggai for Anani son of Azariah in 402 BCE (3.78:24). If the order of witnesses was by age, he and Haggai were young here in 449 and elderly in 402.
[43] In the endorsement of an earlier document, the scribe wrote the name in full ("Mibtah daughter of Mahsah" [3.61:35]).

REFERENCES

Text and translation: *TAD* B2.7; *EPE* B29b. Porten 1968; 1990; Porten and Szubin 1982; Szubin and Porten 1983a; 1988; *TAD*.

WITHDRAWAL FROM GOODS (3.65)
(26 August, 440 BCE)

Bezalel Porten

Mibtahiah (here called Miptahiah) and the Egyptian builder Peu engaged in litigation in Syene regarding silver, grain, clothing, vessels, and a document of wifehood. Mibtahiah won her claim through an oath by the Egyptian goddess Sati and Peu drew up this document of withdrawal, supporting his waiver of all future suit by a standard five *karsh* penalty. We may conjecture that the dispute involved goods left on deposit. The document was drawn up by an Aramean scribe in Syene and attested by four non-Jewish witnesses.

Date

(Recto)(1)On the 14th of Ab, that is day 19 of Pachons, year 25 of Artaxerxes the king,[1]

Parties

said Peu (2)son of Paḥe/Pakhoi,[2] a builder[3] of Syene the fortress, to Mibtahiah daughter of Mahseiah son of Jedania,[4] (3)an Aramean of Syene of the detachment of Varyazata,[5]

Suit

about[6] the suit which we made[7] in Syene,[8] a LITIGATION[9] about silver (4)and grain and clothing and bronze and iron — all goods and property — and (the) wifehood document.[10]

Oath

Then,[11] the oath[12] (5)came[13] upon you and you swore[14] for me about them by Sati the goddess.[15]

Satisfaction

And my heart was satisfied (6)with that oath[16] which you made[17] for me about those goods

Withdrawal

and I withdrew[18] from you from (7)this day and forever.[19]

Waiver of suit

I shall not be able to institute against you suit or process — (against) you or son (8)or daughter of yours — in the name of[20] those goods about which you swore for me.

Penalty

If I institute against you (9)suit or process, or a son of mine or a daughter of mine[21] institute against you (suit) in the name of that oath, I, Peu — or my children — (10)shall give to Mi(b)tah-

[1] Since 14 Ab = August 27 in 25 Artaxerxes II and 19 Pachons = August 26 in that year, we must assume that this contract was written at night; see Porten 1990:21 and Figure 8 in *TAD* B.

[2] Both names are Eg.

[3] Mibtahiah's second husband Esḥor bore the title "builder of the king." We do not know what either of these tasks encompassed; see 3.63, n. 3. The Aram. word *ᵓrdykl* derives from the Akk. *arad ekalli*, lit. "palace slave" which evolved into the specialized meaning "builder"; see Fitzmyer 1979:250.

[4] His name was spelled here with final *aleph* rather than *he*.

[5] This designation, the same as that frequently borne by Mahseiah, would here seem to apply to his daughter Mibtahiah (see 3.59, nn. 3-4). Father and daughter later belonged to the same detachment, as elsewhere husband and wife did (3.72:2-3).

[6] It was unusual for the body of a document to begin with a prepositional clause and not with a verb (see 3.62, n. 3).

[7] For this rare expression "make a suit" (= "undertake a suit"), see 3.61, n. 66.

[8] The litigation was undertaken where Peu was located.

[9] The word *nprt* may be related to Old Persian *parᶦt*, "fight, contend, curse" (*GEA* 372.53 and reference there to Shaked). For an earlier explanation of this word see Porten 1968:247.

[10] This was a kind of all-inclusive list of goods serving as security for loans (3.69:9-10; 3.81:11; *TAD* B4.6:12) or placed on deposit for safekeeping (3.66:5-7). Every item is singular, collective and "document" must have been similarly intended to designate a number of such. Subsequent supralinear addition of the word *ᵓntw*, "wifehood," limited this to a single document. It had long been assumed that this referred to a marriage with Peu which was now dissolving (Porten 1968:245-247), but the new date proposed for 3.63 would mean that Mibtahiah was married at the time to Esḥor. It is, therefore, best to take these goods, including what must have been the document of wifehood with Esḥor, as having been placed on deposit with Peu.

[11] Only here in our documents does this introductory adverb (*ᵓdyn*) occur in the body of the contract. For its regular usage, see 3.66, n. 2.

[12] Aram. *mwmᵓh*; see 3.60, n. 15.

[13] Aram. *mṭᵓh*, also in *TAD* B7.2:7, with the meaning "was imposed."

[14] Probably in a shrine.

[15] Exculpatory oath was a known procedure for resolving a dispute between bailor and bailee in a case of deposit (cf. Exod 22:8; 1 Kgs 8:31-32). Similar disputes at Elephantine were resolved by this type of oath in Byzantine times (*P. Münch.* 1.25-26 [*EPE* D29]; 6.7-8, 54-58 [D35]). Sati was the Eg. goddess at Elephantine and an oath by her would certainly have satisfied the Eg. Peu. It is not clear why the Jewess Mibtahiah would have agreed to take an oath by this pagan deity when her father, mother, and brother had earlier sworn to the Khwarezmian Dargamana by the Jewish God YHW (3.60:4-5). See Porten 1968:151-154.

[16] Just as had been the heart of Dargamana with the oath of Mahseiah (3.60:11-12). For the phrase see 3.63, n. 14.

[17] I.e. the oath which you took for me.

[18] Withdrawal (*rḥq*) followed satisfaction in a loss of suit (see 3.64, n. 17).

[19] A standard expression; see 3.61, n. 29.

[20] See 3.60, n. 34.

[21] The *Waiver* and *Penalty* clauses have been composed with intentional ellipsis. The scribe omitted reference to suit by "son or daughter" in the *Waiver* clause (line 7) because he included it in the *Penalty* clause (lines 7-8) and conversely omitted suit against "son or daughter" in the

iah[22] silver, 5 *karsh*[23] by the stone(-weight)s of the king, without suit and without process,

Reaffirmation

(11)and I am withdrawn from every suit or process.[24]

Scribe and place

Peṭeese son of Nabunathan wrote this document (12)in Syene[25] the fortress at the instruction of Peu son of Paḥe/Pakhoi.

Witnesses

The witnesses herein:[26]

(2nd hand) Naburai son of Nabunathan[27];

(13)(3rd hand) Luḥi son of Mannuki[28];

(4th hand) Ausnahar son of Duma/Ruma[29];

(5th hand) Naburai son of Vishtana.[30]

Endorsement

(Verso)(14)Document (*sealing*) of withdrawal which Peu wrote for Miptah[ia]h.

Penalty clause (line 9) because he included it in the *Waiver* clause (lines 7-8). The clauses limited potential claimants and protected parties to heirs; see Porten and Szubin 1987b:48-51.

[22] The scribe shifted from first to third person, addressed by name (see 3.64, n. 12). Writing "I, Peu," he should have followed up with "you, Mib/ptahiah" (cf. 3.73:5-6). He also omitted the "p/b" in her name.

[23] This penalty lay at the lower end of the scale (see 3.59, n. 15).

[24] See 3.60, n. 39.

[25] The document was written at the site of the litigation by an Aramean scribe whose praenomen was Eg.; see 3.60, n. 41. A mixed Eg.-Aramean onomasticon was characteristic of the Makkibanit letters addressed to Syene and Luxor *TAD* A2.1-7) and the Saqqarah funerary inscriptions (*COS* 2.61-62).

[26] All the witnesses were non-Jews, probably residents of Syene, who appear only here. None prefaced his name with the word "witness." Only four witnesses were required in documents concerning movables, including chattel (3.66:17-18; 3.68:15-16; 3.69:21-22; 3.74:16-17; 3.81:13-14; *TAD* B4.2:12-15; 5.5:12).

[27] Both names are Aram. Might Naburai, the same name as the fourth witness, be a brother of the scribe?

[28] Both names are Akk.

[29] Both names are Arab., a rare phenomenon in the Elephantine onomasticon.

[30] The praenomen is Aram. and the patronym is Persian.

REFERENCES

Text and translation: *TAD* B2.8; *EPE* B30. Fitzmyer 1979; *GEA*; Porten 1968; 1990; Porten and Szubin 1987b; *TAD*.

WITHDRAWAL FROM GOODS (3.66)
(2-30 September, 420 BCE)

Bezalel Porten

It must have been shortly after the death of Esḥor that the brothers Menahem and Ananiah, grandsons of Shelomam, sued Jedaniah and Mahseiah before the Chief and the Troop Commander, claiming that Shelomam had deposited assorted goods with Esḥor, who never returned them. The brothers were interrogated and satisfied the claimants by returning the goods. They then drew up the present document of withdrawal which contains an expanded *Waiver* clause (adding representatives), backed by the standard ten *karsh* penalty.

Date (recto)

(1)In the month of Elul, that is Pay[ni], year 4 of Darius the king,[1]

Place

then in Elephantine the fortress,[2]

Parties

said (2)Menahem and Ananiah, all (told) two,[3] sons of Meshullam son of Shelomam,[4] Jews of Elephantine the fortress of the detachment of Iddinnabu,[5] (3)to Jedaniah and Mahseiah,[6] all (told) two, sons of

[1] There are two documents in our collection, both written by Mauziah son of Nathan in successive months, which lack day dates, but the month dates correspond exactly (3.76:1); Porten 1990:20-21.

[2] It was first in 427 BCE that we find the body of the document opening with the word *ʾdyn* (3.74:1; 3.78:1; 3.79:1; 3.80:1; *TAD* B4.6:1), usually followed by the *Place*, as here (3.66:1; 3.67:1; 3.75:1; 3.76:1; 3.77:1; 3.81:1; *TAD* B5.5:1). Thus a new phrase was added to the documents.

[3] For the practice of tallying two and more persons, see 3.60, n. 9.

[4] Shelomam gave his son Meshullam a name from the same root as his own (*šlm*). The grandfather is cited here so as to indicate the familial links of the claimants with the bailee Shelomam son of Azariah (line 6). For other three-generation genealogies among the parties see 3.64, n. 7.

[5] Along with the Iranians Varyazata (3.64:2 [446 BCE]) and Namasava (3.72:2 [437 BCE]), this Babylonian detachment commander was present during the years of Mibtahiah's activity (*TAD* B6.1:2 [446 BCE]; 3.74:2 [427 BCE]; 3.76:2 [420 BCE]).

[6] The sons were named after the grandfather and father, respectively, of Mibtahiah. They were probably cousins of the Jewish communal leader (see 3.46:3 [*EPE* B13]); Porten 1968:238; 2001:334-335.

Esḥor son of Djeḥo from Mibtahiah daughter of Mahseiah,[7] Jews (4)of the same detachment, saying:

Suit

We brought suit of *np*ᵓ[8] against you before Ramnadaina, Chief[9] (and) Vidranga,[10] (5)the Troop Commander,[11] saying:

"There [are] the(se) goods[12] — woolen and linen garments, bronze and iron utensils, wooden (6)and palm-leaf (5)utensils, (6)grain and other (things)."[13]

Saying:[14]

"Goods Esḥor your father took[15] from Shelomam son of Azariah.[16] Moreover, (7)he[17] said,

'There are (these goods) which[18] [a] were placed on depos[it].'

But he took hereditary possession[19] and did not return (them) to him."

And consequently,[20] we brought (suit) against you.

Interrogation

(8)Afterwards,[21] you were interrogated[22]

Satisfaction

and you, Jedaniah and Mahseiah, sons of Esḥor, satisfied our heart with[23] those goods (9)and our heart was satisfied[24] herein from this d[a]y forever.[25]

Withdrawal

I, Menahem and Ananiah, we are withdrawn[26] from you (10)from this day forever.[27]

Waiver of suit

We shall no[t] be able — we, or our sons or our daughters, or our brothers, or a man who is ours,[28] near (or far), or member of (a detachment or) (11)town[29] — they shall not be able[30] to br[i]ng against [yo]u, you, Jedaniah and Mahseiah, suit or process. And they[31] shall not be able to bring (suit) against your children[32] (12)or your brothers, or a man of yours in the [na]me of (the)[33] goods[34] and silver,[35] grain and other (things) of Shelomam son

[a] Ezra 5:17

[7] Reference to the mother in a filiation is rare in the Aram. documents and limited to Esḥor and Mibtahiah, probably because he had been married before. The practice was standard in the Demotic documents (*P. Berlin* 13614.1 [*EPE* C27], et al.); Roman documents (*P. Paris* 17.3 [*EPE* D14], et al.); and Byzantine documents (*P. Edmonstone* 3 [*EPE* D18]; *P. Lond.* V 1722.3 [*EPE* D22], et al.).

[8] This word is an unresolved crux. It occurs again in the expression, "You complained against me in *np*ᵓ" (*TAD* B7.2:4). No place by this name is known. Also unusual in this expression is the addition of the preposition *beth* preceding *dyn*, "suit." Such addition occurs only once more in a fragmentary text where the following word is missing (*TAD* B5.2:3) Could it have been *np*ᵓ?

[9] Bearing a Persian title (*prtrk*), Ramnadaina was the leading authority in Syene-Elephantine. He was succeeded by Vidranga, presently Troop Commander. The Chief (*frataraka*) was normally stationed in Elephantine and had military as well as judicial authority (see 3.50:4 [*EPE* B17]).

[10] See 3.48, n. 8 (*EPE* B15).

[11] The Persian Troop Commander, here (and in 3.67:2-4; 3.77:2; 3.48:3; *TAD* A5.2:7) written as two words (*rb ḥyl*) but elsewhere as one (*TAD* A3.1v:5; B5.1:3; 3.51:4) was subordinate to the Chief, and was frequently involved in judicial affairs (3.67:2-4; 3.77:2; *TAD* B5.1:3). His station was in Syene (3.67:2-4; *TAD* A5.2:7; 3.51:4). In a Demotic document of 486 BCE, Parnu was entitled "He of Tshetres, to whom the fortress of Syene is entrusted" (*P. Berlin* 13582.2-3 [*EPE* C35]). Did he hold both the posts of *frataraka* and of Troop Commander?

[12] The formulation here and in line 7 does not begin with a transitive verb but with the stative ᵓ*yty*. The focus was to be on the goods (as it was on the house in 3.66:3) and this word recurs twice in initial or near-initial position (lines 5-7). Thus a statement that might have been made in one long, compound sentence was broken down into three distinct statements.

[13] For such generalized lists of property, see 3.65, n. 10.

[14] The recurrence of this word here is most awkward. Actually, it comes after the following word "goods."

[15] Did he "take" them on his own initiative or were they delivered to him for safe-keeping?

[16] Probably the grandson of the witness Shelomam son of Azariah (*TAD* B5.1:10), he was the grandfather of the brothers drawing up the contract. Their father Meshullam must have passed from the scene.

[17] I.e. Esḥor.

[18] The expression here has the meaning "It is (a fact) that" as in Ezra 5:17; *DAE* 198.

[19] He incorporated them into his private estate and passed them on to his sons, the other parties to the contract.

[20] This word (*mnkn*) occurs only here in our documents.

[21] See 3.62, n. 18.

[22] The ordinary word for "ask" (*š*ᵓ*l*) takes on the meaning of "interrogate" in a judicial context (*TAD* A5.2:3; 5.4:5; B7.2:6; 8.7:2, 9; 8.8:5, 8; 8.10:6).

[23] The preposition *beth* indicates that the goods were returned (3.65:5; 3.70:4; 3.72:6-7). See Botta 2001:134, 177-180.

[24] The statement of satisfaction occurs here in its fullest form — "you satisfied our heart ... our heart was satisfied" (see 3.60, n. 28; 3.63, n. 14).

[25] The appearance of this phrase in the satisfaction statement is unique (see on 3.61:8). It would seem to mean "once and for all."

[26] Withdrawal regularly followed on satisfaction (see 3.64, n. 17), though the scribe did not always make it explicit (3.60:11-12).

[27] For this occasional addition to the *Withdrawal* clause, see 3.64, n. 17.

[28] In documents drawn up after 420 BCE, the list of claimants and covered parties was expanded beyond heirs and beneficiaries to include representatives, *viz.* an agent or lessee. The specific terms were variegated — "man who is mine/ours/yours" (lines 10, 13-14); "man/woman of mine/ours/yours" (line 12; 3.67:10-14; 3.77:4-6), and "individual who is mine/yours" (3.68:8, 10).

[29] The truncated phrase "near or civilian" is another indication of scribal ellipsis; for the full phrase, see on 3.59:9.

[30] The awkward syntactical shift in the person of the auxiliary verb ("we shall not be able" > "they shall not be able") resulted from compacting into one clause both the first and third person *Waivers*.

[31] The heirs and representatives after our death.

[32] The Aram. word (*bnn*) was the same as that for "sons" in the preceding sentence (line 10). If "sons" were meant here, then "daughters" would be implicit because it was explicit in the previous and following sentences (lines 10, 13).

[33] See 3.61, n. 37.

[34] This would refer to the garments and utensils mentioned above (lines 5-6).

[35] Strangely, there was no mention of silver in the original list above.

of Azariah.

Penalty
And if we, (13)or our sons or our daughters, or a man who is ours, or the sons of Shelomam son of Azariah,[36] bring (suit) against you or bring (suit) against your sons or your daughters, (14)or a man who is yours, then whoever shall bring su[it] about it[37] shall give you, or your sons or whomever they bring (suit) against, the penalty[38] (15)of silver, ten *karsh* by the stone(-weight)s of the king, silver 2 q(uarters) to 1 *karsh*,

Reaffirmation
and he is likewise withdrawn from these goods[39] (16)about (15)which (16)we brought (suit), without suit and without process,[40]

Scribe
Mauziah son of Nathan[41] wrote this document at the instruction of Menahem and Ananiah, all (told) two, (17)sons of Meshullam son of Shelomam.

Witnesses
(2nd hand) witness Menahem son of Gaddul[42];
(3rd hand) witness Gaddul son of Berechiah[43];
(4th hand) witness Menahem son of Azariah[44];
(18)(5th hand) witness Hodaviah son of Zaccur son of Oshaiah.[45]

Endorsement
(Verso)(19)Document (*sealing*) of [withdrawal] which Menahem and Ananiah, all (told) two, sons of Menahem[46] son of Shelomam, wrote (20)[for Jedania]h and Mahseiah, all (told) two, sons of Eṣhor son of D]jeḥo.[47]

[36] Their uncles, who were presumably not around at the moment or else they might have sued instead of Shelomam's grandchildren.

[37] The "then" clause is introduced by the conjunction *waw* and recapitulates the long protasis before introducing the penalty statement ("shall give you"); see *DAE* 199.

[38] It is first in 427 BCE that we find the introduction of the word ᵓ*bygrn* (< OP **abigarana*) to designate the penalty. It recurs regularly thereafter, with precise formulation following scribal preference — "the penalty of silver" employed by Mauziah son of Nathan (also 3.66:14; 3.67:15; 3.76:31), "the penalty, silver/barley" (3.68:10; *TAD* 7.1:8), or simply "a penalty (of) silver," favored by Haggai son of Shemaiah (3.74:8, 14-15; 3.78:20; 3.79:10, 14; 3.80:30) and other scribes (3.75:17; 3.77:7; *TAD* B5.5:6, 11). Once the order is reversed — "silver, a penalty" (3.71:6; cf. line 7). See Azzoni and Lippert 2000:22-25.

[39] I.e., he has no right to reclaim these goods again from you; Botta 2001:135. Had Jedaniah and Mahseiah retained possession of the goods the language should have been like that in the deed of withdrawal drawn up by Dargamana, who relinquished possession ("and that land is [> and these goods are] likewise yours and you are withdrawn from any suit" [3.60:15]). But the *Reaffirmation* clause in the withdrawal document of Peu did not reaffirm Mibtahiah's rights to the goods (3.65:11). So we are back to square one.

[40] For this addition to the withdrawal statement, see 3.61, n. 40. Here it has the meaning "(withdrawn) absolutely."

[41] He was one of the five leaders of the community (3.53:10 and see 3.47:1, 17; 3.48:2, 12) and a professional scribe who drew up seven or eight more documents in our collection (3.67:17; 3.73:22; 3.76:42; *TAD* B6.1, 6.4:8-9; 7.1:9; and probably D2.25).

[42] His grandfather was Baadiah (3.67:18) and he appears among the first signatories in four documents between 420 and 402 BCE, including the last three in this archive — first (here; 3.68:15), second of eight (3.79:18), and third of eight (3.67:18). The scribe forgot the introductory statement, "The witnesses herein." For the number of witnesses, see 3.65, n. 26.

[43] He also appears in the next document as sixth witness (3.67:19).

[44] He appears as witness a month later in another contract written by Mauziah (3.76:44).

[45] Appears only here. Three-generation genealogies among witness were rare. See 3.64, n. 7.

[46] Influenced, perhaps, by the first Menahem, the scribe wrote Menahem here instead of Meshullam (see line 2).

[47] This is one of three two-line endorsements (see 3.61, n. 83).

REFERENCES

Text, translation and studies: *TAD* B2.9; *EPE* B31. *DAE*; Azzoni and Lippert 2000; Porten 1968; 1990; 2002; *TAD*.

WITHDRAWAL FROM HOUSE (3.67)
(16 December, 416 BCE)

Bezalel Porten

Like the preceding document, this too was drawn up in the presence of the Troop Commander. But unlike that one, there is no mention here of a suit. A nephew of Jezaniah, Mibtahiah's first husband, withdrew from Jezaniah's house in favor of Mibtahiah's children from her second husband, here named Nathan (lines 2-9). Upon Jezaniah's premature death, his house must have passed to his wife. She recently died and her estate required probate. No children of Jezaniah stepped forward, though possible offspring lurked in the background (lines 13, 17), and so the relinquishment by the nephew Jedaniah son of Hoshaiah/Hosea may have been drawn up as part of a probate procedure (cf. an earlier one, likewise in the presence of the Troop Commander [*TAD* B5.1:3]). With other potential heirs in mind, the *Waiver* and *Penalty* clauses were careful to offer protection only against a suit brought "in the name of" Jedaniah, his heirs, and representatives. The standard ten *karsh* penalty was to apply (lines 9-17) and the requisite number of eight witnesses, all Jewish, signed (lines 17-19).

Date

(Recto)(1)On the 3rd of Kislev, year 8, that is day 12 of Thoth, year 9 of Darius the king,[1]

Place

then in Elephantine (2)the fortress,[2]

Parties

Said Jedaniah son of Hoshaiah son of Uriah,[3] an Aramean of Elephantine the fortress,[4] before Vidranga the Troop Commander (3)of Syene,[5] to Jedaniah son of Nathan[6] and Mahseiah son of Nathan his brother, their mother (being) Mibtahiah daughter of Mahseiah son of Jedaniah,[7] before (4)Vidranga the Troop Commander of Syene, saying:

Withdrawal

I withdrew[8] from you

Object

from the house of Jezaniah son of Uriah.

Boundaries I

Behold its boundaries:[9]

(5)above (it) the house of Hosea son of Uriah adjoins it[10]; below it the house of Hazzul son of Zechariah adjoins it[11];

Description

(6)on the (side) below and above windows are open there[12];

Boundaries II

east of it is the Temple of YHW the God and the road of (7)the king is between them;

west[13] of it the house of Mibtahiah daughter of Mahseiah, which Mahseiah her father gave her,[14] (8)adjoins it.

Investiture

That house, whose boundaries are written above,[15] is yours[16] — you, Jedaniah and Mahseiah, all (told) two,[17] (9)sons of Nathan — forever, and your children's after you and to whomever you love you may give it.[18]

Waiver of suit

I shall not be able — I, Jedaniah or my children, (10)or woman or man of mine[19] — I shall not be able to institute against you suit or process. Moreover, we shall not be able to bring (suit) against son or daughter of yours,[20] (11)brother or sister,[21] woman or man of yours, or a person to whom you sell that

---

[1] Between Eg. 1 Thoth and Babyl. 1 Nisan, the scribe, as here, often gave two regnal dates (so in 3.68:1, but absent from 3.69:1 and 3.79:1), since the Egyptian new year began three months earlier than the Babylonian new year. This document must have been written at night since 3 Kislev in 8 Darius II = December 17 while 12 Thoth in 9 Darius II = December 16. See Porten 1990:21 and Figure 8 in *TAD* B.

[2] See 3.66, n. 2.

[3] Jedaniah was a nephew of Mibtahiah's first husband, Jezaniah son of Uriah (lines 4, 13, 17; 3.61:6-7; 3.62:2-4). His grandfather was listed here so as to link him up with the house in question, that of Jezaniah son of Uriah. For other three-generation genealogies, see 3.64, n. 7.

[4] See 3.59, n. 3. His detachment is not listed.

[5] Unlike the previous document (3.66:4) where the alienors had brought suit before the Chief and Troop Commander, here the alienor merely made a declaration in the presence of the Troop Commander of Syene. A similar procedure took place a few months earlier in a case of emancipation-adoption (3.77:2-3). In both cases the name of Vidranga was repeated, once following the name of the alienor and again after that of the alienee. See further on 3.48, n. 8 (*EPE* B15).

[6] In the previous documents the husband of Mibtahiah and the father of Jedaniah and Mahseiah was known as Esḥor (3.63:2, 17-26, 30; 3.66:3, 8, 20). Now, the same scribe who wrote one of those documents ten years earlier referred to him as Nathan. Since he was presumably dead at the time, he must have assumed that second, Jewish name during his lifetime.

[7] For mention of the mother, see 3.66, n. 7. The scribe was the same but the formula was different. Moreover, here he added Mahseiah's patronym to yield a three-generation genealogy. See 3.64, n. 7.

[8] See 3.64, n. 17.

[9] For the formula, see 3.60, n. 19. For the plan, see *TAD* B, Figure 3.

[10] Hosea/Hoshaiah son of Uriah was the brother of Jezaniah and his neighbor. Perhaps both houses had once been united in their father's possession and were divided up between the brothers after his death.

[11] Zechariah was owner of the house back in 471 BCE when Mahseiah first appeared on the scene (3.59:5).

[12] The windows were apparently located in the lower (= southern?) side of Jezaniah's house (for a different view, see Porten 1968:309-310). The presence or absence of windows, and their location, was frequently mentioned in conveyances (3.72:5; 3.73:8; 3.78:13; 3.80:13, 21).

[13] The sitings here are those of the scribe Attarshuri for whom the house of Jezaniah lay east of the house of Mibtahiah (3.61:6-7) and not of Itu for whom it lay "below" that house (3.60:9-10).

[14] In 3.61; see 3.60, n. 22 for explanatory notations.

[15] For this expression, see also 3.72:17; 3.79:11.

[16] Only here is the usually terse *Investiture* statement expanded with reference to the boundaries; see 3.59, n. 8.

[17] For the practice of tallying two and more persons, see 3.60, n. 9.

[18] This clause with its multiple elements (yours ... forever ... children ... love) was the most expansive *Investiture* clause of its type, yet it would appear to limit the right of alienation to heirs and beneficiaries.

[19] Like the previous document (see 3.66, n. 28), this one extended coverage to representatives in addition to heirs.

[20] The scribe has composed separate *Waiver* sentences for the alienee ("not sue you") and for those associated with him ("not sue heirs, representatives, et al.").

[21] Explicitly mentioned in the second sentence, "brother or sister" are to be understood as included in the first sentence and in the following *Penalty* clause (line 14).

house[22] or to whom in love you give (it)[23] — (to bring [suit]) (12)in my name,[24] I, Jedaniah, or in the name of children or woman or man of mine.

Penalty
And if I, Jedaniah, bring (suit) against you, or (13)son of mine or daughter, woman or man (12)bring (suit) against you (13)in my name or in the name of my children — excluding son or daughter of Jezaniah son of Uriah — (14)or they bring (suit) against son or daughter, or woman or man of yours, or persons to whom you sell or to whom in love you give (15)that house, (15)then whoever shall bring suit against you[25] shall give you the penalty[26] of silver, ten *karsh*, that is 10 *karsh*,[27] silver (16)2 q(uarters) to 1 *karsh*, by the stone(-weight)s of the king,

Reaffirmation
and the house is likewise yours forever[28] and your children's after you — excluding (17)children of Jezan son of Uriah — without suit.

Scribe
Mauziah son of Nathan wrote[29] at the instruction of Jedaniah son of Hosea.[30]

Witnesses
And the witnesses (18)herein:[31]
(2nd hand) Menahem son of Shallum[32];
(3rd hand) Mahseiah son of Jedaniah[33];
(4th hand) Menahem son of Gaddul son of Baadiah[34];
(5th hand) Jedaniah son of Meshullam[35];
(19)(6th hand) Islaḥ son of Gaddul[36];
(7th hand) Gaddul son of Berechiah[37];
(8th hand) Jezaniah son of Penuliah[38];
(9th hand) Ahio son of Nathan.[39]

Endorsement
(Verso)(20)Document (*sealing*) of withdrawal which Jedaniah son of Hosea wrote about the house of Jezaniah son of Uriah (21)for Jedaniah son of Nathan and Mahseiah his brother, all (told) two.[40]

[22] Mention here of a potential purchaser, listed even ahead of a beneficiary ("give in love") was designed to indicate that the reference to "give it to whomever you love" in the *Investiture* clause (line 9) was not meant to limit the alienee's right of disposition. See Szubin and Porten 1983a:38-39.

[23] For the meaning of this clause, see 3.61, n. 31.

[24] Emphasis on name here and in the following *Penalty* clause was particularly pertinent because a suit entered in the name of any (at present unknown?) descendant of Jezaniah was not covered under the provisions of this contract (see lines 13, 17).

[25] After a very lengthy protasis, the scribe employed the same kind of apodosis construction here that he had in the previous document (see 3.66, n. 37).

[26] For this term see 3.66, n. 38.

[27] For the numerical repetition, see 3.60, n. 36.

[28] Only here did the scribe add "forever" to the *Reaffirmation* clause. See 3.59, n. 18.

[29] He omitted the usual object "this document." See also on 3.59:15; 3.66:16.

[30] Hosea (also in the endorsement [line 20]) abbreviates Hoshaiah cited in line 2.

[31] Eight witnesses were standard for withdrawal from realty (see 3.59, n. 34). None of them here prefaced his name with the word "witness."

[32] This witness who signed first here in 416 BCE and then again in 402 BCE (3.81:13) was party to two documents himself — an oath text (*TAD* B7 3) and a deed of obligation (for his former[?] wife) in 400 (*TAD* B4.6) — and was recorded in a compilation of memoranda (*TAD* C3.13:46).

[33] According to the handwriting (cf. 3.64:17-18 and 3.70:13) this was not Mahseiah son of Jedaniah who began the archive in 471 BCE (3.59:1). On the basis of papponymy this Mahseiah son of Jedaniah would have been his grandson, son of the earlier witness Jedaniah son of Mahseiah (3.61:31; 3.62:20). It is unlikely that he was son of the Jedaniah in our contract. The latter's father was married in 449 BCE (3.63) and Mahseiah was his second son. Thirty years maximum is hardly enough time to allow for a second generation witness signing second with a skilled hand. Porten 2001:334-335.

[34] Witnessed four documents (see 3.66, n. 42).

[35] Appears only here.

[36] In 420 BCE, he was the second of six witnesses to a document of wifehood drawn up by Mauziah (3.76:43-44) and in 407 BCE he was a creditor designated "Aramean of Syene" (*TAD* B4.5:2).

[37] He also appeared in the previous document as the second witness (3.66:17).

[38] Appears only here; probably son of the witness Penuliah son of Jezaniah of 449 BCE (3.63:38). See Porten 2001:348.

[39] Ahio son of Nathan son of Anani also appeared as the third of eight witnesses in 402 BCE (3.79:18) and in two lists from the end of the century (*TAD* C3.15:131; 4.6:1). He may have been the brother of the professional scribe Mauziah son of Nathan son of Anani. See Porten 2001:339-340.

[40] This is one of three two-line endorsements (see 3.61, n. 83). For the expanded formulation see 3.59, n. 44.

REFERENCES

Text and translation: *TAD* B2.10; *EPE* B32; *EPE*. Porten 1968; 1990; 2001; Szubin and Porten 1983a; *TAD*.

APPORTIONMENT OF SLAVES (3.68)
(10 February, 410 BCE)

Bezalel Porten

Just over five years after the brothers Jedaniah and Mahseiah received clear title to the house of their mother's first husband (3.67), they decided to divide between them two of Mibtahiah's four Egyptian slaves. Both were branded with their mother's name. The present document was drawn up by Mahseiah for his elder brother and he assigned him Peṭosiri, taking Bela for himself (lines 2-6). An identical document must have been drawn up by Jedaniah, assigning Bela to his brother. Inheritance terminology is clearly in evidence ("share," "came to you," and "take hereditary possession"). Mahseiah guaranteed Jedaniah's rights with the usual *Waiver* and *Penalty* clauses, protecting him, his heirs, and his representatives against suits (*sic*!) by Mahseiah and his people, subject to the standard ten *karsh* penalty (lines 7-12). Mother Tabi and her third, presumably small, child Lilu were left for future division (lines 12-14). The scribe was Aramean, though the document was drawn up in Elephantine and attested by four Jewish witnesses (lines 14-16). [For Petosiris, high priest of Thoth in Hermopolis a century later, see Lichtheim AEL 3:44-54. Ed.]

Date

(Recto)(1)On the 24th of Shebat, year 13, that is day 9 of Hathyr, year 14 of Darius the king,[1]

Place

in Elephantine the fortress,[2]

Parties

(2)said Mahseiah son of Nathan, 1, Jedaniah son of Nathan, 1, all (told) two,[3] Arameans of Syene of the detachment of Var[yaza]ta,[4] saying:

Apportionment of slaves

We have acted as equals (3)as one[5] and divided (between) us the slaves[6] of Mibtahiah our mother.[7]

Description

And behold,[8] this is the share which came[9] to you as a share, you,[10] Jedaniah[11]:

(4)Peṭosiri by name,[12] his mother (being) Tabi,[13] a slave, *ywd/r*, 1,[14] branded[15] on his right hand (with) a brand reading (in) Aramaic like this: (5)"(Belonging) to Mibtahiah."

And behold, this is the share which came to me as a share, I,[16] Mahseiah:

Bela by name, his mother (being) Tabi, a slave, *ywd/r*, 1, (6)branded on his right hand (with) a brand reading (in) Aramaic like this: "(Belonging) to Mibtahiah."

Investiture

You, Jedaniah, have right to[17] Peṭosiri, (7)that slave who came to you as a share,[18] from this day and forever and (so do) your children after you and to

[1] For the double regnal year on a document written during the first months of the Julian calendar year, see on 3.67:1. This document must have been written at night since in 13 Darius II 24 Shebat = February 11 while in 14 Darius II 9 Hathyr = February 10. See Porten 1990:21 and Figure 8 in *TAD* B.

[2] See 3.66, n. 2.

[3] For the practice of tallying two and more persons, see 3.60, n. 9.

[4] Their grandfather was listed in identical fashion 55 years earlier (3.59:2), but it is highly improbable that this was the same detachment commander. It was probably his grandson.

[5] In modern legal parlance we would say: "we held equal rights; by the whole and by the half, as tenants in common in an individual estate." Identical terminology is found in an Aram. joint venture agreement from Korobis in 515 BCE (*TAD* B1.1:6); see Szubin and Porten 1992:76.

[6] Actually only two of her four slaves were being divided. All four had Eg. names. A houseborn slave of Zaccur son of Meshullam bore the Heb. name Jedaniah (3.77:3).

[7] Their mother had probably died at least six years earlier when her house from her first husband Jezaniah passed through probate (see introduction to 3.67).

[8] This same interjection, followed by demonstrative pronoun, was used to introduce the *Boundaries* clause (see 3.60, n. 19).

[9] The language here is technical in a situation where property "comes" to an heir as his "portion" of the estate; similar terminology is encountered in biblical, Talmudic, and Demotic texts (see on *TAD* B5.1:4 [*EPE* B47] and Porten and Szubin 1982b:653.

[10] For addition of the independent pronoun as emphatic, see 3.60, n. 17 and *TAD* A3.3:11.

[11] For double reinforcement of the name of an owner ("to you; you, Jedaniah"; "to me; I; Mahseiah"), see 3.60, n. 17.

[12] This word (*šmh*) was regularly attached to the name of a slave (lines 5; 9; 13; *TAD* A6.7:3-5; 3.71:3; 3.74:24; 3.75:3; 3.76:3; 3.77:3); a royal servant (*TAD* A6.3:3; 6.9:2; 6.11:1, 4; 6.12:1; C1.1:1; et al.; 2.1:12; et al.), and even communal leaders in a petition (3.53:1-5).

[13] Slaves were normally known by their mother (cf. Jedaniah son of Taḥe/Takhoi [3.77:3); though the handmaiden Tamet daughter of Patou (3.80:3) was an exception. Who sired our three slave lads? There was no mention of any father.

[14] This inexplicable word, followed by the numeral "1" in a tally, designated an Eg. male head of family where the wife was called "great lady" (*TAD* C3.9:9, 12-14; 3.10:2). Here we have the word + numeral but no tally, perhaps because they were divided up between the two brothers. This word + numeral had hitherto been taken to mean a mark of some kind that was the subject of the following verb, "branded" (see Porten 1968:203-205 for full discussion).

[15] It was customary in Egypt generally (*TAD* A6.10:7) and at Elephantine specifically to brand slaves with the name of their owner (3.74:3 [on the right hand; as here]; 3.77:5-7; 3.87I:3-4).

[16] For addition of the independent pronoun as emphatic, see 3.60, n. 17 and *TAD* A3.3:11 (*EPE* B9).

[17] See note on line 12 below and 3.61, n. 28.

[18] Every reference to Peṭosiri carried the notation that he was an heir's share (lines 9-11).

whomever you desire you may give (him).[19]

Waiver of suit
I shall not be able — (8)I, Mahseiah, son or daughter of mine, brother or sister[20] of mine, or an individual who is mine — to bring[21] suits against you or against your children on account of[22] Peṭosiri (9)by name, the slave who came to you as a share.

Penalty
If we bring suit against you about it — we, Mahseiah or my children[23] — or bring (suit) against son (10)or daughter of yours or against an individual who is yours[24] on account of Peṭosiri, that slave who came to you as a share, afterwards[25] we shall give you the penalty[26] (of) (11)pure (10)silver, (11)ten *karsh* by the weight of the king,

Reaffirmation
and we are withdrawn[27] from you and from your children from (any) suit on account of that Peṭosiri (12)who came to you as a share. Yours shall he be and your children's after you and to whomever you desire you may give him, without suit.[28]

Future apportionment
Moreover, there is Tabi (13)by name, the mother of these lads, and Lilu her son whom we shall not yet divide (between) us.[29] When (the) time will be, we shall divide them (14)(between) us and, (each) person his share, we shall take hereditary possession,[30] and a document of our division[31] we shall write between us, without suit.

Scribe and place
Nabutukulti son of Nabuzeribni[32] wrote (15)this document in Elephantine[33] the fortress at the instruction of Mahseiah and Jedaniah his brother.

Witnesses
The witnesses herein[34]:
(2nd hand) Menahem son of Gaddul[35];
(16)(3rd hand) witness Hanan son of Haggai[36];
(4th hand) witness Nathan son of Jehour[37];
(5th hand) witness Shillem son of Nathan.[38]

Endorsement
(Verso)(17)Document (*sealing*) of division of (the) slave[39] Peṭosiri (which) Mahseiah son of Nathan wrote for Jedaniah son of Nathan his brother.

[19] Virtually the same language was used in the *Investiture* clause drawn up for Mahseiah in 459 BCE by this scribe's grandfather, Attarshuri (3.61:9-10), except that here the right of alienation was not limited ("give to whomever you desire").

[20] Explicit in the *Waiver* clause, "brother or sister" was meant to be implicit in the list of protected parties in the *Penalty* clause (line 10).

[21] The construction here of complementary infinitive plus plural object (*lmršh dynn*) is unique.

[22] For this technical term and its legal overtones, see 3.60, n. 12.

[23] Enumerated in the *Waiver* clause (Mahseiah, children, siblings, representatives [line 8]); the potential claimants are abridged in the *Penalty* clause (Mahseiah, children).

[24] Abridged in the *Waiver* clause (children [line 8]); the protected parties are enumerated (children; representatives) in the *Penalty* clause. All in all, there were four potential claimants (alienor, children, siblings, representatives) and the identical four protected parties.

[25] For this conjunction, see 3.62, n. 18.

[26] See 3.66, n. 38.

[27] See 3.60, n. 39.

[28] The scribe has reiterated and expanded the *Investiture* clause (lines 6-7) — not only do you have right of possession over (*šlyṭ b-*) that slave but also title to him (*lk yhwh*).

[29] Mother and minor child remained joint property, presumably to be divided up when the child could fend for himself.

[30] For this technical term, see 3.61, n. 65.

[31] Much like the present document, but the archive ended before such a document made its way into it.

[32] This scribe with Akk. praenomen and patronym was the grandson of Attarshuri son of Nabuzeribni who drew up two documents for Mahseiah in 459 BCE (3.61:27-28; 3.62:16).

[33] See 3.59, nn. 31 and 33 and 3.60, n. 41.

[34] Four witnesses was the standard number for withdrawal from movables. See 3.65, n. 26.

[35] Witnessed the last three documents in this archive. See 3.66, n. 34.

[36] Appears also in a memorandum of accounts *TAD* C3.13:2).

[37] Appears also in three late documents (404-402 BCE) written by Haggai son of Shemaiah, where he was third of eight (3.78:24); first of eight (3.79:18); and third of four (3.80:34).

[38] Appears only here.

[39] For the formula, see 3.59, n. 44.

REFERENCES

Text and translation: *TAD* B2.11; *EPE* B33. Porten 1968; 1990; Porten and Szubin 1982b; Szubin and Porten 1992; *TAD*.

THE ANANIAH ARCHIVE (456-402 BCE)

Bezalel Porten

In the early part of 1893 the American traveler and collector, Charles Edwin Wilbour acquired at Aswan over a dozen Aramaic papyri that went into storage in Brooklyn, New York, after his death in 1896. Upon the demise of his daughter Theodora in 1947, they were bequeathed to the Brooklyn Museum and were published in 1953 by Emil G. Kraeling. Unprofessional attempts to open three of the intact rolls (3.70, 3.75, and 3.76) reduced each to numerous fragments that had to be restored in jigsaw fashion. This was accomplished with great skill by the technician of the Department of Egyptian Art, Anthony Giambalvo for the original publication, and enhanced in 1987 by Porten and Yardeni for publication in their *Textbook* (1989). The major documents stemmed from the archive of the Temple official Anani(ah) son of Azariah and his Egyptian-born handmaiden wife Ta(p)met, their daughter Jehoishma and her husband Anani(ah) son of Haggai. To this we have added the only intact roll to emerge from the Rubensohn excavations, a contract for a loan made by Meshullam son of Zaccur (3.69), who was slaveowner of Tamet (3.71) and whose son Zaccur gave her daughter's hand in marriage to the above-named son of Haggai (3.76). The archive opens at the beginning of the Egyptian year (456 BCE), before the collapse of the Egyptian revolt against Artaxerxes I[1] and comes to an end at the beginning of the Egyptian year (402 BCE), on the eve of the expulsion of Artaxerxes II.[2] It bears allusion to events in the Egyptian-Jewish clash that led to the destruction of the Jewish Temple (3.78:8-9; 3.79:3-4) and is a disinterested witness to its likely reconstruction (3.80:2, 18-19). Like Mibtahiah, Anani lived across from the Temple, in a piece of abandoned property he bought from a Caspian couple in 437 BCE (3.72), a dozen years after the redaction of his wifehood document with Tamet (3.71). Three years after his purchase he bestows a room in the house upon his wife (3.73), and then in stages another room upon his daughter (420 [3.75]), 404 [3.78], and 402 [3.79]), and the remainder to his son-in-law in sale (402 [3.80]). Unique among the papyri are a document of emancipation and one of adoption. The former is drawn up in 427 BCE by Meshullam for Tamet and her daughter (3.74); the latter for his son Zaccur by one Uriah son of Mahseiah in 416 BCE (3.77). The final document is a loan of grain taken out by Ananiah son of Haggai (3.81).

[1] Briant 1996:592-594.
[2] Briant 1996:653-654.

LOAN OF SILVER (3.69)
(13 December 456 BCE)

Bezalel Porten

This was the only Aramaic document found intact by Otto Rubensohn in excavation. The otherwise unknown woman Jehoḥen borrowed the small sum of four shekels from the well-known Meshullam son of Zaccur at a 5% monthly interest rate (lines 2-5). If the interest went unpaid in any month it became capitalized and bore interest like the principal (lines 5-7). If interest and principal were not returned by the end of the year, Meshullam was entitled to seize any durable or perishable property of the debtor as security toward repayment (lines 7-11). Should she die before repaying the loan, her children inherited the obligation and the same right of seizure from her applied to them as well (lines 14-18). Any attempt to deny the loan or any legal complaint against seizure of security would be thwarted by Meshullam's retention of the document (lines 11-14, 18-20). The contract has been assigned to the Anani archive on the assumption that the loan had never been repaid and some personal possession of Jehoḥen had been seized. This was subsequently passed on to Jehoishma as part of her dowry along with the contract as evidence of title to the items.

Date		*Parties*
(Recto)(1)On the 7th of Kislev, that is day 4 of the month of Thoth, year 9 of Artaxerxes (2)the king,[1]		said Jehoḥen daughter of Meshullach, a lady of Elephantine the fortress, to Meshullam son of

[1] As written, the double dates do not synchronize — 7 Kislev = December 14 = 4 Thoth, 9 Artaxerxes I = December 18, 456 BCE. One way to account for the four-day difference is to assume that the scribe forgot to account for the 5 epagomenal days at the end of the Eg. year so 4 Thoth would be an error for the 4th epagomenal day = December 13. The equation would then be 7 Kislev = December 14 = 4 epagomenal = December 13, 456 BCE. The document was thus written on the night of December 13. The date formula was abridged in another respect. Usually, Eg. dates that fell between 1 Thoth (the Eg. New Year) and 1 Nisan (the Babylonian New Year), carried a double year date, with the Eg. year being one year ahead (so in 3.67:1 and 3.68:1). Here the scribe Nathan, error-prone on chronology (see on 3.64:1), gave only the Babylonian year. See Porten 1990:25 and Figure 8 in *TAD* B.

(3)Zaccur,[2] a Jew of Elephantine the fortress,[3] saying:

Loan

You gave me a loan of silver,[4] (4)4, that is four,[5] (3)shekels (4)by the stone(-weight)s of the king, at its interest.

Interest I

It will increase upon me[6] (5)(at the rate of) silver, 2 hallurs for 1 shekel for 1 month. (That) was silver,[7] 8 hallurs (6)for one month.[8] If the interest (be)come the capital,[9] the interest shall increase like the capital,[10] (7)one like one.[11]

Security I

And if a second year come[12] and I have not paid you your silver (8)and its interest, which is written in this document,[13] you Meshullam or your children have the right (9)to take for yourself any security[14] which you will find (belonging) to me — house of bricks, silver or gold, (10)bronze or iron, slave or handmaiden, barley,[15] emmer[16] — or any food which you will find (belonging) to me (11)until you have full (payment) of[17] your silver and its interest.

Document validity I

And I shall not be able to say (to you) saying[18]:

"I paid you (12)your silver and its interest"

while this document is in your hand. And I shall not be able to complain[19] (13)against you before prefect or judge,[20] saying:

"You took from me a security"

while (14)this (13)document (14)is in your hand.

Obligation of heirs

And if I die and have not paid you[21] this silv(er and its interest), (15)it will be my children (who) shall pay you this silver and its interest.[22]

Security II

And if (16)they do not pay this silver and its interest, you, Meshullam, have the right (17)to take for yourself any food or security which you will find (belonging) to them until you have full (payment) (18)of your silver and its interest.[23]

Document validity II

And they shall not be able to complain against you before prefect (19)or judge while this document is in your hand. Moreover, should they go into a suit,[24] they shall not prevail (20)while this document is in your hand.[25]

Scribe

Nathan son of Anani[26] wrote this document (21)at the instruction of Jehoḥen.

Witnesses

And the witnesses herein:[27]

---

[2] For this prominent property-holder see 3.64, n. 7.

[3] His detachment affiliation was omitted.

[4] An even terser beginning appears in an earlier silver loan contract — "You gave me silver" (*TAD* B4.2:1) — whereas a grain loan from the end of the century began "I came to you in your house in Syene the fortress and borrowed from you and you gave me emmer" (3.81:2-3).

[5] Interestingly, loan contracts and deeds of obligation were often written for very small amounts, two shekels (*TAD* B4.6), 3½ shekels (*TAD* B4.2:2) and four shekels (our document). The largest amount was fourteen shekels (*TAD* B4.5:3). For the numerical repetition see 3.60, n. 36.

[6] I.e. interest will accrue from me (also *TAD* B4.2:2).

[7] A fuller formulation is found in an earlier contract — "And the interest on your silver will be" (*TAD* B4.2:3-4).

[8] That would be 5% monthly.

[9] The earlier contract was more explicit — "And the month in which I shall not give you interest, it will be capital." See next note.

[10] It was to be understood that when the interest was not paid it became capital and bore interest just like the capital (so also in *TAD* B4.2:3-4).

[11] One like the other, both the same.

[12] The earlier loan contract added, "And I shall pay it to you month by month from my allotment which they will give me from the treasury and you shall write me a receipt for all the silver and interest ..." (*TAD* B4.2:5-6).

[13] See 3.59, n. 26. The loan was ordinarily meant for a year. Why was no source of funds for repayment indicated for Jehoḥen? Did she not receive an allotment?

[14] The right to seize any property as security to force payment of a debt was not uncommon (3.81:10-12).

[15] For this grain see on *TAD* A2.4:9 (*EPE* B4).

[16] The "security which you will find (belonging) to me" consisted of durables (house, precious metals, vessels, slaves, and grain) and was distinguished from any "food which you will find (belonging) to me," which were perishables. The two are likewise differentiated below — "any food and security which you will find (belonging) to them" (line 17). A similar list is found in other contracts of loan and obligation (3.81:10-12).

[17] This expression (*ʿd ttmlʾ b-*) is found also in *TAD* B4.4:17 and may be restored in B4.6:13. An alternate formulation (*ʿd tšlm b-*) is found in 3.81:11.

[18] For this construction, see on *TAD* B2.1:11-12 (B23).

[19] For a similar provision in a loan contract, see *TAD* B4.6:14.

[20] See 3.60, n. 14.

[21] A provision typical of loan contracts (3.81:8).

[22] Jehoḥen's heirs inherited her debts.

[23] The same right of seizure of the debtor's property applied to the creditor's heirs until the loan was repaid (lines 8-11).

[24] I.e. take legal action.

[25] The identical sentence appears in a conveyance witnessed three years earlier by Nathan (3.61:22, 32), scribe of this document; also in 3.79:15.

[26] See 3.61, n. 77.

[27] Only four witnesses were necessary in loans and ordinary deeds of obligation (3.81:13-14); see further 3.59, n. 34.

(2nd hand) witness Osea son of Galgul[28];
(22)(3rd hand) Hodaviah son of Gedaliah[29];
(4th hand) Ahio son of Pelatiah[30];
(5th hand) Agur son of Ahio.[31]

Endorsement
(Verso)(23)Document (*sealing*) of silver of the debt[32] which Jehoḥen daughter of Meshullach wrote (24)for Meshullam son of Zaccur.

[28] Appears only here.
[29] Appears only here.
[30] Was he son of the professional scribe Pelatiah son of Ahio? See 3.59, n. 32.
[31] Was he the same as Hagur son of Ahio on an ostracon (*TAD* D9.4:1)?
[32] See reference in *EPE* 204, n. 35.

REFERENCES

Text and translation: *TAD* B3.1; *EPE* B34. *EPE*; Porten 1990; *TAD*.

WITHDRAWAL FROM *HYR*$^{\supset}$ (3.70)
(6 July, 451 BCE)

Bezalel Porten

This is one of the most enigmatic documents in our collection. The object of the contract (*hyr*$^{\supset}$) remains unexplained. The *Waiver* and *Penalty* clauses covered only the party drawing up the contract (lines 4-8). A *Defension* clause covered only brother and sister (lines 8-9). Both parties had entered a complaint about the property; Anani paid Mica five shekels to withdraw. Mica did so, but provided Anani with very limited warranties. It is likely that the object in dispute was a piece of abandoned property to which neither had title and both laid claim.[1] The scribe was Aramean and only one witness was Jewish (line 13). The onomasticon shows how non-Jews within the same family drew freely upon Akkaddian (Nabukaṣir, Aḫushunu, Mannuki), Aramean (Zabdi, Sachael, Attarmalki, Zabbud, Zabidri), Egyptian (Renpenofre, Psami) and Persian (Bagaina) names (lines 11-14).

Date
(Recto)(1)On the 25th of Phamen[o]th, that is day 20 of Sivan, year 14 of Artaxerxes, the king,[2]

Parties
(2)said Mica son of A[hio][3] to Anani son of Azar-[iah],[4] a servitor to YHW in Elephantine,[5] (3)saying:

Transfer
You gave me

Object
silver, 5 shekels

Complaint
as payment[6] of the *hyr*$^{\supset}$[7] of yours[8] (about) which (4)you complained against me[9] herein

Satisfaction
and my heart was satisfied with it[s] payment.[10]

[1] See Szubin and Porten 1983b.
[2] In 14 Artaxerxes I (= 451 BCE), 25 Phamenoth = July 6 while 20 Sivan = July 7. This document was thus written on the night of July 6. Only here and in 3.75:1 did the Eg. month precede the Babyl. month in the date formula.
[3] This name was restored here on the basis of its almost complete, but undoubted, appearance in line 10. Was he the same as the Micaiah son of Ahio, the witness who apparently began to sign second but erased his signature to give way to another witness, and so signed third? The only other person who witnessed his own document was Mahseiah son of Jedaniah, who signed first, adding the expression, "with his own hands" instead of his patronym (3.64:17-18).
[4] Alternately called Ananiah or Anani, this person was party to nine documents in this family archive. His father, with the same title as his son (*lḥn*$^{\supset}$), appeared in another accounts fragment, where he bore a second, unintelligible title (*TAD* C3.13:45).
[5] His title appeared in more different formulations than there were documents — "servitor to YHW the God," "servitor to YHW in Elephantine," "servitor to YH in Elephantine," "servitor to YHW the God in Elephantine the fortress," "the servitor" (always at the end of the contract), "servitor of YHW," "servitor of YHW the God," "the servitor of YHW the God" (always at the end of the contract), "servitor of YHW the God in Elephantine the fortress," or "servitor of YHH the God who is in Elephantine the fortress," while his wife was once designated as "servitor of YHW the God dwelling (in) Elephantine the fortress." For localization of YHWH in Jerusalem, cf. Ezra 1:3-4, 7:15. The Aram. title had its Neo-Assyrian forerunner in such titles as "*laḫḫinu* of Ashur," "*laḫḫinu* of Nabu," "*laḫḫinu* of Ishtar of Arbel," or "*laḫḫinu* of Sin of Harran." In one instance the official was responsible for maintenance and supplies; see Porten 1968:200-201.
[6] This was a negotiated inducement to Mica to withdraw his claim.
[7] A word of uncertain meaning, the *hyr*$^{\supset}$ seems to have been a piece of abandoned property to which neither Mica nor Anani had hereditary right or clear title. Both laid claim and each sued the other. Anani paid Mica five shekels, almost one-third the fourteen shekels he would later have to pay for an abandoned house (3.71:4-6), and Mica withdrew his claim.
[8] The property was "yours," i.e. Anani's, because he paid for it in settlement of the suit.
[9] See 3.60, n. 11.
[10] Satisfaction after the settlement of a suit is usually followed by a statement of withdrawal (see on 3.60:7), but here such a statement was deferred until the retrospect of the *Penalty* clause (line 7).

Waiver of suit
I shall not be able to institute against you,[11] (5)suit or process in the name of[12] this *hyrᵓ* (about) which you complained against me herein.

Penalty
If I complain (6)against you[13] (before) judge or lord in the name of [t]his *hyrᵓ* — (about) which I complained against you[14] (7)herein and you gave m[e] its payment, silver [4+]1 (= 5) shekels and I withdrew from you[15] — (8)I shall give you silver, 5 *karsh*.[16]

Defension[17]
If brother or sister, (9)near or f(a)r,[18] (8)institute (suit) against you (9)in the name of this *hyrᵓ*, I shall cleanse (it) and give (it) to you.

a Neh 9:4; 10:16; 11:15

Scribe
(10)Bunni[a] son of Mannuki[19] wrote at the instruction of Mica son of Ahi[o].

Witnesses
The witnesses herein:[20]
(11)(2nd hand) Zabdi (son of) Nabuzi[21];
(3rd hand) (ERASURE: Micaiah)[22];
(4th hand) Sachael son of Nabukaṣir[23];
(12)(3rd hand) Micaiah son of Ahio[24];
(5th hand) Aḥushunu son of Renpenofre[25];
(13)(6th hand) Mahseiah son of Jedaniah[26];
(7th hand) Mannuki son of Bagaina[27];
(8th hand) Attarmalki son of Psami[28];
(14)(9th hand) Zabbud son of Zabidri.[29]

(endorsement missing)

[11] Both the *Waiver* and *Penalty* clauses limited protection to a suit by Mica only, not by his heirs or beneficiaries. Since the obligation he was willing to spell out was limited, we may deduce that his initial claim was also limited.

[12] See 3.60, n. 34.

[13] This was the only case where the *Waiver* clause promised not to sue (lines 4-5) and the concomitant *Penalty* clause spoke of entering a complaint. But elsewhere the scribe uniquely combined the noun "suit" with the verb "complain" (3.60:16).

[14] If not a scribal error for "you complained against me" (so in line 4), then the case in this document was one of suit counter-suit.

[15] A subordinate clause describing the prior transfer of the object in whose name the present suit was being instituted was common (3.61:12-13; 3.64:9-10; 3.65:8), but none of the clauses was as long as the present one, which summarized the complete proceedings.

[16] The penalty was ten times the value of the object, but a low penalty on the Elephantine scale (see 3.59, n. 15).

[17] *Defension* clauses at Elephantine were third-party suits entered not in the name of the alienor. None of the conveyances of property where title was clear had such a clause. It only occurred in a case of abandoned property (3.72:19-23). Son or daughter were omitted here as potential claimants because as heirs they would sue in their father's name, whereas brother or sister might sue in their own name. The suit was considered a besmirchment of the property which Mica undertook to "clean" and present anew to Anani. There was no time limit to the cleansing or penalty for failure to do so (contrast 3.72:20-23).

[18] See 3.59, n. 22.

[19] The scribe's praenomen is West Semitic and was borne by a lay and one or two Levitical families in Jerusalem (Neh 9:4; 10:16; 11:15 [*plene* as here]) but the patronym was Akk. His script is large and bold and this is his only appearance.

[20] None of the names is preceded by the designation "witness." Since eight witnesses, double the usual number, were elsewhere required for withdrawal from realty (3.67:18-19), we may conclude that the unknown property here was also realty. See 3.59, n. 34.

[21] Alternately, Nabeḥai. This Aramean witness forgot to write "son of" before his patronymic, which was probably Akk.

[22] Judging from the traces of the handwriting, he appears to be the Micaiah who signed third. Here he jumped the cue and was forced back. Was he the same as the party to the contract, Mica son of Ahio?

[23] This Aramean witness with an Akk. patronymic appears only here.

[24] He was also a witness in 427 BCE (3.74:17) and his son Ahio son of Micaiah was among the Jewish leaders imprisoned in Thebes at the end of the century (3.49:7); Porten 2001:352.

[25] Such a name combination, Babylonian son of Egyptian, is rare (*TAD* B5.5:12) and this witness appears only here. Very common in Demotic, the praenomen was always feminine; thus both the mother and wife of a late 6th century BCE Eg. priest, Espmet son of Bokrinf, bore the name Renpenofre (*P. Wien* D 10150.1 [*EPE* C28], 10151:2 [*EPE* C29]). Possibly affiliated to a matronym and not a patronym, was our witness a slave or freedman?

[26] Besides Micaiah, who may have been party to the contract, Mahseiah son of Jedaniah, founder of the Mibtahiah family archive (3.59-65), was the only Jewish witness.

[27] This witness with Akk. name and Persian patronymic appears only here.

[28] This witness with Aram. name and Eg. patronymic appears only here.

[29] Both names are Aramean and the witness appears only here.

REFERENCES

Text and translation: *TAD* B3.2; *EPE* B35. *EPE*; Porten 1968; 2001; Porten and Szubin 1983b.

DOCUMENT OF WIFEHOOD (3.71)
(9 August 449 BCE)

Bezalel Porten

This record of a free man-handmaiden marriage presents a unique opportunity to reconstruct the haggling that went on between groom and master regarding the status of the bride and the rights of the parties to the contract. Tamet's status may be described as comparable to the biblical "slave woman designated for a man" for the purpose of marriage (Lev 19:20). In rabbinic terms she was "part slave and part free." Not yet manumitted, she was not entitled to have *mohar* paid for her from Anani. Her dowry was little more than the garment on her back, the sandals on her feet, and an item or two of toilette (lines 4-7). The customary reciprocal *Repudiation* and *Death* clauses were applied here too (lines 7-13), but the "silver of hatred" was only 5 shekels and not 7½, there was no indication that the repudiating or repudiated wife might go "wherever she desired," and upon the death of either spouse, Meshullam was entitled to half of the couple's joint property. A unique clause entitled Meshullam to "reclaim" the already existing child Pilti should Anani divorce Tamet (lines 13-14). While the clause provided Tamet some protection against rash divorce, it indicated that the child of a handmaiden, even when married, still belonged to her master. But these arrangements were not to the liking of the couple and they achieved revision of the document even as it was being written — at first elimination of Meshullam from any share in the estate of the surviving spouse, and subsequently increase of the "silver of hatred" to the standard 7½ shekels, the imposition of a five *karsh* penalty on Meshullam for unwarranted reclamation of Pilti, and the addition to Tamet's dowry of fifteen shekels cash (line 16).[1]

Dates

(Recto)[(1)][On] the 18th of [A]b, [that is day 30] of the month of Pharmouthi, year 16 of Artaxer(xes) the king,[2]

Parties

said [(2)]Ananiah son of Azariah, a servitor of YHH[3] the God who is in Elephantine the fortress, to Meshullam son of Zaccur, an Aramean of Syene [(3)]of the detachment of Varyazata, saying:

Marriage[4]

I came to you (and asked you) to give me[5] Tamet by name,[6] who is your handmaiden,[7] for wifehood.

Affirmation of status

She is my wife [(4)]and I am her husband from this day and forever.[8]

Dowry

Tamet brought into me in her hand[9]:

7 shekels 1 garment of wool,[10] worth (in) silver [(5)]7 shekels;[11]

.19 shekels 1 mirror, worth (in) silver 7 (and a) half hallurs; 1 PAIR of sandals; (ERASURE: 1 handful of) [(6)]one-half handful[12] of [(5)]balsam oil; [(6)]6 handfuls of castor oil;[13] 1 TRAY.

7.19 shekels All the silver and the value of the goods: (in) silver {silver}, 7 shekels, [(7)]7 (and a) half hallurs.[14]

Repudiation by husband[15]

Tomorrow or (the) next day,[16] should Anani stand up in an assembly and say:

"I hated Tamet my wife,"

[(8)]silver of hatre(d) is on his head. He shall give Tamet silver, 7 shekels, 2 q(uarters) and all that,[17] she brought in in her hand she shall take out, from straw [(9)]to string.[18]

[1] For full treatment of this document, see Porten and Szubin 1995.

[2] 18 Ab = August 11 = 30 Pharmouthi = August 9 in 16 Artaxerxes I (= 449 BCE). If the document was written on the night of August 9 (= 17 Ab), then the gap would be reduced to one day; see Porten 1990:22-23. For other chronological errors by the scribe Nathan son of Anani see on 3.64:1.

[3] For this spelling of the divine name, see 3.64, n. 30.

[4] For this clause, see 3.63, n. 6.

[5] For the terminology and procedure, see 3.59, n. 6.

[6] A qualifier regularly attached to the name of a slave (see 3.68, n. 12).

[7] Forty-seven years later, and in retrospect, Tamet would be called the "MAIN BELOVED of Meshullam" and "(THE ONE BELONGING TO) THE INNER (CHAMBER) of Meshullam" (3.80:11, 24). Here she was simply called a "handmaiden" and was not emancipated by Meshullam until twenty years after the date of this contract (3.74:3-4).

[8] See 3.63, nn. 10-11.

[9] See 3.63, n. 17. A var. formula was "Jehoishma your sister brought in to me to my house" (3.76:5).

[10] Tamet's dowry consisted of little more than the dress on her back. A woolen garment worth seven shekels lay at the lower end of the scale while her bronze mirror was worth one-fifth that of her daughter Jehoishma. She was endowed with a handful more castor oil than her daughter but of the many vessels her daughter would have she had only a TRAY (3.76:6-21). For the oils, see Porten 1968:91-93.

[11] The scribe originally valued the garment at 5 shekels, but shortly after he wrote down the amount he added, presumably at the insistence of Meshullam, two more strokes to the figure to raise it to 7 shekels.

[12] The balsam oil, on the other hand, written at the end of line 5, was measured at "1 handful" but this quantity was erased, no doubt at the insistence of one of the parties, and "a half handful" was written at the beginning of line 6.

[13] See on *TAD* A2.1:7 (*EPE* B1).

[14] The meager amount was duly totaled (7.19 shekels) but there was no statement of receipt and satisfaction as in the document of Mibtahiah (3.63:15).

[15] The wording of the two *Repudiation* clauses in our document was almost identical, with the single word *bᶜdh*, "in an assembly," absent from the second one, no doubt due to scribal ellipsis, and the word order "Tamet my wife" chiastically reversed in the second clause to "my husband Anani" (cf. reversal in 3.63:23, 27 and see there, lines 22-26, for the details of this clause).

[16] See 3.59, n. 12.

[17] The original amount assessed was 5 shekels but haggling raised it to 7½. In the Code of Hammurabi the lower class *muškenum* paid his repudiated wife only ⅓ maneh whereas the upper class *awelum* had to pay a full maneh (CH §§139-40; *COS* 2.131, p. 344).

[18] The document did not accord Tamet the option of going wherever she wished (cf. 3.63:25, 28-29; 3.76:24) or of returning to her father's house (cf. 3.76:28), steps which were not viable for a handmaiden like Tamet. She was apparently not forced to leave Anani's domicile but might

Repudiation by wife
Tomorrow or (the) next day, should Tamet stand up and say:
"I hated my husband Anani,"
silver of ha(t)red is on her head. (10)She shall give to Anani silver, 7 shekels, 2 q(uarters) and all that she brought in in her hand she shall take out, from straw to string.

Death of husband
Tomorrow or (11)(the) next (10)day, (11)should Ananiah die (ERASURE: [It is Meshullam son of Zaccur (who)] has right to half), it is Tamet (who) has right to all goods which will be between Anani and Tamet.[19]

Death of wife
(12)Tomorrow or (the) next day, should Tamet die, it is Anani, he, (who) has right[20] (ERASURE: to half) to all goods which will be between (ERASURE: between) (13)Tamet and between[21] Anani.

Rights to child[22]
And I, Meshullam,[23] tomorrow or (the) next day, shall not be able to reclaim[24] Pilti from under (14)your heart unless you expel his mother Tamet. And if I do reclaim him from you I shall give Anani silver 5 *karsh*.

Scribe
Wrote Nathan son of Ananiah this document.

Witnesses
And the witnesses (15)herein[25]:
witness Nathan son of Gaddul[26];
Menahem son of Zaccur[27];
Gemariah son of Mahseiah.[28]

Dowry addition
15 Shekels (Verso)(16)Tamet brought in to Anani in her hand silver, 1 *karsh*, 5 shekels.[29]

Endorsement
(17)Document (*sealing*) of wi[fehood[30] which Anani wrote for Ta]met.

remain in his household as a married woman, albeit demoted in status (akin to the "hated" Leah [Gen 29:31] and the hated wife of Deut 21:15-17).

[19] The name of the deceased party whose estate was the subject of the clause was judiciously placed first in the respective clauses — "all goods which will be between Anani and Tamet" in the *Death* clause of Anani but the reverse order in the *Death* clause of Tamet, "all goods which will be between Tamet and between Anani" (lines 12-13). Since initially Meshullam was given property rights in the event of Anani's predecease, the scribe was careful to avoid the language used in the parallel clause in the other wifehood documents, namely that the surviving spouse had rights to her dead husband's "house, goods, property" and everything else (3.63:17-20; 3.76:28-30). Such a clause would have given Meshullam rights to half of Anani's property acquired before their marriage. The revised document allocated the marital property solely between husband and wife, thereby eliminating Meshullam's benefits. For the expression "between ... between" to designate jointly held property see *TAD* A3.10:2.

[20] The scribe here used the term "have right to" (*šlyṭ*) and not "inherit" (*yrt*), the term judiciously used for Esḥor (3.63:21) and Anani son of Haggai (3.76:35) should they survive their respective spouses. The latter term would have been inappropriate since, in the original version, Meshullam was to get half. As he was not a natural heir, under no circumstances could the clause be formulated to have him inherit. Anani, who would have inherited from Tamet were she completely manumitted, lost her share to Meshullam under the original terms, retaining control only over his own half. Even under the revised terms, Meshullam's proprietary rights to Tamet remained in effect and Anani could still not aspire to inherit Tamet.

[21] The scribe duplicated the preposition "between" when describing the property of Tamet since he was cognizant of the distinction between her individual property (the dowry) recorded in this document and their post-nuptial, jointly acquired property, the subject of this clause. No such distinction was necessary for Anani since the document omitted any reference to his individual property (cf. *hyrʾ* mentioned in 3.70). So conscious was the scribe of the need to distinguish between the individual and joint property that he prematurely wrote a second *byn* (end of line 12), an anticipatory dittography, so to speak, which he subsequently erased.

[22] This clause had a two-fold thrust: (1) deterrence against peremptory expulsion; (2) provision of child custody in case of said expulsion. Born of a union between a free man and a slave, Pilti remained a slave. Meshullam's ultimate control of him was also his check on Anani's behavior vis-a-vis Tamet. He could not prevent him from expelling (*trk*) Tamet just as Abraham had expelled (*grš* = *tryk* [Onkelos]) Hagar (Gen 21:10), but he could discourage Anani from doing so under threat of loss of his child. The supralinearly added compensation clause actually served to elevate Pilti's status from mere chattel, easily recoverable and reverting to bondage, to that of a son with protected rights and the prospects of attaining complete freedom. The shift in persons from second ("reclaim from you") to third ("give Anani") was commonplace, particularly in clauses of recovery (see 3.79:10). See Szubin and Porten 1988:38-39.

[23] Only rarely did the party of the second part also appear in direct speech in the contracts; a small vertical marginal line marked the change of speaker. See also 3.74:11. Still, the contract was drawn up only at the instruction of the party of the first part.

[24] The word *nṣl* means "to recover, retrieve that which rightfully belongs to one;" see 3.61, n. 50.

[25] See 3.63, n. 65.

[26] Appears only here.

[27] He also witnessed the wifehood document of Mibtahiah drawn up by the same scribe two months later (3.63:38).

[28] The last witness here, he was first in a bequest of Mahseiah (see 3.61, n. 70).

[29] This was an addition of cash to Tamet's dowry written on the *verso* after the document had been all but tied and sealed (see 3.63, n. 15).

[30] Cf. the Demotic *sẖ n ḥm.t*, "writing concerning a wife" (*P. Berlin* 13614 [*EPE* C27], 13593 [*EPE* C33], though the term does not occur in these documents) and the Greek *syngraphē synoikisias*, "contract of cohabitation" (*P. Eleph.* 1.2 [*EPE* D2]).

REFERENCES

Text and translation: *TAD* B3.3; *EPE* B36. *EPE*; Porten 1968; 1990; Porten and Szubin 1995; Szubin and Porten 1988; *TAD*.

SALE OF ABANDONED PROPERTY (3.72)
(14 September, 437 BCE)

Bezalel Porten

Twelve years after the redaction of his document of wifehood (3.71), Anani paid fourteen shekels for the run-down house of the Caspian ᵓ*pwly* which was held in adverse possession by the Caspian couple Bagazushta and *Wbyl*. It lay across from the Temple on one side and next to the house of *Wbyl*'s father, Shatibara, who may have facilitated the couple's occupation of the property (lines 2-11). The double *Waiver* clauses (we, children) protected heirs and beneficiaries of the buyer with a stiff twenty *karsh* penalty (lines 11-19). But the *Defension* clause provided a limited warranty in case of third-party suit, i.e. replacement; and reimbursement in case of inability to turn back a suit by heirs of the original owner (lines 19-23). The four witnesses were Persians and Caspians (lines 23-24).[1]

Date
(Recto)(1)On the 7th of Elul, that is day 9 of the month of Payni, year 28 of Artaxerxes the king,[2]

Parties
said (2)Bagazushta son of Bazu, a Caspian[3] of the detachment of Namasava,[4] and lady[5] *Wybl* daughter of Shatibara, a Caspian of Syene of the detachment of Namasava,[6] (3)all (told) 1 (ERASURE: 1) lady 1 man (3)to Ananiah son of Azariah, a servitor to YHW the God, saying:

Transfer I
We sold and gave (4)you[7]

Object
the house

Pedigree
of ᵓ*pwly* son of Misdaya[8]

Location
which is in Elephantine the fortress,

Description
whose walls are standing but (who)se courtyard (5)is (barren) land and not built[9]; and windows are in it but beams it does not contain.[10]

Transfer II
We sold it to you

Price
and you gave (6)us its payment (in) silver, 1 *karsh*, 4 (ERASURE: [+]1)[11] shekels by the stone(-weight)s of the king, silver zuz[12] to 1 *karsh*,

Satisfaction
and our heart was satisfied[13] (7)with the payment which you gave us.

Boundaries
And behold these are the boundaries[14] of that house which we sold you:
above (8)it is the house of Shatibara;[15]
below it is the town/way of Khnum[16] the god and the street of the king is between them;
(9)east of it the treasury of the king[17] adjoins it;
to the west (of it) is the Temple of (10)YHW the God and the street of the king is between them.[18]

Transfer III
I, Bagazushta and ᵓ*wbl*, all (told) two, we sold and

[1] For comprehensive discussion of this document see Porten and Szubin 1982a:123-131.

[2] In 28 Artaxerxes I, 7 Elul = September 15 while 9 Payni = September 14, so this document was written on the night of September 14, 437 BCE; Porten 1990:21; *TAD* B 186-187.

[3] Caspians appeared occasionally as witnesses to the documents of Mahseiah (3.64:18-19 and probably also 3.59:18).

[4] This Iranian detachment commander is mentioned only here and was one of three commanders mentioned during the period of Mibtahiah's activity; see 3.66, n. 5.

[5] See 3.61, n. 7.

[6] Husband and wife belonged to the same detachment just as father Mahseiah and daughter Mibtahiah did (3.64:1-2; 3.65:2-3).

[7] The regular formula for sale; see also 3.80:3, 12.

[8] Of which they had only possession and not title.

[9] A Byzantine courtyard in Syene was described as "ruined ... single-storied and unroofed" (*P. Münch*. 13.20-21 [*EPE* D47]).

[10] This was a typical description of a piece of property in a state of disrepair, in our case also abandoned. See Porten 1968:97.

[11] The scribe mistakenly wrote five strokes, erased the fifth one immediately, and continued writing without a break. The house cost him just a little less than a third of what was the value in goods of a house given Mibtahiah by her father Mahseiah in 446 BCE (3.64:6).

[12] The zuz was equivalent to one-half shekel, i.e. 2 quarters, and the scribe sometimes preferred it to "2 q(uarters)" in this monetary formula (lines 15, 18; 3.76:17; 3.77:8).

[13] See 3.63, n. 14.

[14] See 3.64, n. 27.

[15] Father of the woman who was partner to the sale.

[16] The phrase *tm*ᵓ*/tmy zy ḥnwm* (3.73:10), and its relationship to *tmw*ᵓ*nty* "way of the god" (3.78:9), has been much discussed and the options are left open here for both explanations; see Porten 1968:309; *TAD* B 177; *GEA* 375.28, 30.

[17] This was most likely the same building as the "royal BARLEY-HOUSE" partially cut away by the Khnum priests in 410 BCE (3.50:5) and replaced by a "protecting" (wall) of a ceremonial way (3.79:3-4).

[18] Anani was buying a house across the street from his place of employment.

gave (it) (11)to you

Withdrawal

and withdrew from it from this day and forever.[19]

Investiture

You, Ananiah son of Azariah, have right (12)to that house and (so do) your children after you and anyone whom you desire to give (it) to.[20]

Waiver of suit I

We shall not be able to institute against you suit (13)or process in the name of[21] this house which we sold and gave you and from which we withdrew. And (ERASURE: he) we shall not be able (14)to institute (suit) against son of yours or daughter or anyone whom you desire to give (it) to.[22]

Penalty I

If we institute against you suit or process or institute (suit) (15)against son in/with (SCRIBAL ERROR FOR: or) daughter of yours or anyone whom you desire to give (it) to, we shall give you silver, 20 *karsh*,[23] silver zuz (16)to the ten,[24]

Reaffirmation I

and the house is yours likewise and your children's after you and anyone whom you desire to give (it) to.[25]

Waiver of suit II

And (17)son or daughter of ours shall (16)not (17)be able to institute against you[26] suit or process in the name of this house whose boundaries are written (18)above.[27]

Penalty II

If they institute (suit) against you or institute (suit) against son or daughter of yours, they shall give you silver, 20 *karsh*, silver zuz to the 10,

Reaffirmation II

(19)and the house is yours likewise and your children's after you.

Defension[28]

And if another person institute (suit) against you or institute (suit) (20)against son or daughter of yours, we shall stand up[29] and cleanse (it) and give (it) to you within 30 days. And if we do not cleanse (it), (21)we or our children shall give you a house in the likeness of your house and its measurements, unless a son male or female of *ᵓpwly*, (22)or a daughter of his should come and we not be able to cleanse (it.[30] Then) we shall give you your silver, 1 *karsh*, 4 shekels and (the value of) the building (improvements) which you will have built in it (23)and all the FITTINGS[31] that will have gone into that house.[32]

Scribe

(23sl)Haggai son of Shemaiah wrote at the instruction of Bagazushta and *ᵓbl*.[33]

Witnesses

And witnesses herein[34]:

(23)(2nd hand) Mithradata son of Mithrayazna;

(3rd hand) witness *Ḥyḥ/Ḥyrw* son of *ᵓtrly*, a Caspian;

(24)(4th hand) house of *Wyzbl*, a Caspian[35];

(5th hand) witness Aisaka son of Zamaspa.

---

[19] The scribe did not directly juxtapose the *Withdrawal* clause to the *Satisfaction* clause, as elsewhere (3.65:6), but tacked it onto the *Transfer* formula to form an inclusion around the *Boundaries* clause. See also 3.64, n. 17.

[20] The somewhat awkwardly formulated *Investiture* and *Reaffirmation* clauses gave him unlimited right of alienation; Szubin and Porten 1983a:38.

[21] See 3.60, n. 34.

[22] In two separate clauses, the seller granted protection first to the buyer and then to his heirs and beneficiaries; for this split of clauses see also 3.67:9-12; 3.80:24-26.

[23] The penalty of twenty *karsh* (= 200 shekels) was stiff but recurs four more times regarding this property (line 18; 3.73:16; 22:30); see 3.59, n. 15. In contrast to this heavy penalty for a suit by the seller and his heirs is the limited warranty offered in case of a third-party suit (lines 19-23).

[24] The *Penalty* clause combined into one both the buyer and his heirs and beneficiaries.

[25] Repeating the same awkward formulation in the *Investiture* clause (lines 11-12).

[26] Omitted here, "son or daughter of yours" was implicit because it was included in the *Penalty* clause (line 18). Beneficiary was omitted from both clauses but was implicit because it was explicit in the first set of *Waiver-Penalty* clauses (lines 12-16).

[27] For this expression cf. 3.67:8 and see 3.59, n. 26.

[28] In case of a third party suit, the sellers provided Anani with a limited three-phase warranty, promising in succession to cleanse the property of all challenge, to replace it in case of failure to cleanse, and to refund the purchase price in case of failure to cleanse because the challenge came from an heir of the original owners.

[29] Cf. *TAD* B1.1:10, but ordinarily this auxiliary verb introduces a negative act: "repudiate" (3.63:22, 26; 3.71:7, 9; 3.74:13; 3.76:21), "evict" (3.63:29; 3.75:16; 3.76:30), "reenslave" (3.74:7; 3.77:6-7).

[30] The ability of the sellers to cleanse the property in case of a suit by the heirs of the original owners might depend upon whether the heirs had filed public protest according to accepted procedure in Eg. law.

[31] For this word see on *TAD* A6.2:5 (*EPE* B11).

[32] Reimbursement for improvements installed prior to eviction is provided by a Byzantine contract (*P. Lond.* V 1735.17-18 [*EPE* D50]) and is found in Talmudic law (*Tosefta Ketubot* 8:10).

[33] Surprisingly, the scribe Haggai forgot to sign his name before the signature of the first witness and so had to squeeze it in between the lines; see 3.64, n. 41.

[34] Only the standard number of four witnesses was required for sale (see 3.59, n. 34) and they were all Caspians (3rd and 4th hands) and Iranians. None appear elsewhere.

[35] A similar name appears among the witnesses to two documents in the Mibtahiah archive (3.63:39; 3.64:18). The initial word "house of"

Endorsement
(Verso)(25)Document (*sealing*) of a house which Bagazushta and *Ybl* sold[36] to Ananiah, a servitor to YH[37] in Elephantine.

appears to have been written by the scribe and is most puzzling.

[36] Sale contracts had the word "sold" rather than "wrote" (3.80:35); see 3.59, n. 44.

[37] The divine name was uniquely abbreviated here.

REFERENCES

Text and translation: *TAD* B3.4; *EPE* B37. *EPE*; *GEA*; Porten 1968; 1990; Porten and Szubin 1982a; Szubin and Porten 1983a; *TAD*.

BEQUEST OF APARTMENT TO WIFE (3.73)
(30 October, 434 BCE)

Bezalel Porten

Anani refurbished the house of ᵓ*pwly* which he had bought from the Caspians Bagazushta and *Wbyl*. Three years after purchase date, the requisite period according to Egyptian law for establishing right to abandoned property, he bestowed a room therein (measuring 11 x 7⅓ cubits = 81 square cubits, see note 14 below) upon his wife Tamet, perhaps on the occasion of the birth of their daughter Jehoishma (lines 2-12). The *Investiture* clause did not seek to preempt Tamet's right to dispose of the property during her lifetime. But Anani treated his house as a family estate and should the couple die intestate, it was to pass on to their mutual children, Jehoishma and Pilti (lines 4-5, 16-20). Thirty-two years later, Tamet and Anani sold their share to their son-in-law (No. 22), an act which would have been in violation of this contract had it been a bona fide gift and not a bequest. Uncharacteristically, each challenge in our document carried a distinct penalty — five *karsh* for a suit by Anani, twenty *karsh* for one by his heirs, and ten *karsh* for attempted reclamation by his heirs after his death (lines 12-22). Two of the four witnesses were Magians (line 24).

Date
(Recto)(1)On the 25th of Tishri, that is day 25 of the month of Epeiph, year 31 of Artaxerxes the king,[1]

Parties
said Ananiah (2)son of Azariah, a servitor of YHW the God in Elephantine the fortress, to lady Tamet his wife, saying:

Transfer I
I gave (3)you

Object
half of the large room,[2] and its chamber, of the house

Pedigree[3]
which I bought from ᵓ*wbyl* daughter of Shatibara and from Bagazushta, (4)Caspians of Elephantine the fortress.

Transfer II
I, Ananiah, gave it to you in love.[4]

Investiture
Yours it is[5] from this day (5)forever[6] and your children's, whom you bore me,[7] after you.

Measurements
And behold the measurements of that house[8] which I, (6)Ananiah, gave you, Tamet,[9] from[10]

[1] An exact synchronism for October 30, 434 BCE; Porten 1990:20 and *TAD* B 186-187.

[2] This is a fem. noun loanword from Eg.: *try* = *t*ᵓ *ry.t*; *GEA* 375.36.

[3] See 3.64, n. 6.

[4] The *Transfer* clause was repeated as an inclusion to the *Pedigree*. Dowries and bequests made *inter familium* were regularly stated as being given "in love" (*brḥmn* [line 12; 3.66:41; 3.78:5, 12, 17; 3.79:9]; *brḥmh* [3.75:14] *rḥmt* [3.81:26, 31]); see Szubin and Porten 1983a:36.

[5] See 3.59, n. 8

[6] See 3.61, n. 29.

[7] Anani was treating his house as an estate, to pass on only to his children with Tamet. There was no clause authorizing transfer to a third party, as there was in 3.61:9-10; 3.64:8, 16; 3.72:11-12; 3.80:22-24; see Szubin and Porten 1983a:42.

[8] The word "house" was often used in these documents to designate no more than a room or so (lines 12, 14, 25; 3.78:5, 8, 11-12, 16, 27; 3.79:2, 7, 11, 13-15, 21; 3.80:3-4, 12-13, 15, 17, 22, 25, 28-30, 35). Correspondingly, plural "houses" might mean "rooms" or even upper and lower structures (3.75:14, 16). See Szubin and Porten 1988:37.

[9] When adding the name of the first person donor ("Ananiah") in a second person address ("you") it was good form to add the name of the donee ("Tamet") as well (absent in 3.59:11-12).

[10] I.e. consisting of.

half of the large room and its chamber was[11]:
from above to below, (7)11 (6)cubits (7)by the measuring rod;
in width, cubits[12] from east to west, 7 cubits 1 h(and)[13] by the measuring rod;
IN AREA,[14] (8)81 cubits.

Description

Built is (the) lower house,[15] new, containing beams[16] and windows.[17]

Boundaries

And behold this is[18] the boundaries of that house[19] (9)which I gave you:
above it the portion of mine, I,[20] Ananiah,[21] adjoins it;
below it (10)is the Temple of YHW the God and the street of the king is between them;
east of it is the town/way of Khnum the god (11)and the street of the king is between them;
west of it the house of Shatibara, a Caspian, adjoins it.

Transfer III

This share of (12)the house who(se) measurements are written and whose boundaries (are written above)[22] — I, Ananiah, gave it to you in love.[23]

Waiver of suit

I shall not be able, (13)I, Ananiah, to bring (suit) against you on account of it.[24] Moreover, son of mine or daughter, brother or sister shall not be able (14)to institute (suit) against you in the name of[25] that house.[26]

Penalty

And if I institute suit against you in the name of that house, I shall be obligated[27] (15)and I shall give you silver, 5 *karsh*, that is five,[28] by the stone(-weight)s of the king, silver 2 q(uarters) to 1 *karsh*, without suit. (16)And if another person[29] institute against you suit, he shall give you silver, 20 *karsh*,[30]

Reaffirmation I

and the house likewise is yours.

Succession[31]

But (17)if you die at the age of 100 years,[32] it is my children whom you bore me (that) have right to it after (18)your death. And moreover, if I, Anani, die at the age of 100 years, it is Pilti and Jehoishma,[33]

---

[11] Instead of the grammatically correct "were." The formula is unusually long; see 3.61:3-4 and *DAE* 222. An alternate rendering would attach "from half of the large room ..." to the beginning of the following measurements. That rendering would eliminate the non-congruence between plural "measurements" and singular "was" by assuming a double introduction — "And beho[d the measurement ... its chamber. It was:" This singular verb (*hwh*) elsewhere preceded the term "length" in a measurement formula (3.63:8-10; 3.75:4).

[12] The word here was an anticipatory redundancy.

[13] Aram. has the single letter *kaph*, which probably abbreviates *kp*, "hand" (measured from the tip of the middle finger to the wrist joint) = ⅓ cubit; see *TAD* B 177, also for next note.

[14] Arrived at by multiplying the length by the width and rounding off (11 x 7⅓ = 80⅔, rounded off to 81).

[15] I.e. the bottom floor.

[16] Beams might be bought for grain and stored for future use. See on *TAD* A2.2:14 (*EPE* B2).

[17] The house Anani bought from Bagazushta and his wife contained windows but no beams (3.62:5). He had since made it "like new."

[18] Instead of the grammatically correct "these are."

[19] For the *Boundaries* clause see 3.60, nn. 18-19. Three of the four boundaries of the house as acquired from Bagazushta are the same. Anani gave Tamet a room which lay "below" his. "Above" that room lay the royal treasury. But the location of the neighbors has shifted 90°. In the previous document Haggai listed the neighbors Shatibara-treasury-Khnum-Temple in the order above-east-below-west (so too in 3.78-80). But here they were west-above-east-below. As in the shift of orientation in the Mahseiah archive (see 3.61, n. 19) so here true location lay midpoint. See *TAD* B 177 and figure 4.

[20] For addition of the independent pronoun as emphatic, see on *TAD* A3.3:11 (*EPE* B8) and 3.60:7.

[21] Such a double reenforcement ("mine, I, Ananiah") also appears in line 19; see 3.60, n. 17.

[22] The clause here is elliptical. See 3.59, n. 26.

[23] The *Transfer* clause is again repeated, this time as an inclusion to the *Measurements*, *Description*, and *Boundaries* clauses. The scribe also took the opportunity to add to two of those clauses the statement "of that house which I gave you," bringing to five the number of occurrences of the key word "gave."

[24] See 3.60, n. 12.

[25] See 3.60, n. 34. The scribe varied his terminology, alternating "on account of" and "in the name of."

[26] In two separate clauses, the donor first obligated himself and then his heirs not to sue.

[27] The verb *ḥwb* occurs here for the first time in our archives and is followed by (a verb to "give") money (3.74:14; 3.79:10, 13; 3.80:29; 3.81:6; but see already *TAD* B4.4:15 [483 BCE]) = "We shall be obligated to you for silver, 100 *karsh*." In the stative form (*ḥyb*) the verb occurs twice in *Waiver of reclamation* of dowry clauses without stated monetary consequences for violation (3.76:40-42; *TAD* 6.4:7-8).

[28] For the numerical repetition, see 3.60, n. 36.

[29] "Another person" here is a collective term referring to the children and siblings singled out in the second half of the *Waiver* clause (line 13). It has similar collective meaning in the line 19 below.

[30] In contrast to the moderate, five *karsh* penalty Anani imposed on himself in case of suit is the heavy twenty *karsh* penalty imposed on a suit by his heirs. See 3.59, n. 7; 3.72, n. 23.

[31] This paragraph spelled out what was implicit in the *Investiture* clause — the couple's children, *and only the couple's children*, were to control the property, in whole or in part, after their death.

[32] Clauses anticipating death in the legal contracts ("If PN should die tomorrow or the next day" [3.59:8; 3.63:17, 20; 3.71:10-12; 3.76:28-29, 34-35] or "If I should die" (3.69:14; 3.81:8]) were not infrequent. Only here, however, did "next day" give way to "100 years" in an apparently apotropaic statement. See Porten 1968:185 and 3.59, n. 20.

[33] Pilti, later known as Pelatiah (3.75:11-12), was present at the time of the redaction of Tamet's document of wifehood fifteen years earlier

all (told) two, my children, (who) (19)have right to my other portion, I, Anani.[34] Another person[35] — my mother or my father, brother or sister, or (20)another (19)man[36] — (20)shall not have right to the whole house, but (only) my children whom you bore me.

Reclamation

And the person[37] who shall reclaim[38] (21)my house after my death from Pilti and Jehoishma

Penalty

shall give them silver, 10 *karsh* by the stone(-weight)s of (22)the king, silver 2 q(uarters) to 1 *karsh*,

Reaffirmation II

and my house is theirs likewise, without suit.

Scribe

Mauziah son of Nathan[39] wrote at the instruction of (23)Ananiah son of Azariah the servitor.

Witnesses

And the witnesses herein:[40]

(1st hand) Gemariah son of Mahseiah[41];
(24)(2nd hand) Hoshaiah son of Jathom[42];
(3rd hand) Mithrasarah the Magian[43];
(4th hand) Tata the Magian.[44]

Endorsement

(Verso)(25)(sealing) Document of a house which Ananiah wrote for Tamet his wife.[45]

(3.71:13). Perhaps the present bequest was made on the occasion of Jehoishma's birth. These are the same children meant in line 17, only here their names are spelled out.

[34] This double reinforcement also occurs in line 9. See 3.60, n. 17.

[35] Proper punctuation of this sentence is important for correct interpretation. "Another person" was, as above (line 13), a collective term (also in 3.74:9), here covering the following specific persons (parent, sibling, beneficiary). But the term could be ambiguous, referring in one and the same document to a specific beneficiary, equivalent to "another man," and, as here, a collective of beneficiaries (3.64:8-9, 11). See Porten and Szubin 1987b:51-58.

[36] "Another man" was a beneficiary, as elsewhere in these legal texts. See 3.61, n. 33.

[37] This "person" = "another person" (line 19) refers to the potential claimants in the *Succession* clause.

[38] Property given "in love," as was this one, was particularly vulnerable to reclamation, either by the donor or his heirs, but only here was such an attempt penalized. See 3.61, n. 50.

[39] For this professional scribe, see 3.66, n. 41.

[40] In the subsequent bequests of part of this property to the daughter Jehoishma, eight witnesses were required (3.78:23-26; 3.79:18-20).

[41] Probably son of Mahseiah son of Jedaniah, he witnessed four documents. See 3.61, n. 70.

[42] See 3.49:7 (*EPE* B16).

[43] A Mithrasarah son of Mithrasarah witnessed a contract of Mahseiah in 446 BCE (3.64:18).

[44] The two Magians must have come together. This second one appears only here.

[45] Uniquely, the endorsement was not written on either side of the seal, beginning from the right edge of the papyrus, but to the left of the bulla, beginning at the left edge of the papyrus roll, which had been turned 180° for the purpose.

REFERENCES

Text and translation: *TAD* B3.5; *EPE* B38. *DAE*; *EPE*; *GEA*; Porten 1990; Porten and Szubin 1987b; Szubin and Porten 1983a; 1988; *TAD*.

TESTAMENTARY MANUMISSION (3.74)
(12 June 427 BCE)

Bezalel Porten

In a document drawn up in contemplation of death, at least twenty-two years after Tamet's marriage to Anani, her master Meshullam manumitted wife and daughter Jehoishma upon his death. The contract was designated on the endorsement "document of withdrawal" (line 18) and its format was that of the conveyance, freedom here being the commodity conveyed and a stiff fifty *karsh* penalty imposed on any heir or related party seeking to deny it. The emancipation formula was threefold, each time expanding the word "release" — "free," "from the shade to the sun," "to God/the god" (lines 2-10). The pair did not go scot-free, however, but became part of Meshullam's family, his adoptive children and the adoptive sisters of Meshullam's son Zaccur. In consideration of emancipation they pledged continued service as children, to Meshullam till his death and afterwards to Zaccur, again under heavy fifty *karsh* penalty for future refusal (lines 11-15). The procedure was not drawn up in the presence of any government official (contrast 3.77:2-3) and only four witnesses were required, one of whom was a Mede (line 17). The scribe Haggai introduced four Persian loanwords — one specific to this transaction (ᵓ*zt*, "free" [line 4]) and the other three words that would recur in subsequent contracts (*hngyt*, "partner in chattel," *hnbg*, "partner in realty," and ᵓ*bgrn*, "penalty" [lines 5, 8, 14).

Date

(Recto)(1)On the 20th of Sivan, that is day 7 of Phamenoth, year 38 of Artaxerxes the king,[1]

Parties

then[2] (2)said Meshullam son of Zaccur,[3] a Jew of Elephantine the fortress of the detachment of Iddinnabu,[4] to lady Tapmet[5] by name[6] (3)his handmaiden, who is branded[7] on her right hand like this: "(Belonging) to Meshullam," saying:

Manumission

I thought of you (4)in my lifetime.[8] (To be) free[9] I released you at my death and I released Jeh(o)ishma[10] by name your daughter, whom (5)you bo(r)e me.[11]

No reenslavement

Son of mine or daughter or brother of mine or sister, near or far,[12] partner-in-chattel or partner-in-land[13] (6)does not have right to you or to Jeh(o)ishma your daughter, whom you obre (ERROR FOR: bore) me; does not have right to you, (7)to brand you or TRAFFIC WITH you (for) PAYMENT[14] of silver.[15]

Penalty

Whoever[16] shall stand up against you[17] or against Jeh(o)ishma your daughter, (8)whom you bo(r)e me, shall give you a penalty[18] of silver, 50 *karsh*[19] by the stone(-weight)s of the king,

Reaffirmation[20]

and you (9)are released from the shade to the sun[21] and (so is) Jeh(o)ishma your daughter and another person[22] does not have right (10)to you and to Jeh(o)ishma your daughter but you are released to God.[23]

Obligation of support

(11)And said Tapmet and Jeh(o)ishma her daughter[24]: We, he (ERROR FOR: we) shall serve[25] [a] you, (a)s a son or daughter supports[26] [b] his father, (12)in your lifetime.[27] And at your death we shall support Zaccur your single[28] son (ERASURE: w[ho]) like a son who supports his father, as we shall have been

a Mal 3:17; Ruth 4:17

b Isa 46:4; Ruth 4:15

[1] The double date yields a perfect synchronism for June 12, 427 BCE. See Porten 1990:20.

[2] See 3.66, n. 2.

[3] See 3.64, n. 7.

[4] For the years of his activity (446-420 BCE) see 3.66, n. 5.

[5] This was the way the scribe Haggai wrote her name (lines 11, 18; 3.80:1 3, 11, 24, 33, 35) in contrast to the other scribes who wrote Tamet (3.71 [Nathan]; 3.73:2, 6, 25 [Mauziah]; 3.75:3).

[6] A qualifier regularly attached to the name of a slave (line 4 and see 3.68, n. 12).

[7] See 3.68, n. 15.

[8] This was an expression appropriate to a gift in contemplation of death (3.78:2), here emancipation.

[9] Aram. *ʾzt* is an Old Persian loanword from **azātā-* (*GEA* 370.11); for a Greek parallel see *P. Edmonstone* 7 (*EPE* D18).

[10] Throughout the document her name was written without the letter waw.

[11] I.e. "whom you bore me" in a legal sense, as handmaiden, since Jehoishma's biological father was Anani (3.73:17-18).

[12] See 3.59, n. 22.

[13] These two Persian loanwords (*hngyt* = **hangaitha*, "partner in chattel" and *hnbg* = *hanbāga-*, "partner in realty") appears for the first time here (*GEA* 371.34-35) and recur in all subsequent contracts drawn up by Haggai for Anani (3.78:18; 3.79:12; 3.80:27) and in a document by an unknown scribe (*TAD* B5.5:9). Describing categories of joint ownership, they displace but do not exclude, the terms "another man" (= beneficiary) and "man of mine" (= representative). They illustrate the striving for precision in the formulation of the *Waiver* clauses. See Porten and Szubin 1987b:62-63.

[14] Aram. *lmzlky mndt* is difficult to translate precisely.

[15] With the term "have right to" put in the negative this clause is equivalent to a *Non-* or *Disinvestiture* clause. It is comparable to the second half of the first *Investiture* clause in Mahseiah's bequest to Mibtahiah, "I have no child, sibling or beneficiary who has right to that land but you" (3.61:10-11).

[16] Whoever among those enumerated in the *No-reenslavement* clause (line 5).

[17] The expression is elliptical for "stand up against you to brand you" (3.77:7; cf. 3.63:29; 3.75:16; 3.76:30).

[18] See 3.66, n. 38.

[19] This was the stiffest penalty recorded, indicating the importance attached to preservation of the rights of an emancipated slave.

[20] Repeating and expanding the tenn of the *Manumission* clause ("released"), this clause, following as it does the *Penalty* clause, is comparable to the *Reaffirmation of investiture* clause in conveyances (see 3.59, n. 18).

[21] A metaphorical expression with its counterpart in the Passover Haggadah on the Israelites' release from "darkness to light."

[22] Here once more this term is used as a collective (see 3.73, n. 35), to refer to the enumerated parties in the *No-reenslavement* clause (line 5).

[23] Or to "the god." Release to deity was well-known in Babyl. manumission documents. See Porten 1968:220 for references. In an Elephantine Greek manumission document the freed person was released "under (= subject only to) earth and sky" (*P. Edmonstone* 7 [*EPE* D18).

[24] See 3.71, n. 23. The declaration begins on a new line with a short marginal stroke drawn to indicate the change in speakers.

[25] Aram. *plḥ* = Heb. *ʿbd* (Mal 3:17) would be a standard term to describe the "service" a son rendered to a father. Thus the child of Ruth and Boaz who was to support Naomi in her old age was called Obed, "Server" (Ruth 4:17).

[26] Aram. *sbl* = Heb. *klkl* (Ruth 4:15) was the normal term for old-age support (3.78:17 and probably *TAD* B5.5:4; Isa 46:4). See also *TAD* A2.3:5.

[27] Though not emancipated until Meshullam's death, mother and daughter were already to relate to him as an adoptive father, and to his son Zaccur in the same fashion after his death.

[28] If this thick stroke is correctly read it would give the numeral "1" the meaning of "single, only." Elsewhere it has the meaning "alone" (*TAD* A2.4:4). Zaccur bore the same name as his grandfather (line 2).

doing (13)for you in your lifetime.

Penalty
(ERASURE: If stand up) We, if we stand up,[29] saying:
"We will not support you as a son supports (14)his father, nor Zaccur your son after your death,"
we shall be obligated[30] to you and to Zaccur your son (for) a penalty of (15)silver, 50 *karsh* by the stone(-weight)s of the king, pure silver,[31] without suit and without process.[32]

Scribe and place
Haggai[33] wrote (16)this document in Elephantine at the instruction of Meshullam son of Zaccur.

Witnesses
And the witnesses herein[34]:
(2nd hand) Atrpharna son of Nisaya, (17)a Mede[35];
(3rd hand) witness Micaiah son of Ahio[36];
(4th hand) witness Berechiah son of Miptah[37];
(5th hand) Dalah son of Gaddul.[38]

Endorsement
(Verso)(18)[Document] (sealing) of withdrawal which Meshullam son of Zaccur wrote for Tapmet and Jeh(o)ishm(a).

[29] Particularly in the documents of wifehood, the act of "standing up" was introductory to a declaration of legal import with negative consequences (3.63:22, 26; 3.71:7, 9; 3.76:21); see 3.72, n. 29.
[30] See 3.73, n. 27.
[31] See 3.59, n. 18.
[32] See 3.61, n. 40.
[33] According to the handwriting he was Haggai son of Shemaiah who was once a witness for Mahseiah and wrote most of the documents for Amaniah. See 3.64, n. 41.
[34] The normal number of four witnesses sufficed for this transaction. See 3.59, n. 34; 3.65, n. 26.
[35] Appeared only here
[36] See 3.70, n. 24.
[37] Appeared only here.
[38] Appeared only here.

REFERENCES

Text and translation: *TAD* B3.6; *EPE* B39. Porten 1990; Porten and Szubin 1987b; *TAD*.

A LIFE ESTATE OF USUFRUCT (3.75)
(11 July, 420 BCE)

Bezalel Porten

Written by an unknown scribe, this document was much corrected and bore unique terms and formulae.[1] It was the first of three deeds drawn up by Anani for the bequest of room(s) in his house which he was bestowing upon his daughter Jehoishma. This one was in contemplation of her marriage, which was to be recorded in a document of wifehood drawn up three months later (3.76:1). Absence of certain provisions, such as right of devolution and alienation and penalty for non-reclamation, indicated that Anani, who had already bestowed upon his son Pilti/Pelatiah part of a courtyard in his house (lines 10-12), was now creating a life estate of usufruct for his daughter in another part. This consisted of the upper and lower parts of a room (7 x 6? cubits) which lay "above" Anani's quarters, the other half of the courtyard, and access rights to Anani's stairway and exit from the property (lines 3-14). While his pledge of non-reclamation was not subject to penalty, attempted eviction after his death was penalized at ten *karsh*. The document broke off just where the fate of the property after Jehoishma's death was laid down (lines 15-18).

Date
(recto)(0)(ERASURE: of Pharmouthi, that is d[ay])
(1)On the 8th of Pharmouthi, that is d[a]y 8 of Tammuz, year 3 of Darius the king,[2]

Place
then (2)[in Elephantine] the [fort]ress,[3]

Parties
say I,[4] Anani son of Azariah, a servitor of YHW

[1] Discussed at length in Szubin and Porten 1988:29-45.
[2] If we assume that the scribe omitted a fourth stroke in the year date, then we get an exact synchronism for July 11, 420 BCE. Otherwise there would be a twelve day discrepancy for 421 (= 3 Darius II), when 8 Pharmouthi = July 11 and 8 Tammuz = July 23; Porten 1990:24. For precedence of the Eg. month to the Babyl. month see on 3.70:1.
[3] See 3.66, n. 2.
[4] Only here does the *Parties* clause begin in the 1st person present tense. See Szubin and Porten 1988:36.

the God, to Jeh(o)ishma (3)by name,[5] my child,[6] her mother (being) Tam[et] my wife, saying:

Transfer I
I, Anani, g[av]e you

Object I
a[7] house,[8]

Description
built, (4)containing beams,[9] —

Measurements
it was:[10] l[ength] seven, that is 3[+4] (= 7),[11] cubits by the measuring rod [by six;

Object II
and half the courtyard], (5)(which) they call (in) Egyptian[12] [the *hyt*; and half the stairway].

Boundaries
These are the boun[da]ries of [th]at house[13]:
below i[t] is (6)the house[14] of Anani son of Azariah [...] ... between them;
a[bo]ve it is (7)the treasury of the king;
west [of it the house of Shatibara adjoins i]t[15];
east of it is (ERASURE: the house of) (8)the house of Ḥor, a servant of Kh[num the god].

Transfer II
[I gave it to yo]u.[16]

Investiture I
You, Jehoishma my daughter, (9)have right to [this] hous[e, who]se boundaries are written in [t]h[is] document,[17] below and a[bo]ve.[18] (10)And yo[u] have right [to] ascend and to descend by th[at] stairway [of] my [h]ouse. And [that] courtyard [which is] (11)bet[w]een them,[19] the bottom and th[at a]bove,[20] between Pelatiah my son and [Jehoi]shma my daughter — [half] (12)to Pelat[ia]h and half to [Je]h[oishma ...] ...[21]

Transfer III
I, Anani, [ga]ve you this hous[e] (13)and half the courtyard and half the stair[way].

Investiture II
[And] you [have right] to them to ascend above and descend (14)and go out outside.

Transfer IV
I, Anani, gave you these houses[22] in love.[23]

Waiver of reclamation[24]
(15)I, Anani, (14)shall not be able (15)to reclaim (them)[25] from you. And I shall not be able to say:[26] "My soul[27] desired (them). I shall reclaim (them) from you."[28]

Penalty for expulsion
(16)Whoever shall stand up against you[29] to expel

[5] Jehoishma was still tagged "by name," the designation of a slave.

[6] Aram. *bry*, narrowly "my son" but possible as "my child." The scribe had apparently begun to write *brty*, "my daughter" (which he did write in line 11) but erased the *taw* and wrote *bry* instead.

[7] For the indefinite article, see 3.59, n. 7.

[8] For "house" = room, see 3.73, n. 8.

[9] There was no window in this room as there was in Tamet's room (see on 3.73:8).

[10] With merely the verb *hwh* the formula was elliptical for "its measurements was (= were)." See on 3.63:8-10.

[11] For the numerical repetition, see 3.60, n. 14.

[12] This lexicographical observation was also made for this word in the only other document where it occurred (3.79:4).

[13] See 3.60, n. 19. The orientation here was the same as that in the document drawn up by Mauziah (3.73:9-11).

[14] I.e. his remaining room(s).

[15] For justification of this restoration, see Szubin and Porten 1988:36.

[16] At first glance this clause would appear merely to establish an inclusion around the *Measurements*, *Description*, and *Boundaries* clauses, as frequently in our documents (3.61:3-8; 3.72:3-11; 3.79:2-8). Actually it was the second link in a sevenfold chain interweaving the *Transfer* and *Investiture* clauses (gave [line 3], [gave {8}], right to [9], right to [10], gave [12], right to [13], gave [14]). See Szubin and Porten 1988:40-41.

[17] See 3.59, n. 27.

[18] I.e. the ground floor and the upper story, to be reached by the stairway in Anani's apartment.

[19] I.e. which lay between the property of Anani and Jehoishma.

[20] The courtyard which was barren when the property was bought from the Caspian couple (3.72:4-5) had since been built up and contained some sort of upper structure.

[21] Pelatiah, known earlier as Pilti (3.71:13; 3.73:18), must have been given a document, similar to that of Jehoishma, which guaranteed his rights to a half share of the courtyard.

[22] Anani referred to the upper and lower structures he was giving as plural items, houses; see 3.73, n. 8.

[23] See 3.73, n. 4.

[24] While the first statement prohibited the act, the second prohibited the intention. A similar prohibition appears in a Byzantine bequest, "But if I should wish in same way to change my mind ..." (*P. Münch* 8.30-32 [*EPE* D23]). Absence of penalty was indicative of the nature of the bequest; see 3.61, n. 50. The last three final clauses (*Waiver*, *Penalty*, *Reversion*) follow a life sequence: benefactor's lifetime, benefactor's death, beneficiary's death. See Szubin and Porten 1988:41.

[25] See 3.61, n. 50.

[26] This self-restriction also occurs, expanded and with implicit penalty, in documents of wifehood with regard to the dowry (3.76:41-42; *TAD* B6.4:7-8).

[27] The two parallel passages had simply "I;" see previous note.

[28] Alternately translate: "My soul desired to reclaim them from you" — complementing a verb by means of a finite verb (cf. 3.76:41).

[29] See 3.74, n. 17.

you[30] from the houses which I wrote[31] and ga[ve you shall give to Jehoishma][32] (17)my daughter a penalty[33] of silver, 10 *karsh*[34] [by the stone(-weight)s of the king, silver 2 q(uarters)/zuz to the ten/1 *karsh*, without suit].

Reversion
(18)If Jehoishma die at the age of [100] y[ears ... (19)...][35] ... will be ... [...] (20)... Hosha[iah ...,

[two unplaced fragments remain; bottom missing]

[30] An action that would take place after Anani's death, as in 3.76:28-32.

[31] Unique in our documents, the expression means "assign property" in Tannaitic texts (Peah 3:7-8; Baba Bathra 8:5). See Szubin and Porten 1988:33.

[32] The scribe switched from 2nd to 3rd person address in the same sentence. See 3.64, n. 12.

[33] See 3.66, n. 38.

[34] This is the same penalty as for an attempt at reclamation of Anani's bequest to Tamet after his death (3.73:20-22). Otherwise, penalties for violation of Anani's purchase and bequests were twenty and thirty *karsh*. See 3.59, n. 15.

[35] As in Anani's bequest to Tamet (3.73:16-20), so here this clause would detail the fate of the property, presumably reverting to the donor, Anani. See Szubin and Porten 1988:41-42.

REFERENCES

Text and translation: *TAD* B3.7; *EPE* B40. *EPE*; Porten 1990; Szubin and Porten 1988; *TAD*.

DOCUMENT OF WIFEHOOD (3.76)
(2-30 October 420 BCE)

Bezalel Porten

At forty-five lines, this is the longest contract in our collection. Emancipated and adopted seven years earlier (3.74), Jehoishma was given away not by her father Anani but by her adoptive brother Zaccur, who furnished her with a handsome dowry of 78.125 shekels plus seventeen unevaluated items (lines 4-21). This included a *mohar* of one *karsh* paid by the groom Anani son of Haggai. The customary *Death* and *Repudiation* clauses were expansively formulated and subtly structured. The repudiation statement was expanded and the amount of the dowry spelled out; loss of *mohar* and 7½ shekel compensation were the price for repudiation (lines 21-28). The *Non-expulsion* clause was tacked onto the *Death of husband* clause directly and violation assessed at twenty *karsh* (lines 30-32). The *Death* clauses are intertwined with the *Repudiation* clauses in symmetric fashion:

A Repudiation by declaration; by husband (lines 21-24)

B Repudiation by declaration; by wife (24-28)

C Death of husband (28-32)

B′ Repudiation by conduct; by wife (33-34)

C′ Death of wife (34-36)

A′ Repudiation by conduct; by husband (36-37).

The "law of hatred" was equally applicable to *Repudiation by Declaration* and *Repudiation by conduct*, that is, taking an additional spouse; though the language was distinctive the penalty was identical. Unique among the documents was the euphemistic and cryptic double negative prohibition on either spouse against "not not" doing the right of one or two of his/her colleagues' spouses. This refusal of conjugal rights was likewise "hatred," that is, tantamount to repudiation by conduct, and it too resulted in application of the "law of hatred" (lines 37-40). Concluding the document was a *Waiver* by Zaccur of the right to reclaim the dowry (lines 40-42). The scribe was the professional Mauziah and at least six Jewish witnesses signed (lines 42-44).[1]

[1] For full discussion, see Szubin and Porten forthcoming.

Date
(recto)(1)In the month of Tishri, that is Epeiph, [y]ear [3+]1 (= 4) of Darius the [king],[2]

Place
[then] in Elephantine the fortress,[3]

Parties
said Ananiah son of Haggai, (2)an Aramean of Elephantine the fortress [of] the detachment of [Iddin]nabu,[4] (2)to Zaccur son of Me[shullam,[5] an Ara]mean of Syene of the same detachment, saying:

Marriage[6]
(3)I came to y[ou in] your [hou]se and asked you for the lady Jehoishma by name,[7] your sister, for wifehood and you gave her[8] (4)to me.

Affirmation of status
She is my wife and I am [her] husband from this day forever.[9] [a]

Mohar
And I gave you (as) *mohar*[10] (for) your sister Jehoishma:

[10]shekels (5)silver, [1] kar[sh].[11]

Satisfaction
It came into you[b] [and] your [heart was satis]fied herein.[12]

Dowry
Jehoishma your sister brought in to me to my house:[13]

22.125 shekels money[14] (6)of silver two *karsh*, 2 she[ke]ls, 5 hallurs;

12.0 shekels 1 new garment of wool,[15] at[16] 7 cubits, 3 handbreadths (and in) width (7)4 cubits, 2 q(uarters),[17] worth (in) silver 1 *karsh*, 2 shekels;

10.0 shekels 1 new GARMENT of wool, at 6 cubits by 4, striped (8)with dye, doubly-well,[18] (for) 1 handbreadth on each edge, worth (in) silver 1 *karsh*;

7.0 shekels 1 new FRINGED garment, at 6 cubits by 4, valued (in) silver (9)(at) 7 shekels;

8.0 shekels [1] new SHAWL[19] of woo[l], at 6 cubits by 3[+2](= 5), 2 q(uarters), [*striped with dye doubly-well*[20] ..., (for)] (10)2 fingerbreadths on each edge, worth (in) silver 8 she[ke]ls;

1.5 shekels [1] worn garme[nt], worth [(in) silver 1 *shekel*, 20 *hallurs*];

[1.0] sheke[l] (11)1 new SKIRT/ROBE of linen, (in) length [6 *cubits* by 4 (in width)], worth (in) silver [1] shek[el;

[1.0 shekel] 1 *new garment of linen*], (12)(in) length 6 cubits by 3 (in width), worth (in) silv[er] 1 [shekel];

1.0 shekel 1 worn and [...] linen [GARMENT, va]lued (in) silver (at) 1 shekel.

Total (13)All garments of wool and linen: 8[21]

Bronze utensils:

1.0 shekel 1 mirror, valu[ed] (in) silv[er] (at) 1 [shekel];

1.25 shekels 1 bowl of bronze, (14)valued (in) silver (at) 1 shekel, 10 h(allurs);

1[.25] shekels 1 cup of bronze, valued (in) silver (at) 1 shekel, [10 h(allurs);

.50 shekel 1] cup, [valued] (in) silver (at) 20

[a] Hos 2:4

[b] Gen 43:23; Num 32:19

[2] See 3.66, n. 1; Porten 1990:20-21, written a month earlier by the same scribe for the heirs of the Mibtahiah archive.

[3] See 3.66, n. 2.

[4] See 3.66, n. 5.

[5] He was son of the bride Jehoishma's former master and later adoptive father (3.74:12) and hence her adoptive brother; see 3.77, n. 6.

[6] See 3.63, n. 6.

[7] As an ex-slave with filial support obligations vis-a-vis the son of her former master Meshullam, Jehoishma bears the appendage *šmh*, "her name" (= "by name" [see 3.68, n. 12]) and is associated with the son Zaccur as your sister." Like her mother in 434 BCE she is also designated *nšn*, "lady."

[8] For the terminology "came ... (asked) ... gave," see 3.59, n. 6.

[9] Reminiscent of the negative biblical formulation, "She is not my wife and I am not her husband" (cf. Hos 2:4), the affirmative Elephantine formula "She is my wife and I am her husband" may have been publicly pronounced but as incorporated into our documents of wifehood written in contemplation of marriage, its main thrust was to introduce the events that would trigger the contractual obligations of the respective parties. See 3.63, n. 12; Porten and Szubin 1995:48-50.

[10] See 3.63, n. 12.

[11] The *mohar* for the widow Mibtahiah was half that amount (3.63:5).

[12] Payment of the ten-shekel *mohar is* duly receipted by the bride's representative as recorded by the technical terms *ʿll ʿl* = Heb. *bʾ ʾl* (Gen 43:23; Num 32:19), meaning "received" and *ṭyb lbb* meaning "fully satisfied"; Muffs 1973; see 3.63, n. 14.

[13] See 3.63, n. 17.

[14] This cash amount of 22.125 shekels was almost twice the 12 shekels received by Mibtahiah (3.63:6-7).

[15] For discussion of these garments see Porten 1968:88-89. The objects were listed more or less in descending order of value.

[16] For the first four woolen garments (lines 6-9) the scribe Mauziah wrote the dimension formula slightly differently than his father Nathan. He did not include the term "it was" (*hwh*), omitted the word "length" from the formula "length cubits" (*ʾrk ʾmn* [3.63:8-11]), and prefixed a *lamed* to the word for "cubits," yielding something like "at cubits."

[17] For the measurements for this and the following garments see on 3.63:8-11.

[18] Alternately, "two-toned."

[19] See 3.63, n. 23.

[20] Alternately, "two-toned."

[21] The supralinear numeral "5" is very puzzling.

hallurs;

.50 shekel (15)1 jug, valued (in) silver (at) 20 h(allurs).

All [ut]ensil[s] of bronze: [5.

Total All the garments and the br]onz[e utensils] and the mo[n]ey and the *mohar*:[22]

78.125 shekels (16)(in) silver seven *karsh*, that is [7], eight [she]ke[l]s, that is 8, 5 hallurs by the stone(-weight)s of (17)the king, silver zuz to the ten.[23]

17 Unpriced Items 1 CHEST of palm-leaf for her garments;

1 new ... of papyrus-reed on which are (18)... alabaster stone INLAYS [...] ...;

2 jug(s);

2 TRAYS of *slq*, herein:

1 [...] ...;

1 *d/rmn* of *slq*;

(19)ladles to carry oil:

2 of [pottery],

2 of wood,

1 of stone,

all (told) 5;

1 CHEST of wood for her jewels;

(20)a PAIR of Persian leather (sandals);

2 [hand]fuls of oi[l];

4 handfuls of olive oil;

1 handful of s[ce]nted oil;

(21)5 handfuls of (20)castor oil.[24]

Repudiation by declaration by husband

(21)Tomorrow or (the) next day[25] should Ananiah stand up in an assembly[26] and say:

"I hated my wife Jehoishma; (22)she shall not be to me a wife,"[27]

silver of ha[tr]ed is on his head.[28] All that she brought in in(to) his house he shall give her[29] — her money[30] (23)and her garments, valued (in) silver (at) seven *karsh*, [eight] sh[ekels, 4+]1 (= 5) [hallurs], and the rest[31] of the goods which are written (above).[32] (24)He shall give her on 1 day at 1 stroke[33] [and] she may go [away[34] [c] from him] wher[ever] she [desires].

c Gen 12:1; Cant 2:10-11

Repudiation by declaration by wife

And if Jehoishm[a] hate her husband (25)Ananiah and say to him.[35]

"I hated you; I will not be to you a wife,"[36]

silver of hatred is on her head (and) her *mohar* will be lost.[37] (26)She shall PLACE UPON[38] the balance scale and give her husband Ananiah silver, 7 shekels, [2] q(uarters), and go out from him with[39] the rest[40] of (27)her money and her goods and her property,[41] [valued (in) silver (at) 6 *karsh*, 2+]6 (= 8) [shekels], 5 h(allurs), and the rest[42] of her goods (28)which are written (above). He shall give

[22] None of the documents includes realty or chattel. Acknowledgment of receipt of dowry is absent in our document, albeit present for the evaluated items in the document of Mibtahiah (3.63:14-15).

[23] The grand total of 78.125+ shekels is quite a handsome amount when we recall that her mother, still a handmaiden, received only 7.19 shekels (3.71:6-7).

[24] See on *TAD* A2.1:7 (*EPE* B 1).

[25] See 3.59, n. 12.

[26] See 3.63, n. 41.

[27] The repudiation statement was spelled out most fully in this contract. See 3.63, n. 43.

[28] In order to safeguard the spouses' respective status and discourage infringement thereof, the contract stipulated a payment of *ksp śnʾh*, "silver of hatred." Though compensatory in nature, it carried the clout inherent in fines and penalties associated with breach of contract. See also 3.63, nn. 44-45.

[29] In the other two documents of wifehood it was stated that "she shall take out" not that "he shall give her." Nor were the items listed and the total evaluated (3.63:27-28; 3.71:8).

[30] This was the 22.125 shekels in cash (lines 5-6).

[31] This included the five bronze vessels and the seventeen *Unpriced items* (lines 13-21).

[32] See 3.59, n. 26.

[33] Neither in phases nor in stages; see 3.63, n. 54.

[34] Since this new status was short of divorce we must understand the final verbs in the respective clauses as optative and not obligatory — "she may go (*away*]" (*thk* [*lh*] and not "she shall/must go [away]." It is this same sense which the verb *alāku* has in the parallel provision in CH §142 (*COS* 2.131, p. 344). As restored, the Aram. verb combination is the equivalent of Heb. *hlk* followed by the ethical dative *l-* with pronominal suffix with the meaning "leave, depart" (Gen 12:1; Cant 2:10-11).

[35] As he reversed the word order ("wife Jehoishma :: husband Ananiah"), so the scribe varied the formulation for Jehoishma (similarly for Tamet [3.71:9]), but the analogy of the contract of Mibtahiah (3.63:22) would indicate that in any case the woman had to make her declaration in an assembly just like the man.

[36] This formulaic divergence indicates that her powers were not equal to his; though she can repudiate her own status as first-ranking wife, relinquishing privileges and shedding obligations, she lacks power to repudiate *his* absolute status as husband (*bᶜl*, lit. "master"). See 3.63, nn. 42-43.

[37] I.e. forfeit.

[38] See 3.64, n. 46.

[39] The other contracts say "she shall take out" all that she brought in (3.63:24-25; 3.71:10).

[40] I.e. minus the one *karsh mohar* which was returned to Anani.

[41] The money was the 22.125 shekels in cash, while the "goods and property" included the garments and bronze vessels (lines 5-17).

[42] These included the *Unpriced Items* (lines 17-21).

her on [1] da[y] at 1 stroke and she may go to her father's house.[43]

Death of husband
And i[f] Ananiah die (29)not having (28)a child, male (29)or female, by [Je]ho[i]shma his wife, it is Jehoishma (who) [HOL]DS ON[44] to it (namely), his house[45] and his goods (30)and his property [and his money and every]thing [which] h[e has].

Expulsion[46]
And whoever shall stand up against [Jehoishma] to expel her from the house (31)[of A]nan[iah, and his] good[s and] his [property] and all that [h]e has

Penalty
[shall g]ive he[r the pe]nalty of silver, (32)twenty *karsh* by the stone(-weight)s of the king, silver 2 q(uarters) to the 10,

Reaffirmation
and do [to her] the law of this document,[47] without suit.[48]

Repudiation by conduct by wife[49]
But Jeho[ishma] does not have right [to] ACQUIRE[50] another husband be[sides] Anani. And if she does thus, (34)hatred it is; they[51] shall do to her [the law of ha]tred.[52]

Death of wife
And if [Jehoishma] die not (35)having (34)a child, ma[le] or female, (35)from Anani [her] husba[nd, it is Anani her husband (who) shall inherit[53] from her her [mo]n[ey] and her goods and her property and all (36)that she has.[54]

Repudiation by conduct of husband[55]
Moreover, [Ananiah shall] n[ot be able[56] to] take anoth[er] woman [besides Jehoishma] (37)for himself for wifehood.[57] If he does [thus, hatred it is. H]e [shall d]o to her [the la]w of [ha]tred.[58]

Refusal of conjugal rights
And moreover, (38)Ananiah (37)shall not be able (38)not to do[59] the law of [one] or two of his colleagues' wives[60] to Jehoishma his wife. And if (39)he does not do thus,[61] hatred [it is].[62] He shall do to her the law of hatred. And moreover, Jehoishma shall not be able (40)not to do the law of one or [t]wo (of her colleagues' husbands) to Ananiah her husband. And if she does not do (so) for him, hatr(ed) (it) is.

Waiver of reclamation
Moreover (41)Zaccur shall (40)not (41)be able to say to his sist[er]:[63]

"These go[o]ds in love I gave to Jehoishma. Now, I[64] desired (them); (42)I shall reclaim[65]

---

[43] See on line 24.
[44] See 3.63, n. 36.
[45] There was an imbalance in favor of the rights of the surviving wife to the house of her husband. Anani was assigned no specific rights (line 35) to the apartment held by Jehoishma (3.75).
[46] See 3.63, n. 55.
[47] See 3.63, n. 59.
[48] See 3.61, n. 40.
[49] Since a universally prohibited act (e.g. theft, murder, adultery) would not be contractually stipulated, the formulation of the negative reveals the norm — the man may normally "take" (*ylqḥ* [lines 36-37]) another wife but the woman would normally be "entitled" (*šlyṭh*) to have another husband only under special circumstances, e.g. her husband's extended absence or unjustified abandonment (cf. 1 Sam 25:44; CH §136 [*COS* 2.131, p. 344], LE 30 [*COS* 2.130, p. 334]; MAL A 36, 45 [*COS* 2.132, pp. 357-358]). In such a case, Jehoishma would be invoking "the law of repudiation," i.e. demotion/diminution of status with all the pecuniary consequences.
[50] The *haphel* form ([*l*]*hb*ᶜ*lh*) of the verb *b*ᶜ*l* occurred only here and its precise nuance is uncertain.
[51] Assuming that Anani's prolonged absence was the occasion for Jehoishma having contracted a relationship of primacy with another husband/lord, the authorities would consider this tantamount to repudiation by declaration and apply to her the law of hatred.
[52] Presumably this included her demotion, relinquishment of *mohar,* and payment to his estate of the 7½ shekel monetary compensation.
[53] See 3.63, n. 36.
[54] Would this include rights to the apartment her father gave her (3.75), even though such was not made explicit as in the case of her succession (line 29)?
[55] Should Anani follow the norm and take another ᵓ*nth* ([first-ranking] wife) for wifehood (*l*ᵓ*ntw*), it would be tantamount to repudiation by declaration and the pecuniary consequences would be the same as in the case of Jehoishma.
[56] Should this gap be restored as in lines 37 and 39 or in parallel with line 33 (restoring ["Anani does not have right"])?
[57] The early Elephantine Greek marriage document stated, "Let it not be permitted to Herakleides to bring in another woman as an outrage to Demetria ..." (P. *Eleph.* 1.8-9 [*EPE* D2]).
[58] The proposed restoration here of [*y*ᶜ]*b*[*dwn*], "[they shall] d[o]" (Hugenberger 1994:228) is palaeographically untenable and legally inappropriate (see form in line 9). Unlike the case of Jehoishma acquiring another husband in Anani's absence, Anani would presumably be taking another wife in Jehoishma's presence and thus be able himself to "do the law of hatred."
[59] I.e. to refuse.
[60] This circumlocution was probably a euphemism for "sexual intercourse"; Porten 1968:224.
[61] I.e. if he refuse.
[62] For either spouse to deny the other conjugal rights was tantamount to repudiation by conduct and required the requisite compensation encompassed by "the law of hatred" (see n. 52 above).
[63] See 3.61, n. 50.
[64] The parallel passage in a conveyance has "my soul" as subject (3.75:15).
[65] See 3.61, n. 50.

them."[66]

Consequences
If he says thus, he shall not be heard[67]; he is obligated.[68]

Scribe
Mauziah son of Nathan[69] wrote (43)this (42)document (43)at the instruction of Ananiah son of Haggai [and] Zaccur son of Meshullam.[70]

Witnesses
And the witnesses herein:[71]

Haggai son of Shemaiah[72];
Islah son of (44)Gaddul[73];
[PN son of PN];
Haggai son of Azzul[74];
Menahem son of Azariah[75];
Jedaniah son of Gemariah[[76]

(bottom right band missing)

Endorsement
(Verso)(45)Document (*sealing*) of wifehood which Ananiah son of Meshullam[77] wrote for Jehoishma.

[66] Alternately translate, "Now, I desired to reclaim them" (cf. 3.75:15).

[67] This reaction occurs only in relation to *Waiver of reclamation* of dowry (*TAD* B6.4:8). Neo-Assyrian contracts have the clause "the judge will not hear his case."

[68] Reclamation of the dowry did not incur a monetary penalty since it was a gift in contemplation of marriage providing only benefits of enjoyment and not full title; Szubin and Porten 1988:38-39. The word here is a stative (*ḥyb*); when it occurs in the imperf. (*ʾ/y/nḥwb*) it is always followed by a monetary payment. See 3.73, n. 27.

[69] See 3.66, n. 41.

[70] Only this and another, fragmentary, wifehood document, also by Mauziah, were drawn up at the behest of the groom and the party responsible for the bride (*TAD* B6.4:8-9}

[71] Five of six names survive; two more may have been on the missing band, bringing the total to eight. See 3.63, n. 65.

[72] For this professional scribe, see 3.64, n. 41.

[73] See 3.67, n. 36.

[74] Appears only here.

[75] He appears as witness a month earlier in another contract written by Mauziah (3.66:17).

[76] The leader of the Jewish community during the traumatic events of the last decade, he modestly signed last (see on 3.46, n. 3 [*EPE* B13]).

[77] The scribe sometimes skipped a generation in a genealogy: Ananiah son of Meshullam or Anani son of Haggai son of Busasa (3.80:11) for Anani son of Haggai son of Meshullam son of Busasa (3.80:2).

REFERENCES

Text and translation: *TAD* B3.8; *EPE* B41. *EPE*; Hugenberger 1994; Porten and Szubin 1995; Szubin and Porten forthcoming; *TAD*.

ADOPTION (3.77)
(22 September or 22 October, 416 BCE)

Bezalel Porten

Somehow a document made out to Zaccur, Jehoishma's adoptive brother, found its way into her archive. He had "given," together with written contract, a houseborn slave to Uriah, though under what circumstances was not indicated (lines 3-4) and Zaccur's contract was not found. Uriah then made a fourfold declaration that Jedaniah was to be his son and that neither he nor his heirs, beneficiaries or representatives would press him into slavery, brand him, or make him a slave, subject to a thirty *karsh* penalty (lines 4-9). As in the earlier case of Tamet and Jehoishma (3.74), emancipation and adoption went hand in hand. However, on the basis of our documents, the former transaction was private while the present one was drawn up in Syene by an Aramean scribe, in the presence of the Troop Commander of Syene, Vidranga (lines 2-3), and attested by eight Aramean witnesses (lines 9-12). Notably, both parties were designated "Arameans of Syene" (lines 2-3).

Date
(Recto)(1) On the 6th of Tishri, that is day 22 of Payni, year 8 of Darius the king,[1]

Place
then in Syene the fortress,[2]

[1] The scribe erred in the month, writing Payni when he meant the month of Epeiph or writing Tishri when he meant the previous month of Elul. Switching either will give a synchronism: 6 Tishri = 22 Epeiph [not Payni] = October 22 and 6 Elul [not Tishri] = 22 Payni = September 22 in 8 Darius II (416 BCE); Porten 190:23-24.

[2] See 3.66, n. 2.

Parties

said ⁽²⁾Uriah son of Mahseiah,[3] an Aramean of Syene, before Vidranga,[4] the Guardian of the Seventh,[5] the Troop Commander of Syene, to Zaccur son of Meshullam,[6] ⁽³⁾an Aramean of Syene, before Vidranga the Guardian of the Seventh, the Troop Commander of Syene, saying:

Non-enslavement and adoption[7]

Jedaniah by name[8] son of Taḥe/Takhoi,[9] [you]r la[d] ⁽⁴⁾whom you gave me and a document you wrote for me about him[10] — I shall not be able, I, Uriah, or son or daughter of mine, brother or sister of mine, or man ⁽⁵⁾of mine, he (shall not be able) to press him (into) slave(ry).[a] My son he shall be. I, or son or daughter of mine, or man of mine,[11] or another individual[12] do not have right ⁽⁶⁾to brand him.[13] I shall not be able — I, or son or daughter of mine, brother or sister of mine, or man of mine — we (shall not be able) to stand up[14] to make him a s[lave] ⁽⁷⁾or brand him.

Penalty

Whoever[15] shall stand up against that Jedaniah to brand him or make him a slave shall give you a penalty[16] of silver, ⁽⁸⁾thirty *karsh*[17] by the weight of the king, silver zuz to the ten,

Reaffirmation

and that Jedaniah, my son shall he be likewise.[18] And an individual does not ⁽⁹⁾have right to brand him or make him a slave, but my son he shall be.

Scribe

Wrote Raukhshana son of Nergal(u)shezib[19] at the instruction of Uriah.

Witnesses

⁽¹⁰⁾The witnesses herein:[20]

(2nd hand) Attarmalki son of Kilkilan;
(3rd hand) Sinkishir son of Shabbethai[21];
(4th hand) Saharakab son of Cepha;
⁽¹¹⁾5th hand) Nabushillen son of Bethelrai;
(6th hand) Eshemram son of Eshemshezib;
(7th hand) Varyazata son of Bethelzabad[22];
⁽¹²⁾(8th hand) Heremnathan son of Paḥo[23];
(9th hand) Eshemzabad son of Shawyan.

(endorsement missing)

a Jer 34:11, 16; Neh 5:3, 5

[3] He was father of Didi in a name list (*TAD* C4.6:14).
[4] See 3.48, n. 8 (*EPE* B 15).
[5] For this Persian title (*hpthpt*ᵓ = **haftaxᵘwapāta*) see Porten 1968:44; *GEA* 372.40.
[6] Son of the householder, creditor and slaveowner Meshullam son of Zaccur (3.64:3; 3.69:2-3; 3.71:2-3; 3.74:2) and adoptive brother of Tamet and Jehoishma (3.74:11-12; 3.76:2), Zaccur was here divesting himself of another slave.
[7] This contract lacked *Transfer* and *Investiture* clauses and began, so to speak, with the final clauses. The prohibited act was repeated three times, with varying terminology — "press (into) slave(ry)," "brand," "make a slave/brand." In between the first and second promise was inserted a positive affirmation of sonship. Had the contract begun with an affirmative statement, we would be able to compare it to the earlier manumission document and consider the *Non-enslavement* clause as equivalent to a *Non-* or *Disinvestiture* clause, as we did there for the *No-reenslavement* clause (3.74:7).
[8] See 3.68, n. 12.
[9] The boy had a Jewish name popular at Elephantine but he was filiated with an Eg. mother, and so was probably a houseborn slave.
[10] For the procedure and formula "gave" and "wrote," cf. 3.64:3.
[11] I.e. a representative; see 3.66, n. 28.
[12] I.e. a beneficiary; see 3.61, n. 33.
[13] Potential claimants included children, siblings, representative, and beneficiaries — in that order; see Porten and Szubin 1987b:61.
[14] See 3.72, n. 29.
[15] Whoever among the parties listed in the previous paragraph.
[16] See 3.66, n. 38.
[17] The penalty for attempted reenslavement of the freed women Tamet and Jehoishma was fifty *karsh* (3.74:8).
[18] This term is normally found in the *Reaffirmation* clause in conveyances. See 3.59, n. 18.
[19] The scribe's name is Persian and his patronym either Akk. or Aram. He appears only here.
[20] All the witnesses were non-Jews and none appear elsewhere. Most of the names were Aram. theophorous and indicate the deities worshipped by the Arameans of Syene — Attar, Bethel, Eshem, Ḥerem, Nabu, and Sahar. For the witness total of eight, see 3.59, n. 34.
[21] Though Shabbethai was originally a Heb. name meaning "(Born on the) Sabbath," in the vicinity of Elephantine it was apparently adopted by non-Jews as well; see Porten 1969:116-121.
[22] Varyazata was a Persian name borne by two detachment commanders, perhaps grandfather and grandson (see 3.59, n. 4 and 3.68, n. 4).
[23] The father's name was Eg.

REFERENCES

Text and translation: *TAD* B3.9; *EPE* B42. *GEA*; Porten 1969; 1990; *TAD*.

BEQUEST IN CONTEMPLATION OF DEATH (3.78)
(25 November, 404 BCE)

Bezalel Porten

Sixteen years after his grant of a life estate of usufruct (3.75), Anani granted his daughter title to the apartment, but only to take effect upon his death. To reassure her in the interim, the scribe repeated the operative word "gave" eight times, doubled the formulae in both the *Pedigree* ("bought" and "gave") and *Investiture* ("yours" and "right") clauses (lines 3, 11), granted her rights of ownership to half the courtyard (as distinct from shared rights [lines 13-14]), and assimilated the bequest to a sale by reference to old-age support as consideration (line 17). Concomitantly, he held back in the formulation of several clauses just because the bequest was to take effect only upon his death — omission of rights of heirs and beneficiaries in the *Investiture* clause (line 11); omission of *Warranty* and *Penalty* clauses in the name of the alienor; and omission of a *Reclamation* Waiver. The several *Transfer* and *Investiture* clauses artfully intertwine as the first half of the contract builds up to a climax — at my death, in affection, in consideration of old-age support (lines 15-18). Penalty for suit or complaint by heirs and related parties was a hefty thirty *karsh* and the new-or-old document clause substituted the word "made" (=prepared) for "wrote" (lines 21-22), a further indication of the deferred character of the bequest.[1] The eight witnesses were Jewish and all but one appear elsewhere (lines 23-26).

Date

(Recto)(1)On the 24th of Marcheshvan, that is day 29 of Mesore, year 1 of Artaxerxes the king,[2]

Parties

then said Anani son of Azariah, (2)a servitor to YHW the God in Elephantine the fortress,[3] to lady[4] Jehoishma his daughter, saying:

Transfer I

I thought of you in my lifetime[5] and gave (3)you

Object I

part[6] of my house

Pedigree

which I bought for money and its value I gave.[7]

Transfer II

I gave it to you —

Object II

that is the southern room,[8] east of (4)the large room of mine;[9] and half the courtyard, that is half the *hyt* (as it is called in) Egyptian;[10] and half the stairway, beneath which is the *peras*(-sized) STORAGE AREA.[11]

Measurements

(5)This is[12] the measurements of the house which I gave Jehoishma my daughter in love; this is the measurements of the house which I, Anani, (6)gave Jehoishma my daughter:[13]

from below to above, 8 and one-half cubits by the measuring rod; and from east to west, (7)7 cubits by the measuring rod[14]; IN AREA, 98 cubits by the measuring rod and[15] half the courtyard and half the stairway and (8)the (7)*pe-*

[1] For full discussion see Porten and Szubin 1987a:179-192.

[2] This document was written at night since 24 Marcheshvan = November 26 while 29 Mesore in 1 Artaxerxes II = November 25, 404 BCE; see Porten 1990:21.

[3] See 3.70, n. 5.

[4] She was no longer designated by the customary slave appellative "by name" (3.76:3) but simply "lady," the customary female tag; see 3.61, n. 7.

[5] A formula for a gift in contemplation of death (3.74:3-4), but the reference to death was deferred to one of the last *Transfer* clauses.

[6] The terminology here is more precise and less confusing than that in the first document Anani drew up where he called the property simply "a house" (3.75:3).

[7] In this formula the scribe both abridged, omitting the name of the seller, and expanded, stating both "bought" and "gave." See Porten and Szubin 1987a:184-185.

[8] The expression is Eg., here written as one word (*dryrsy* = *tʾ ry.t rsy.t*). It occurs again (3.79:3) as two words with the expected *taw* instead of *daleth* (*try rsy*). *GEA* 373.4.

[9] As indicated, Haggai described the house's orientation from a perspective different from that in the first document for this property which accorded with Mauziah's orientation (see 3.73, n. 19; 3.75, n. 13). Thus, what lay east of Anani's large room here lay above it there (3.75:5-6 ["'below' it the house {= large room} of Anani"]). On the Eg. word for room see 3.73, n. 2.

[10] The same linguistic gloss as in the previous document (3.75:4-5), but abbreviated.

[11] The area beneath the stairway was not mentioned in the earlier document. Similar areas were found in the Byzantine houses and were given an Eg. name (*P. Lond* 1722:20 [*EPE* D22]; *P. Münch* 11.27 [*EPE* D45], 12.22 [*EPE* D46]).

[12] Grammatical mistake for "these are."

[13] This was a unique repetition of the *Measurements* caption. It presented the opportunity for repetition of "gave" and the addition of "in love." So, too, each statement varied slightly from the other (addition of "Anani" and omission of "in love" in the second). For the usual formula, see 3.61:4.

[14] In the earlier document the measurements were a cubit or so less (7½ x 6? [3.75:4]).

[15] I.e. including.

ras(-sized) STORAGE AREA its half.[16]

Boundaries

(8)And behold the boundaries of the house[17] which I, Anani, gave Jehoishma my daughter:

east of it is the (9)protecting (8)wall[18] (9)which the Egyptians built, that is the way of the god;[19] above it the house of the shrine of the god[20] adjoins it wall to wall;[21] (10)below it is the wall of the stairway[22] and the house of Ḥor son of Peṭeese, a gardener of Khnum the god, adjoins that stairway; (11)west of it is the wall of the large room.

Investiture I

Yours it is: you have right to it.[23]

Transfer III

This house whose measurements (12)and boundaries are written in this document[24] — I, Anani son of Azariah, gave it to you in love.[25]

Description

Renovated[26] is (the) (13)lower (12)house.[27] (13)It contains beams[28] and 3 windows are in it. One door is in it, shutting and opening.[29]

Investiture II

Moreover, you have right to the *ḫyt*, (14)that is the courtyard, right to prop up (what is) knocked down and its beam in the half of yours.[30] Moreover, you have right to go out (15)through the gateway of the *ḫyt*, that is the courtyard. Moreover, you have right to half the stairway to ascend and descend.[31]

Transfer IV

This (16){this}[32] house whose boundaries and measurements are written and whose words[33] are written in this document[34] — I, Anani, gave it to Jehoishma (17)my daughter at my death[35] in love. Just as she supported[36] me while I was old of days — I was unable (to use) my hands[37] and she supported me — also I (18)gave[38] (it) to her at my death.[39]

Waiver of suit

Son of mine or daughter of mine,[40] partner-in-chattel who is mine or partner-in-land or guarantor[41] who is mine shall not be able to bring against

[16] The area of the "southern room" would have been (8½ x 7 =) 59½ cubits, leaving 38½ cubits for the area of half the courtyard and "half" the stairway. See *TAD* B 177 and figure 6.

[17] The order of the *Boundaries* (east-above-below-west) was quite irregular in order to give prominence to the structural changes that took place since the last document was drawn up sixteen years earlier (3.75; see 3.60, n. 18).

[18] Aram. *hnpnʾ* is an Old Persian loan word (**hanpāna-*); *GEA* 371.39.

[19] Aram. *tmwʾnty* is an Eg. loan word of uncertain derivation. Either *tʾ mʾy.t nṯr*, "'island' of the god" or error for *tʾ my.t nṯr*, "way of the god"; see Porten 1968:284-285, also for following notes; *GEA* 375.30. This wall came in place of the treasury which had been the eastern border in the earlier documents (3.72:9; 3.75:7).

[20] Aram. *qnḥnty* is an Eg. loanword *qnh ntr*; *GEA* 374.22.

[21] Some time after 420 BCE the Eg. priests took over the property of Shatibara and converted it into an adjoining shrine. In the summer of 410, when Arsames left the country, they cut off part of the royal treasury (3.50:4-5) to build an approach way.

[22] This may have been a newly constructed stairway that went along with the other structural changes in the adjacent buildings; see Szubin and Porten 1988:38.

[23] This double formula in a single *Investiture* clause is unique (see 3.61, n. 28) and comes to reassure Jehoishma of full title to the property, even though it would only take effect at his death. On the other hand, the customary devolution of the property upon "your children after you" (see 3.61, n. 30) was omitted as premature since the bequest did not take effect until after Anani's death; Porten and Szubin 1987a:185-186.

[24] See 3.59, n. 26.

[25] *Transfer III* is chiastic inclusion to *Transfer I*, enclosing the *Measurements* and *Boundaries* clauses.

[26] The Aram. is the unusual *pael* pass. ptc. *mbny*, with the expanded meaning of "renovated, restored" (also in 3.79:2-3; 3.80:12-13); see Hoesterman 1992:7-15.

[27] I.e. the bottom floor.

[28] See 3.73, n. 16.

[29] The description is most elaborate. The earlier document mentioned only beams (3.75:3-4). The third bequest mentioned three doors and no windows (3.79:2-3).

[30] As Jehoishma's rights were expanded from usufruct to ownership, she was granted the further right to maintain the structure in her half of the courtyard without requiring specific permission.

[31] This was the newly constructed stairway mentioned in line 10. Rights to half a stairway meant shared rights with others using that stairway.

[32] Redundantly repeated at the beginning of a new line.

[33] I.e. stipulations.

[34] See 3.59, n. 26.

[35] Repeated twice in this paragraph, the reference to "gave at my death" was a feature of the inclusion that harked back to *Transfer I* where Anani affirmed that "I thought of you in my lifetime."

[36] See on *TAD* A2.3:5 (*EPE* B3) and 3.74:11. The reference to support as consideration in the concluding *Transfer* clause added a feature not materially required to effect the transaction but designed to strengthen the bequest by assimilating it to a bona fide sale; cf. *P. Münch*. 8.1-5, 24-25 (*EPE* D23), *P. Lond*. V 1729.16-33 (*EPE* D37) and Porten and Szubin 1987a:189-191.

[37] Alternately translate "(to exist) by my (own) means."

[38] These last two references to "gave" provide a second inclusion to *Transfer I* by adding to *Measurements* and *Boundaries* the stipulations of *Investiture II*.

[39] For this "just as ... also/so" construction, see Dan 6:23 and reference in *EPE* 240 n. 39.

[40] Since the bequest came into effect only after Anani's death, he had omitted reference to potential suit by himself; Porten-Szubin 1987a:187.

[41] To the earlier introduction of specified parties (partner-in-chattel and partner-in-realty) the scribe Haggai now added the guarantor (*ʾdrng* < Old Persian **ādranga-*); see Porten and Greenfield 1969:153-157; *GEA* 370.4. The trilogy recurs in the last three documents concerning

you suit (19)or process, or bring (suit) against your children after you,[42] or complain against you to prefect or lord,[43] or against your children after you.

Penalty
Whoever[44] shall bring against you suit (20)or process or complain against you or against your children shall give you a penalty[45] of silver, 30 *karsh*[46] by the stone(-weight)s of the king, pure silver,[47]

Reaffirmation
and you, (21)Jehoishma, likewise have right[48] and your children have right after you[49] and you may give (it) to whomever you love.[50]

Document validity
Moreover, they shall not be able to take out (22)against you a new or old document, but it is this document which I made[51] for you (that) is valid.[52]

Scribe and place
Haggai son of Shemaiah[53] wrote (23)this (22)document (23)in Elephantine the fortress at the instruction of Anani son of Azariah, the servitor of YHW the God.[54]

Witnesses
The witnesses herein:[55]
(2nd hand) witness Hoshaiah son of (24)Jathom[56];
(3rd hand) Zaccur son of Shillem[57];
(4th hand) witness Nathan son of Jehour[58];
(5th hand) witness Hoshaiah son of Nathan[59];
(25)(6th hand) witness Meshullam son of Mauzi[60];
(7th hand) Pilti son of Jaush (ERASURE: s[on of])[61];
(8th hand) Jashobiah son of Jedaniah[62];
(26)(9th hand) witness Haggai son of Mardu.[63]

Endorsement
(Verso)(27)Document (*sealing*) of a house which Anani son of Azariah the servitor wrote for Jehoishma his daughter.

Anani's estate (3.79:12; 3.80:27) and the guarantor alone appears as a potential recipient of payment along with the debtor's children in a loan contract and a deed of obligation (3.81:8-9; *TAD* B4.6:10).

[42] Omitted from the *Investiture* clause as premature, "your children after you" was pertinent when referring to suits initiated after the death of the benefactor; Porten and Szubin 1987a:186.

[43] The addition of a "complaint" clause is a common feature in the contracts by Haggai (3.79:12-13; 3.80:28), not shared by his contemporary Mauziah son of Nathan (contrast 3.66:11-15; 3.67:9-16; 3.73:12-16).

[44] I.e. among the above enumerated potential claimants.

[45] See 3.66, n. 38.

[46] Such a stiff penalty is found only for this and the following bequest (3.79:10) by Anani to Jehoishma.

[47] A notation used regularly by Haggai but not by every other scribe; see 3.59, n. 17.

[48] The *Reaffirmation* clause generally affirmed "it is yours" (see 3.59, n. 18).

[49] The scribe deferred until the *Reaffirmation* clause the rights of devolution and alienation (see next note) which took on meaning only after Anani's death, for only then did she take full possession of the property. See Porten and Szubin 1987a:187-188.

[50] See 3.61, n. 31.

[51] The usual word in this slot is "wrote" (3.64:12; 3.79:16-17). The unusual *ᶜbdt*, "I made" indicates that the document was being prepared for some future occasion, namely the death of the benefactor; Porten and Szubin 1987a:187-188.

[52] For the new-or-old document clause, see 3.61, n. 43.

[53] See 3.64, n. 41.

[54] See 3.70, n. 5.

[55] For the number of witnesses see 3.59, n. 34. There are eight here and in the following bequest (3.79:18-20).

[56] The second witness for Anani in 434 BCE (3.73:24), see 3.49, n. 18 (*EPE* B16).

[57] The last witness to a contract of Mahseiah in 446 BCE (3.64:20), he failed to preface his name with the word "witness."

[58] A witness for the grandsons of Mahseiah, he witnessed two more documents for Anani (see 3.68, n. 37).

[59] He was the author of a letter to Pilti, the sixth witness here, and possibly of two more (*TAD* A3.6:5; 3.7:1, 5; 3.8:1); Porten 1968:272-274. He was probably also identical with the person whose name is restored in the Collection Account — Hosh[aiah son of Nathan] son of Hoshaiah son of Zephaniah (*TAD* C3.15:7) — and his father Nathan with the debtor Nathan son of Hosea in 407 BCE (*TAD* B4.5:1); Porten 2001:342.

[60] He was first witness in another document of Anani (where his father's name was written Mauziah [3.80:34]) and a contributor to YHW (*TAD* C3.15:112).

[61] Father of the female contributor Jaḥmol (*TAD* C3.15:92) and recipient of a letter from Hoshaiah, the fourth witness above, he failed to preface his name with the word witness."

[62] The only witness not to appear elsewhere, he failed to preface his name with the word "witness."

[63] Witnessed two more documents (3.79:20; 3.81:14).

REFERENCES

Text and translation: *TAD* B3.10; *EPE* B43. *EPE*; *GEA*; Hoesterman 1992; Porten 1968; 1990; 2001; Porten and Greenfield 1969; Porten and Szubin 1987a.

DOWRY ADDENDUM (3.79)
(9 March, 402 BCE)

Bezalel Porten

Less than a year and one-half after Anani had written for his daughter a bequest in contemplation of death, he upgraded it to one to take effect immediately. Assigning title to courtyard and stairway, Anani had no need to spell out specific rights, as earlier (3.78:13-15). Omission of the right of alienation to anyone other than her own children, however (lines 8-9), indicated that Anani intended the property to remain a family estate. Uniquely designating it an "after-gift" to her marriage contract (line 7), i.e. a dowry addendum to which her husband naturally enjoyed rights of usufruct, he had to reassure her against claims of reclamation by himself (lines 9-11) and removal by his heirs and associated parties (lines 11-15), whether in his lifetime or after his death. Any such attempts were subject to a stiff thirty *karsh* penalty. The eight witnesses were Jewish and all but one appeared elsewhere (lines 18-20).

Date

(Recto)(1)On the 20th of Adar, that is day 8 of Choiak, year 3 of Artaxerxes the king,[1]

Parties

then said Anani son of Azariah, a servitor of (2)YHW the God in Elephantine the fortress, to Jehoishma his daughter, saying:

Transfer I

I gave you

Object

a[2] house.[3]

Description

Renovated[4] is (the) lower house[5] — containing beams[6] (3)and 3 doors[7] — that is the southern room. Built is its stairway and its court yard,[8] that is its gate (through which) to go out.

Boundaries

And this is[9] its boundaries:[10]

east of it (4)the treasury of the king adjoins wall to wall the protecting (wall) which the Egyptians built[11]; west of it is the gate of yours (through which) to go out and the street of (5)the king is (in) between[12]; above it the house of the shrine of the god adjoins it wall to wall and the wall of its house adjoins it, (6)that is the large room of mine, (5)wall to wall;[13] (6)below it the house of Ḥor son of Peṭeese,[14] a gardener of Khnum the god, adjoins it wall to wall.

Transfer II

(7)This house whose boundaries are written in this document — I, Anani son of Azariah, gave it to you (as) an after-gift[15] (ERASURE: *t[o your] docum[ent] of wifehood*) written on your document of wifehood) since it is not written on your document of wifehood (8)with Anani son of Haggai son of Meshullam son of Busasa.[16]

Investiture

You, Jehoishma my daughter, have right to it from

[1] This is one of the few intact documents with a perfect, non-problematic synchronism for daytime redaction (also 3.59; 3.66; 3.73; 3.74); Porten 1990:20-21.

[2] For the indefinite article written as the number "one" or the cipher "1," see 3.59, n. 7.

[3] For "house" = room, see 3.73, n. 8.

[4] For the unusual *pael* pass. ptc. *mbny*, with the expanded meaning of "renovated, restored," see 3.78, n. 26.

[5] I.e. the bottom floor.

[6] See 3.73, n. 16.

[7] The description here is not identical with that given some fifteen months earlier. There it mentioned three windows and one door, shutting and opening (3.78:13).

[8] The scribe dropped the Eg. word for courtyard (*tḥyt* [3.75:5, 10, 13; 3.78:4, 13, 15]), using only the Aram.

[9] Grammatical error for "these are."

[10] For this caption see 3.60, n. 19.

[11] Awareness of the Eg. construction was still present. Rather than equating this construction with the "divine way," as fifteen months earlier (3.78:8-9), the scribe here indicated that the royal treasury, present in 420 BCE (3.75:6-7), had not been torn down, but was foreshortened on its western side.

[12] In the previous document the wall of Anani's large room was given on the west (3.78:11). Here the boundary was the implied courtyard with the specified exit gate to the street. Earlier, Jehoishma was granted only half the courtyard and it was necessary to spell out her right of exit therefrom (3.78:14-15). Here she was implicitly given complete dominion over the whole courtyard (line 3), no specification of rights was necessary, and reference to the courtyard as a boundary would further confirm her ownership thereof; see Porten and Szubin 1987c:235.

[13] The language is awkward but must mean that the shrine of the god adjoined the rooms of both Jehoishma and Anani.

[14] He was the same neighbor as earlier, but reference to the stairway was omitted (3.78:10).

[15] For the Old Persian loanword *psšdt* < **pasča dāti-*, see *GEA* 372.57. The gift was to be considered as an addition to Jehoishma's dowry (given to her by her adoptive brother Zaccur son of Meshullam [3.76]), to which her husband Anani son of Haggai would have rights of usufruct (cf. 3.80:9-9a, 17-18), just as Jezaniah son of Uriah had in the property his father-in-law Mahseiah bestowed upon his wife Mibtahiah (3.60.4).

[16] This four-generation genealogy is quite unique (see also 3.80:2, 11 [abbreviated] and 3.64, n. 7). The great grandfather's name is unknown in the Hebrew onomasticon; cf. Zadok 1988:104. It has been suggested that Busasa was born abroad and entered Egypt with his parents at the time of the Persian conquest; Cohen 1966-67:104.

this {this}[17] day forever[18] (9)and your children have right after you.[19]

Waiver of reclamation

(ERASURE: I) I, Anani son of Azariah the servitor, shall not be able to say:

"I gave it to you in affection (as) an after-gift to (10)your (9)document (10)of wifehood until later."[20]

Penalty I

If I say:

"I shall reclaim (it) from you,"

I shall be obligated[21] and I shall give Jehoishma a penalty[22] of silver, 30 *karsh*[23] (11)pure (10)silver[24] (11)by the stone(-weight)s of the king,

Reaffirmation I

and you likewise have right[25] to this house whose boundaries are written above,[26] in my lifetime and at my death.[27]

Waiver of suit

Moreover, (12)son of mine or daughter of mine, brother or sister, partner-in-chattel or partner-in-land or guarantor[28] shall not be able (to sue).[29]

Penalty II

Whoever[30] shall bring against you suit or process or complain against you (13)or against your children to prefect or lord to remove[31] this house from before you in my lifetime[32] or at my death shall be obligated and shall give you (14)or your children a penalty of silver, 30 *karsh* by the stone(-weight)s of the king,

Reaffirmation II

and you likewise have right to this house whose boundaries (15)are written in this document.[33]

Document validity

And should he go into a suit,[34] he shall not prevail.[35] Moreover, they shall not be able to take out against you a new or old document in the name of (16)this (15)house (16)whose (ERASURE: w[ritten]) boundaries above is[36] written in this document. (That document) which he shall take out is false. It is this document which I, Anani, wrote for you (17)(that) is valid.[37]

Scribe and place

Haggai son of Shemaiah[38] wrote this document in Elephantine at the instruction of Anani son of Azariah, the servitor of YHW the God.[39]

Witnesses

(18)The witnesses herein:[40]

---

17 Scribal dittography.

18 The bequest was not to take effect upon Anani's death but immediately; see further 3.61, n. 29.

19 Alienation to a beneficiary or to an unrelated third party was omitted because Anani intended the property to be treated as a family estate to be passed on only to his daughter's legitimate heirs. See Porten and Szubin 1987c:235.

20 The formulation of this *Waiver of reclamation* clause follows most closely the pattern in Jehoishma's document of wifehood (3.76:40-42) with a double unique addition ("after-gift" and "until later"). The second addition may have come to dispel the concern that the newly acquired rights to the other half of the courtyard and stairway might be phased (usufruct now and title upon death) just as were the original rights, made at the time of her marriage (3.75) and subsequently (3.78). Nothing was to be "later"; it was all now.

21 See 3.73, n. 27.

22 See 3.66, n. 38.

23 In the only other conveyance with such a clause, the penalty was just ten *karsh* (3.73:20-22), but thirty *karsh* is also the penalty here (line 14) and in the earlier document for violation of the *Waiver* clause by heirs or related parties (3.78:19-20).

24 For this designation favored by the scribe Haggai, see 3.59, n. 17.

25 When all was said and done, Jehoishma had only shared rights (with her husband [see note 15 above]) and not "absolute, unconditional, fee simple ownership;" see Porten and Szubin 1987c:236-237.

26 See 3.59, n. 26.

27 Most natural in one of the *Transfer* clauses, either as a single phrase (3.61:3), or distributed between two clauses ("I thought of you in my life time ... I gave/released you at my death" [3.74:3-4; 3.78:2, 16-18]), this phrase is unusual here and in the *Penalty* clause below (line 13).

28 This trilogy is found in the last three documents concerning Anani's estate (3.78:18; 3.80:27).

29 The verb was omitted by oversight; Porten and Szubin 1987b:64.

30 Of the above enumerated parties.

31 This is one of two instances in the contracts where a complaint is spelled out. The other is in a loan contract and asserted that a security is seized illegally (3.69:13). Here the complaint sought to "remove" the disputed property from the defendant, probably for alleged breach of contract (see Porten and Szubin 1987c:237). A complaint differed from a suit, which sought to make the loss retroactive (see 3.61, n. 55). The fear of "removal" is also addressed in a document of wifehood (3.63:35). The same formula is found in a Ptolemaic Demotic contract of matrimonial arrangements (*P. Berlin* 13593.7-8 [*EPE* C33]).

32 A suit by an heir, beneficiary, or associated party, challenging title, would normally be entered in the name of the alienor and brought only after his death (see on 3.59:8). But an attempt at "removal," as here, depended upon changing circumstances and might be entered at any time; see Porten and Szubin 1987c:237.

33 See 3.59, n. 26.

34 I.e. take legal action.

35 This statement occurs twice elsewhere and both times it concludes with the statement "while this document is in your hand" (3.61:22; 3.69:19-20).

36 Singular mistakenly written for plural.

37 For this clause, see 3.78:22 and 3.61, n. 44.

38 See 3.64, n. 41.

39 See 3.70, n. 5.

40 The number of witnesses in Anani's bequests is double that normally required; see 3.59, n. 34.

(2nd hand) witness Nathan son of Jehour[41];
(3nd hand) witness Menahem son of Gaddul[42];
(4th hand) witness Ahio son of Nathan[43];
(19)(5th hand) witness Nahum the houseborn[44];
(6th hand) witness Nathan son of Mauziah[45];
(7th hand) witness Shammua son of Peluliah[46];
(20)(8th hand) witness Haggai son of Mardu[47];
(9th hand) witness Jedaniah son of Gemariah.[48]

Endorsement

(Verso)(21)Document (*sealing*) of a house which Anani son of Azariah wrote for Jeh[o]ishma his daughter.

[41] He is a witness in Anani's last three documents and in the last document of Mahseiah's grandsons; see 3.68, n. 37.

[42] He witnessed four documents; see 3.66, n. 42.

[43] He appeared in three other documents; once in a list where he was followed directly by Nathan son of Mauziah, here the witness after the following; see 3.67, n. 39.

[44] Here the fourth of eight witnesses, he also appeared in three other documents — second of four (3.80:34); third of four (3.81:14), where the fourth and last was Haggai son of Mardu, here the seventh witness (line 20); and last of four (*TAD* B4.6:20), where the first witness was Nathan son of Mauziah, who followed him here. His epithet is unique. Was he a(n emancipated) houseborn slave lacking patronymic?

[45] As noted, he appeared elsewhere with two of the witnesses from here, Ahio and Nahum.

[46] The only witness not to appear elsewhere.

[47] Elsewhere the last of eight witnesses (3.78:26) and the last of four (3.81:14); he must have been a junior.

[48] The leader of the Jewish community (see 3.46, n. 3 [*EPE* B13]), Jedaniah waited to sign last, as he had done elsewhere (3.76:44).

REFERENCES

Text and translation: *TAD* B3.11; *EPE* B44. Cohen 1966-67; *EPE*; *GEA*; Porten 1990; Porten and Szubin 1987b; 1987c; *TAD*; Zadok 1988.

SALE OF APARTMENT TO SON-IN-LAW (3.80)
(13 December 402 BCE)

Bezalel Porten

Barely nine months after Anani's final bequest to his daughter Jehoishma, he and his wife sold their remaining share in the house (the large room plus appurtenances [151⅓ square cubits]) to their son-in-law Anani son of Haggai for thirteen shekels (also denominated in Ionian staters), a price that took into account the father's building improvements. The document was remarkable for the fact that after writing 9½ lines, the scribe erased his last unfinished line and began the text anew, making numerous slight changes in formulation. Certain terms were employed to perfect title to the property, originally acquired from a couple who held it in adverse possession: (1) Particular prominence was given to Tamet (here written Tapmet and even Tapmemet [line 33]) by the titles accorded her (lines 2, 11, 24) and it was made to appear as if the house which Anani alone had bought from Bagazushta and his wife (3.72:2-3) was actually acquired jointly by Anani and Tapmet (lines 12, 32). (2) The original owner of the house was pointedly called a "hereditary-property-holder" (lines 4-5). (3) Special reference was made to the fact that Jehoishma's existing share in the house had been an after-gift on her document of wifehood. In fact, it was the imprecision as to whether this had been given originally to Jehoishma or directly to her husband Anani which led the scribe to rewrite the document from scratch (cf. lines 9-9a with 17-18). The son-in-law was given complete right of alienation (lines 22-24) and a suit or complaint by heirs or related parties was subject to a twenty *karsh* penalty (lines 24-31). The original sale document of Bagazushta was handed over (lines 31-32) and the usual four witnesses appended their signatures (lines 33-34).

Date

(Recto)(1)On the 12th of Thoth, year 4 of Artaxerxes the king,[1]

Parties

then said Anani son of Azariah, a servitor of YHW and lady Tapmet[2] (2)his wife, a servitor[3] of YHW the God dwelling[4] [a] (in) Elephantine the fortress, to Anani son of Haggai son of Meshullam son of Busasa[5] an Aramean of (3){of} Elephantine the fort-

[a] Exod 25:8; 29:46; Num 5:3; Deut 33:16; 1 Kgs 8:12; Isa 33:5; 57:15; Ps 135:21; etc.

[1] Most of the contracts at the end of the century (413 BCE on) bore only an Eg. date (3.79; *TAD* B4.5; 4.6; 5.5; 7.1; 7.2), Porten 1990.16-19.

[2] The form of Tamet's name preferred by the scribe Haggai (see 3.74, n. 5).

[3] Manumitted at the death of Meshullam (3.74:3-4), she no longer bore the slave designation *šmh*, "her name." Instead, she was given the feminine form of Anani's title (*lḥnh*), much as the wife of the prophet Isaiah was called *nbyʾh*, "prophetess" (Isa 8:3). The titles bestowed on Tamet here and below (lines 11, 24) were designed to give her status and thereby perfect title to the property which Anani had acquired from Bagazushta who held it in adverse possession.

[4] It is further striking that this quality of divine immanence was attached to the title given Tamet and had never been attached to the title of Anani which was repeated in each of his documents (see 3.70, n. 5). The same term *škn*, indicating YHW's residence at Elephantine, was used to apply to his presence in Jerusalem (Ezra 6:12).

[5] For this unique four-generation genealogy see 3.64, n. 7 and 3.79, n. 16. In line 11 it was abbreviated to three generations by omission of the name of the grandfather Meshullam.

ress of the detachment of Nabukudurri,[6] saying:

Transfer I
I, 1 (and) Tapmet daughter of Patou,[7] all (told) two — we sold and gave you[8]

Object I
our house

Pedigree I
which (4)we bought[9] for silver from Bagazushta son of Friyana/Palliya[10] the Caspian — that is the house of *Ynbwly*[11] son of Misday(a), a Caspian who in Elephantine is (5)hereditary-property-holder,[12] —

Price I
and you gave us the price of our house (in) silver, one, that is 1, *karsh*,[13] three, that is 3, shekels — (in) Ionian silver 6 staters, (6)one shekel[14] —

Satisfaction I
and our heart was satisfied[b] herein that there did not remain to us (incumbent) upon[15] you (any) of the price.[16]

Measurements I
This is[17] the measurements of the house which we sold (7)and gave you:[18]

from east to west {to west}, length, 16 cubits, 2 h(ands)[19] by the measuring rod; (8)and from below to above, width, 5 cubits, 2 h(ands) by the measuring rod; IN AREA, 150 cubits.[20]

Boundaries I
And behold, this is (9)the boundaries of the house which we sold and gave you:[21]
east of it is the house which I gave you[22] (as) an after-gift (9a)(ERASURE: on the document of wifehood of Jehoishma)

Date
(10)On the 12th of Thoth, year 4 of Artaxerxes, the king,

Parties
then said Anani son of Azariah, a servitor of YHW (11)the God, 1 (and) lady
Tapmet his wife, CHIEF OF THE BELOVED of Meshullam son of Zaccur,[23] all (told) 2 as one mouth[24] to Anani son of Haggai son of Busasa, (12)saying:

Transfer II
We sold and gave you

Object II
our house

Pedigree II
which we bought from Bagazushta son of Fri-

[b] Ruth 3:7

[6] Five different persons were affiliated with the detachment of this person bearing an Akk. name (*TAD* B4.5:1-2 [407]; 7.2:2-3 [401]; our document and 3.81:1-2 [402]; *TAD* B4.6:2-3 [400]). This was one of three detachments attested for the last decade of the century — Var[yaza]ta (3.79:2 [410]) and Marya (*TAD* D2.12:3 [403], B7.2:3 [401]).

[7] With a patronymic, Tamet was apparently born free and sold into slavery by/with her father.

[8] The regular sale formula; see 3.72:3-4.

[9] Only Anani not Tamet, "bought" the house. He later bestowed upon her a room in it (3.72-3.73).

[10] The non-Semitic name of the father Bagazushta was given in 437 BCE as Bazu (3.72:2). Was the name incorrectly recalled or was one of the names that of a grandfather?

[11] In the earlier document this Caspian was called *ʾpwly* (3.72:4).

[12] This Caspian here was given the same designation (*mhḥsn*) as that applied to Mahseiah when he transferred to his daughter Mibtahiah a piece of property for which he had no evidence of acquisition (3.61). His status had to serve as evidence of his title. Similarly, Anani had acquired the property of *Ynbwly* from Bagazushta without evidence of title and so the strongest statement he could make for his son-in-law as purchaser was to assert that *Ynbwly* himself had held the property as part of his ancestral estate. Interestingly, he was presented as currently (*hw*) holding the designation. See Szubin and Porten 1982:4-5.

[13] For the numerical repetition, see 3.60, n. 36.

[14] The Ionian stater appears only at the end of the century as the equivalent of two shekels (line 14; *TAD* A4.2:12; B4.5:3; 4.6:7). Anani was here selling for thirteen shekels two-thirds of the property which he had bought thirty-two years earlier for a negotiated price of fourteen shekels (3.72:6). The almost four-shekel difference was due at least in part to his property improvements.

[15] Aram. *ʾštʾr ʿl* = Arabic *baqiya ʿalā* in a 10th century parchment probably from Aswan (*P. Or. Inst.* 10552r.5 [*EPE* F2]).

[16] This explanatIon of the reason for satisfaction takes us back to a pre-legal meaning of satisfaction after a full meal (cf. Ruth 3:7); cf. too, the Demotic receipt of dowry, "I received them from you; they are complete without any remainder; my heart is satisfied with them" (*P. Berlin* 13593.7 [*EPE* C33]); Westbrook 1991b:222.

[17] Singular instead of plural "these are."

[18] See 3.61, n. 10.

[19] Aram. has the single letter *kaph*, which probably abbreviates *kp*, "hand" (measured from the tip of the middle finger to the wrist joint) = $\frac{1}{3}$ cubit; see also 3.73:7 and *TAD* B 177.

[20] $16\frac{2}{3} \times 5\frac{2}{3} = 94\frac{4}{9}$. The difference was due to (1) the greater width of the apartment of Tamet ($7\frac{1}{3}$ cubits [3.73:7]), which meant that one had to add the sum of $18\frac{1}{3}$ cubits (= $11 \times 1\frac{2}{3}$); (2) the calculated sum of just over 38 cubits for the other half of the courtyard and stairway, even though these were not mentioned. See *TAD* B 177 and Fig. 6.

[21] See 3.60, n. 19.

[22] Actually Anani gave the house to his daughter Jehoishma, with implied rights of usufruct for her husband (see lines 17-18); and this may have been the reason he stopped here. Needing to make other changes, the scribe decided to rewrite the document from scratch.

[23] In the rewrite Tamet was not designated "servitor" but *prypt*, Old Persian **friya-pati-*, which means something like "chief concubine" (*GEA* 372.58). As the scribe reached back into the past in the first version to designate the earlier owner *Ynbwly* "hereditary property-holder," he revealed here for the first time Tamet's preferred status in the household of her former master Meshullam. The Aram. equivalent is in line 24.

[24] I.e. of one accord. Cf. the parallel Demotic phrase "total 2 people, who speak (with) one mouth" (*P. Moscow* 135.1 [*EPE* C30]).

yana/Palliya the Caspian[25] —

Description I

a lower house,[26] renovated,[27] (13)containing beams,[28] windows and 2 doors; renovated is (the) lower house, that is the large room of mine[29] —

Price II

and you gave us its price[30] (14)(in) silver, one *karsh*, 3 shekels — Ionian silver in the amount of 6 staters, 1 shekel —

Satisfaction II

and our heart was satisfied with the price which (15)you gave us.[31]

Measurements II

This is the measurements of the house which we sold and gave you:

from east to west, length, (16)16 (15)cubits, (16)2 h(ands) by the measuring rod;

and from above to below, width, 5 cubits, 2 h(ands);

(ERASURE: in) IN AREA, 151 cubits 1 h(and).[32]

Boundaries II

This is (17)its boundaries, (those of) the house which we sold and gave you:[33]

(ERASURE: from east) east of it your house,[34] you,[35] Anani son of Haggai, which we gave[36] (18)to Jehoishma our daughter (as) an after-gift on her document of wifehood, adjoins wall to wall;

west of it is the Temple (19)of YHW[37] and the street of the king is between them;

above it the house of Parnu son of Ziliya and Mrdava his brother adjoins it (20)wall to wall;[38]

below it is the house of Paḥe/Pakhoi and Pamet his brother, boatmen of the (rough) waters, sons of Tawe,[39] (21)and the street of the king is between them.

c Esth 2:9

Description II

And its 1 window is open toward[40] the large room.[41] And its gateway is open toward the street of the king; (22)from there you may go out and come in.

Investiture[42]

This house whose measurements and whose boundaries is written in this document — you, Anani,[43] (23)have right to it from this day and forever and your children have right after you and (so does) anyone whom you give it to lovingly[44] or (24)whom you sell it to for silver.[45]

Waiver of suit[46]

I, Anani, and Tapmet[47] my wife, who was THE INNER ONE[48] c of Meshullam son of Zaccur[49] and he

[25] The scribe did not repeat the additional notice that the house had belonged to *Ynbwly*, but he did add a property *Description*.

[26] I.e. bottom floor.

[27] See 3.78, n. 26.

[28] See 3.73, n. 16.

[29] In 434 BCE Anani had given Tamet half of his large room, which half he had measured at 11 x 7⅓ cubits. The document alternated between speaking of the property as "our house" (lines 3, 5, 12) and "the large room of mine."

[30] A variation on the language above ("the price of our house" [line 5]).

[31] Above the scribe wrote "herein that there did not remain to us from you (any) of the price" [line 6]).

[32] The AREA measurements increased from 150 cubits (line 8) to 151⅓ cubits.

[33] The formulatlon of the *Boundaries* clause is grammatically awkward, blending two distinct formulae; see 3.60, n. 20.

[34] The formulation "your house" corrected the earlier "which I gave you." Given to Jehoishma, it was her husband's by implicit or explicit right of usufruct; see Jezaniah's document granting him building rights in the house of his wife Mibtahiah (3.62).

[35] For addition of the independent pronoun as emphatic, see on *TAD* A3.3:11 (*EPE* B8) and 3.60, n. 17.

[36] It was only Anani who had given (3.79:7-8) the property to Jehoishma, as was correctly stated in the version above (line 9).

[37] This was the Temple that was destroyed by the Khnum priests in connivance with the Persian Chief Vidranga in the summer of 410 BCE (3.51). Some time after late November, 407 BCE, the governors of Judah and Samaria gave their qualified approval for its reconstruction (3.52). Does this routine boundary description, as well as Tamet's title above ("servitor of YHW the God dwelling [in] Elephantine" [line 2]) mean that the Temple had indeed been, or was being, rebuilt?

[38] The previous neighbor here had been Shatibara, father of the woman, who together with her husband Bagazushta, had originally sold the property to Anani (3.72:2, 1-8; 3.73:11, and probably 3.75:7). Had he sold his property to the brothers bearing Iranian names (perhaps also Caspians) or had he like *Ynbwly*, departed and so the property was appropriated as abandoned?

[39] These Eg. boatmen, apparently filiated to their mother, shared the southern border of Anani's house with an Eg. gardener of Khnum (3.75:7-8; 3.78:10; 3.79:6).

[40] I.e. it looks into.

[41] It is not clear how this "1 window" relates to the "windows" mentioned above in line 13.

[42] Son-in-law Anani was given full rights of alienation — to heirs ("your children after you"), beneficiaries ("any-one whom you give it to lovingly"), and purchasers ("sell it to for silver). See Szubin and Porten 1983a:44.

[43] For the addition of the name, see on 3.59:11-12.

[44] For all these phrases and formulae, see on 3.61:9-10.

[45] The explicit right to "sell for silver" appears only in this document.

[46] The scribe has unusually compacted three statements in the *Waiver* clause (we shall not sue you; we shall not sue your heirs, buyers, or beneficiaries; our heirs or associated parties shall not sue you [lines 24-27]), followed by a single *Penalty* clause (lines 27-31). See Porten and Szubin 1987b:64.

[47] See 3.59, n. 29.

[48] Aram. *gwʾ* = *gwʾh*, with the same meaning as Old Persian *prypt* (line 11).

[49] This special status is strikingly reminiscent of the "insider" (*pnymh*) status which a princess (*bt mlk*) or consort (*šgl*) enjoyed in the royal household (Ps 45:10, 14). Cf. also Middle and New Persian *andarōn*, "the inner chamber," i.e. the women's quarter (Esth 2:9) (S. Shaked orally).

gave her to me (25)for wifehood[50] — we shall not be able to bring against you suit or process in the name of[51] this house which we sold and gave you and (for which) you gave us its price (26)(in) silver and our heart was satisfied herein. Moreover, we shall not be able to bring (suit) against your sons or your daughters or (anyone) whom you give it to for silver or lovingly.[52] Moreover, (27)son of ours or daughter, brother or sister of ours, partner-in-chattel or partner-in-land or guarantor[53] of ours shall (26)not (27)be able (to sue).[54]

Penalty

Whoever shall bring against you suit[55] or bring (suit) (28)against your sons or against a man whom you give (it) to or whoever shall complain[56] against you to prefect or lord or judge[57] in the name of this house who(se) measurements (29)is written above[58] or whoever shall take out against you a new or old document in the name of this house[59] which we sold and gave you shall be obligated[60] (30)and shall give you or your children a penalty[61] of silver, 20 *karsh*[62] by the stone(-weight)s of the king, pure silver,[63]

Reaffirmation

and the house is (likewise) yours or your children's (31)or his whom you give (it) to lovingly.[64]

Document transfer

Moreover, we gave you the old document which Bagazushta wrote for us, the document of purchase/sale (of the house) (32)which he sold us and (for which) we gave him its payment (BLANK SPACE) (in) silver.[65]

Scribe and place

Haggai son of Shemaiah wrote this document in Elephantine the fortress (33)at the instruction of Anani, the servitor of YHW the God, (and) Tapmemet[66] daughter of Patou, his wife, all (told) 2 as one mouth.

Witnesses[67]

(1st hand) witness Meshullam (34)son of Mauziah[68];
(2nd hand) witness Nahum the houseborn[69];
(3rd hand) witness Nathan son of Jehour[70];
(4th hand) Magir.[71]

Endorsement

(Verso)(35)Document (*sealing*) of a house which Anani son of Azariah and Tapmet his wife sold.[72]

---

[50] It is not readily evident why the scribe at this point described Tamet's special status in the household of Meshullam.

[51] See 3.60, n. 34.

[52] The scribe chiastically reversed the word order of the *Investiture* clause (lovingly: silver:: silver: lovingly), omitted the word "sell," and subsumed both modes of transfer under the generic term "give."

[53] For this trilogy of associated parties, see 3.78, n. 41.

[54] The scribe fell into ellipsis and failed to complete the sentence.

[55] See 3.61, n. 35.

[56] This feature was introduced into the *Penalty* clause without having been mentioned in the *Waiver* clause. See 3.60, n. 11.

[57] This triumvirate of officials appears also in *TAD* B4.6:14.

[58] See 3.59, n. 26.

[59] See 3.61, nn. 42-43. It is clear from the incorporation of this provision in the *Penalty* clause that the party expected to produce such a document was one of those mentioned in the *Waiver* clause.

[60] See 3.73, n. 27.

[61] See 3.66, n. 38.

[62] This was the penalty for suit in the original sale document for this property (3.72:15, 18); see further 3.59, n. 15.

[63] A term regularly used by the scribe Haggai (see 3.59, n. 17).

[64] The clause is elliptical, omitting "sell/give for silver" explicitly recorded in the *Investiture* and *Waiver* clauses. See Szubin and Porten 1983a:44.

[65] For the standard procedure of *Document transfer*, see 3.61, n. 64. The scribe did not know the amount of the original sale and so left the space blank.

[66] The expanded (and incorrect?) spelling here of Tamet's name would accord with the enhanced status given her elsewhere in this document (lines 2 11, 24).

[67] The scribe omitted the customary heading, "The witnesses herein" (so too in 3.66). Four was the customary number of witnesses for sales; see 3.69, n. 27.

[68] He was the fifth witness in an earlier document of Anani (3.78:25) and a contributor to YHW (*TAD* C3.15:112). In both documents the father's name was abbreviated to Mauzi.

[69] He witnessed three other documents (see 3.79, n. 44), in one of which he followed the next witness, Nathan.

[70] Nine months earlier Nathan appeared as the first witness and Nahum as the fourth (3.79:18-19); see further 3.68, n. 37.

[71] Lacking patronymic, this witness with a Babylonian name appeared only here.

[72] Unusually, the endorsement lacked the name of the alienee, Anani son of Haggai; see 3.59, n. 44.

REFERENCES

Text and translation: *TAD* B3.12; *EPE* B45. *EPE*; *GEA*; Porten 1990; Szubin and Porten 1982; 1983a; Porten and Szubin 1987b; *TAD*.

LOAN OF GRAIN (3.81)

(2-31 December 402 BCE)

Bezalel Porten

This is the only loan document for grain and we cannot tell for certain whether it was drawn up after Anani son of Haggai bought his in-laws' apartment or before (3.80), since it lacked day date. In the middle of December, in the first month of the Egyptian year, Anani went to Syene to borrow from the Egyptian-named Aramean, Pakhnum son of Besa, 2 *peras* 3 seah of emmer (approximately a double ration for a month) which he promised to repay as soon as he received his government ration (lines 2-4). If he failed to repay within twenty days, he was given a one *karsh* penalty (lines 5-8). Should he die before making payment, then the burden fell on his children or guarantors. Should they not pay the fine, then Pakhnum was entitled to seize as security for payment any item of Anani's property, wherever found (lines 8-12). Though the document was silent about repayment of the grain, the terminology ("penalty," "without suit") does not argue for conversion of a loan in kind to a loan in silver. Though drawn up in Syene by an Aramean scribe, the document's requisite four witness were well-known Jews (lines 12-14).

Date

(Recto)(1)(In the) month of Thoth, year 4 of Artaxerxes the king,[1]

Place

then in Syene the fortress,[2]

Parties

said Anani son of Haggai son of Meshullam,[3] (2)a Jew of the detachment of Nabukudurri,[4] to Pakhnum son of Besa,[5] an Aramean of Syene of that detachment likewise, saying:

Loan

I came to you (3)in your house[6] in Syene the fortress and borrowed from you and you gave me[7] emmer,[8] 2 *peras*, 3 seahs.[9]

Repayment

Afterwards,[10] I, Anani son of Haggai,[11] (4)shall pay and give you that emmer, e(mmer), 2 *p(eras)*, 3 seahs from the ration which will be given me from the treasury of the king.[12]

Penalty

(5)And if I do not pay and give you that emmer which above is written[13] when the ration is given me (6)from the (store-)house of the king,[14] afterwards I, Anani, shall be obligated[15] and shall give you silver, a penalty[16] of one, 1, *karsh*[17] pure silver. (7)Afterwards, I, Anani, shall pay and give you the penalty which is above written within 20, that is twenty, days,[18] (8)without suit.[19]

[1] This was one of seven contracts from the end of the century that gave only an Eg. date and one of four contracts that, in Eg. fashion, gave only the month and no day date (3.66:1; 3.76:1; *TAD* B7.1:1); Porten 1990:18-19. If the thirteen shekels paid for his father-in-law's house (3.80:1, 5) emptied Anani's coffers, then this document was drawn up between December 14 and 31.

[2] The document was written in the town of the Aramean creditor (line 3) by an Aramean scribe (line 12); see on further 3.66, n. 2.

[3] He appears regularly in his last three documents in a three- and four-generation genealogy (3.79:8; 3.80:2, 11).

[4] See 3.80, n. 6.

[5] Eg. names borne by Arameans were characteristic of the correspondents in the Makkibanit letters (*TAD* A2.1-7).

[6] This opening occurs in the first contract of the Mibtahiah archive (see 3.59, n. 6).

[7] The opening statement in loans of silver is much more laconic (see 3.69, n. 4).

[8] This was the grain widely cultivated in Egypt during the Persian period; Porten 1968:83.

[9] The value of the *peras* is uncertain; the largest subdivision so far known was four seahs (*TAD* C13:37); Porten 1983:569. One seah was roughly ten quarts; Porten 1968:71.

[10] Rare in contracts, this word recurs here five times (lines 3, 6, 7, 8, 10); see 3.62, n. 18.

[11] See 3.59, n. 29.

[12] Two Egyptian Aramaic texts from the end of the fifth century record royal grain disbursements, one of barley designated "ration" (*ptpʾ* [*TAD* C3.14:41; *GEA* 373.68]; see also B5.5:7-8, 10) as here and another of emmer designated "allotment" (*prsʾ*) (*TAD* C3.26:4-19). The latter term was usually reserved for payment in silver (*TAD* A2.3:8; B4.2:6). Unfortunately for the understanding of our text, the disbursements were always calculated in ardabs and the ratio of the *peras* to the ardab has not been determined. The most frequent emmer ration was 2½ ardabs and multiples thereof (5, 10, 15, 25). An ardab was three seahs and there were at least four seahs in a *peras*, so the loan here was about four ardabs (or more), i.e. something like a double monthly ration. The loan was interest-free if repaid within a month, i.e. at the time of the monthly ration distribution.

[13] This expression recurs here six times (lines 5, 7, 8, 9, 10, 11-12); see 3.59, n. 26.

[14] Apparently, "treasury" (line 4) and "(store-)house" were synonymous; Porten 1968:60.

[15] See 3.73, n. 27.

[16] Since this term was used only to connote a monetary fine (see 3.66, n. 38), it would be strange to find it here being used for substitution repayment of the loan in silver rather than grain. Still, the document is reticent about the obligation to repay the loan despite the penalty.

[17] For the numerical repetition, see 3.60, n. 36. The penalty was the smallest recorded; see 3.59, n. 15. There is no data available that would indicate the relationship of the penalty to the value of the loan.

[18] The scribe composed a whole additional sentence to state that the fine was to be paid within twenty days of receipt of rations.

[19] This expression invariably occurs after penalties (see 3.61, n. 15) and is further evidence that the one *karsh* sum was not meant as debt repayment.

Obligation of heirs
And if I die and have not yet paid[20] and given you the silver of yours which is above written, afterwards my children (9)or my guarantors[21] shall pay you your silver which is above written.

Security
And if my children or my guarantors do not pay you (10)this silver which is above written, afterwards you, Pakhnum, have right to my security[22] to seize (it) and you may take for yourself from (among) (11)a house of bricks, slave or handmaiden, bronze or iron utensils, which you will find of mine in Elephantine or in Syene or in the province, raiment or grain until you are paid your silver which above (12)is written without suit.[23]

Scribe and place
Shaweram son of Eshemram son of Eshemshezib[24] wrote this document in Syene the fortress at the instruction of (13)Anani son of (ERASURE: Meshullam)[25] Haggai son of Meshullam.

Witnesses
The witnesses herein:[26]
(2nd hand) witness Menahem son of Shallum[27];
(3rd hand) witness Haggai[28];
(4th hand) (14)witness Nahum the houseborn[29];
(5th hand) witness Haggai son of Mardu.[30]

Endorsement
(Verso)(15)[Do]cument of grain [which Anani son of Haggai] son of Meshullam [wrote] for Pakhnum son of Besa.

[20] A provision typical of loan contracts (3.69:14); see further 3.59, n. 20 and 3.73, n. 32.
[21] See 3.78, n. 41. It is surprising to find this recently introduced Iranian word so acclimatized to Aram. that it could take a possessive suffix ending the first person (ʾ*drngy*) and in the third person (ʾ[*drn*]*gyky* [*TAD* B4.6:10]).
[22] See 3.69:9.
[23] For the right to seize personal property as security to force debt payment, see 3.69, n. 14.
[24] This Aramean scribe appears only here.
[25] The scribe initially wrote the name of Anani's grandfather, then erased it and wrote right over it the name of his father.
[26] See 3.69, n. 27 and 3.59, n. 34.
[27] See 3.67, n. 32.
[28] This might be the well-known professional scribe Haggai son of Shemaiah; see 3.64, n. 41.
[29] See 3.79, n. 44. In that document he appears together with Haggai son of Mardu, who follows here.
[30] See 3.79, n. 47.

REFERENCES

Text and translation: *TAD* B3.13; *EPE* B46. *EPE*; *GEA*; Porten 1968; 1983; 1990; *TAD*.

C. ACCOUNTS

1. THE TITHE IN UGARIT

The tithe in Ugarit is known from legal and economic documents dating from the fourteenth century to the beginning of the twelfth century BCE. The Akkadian term for tithe in Ugarit is *ma-ᵓa-ša-ru* or *êšrêtu* (cf. Hebrew *maᶜaśer*). [These two documents should, strictly speaking, appear with the Akkadian contracts (*COS* 3.107-110) and accounts (*COS* 3.125-126) respectively. WWH]

LAND GRANT ALONG WITH TITHE OBLIGATIONS (3.82)
(*PRU* III 16.276)

Michael Heltzer

From the present day[1] Niqmadu, son of Ammistamru king of Ugarit[2] gave (donated) the village[3] Uḫnappu to Kar-Kushuḫ, son of Ana[nu] and to Apapa, the king's daughter, with its tithe (*êšrêtu*) with its custom-duties (*miksu*)[4] with its gifts (*širku*). Nobody shall raise claims concerning Uḫnappu against Kar-Kushuḫ and Apapa and against the sons of Apapa. He (the king) donated Uḫnappu. Further: Kar-Kushuḫ is pure like the sun forever.[5] Later he is (also) pure. The temple of Baᶜal of the Ḫazi mountain[6] and its priests shall not have claims to Kar-Kushuḫ.[7]

[1] Standard beginning of legal texts of Ugarit.
[2] Niqmaddu III reigned ca. 1225/1220-1215 BCE.
[3] *ālu* lit. "town, city," but in texts from Ugarit "village."
[4] *Uḫnappu* was at the seashore.
[5] Formula of freeing from obligations.
[6] Sacred mountain of Ugarit, Ug. *Ṣpn*, classic *Mons Casius*, modern Jebel-el-Aqra.
[7] Note that Kar-Kushuḫ and Apapa, the daughter of the king, receive the obligations from Uḫnappu for themselves from the king. The whole village had to pay the tithe.

REFERENCES

Text: *PRU* III 16.276.

VILLAGE TITHE PAYMENTS AT UGARIT (3.83)
(*PRU* III 10.044)

Michael Heltzer

Despite the fact that the text is in a damaged state, we see here payments to the authorities, which could be the tithe from a number of villages of the kingdom of Ugarit. The text is written in Akkadian and shows the tax (tithe) payments by the villages in kind: barley (flour), oxen and wine.

1′ [the village... *kùr*][1] barley or (flour)[2]
2′ The village[3] [...] *kùr* barley (or flour), 1 [ox][4]
3′ The village Araniya 2 *kùr* barley (or flour),
4′ The village Uburᵓa 18 *kùr* barley (or flour), 1 ox [...
5′ The village Biru [1] 6 *kùr* barley (or flour), 1 ox [...
6′ The village Inuqapaᵓat 6 *kùr* barley (or flour), [...
7′ The village Beqani 50 *kùr* barley (or flour), [...
8′ The village Ilishtamᵓi 18 *kùr* barley (or flour), [...
9′ The village Shubbani 5 *kùr* barley (or flour), [...
10′ The village Tebaqu 5 *kùr* barley (or flour), [...
11′ The village Riqdi 18 *kùr* barley (or flour), [... — o[x ...

[1] 1 *kùr* cf. Heb. *kōr* consisted in Ugarit of 300 *qû* and at that time had the volume of ca. 250 liters.
[2] ZI KAL.MEŠ.
[3] *ālu* = URU.
[4] *alpu* = GUD.

12′ The village Shurashi 6 *kùr* barley (or flour), [...] 11[5] jars w[ine], 1 ox;
13′ The village Iṣṣuru 6 *kùr* barley (or flour), [...] 11 jars w[ine],
14′ [The village...] *kùr* barley (or flour), [...] 12 jars w[ine], 1 ox;
15′ [The village] *kùr* barley (or flour), 7 jars w[ine],
16′ [The village], 1 ox [...];
17′ [The village]

[5] *karpātu* (DUG) "jar"; ca. 21-23 liters; Heltzer 1991.

REFERENCES

Text, translations and studies: *PRU* III; Heltzer 1975; 1976; 1982; 1991.

2. AMMONITE OSTRACA FROM ḤESBÂN

Walter E. Aufrecht

Between 1968 and 1978, the Tell Ḥesbân excavations produced eight ostraca with writing in the cursive Ammonite or Aramaic scripts.[1] Four of these, A3, A4, A5 and A6, are lists of names; two, A7 and A8, are graffiti; and two, A1 and A2, are accounts presented below.[2]

ḤESBÂN OSTRACON A1 (3.84)

This ostracon, discovered in 1973, is from a body sherd of a large, rough storage jar. It measures 10.6 x 6.5 x 1.6 cm. The upper left side of the sherd is missing, but the right margin is intact. The surface is not smooth and contains large calcium grits, causing the pen strokes to be broad and sometimes distorted or blurred. The text is a record kept by a royal steward of the assignment or distribution from the royal stores of foodstuffs and other goods to courtiers and others to whom the crown is under obligation (Cross 2002), written in Ammonite cursive script with numerals written in Hieratic.[3] The ostracon is in the Amman Archaeological Museum, Ḥesbân No. H73.1657.[4] It has been dated paleographically to ca. 600 BCE.[5]

To the] king: 35 (jars) of grain[a] [ ]
and 8 sheep and goats; [ ]
and to Nadabʾil son of Naʿamʾil f[rom]
To Z[ ] from ʾIlat[6]: 12 (measures) of gum[7b]; (x jars) of gr[ain
To [ ]: 2 (measures) of gum; a two-year old cow and [ ]
To Baʿša[ʾ][8c] 40 (pieces) of silver which he gave to [ ]
22 (jugs) of wine; and 10 sheep and goats; (x measures) of fine flour [ ]
8 (jugs) of wine; and 6 (jars) of grain.
To Yatib: hay; 24 (jars) of grain;
9 sheep and goats;
a three-year-old cow.

a Gen 41:35, etc.
b Gen 37:25, 43:11
c 1 Kgs 15:16, etc.

[1] The Ḥesbân ostraca were published in the sequence of their discovery. Cross (1986; 2002) has rearranged the series in the order of their date: A1 (old #4 = *CAI* 80), dated ca. 600 BCE; A2 (old #11 = *CAI* 94), dated ca. 575 BCE; A3 (old #12 = *CAI* 137) is a list of names, dated ca. 550-525 BCE (the end of the Ammonite cursive series); A4 (old #2 = *CAI* 76), inscribed in Aram. cursive but probably written in the Ammonite language (Shea 1977), may be a docket recording the distribution of tools or a letter giving instructions to agricultural workers, dated ca. 525 BCE; A5 (old #1 = *CAI* 65) and A6 (Cross 2002; Aufrecht 1999 #214) are lists of Ammonite names written in Aram. script, dated to the end of the 6th century BC; and A7 (old #5 = *CAI* 81) and A8 (old #6) are Ammonite graffiti dated to the 7th century BCE.

[2] There are other Ammonite ostraca. Tell el-Mazār Ostracon 3 (*CAI* 144) is a personal letter, dated by Cross (2002) ca. 575 BCE. An ostracon from Tell el-'Umeiri (Aufrecht 1999 #211) may be a letter or a docket, also dated ca. 575 BCE (Sanders 1997). Nine ostraca contain only names: Tell el-Mazār Ostraca 4, 5 and 7 (*CAI* 145-147), the Khirbet Umm ed-Danānīr Ostracon (Aufrecht 1999 #150), the Amman Ostracon (*CAI* 77), two Tell el-'Umeiri Ostraca (Aufrecht 1999 ##171-172), and the Nimrud Ostracon (*CAI* 47). Finally, in addition to Ḥesbân A8 (above n. 1), there are five ostraca which contain only one- or two-letter inscriptions: the Sahab Ostracon (Ibrahim 1975:73); the Tell es-Sa'idiyeh Ostracon (Tubb 1988:31, 33); two ostraca from the Amman Citadel (Dornemann 1983:103); and an ostracon from Tell el-'Umeiri (Herr 1992:195-96).

[3] Cross 2002. Hübner (1988; 1992) has argued that this ostracon is Moabite.

[4] For the most recent discussions, see *CAI* 214-19 (#80); and Cross 2002.

[5] See Cross 1975:17; 2002.

[6] Cross (1975, 2002) notes that this is probably the name of the port and caravan city on the Gulf of Aqabah (Heb. ʿElat).

[7] The word translated as "gum" is vocalized in Biblical Heb. as *nĕkōʾt*.

[8] The name is the same as that of the king of Israel.

ḤESBÂN OSTRACON A2 (3.85)

This ostracon, discovered in 1974, is a body sherd from a heavy storage jar. Its maximum dimensions are 8.4 x 5.4 cm. It was, however, originally larger than its present version as evidenced by a modern break along its top. The text is a list of goods, written in Ammonite cursive script.[9] The ostracon is in the Amman Archaeological Museum, Ḥesbân No. H74.2092.[10] It has been dated paleographically to ca. 575 BCE.[11]

[ ] figs[d] [ ]
[ ] figs from[12] [ ]

d Num 13:23, etc.
e Exod 22:4

[ ] work animals[e] [ ]
[ ] ropes

[9] Hübner (1988) suggested that this ostracon is Moabite, but subsequently (1992:32 n. 67) he identified it as possibly Ammonite.
[10] For the most recent discussions, see *CAI* 245-46 (#94); Cross 2002.
[11] See Cross 1976:148; 2002.
[12] An alternate reading suggested by Cross (2002) is "figs, one talent."

REFERENCES

Text, translations, and studies: *CAI* 214-219 (#80); *CAI* 245-246 (#94); Aufrecht 1999; Cross 1975; 1976; 1986; 2002; Dornemann 1983; Herr 1992; Hübner 1988; 1992; Ibrahim 1975; Sanders 1997; Shea 1977; Tubb 1988.

3. HEBREW OSTRACA

OPHEL OSTRACON (3.86)

K. Lawson Younger, Jr.

This fragmentary ostracon (10 x 8 cm) was discovered during excavations on the Ophel (area south of the temple mount in Jerusalem) by J. G. Duncan in 1924, although in an unstratified context. It can be dated on palaeographic grounds to the end of the seventh or the beginning of the sixth century BCE. While the ostracon appears to have contained eight lines, the left side of the inscription and lines 4-7 are no longer legible. Moreover, some of what is extant contains difficult readings.[1] Nonetheless, the text appears to be a list of personal names that probably served some administrative purpose.

(1) ⌜Ḥiz⌝qîyāhû (Hezekiah),[2] son of Qōrʾēh,[3] [a] from the stock[b] of ⌜Buqqî⌝yāhû[4] [c]
(2) ʾAḥîyāhû,[5] son of Haśśōrēq,[d] in the valley of st⌜elae⌝[6] [e]

(3) ⌜Ṣapan⌝yāhû,[7] son of Qāra⌜y⌝,[8] in the valley of

a 1 Chr 9:19; 26:1; 2 Chr 31:14 *b* Deut 29:17; Isa 5:24; 11:1, 10; 14:29, 30; 53:2 *c* Num 34:22; Ezra 7:4; 1 Chr 5:31; 6:36; 25:4, 13 *d* Zech 1:8(?) *e* Jer 31:40

[1] The best photo of the ostracon is found in Hestrin 1973 #138.
[2] Some scholars read: *yḥ*[*z*]*qyhw*. As Renz (*HAE* 1:310) rightly notes, the photo in Hestrin 1973 reveals practically nothing before the *qyhw*. For a discussion of *ḥ*[*z*]*qyhw*, see Zadok 1988:287.
[3] Gibson (following Avigad 1966) argues that the second names are not patronymics in the narrow sense, but family or clan names of the kind that frequently appear in the statistical records embedded in Numbers, Chronicles, Ezra and Nehemiah and which are typically names of animals, insects, plants, etc. (*SSI* 1:25). See also Hestrin 1973:62.
[4] A number of interpreters since Milik 1959 have understood the last words of line 1 as *bśd śrqm* "in the field of the wool-carders." See Lipiński 1975b:268; Lemaire 1977:239. However, Renz has recently argued that the reading of *bśd śrqm* is problematic since *śd* is written defectively while one would perhaps expect a plene writing of the word in the construct. His argument is reinforced now by the plene writing of the construct of *śdh* in the roughly contemporary Widow's Plea Ostracon (*COS* 3.44 above) which has in line 6: *wʿt . śdh . hḥṭm* "And now, the wheat field ...."
[5] For *ʾḥyhw bn hšrq/hśrq*, see Zadok 1988:287.
[6] The reading of the word is difficult. A number of scholars have read *yhw*[ ] with some restoring *ʿmq yhw*[*špṭ*] "the valley of Jehoshapat" (see also Torczyner 1939; *SSI* 1:26; and Hestrin 1973). If this is the correct reading, then Joel 4:2, 12 might be in view. But since Milik's suggestion (1959:551-553), a number of scholars have read *ydt* "hands" (fem. pl. of *yd* "hand") with the nuance of "stelae" (cf. 1 Sam 15:12; 2 Sam 18:18; Isa 56:5; cf. Ezek 21:24). On the phrase "valley of the stelae," cf. the phrase *bqʿt ydyn* in the Babylonian Talmud (Giṭṭin 57). Lipiński (1975b:268) suggests this valley is referred to in Jer 31:40.
Recently, A. Schüle (2000:74, n. 2) argued that the phrase must be read *bʿmq yhw*[*šapaṭ*]. The phrase *ʿmq ydt* is grammatically unlikely since the feminine plural of *yd* has the meaning of hand mostly with the sense of "grasp, hold"; as a description for the body part, the dual is expected. However, this is more of a lexical than a grammatical argument. The word *yd* is clearly used with the meaning of "monument" (*KBL*[2] 363, usage 6).
[7] Ṣpnyhw, son of Qry. See Zadok 1988:287.
[8] Scholars have read either *qrṣ* (Torczyner, SSI, Hestrin) or *qry* (Sukenik, Milik, Lipiński, Smelik, *HAE*); some have given both possibilities:

the st⌈elae⌉;
(4) ⌈Ṣidqîyāhû⌉[9]
(lines 5-7 missing)
(8) ⌈the son of ᵓUrî⌉yāhû[10] *f*

f 2 Sam 11:3-26; 12:9-10, 15; 23:39; 1 Kgs 15:5; 2 Kgs 16:10-16; Isa 8:2; Jer 26:20-21, 23; Ezra 8:33; Neh 3:4, 21; 8:4; 1 Chr 11:41

qry/ṣ (Moscati), *qrṣ/y* (*KAI*).

9 Ṣdqyhw. See Zadok 1988:287.

10 [..]⌈*bn* ᵓ*wryhw*⌉ (*HAE* 1:311). Others read: *hwdyhw* Hodiyahu, the [...] (Milik 1959; Lipiński 1975b:268); or [*yḥ*]*zqyhw* (*KAI*). For the name ᵓUrîyāhû, see also Zadok 1988:287.

REFERENCES

Text, translations and studies: Cook 1924; Albright 1926; Diringer 1934:74-79; Torczyner 1939; Sukenik 1947; Moscati 1951:44-46, pl. x; Milik 1959; *KAI* #190; *SSI* 1:25-26; Hestrin 1973:62, #138 (best photo); Lipiński 1975b; Lemaire 1977:239-243; Jaroš 1982 #50; Smelik 1991; *AHI* 4.101; *HAE* 1:310-311.

D. MISCELLANEOUS TEXTS

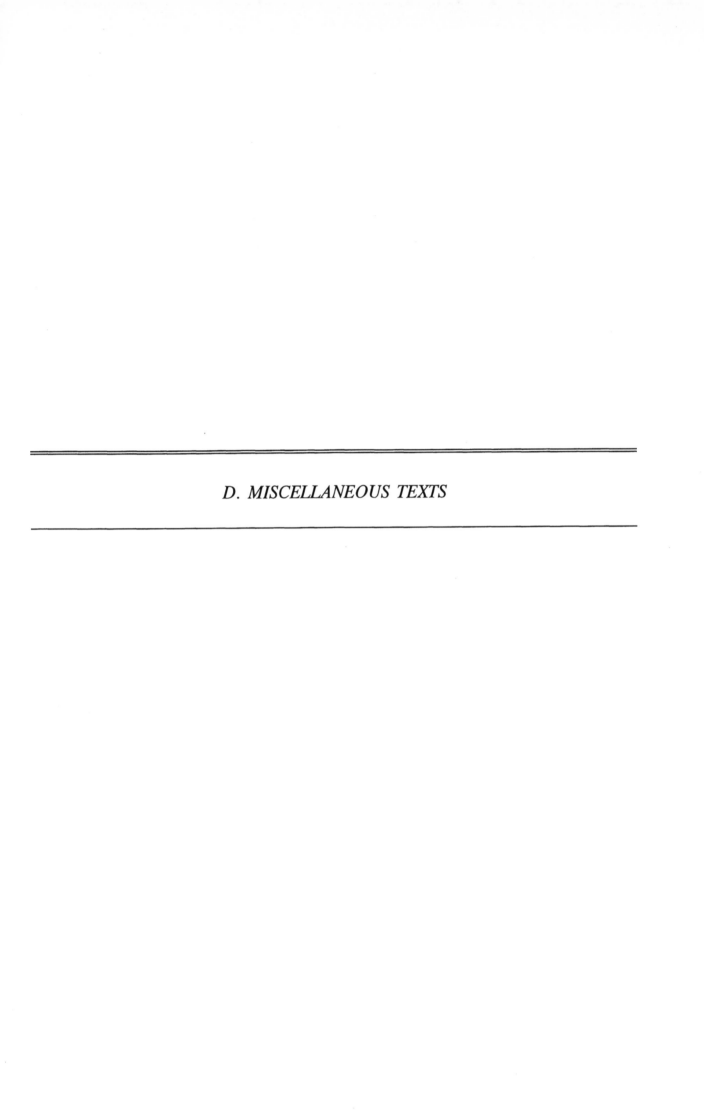

1. ARAMAIC OSTRACA
(ca. 475 BCE)

Bezalel Porten

Egyptian Aramaic ceramic inscriptions are scattered in over a dozen different places throughout the world (New York, Oxford, Cambridge, London, Paris, Strasbourg, Munich, Berlin, Vienna, Moscow, Cairo, Elephantine, and Jerusalem). So far 118 have been published, almost all from Achaemenid Elephantine, and these may be divided into six categories: letters (*TAD* D7.1-57), accounts (*TAD* D8.1-13), lists (*TAD* D9.1-15), abecedaries (*TAD* D10.1-2), jar inscriptions (*TAD* D11.1-26), and mummy labels (*TAD* D19.1-5). The ostraca letters were randomly shaped, measured, say, 7 x 10 cm more or less, and were written on both sides, beginning on the concave and continuing on the convex side. Palaeographically, most of them were written by a single scribe (ca. 475 BCE)[1] who we may imagine sat on the wharf at Syene, available to soldiers writing to their family and friends on Elephantine island. The extant ostraca were addressed to at least ten different persons, among them three women — Hoshaiah (*COS* 3.87A), Uriah (3.87B), Micaiah (3.87C), Haggai (3.87D-E), Jedaniah (*TAD* D7.10), Meshullach (*TAD* D7.31), Nathan (*TAD* D7.28); Kaviliah (3.87F), Islaḥ (3.87G), and Aḥutab (3.87H; *TAD* D7.3-5). Only rarely did the writer give his name — Giddel to Micaiah (3.87C:1-2) and Jarḥu to Haggai (3.87E:1-2) — and frequently he even omitted the name of the addressee (3.87J-K). The messenger doubtless knew each one personally. The language of the letters was terse, allusive, and often cryptic. Formerly compared to the modem telegram,[2] it may now be compared to an e-mail message.

The opening salutation or blessing, a regular feature in papyrus letters, was included in the ostraca letters only infrequently and included the unique formula, *šlmk yhh [ṣbʾt yšʾ]l bkl ʿdn*, "Your welfare may the Lord of [Hosts seek aft]er at all times" (*TAD* D7.35:1-2). In the letter to Hoshaiah it was abbreviated down to a single word, *šlmk*, "Your welfare" (*COS* 3.87A:2). More representative was the compact, two-word *šlm* + Address, "Greetings, PN" (3.87B:1; 3.87G:1; 3.87H:1). Strikingly, the two letters that have the full "to-from" address formula also have a polytheistic salutation — *šlm wḥyn šlht lk brktk lyhh wlḥnwm*, "(Blessings) of welfare and life I sent you. I blessed you by YHH and Khnum" (3.87C:1-3; 3.87E [see below]). Otherwise, the scribe simply began his letter with a clause-initial adverbial followed by a presentative, for example, *kʿnt hlw*, "Now, lo" (Aramaic Dream Report, *COS* 3.88:1) or went straight to the body of the letter, with or without the adverbial, *kʿnt ḥzw*, "Regard ..." (3.87I:1 3.87K:1 [without]); "I dispatched" (3.87K:1 [without]). Whereas the terms *hʾ* and *hlw* introduced statements conveying information (3.87B:2; 3.87F:2; 3.87G:1; 3.87J:1), *ḥzw* introduced a directive, which might be expanded by the preposition *ʿl*, yielding "Look after" (3.87A:2-3).

The two verbs occurring most frequently in the letters are *šlḥ*, which was used for the sending of a message or a letter, and *hwšr*, which was used for the dispatch of an object. PN_1 would write to PN_2 to give him information (Aramaic Dream Report, *COS* 3.88) or instructions (3.87A:2-8; 3.87B:1-8; 3.87D:7-10; 3.87F:5-15; 3.87J); to announce the dispatch of an object (3.87K) or to give him instructions on handling a dispatched object (3.87G:1-4); and requested that PN_2 send him or PN_3 information (3.87A:8-9; 3.87B:9-11; 3.87I:10-13) or some object (3.87C:4; 3.87H:1-5); or that PN_2 get some object from PN_3 (3.87D:7-10). The objects of the requests included salt (3.87H:1-2), a garment that needed to be sewn (3.87C:4-5), and money for the *marzeaḥ* (3.87D:7-10), while among the objects being dispatched were wood (3.87K) or legumes (*bqlʾ*), which were to be exchanged for barley (3.87G:1, 5). A recurrent theme is the provision of bread and/or flour (3.87A:6; 3.87B:13, 15; 3.87F:13; 3.87H:6). Between Syene and Elephantine, then as today, there seems to have been a regular ferry service and correspondents assumed a system of immediate delivery — three of our messages speak of action to be done "today" (3.87B:9-10; 3.87F:5-7; 3.87H:1-2). Personal matters ranged from solicitude for the children (3.87A:2-8, 10-11) or concern that one's slave be properly branded (3.87I:3-8) to a report of a feverish dream. In fact, one side of the ostracon might tell of the dream and the other give advice on food for the children (Aramaic Dream Report, 3.88). Occupations and tasks unknown to the papyri, such as shepherds and sheep, are strikingly attested in two ostraca (3.87B, 3.87F). Matters sacred as well as profane are recorded in these ordinary missives — Sabbath (3.87G:2) and Passover (3.87A:9); an oath by YHH (3.87G:3, 7); donations of beer for libation (3.87I:1-3) and wood for the altar (3.87K); a tunic left at the House of YHH (3.87J:1-3); and, most intriguingly, funds for the *marzeaḥ* association (3.87D).

[1] Naveh 1970:37-38.

[2] Degen 1972:26; see too Dion 1982a:534; Alexander 1978:169.

The cosmopolitan nature of the Elephantine community is attested by the one letter not written by our "wharf scribe." Sent by Jarḥu to Haggai, it contained only a salutation: "The welfare of my brother may Bel and Nabu, Shamash and Nergal (seek after)" (3.87E).[3]

All of the ostraca have been copied at source by Ada Yardeni and many new readings have been attained (*TAD* D7).

[3] For a fuller survey of the ostraca letters see Porten 1994 and for the bibliography of each ostracon, see Fitzmyer and Kaufman 1992 and *TAD* D, pp. xxix-xxx.

INSTRUCTIONS REGARDING CHILDREN AND INQUIRY REGARDING PASSOVER (*TAD* D7.6) (3.87A)

Bezalel Porten

Published by Archibald Henry Sayce in 1911 (Bodleian Aramaic Inscription 7) and variously dubbed the Oxford Ostracon (*DAE* 94) or the Passover Ostracon (Fitzmyer and Kaufman 1992), this piece is an unexpected blend of concern for the care and diet of the children of Aḥutab during her absence and inquiry into when the Passover was to be observed. Attaching this query to matters banal leaves the impression that the paschal sacrifice was a family affair (as in Exod 12:1-28), and not confined to the Temple. On this last question see the Passover Letter (*COS* 3.46).

Address

(Concave)(1)To Hoshaiah.[1]

Salutation

(2)Your welfare[2] (may DN seek after at all times).

a Gen 18:6; 1 Sam 28:24; 2 Sam 13:8; Jer 7:18; Hos 7:17

Instructions

Now,[3] singly[4] look (3)after[5] the children until (4)Aḥutab[6] (3)come(4)s. Do not entrus(5)t[7] them to others. (Convex) (6)If their bread[8] is ground,[9] (7)knead[10] [a] for them 1 *qab*[11] before (8)their mother comes.[12]

[1] This Heb. name ("Deliver, O YH") occurs often in the Elephantine papyri and in a contract of 471, the period of our ostraca, appears as the father of the witness Shillem (3.59:19).

[2] This one-word greeting (*šlmk/šlmky*) occurs once more in these letters (*TAD* D7.5:1)

[3] This clause-initial adverbial was the normal transition marker between the *praescriptio* and the body of the letter (3.87B:1, 13; 3.87C:4; 3.87F:2; 3.87G:1; 3.87H:1), introduced the letter even when the *praescriptio* was absent (3.87I:1; 3.87J:1), and often served as a paragraph head (3.87B:5; 3.87D:5; 3.87F:11; 3.87G:5, 6; 3.88:8); *GEA* 310.

[4] That is, alone, expressed by the stroke for the numeral 1; similarly in one of the Makkibanit letters (*TAD* A2.4:4); *GEA* 240.

[5] The expression *ḥzy* ^{c}*l*, "look after" was used especially in connection with family members (*TAD* A2.3:11), particularly children (*TAD* A2.7:3; 3.5:6, 6:3).

[6] The mother in line 8, she is the main personality in these letters. Aram. Aḥutab = Heb. Ahitub, "(My Divine) Brother is Goodness," a name current during the United Monarchy (1 Sam 14:3; 2 Sam 8:17). Not found in the papyri, this female name was the one most mentioned in the ostraca. Five published texts were addressed to her (3.87B:12; 3.87H:1; *TAD* D7.3-5) and three unpublished ones (Clermont-Ganneau ##78, 135, 157), while she was cited in three published texts (here; *TAD* D7.7:9, 10:4) and in two unpublished ones (Clermont-Ganneau ##214, 255), thirteen texts in all; Dupont-Sommer 1942-45:66. Three ostraca to her were anonymously written (3.87H; *TAD* D7.3-4) and one was sent by Micaiah (*TAD* D7.5). Of the other three ostraca mentioning her, one was addressed to Uriah and secondarily to her (3.87B:12) and a second to Jedaniah (*TAD* D7.10:4).

[7] The last letter of the word is written at the beginning of the next line; for this use of *ykl*, see *DNWSI* 456; *GEA* 123. The same caution with regard to the children was expressed by the cognate root *tkl*, with ^{c}*l* as here, "rely upon" (*TAD* A2.7:2; also 3.87G:4).

[8] The word *lhm* here has the meaning of grain (Isa 28:28); Sukenik and Kutscher 1942:55.

[9] Pass. ptc. *grs* written defectively. Grain was ground in millstones (Num 11:8; Isa 47:2).

[10] I.e., mix the meal with salt and water in a wooden kneading bowl (Exod 7:28, 12:34; Deut 28:5, 17) and make it into dough.

[11] A fragmentary ostracon has "Dispatch to me 1 *qab* of barley" (*TAD* D7.45:7-8). On a scale of 6 *qabs* to a seah, a half or third of a *qab* sufficed for a loaf of bread (M. Erubin 8:2; Kelim 17:11). But two Ptolemaic texts (from Edfu?) project a seah of more than 8½ or 9 *qabs* (*TAD* C3:28; D8.11:4). Another fragmentary ostracon speaks of "the large *qab*" (*TAD* D7.46:2). Abraham had his wife knead three seahs of fine wheat to feast his angelic guests (Gen 18:6). The children here were to receive a fraction of that amount. The word for "knead" is a plural imperative (*lšw* [*GEA* 131,298]) as *t*^{c}*bdn* in line 9 is 2nd person plural imperfect, though the rest of the letter is addressed in the sing. Sukenik and Kutscher 1942:55 suggested a scribal metathesis for *lwš* in the sing. But letters often shift from sing. to plural.

[12] Plural. Presumably she would then bake the bread.

Request I

Send[13] (word) (9)to me when[14] you will make[15] (10)the (9)Passover.[16] [b]

b Exod 12:47-48; Num 9:2-14; Deut 16:1; Josh 5:10; 2 Kgs 21-23; 2 Chr 30:1-5; 35:1, 16-19

Request II

(10)Do send greetings[17] (= news) of (11)the child.

---

[13] As sometimes in the Bible (e.g. 1 Kgs 5:16, 22 [cf. 2 Chr 2:10; Josephus, Ant. viii.2.6-8]) and consistently in the papyri, *šlḥ* by itself means "send word in a letter" (3.87B:10; 3.87I:5, 12).

[14] For thirty years the word *ʾmt* was understood as "handmaiden" and the sentence taken to mean, "Send me a maid to prepare the Passover." Almost concurrently and independently Sukenik and Kutscher 1942:55-56 and Dupont-Sommer 1946-47b:47-49 recognized the word as the interrogative particle. It is a subordinate conjunction introducing an indirect question; *GEA* 59, 94. Without calendar, or guided only by the Eg. calendar, the writer may have sought to know the day of the festival, or more probably, the hour at which the sacrifice would take place. Perhaps he wanted to get home in time. The Bible speaks once of "between the two evenings" (Exod 12:6), the same time as the daily regular offering (Exod 29:39; Num 28:40), but elsewhere as "in the evening, at sundown" (Deut 16:6). The Mishnah determined that the regular offering was slaughtered at 7½ hours and sacrificed at 8½ hours, to be followed by the paschal sacrifice (Pes. 5:1). Our question is reminiscent of that in the opening Mishnah, "From when do they read the *shema* at night" (Ber. 1:1). Alternately, the inquirer may want to know if a second Adar was to be intercalated and Passover delayed by a month. Such leap years occurred in 482, probably 479 and 476, 474, 471, 468, and 463; Parker and Dubberstein 1946:31-32. See also Porten 1968:131-132.

[15] Shift between sing. and plural (*tʿbdn*) in letters is not unusual; see below 3.87F:3-4; 3.87H:1, 4; 3.87I:1, 3, 13 (plural) vs 3.87I:2-3, 9, 11-12, 16 (sing.); 3.87J:1, 3.

[16] *ʿbd psḥ* = Heb. *ʿśh psḥ*, which occurs some 30 times in the Bible in eight different contexts. It is immaterial whether we translate these passages neutrally, with the RSV, "keep the Passover" or explicitely (with NJPS) as "perform the paschal sacrifice." The essence of observing this festival is performing the paschal sacrifce, as all the biblical sources make clear, explicating the expression with the verbs *hqryb*, "offer up" (Num 9:7, 13), *zbḥ*, "sacrifice" (Deut 16:2, 4-6), and *šḥṭ*, "slaughter" (2 Chr 35:1, 6, 11). For the syntax of the last two sentences, see *GEA* 313.

[17] The periphrastic imperative (*hwy šlḥ*) denotes a sense of urgency and appears in an identical context in a papyrus letter (*TAD* A2.3:11); *GEA* 205, 298.

REFERENCES

Text, translations and studies: *DAE* #94; Dupont-Sommer 1946-47b; Fitzmyer and Kaufman 1992 B.3.c.20; *GEA*; Lindenberger 1994 #19; Parker and Dubberstein 1946; Porten 1968; RES 1793; Sukenik and Kutscher 1942; *TAD* D.

INSTRUCTIONS TO SHEAR EWE (3.87B)
(*TAD* D7.8)

Bezalel Porten

Discovered in the Rubensohn excavations of 1906-1907, published in 1911 by Sachau (plate 63,1) but properly understood only by Lidzbarski and Perles, this ostracon was made over to the Egyptian Museum, Cairo (JE 43464B). The anonymous writer informed Uriah that it was time for him to shear his big ewe (3-4 years old) lest its wool get torn by thorns. Moreover, the shearing should follow hard upon the washing. Should Uriah not be able to come today, the writer offered to wash the ewe for him, so that it would be ready for his arrival. He then informed Aḥutab that he and his companions had bread to eat until evening of the next day. Whether this was the same as, or in addition to, the remaining ardab of flour is uncertain.

Greetings + Address

(Concave)(1)Greetings, Uriah.[1]

a Deut 15:9; Isa 53:7; Cant 4:2

Instructions

Now, (2)lo,[2] (3)the big (2)ewe[3] which is yours[4] (3)has arrived (for you) to shear[5] (4)the wool of hers[a]

---

[1] Uriah is mentioned in two other ostraca in connection with cultic matters (3.87I:1, 3, 10; 3.87J:3). A Uriah father of Jezaniah appeared in the same time frame as our ostracon (3.61:6-7; 3.62:2). At the end of the century, among the communal leaders there appeared a Uriah who may have been a priest (*COS* 3.47:1).

[2] This introductory pair occurs also in the Aramaic Dream Report, *COS* 3.88:1; *GEA* 329.

[3] For the word *tʾtʾ*, see *DNWSI* 1094-1095; *GEA* 7.

[4] The Aram. exceptionally positions the possessive pronoun *zy lk* in between noun and adjective; see *GEA* 56, 214. How many sheep did Uriah have?

[5] I.e., "has reached the time for shearing"; *GEA* 208; for the form of the verb *lmgz*, see *GEA* 133. Sheep shearing occurs a half-dozen times in the Bible — in narratives (see below) as well as legal and prophetic texts (Deut 15:19; Isa 53:7) — and is perhaps alluded to in Cant 4:2.

before[6] (5)it is torn on the thorn(s). Now, (6)come[7] and shear her.[8] *b* On the day (7)that[9] you will wash her (8)you should shear her.[10] (Convex) (9)And if you do not go out[11] (10)this day, send (word) (11)to me so that I may wash her[12] before (12)you go out.

Greetings + Address
Greetings, Aḥutab.

b Gen 31:19; 38:12-13; 1 Sam 25:2, 4, 7, 11; 2 Sam 13:23-24

Report
(13)Now, about this[13] bread — (14)we shall eat (it) until tomorrow (15)evening.[14] An a(rdab)[15] of flour[16] (16)remains here.

[6] The form *qdm*ᵓ does not occur elsewhere and the translation here follows Lidzbarski (*ESE* 3:255-256) and Perles 1911:503; it may also mean "its early wool" (*GEA* 214) or "already" (Greenfield 1960:99100). For the word order infinitive (*lmgz*) — object (ᶜ*mr*ᵓ), see *GEA* 308.

[7] This is the only *lamed-yod* imperative spelled with final he (ᵓ*th*) and not *yod*; *GEA* 138, 147.

[8] An *ayin-ayin* verb imperative with 3rd fem. sing. suffix (*gzh*); *GEA* 133. It was customary for the owner of the sheep to be present at the shearing; so Laban (Gen 31:19), Judah (Gen 38:12-13), Nabal (1 Sam 25:2, 4, 7, 11), and Absalom (2 Sam 13:23-24); Greenfield 1960:101.

[9] For this *bywm zy* construction, see *GEA* 227, 313.

[10] As expected, both imperfect verbs are spelled with energic *nun* — *trḥ*ᶜ*nh* and *tgznh*; *GEA* 145. Sheep were generally washed before shearing so that the wool would be clean (Cassin 1959). These activities took place in mid-spring, in Egypt, according to a late Roman text, ca. 15 May (Schwartz 1960:102).

[11] One "went out" (*npq*) from Elephantine and "came" (ᵓ*th* [line 6]) to Syene (Porten-Yardeni 1991:209).

[12] A volitive (*šlḥ*) followed by a jussive (ᵓ*rḥ*ᶜ*h*) was a standard formula with this scribe (3.87C:4-5; 3.87D:7-10; 3.87J:3-4); *GEA* 104, 146.

[13] For the expression ᶜ*l znh*, "about this" at the end of a letter, see 3.51:28-30. Here it must be a reply to an earlier query of Aḥutab about their food supply. In 3.87H, the anonymous writer asked Aḥutab to send him some salt to put in the flour. Bread itself was also dispatched from Elephantine on a regular basis (*TAD* D7.44, 48:2-3 ["send me today"]); see further 3.87A:6; 3.87F:13; *TAD* D7.10:3, 7.19:5. A first century CE Judean ostracon records for a five-day period the delivery of a loaf of bread a day to a certain Judah (Yardeni 1990:144 [#4:12-14]).

[14] The form ᶜ*rwbh* is either feminine absolute (*DNWSI* 887) or masculine determinative with final *he* instead of *aleph* (*GEA* 63). In later Aram. the feminine determinative ᶜ*rwbt*ᵓ means eve of the Sabbath or of some other holy day (Jastrow s.v.); see Dupont-Sommer 1960:68-71, who cites unpublished Clermont-Ganneau ostracon #204; Porten 1968:132.

[15] An ardab held three seahs; Porten 1968:71.

[16] See also 3.87H:7.

REFERENCES

Text, translations and studies: Cassin 1959; *DAE* #95; *DNWSI*; Dupont-Sommer 1960; *ESE*; Fitzmyer and Kaufman 1992 B.3.c.22; *GEA*; Lindenberger 1994 ##15-16; Perles 1911; Porten 1968; Porten-Yardeni 1991; Schwartz 1960; *TAD* D; Yardeni 1990.

OFFER TO SEW A GARMENT (3.87C)
(*TAD* D7.21)

Bezalel Porten

Discovered by Jean Clédat on March 20, 1907 and published by Dupont-Sommer in 1945 (Clermont-Ganneau 70), this is the only ostracon letter addressed "to my lord" by "your servant." For this reason it contains not only one but two opening blessings and a concluding wish for well-being. All three formulae are closely paralleled in the nearly contemporary Makkibanit (Hermopolis) letters, written by Arameans. Probably an Aramean, Giddel blessed Micaiah by Egyptian Khnum (alongside YHH), much as the Aramean writers of the Makkibanit letters blessed their recipients by Egyptian Ptaḥ.

Address (Concave)
(1)To my lord Micaiah,[1] your servant (2)Giddel.[2] *a*

a Ezra 2:47, 56; Neh 7:49, 58

Salutation
(Blessings of) welfare and life I sent[3] (3)you.[4] I

[1] He is the most frequently mentioned male in the ostraca. Besides this one, another is addressed to him by Nathan b. Gemariah on the concave and by Jedaniah on the convex side (*TAD* D7.20:1, 6). He himself writes one (*TAD* 7.22:1) and is mentioned in two others (*TAD* D7.23:5, 7.24:13). The earliest namesake is Mica/Micaiah b. Ahio, a generation later (3.70:2, 10, 12?, 3.74:17 [451-427 BCE]).

[2] As here vocalized, this name in the Bible was borne only by those originally non-Israelites (Ezra 2:47, 56 ‖ Neh 7:49, 58). Written *gdl*, it occurs nowhere else in the papyri.

[3] This and the following "blessed" have been called both the "epistolary perf." (Dempsey 1990) and the "performative perf." (*GEA* 193-194). According to the fomer explanation, the verb assumes the perspective of the recipient; according to the latter the verb in the perf. is tantamount to performing the act — "I hereby send you."

[4] See the parallels in the Makkibanit letters (*TAD* A2.4:5, 2.7:1).

blessed you by YHH[5] and Khnum.[6]

Request
(4)Now, send me[7] the garment[8] (Convex) (5)which is upon you[9] *b* so that I/they may sew it.[10]

b Gen 37:23; 1 Kgs 11:30

Welfare
(6)(To inquire) about your welfare I sent (this) letter.[11]

[5] The name YHW was spelled this way in the ostraca (3.87G:3, 7; 3.87J:3; *TAD* D7.35:1), in contracts by the scribe Nathan son of Anani (3.71:2 [449 BCE] and 3.64:14 [446 BCE]), and even in personal names (*TAD* B5.1:2 [495 BCE] and 3.47:13 [ca. 487 BCE]). Originally Heb., the spelling YHH indicates a pronunciation Yaho; cf. *yryḥh*, Jericho (1 Kgs 16:34), *šlh*, Shiloh (Josh 18:1 etc), *prʿh*, Pharaoh. The spelling YHW is first attested at Elephantine in 464 BCE (3.60:4, written by the Aramean scribe Itu son of Abah). See *GEA* 30.

[6] Abbreviated from the fuller Makkibanit formula, "I blessed you by DN that he may show me your face in peace" (*TAD* A2.1:2, 2.2:2, 2.3:2, 2.4:1-2, 2.5:1-2, 2.6:1-2). For fuller discussion, see *EPE* 90, n. 6. The *waw* of *ḫnwm* is squeezed in above the line. Khnum was the Eg. god of the island whose priests later conspired to destroy the Jewish Temple (3.51:5-6).

[7] Written as one word, *šlḥly*, the usage is unique. The regular word in these texts for dispatching an object other than a letter was *hwšr*. Only in the Bisitun inscription, in the Ahiqar narrative, and in texts of the Ptolemaic period do we find *šlḥ* with that meaning (*TAD* C1.1:62; 2.1:39, 40; D7.57:4).

[8] The most frequently mentioned garment in the ostraca is the tunic (*ktwn*); 3.87J:1; *TAD* D7.7:7, 7.14:2, 6, 7.55:2 (Edfu).

[9] Idiomatically translated by Lindenberger 1994 #20 as "the garment you have on" with an alternate translation in the footnotes, "the garment you have on account"; for a similar use of *ʿl*, see, in the Makkibanit letters, *TAD* A2.2:9. Moriya (1995:236) translates, "that is charged upon you."

[10] It is not certain whether we are to read *wʾḥṭnh* or *wyḥṭnh*. If the latter, it may be defective spelling for *yḥṭwnh*, plural as imperfect (Dupont-Sommer 1945:25; *ANET* 491). Lindenberger 1994 #20 paraphrased, "so it can be re-stitched." Who was the tailor? For the volitive (*šlḥ*) — jussive (*wʾḥṭnh* or *wyḥṭnh*) construction, see on 3.87B:10-11.

[11] A standard conclusion in the Makkibanit letters (*TAD* A2.1:11-12, 2.2:17, 2.3:12-13, 2.4:13, 2.5:9, 2.6:10, 2.7:4); *EPE* 92, n. 26. The scribe here omitted the demonstrative *znh*.

REFERENCES

Text, translations and studies: *DAE* #87; Dempsey 1990; *DNWSI*; Dupont-Sommer 1942-45; Dupont-Sommer 1945; *EPE*; Fitzmyer and Kaufman 1992 B.3.c.33:70; *GEA*; Lindenberger 1994 #20; Moriya 1995; Porten 1968; Rainey 1996; *TAD* D.

INSTRUCTIONS REGARDING SILVER FOR MARZEAḤ (3.87D)
(*TAD* D7.29)

Bezalel Porten

Discovered in 1902 by Sayce, published by him in 1909 (RES 1295), deposited in the Egyptian Museum, Cairo (JE 35468A), and recopied by Lidzbarski in 1915, though without plate (*ESE* III 119-121), this ostracon is the only Elephantine document to mention this institution, so widely known in the world of West-Semitic inscriptions for over a millennium. It was a funerary association that held periodic banquets. Asked by the anonymous writer about the money for the *marzeaḥ*, the Aramean Ashian replied that the till was empty but that he would forward funds to Haggai or Igdal, persons bearing Jewish names. The writer herein instructs Haggai to get the money from Ashian. It is not apparent what role each of the four parties played in the association, and different combinations are possible.

Address
(Concave)(1)To Haggai.[1]

Report
I spoke[2] (2)to Ashian[3] about the silver of (3)the *marzeaḥ*,[4] *a* Thus he said (4)to me, saying:[5] "There is none.[6] (5)Now, I shall give it (6)to Haggai or (7)Igdal."[7]

a Amos 6:7; Jer 16:5

[1] The writer is anonymous. Haggai is addressed in another ostracon (3.87E) by the Aramean Jarḥu and sent blessings by four pagan deities. The name was very popular at Elephantine but the earliest Haggai is the scribe, son of Shemaiah, who first appears in 446 (3.64:19).

[2] Aram. *ʾmrt*, lit. "I said."

[3] A daughter of an Ashian is designated "Aramean" in a contract fragment from the middle of the fifth century (*TAD* D2.4:2). The name may be Old Persian Ashina (Hinz 1975:22) or a West-Semitic hypocoristicon from the root *ʾwš* (Ran Zadok, orally).

[4] As new material accumulates, the *marzeaḥ* receives ongoing scholarly treatment; see Porten 1968:179-186; Greenfield 1974:451-455; Barstad 1984:127-142; Lewis 1989:80-98.

[5] The particle *lm* introduces direct speech; *GEA* 339.

[6] Lit., "there is not" (*lʾyty* and not *lʾytw*, "to Ito," as formerly read [*ESE* III 119-121]). This apocopated construction occurs also in 3.87H:6 and 3.76:29; see *GEA* 41, 95.

[7] Hypocoristicon of Igdaliah ("May YH Be/Do Great{ly}" [Hestrin and Dayagi 1979:85]), the name occurs once more in a fragmentary ostracon (*TAD* D7.11:3). An Igdal father of Gaddul appears in a contract of 464 (3.60:18) and an Igdal father of Hosea in 459 (3.61:34, 3.62:22). For omission of the preposition "to" before Igdal in our text, see *GEA* 317.

Instructions Get[8] (8)to him (9)so that he may give it[9] (10)to you.[10]		

[8] Aram. *dbr*, translated "speak" by Lidzbarski, is used here idiomatically for "lead the way to someone, betake oneself, repair to."

[9] For this volitive (*dbr*) — jussive (*wyntnhy*) sequence, see on 3.87B:10.

[10] For the double pronominal object construction, see *GEA* 267, 309.

REFERENCES

Text, translations and studies: Barstad 1984; *DAE* #92; *DNWSI*; Dupont-Sommer 1945; Fitzmyer and Kaufman 1992 B.3.c.30; *GEA*; Greenfield 1974; Hestrin and Dayagi 1979; Hinz 1975; Lewis 1989; Lindenberger 1994 #13; Porten 1968; *TAD* D.

GREETINGS FROM A PAGAN TO A JEW (3.87E)
(*TAD* D7.30)

Bezalel Porten

Discovered by Gautier in the 1908/09 season and published by Dupont-Sommer in 1944 (Clermont-Ganneau 277), this ostracon was not written by the popular wharf scribe. It is a palimpsest and is unique in being written on only one side and containing no message beyond an elaborate blessing by four pagan deities. Leading gods in the Babylonian pantheon (cf. Sefire A8-9 = *KAI* 222; *COS* 2.82), all four were prominently featured among the Arameans of Egypt.

Address (Concave)(1)To my brother[1] Haggai,[2] your brother (2)Jarḥu.[3]	*a* Jer 50:2; 51:44; Isa 46:1 *b* Isa 46:1 *c* 2Kgs 17:30	*Salutation* The welfare of my brother (3)may Bel[4] [a] and Nabu,[5] [b] Shamash[6] and Nergal[7] [c] (seek after at all times).[8]

[1] Term of address between peers.

[2] This Haggai is probably the same as the one addressed in 3.87D.

[3] The moon-god *Yrḥ* figures prominently at Ugarit (*DDD* 1101) and in personal names there (e.g. *ᶜbdyrḫ* [Gröndahl 1967:105]), and in Ammonite (*yrḥᶜzr* [Aufrecht 1989:106-109]), Phoen. and Punic (*yrḥ*, *ᶜbdyrḥ* [Benz 1972:326]), and Palmyrene (*yrḥy* [Stark 1971:91]). Related are the biblical PNs Jerah and Jaroah (Gen 10:26; 1 Chr 5:14) and the GN Jericho. Hypocoristic endings with *-u* were not infrequent among the Arameans at Elephantine (e.g. Itu [3.60:16], Jaulu [*TAD* C3.14:16], Palṭu [3.64:15]).

[4] The deity appears in two fragmentary papyri (*TAD* D1.22:1; Segal 1983:23b:5) and in the personal names Belhabeh ("Bel, Give Her/Him" [*TAD* D22.13:1]), and *Blbn* = Belbani/Belibni (*TAD* C3.14:14). The earliest Aram. monument in Egypt is a statuette of Belsharuṣur (*TAD* D 16.1).

[5] A Temple to Nabu was established in Syene (*TAD* A2.3:1) and one of its priests, Sheil, was buried in Saqqarah (*TAD* D18.1; see, too, D11.24:1). The deity figures in the fragmentary cave narrative from Sheikh Fadl (*TAD* D23.1:6:7, 1:16:2) and appears in numerous personal names, both Aramean (e.g. Nabuyehab [*TAD* C4.9:2], Nabunathan [*TAD* A2.3:14; 3.65:12, et al.], Nabuakab [*TAD* A6.2:23, C3.13:54, et al.]) and Babylonian (e.g. Nabuzeribni [3.61:28, 3.62:16, et al.], Nabukudurri [3.59:18, 3.81:2, et al.], Nabusumiskun [3.60:19]).

[6] Shamash was the main deity adored in several Aram. graffiti incised on an ancient stela in Wadi el-Hudi, south of Aswan (*TAD* D22.47:4, 22.48, 22.49:2). He appears in the personal names Shamashnuri (*TAD* B4.2:12; D 18.16:1) and Nurshawash (*TAD* C3.14:24), in the Words of Ahiqar (*TAD* C 1.1:107, 187-188) and perhaps in the Sheikh Fadl narrative as well (*TAD* D23.1.2:7, 1.3-4:2, 1.6:2)

[7] The last two letters of the name (*gl*) were written below the line. Nergal migrated to Samaria with the inhabitants exiled from Cutha (see further *DDD* 1169-1172). At Elephantine there appeared a Nergal(u)shezib father of an Aramean scribe with the Persian name Raukhshana (3.77:9). The name Nargi may be a hypocoristicon (*TAD* B 1.1:17).

[8] The blessing was formulaic (see 3.46:1-2; 3.47:1-2; 3.48:2; 3.51:1-2) and its conclusion implicit.

REFERENCES

Text, translations and studies: *ANET* 491; Aufrecht 1989; Benz 1972; *DAE* #88; *DDD*; *DNWSI*; Dupont-Sommer 1944; Fitzmyer and Kaufman 1992 B.3.c.33:277; *GEA*; Gröndahl 1967; *KAI* #222; Moriya 1995; Porten 1968; Segal 1983; Stark 1971; *TAD* D.

INSTRUCTIONS TO AID SHEPHERD (3.87F)
(*TAD* D7.1)

Bezalel Porten

Donated by Sir Henry Thompson to the Cambridge University Library (Cambridge 131-33) and published by Cowley in 1929, this is the only ostracon addressed to a mother. Threading the word *ṭbh*, "goodness" through his letter, the anonymous son informs her that her *bᶜl ṭbh*, a certain shepherd, is coming to Syene to sell sheep. If she does *ṭbh* by him, he will do right by the son. She could further do *ṭbh* for him and his family if she would provide them with food, for they are hungry. The reading on the convex differs markedly here from that in Cowley 1929.

Address
(Concave)(1)To my mother[1] Kaviliah.[2]

Salutation
Blessings of [...] (2)I sent you.

Instructions I
Now, lo, behold[3] (3)*Npnᵓ* the shepherd of sheep[4] [a] of Sekhmere,[5] (4)your (3)obli(4)gee,[6] [b] is coming (to)[7] Syene with the sheep (5)to sell.[8] Go, stand[9] (6)with him[10] in Syene (7)this (6)day.[11] (7)If you do (Convex) (8)[for him g]ood[c] in Syene, (9)[also h]e (8)will do (good) for me.[12] (9)Lo, tomorrow I have to go[13] (10)[to] my house, so let them give you 1 goat before (11)I reach you.[14]

Instructions II
Now, regard[15] (that) which is a good (thing) (12)to do for him. Lo, they are hungry.[16] (13)Both bread and flour[17] giv[e] (14)to him and ask him, (15)*saying*: "*What* do you seek?"[18] (or: To ... you seek)

a Gen 4:2, 46:34, 47:3
b Prov 3:27
c Judg 9:16; 1 Sam 24:18

[1] Three papyrus letters were addressed to "my mother" (*TAD* A2.6:11, 2.7:1; 3.4:1) but two of these alternate in the internal and external addresses between "my mother" and "my sister" (*TAD* A2.6:1, 11, 2.7:1, 5).

[2] This woman occurs only here. Her name means "Wait for the Lord" (cf. Ps 27:14) and belongs to the category of Names of Encouragement (Porten 1968:144-145).

[3] This is the only ostracon that has this threefold combination (*kᶜnt hlw hᶜ* [the last letter partially restored]).

[4] The word *qn* was inserted supralinearly, creating an idiom known from the Bible and with links to Egypt.

[5] The construction is "PN (*Npnᵓ*), occupation (shepherd), origin (Sekhmere);" cf. the similar "Peu son of Paḫe, a builder of Syene the fortress" (3.65:1-2). The GN may be explained as *Sḫ.t-mry*, "Field of M..." (cf. Gauthier V:53 who cites a Sokhit mour from Edfu. References from Günter Vittmann and Janet Johnson).

[6] The precise nuance of this construct phrase (*bᶜl ṭbtkm*) eludes us. The sense assumed here is that the "owner of goodness" is the beneficiary who is obligated to the benefactor (*DAE* 23:3-4). Others rendered "friend" (Cowley 1929; *GEA* 225-226, 230) with the meaning "those who are entitled to your goodness" (*DNWSI* 418) or "partner" (Lindenberger 1994 #17:3-4 [inconsistent with his rendition "client" for 3.51:23-24; for fuller discussion see there]). The shift between plural (*-km*) and sing. address is not unusual in letters; see 3.87A:8-10.

[7] Aram. often omits the preposition *lamed* with the verb *ᵓth* (*GEA* 268).

[8] Was this a market day? For elision of the object ("them"), see *GEA* 273; for the form of the infinitive, *GEA* 109.

[9] Asyndesis, where the first verb is one of motion (*ᵓzly*), is a common feature in our texts; *GEA* 257-258.

[10] The expression *qwm ᶜm* appears in Old Aram. inscriptions with deity as subject assisting his protégés (Baalshmayin with Zakkur [*KAI* 202A:3, 13-14; *COS* 2.35] and the pantheon with Panamuwa [the Hadad Inscription: *KAI* 214:21; *COS* 2.36). For full discussion of the idiom, see Tawil 1974:43-45.

[11] For the adverbial at the end of the sentence, see *GEA* 313.

[12] For the protasis-apodosis sentence construction, see *GEA* 325g. If the benefactor does good (*ṭbh*) for her beneficiary (*bᶜl ṭbtᵓ*), he will reciprocate toward her son, the letter writer. There existed norms of proper behavior and such was to be rewarded by the recipient (*TAD* C1.1:52) or by the deity (*TAD* A2.3:7; 1 Sam 24:19). Correspondingly, improper behavior was to be severely punished (Judg 9:16-20).

[13] The infinitive (*lmᵓzl*) as subject of a nominal clause is rare; *GEA* 210.

[14] A parade example of a cryptic sentence whose meaning was clear to the parties but whose thrust eludes us. Does "them" (*wyntnw*) refer to the shepherd? What is the nature of the "gift" and how is its timing linked to his cominmg to her? Finally, what does it have to do with his going to his house?

[15] The imperative *ḥzy*, like its Heb. counterpart *rᵓh*, was regularly used with direct object to introduce an object or person which required specific attention (see 3.87I:1; 3.87J:1; *TAD* A3.10:2; 3.51:23; 6.15:4; 2 Sam 24:22; Pss 25:18-19; 119:153); see *GEA* 329.

[16] The root *kpn* occurs once, in a fragmentary aphorism from Ahiqar — "Hunger will sweeten bitterness" (*TAD* Cl. 1:123): anything tastes good when you're hungry.

[17] The "both ... and" sequence is expressed by reduplication of the particle *ᵓp*; *GEA* 336.

[18] I.e. what do you need? The first four letters in the last line are not clear and may be read *lm*[ ]*h*; see drawing in *TAD* D7.1:15.

REFERENCES

Text, translations and studies: Cowley 1929; *DAE* #23; *DNWSI*; Fitzmyer and Kaufman 1992 B.3.c.34; *GEA*; *KAI*; Lindenberger 1994 #17; Moriya 1995; Porten 1968; *TAD* D; Tawil 1974.

INSTRUCTIONS REGARDING LEGUMES AND BARLEY, ETC. (3.87G)
(*TAD* D7.16)

Bezalel Porten

Discovered by Charles Clermont-Ganneau in 1908, published in 1949 by Dupont-Sommer (Clermont-Ganneau 152), and correctly interpreted by Franz Rosenthal in 1966 (letter of April 24; Rosenthal 1967:12-13), the end of the concave and the first half of the convex still remain obscure. The anonymous writer is sending some legumes by boat on the Sabbath, to be exchanged for barley, and orders the addressee to receive the shipment personally and not rely on others. Moreover, he threatens to kill her should they get lost. Since the boatman would have been Egyptian (3.59:13; 3.80:12; *TAD* C3.26:29; D7.13, 24:2), there would not necessarily have been any Sabbath violation. Two generations later Nehemiah banned Tyrian merchants from selling fish at the gates of Jerusalem (Neh 13:14-22).

Greetings

(Concave)(1)Greetings, Islaḥ.[1]

Instructions I

Now, behold, legumes[2] I shall dispat(2)ch[3] tomorrow. Meet the boat[4] tomorrow on Sabbath.[5] (3)Lest,[6] [a] if they get lost, by the life of YHH,[7] [b] if not[8] [c] yo[ur] soul (4)I shall take.[9] [d] Do not rely on Meshullemeth[10] [e] (5)or on Shemaiah.[11]

Instructions II

Now, exchange for me barley.[12] (6)And seek someone[13] and I shall ... (with) them legumes (or: and I will set them up in *ql*).

Warning

Now, (7)by the life of YHH, if not(,) on (8)your soul

Report (Convex) (9)... on account of *ṭqbḥ*. That which (10)you dispatched instead of *ḥmy*[14] to/for ... (11)you dispatched it.

Rebuke

If Meshullemeth is not concerned (12)about me, you, what will you say?![15]

Hope

You will see my face (in peace) (13)and I shall see your face (in peace).[16] [f]

a Ezra 4:22, 7:23 *b* 1 Sam 14:39; 25:34; 26:16; 2 Sam 4:9-11; 12:5; 1 Kgs 2:24 *c* Gen 24:37-38; Num 14:28; Ps 137:6 *d* 1 Kgs 19:4; Jon 4:3; Ps 31:14; Prov 1:19 *e* 2 Kgs 21:19 *f* Gen 32:21; 33:10; 43:3, 5; 44:23, 26; 46:30; 48:11; Exod 10:28-29; 2 Sam 3:13; 14:24, 28, 32

[1] A popular masculine hypocoristicon ("May [DN] Forgive") at Elephantine (3.49:1, 5, 10; 3.67:19; 3.76:43; *TAD* A3.9:[1], 9; 4.5:2; C3.15:106; D3.17:9; 4.25:3; 9.6:1, 9.14:2), it occurs in only one other text from our period, a fragmentary ostracon (*TAD* D9.2:1). On the basis of the gender of the verbs, the name here must be feminine.

[2] As noted by Milik (1967:535) the word *bql* is "pan-Semitic" but occurs only here in Eg. Aram.

[3] Hafel *hwšr* is the regular term in the Elephantine documents for sending an object (3.87H:1; 3.87I:14, 16). It is cognate with Akk. D [= Aram. pael] *wuššuru*, occurring frequently as a Canaanism in the Amarna tablets (Dupont-Sommer 1942-45:70, n. 7; Rainey 1996 2:159-168).

[4] An instruction that appears in three other unpublished ostraca (Clermont-Ganneau 42, 104, 157), as reported by Dupont-Sommer 1949:32. Otherwise the root is known from the preposition *lᶜrq/lᶜrᶜ*, "toward," recurrent in Bisitun (*TAD* C2.1:9, 15, 22, 42, 45, et. al.)

[5] For discussion of the absolute state of *šbh*, see *DNWSI* 1107 with references. The word occurs in five or six ostraca (*TAD* D7.10:5, 12:9, 28:4, 35:7, and perhaps 48:5). Presumably to obviate any hint of Sabbath desecration, Grelot translated *bšbh*, "for the Sabbath," as if the boat was being sent before the Sabbath.

[6] The word *lmh* introduces a threat, which may be prefaced by a circumstantial or (as here) a conditional clause (see *TAD* A6.15:7-8).

[7] This unique oath formula is written as one word, here and in line 7 (*ḥylyhh*). For this spelling of the divine name, see on 3.87C:3. Several biblical passages underpin death threats with divine oath. Structurally apposite is Saul's oath, "By the life of YHWH ... if it was through my son Jonathan, he shall be put to death" (1 Sam 14:39).

[8] This is the negative oath particle (*hn lᵓ* = Heb. *ᵓm lᵓ*), with numerous biblical examples. Lit., it means, "If I do not kill you, may I be killed" (or the like). It may be paraphrased "surely."

[9] A familiar biblical idiom (*lqḥ npš*), used by Elijah and Jonah pleading for death. We may paraphrase the sentence as follows, "If they get lost, I swear I'll kill you."

[10] A feminine form of Meshullam (< Meshelemiah [1 Chr 9:21, 26:1-2, 9]) the name Meshullemeth was well-known at Elephantine in documents from the end of the century (*TAD* A3.7:3; C3.13:38, 3.15:2, 85, 96, 113)

[11] A popular name at Elephantine, there is a Shemaiah son of Hosea from 471 BCE (3.59:17).

[12] Send me barley in return for the legumes; *DNWSI* 377. A contemporary papyrus letter from Memphis to Syene requests castor oil so as to exchange it for another, unspecified oil (*TAD* A2.1:7).

[13] Lit., "1." [For a different reading of this line see *COS* 3.88, n. 11. WWH]

[14] This unknown word occurs also in a fragmentary papyrus list in the enigmatic expression, *zy ᶜbdw ḥmy*, "(Those) who did/made *ḥmy*: PN son of PN for PN" (*TAD* D3.17:1, 3, 5).

[15] Meshullemeth's lack of concern explains the writer's unwillingness to trust her with the shipment of legumes. Islaḥ is being rebuked for remaining silent. Contemporary papyrus letters repeat some form of the refrain, "Do not be concerned about me; I am concerned about you" (*TAD* A2.1:8; 2.2:3, 2.3:4, 2.4:3, 12, 2.6:9; 3.9:6).

[16] A prayer "to see one's face in peace" was the recurrent salutation in the contemporary papyrus letters (*TAD* A2.1:2, 2.2:2, 2.3:2, 2.4:2, 2.5:2, 2.6:2; 3.3:3; also ⌜3.5:8; 3.52:9⌝). In biblical parlance "to see the face" was often used in the context of coming from afar to see someone. Here *tḥzyn* is in the indicative so we may not translate the statement as jussive, "May you/I see my/your face." See *EPE* 90. n. 6.

REFERENCES

Text, translations and studies: *DAE* #91; *DNWSI*; Dupont-Sommer 1949; *EPE*; Fitzmyer and Kaufman 1992 B.3.c.33; *GEA*; *KAI*; Lindenberger 1994 #22; Milik 1967; Porten 1968; Rosenthal 1967; *TAD* D.

REQUEST FOR SALT (3.87H)
(*TAD* D7.2)

Bezalel Porten

Discovered by Charles Clermont-Ganneau in 1908 and published in 1945 by Dupont-Sommer (Clermont-Ganneau 169), this ostracon is concerned with one thing — getting salt for making bread. Elsewhere, we learn that bread itself was dispatched from Elephantine to Syene (*TAD* D7.44).

Greetings
(Concave)(1)[Gr]eetings, Aḥutab.

Request
Now, dispatch (2)to me a little[1] salt[2] [a] this day.[3] (3)And if there isn't[4] [b] salt in the house (4)buy[5] from the boats of grain[6] [c] (5)which are in Elephantine.

Report
Lo,[7] (6)I don't have (Convex) (7)any salt to put[8] in the flour.[9]

a Ezra 4:14; 7:22
b Dan 2:10-11; 3:25, 29; 4:32; Ezra 4:16
c 2 Sam 19:19

[1] As quantifier, *zᶜyr* precedes the noun it modifies (*GEA* 242).

[2] Salt was a frequent object of request. One ostracon asked for "2 *qabs*, fine and coarse (with) the basket over it" (*TAD* D7.7:2-4). An Aram. ostracon, probably of March 23, 252 BCE, records the payment of the salt tax (*TAD* D8.13).

[3] Perhaps with the person who delivered the letter, in the return ferry to Syene.

[4] The contracted English reflects the elided *aleph* and the writing as one word and contraction of *lʾ ʾyty* → *lʾyt*; similarly in line 6: *lʾty*. For the grammatical construction, see *GEA* 290, 322-323.

[5] The opening command, "dispatch" (*hwšry*), is in the feminine sing., while "buy" (*zbnw*) is in the plural; see on 3.87A:8-9.

[6] Alternately, "ferryboats." Aram. *ᶜbwr* = "grain" and conceivably may be related to the root *ᶜbr*, "pass over" (*DAE* #19). Milik (1967:555) surmised that these grain boats were commissioned by the government to supply the garrison. In a document of 483, Hosea and Ahiab receive a shipment of barley and legumes from Espemet, probably the boatman and somehow associated with Taḥpanhes, and undertake to deliver it to the royal storehouse (*TAD* B4.3-4). Apparently salt, transported from Lower Egypt (Lucas 1989:268), was not part of the government ration (*ptpʾ*), but had to be paid for separately out of the monthly allotment (*prs*); see 3.87I:11.

[7] For the presentative *hʾ*, see *GEA* 329.

[8] For the infinitive as noun modifier, see *GEA* 209

[9] And how will the bread taste without salt?!

REFERENCES

Text, translations and studies: *DAE* #19; Dupont-Sommer 1942-45; *GEA*; Lucas 1989; Milik 1967; *TAD* D.

LETTER REGARDING GIFT, HANDMAIDEN, ALLOTMENT, AND POTS (*TAD* D7.9) (3.87I)

Bezalel Porten

Discovered by Sayce in 1901 and published by Sayce and Cowley in 1906 (Bodleian Aramaic Inscription 1), this palimpsest, dubbed the Uriah Ostracon (Fitzmyer and Kaufman 1992 B.3.C.36), has since disappeared. Though two or three commands are in the plural (*wblwh*, *yktbwh*, *hwšrwhy*), the letter is essentially addressed to a female (*hbyh*, *ḥzy* [masculine or feminine], *hzdhry*, *tšmᶜyn*, *šlhy*, *ḥzy* [masculine or feminine], *hwšry*). Uriah had given the anonymous writer beer for the libation. The latter was now calling upon an anonymous female to forward it to Gemariah b. Aḥio to prepare it and then have it returned to Uriah. The writer further expressed Uriah's concern that a recently acquired Egyptian handmaiden be branded with the latter's name. The writer asked to be informed when government allotment would be distributed at Syene and to be sent various pots.

Instructions I (Concave)
(1)Now, regard[1] the GIFT[2] which Uriah[3] gave me for the libation,[a] (2)Give it to Gemariah son of Ahio[4] so that he may prepare[5] it from (3)the beer,[6]

a Num 28:7

[1] See on 3.87F:11.

[2] This word occurs once or twice more in the ostraca (3.87K:2, *TAD* D7.40:3). Stephen Kaufman (orally) proposed a derivation from *ḥn*, "favor, grace," *ḥnn*, "give as a favor" (Shmuel Safrai orally [Gen 33:5, 11; Num 6:25]), *ḥnm*, "gratis," hence Aram. **ḥnh*, "gift." This would be a cultic term, here referring to fermented drink for the daily libation and in 3.87K to wood for burning on the altar.

[3] The name is spelled here with final *he* but in line 3 with final *aleph*. Is he the same one (name spelled *ʾryh*) associated with the Temple in 3.87J? See on 3.87B:1.

[4] He was scribe of his own loan contract in 487 BCE (*TAD* B4.2:1, 16) and contract witness in 464 BCE (3.60:18).

[5] The thrust of the verb *ᶜrk* here eludes us. The same verb in Heb. occurs frequently in cultic contexts with regard to arranging wood and sacrifice on the altar (Gen 22:9; Lev 1:7; 1 Kgs 18:33), lamps in the lampstand (Exod 27:21; Lev 24:34), and bread of display on the table (Exod 40:23; Lev 24:8).

[6] As part of the twice daily regular offering in the Tabernacle, this fermented drink (*škr*) constituted the libation on the altar of incense (Milgrom

and bring it to Uria.[7]

Instructions II
Moreover, regard (4)our (3)Teṭosiri.[8] (4)Let them mark[9] *b* her on her arm[10] above the mark (5)which is on her arm.[11] Lo, thus he (i.e. Uriah) sent, saying that[12] (6)they might not find his lass (7)marked according to[13] (8)his[14] name.[15]

Instructions III
(Convex)(9)Now, [...]. And moreover, take heed[16] (10)... to mark.

b Isa 44:5

Request I
Moreover, when (11)you will hear[17] saying:[18] "We have begun giving[19] (out) allotment[20] (12)at Syene," send (word) to me.

Request II
Regard the STAND of the pot[21] (13)which I brought in my hand. Dispatch it to me.[22] And the pot which (14)I dispatched to you from ... the river (15)and the [1] big pot[23] which (16)Malchiah[24] (15)gave (16)[to you] — dispatch (17)them to me.

1990:240).

[7] A completely different interpretation of this text is to be found in Lindenberger 1994 #18. Moreover, he placed the convex side first.

[8] For this phrase (*T. zyln*) with the disjunctive personal pronoun, see *GEA* 232-33. Teṭosiri was Eg. (*tꜣ-dy-Wsir*, "The {One} whom Osiris Gave") as were most of the other slaves owned by the Elephantine Jews — Peṭosiri, Bela, Lilu and their mother Taba owned by Mibtahiah (3.68), Tamet owned by Meshullam (3.71:2-3), and probably the houseborn Jedaniah son of Taḥo owned by Meshullam's son Zaccur (3.77).

[9] Slaves at Elephantine, and elsewhere in Egypt (*TAD* A6.10:7), were marked on the right arm with the owner's name, e.g. "(Belonging) to Mibtahiah" (3.68:5-6) or "(Belonging) to Meshullam" (3.74:3). The verb *ktb* in this text is in *pael* (*GEA* 108-109, n. 504, 120, 190).

[10] Spelled here with *dalet* (*drᶜ*), the homonym, meaning "seed," is spelled elsewhere with a *zayin* (*zrᶜ* [*TAD* B 1.1:4; 3.64:8]).

[11] That is, the mark of her former owner, from whom she was recently acquired.

[12] For this construction introduced by *zy* and expanded with an object complement, see *GEA* 271-272.

[13] Lit. *ᶜl*, "on."

[14] That is, Uriah's.

[15] See Porten 1968:204.

[16] See *GEA* 116, 118.

[17] Aram. plene spelling *tšmᶜyn*, 2 fem. sing.; *GEA* 140, n. 659.

[18] For *lꜣmr*, see *GEA* 209, 328.

[19] Aram. *šryn yhbn* (*DAE* #22, note *f*); *GEA* 139, 260.

[20] The allotment was distributed monthly from the royal treasury (*TAD* B4.2:5-6) or store-house (*TAD* B4.4:16), known from the conveyances to have been located in Elephantine (e.g. 3.72:9). But there is also an epistolary allusion to allotment being taken at Syene (*TAD* A2.3:8-9; *EPE* 98). In our case, the authorization may have come from Elephantine, while the payment would have been made in Syene to those on duty there (Porten 1968:277). Withholding allotment from the families of soldiers on duty away from home was a disturbing practice (*TAD* A3.3:3-5).

[21] Aram. *qpyr* = Akk. *qapiru*, "a container" (*CAD* Q 91; reference courtesy of Stephen Kaufman).

[22] For the verb with double object, see also lines 16-17 and *GEA* 266-268.

[23] For the construction in absolute state, see *GEA* 241.

[24] Malchiah appears in an ostracon listing Eg. boat captains (*TAD* D7.13:17) and perhaps in a letter (*TAD* D7.27:10). A Malchiah son of Zechariah appears as a witness ca. 487 BCE (*TAD* B4.2:15) and a Malchiah was father of the witness Maaziah in 459 (3.61:30-31; 3.62:19).

REFERENCES

Text, translations and studies: *DAE* #22; *EPE*; Fitzmyer and Kaufman 1992 B.3.C.36; *GEA*; Lindenberger 1994 #18; Milgrom 1990; Porten 1968; *TAD* D.

INSTRUCTIONS REGARDING TUNIC (3.87J)
(*TAD* D7.18)

Bezalel Porten

Discovered in 1925 and published in 1926 by Aimé-Giron, this ostracon is housed in the Cairo Egyptian Museum (Cairo 49624). The attempt to interpret the text as an instruction to Uriah to dedicate a tunic to the Temple is based on both erroneous reading and assumption. Uriah is simply called upon to take it from the Temple and, in somewhat idiomatic language, "drop it off" at the house of the woman Salluah. Perhaps the writer was a priest who had changed into and out of officiating garb at the Temple.

Instructions (Concave)
(1)Regard[1] my tunic[2] [a] which (2)I left[3] at the house[4] of the House of (3)YHH.[5] [b] Tell[6] Uriah[7] (4)[that] he *should drop it off*[8] at Salluah('s).[9]

a Gen 3:21; 37:3; Exod 29:5; 2 Sam 13:18; Isa 22:21; Cant 5:3; Ezra 2:69; Neh 7:69, 71; etc.
b 1 Kgs 7:12, 40, 45, 48, 51, etc.

[1] Like 3.87I, this ostracon opens with *ḥzw* in the plural and then shifts to an imperative in feminine sing. (*ʾmry*); see further on 3.87A:9. For the verb, see on 3.87F:11.

[2] The buying and sending of tunics was a frequent subject in the papyrus and ostraca letters (*TAD* A2.1:4, 6; 2.2:4, 6, 2.2:11; 3.3:8-9, 11, 3.8:10, 13; 6.16:3; D7.7:7, 7.14:2, 6); Porten 1968:90. It is the most common garment mentioned in the Bible, worn by male and female alike, and figures prominently among the priestly garb.

[3] The root *šbq* is very supple — abandon an elder or a guardpost (*TAD* A2.4:4; 4.5:1), release a slave (3.74:4, 9-10), allow an act to take place (*TAD* A4.7:23), deposit beams (*TAD* A2.2:15, 2.4:10), and let go of a garment seized by a wicked person (*TAD* C1.1:107). Did the writer leave his garment at the Temple intentionally or simply forget it?

[4] Is the duplication of *byt* a dittography or does the first occurrence have the meaning of "building," an annex perhaps?

[5] The term for the Jewish Temple employed in the contracts and in official letters was *ʾgwrʾ* (3.51 and *TAD* A4.8 passim; 3.64:14, 3.67:6; 3.72:9, 3.73:10, 3.80:18). Yet once elsewhere we find the term *byt Yhw* in a papyrus letter (*TAD* A3.3:1); Porten 1968:105-110. It is the regular term for temple in the Bible. For the spelling YHH, see on 3.87C:3.

[6] Lit. *ʾmry l-*, "say to."

[7] The name is written here defectively — *ʾryh*. Was he associated with the cult? See 3.87B:1.

[8] The word *yrmh* = √*rmy* + object suffix. The basic meaning is "to throw down" and thus a colloquial meaning "drop something off at someone's place" might develop. Alternately, the term occurs with the meaning "put on" four threads (Shab. 10a); see Jastrow 1482. The word cannot be read *yḥrmh*, "dedicate it," as desiderated by Dupont-Sommer 1946-47a:82. For the volitive (*ʾmry*) — jussive (*yrmh*) sequence, see on 3.87B:10.

[9] Salluah is a well-attested female name. In 495 BCE it was borne by a daughter of Kenaiah (*TAD* B5.1:1-2). Nowhere else does the address on the ostraca appear at the end of the letter, as proposed by Dupont-Sommer 1946-47a:82.

REFERENCES

Text, translations and studies: *DAE* #90; Dupont-Sommer 1946-47a; Fitzmyer and Kaufman 1992 B.3.C.28; Lindenberger 1994 #21; Porten 1968; *TAD* D.

NOTICE OF DISPATCH OF WOOD (3.87K)
(*TAD* D7.36)

Bezalel Porten

Discovered on November 1, 1979 in the eighth season of the German Institute of Archaeology, this ostracon was published in 1987 by Mohammed Maraqten. Collated at source, it has yielded several new readings. It may be interpreted to mean that the writer has made a donation (*ḥntʾ*) of as much as 70 pieces of wood for the Temple altar, being sent by boat from Syene.

Report (Concave)
(1)I dispatched[1] in the hand of[2] [a] (= with) (2)Peṭekhnum[3] as GIFT[4] (3)3 loads[5] (4)in which (there are) wood,[6] (5)70/61 (pieces).

a Lev 16:21; 1 Sam 11:7; 16:20; 2 Sam 10:2; 11:14; 12:25; etc.

[1] Other ostraca report the dispatch of wood (*TAD* D7.37:3, 54:2 [20 pieces]); one, as here, "in the hand of" an Eg. boatman, Pamun (*TAD* D7.5:6-7).

[2] The expression *hwšr byd* means "to send (something) with somebody."

[3] This Eg. name (*pʾ-dy-Ḫnm*, "The {One} whom Khnum Gave") was popular at Elephantine (*TAD* C4.6:9; D9.9:4); a Peṭekhnum appeared as father of the Arameans Nabushezib (*TAD* A2.1:15, 2.5:10) and Ashah (*TAD* A2.1:11-12) and of the Jew Hosea (3.60:17). Our person is most likely an Eg. boatman.

[4] See on 3.87I:1.

[5] It is not clear how the pieces were distributed among the three loads; see also *TAD* D7.53:4. In the fourth century BCE Idumean Aram. ostraca "a load of wood" appears frequently among the delivered objects (Ephʿal and Naveh 1996 ##25:1, 129:2, 158:1, 167:2-3 [3 loads]). The term *mwbl* applied also to an ass's burden (*TAD* C1.1:185). Among the tales in later Jewish lore about a load of wood is one of a priest who learned from his altar experience how much of the wood goes up in smoke (Lam Rab. 49:2023; further references in Sokoloff 1990:294).

[6] The Pact enacted under Ezra and Nehemiah included a clause assigning by lot the obligation to bring at fixed times the wood offering to provide fuel for the altar (Neh 10:35; 13:31). The same selected parties carried on the tradition throughout Second Temple times and their names were recorded in the Mishnah (Taanith 4:5). For details, see Safrai 1976:253-255.

REFERENCES

Text, translations and studies: Ephʿal and Naveh 1996; Maraqten 1987; Safrai 1976; Sokoloff 1990; *TAD* D.

AN ARAMAIC DREAM REPORT FROM ELEPHANTINE (3.88)

Baruch A. Levine and Anne Robertson

This Aramaic ostracon from Elephantine is registered as *CIS* 2.137, and has been variously dated as early as the fifth century BCE and as late as ca. 300 BCE (Fitzmyer and Kaufman 1992:109-110). It was first published by Euting (1887), and has recently received two very different treatments by A. Dupont-Sommer (1948a) and B. A. Levine (1964). See also J. Teixidor (1967:178) and B. Porten (1968:275). It is a letter, written with a reed pen on both sides of a piece of pottery, and consists of thirteen brief but almost completely preserved lines. The reference to beholding a dream, a theme prominent in the narratives of the Book of Daniel, has drawn unusual attention to this enigmatic ostracon.

The writer, probably the head of a family, was detained away from home and, fearing that he would be further delayed in his return, wrote to his wife with interim instructions. He reports that he experienced an anxiety dream which had made him feverish, adding, however, that he was soon reassured by a vision whose message was: "Peace!" This report comes across as a symbolic characterization by the writer of his actual plight, intended to assuage his wife's probable apprehensions. The writer then instructed his wife to sell stored bundles of grain for coins, with the proceeds to be used to purchase food for the young children of the family.

[Collation of the original led Porten and Yardeni in *TAD* 4 (1999) 169 (D7.17) to some rather different readings and translations, here identified as *TAD*. Ed.]

An Anxiety Dream, and Prompt Reassurances
(Concave: lines 1-7)
Now,[1] indeed,[2] I beheld a dream,[3] [a] and from that time on,[4] I was exceedingly feverish.[5] Then a vision appeared[6] [b]; its words: "Peace!"[7] [c]

a Dan 2:26, 4:2,6, 15, 7:1 *b* Dan 2:19, 28, 4:2, 6-8, 10, 15, 17, 7:1-2, 7, 13 *c* Ezra 4:17, 5:7 *d* Ruth 2:14

Practical Instructions from a Man to His Wife
(Convex: lines 8-13)
Now, if my bundles of grain,[8] [d] all (of them),[9] you will sell, the small children[10] may eat. Indeed, there is no balance of coins.[11]

[1] Aram. *kᶜn* "Now," and the var. *kᶜnt*, are conventional in biblical Aram. (Dan 3:15, 4:34, 5:12; Ezra 4:10), and in epigraphic Aram. epistolary style.

[2] Aram. *hlw* "Indeed!" is cognate with Heb. *hinnēh*, and other Heb. and Aram. forms such as *harê*, *ᵓarê*, and *ᵓarû*, and also with Ugaritic *hl* (Brown 1987). See *DNWSI* 280.

[3] The idiom "to behold a dream" (*ḥlm ḥzy*) occurs regularly in the book of Daniel (2:26, 4:2, 6, 15, 7:1). For the related noun *ḥzw* "vision, apparition," see below, in note 5. As the ostracon is inscribed, we actually have the noun followed by an ideographic numeral, producing *ḥlm 1*. This is conventional in Aram. documents of the period.

[4] Aram. *ᶜdnᵓ* "time, season" is also characteristic of the vocabulary of the book of Daniel (Dan 2:8-9, 9, 21, 3:5, 15, 7:12, 25).

[5] The sense of feverishness is expressed as *ḥmm śgᵓ* (*ḥammîm śaggîᵓ*), lit.: "excessively hot." Cf. Dan 7:28: "And as for me, Daniel, my thoughts alarmed me exceedingly (*śaggîᵓ*), and my face darkened."

[6] We restore: [ᵓ]*tḥzy ḥz*[*w*] "a vision appeared." Compare the similar idiom in the Genesis Apocryphon from Qumran, where we read: *wᵓtḥzy ly ᵓlhᵓ bḥzyᵓ dy lylyᵓ* "and God appeared to me in a nocturnal vision" (Avigad and Yadin 1956 col. xxi, line 8). The term *ḥzw* occurs in Dan 2:19, 4:6-7, 7:2, 20, and elsewhere in the plural. See *DNWSI* 357-359 s.v. *ḥzy*$_1$.

[7] [*TAD*: "May Iahmaliah regard (= attend to) my welfare" (assigning the final *y* to the end of line 7 not line 6). Ed.]

[8] Read *ṣbty kl*, lit.: "my bundles, all," comparing Heb. *ṣebātîm* "bundles (of grain)" in Ruth 2:16, as first suggested by Hoffmann 1896. The syntax is well attested in Elephantine Aram., as in AP 30:15: *ᵓgwryᵓ ᵓlhy mṣryn kl* "the temples of the gods of Egypt, all"; AP 30:26: *yhwdyᵓ kl* "the Jews, all;" AP 39:1: *ᵓlhyᵓ kl* "the gods, all." See *DNWSI* 505 s.v. *kl* (1, c): "in absolute state as last element of an appositional group."

[9] The Aram. reads: *tzbny hmw* "you (fem. sing.) will sell them." The antecedent is *ṣbty* "my bundles (of grain)." [*TAD*: "Now, if you wish, do not sell them" (reading *ᵓl* not *kl* in line 9. Ed.]

[10] Aram. *ynqyᵓ* "young children," recalls Heb. *yônēq* "suckling, young child," often used collectively (Deut 32:25, Jer 44:7). The very form occurring here, the determined plural, is attested in Aram. texts from fifth century BCE Egypt. See *DNWSI* 462 s.v. ynq$_2$.

[11] Aram. *qṭyn* is taken to mean "pieces," namely, "pieces of silver, coins," from the root "to cut." Aram. *qṭ* is attested in another Elephantine ostracon, the so-called "Ostracon Araméen du Sabbat" (*COS* 3.87G), which also reports on an exchange of grain. In concave, line 6, of that inscription we read: *ḥṭ hnw bqṭ* "he weighs them out in coin. See Levine 1964:20. [*TAD*: "Lo, there do not remain (any) cucumbers." Note that in 3.87G (above), Porten reads *wᵓht hmw bgl*. Ed.]

REFERENCES

Text, translations and studies: *DAE* #21; Dupont-Sommer 1948a; 1949; Fitzmyer and Kaufman 1992 B.3.c.47; *KAI* #270; Levine 1964; Lindenberger 1994 #12; Porten 1968; *TAD* D; Teixidor 1967.

2. ARAMAIC STELA FRAGMENT

THE BUKĀN INSCRIPTION (3.89)

K. Lawson Younger, Jr.

This inscription was discovered in two fragments: the major piece was found in archaeological excavations in 1985 at Tapeh Qalâychi near Bukān, southeast of Lake Urmia in Azerbaijan, Iran; the other, smaller piece, was recovered on the antiquities market in 1990.[1] Together the fragments (.8 x 1.5 m) preserve only the last thirteen lines of an Old Aramaic inscription. Although much of the original text that was above the fragments is missing, it is clear that this was a memorial or dedicatory inscription set up by the local ruler of the land of Mannaea,[2] whose native language was certainly not Aramaic.

The text appears to date palaeographically to c. 700 BCE (Lemaire 1998a:27). The extant lines contain curses to be inflicted by the gods Hadad and Haldi on the country[3] of the king who would remove the stela. On these curses see further above, pp. xli-xlii.

(1) Whoever will remove[4] this stela,
[...] (2) in war or in peace,
whatever[5] the pestilence[6] [...] (3) which was in all the land,
may the gods impose[7] it on the [coun]try (4) of that king.
And may he be accursed[8] [a] to the gods,
and may he be accursed (5) to Ḫaldi who is in Zᶜtr.[9]
May seven (6) cows nurse one calf,[10]
but may it not be sated.
May seven (7) women bake (bread) in one oven,[11] [b]
but may they not fill (8) it.
May the smoke of its (cooking) fire and the sound of (9) a mill[12] [c] vanish from his country.
May his soil be salted,[d]
and (10) may it make him bitter from poisonous weeds.[13]
And that king who [...] (11) on this stela,
may Hadad and Ḫaldi overturn[14] [e] his throne.
(12) And seven years may Hadad not give his thunder[f] (lit. "voice") (13) in his country,
and may the entire curse[15] of this stela smite him.

a 1 Sam 26:19 *b* Lev 26:26a *c* Jer 25:10 *d* Deut 29:22; Judg 9:45; Jer 17:6; Zeph 2:9; Job 39:6 *e* Ps 89:45 *f* 2 Sam 22:14 = Ps 18:14

[1] The text was first published in Iranian by Bashash Kanzaq 1996. See now Lemaire 1998a 1998b; and Sokoloff 1999.

[2] For the Mannaeans, see Postgate 1987-90.

[3] Ephᶜal (1999:116, n.2) points out that in the ancient Near Eastern curses on potential mutilators of comemmorative inscriptions are generally directed against persons, and not against their countries. This may reflect the geopolitical situation of Mannaea, which was constantly under threat by its neighbors, the Urartaeans and the Assyrians.

[4] Most likely a Qal of *hns* "to remove" (*DNWSI* 290 s.v. *hns*). See e.g. Zakkur (*KAI* 202b:20): *wyhnsnh m*[*n*] [*ʾš*]*rh* "and takes it away from its place" (see *COS* 2.35). Sokoloff (1999:108) suggests a Hafᶜel of *nss* "to upset."

[5] *DNWSI* 504 s.v. *kl* (esp. *kl mh* = "whatever, every case, whatsoever"). See Lemaire 1998a:19. cf. Sefire I A 24-25. Sokoloff argues that while *kl mh* (or *klmh*) is well-attested in Old Aramaic it is always followed by a noun in the absolute state. Since *mwtnʾ* is a determined noun, this is problematic to Lemaire's restoration. Nonetheless, the reading [ ]*l* . *mh* is clear. So the restoration seems best and possibly our understanding is incomplete.

[6] See *DNWSI* 607 s.v. *mwtn* "pest."

[7] Two understandings of *yšmwh* have been proposed: 1) editio princeps and Sokoloff (p. 110) Peᶜal √ *śym* "to set, place"; 2) Lemaire 1998a:20 Haphᶜel (perhaps Qal?) √ *šmm* "destroy."

[8] From the √ *lwṣ/lwṭ* "curse." Understood here as a pass. ptc. (see Sokoloff 1999:111).

[9] Haldi was a deity of warfare among the Urartaeans (see Zimansky 1995:1144) and may have played such a role among the Mannaeans. Lemaire identifies *Zᶜtr* with the city *Zirtu/Izirtu* (1998a:21). Ephᶜal (1999:120) raises doubts concerning the metathesis of *tr/rt*. S. Kaufman (cited in Sokoloff 1999:111, n. 36) also raises doubts about this metathesis and questions the Semitic *ᶜayin* in a non-Semitic name.

[10] Cf. Tel Fakhariyah 20-21. See *COS* 2.34.

[11] See Cathcart 1996:144-145 and West Semitic introduction above (3.xxxv-xlii).

[12] See Lemaire 1997b; Sokoloff 1999:112-113.

[13] See Sokoloff 1999:107.

[14] For the verb *yhpkh*, cf. the Aḥiram inscription (*KAI* #1:2; Teixidor 1987; *COS* 2.55).

[15] See Sokoloff 1999:114.

REFERENCES

Text, translations and studies: Bashash Kanzaq 1996; Ephᶜal 1999; Lemaire 1997b; 1998a, photo p. 17; 1998b; Sokoloff 1999.

WEST SEMITIC BIBLIOGRAPHY

AHARONI, Y.

1966 "Hebrew Ostraca from Tel Arad." *IEJ* 16:1-7.

1970 "Three Hebrew Ostraca from Arad." *BASOR* 197:16-42.

AHARONI, Y., J. NAVEH, A. RAINEY, M. AHARONI, B. LIFSHITZ, M. SHARON, and Z. GOFER

1981 *Arad Inscriptions*. Judean Desert Studies. Jerusalem: Israel Exploration Society (English translation of Aharoni and Naveh 1981, including three new Hebrew inscriptions and new information on inscribed weights and jar handles).

AHARONI, Y., and J. NAVEH

1975 *Arad Inscriptions*. Jerusalem: Bialik Institute and Israel Exploration Society (in Hebrew).

AHL, S. W.

1973 "Epistolary Texts from Ugarit: Structural and Lexical Correspondences in Epistles in Akkadian and Ugaritic." Ph.D. dissertation, Brandeis University; Ann Arbor, MI: University Microfilms.

ALBRIGHT, W. F.

1926 "Notes on Early Hebrew and Aramaic Epigraphy." *JPOS* 6:88-93.

1958 "Specimens of Late Ugaritic Prose." *BASOR* 150:36-38.

ALEXANDER, P. S.

1978 "Remarks on Aramaic Epistolography in the Persian Period." *JSS* 23:155-170.

ASTOUR, M. C.

1965 "New Evidence on the Last Days of Ugarit." *AJA* 69:253-258.

1969 "The Partition of the Confederacy of Mukiš-Nuḫašše-Nii by Šuppiluliuma. A Study in Political Geography of the Amarna Age." *Or* 38:381-414.

1981 "Ugarit and the Great Powers." Pp. 3-29 in *Ugarit in Retrospect. Fifty Years of Ugarit and Ugaritic*. Ed. by G. D. Young. Winona Lake: Eisenbrauns.

AUFRECHT, W. E.

1989 *CAI*.

1999 "Ammonite Texts and Language." Pp. 163-188 in *Ancient Ammon*. Ed. by B. MacDonald and R. W. Younker. Leiden: E. J. Brill.

AVIGAD, N.

1966 "A Hebrew Seal with a Family Emblem." *IEJ* 16:50-53.

AVIGAD, N., and Y. YADIN.

1956 *A Genesis Apocryphon*. Jerusalem: Magnes Press and Heikal Ha-Sefer.

AZZONI, A., and S. L. LIPPERT.

2000 "An Achaemenid Loanword in the Legal Code of Hermopolis ᵓ*bygrn*." *Enchoria* 26:20-30.

BARNETT, R. D.

1969 "Ezekiel and Tyre." Pp. 6-13 and pl. iv in *W. F. Albright Volume*. Eretz-Israel 9. Jerusalem: Israel Exploration Society.

BARSTED, H. M.

1984 *The Religious Polemics of Amos*. VTSup 34. Leiden: E. J. Brill.

BASHASH KANZAQ, R.

1996 "A Complete Reading of the Inscription from Bukān." Pp. 25-39 in *Collection of Articles from the First Colloqium: Languages, Inscriptions and Ancient Texts. Shiraz 12-14 Esfand 1370 (March 2-4, 1991)*. Teheran, 1375/1996 (in Iranian).

BAUMGARTEN, A. I.

1981 *The Phoenician History of Philo of Byblos*. Leiden: E. J. Brill.

BEIT-ARIEH, I., and B. C. CRESSON

1991 "Ḥorvat ᶜUza: A Fortified Outpost on the Eastern Negev Border." *BA* 54:126-135.

BENZ, F. L.

1972 *Personal Names in the Phoenician and Punic Inscriptions*. Studia Pohl 8. Rome: Pontifical Biblical Institute.

BERLEJUNG, A., and A. SCHÜLE

1998 "Erwägungen zu den neuen Ostraka aus der Sammlung Moussaïeff." *ZAH* 11:68-73.

BONNET, C.

1988 *Melqart. Cultes et mythes de l'Héraclès tyrien en Méditerranée*. Studia Phoenicia 8. Leuven: Uitgeverij Peeters; Namur: Presses Universitaires de Namur.

1992 "Baal kr." P. 58 in *DCPP*.

BOOIJ, Th.

1986 "The Yavneh Yam Ostracon and Hebrew Consecutive Imperfect." *BiOr* 43:642-647.

BORDREUIL, P.

1982 "Quatre documents en cunéiformes alphabétiques mal connus ou inédits (U.H. 138, RS 23.492, RS 34.356, Musée d'Alep M. 3601)." *Semitica* 32:5-14, pls. i-ii.

1984 "Arrou, Ǵourou et Ṣapanou: Circonscriptions administratives et géographie mythique du royaume d'Ougarit." *Syria* 61:1-10.

1991 "Les circonstances de la découverte épigraphique de 1973." Pp. 7-9 in RSOu 7.

BORDREUIL, P., and A. CAQUOT.

1980 "Les textes en cunéiformes alphabétiques découverts en 1978 à Ibn Hani." *Syria* 57:343-373.

BORDREUIL, P., and F. MALBRAN-LABAT.

1995 "Les archives de la maison d'Ourtenou." Pp. 443-456 in *Académie des Inscriptions et Belles-Lettres: Comptes Rendus*. Paris: Boccard.

BORDREUIL, P., and D. PARDEE.
1982 "Le rituel funéraire ougaritique RS 34.126." *Syria* 59:121-128.
1989 RSOu 5/1.
1991 "Les textes en cunéiformes alphabétiques." Pp. 139-172 in RSOu 7.
in press "Textes ougaritiques," in *Études ougaritiques, Travaux 1985-1995* [*editio princeps* of Ugaritic texts from excavations of 1986-1992].
in preparation "Textes ougaritiques" [*editio princeps* of Ugaritic texts from excavations of 1994-2000].
BORDREUIL, P., F. ISRAEL, and D. PARDEE
1996 "Deux ostraca paléo-hébreux de la collection Sh. Moussaïeff: I) Contribution financière obligatoire pour le temple de YHWH, II) Réclamation d'une veuve auprès d'un fonctionnaire." *Semitica* 46:49-76, pls. 7-8.
1998 "King's Command and Widow's Plea: Two New Hebrew Ostraca of the Biblical Period." *Near Eastern Archaeology* 61:2-13.
BORGER, R.
1956 *Asarh.*
BOTTA, A. F.
2001 *Interrelationships between Aramaic and Demotic Legal Traditions. An Egyptological Approach to the Withdrawal Clause in the Elephantine Aramaic Documents*. Ph.D. Dissertation, Hebrew University. Jerusalem.
BOUNNI, A., J. LAGARCE, and E. LAGARCE.
1998 *Ras Ibn Hani, I. Le palais nord du Bronze récent, fouilles 1979-1995, synthèse préliminaire*. Bibliothèque Archéologique et Historique 151. Beirut: Institut Français d'Archéologie du Proche-Orient.
BRIANT, P.
1996 "Une curieuse affaire à Éléphantine en 410 av. n.è.: Widranga, le sanctuaire de Khnûm et le temple de Yahweh." Pp. 115-131 in *Égypte pharaonique: pouvoir, societé*. Méditerranées 6/7. Ed. by B. Menu. Paris: L'Harmattan.
BRON, F., and A. LEMAIRE
1980 "Notes de lexicographie ouest-sémitique." *Comptes Rendus du Groupe Linguistique d'Études Chamito-Sémitiques* 24-28:7-17.
BROOKE, G. J.
1979 "The Textual, Formal, and Historical Significance of Ugaritic Letter RS 34.124 (= *KTU* 2.72)." *UF* 11:69-87.
BROWN, M. L.
1987 "'Is it not?' or 'Indeed!': *HL* in Northwest Semitic." *Maarav* 4:201-219.
CALLOT, O.
1983 RSOu 1.
1994 RSOu 10.
CAQUOT, A.
1975 "Hébreu et Araméen." *ACF* 75:423-432.
1978a "La lettre de la reine Puduḫepa." Pp. 121-134 in *Ugaritica* 7.
1978b "Correspondance de ᶜUzzin fils de Bayaya (RS 17.63 et 17.117)." Pp. 389-398 in *Ugaritica* 7.
CASSIN, E.
1959 "Le bain des brebis." *Or* 28:225-229.
CATHCART, K. J.
1996 "The Curses in Old Aramaic Inscriptions." Pp. 140-152 in *Studies McNamara*.
COATS, G. W.
1970 "Self-Abasement and Insult Formulas." *JBL* 89:14-26.
COHEN, N.
1966-67 "Historical Conclusions Gleaned from the Names of the Jews of Elephantine." *Lešonénu* 31:97-106.
COOK, S. A.
1924 "Inscribed Hebrew Objects from Ophel." *PEFQS* 56:180-186, pl. vi.
COURTOIS, J.-C.
1990 "Yabninu et le Palais sud d'Ougarit." *Syria* 67:103-142.
COWLEY, A. E.
1923 *AP*.
1929 "Two Aramaic Ostraka." *JRAS* 107-111.
CROSS, F. M.
1956 "Lachish Letter IV." *BASOR* 144:24-26.
1962 "Epigraphic Notes on Hebrew Documents of the Eighth-Sixth Centuries B.C.: II. The Murabbaᶜât Papyrus and the Letter Found Near Yabneh-Yam." *BASOR* 165:34-46.
1975 "Ammonite Ostraca From Heshbon, Heshbon Ostraca IV-VIII." *AUSS* 13:1-22, pls. 1-2.
1976 "Heshbon Ostracon XI." *AUSS* 14:145-148, pl. 15:A.
1986 "An Unpublished Ammonite Ostracon from Ḥesbān." Pp. 475-489 in *Studies Horn*.
2002 "Ammonite Ostraca from Tell Hesbân." *Leaves From an Epigrapher's Notebook: Collected Papers in Hebrew and West Semitic Palaeography and Epigraphy*. HSS 50. Cambridge, MA: Harvard University.
CROSS, F. M., Jr., and D. N. FREEDMAN.
1952 *Early Hebrew Orthography*. New Haven: American Oriental Society.
CUNCHILLOS, J.-L.
1988 "Mes affaires sont terminées! Traduction et commentaire de KTU 2.13." *SEL* 5:45-50.
1989 "Correspondance." Pp. 239-421 in *Textes ougaritiques*. Tome II: *Textes religieux, rituels, correspondance*. LAPO 14. Paris: Cerf.
1999 "The Ugaritic Letters." Pp. 359-374 in *HUS*.
DALLEY, S., and J. N. POSTGATE.
1984 *The Tablets from Fort Shalmaneser*. CTN 3. Oxford: British School of Archaeology.
DEGEN, R.
1972 "Zum Ostracon *CIS* II 138." *NESE* 1:23-37.
DEMPSEY, D.
1990 "The 'Epistolary Perfect' in Aramaic Letters." *BN* 54:7-11.

DHORME, E.
1933 "Deux tablettes de Ras-Shamra de la campagne de 1932." *Syria* 14:229-237.
1938 "Nouvelle lettre d'Ugarit en écriture alphabétique." *Syria* 19:142-146.
DIETRICH, M., and O. LORETZ.
1964-66 "Der Vertrag zwischen Šuppiluliuma und Niqmandu. Eine philologische und kulturhistorische Studie." *WO* 3:206-245.
1974 "Eine briefliche Antwort des Königs von Ugarit auf eine Anfrage: PRU 2,10 (= RS 16.264)." *UF* 6:453-455.
1984 "Der Brief KTU 2.70 (RS 29.93)." *UF* 16:63-68.
1994 "Ugaritisch *iṯ*, *ṯyndr* und hebräisch *ʾšh*, *šy*, (KTU 1.14 IV 38; 2.13:14-15; 2.30:12-14a)." *UF* 26:63-72.
DIETRICH, M., O. LORETZ, and J. SANMARTÍN.
1976 *KTU.*[1]
1995 *KTU.*[2]
DIJKSTRA, M.
1976 "Two Notes on PRU 5, No. 60." *UF* 8:437-439.
1994 "The Myth of Astarte, the Huntress (KTU 1.92): New Fragments." *UF* 26:113-26.
DIJKSTRA, M., J. C. DE MOOR, and K. SPRONK.
1981 "Review of Dietrich, Loretz, and Sanmartín 1976." *BiOr* 38:371-380.
DION, P.-E.
1982a "La lettre araméenne passe-partout et ses sous-espèces." *RB* 89:528-575.
1982b "The Aramaic 'Family Letter' and Related Epistolary Forms in Other Oriental Languages and in Hellenistic Greek." Pp. 59-76 in *Ancient Letter Writing*. Ed. by J. L. White. Semeia 22. Chico, CA: Scholars Press.
1983 "Review." *JAOS* 103:470-472.
1992 "Les *KTYM* de Tel Arad: Grecs ou Phéniciens?" *RB* 99:70-97.
DION, P.-E., D. PARDEE, and J. D. WHITEHEAD
1979 "Les types épistolaires hébréo-araméens jusqu'au temps de Bar-Kokhbah." *RB* 86:544-579.
DIRINGER, D.
1934 *Le iscrizioni antico-ebraiche palestinesi*. Florence: Le Monnier.
1953 "Early Hebrew Inscriptions." Pp. 331-359 (ch. 10) in *The Iron Age* (Lachish III). Ed. by Olga Tufnell, et al. London: Oxford University Press.
DOBBS-ALLSOPP, F. W.
1994 "The Genre of the Meṣad Ḥashavyahu Ostracon." *BASOR* 295:49-55.
DORNEMANN, R. H.
1983 *The Archaeology of the Transjordan in the Bronze and Iron Ages*. Milwaukee: Milwaukee Public Museum.
DRINKARD, J. F., Jr.
1988 "Epigraphy as a Dating Method." Pp. 417-39 in *Benchmarks in Time and Culture. An Introduction to Palestinian Archaeology Dedicated to Joseph A. Callaway*. Ed. J. F. Drinkard, Jr., et al. ASOR, SBL, Archaeology and Biblical Studies 1. Atlanta: Scholars Press.
DUPONT-SOMMER, A.
1942-45 "Un ostracon araméen inédit d'Éléphantine adressé à Aḥuṭub." *RES* 65-75.
1944 "'Bêl et Nabû, Šamaš et Nergal' sur un ostracon inédit d'Éléphantine." *RHR* 128:28-39.
1945 "Le syncrétism religieux des Juifs d'Éléphantine d'après un ostracon araméen inédit." *RHR* 130:17-28.
1946-47a "'Maison de Yahvé' et vêtements sacrés à Éléphantine d'après un ostracon araméen du Musé du Caire." *JA* 235:79-87.
1946-47b "Sur la fête de la Pâque dans les documents araméens d'Éléphantine." *REJ* 107:39-51.
1948a "Ostraca Araméens d'Éléphantine." *ASAE* 48:109-130 and pls.
1948b "Un papyrus araméen d'époque saïte découverte à Saqqarah." *Semitica* 1:43-68.
1949 "L'ostracon araméen du Sabbat (Collection Clermont-Ganneau No. 152)." *Semitica* 2:29-39.
1950 "Sabbat et parascève à Éléphantine d'après des ostraca araméens inédits." *MAIBL* 15:67-88.
DUSSAUD, R.
1938 "Le prophète Jérémie et les lettres de Lakish." *Syria* 19:256-271.
ELAYI, J.
1988 "A Phoenician Vase Representing the God Milqart?" *BaM* 19:549-555.
1990 *Sidon, cité autonome de l'empire perse*. 2nd ed. Paris: Editions Idéaphane.
EPHᶜAL, I.
1999 "The Bukān Aramaic Inscription: Historical Considerations." *IEJ* 49:116-121.
EPHᶜAL, I., and J. NAVEH.
1996 *Aramaic Ostraca of the Fourth Century BC from Idumaea*. Jerusalem: Magnes Press.
1998 "Remarks on the Recently Published Moussaieff Ostraca." *IEJ* 48:269-73.
EUTING, J.
1887 "Epigraphische Miscellen." SPAW 23:407-422.
FALES, F. M.
1986 *AECT.*
1987 "Aramaic Letters and Neo-Assyrian Letters: Philological and Methodological Notes." *JAOS* 107:451-469.
FALES, F. M., and J. N. POSTGATE.
1995 *Imperial Administrative Records, Part II. Provincial and Military Administration*. SAA 11. Helsinki: Helsinki University Press.
FANTALKIN, A.
2001 "Meṣad Ḥashavyahu: Its Material Culture and Historical Background." *Tel Aviv* 28:3-165.
FITZMYER, J.
1965 "The Aramaic Letter of King Adon to the Egyptian Pharaoh." *Biblica* 46:41-55.
1979 *A Wandering Aramean: Collected Aramaic Essays*. Missoula: Scholars Press.
FITZMYER, J., and S. A. KAUFMAN.
1992 *An Aramaic Bibliography, Part I: Old, Official and Biblical Aramaic*. Baltimore: Johns Hopkins University Press.

FOLMER, M.
1995 *The Aramaic Language in the Achaemenid Period: A Study in Linguistic Variation*. OLA 68. Leuven: Peeters.
FREU, J.
1999 "La fin d'Ugarit et de l'empire hittite: données nouvelles et chronologie." *Semitica* 48:17-39.
FRIEDRICH, J., et al.
1940 *TH*.
FRYMER-KENSKY, T.
2001 "Israel." Pp. 251-263 in *Security For Debt in Ancient Near Eastern Law*. CHANE 9. Ed. by R. Westbrook and R. Jasnow. Leiden: E. J. Brill.
GALÁN, J. M.
1993 "What is He, the Dog?" *UF* 25:173-180.
GIBSON, J. C. L.
1975 *SSI* 2:110-116.
GINSBERG, H. L.
1940 "King of Kings and Lord of Kingdoms." *AJSL* 57:71-72.
1948 "An Aramaic Contemporary of the Lachish Letters." *BASOR* 111:24-27.
GITIN, S.
1998 "The Philistines in the Prophetic Texts: An Archaeological Perspective." Pp. 273-290 in *Studies Frerichs*.
GORDON, C. H.
1947 *Ugaritic Handbook: Revised Grammar, Paradigms, Texts in Transliteration, Comprehensive Glossary*. AnOr 25. Rome: Pontifical Biblical Institute.
GREENFIELD, J. C.
1960 "'Le bain des brebis.' Another Example and a Query." *Or* 29:98-102; repr. Greenfield 2001:1-5.
1974 "The *Marzeaḥ* as a Social Institution." *Acta Antiqua* 22:451-455; repr. Greenfield 2001:907-911.
1990 "Some Phoenician Words." *Semitica* (= *Hommages à Maurice Sznycer*, Volume 1) 38:155-158; repr. Greenfield 2001:799-802.
2001 *ᶜAl Kanfei Yonah: Collected Studies of Jonas C. Greenfield on Semitic Philology*. 2 vols. Ed. by S. M. Paul, M. E. Stone and A. Pinnick. Leiden: Brill; Jerusalem: Magnes Press.
GRÖNDAHL, F.
1967 *Die Personennamen der Texte aus Ugarit*. Studia Pohl 1. Rome: Pontifical Biblical Institute.
HAWKINS, J. D.
1972-75 "Ḫilakku." *RlA* 4:402-403.
HELCK, W.
1963 "Urḫi-Tešup in Ägypten." *JCS* 17:87-97.
HELTZER, M.
1975 "On Tithe Paid in Grain in Ugarit." *IEJ* 25:124-128.
1976 *The Rural Community of Ancient Ugarit*. Wiesbaden: Reichert-Verlag.
1982 *The Internal Organization of the Kingdom of Ugarit*. Wiesbaden: Reichert Verlag.
1991 "Vineyards and Wine in Ugarit (Property and Distribution)." *UF* 22:119-135.
HERDNER, A.
1963 *CTA*.
1978 "Lettre de deux serviteurs à leur maître." Pp. 75-78 in *Ugaritica* 7.
HERR, L. G.
1992 "Epigraphic Finds from Tell El-'Umeiri During the 1989 Season." *AUSS* 30:187-200.
HERZOG, Z., M. AHARONI, A. F. RAINEY, and S. MOSHKOVITZ
1984 "The Israelite Fortress at Arad." *BASOR* 254:1-34.
HESTRIN, R.
1973 *Inscriptions Reveal: Documents from the time of the Bible, the Mishna and the Talmud*. Jerusalem: Israel Museum.
HESTRIN, R., and M. DAYAGI-MENDELS.
1979 *Inscribed Seals: First Temple Period*. Jerusalem: Israel Museum.
HINZ, W.
1975 *Altiranisches Sprachgut der Nebenüberlieferungen*. Göttinger Orientforschungen 3. Iranica 3. Wiesbaden: Harrassowitz.
HOFFMANN, G.
1896 "Aramäische Inschriften aus Nerab bei Aleppo: Neue und alte Götter." *ZA* 11:207-292.
HOFFNER, H.
1998 *Hittite Myths*. SBLWAW. Second edition. Atlanta, GA: Scholars Press.
HOFTIJZER, J.
1967 "Das sogenannte Feueropfer." Pp. 114-134 in *Studies Baumgartner*.
1979 "Une lettre du roi de Tyr." *UF* 11:383-388.
1982 "Une lettre du roi hittite." Pp. 379-387 in *Studies van der Ploeg*.
1986 "Frustula Epigraphica Hebraica." Pp. 85-93 in *Studies Hospers*.
HORN, S. H.
1968 "Where and When Was the Aramaic Saqqara Papyrus Written?" *AUSS* 6:29-45.
HÜBNER, U.
1988 "Die ersten moabitischen Ostraca." *ZDPV* 104:68-73.
1992 *Die Ammoniter: Untersuchungen zur Geschichte, Kultur und Religion eines transjordanischen Volkes im 1. Jahrtausend v. Chr.* Wiesbaden: Otto Harrassowitz.
HUFFMON, H. B., and S. B. PARKER.
1966 "A Further Note on the Treaty Background of Hebrew *yādaᶜ*." *BASOR* 184:36-38.
HUG, V.
1993 *Altaramäische Grammatik der Texte des 7. und 6. Jahrhunderts v. Chr.* Heidelberg: Orientverlag.

HUGENBERGER, G. P.
1994 *Marriage as a Covenant: A Study of Biblical Law and Ethics Governing Marriage, Developed from the Perspective of Malachi.* VTSup 52. Leiden: E. J. Brill.
HURVITZ, A.
1995 "Terms and Epithets Relating to the Jerusalem Temple Compound." Pp. 165-183 in *Studies Milgrom.*
IBRAHIM, M. M.
1975 "Third Season of Excavations at Sahab, 1975 (Preliminary Report)." *ADAJ* 20:69-82, pls. 25-29.
JAROŠ, K.
1982 *Hundert Inschriften aus Kanaan und Israel.* Fribourg: Verlag Schweizerisches Katholisches Bibelwerk.
JIDEJIAN, N.
1969 *Tyre through the Ages.* Beirut: Dar el-Mashreq.
DE JONG, T., and W. H. VAN SOLDT
1987-88 "Redating an Early Solar Eclipse Record (KTU 1.78). Implications for the Ugaritic Calendar and for the Secular Accelerations of the Earth and Moon." *JEOL* 30:65-77.
JOÜON, P.
1934 "Notes grammaticales, lexicographiques et philologiques sur les papyrus araméens d'Égypte." *Mélanges de l'Université Saint-Joseph* 18:1-90.
KAISER, O.
1970 "Zum Formular der in Ugarit gefundenen Briefe." *ZDPV* 86:10-23.
KAUFMAN, S.
1974 *The Akkadian Influences on Aramaic.* AS 19. Chicago and London: The University of Chicago.
1977 "An Assyro-Aramaic *egirtu ša šulmu.*" Pp. 119-127 in *Studies Finkelstein.*
1989 "Assyro-Aramaica." *JAOS* 109:97-102.
KITZ, A. M.
2000 "Undivided Inheritance and Lot Casting in the Book of Joshua." *JBL* 119:601-618.
KLENGEL, H.
1974 "'Hungerjahre' in Ḫatti." *AoF* 1:165-174.
1992 *Syria 3000 to 300 B.C.: A Handbook of Political History.* Berlin: Akademie Verlag.
KLETTER, R.
1998 *Economic Keystones: The Weight System of the Kingdom of Judah.* JSOTSup 276. Sheffield: Sheffield Academic Press.
KORNFELD, W.
1978 *Onomastica Aramaica aus Ägypten.* Phil.-hist. Klasse 333. Vienna: Verlag der Österreichische Akademie der Wissenschaften.
KRAELING, E. G.
1953 *The Brooklyn Museum Aramaic Papyri: New Documents of the Fifth Century B.C. from the Jewish Colony at Elephantine.* New Haven: Yale University Press.
KRAHMALKOV, C. R.
1981 "The Historical Setting of the Adon Papyrus." *BA* 44:197-198.
2000 *Phoenician-Punic Dictionary.* OLA 90. Studia Phoenicia 15. Leuven: Peeters.
KRISTENSEN, A. L.
1977 "Ugaritic Epistolary Formulas: A Comparative Study of the Ugaritic Epistolary Formulas in the Context of the Contemporary Akkadian Formulas in the Letters from Ugarit and Amarna." *UF* 9:143-158.
KUTSCHER, E. Y.
1977 *Hebrew and Aramaic Studies.* Ed. by Z. Ben-Ḥayyim, A. Dotan, and G. Sarfatti. Jerusalem: Magnes Press.
LACKENBACHER, S.
1989 "Trois lettres d'Ugarit." Pp. 317-320 in *Studies Sjöberg.*
LAROCHE, E.
1966 *Les noms des Hittites.* Études linguistiques 4. Paris: C Klincksieck.
LAWTON, R. B.
1992 "Arad Ostraca." *ABD* 1:336-337.
LEBRUN, R.
1992 "Cebelireis Daği." P. 96 in *DCPP.*
LEMAIRE, A.
1977 *Inscriptions hébraïques.* Tome I: *Les ostraca.* Littératures Anciennes du Proche-Orient 9. Paris: Le Cerf.
1983a "Review." *Or* 52:444-447.
1983b "L'inscription phénicienne de Hassan-Beyli reconsidérée." *RSF* 11:9-19.
1986 "Review." *JNES* 45:152-154.
1989 "Une inscription phénicienne découverte récemment et le mariage de Ruth la Moabite." Pp. 124-129 in *Y. Yadin Volume.* Eretz-Israel 20. Jerusalem: Israel Exploration Society.
1997a "Arad Inscriptions." *OEANE* 1:176-77.
1997b "Jérémie xxv 10b et la stèle araméenne de Bukân." *VT* 47:543-545.
1998a "Une inscription araméenne du VIIIe s. av. J.-C. trouvée à Bukân." *Studia Iranica* 27:15-30, photo p. 17.
1998b "L'inscription araméenne de Bukân et son intéret historique." *CRAI* 293-299.
1999 "Veuve sans enfants dans le royaume de Juda." *Zeitschrift für Altorientalische und Biblische Rechtsgeschichte* 5:1-14.
2001 *Nouvelles tablettes araméennes.* Hautes études orientales 34. Geneva: Droz.
LEVINE, B. A.
1964 "Notes on an Aramaic Dream Text from Egypt." *JAOS* 84:18-22.
1983 "In Praise of the Israelite *Mišpaḥah*: Legal Themes in the Book of Ruth." Pp. 95-106 in *Studies Mendenhall.*
LEWIS, T. J.
1989 *Cults of the Dead in Ancient Israel and Ugarit.* Atlanta: Scholars Press.

LIDZBARSKI, M.
1921 *AUA*.

LINDENBERGER, J. M.
1994 *Ancient Aramaic and Hebrew Letters*. SBLWAW 4. Atlanta: Scholars Press.
2001 "What Ever Happened to Vidranga? A Jewish Liturgy of Cursing from Elephantine." Pp. 134-157 in *The World of the Aramaeans III: Studies in Language and Literature in Honour of Paul-Eugène Dion*. Ed. by P. M. M. Daviau, J. W. Wevers and M. Weigl. Sheffield: Sheffield Academic Press.

LIPIŃSKI, E.
1970 "La fête de l'ensevelissement et de la résurrection de Milqart." Pp. 30-58 in *Actes de la XVIIe Rencontre assyriologique internationale*. Harm-sur-Heure: Comité belge de récherches en Mésopotamie.
1975a *Studies in Aramaic Inscriptions and Onomastics*. OLA 1. Leuven: Leuven University.
1975b "Ophel Ostrakon." P. 268 in *Religionsgeschichtliches Textbuch zum Alten Testament*. Ed. by W. Beyerlin. Göttingen: Vandenhoeck & Ruprecht (= p. 252 in *Near Eastern Religious Texts Relating to the Old Testament*, 1978).
1994 *Studies in Aramaic Inscriptions and Onomastics*. 2. OLA 57. Leuven: Peeters.
1995 *Dieux et déesses de l'univers phénicien et punique*. OLA 64. Leuven: Peeters.

LIVERANI, M.
1962 *Storia di Ugarit nell'età degli archivi politici*. Studi Semitici 6. Rome: Università di Roma, Istituto di Studi del Vicino Oriente.
1964a "Elementi innovativi nell'ugaritico non letterario." *Atti della Accademia Nazionale dei Lincei, Rendiconti della Classe di Scienze morali, storiche e filologiche* 8/19:173-191.
1964b "Un tipo di espressione indefinita in accadico e in ugaritico." *RSO* 39:199-202.
1979 "Ras Shamra: Histoire." Cols. 1295-1348 in *SDB*, vol. 9.
1995 "La fin d'Ougarit. Quand? Pourquoi? Comment?" Pp. 113-17 in RSOu 11.
1997 "A Canaanite Indefinite Idiom in the Amarna Letters." *NABU* 1997:119-120.

LOEWENSTAMM, S. E.
1967 "Prostration from Afar in Ugaritic, Akkadian and Hebrew." *BASOR* 188:41-43.

LONG, G. A.
1991 "A Kinsman-Redeemer in the Phoenician Inscription from Cebel-Daği." *ZAW* 103:421-424.

LONG, G. A., and D. PARDEE.
1989 "Who Exiled Whom? Another Interpretation of the Phoenician Inscription from Cebel Ires Daği." *AO* 7:207-214.

LUCAS, A.
1989 *Ancient Egyptian Materials and Industries*. London: E. Arnold & Co.

MALAMAT, A.
1988 "The Kingdom of Judah Between Egypt and Babylon: A Small State Within a Great Power Confrontation." Pp. 117-129 in *Studies Fensham*.

MALBRAN-LABAT, F.
1991 "Lettres." Pp. 27-64 in RSOu 7.
1995a "La découverte épigraphique de 1994 à Ougarit (les textes akkadiens)." *SMEA* 36:103-111.
1995b "L'épigraphie akkadienne. Rétrospective et perspectives." Pp. 33-40 in RSOu 11.

MALININE, M. (Editor).
1953 *Choix de textes juridiques en hiératique "anormal" et en démotique (XXVe-XXVIIe dynasties)*. Bibliothèque de l'École des Hautes Études 300. Paris, H. Champion.

MANDER, P.
1990 *Administrative Texts of the Archive L. 2679*. MEE 10. Materiali per il vocabolario sumerico 1. Rome: Università degli studi di Roma "La Sapienza."

MANOR, D. W., and G. A. HERION
1992 "Arad." *ABD* 1:331-336.

MARAQTEN, M.
1987 "Neue aramäische Ostraka aus Elephantine." *MDAIK* 43:170-171.
1988 *Die semitischen Personennamen in den alt- und reichsaramäischen Inschriften aus Vorderasien*. Texte und Studien zur Orientalistik 5. Hildesheim and New York: G. Olms.

MILANO, L.
1983 "Gli epiteti del faraone in una lettera ugaritica da Ras Ibn Hani." Pp. 141-158 in *Studies Pintore*.

MILGROM, J.
1990 *Numbers, JPS Torah Commentary*. Philadelphia: Jewish Publication Society.

MILIK, J. T.
1959 "Notes d'épigraphie et de topographie palestiniennes." *RB* 66:550-575.
1967 "Les papyrus araméens d'Hermopolis et les cultes syro-phéniciens en égypte perse." *RB* 48:546-622.

DE MOOR, J. C.
1965 "Frustula Ugaritica." *JNES* 24:355-364.
1996 "Egypt, Ugarit and Exodus." Pp. 213-247 in *Studies Gibson*.

MORIYA, A.
1995 "Aramaic Epistolography; The Hermopolis Letters and Related Material in the Persian Period." Ph.D. Dissertation, Hebrew Union College. Cincinnati.

MOSCA, P. G., and J. RUSSELL.
1983 "A New Phoenician Inscription from Rough Cilicia." *AJA* 87:246.
1987 "A Phoenician Inscription from Cebel Ires Daği in Rough Cilicia." *Epigraphica Anatolica* 9:1-28.

MOSCATI, S.
1951 *L'epigrafia ebraica antica, 1935-1950*. Biblica et Orientalia 15. Rome: Pontificial Biblical Institute.

MUFFS, Y.
1973 "Two Comparative Lexical Studies." *JANES* 5:287-294.

MURAOKA, T., and B. PORTEN.
1998 *GEA*.
NAVEH, J.
1960 "A Hebrew Letter from the Seventh Century BC." *IEJ* 10:129-139.
1962 "More Hebrew Inscriptions from Meṣad Ḥashavyahu." *IEJ* 12:27-32.
1964 "Some Notes on the Reading of the Meṣad Ḥashavyahu Letter." *IEJ* 14:158-159.
1970 "The Development of the Aramaic Script." *Proceedings of the Israel Academy of Sciences and Humanities* 5/1:1-69.
1992 "The Numbers of *Bat* in the Arad Ostraca." *IEJ* 42:52-54.
NAʾAMAN, N.
1991 "The Kingdom of Judah under Josiah." *Tel Aviv* 18:3-71.
NOUGAYROL, J.
1955 *PRU* 3.
1956 *PRU* 4.
1968 "Textes suméro-accadiens des archives et bibliothèques privées d'Ugarit." Pp. 1-446 in *Ugaritica* 5.
OWEN, D. I.
1981 "An Akkadian Letter from Ugarit at Tel Aphek." *Tel Aviv* 8:1-17.
PARDEE, D.
1975 "The Ugaritic Text 2106:10-18: A Bottomry Loan?" *JAOS* 95:612-619.
1977 "A New Ugaritic Letter." *BiOr* 34:3-20.
1978a "The Judicial Plea from Meṣad Ḥashavyahu (Yavneh-Yam): A New Philological Study." *Maarav* 1:33-66.
1978b "Letters from Tel Arad." *UF* 10:289-336.
1979-80 "La lettre de *pnḥṯ* et de *yrmhd* à leur maître." *Annales Archéologiques Arabes Syriennes* 29-30:23-35.
1981 "A Further Note on *PRU V*, No. 60, Epigraphic in Nature." *UF* 13:151-156.
1981-82 "Ugaritic." *AfO* 28:259-272.
1982 "New Readings in the Letters of ʿ*zn bn byy*." *AfO* Beiheft 19:39-53.
1983 "The 'Epistolary Perfect' in Hebrew Letters." *BN* 22:34-40.
1983-84 "Ugaritic: The Letter of Puduḫepa: The Text." *AfO* 29-30:321-329.
1984 "Ugaritic: Further Studies in Ugaritic Epistolography." *AfO* 31:213-230.
1985 "Review." *JNES* 44:67-71.
1986 "Epigraphic Notes to Articles in *UF* 16." *UF* 18:454.
1987a "Ugaritic Bibliography." *AfO* 34:366-471.
1987b "Epigraphic and Philological Notes." *UF* 19:199-217.
1987c "'As Strong as Death.'" Pp. 65-69 in *Studies Pope*.
1988 RSOu 4.
1990 Review. *Journal of Near Eastern Studies* 49:88-94.
1997a "Ugaritic." *OEANE* 5:262-264.
1997b "Ugarit Inscriptions." *OEANE* 5:264-266.
1997c "Lachish Inscriptions." *OEANE* 3:323-324.
2000a *Les textes rituels*. Paris: Éditions Recherche sur les Civilisations.
2000b "Ugaritic Studies at the End of the 20th Century." *BASOR* 320:49-86.
forthcoming a "Un « nouveau » mot ougaritique"
forthcoming b "Trois comptes ougaritiques." Forthcoming in *Syria*.
forthcoming c "Une formule épistolaire en ougaritique et accadien." Forthcoming in *Fronzaroli Festschrift*.
forthcoming d *Les textes épistolaires*. Paris: Éditions Recherche sur les Civilisations.
PARDEE, D., S. D. SPERLING, J. D. WHITEHEAD, and P.-E. DION.
1982 *Handbook of Ancient Hebrew Letters*. SBL Sources for Biblical Study 15. Chico: Scholars Press.
PARDEE, D., and R. M. WHITING.
1987 "Aspects of Epistolary Verbal Usage in Ugaritic and Akkadian." *BSOAS* 50:1-31.
PARKER, R. A., and W. H. DUBBERSTEIN.
1946 *Babylonian Chronology 626 B.C.-A.D. 45*. 2nd Edition. SAOC 24. Chicago: University of Chicago Press.
1956 *Babylonian Chronology 626 B.C.-A.D. 75*. Brown University Studies 19. Providence: Brown University Press.
PARKER, S. B.
1994 "The Lachish Letters and Official Reactions to Prophecies." Pp. 65-78 in *Uncovering Ancient Stones. Essays in Memory of H. Neil Richardson*. Ed. by L. M. Hopfe. Winona Lake: Eisenbrauns.
1997 *Stories in Scripture and Inscriptions: Comparative Studies on Narratives in Northwest Semitic Inscriptions and the Hebrew Bible*. New York, Oxford: Oxford University Press.
PARPOLA, S.
1970 *Neo-Assyrian Toponyms*. AOAT 6. Kevelaer: Butzon & Bercker.
PEDERSÉN, O.
1986 *Archives and Libraries in the City of Assur: A Survey of the German Excavations* II. Acta Universitatis Upsaliensis, Studia Semitica Upsaliensia 8. Uppsala: Uppsala University.
PERLES, F.
1911 "Zu Sachaus 'Aramäische Papyrus und Ostraka.'" *OLZ* 14:497-503.
PETTINATO, G.
1979 "Culto ufficiale ad Ebla duranto il regno di Ibbi-Sipiš." *OA* 18:85-215, pls. i-xii.
VON PILGRIM, C.
1998 "Textzeugnis und archäologischer Befund: Zur Topographie Elephantines in der 27. Dynastie." Pp. 485-497 in *Stationen: Beiträge zur Kulturgeschichte Ägyptens: Rainer Stadelmann Gewidmet*. Ed. by H. Guksch and D. Polz. Mainz: P. von Zabern.
1999 "Der Tempel des Jahwe." *MDAIK* 55:142-145.

POMPONIO, F., and P. XELLA.
1997 *Les dieux d'Ebla. Étude analytique des divinités éblaïtes à l'époque des archives royales du IIIe millénaire*. AOAT 245. Münster: Ugarit-Verlag.
PORTEN, B.
1968 *Archives from Elephantine*. Berkeley and Los Angeles: University of California Press.
1979 "Aramaic Papyri and Parchments: A New Look." *BA* 42:74-104.
1981 "The Identity of King Adon." *BA* 36-52.
1983 "An Aramaic Oath Contract: A New Interpretation (Cowley 45)." *RB* 90:563-575.
1990 "The Calendar of Aramaic Texts from Achaemenid and Ptolemaic Egypt." Pp. 13-32 in *Irano-Judaica II: Studies Relating to Jewish Contacts with Persian Culture throughout the Ages*. Ed. by S. Shaked and A. Netzer. Jerusalem: Ben-Zvi Institute for the Study of Jewish Communities in the East.
1992 "Aramaic-Demotic Equivalents: Who is the Borrower and Who the Lender?" Pp. 259-264 in *Life in a Multi-Cultural Society: Egypt from Cambyses to Constantine and Beyond*. Studies in Ancient Oriental Civilization 51. Ed. by J. Johnson. Chicago: Oriental Institute of the University of Chicago.
1994 "A Survey of Aramaic Ostraca Letters." *EI* (Malamat Volume) 24:164-174 (in Hebrew).
1995 "The Status of the Handmaiden Tamet: A new Interpretation of Kraeling 2 (TAD B3.3)." *ILR* 29:43-64.
1998 "The Revised Draft of the Letter of Jedaniah to Bagavahya (*TAD* A4.8 = Cowley 31)." Pp. 230-242 in *Studies Gordon 1998*.
2001 "Jews of Elephantine who were Named after their Ancestors." Pp. 332-361 in *Homage to Shmuel: Studies in the World of the Bible*. Ed. by Z. Talshir, S. Yona, and D. Sivan. Jerusalem: Ben Gurion University of the Negev (in Hebrew).
PORTEN, B., and H. Z. SZUBIN.
1982a "'Abandoned Property' in Elephantine: A New Interpretation of Kraeling 3." *JNES* 41:123-141.
1982b "Exchange of Inherited Property at Elephantine (Cowley 1)." *JAOS* 102:651-654.
1987a "An Aramaic Deed of Bequest (Kraeling 9)." Pp. 179-192 in *Community and Culture: Essays in Jewish Studies in Honor of the Ninetieth Anniversary of the Founding of Gratz College 1895-1985*. Ed. by N. M. Waldman. Philadelphia: Gratz College.
1987b "Litigants in the Elephantine Contracts: The Development of Legal Terminology." *Maarav* 4:45-67.
1987c "A Dowry Addendum: Kraeling 10." *JAOS* 107:231-238.
1995 "The Status of the Handmaiden Tamet: A New Interpretation of Kraeling 2 (*TAD* B3.3)." *ILR* 29:43-64.
PORTEN, B., and A. YARDENI.
1991 "Three Unpublished Aramaic Ostraca." *Maarav* 7:207-227.
POSTGATE, J. N.
1976 *Fifty Neo-Assyrian Legal Documents*. Warminster: Aris & Phillips.
1987-90 "Mannäer." *RlA* 7:340-342.
RAINEY, A. F.
1974 "The Ugaritic Texts in *Ugaritica* 5." *JAOS* 94:184-94.
1987 "Watching Out for the Signal Fires of Lachish." *Palestine Exploration Quarterly* 119:149-151.
1996 *Canaanite in the Amarna Tablets*. 4 vols. Leiden: E. J. Brill.
RENZ, J.
1995 *HAE*.
RÖLLIG, W.
1999 "Appendix 1: The Phoenician Inscriptions." Pp. 50-81 in *CHLI 2*.
ROSENTHAL, F.
1967 *An Aramaic Handbook*. Part I/1. Wiesbaden: Harrassowitz.
SAADÉ, G.
1995 "Le port d'Ougarit." Pp. 211-25 in RSOu 11.
SACHAU, E.
1911 *Aramäische Papyrus und Ostraka aus einer jüdischen militär-kolonie zu Elephantine, altorientalische Sprachdenkmäler des 5. Jahrhunderts vor Chr.* Leipzig, J. C. Hinrichs.
SAFRAI, Sh.
1976 "Wood Offering." *Encyclopaedia Biblica* 7:253-255 (in Hebrew).
SANDERS, T. K.
1997 "An Ammonite Ostracon from Tall al-'Umayri." Pp. 331-36 in *Madaba Plains Project 3*. Ed. by L. G. Herr, et al. Berrien Springs, MI: Andrews University Institute of Archaeology.
SASSON, V.
1982 The Meaning of *whsbt* in the Arad Inscription." *ZAW* 94:105-111.
SCHÜLE, A.
2000 *Die Syntax der althebräischen Inschriften. Ein Beitrag zur historischen Grammatik des Hebräischen*. AOAT 270. Münster: Ugarit-Verlag.
SCHWARTZ, J.
1960 "Note sur le bain des brebis." *Or* 29:102.
SEGAL, J. B., and H. S. SMITH.
1983 *Aramaic Texts from North Saqqâra with Some Fragments in Phoenician*. Texts from Excavations. 6th memoir. Excavations at North Saqqâra Documentary Series 4. London: Egypt Exploration Society.
SHEA, W. H.
1977 "Ostracon II from Heshbon." *AUSS* 15:117-125.
1985 "Sennacherib's Second Palestinian Campaign." *JBL* 104:410-418.
SINGER, I.
1991 "A Concise History of Amurru." Pp. 134-195, "Appendix III," in S. Izre'el, *Amurru Akkadian: A Linguistic Study*. Vol. 2. HSS 41. Atlanta: Scholars Press.
1999 "A Political History of Ugarit." Pp. 603-733 in *HUS*.

SIVAN, D.
1984 "Diphthongs and Triphthongs in Verbal Forms of Verba Tertiae Infirmae in Ugaritic." *UF* 16:279-293.
SMELIK, K. A. D.
1990 "The Riddle of Tobiah's Document: Difficulties in the Interpretation of Lachish III, 19-21." *PEQ* 122:133-138.
1991 *WAI* 75.
1992 "The Literary Structure of the Yavneh-Yam Ostracon." *IEJ* 42:55-61.
SOKOLOFF, M.
1990 *A Dictionary of Jewish Babylonian Aramaic*. Ramat Gan: Bar Ilan University Press.
1999 "The Old Aramaic Inscription from Bukān: A Revised Interpretation." *IEJ* 49:105-115.
VAN SOLDT, W. H.
1983 "Review of G. D. Young, ed., *Ugarit in Retrospect*." *BiOr* 40:692-697.
1985-86 "The Queens of Ugarit." *JEOL* 29:68-73.
1990 "Fabrics and Dyes at Ugarit." *UF* 22:321-357.
1991 *Studies in the Akkadian of Ugarit: Dating and Grammar*. AOAT 40. Kevelaer: Butzon & Bercker; Neukirchen-Vluyn: Neukirchener Verlag.
1996 "Studies in the Topography of Ugarit (1). The Spelling of the Ugaritic Toponyms." *UF* 28:653-692.
1998 "Studies in the Topography of Ugarit (3). Groups of Towns and their Locations." *UF* 30:703-744.
STARK, J. K.
1971 *Personal Names in Palmyrene Inscriptions*. Oxford: Oxford University Press.
STARKE, F.
1990 *Untersuchung zur Stammbildung des keilschrift-luwischen Nomens*. StBoT 31. Wiesbaden: O. Harrassowitz.
SUKENIK, Y.
1947 "The 'Ophel Ostracon'." *BJPES* 13:115-118 (in Hebrew).
SUKENIK, E. L., and E. Y. KUTSCHER.
1942 "A Passover Ostracon from Elephantine." *Qedem* 1:53-56.
SZUBIN, H. Z., and B. PORTEN.
1982 "'Ancestral Estates' in Aramaic Contracts: The Legal Significance of the Term *mhḥsn*." *JRAS* 3-9.
1983a "Testamentary Succession at Elephantine." *BASOR* 252:35-46.
1983b "Litigation concerning Abandoned Property at Elephantine (Kraeling 1)." *JNES* 42:279-284.
1988 "A Life Estate of Usufruct: A New Interpretation of Kraeling 6." *BASOR* 269:29-45.
1992 "An Aramaic Joint Venture Agreement: A New Interpretation of the Bauer-Meissner Papyrus." *BASOR* 288:67-84.
forthcoming "The Status of a Repudiated Spouse: A New Interpretation of Kraeling 7 (*TAD* B3.8)."
TAWIL, H.
1974 "Some Literary Elements in the Opening Sections of the Hadad, Zākir, and Nērab II Inscriptions in Light of East and West Semitic Royal Inscriptions." *Or* 43:40-65.
TEIXIDOR, J.
1967 "Bulletin d'épigraphie semitique." *Syria* 44:163-195.
1987 "L'inscription d'Ahiram à nouveau." *Syria* 64:137-140.
THUREAU-DANGIN, F.
1937 "Trois contrats de Ras-Shamra." *Syria* 18:245-255.
TOMBACK, R. S.
1978 *A Comparative Semitic Lexicon of the Phoenician and Punic Languages*. SBLDS 32. Missoula, Montana: Scholars Press.
TORCZYNER, H. (TUR-SINAI)
1938 *The Lachish Letters*. Lachish I. London: Oxford University Press.
1939 *BJPES* 7:6-8.
1940 *Tᶜ WDWT LKYŠ: MKTBYM MYMY YRMYHW HNBYᵓ*. Jerusalem: Jewish Palestine Exploration Society (republished in 1987 by the Bialik Institute and the Israel Exploration Society, with an introduction by Shmuel Aḥituv) (in Hebrew).
TROPPER, J.
2000 *Ugaritische Grammatik*. AOAT 273. Münster: Ugarit-Verlag.
TUBB, J. N.
1988 "Tell es-Sa'idiyeh: Preliminary Report on the First Three Seasons of Renewed Excavations." *Levant* 20:23-88.
USSISHKIN, D.
1978 "Excavations at Tel Lachish — 1973-1977." *Tel Aviv* 5:1-97.
VATTIONI, F.
1970 "Epigrafia aramaica." *Augustinianum* 10:493-552.
1971 "Epigrafia aramaica." *Augustinianum* 11:18-190.
1979 "Epigrafia aramaica." *Or* 48:140-145.
DE VAUX, R.
1946 "Review." *RB* 53:456-459.
VIROLLEAUD, C.
1938 "Textes alphabétiques de Ras-Shamra provenant de la neuvième campagne." *Syria* 19:127-141.
1940 "Lettres et documents administratifs provenant des archives d'Ugarit." *Syria* 21:247-276.
1957 *PRU* 2.
1965 *PRU* 5.
1968 "Les nouveaux textes mythologiques et liturgiques de Ras Shamra (XXIVᵉ campagne, 1961)." Pp. 545-606 in *Ugaritica* 5.
VITA, J-P.
1995 *El Ejército de Ugarit*. Banco de Datos Filológicos Semíticos Noroccidentales, Monografías 1. Madrid: Consejo Superior de Investigaciones Científicas.
VITA, J.-P., and J. M. GALÁN.
1997 "Šipṭi-baᶜalu, un 'égyptien' à Ougarit." *UF* 29:709-713.

VLEEMING, S. P.
1985 "Demotic Measures of Length and Surface." Pp. 208-229 in *Textes et études de papyrologie grecque, démotique et copte*. Papyrologica Lugduno-Batava 23. Ed. by P. W. Pestman. Leiden: E. J. Brill.
WATSON, W. G. E., and N. WYATT, Editors.
1999 *HUS*.
WENNING, R.
1989 "Mesad Hasavyahu. Ein Stützpunkt des Jojakim?" Pp. 169-196 in *Vom Sinai zum Horeb. Stationen alttestamentlicher Glaubensgeschichte*. Ed. F.-L Hossfeld. Würzburg: Echter Verlag.
WESTBROOK, R.
1988 *Studies in Biblical and Cuneiform Law*. Cahiers de la Revue Biblique 26. Paris: Gabalda.
1991a *Property and the Family in Biblical Law*. JSOTSup 113. Sheffield: Sheffield Academic Press.
1991b "The Phrase 'His Heart is Satisfied' in Ancient Near Eastern Legal Sources." *JAOS* 111:219-224.
WILHELM, G.
1970 "Ta/erdennu, ta/urtannu, ta/urtānu." *UF* 2:277-282.
WISEMAN, D. J.
1956 *Chronicles of Chaldaean Kings (626-556 B.C.) in the British Museum*. London: British Museum.
XELLA, P.
1991 *Baal Hammon. Recherches sur l'identité et l'histoire d'un dieu phénico-punique*. Collezioni di Studi Fenici 32. Contributi alla Storia della Religione Fenicio-Punico 1. Rome: Consiglio Nazionale delle Ricerche.
YADIN, Y.
1976 "The Historical Significance of Inscription 88 from Arad: A Suggestion." *IEJ* 26:9-14.
1981 "The Lachish Letters — Originals or Copies and Drafts?" Pp. 179-186 in *Recent Archaeology in the Land of Israel*. Ed. by H. Shanks. Washington, D.C.: Biblical Archaeology Society.
YARDENI, A.
1990 "New Jewish Aramaic Ostraca." *IEJ* 40:130-152.
YARON, R.
1958 "Aramaic Marriage Contracts from Elephantine." *JSS* 3:1-39.
YON, M.
1992 "The End of the Kingdom of Ugarit." Pp. 111-122 in *The Crisis Years: The 12th Century B.C. From Beyond the Danube to the Tigris*. Ed. by W. A. Ward and M. S. Joukowsky. Dubuque, IA: Kendall/Hunt.
1995 "La maison d'Ourtenou dans le Quartier Sud d'Ougarit (fouilles 1994)." Pp. 427-443 in *CRAIBL*.
1997 "Ugarit." in *OEANE* 5:255-262.
YOUNGER, K. L., Jr.
1998a "The Phoenician Inscription of Azatiwada. An Integrated Reading." *JSS* 43:11-47.
1998b "Two Comparative Notes on the Book of Ruth." *JANES* 26:121-132.
YURCO, F. J.
1991 "The Shabaka-Shebitku Coregency and the Supposed Second Campaign of Sennacherib Against Judah: A Critical Assessment." *JBL* 110:35-45.
ZADOK, R.
1985 *Geographical Names According to New- and Late-Babylonian Texts*. Répertoire Géographique des Textes Cunéiformes 8. Wiesbaden: Harrassowitz.
1988 *The Pre-Hellenistic Israelite Anthroponymy and Prosopography*. OLA 28. Leuven: Peeters.
ZGUSTA, L.
1964a *Kleinasiatische Personennamen*. Monografie Orientálního Ústavu 19. Prague: Verlag der Tschechoslowakischen Akademie der Wissenschaften.
1964b *Anatolische Personennamesippen*. Dissertationes Orientales 2. Prague: Verlag der Tschechoslowakischen Akademie der Wissenschaften.
ZIMANSKY, P. E.
1995 "The Kingdom of Urartu in Eastern Anatolia." Pp. 1135-1146 in *CANE*.

AKKADIAN ARCHIVAL DOCUMENTS

A. LETTERS

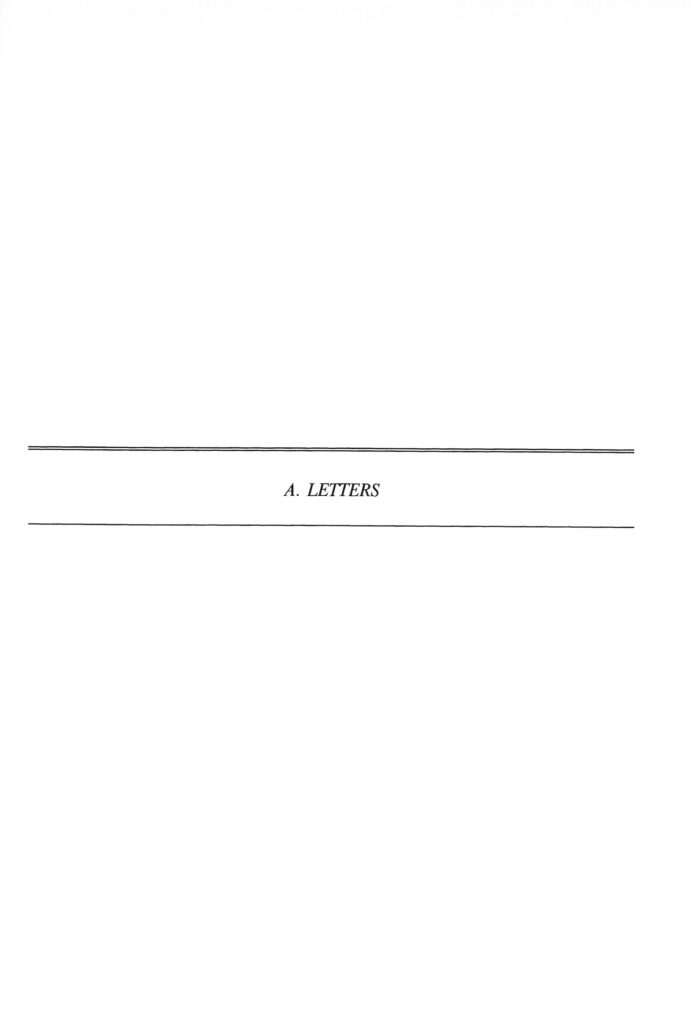

1. EBLA

A LETTER OF ENNA-DAGAN (3.90)

William W. Hallo

The city of Ebla ruled a considerable territory in western Syria during the third millennium; for an overview of its history and a brief bibliography see Milano 1995. For fuller bibliographies see Beld, Hallo and Michalowski 1984; Baffi Guardata, Baldacci and Pomponio 1987, 1989, 1993, 1997. The language of Ebla was neither purely Akkadian (East Semitic) nor certifiably West Semitic. It combined elements of both, but was different from both. It may thus represent an earlier stage of Semitic, before the strict separation into East and West Semitic, and has been called North Semitic (von Soden 1981). It employed the cuneiform script of Mesopotamia which was developed to write Sumerian, and most of its texts were in fact written in Sumerian. Many of these texts are lexical, equating Sumerian with the local Eblaite dialect of Semitic. Others are elaborate accounts from the royal archives. A number of letters are also preserved, among them some that deal with high matters of state. One of these is the "Enna-Dagan letter." It recounts the history of a dispute between Ebla and Mari concerning lands lying between them along the middle course of the Euphrates River. The letter was found at Ebla; in language, orthography and appearance it closely resembles the contemporary texts originating in Ebla (see the photographs in Pettinato 1980 and Matthiae 1981, 9th page after p. 112). Its writer has been variously seen as an Eblaite commander (so Pettinato 1980; 1995; Kienast 1980b; 1984) and as a king of Mari (so Edzard 1981; 1994). Admittedly his name is not attested as such in the newly recovered Sumerian king List from Shubat-Enlil which preserves the names of the six Early Dynastic rulers of Mari (Vincente 1995). Neither are any of the other names regarded by Edzard as identifying rulers of Mari in the Enna-Dagan letter with the possible exception of *a-nu-bu*$(_x)$ at the beginning of the letter if he is in fact to be equated with the first Mari king Anbu (Alberti 1990). Geller's attempt (1987) to restore the name *sa-ʾu-me* in the Weld-Blundell prism must be rejected in light of collation of the prism (Hallo 1971) and the Shubat-Enlil list. Iblul-il, however, has long been known as a ruler of Mari by the find of his inscribed statue there, and it may be argued that the King List simply does not preserve this and a number of other royal names. In the translation that follows, Edzard's interpretation has been largely followed, with Pettinato's mostly recognized in the footnotes.

(1)Thus says Enna-Dagan, ruler of Mari, to the ruler of Ebla[1]: The cities Aburu and Ilgi, the lands of Belan, Anbu[2] the ruler of Mari defeated; tells and ruins in the mountain of Lebanon he left.

(2)The cities Tibalat and Ilwi, Sa'umu[3] the ruler of Mari defeated; in the mountain terrain of Anga'i-x he left tells and ruins.

(3)The lands of Ra'ak and Irum, Ash'aldu and Badul, Sa'umu the ruler of Mari defeated, in the border of x-an, in Nahal, he left tells and ruins.

(4)And the cities Emar and Lalanium and the canebrake(?),[4] (that) of Ebla, Ishtup-shar, the king of Mari, defeated; in Emar and in Lalanium he left tells and ruins.

(5)And the city Gallabi [and x] the liberated canebrake(?), Iblul-il, the ruler of Mari and Apishal(?),[5] defeated; in Zahiran he left also seven tells and ruins.

(6)Iblul-il, the ruler of Mari and Shada and Addali and Arisum, the lands of Burman which (include) the city Sugurum, Iblul-il defeated and left (in) tells and ruins.

(7)Also the cities Sharan and Dammium, Iblul-il the king of Mari, defeated; he left two tells and ruins.

(8)Against the city Nerad and against the fortress[6] of Hazuwan Iblul-il, the king of Mari, went forth. And he received the tribute[7] of Ebla in its midst, (in) Nema.

(9)Also Emar he defeated(?), he left tells and ruins, did Iblul-il, the king of Mari.[8]

---

[1] The unnamed ruler of Ebla must have been Ar-Ennum (Arru-LUM) according to Matthiae (1981:171) to judge by the frequency with which his name occurs together with Enna-Dagan's in administrative documents.

[2] Written A.NU.KA and interpreted respectively as the royal name Anbu (A-nu-bu_x) by Alberti (1990), or as a verbal clause (a nu-du_{11} = "non hanno fornito acqua," 'he did not furnish water') by Pettinato (1995:79).

[3] Pettinato takes *sa-ù-mu* here and elsewhere as a verb, "ho marciato" ('he marched, advanced') rather than as a personal name.

[4] So Pettinato; Edzard considers GA.NU.UM possibly a toponym. In light of Apum the toponym and *apum*, "canebrake," the two interpretations are not irreconcilable. Kienast (1980b:256) suggests "colony"; Geller (1987:144, n. 11) "border."

[5] Written A.BAR.$SILA_4$. The exact reading is in dispute, but was probably *not* Ashur.

[6] Taking é-na for é-na_4, lit. "house of stone" (so Pettinato). But note that, at least in Hittite, é-na_4 means "mausoleum."

[7] mu-túm, ordinarily "delivery" (so Pettinato). Edzard prefers "gift" or the like.

[8] The division into paragraphs (not indicated on the tablet!) hereafter follows Pomponio 1999-2000:47.

(10) And Nahal and Nubat and Shada, the lands of Gasur(?), he defeated in Kanane[9]; he also left seven tells and ruins.
(11) Iblul-il, the king of Mari, both Barama — for the second (time) — and Aburu and Tibalat, the lands of Belan, defeated; Enna-Dagan, the ruler of Mari, left tells and ruins.
(12) The two nations(?) in oil, the(ir) lands I bound.[10]
(13) ... Iblul-il, the king of Mari, ...[11]

[9] Pettinato wants to read this as Cana'an, for which other and later equivalents have been proposed by Dossin 1957; Moscati 1959; de Vaux 1968.

[10] Possibly a reference to a treaty accord ratified by unction. Note that near the end of the long treaty between Ebla and Apishal(?), for which see Sollberger 1980, Lambert 1987, there is reference to oil and binding, admittedly in connection with *maš*, "interest(?)," as frequently in this text.

[11] This paragraph is largely unintelligible, but it appears to be the conclusion of the text, since the remainder of the tablet is blank.

References

Text and studies: Pettinato 1980; 1981:99-102; 1995; Kienast 1980b; 1984; Edzard 1981; 1994; Michalowski 1993:14-18; Pomponio 1999-2000.

---

2. ALALAKH

LETTER ASKING FOR THE RETURN OF STOLEN DONKEYS (*AT* 116) (3.91)

Richard S. Hess

This letter exemplifies the small collection of epistolary literature from Alalakh (Akkadian *AT* 106 - *AT* 117; Hittite *AT* 125), all from Level IV. The introduction compares with letters from other Late Bronze Age collections at Ugarit and Amarna. The writer, Ianḫe, is concerned about donkeys that belonged to him but have been seized by his servant. This concern recalls the search of Saul in 1 Samuel 9.

Formulaic Introduction (lines 1-7)

1 To Šani [ ]
2 Speak!
3 Ian[ḫe] writes as follows:
4 Live w[ell!]
5 May Teššub keep you,
6 your children,
7 and your lands well.

Content (lines 8-17)

8 Now the servant of Ianḫe:
9 Judge his case
10 there
11 in your presence.
12 Bring forward his case.
13 Concerning his affairs
14 make a good enquiry.
15 Why should
16 they seize
15 the donkeys belonging to Ianḫe's servants?
17 Ask th[em!]

Additional note(?) (lines 18-19)

18 Mazianu[1]
19 stays there.

[1] Is Mazianu the servant? It is not clear from this letter.

REFERENCES

Copy: *AT* pl. xxv. Transliteration: *AT* 60. Translation: *AT* 60.

---

3. TELL EL-AMARNA

LETTER OF ABDI-HEBA OF JERUSALEM (*EA* 286) (3.92A)

William Moran

This letter is one of six (*EA* 285-290) in the Amarna archive from Abdi-Heba,[1] ruler of Jerusalem, to the Pharaoh, probably Amenophis IV (ca. 1350-1334 BCE).[2]

(lines 1-4)
Say to the king, my lord: Message of Abdi-Heba, your servant. I fall at the feet of my lord, the king, seven times and seven times.[3] [a]

(lines 5-15)
What have I done to the king, my lord?[4] [b] They denounce me: I am slandered[5] before the king, my lord, "Abdi-Heba has rebelled against the king, his lord."[6] Seeing that, as far as I am concerned, neither my father nor my mother put me in this place, but the strong arm[c] of the king brought me into my father's house,[7] why should I of all people commit a crime against the king, my lord?

(lines 16-21)
As truly as the king, my lord, lives,[d] I say to the commissioner[8] of the king, my lord, "Why do you love[e] the Apiru[9] but hate the mayors?"[10] Accordingly, I am slandered before the king, my lord.

(lines 22-31)
Because I say, "Lost are the lands of the king, my lord," accordingly, I am slandered before the king, my lord. May the king, my lord, know (this). Though the king, my lord, stationed a garrison (here), Enhamu[11] has taken i[t al]l (?) away. [...] ...

(lines 32-43)
Now, O king, my lord, there is no garrison, and so may the king provide for his land.[12] May the king [pro]vide (?) for his land! All the lands of the king, my lord, have deserted. Ili-Milku[13] has caused the loss of all the land of the king, and so may the king, my lord, provide for his land. For my part, I say, "I would go in to the king, my lord, and visit the king, my lord."[14] But the war against me is severe, and so I am not able to go in to the king, my lord.

(lines 44-52)
And may it seem good in the sight of the king, my lord, and may he send a garrison so I may go in and visit the king, my lord. *In truth*, the king, my lord, lives:[d] whenever the commissioners have come out, I would say (to them), "Lost are the lands of the king," but they did not listen to me. Lost are all the mayors; there is not a mayor remaining to the king, my lord.

(lines 53-60)
May the king turn his attention to the archers[15] so that archers of the king, my lord, come forth. The king has no lands. (That) Apiru[16] has plundered all the lands of the king. If there are archers this year, the lands of the king, my lord, will remain. But if there are no archers, lost are the lands of the king, my lord.

(lines 61-64)
To the scribe[17] of the king, my lord: Message of Abdi-Heba, your servant. Present eloquent words to the king, my lord. Lost are all the lands of the king, my lord.

a Gen 43:28; 1 Sam 24:9; Isa 60:14
b Jer 2:5; Mic 6:3
c Deut 4:34; 5:15; Jer 21:5, etc
d Gen 42:15-16; 2 Sam 15:21
e Deut 6:5; Judg 5:31; 1 Sam 18:1, 3; 20:17; 2 Sam 19:7; 1 Kgs 5:15

[1] The name means "Servant of (the Hurrian goddess) Heba (Hepat)" (Hess 1993a:176); for this king and scribe, see Moran 1975.

[2] For an introductory survey of the archive, see Moran 1992:xiii-xxxix.

[3] "Seven times and seven times," i.e., "over and over." One prostrates oneself before an official, but before the king "seven times and seven times," in Palestinian letters often with the amplification "both on the belly and on the back." For a representation, see *ANEP*[2] fig. 5. For the comparable salutation in Ug. letters to the king or queen, cf. above *COS* 3.92T-V, Y (nos. 20-22, 25).

[4] Abdi-Heba's defense begins with a rhetorical question, as was perhaps customary in lawsuits.

[5] Gloss to previous expression (cf. its Aram. form in Dan 3:8, 6:25) in Western Peripheral Akk., which makes clear that the charges are false.

[6] Similar charges are made in *EA* 280.

[7] When said of kings, entry into the father's house means succession to the throne.

[8] "Commissioner" (Akk. *rābiṣu*) designates the head of an Eg. province.

[9] Here, as usually in *EA*, a pejorative term for those rejecting Eg. authority. See Naʾaman 1986.

[10] "Mayor" (Akk. *ḫazannu*) refers in *EA* to the local rulers and makes of them as so designated royal appointees incorporated in the peripheral administration; for this and other terms used of them, see Moran 1992:xxvii, nn. 73-74.

[11] Enhamu (dialectal form of Yanhamu), mentioned frequently in *EA*, was at the time the provincial "commissioner." See Hess 1993a:82-84.

[12] Naʾaman (1995:36): "May the king exercise power/rule over his land."

[13] Ili-Milku, usually Milk-ilu, was the ruler of Gezer (Gazru) and, according to Abdi-Heba, the leader of a disloyal coalition, 3.92B (*EA* 289) lines 5, 11, 25 (see next letter); 290:6, 26. For the personal name, see Hess 1993a:86-88, 112-114.

[14] Visiting the king (here lit. "see his eyes") was a vassal's duty but one which, as here, perhaps fearing long detention at court as quasi-hostages, they frequently shied away from, pleading an unfavorable situation.

[15] Designation of regular army-units as distinct from auxiliaries and garrison-troops.

[16] Ili-Milku (Milk-ilu).

[17] The scribe at the Eg. court, as the one responsible for communicating the letter to the illiterate addressee, is asked to gloss the message with special eloquence; see also *EA* 287-289 (next letter), 316, and for this and similar practices, see Moran 1992:xxiii-xxiv, n. 58.

REFERENCES

Text, translations and studies: *EA* (VAB 2) 858-863; *ANET* 487-488; Liverani 1998-99 1:94-96; Moran 1975; 1992; Naʾaman 1986; 1995.

LETTER OF ABDI-HEBA OF JERUSALEM (URUSALIM) (*EA* 289) (3.92B)

William Moran

This letter pursues the charges in *EA* 286 against Milk-ilu[1] of Gezer (Gazru) and names his fellow-traitors. The lack of a garrison, also mentioned in the earlier letter, is further stressed.

(lines 1-4)
Say to the king, my lord: Message of Abdi-Heba, your servant. I fall at the feet of my lord, the king, seven times and seven times.[2] [a]

(lines 5-10)
Milk-ilu does not break away from the sons of Labʾayu[3] and from the sons of Arsawa,[4] as they desire the land of the king for themselves. As for a mayor[5] who does such a deed, why does the king not <c>all him to account?

(lines 11-17)
Such was the deed that Milk-ilu and Tagi[6] did: they took Rub(b)utu.[7] And now as for Urusalim, if this land belongs to the king, why is it <not> of concern (?) to the king like Hazzatu?[8]

(lines 18-24)
Gintikirmil[9] belongs to Tagi, and men of Gintu are the garrison in Bitsanu.[10] [b] Are we to act like Labʾayu when he was giving the land of Šakmu (Shechem)[c] to the Hapiru?[11]

(lines 25-36)
Milk-ilu has written to Tagi and the sons <of Labʾayu> (?), "Be both of you (?) a protection(?).[12] [d] Grant all their demands to the men of Qiltu,[13] [e] and let us isolate Urusalim."[14] Addayu[15] has taken the garrison that you sent in the charge of Haya,[16] the son of Miyare; he has stationed it in his own house in Hazzatu and has sent 20 men to Egypt.[17] May the king, my lord, know (that) no garrison of the king is with me.

(lines 37-44)
Accordingly, as truly as the king lives,[f] his irpi-official, Puʾuru,[18] has left me and is in Hazzatu. May the king call (this) to mind when he arrives (?). And so may the king send 50 men as a garrison to protect the land. The entire land of the king has deserted.

(lines 45-51)
Send Yenhamu[19] that he may know about the land of the king, my lord. To the scribe of the king, my lord: Message of Abdi-Heba, your servant. Offer eloquent words to the king: I am always, utterly yours(?).[20] I am your servant.

a Gen 43:28; 1 Sam 24:9; Isa 60:14
b Judg 1:27, etc.
c Gen 12:6, etc.
d Num 14:4; Jer 48:45; Ps 91:1; Isa 30:2-3; Lam 4:20
e 1 Sam 23:1-13
f Gen 42:15-16; 2 Sam 15:21

[1] See above 3.92A (*EA* 286), n. 13.
[2] See above 3.92A (*EA* 286), n. 3.
[3] The former ruler of Šakmu (biblical Shechem), now followed by two sons. See also below, n. 11. For the name, see Hess 1993a:102-103.
[4] Identity unknown; the name is not Semitic. See Hess 1993a:40-42.
[5] See above 3.92A (*EA* 286), n. 10.
[6] Name, probably Hurrian, of Milk-ilu's father-in-law. See Hess 1993a:153-155.
[7] A town probably somewhere between Urusalim (Jerusalem) and Gazru (Gezer).
[8] Modern Gaza, administrative center of the Eg. province.
[9] Probably a town in the Carmel region, perhaps a recent acquisition. Abbreviated form: Gintu.
[10] Biblical Bethshean.
[11] Adamthwaite (1992:4): "'But (they say) let us act like Labʾaya!' So the land of Šakmi they have given to the ʿ*Apîrû*." In this version, for which Adamthwaite makes a good case, the speakers and donors are Milk-ilu and Tagi. For the pros and cons, see Rainey 1995-96:119-120. On the Apiru, see above 3.92A (*EA* 286), n. 9.
[12] For other readings and interpretations, see Moran 1992:333, n. 3 ("Protection," *ṣillu*).
[13] Probably biblical Keilah.
[14] Perhaps "let us desert."
[15] A high Eg. official (commissioner) mentioned also in *EA* 254 (3.92G), 285, 287. See Hess 1993a:19-21.
[16] Eg. official; more than one bearer of this name in the Amarna letters. See Hess 1993a:75-76.
[17] The men sent to Egypt were perhaps drawn from the transferred garrison.
[18] According to *EA* 287:45, a commissioner; on his death, see below 3.92E (*EA* 362). See Hess 1993a:125-126.
[19] See above 3.92A (*EA* 286), n. 11.
[20] An abbreviated form (without "utterly") of this problematic expression occurs at the end of *EA* 287. For other renderings, see Moran 1992 *EA* 287, n. 20.

REFERENCES

Text, translations and studies: *EA* (VAB 2/10) 872-877; *ANET* 489; Adamthwaite 1992; Liverani 1998-99 1:89-91; Moran 1992; Rainey 1995-96.

LETTER OF THE RULER OF GEZER (GAZRU) (*EA* 292) (3.92C)

William Moran

This letter and *EA* 293 were sent by the ruler of Gazru, whose name is written logographically and remains of uncertain interpretation. The scribe who wrote these two letters also wrote *EA* 294, and probably for the same ruler.

(lines 1-7)
Say to the king, my lord, my god, my Sun: Message of Adda-danu(?),[1] your servant, the dirt at your feet. I fall at the feet of the king, my lord, my god, my Sun, seven times and seven times.[2]

(lines 8-13)
I looked this way, and I looked that way, and there was no light. Then I looked towards the king, my lord, and there was light.[3] [a]

(lines 13-17)
A brick may move from under its partner, still I will not move from under the feet of the king, my lord.[4]

(lines 17-26)
I have heard the orders that the king, my lord, wrote to his servant, "Guard your commissioner, and guard the cities of the king, your lord."[5] I do indeed guard, and I do indeed obey the orders of the king, my lord, day and night.

(lines 26-40)
May the king, my lord, be informed about his servant. There being war against me from the mountains, I have erected/built (?) a house — its (the village's) name is Manhatu[b] — to make preparations before the arrival of the archers of the king, my lord, and Maya[6] has just taken it away from me and placed his commissioner in it. Enjoin Reanap,[7] my commissioner, to restore my village to me, as I am making preparations before the arrival of the archers of the king, my lord.

(lines 41-52)
Moreover, consider the deed of Peya, the son of Gulatu,[8] against Gezer (Gazru),[c] the maidservant of the king, my lord. How long has he gone on plundering it so that it has become, thanks to him, like a pot held in pledge. People are ransomed from the mountains for 30 shekels of silver, but from Peya for 100 shekels. Be informed of these affairs of your servant.

a Exod 24:17; 34:27-35; Num 6:25 Ezra 48:3
b 1 Chr 8:6
c Josh 10:33; 12:12; 16:3, 10; 21:21; Judg 1:29; 2 Sam 5:25; 1 Kgs 15-17; 1 Chr 6:52; 7:28; 14:16; 20:4

[1] [Id]IM-DI.KUD. For this much discussed personal name, see Hess 1993a:53-54.
[2] See above 3.92A (*EA* 286), n. 3.
[3] This brief celebration of the royal effulgence, with its poetic parallelisms, is found also at the beginning of *EA* 266 and 294.
[4] The comparison with a brick also follows in *EA* 266 and 294. The first part should be understood as an impossibility (cf. the use of *adynata* in classical literature), making what follows an even greater impossibility.
[5] Cf. *EA* 294:8-11: "Obey your commissioner, and guard the cities of the king, your lord, where you are." The most frequent injunction is "Guard yourself, and guard the city/place of the king where you are." For underlying Eg. models, see Moran 1992:xxvii-xxxi.
[6] Eg. commissioner. See Hess 1993a:105-106.
[7] Eg. commissioner. See Hess 1993a:132.
[8] Peya, identified here by his mother, is charged in *EA* 294:23-24 with another attack. He is otherwise unknown. See Hess 1993a:123.

REFERENCES

Text, translations and studies: *EA* (VAB 2) 878-883; *ANET* 489-490; Liverani 1998-99 1:103-104; Moran 1992.

LETTER OF TUŠRATTA, KING OF MITANNI (*EA* 17) (3.92D)

William Moran

In one of the earliest letters of the Amarna archive, the king of Mitanni tries to patch up relations with Egypt and renew an earlier alliance.

(lines 1-10)
Say to Nibmuareya,[1] the king of Egypt, my brother: Thus Tušeratta,[2] the king of Mitanni,[3] your brother. For me all goes well. For you may all go well. For Kelu-Heba[4] may all go well. For your household, for your wives, for your sons, for your magnates, for your warriors, for your horses, for your chariots, and in your country, may all go very well.

(lines 11-20)
When I sat on the throne of my father, I was young,[5] and UD-hi[6] had done an unseemly thing to my country and had slain his lord. For this reason he would not permit me friendship with anyone who loved me.[7][a] I, in turn, was not remiss about the unseemly things that had been done in my land, and I slew the slayer of Artašumara, my brother, and everyone belonging to them.

(lines 21-29)
Since you were friendly with my father, I have accordingly written and told you so that my brother might hear of these things and rejoice. My father loved you, and you in turn loved my father. In keeping with this love, my father gave you my sister. And who else stood with my father as you did?

(lines 30-35)
[The ver]y next year (?), moreover, my brother's ... all the land of Hatti. When the enemy advanced against my country, Teššup,[8] my lord, gave him into my hand,[b] and I defeated him. There was not one of them who returned to his own country.[c]

(lines 36-38)
I herewith send you 1 chariot, 2 horses, 1 male attendant, 1 female attendant, from the booty from the land of Hatti.

(lines 39-40)
As the greeting-gift of my brother, I send you 5 chariots, 5 teams of horses.

(lines 41-45)
And as the greeting-gift of Kelu-Heba, my sister, I send her 1 set of gold toggle-pins, 1 set of gold (ear)rings, 1 gold *mašhu*-ring, and a scent container that is full of "sweet oil."

(lines 45-50)
I herewith send Keliya, my chief minister, and Tunip-ibri.[9] May my brother let them go promptly so they can report back to me promptly, and I hear the greeting of my brother.

(lines 51-54)
May my brother seek friendship with me, and may my brother send his messengers to me that they may bring my brother's greetings to me and I hear them.

a Deut 6:5; Judg 5:31; 1 Sam 18:1, 3; 20:17; 2 Sam 19:7; 1 Kgs 5:15

b Deut 1:27; Josh 6:2; 7:7, 24; 1 Kgs 22:6; 2 Kgs 18:30; 19:10

c Exod 14:28; Deut 2:15; Josh 7:24

[1] Of this Pharaoh, the *prenomen*, fourth in the royal titulary, is *Nb-m*$^{\supset c}$*t-R*^{c} "lord of truth is Re^{c}," followed by the *nomen*, *Imn-htp*, the third so called in this dynasty, whence Amenhotpe (Amenophis) III. See Hess 1993a:117-118.

[2] An aberrant spelling of Tušratta. "Brother," either as claiming equal status, or as ally again and thus member of the same household; on the latter metaphor, see Moran 1992:24-25, n. 61.

[3] Also called Hana/igalbat and "Hurrian land," the region between the Upper Euphrates and Upper Tigris Rivers, political center between Balih and Habur Rivers.

[4] Tušratta's sister; see lines 21-29, 41-45. See Hess 1993a:99.

[5] Exact implications of term — legally a minor or something less precise? — are not clear.

[6] Identity uncertain. For a discussion, see Hess 1993a:123-124.

[7] "Love" belongs to the political lexicon of the first and second millennia BCE, denoting the bond between independent allies, vassal to suzerain, at times suzerain to vassal; for the evidence and biblical relevance, see Moran 1963.

[8] Hurrian storm-god.

[9] The two-man embassy is a variant of the standard two-man messenger-team; on the latter, see *EA* 1:85-86 and Rainey 1995-96:110.

REFERENCES

Text, translations and studies: *EA* (VAB 2/1) 130-135; Adler 1976; Liverani 1998-99 2:366-367.

LETTER OF RIB-HADDI OF BYBLOS (GUBLA) (*EA* 362) (3.92E)

William Moran

The most diligent — and most wearisome — of the Pharaoh's vassal correspondents, Rib-Hadda (here Rib-Haddi) continues his litany of requests for action against the rising state of Amurru to the north, earlier under Abdi-Aširta, now under his sons, especially Aziru. The Pharaoh is Amenophis IV (Akhenaten).

(lines 1-4)
Rib-Haddi.[1] Say to the king, my lord: I fall beneath the feet of my lord seven times and seven times.[2] [a]

(lines 5-20)
I have indeed heard the words of the king, my lord, and my heart is overjoyed. May my lord hasten the sending of the archers with all speed. If the king, my lord, does not send archers, then we ourselves must die, and Gubla[b] will be taken. He was distraught (?) recently, he is also distraught (?) now. Recently they were saying, "There will be no archers," but I wrote with the result that archers came out and took their father.[3]

(lines 21-30)
Now indeed they are saying, "Let him (Rib-Haddi) not write or we will certainly be taken." They seek to take Gubla, and they say, "If we take Gubla, we will be strong." If they take Gubla, they will be strong; there will not be a man left, (and) they (the archers) will certainly be too few for them.

(lines 31-39)
I, for my part, have guarded Gubla, the city of the king, night (and) day. Should I move to the (outlying) territory, then the men will desert in order to conquer territory for themselves, and there will be no men to guard Gubla, the city of the king, my lord.

(lines 40-50)
So may my lord hasten the archers or we must die. Because my lord has written to me, they know indeed that they are going to die, and so they seek to commit a crime. As to his having said before the king, "There is a pestilence in the lands," the king, my lord, should not listen to the words of other men. There is no pestilence in the lands,[c] It has been over for a long t<i>me.[4]

(lines 51-59)
My lord knows that I do not write lies to my lord.[d] All the mayors are not in favor of the archers' coming out, for they have peace. I am the one who wants them to come out, for I have distress.

(lines 60-65)
May the king, my lord, come out, visit his lands, and take all. Look, the day you come out, all the lands will be (re)joined to the king, my lord. Who will resist the troops of the king?

(lines 66-69)
May the king, my lord, not leave this year free (?) for the sons of Abdi-Aširta,[5] for you know (?) all their acts of hatred (?) against the lands of the king.[6] Who are they that they have committed a crime and killed the commissioner, Pewure?

a Gen 43:28; 1 Sam 24:9; Isa 60:14
b Ezek 27:9
c Exod 5:3; 9:15; Lev 26:25; Num 14:12; Deut 28:21; 2 Sam 24:13, 15; Hab 3:5
d Judg 16:10, 13; Hos 7:13; Zeph 3:13; Pss 5:7; 58:4 Dan 11:27;

[1] For the name, see Hess 1993a:132-134.
[2] See above 3.92A (*EA* 286), n. 3.
[3] See *EA* 117:21-28.
[4] For other versions, see Moran 1992:361, n. 10.
[5] For this personal name, see Hess 1993a:10-12.
[6] For the reading and other versions, see Moran 1992:361, n. 11.

REFERENCES

Text, translations and studies: Thureau-Dangin 1922; Rainey 1970a; 1978; Liverani 1998-99 1:207-208; Moran 1992.

LETTER OF LABʾAYU OF SHECHEM (ŠAKMU) (*EA* 253) (3.92F)

William Moran

The Amarna archive preserved three letters from Labʾayu (*EA* 252-254). In the first, he agrees, very reluctantly, to obey orders of the king he finds very distasteful; in the others, both apparently in reply to a letter from the Pharaoh questioning his loyalty, especially in his dealings with Gezer (Gazru),[1] he sets the record straight.

(lines 1-6)
To the king, my lord and my Sun: Thus Labʾayu, your servant and the dirt on which you tread. I fall at the feet of the king, my lord, seven times and seven times.[2] [a]

(lines 7-10)
I have obeyed the orders that the king, my lord, wrote to me on a tablet.

(lines 11-17)
As [I am] (?) a servant of the king [like] (?) my [fathe]r (?) and my grandfather, a servant of the king from l[on]g a[g]o (?), I am not a rebel and I am not delinquent in duty.

(lines 18-25)
Here is my act of rebellion and here is my delinquency: when I entered Gezer (Gazru),[b] I (spoke)

a Gen 43:28; 1 Sam 24:9; Isa 60:14
b Josh 10:33; 12:12; 16:3, 10; 21:21; Judg 1:29; 2 Sam 5:25; 1 Kgs 15-17; 1 Chr 6:52; 7:28; 14:16; 20:4

[1] See above 3.92B (*EA* 289).
[2] See above 3.92A (*EA* 286), n. 3.

as follows: "The king treats us kindly."[3] [c]

(lines 25-31)
Now there is indeed no other purpose (for me) except the service of the king, and whatever the king orders, I obey.

(lines 32-35)
May the king keep me in [the char]ge (?) of my commissioner in order to guard the c[it]y (?) [of the king]. (?)

c Gen 33:11; 43:29; Num 6:25; 2 Sam 12:22

[3] For another interpretation, see Moran 1992:307, n. 2.

REFERENCES

Text, translations and studies: *EA* (VAB 2/1) 808-811; Hess 1993b:103-106; Liverani 1998-99 1:116; Moran 1992.

LETTER OF LAB᾿AYU OF SHECHEM (ŠAKMU) (*EA* 254) (3.92G)

William Moran

Lab᾿ayu again protests his utter loyalty, further elaborating the rhetoric of *EA* 253 (3.92F).

(lines 1-5)
To the king, my lord and my Sun. Thus Lab᾿ayu, your servant and the dirt on which you tread. I fall at the feet of the king, my lord and my Sun, seven times and seven times.[1] [a]

(lines 6-10a)
I have obeyed the order that the king wrote to me.

(lines 10b-15)
The fact is that I am a loyal servant of the king! I am not a rebel and I am not delinquent in duty. I have not held back my payments of tribute; I have not held back anything requested by my commissioner.

(lines 16-29)
He denounces me unjustly, but the king, my lord, does not examine my (alleged) act of rebellion. Moreover, my act of rebellion is this: when I entered Gezer (Gazru),[b] I kept on saying, "Everything of mine the king takes,[c] but where is what belongs to Milk-ilu?" I knew the actions of Milk-ilu against me!

(lines 30-37)
Moreover, the king wrote for my son.[2] I did not know that my son was consorting with the Apiru.[3] I herewith hand him over to Addaya.

(lines 38-46)
Moreover, how, if the king wrote for my wife, how could I hold her back? How, if the king wrote to me, "Put a bronze dagger into your heart and die," how could I not execute the order of the king?[4]

a Gen 43:28; 1 Sam 24:9; Isa 60:14

b Josh 10:33; 12:12; 16:3, 10; 21:21; Judg 1:29; 2 Sam 5:25; 1 Kgs 15-17; 1 Chr 6:52; 7:28; 14:16; 20:4

c 1 Sam 8:11-17

[1] See above 3.92A (*EA* 286), n. 3.
[2] On the reading, see Moran 1992, *EA* 254, n. 4.
[3] See above 3.92A (*EA* 286), n. 9.
[4] On the hieratic document that follows, and its bearing on the chronology of the Amarna letters, see Moran 1992:xxxvii.

REFERENCES

Texts, translations and studies: *EA* (VAB 2/1) 810-813; *ANET* 486; Hess 1993b:107-111; Liverani 1998-99 1:116-117; Moran 1992.

3. KUMIDI

A LETTER TO ZALAIA (3.93)

William W. Hallo

While most of the diplomatic correspondence of the Amarna period was found at Amarna itself (see above 3.92A-G), some of it has turned up in excavations in the Levant. The following letter is known in two versions found in Lebanon at Kamid-el-Loz, the ancient Kumidi. (For other texts from the same site, see Huehnergard 1996:98). Judging by its conclusion, its royal author was presumably the pharaoh.

To Zalaia, the "man" (ruler) of Damascus,[a] speak[1]:
Thus (says) the king.[2]
Now I have had this letter (lit.: tablet) brought to you, my speaking (is) unto you.
Further: send me the Habiru's[3] [b] (of) Amurru(?) about whom I wrote to you saying "I will assign them to the cities of the land of Kush[4] [c] for settling them in its midst in place of those (that) I had forcibly removed (from there)."
Moreover: may you know that the king is well, like the sun in heaven, his many (foot-)soldiers (and) his chariot (forces) are very well, from the Upper Land to the Lower Land, (from) sunrise to sunset.[5] [d]

a Gen 15:2 etc. *b* Gen 14:13 etc. *c* Gen 10:6 etc. *d* Mal 1:11; Pss 50:1; 113:3

[1] The other version has: "To Abdi-Milki, the 'man' of Shaza'ena, speak." Otherwise it is identical with the first version as far as preserved. Edzard weighs the possibility that this addressee is identical with the author of another Amarna letter (EA 203), Abdi-Milki of Shazhimi, a town east of the Sea of Galilee acording to Moran 1992:392.

[2] I.e., the pharaoh, probably Amenophis III.

[3] See above, *COS* 3.92A, n. 9.

[4] *mat ka-a-ša* in the text. For the equation with Kush (= Nubia) in Amarna texts, see in detail Edzard 1970:58-60.

[5] I.e. from south to north and from east to west. The whole conclusion is standard in Amarna letters from the Pharaoh to his vassals; cf. EA 99, 162, 367, 369f.

REFERENCES

Text: Edzard 1970.

4. APHEK

THE LETTER OF TAKUHLINA (3.94)

William W. Hallo

Relatively few cuneiform documents have so far been recovered from the soil of Israel/Palestine, but excavations continue to turn up more; see Hallo, *Origins* 161, for a provisional list.[1] The site of ancient Aphek, for example, has yielded eight texts and fragments dating to the very end of the Bronze Age (ca. 1200 BCE) as the following letter indicates. It originated in Ugarit and was destined for the Egyptian vizier who may have been stationed at Aphek. The writer of the letter may well be identical with Takuhlu/i known from documents found at Ugarit as the representative of Ugarit to the Hittite court at Hattusha, as well as with Takhulinu/a known from Ugarit as residing there and in Karkemish. The addressee may well be identical with the Ḥ(w)y who, among many other high offices, held the post of vizier and royal messenger to foreign lands under Ramesses II. In the last capacity, he may have served in Hattusha and could have met Takuhlina there. If both men had returned to their native lands by the time this letter was written, it may be that it never reached its destination, its journey to Egypt interrupted at Aphek during the unsettled days at the end of the 13th century.

To Haia the Great Man,[2] my father, my lord, speak:
Thus says Takuhlina the governor(?) of the land of Ugarit-city, your son, your servant.
At the feet of my lord I fall.

With my father, my lord, may it be well!
May the gods of the Great King your lord
and the gods of the land of Ugarit-city
bless you and protect you![a]

My father — my wheat, 250 2/6 (bushels of) wheat
which Adduia gave in(to) the hand of Dur-shimati,
in the city of Jappo[b]
and my fathers ordered thus — 250 2/6 (liters of) wheat let him give in(to) the hands of Adduia!

Secondly: My father - the wheat which you desire
and which I have shipped to you
and my request (requisition) which came before my father
you have not (yet) given out.

Now my father - my (most urgent) needs within my request ship to me!
And my wheat may my lord give in(to) the hands of Adduia my emissary.

And now: the money of Adduia the enemies have taken away,
and may he appear before my father!
and may my father investigate them!
Now as a gift of greeting[3] [c] for my father

a Num 6:24 *b* Josh 19:46; Jon 1:3, etc. *c* Isa 1:23

[1] This list can be augmented by a find from Ashkelon; see Huehnergard and Van Soldt 1999. See also below, *COS* 3.115-118, 120, 122.

[2] The great man (LÚ.GAL) is the title of the local ruler, probably under Egyptian suzerainty, as at Kumidi; cf. above, and Edzard 1976:64.

[3] Akk. *šulmānu*; cf. Finkelstein 1952.

100 (shekels of) blue wool and 10 (shekels of) red wool I am sending you.

REFERENCES

Owen 1981; Huehnergard and van Soldt 1999.

5. ASSYRIA

THE MURDER OF SENNACHERIB (3.95)

William W. Hallo

About three thousand letters have been recovered from the royal archives of the Sargonid Dynasty (721-609 BCE) at Nineveh. Half of them were published by Harper (1892-1914) under the title of *Assyrian and Babylonian Letters* (hence *ABL*), and translated by Waterman (1930-36) and, in part, by Pfeiffer (1935). The whole corpus is being reedited by the State Archives of Assyria (SAA) project (Helsinki); see for now SAA 1, 5, 8, 10, 13 and 15. From the contextual perspective, one of the most interesting is *ABL* 1091. Although published by Harper as long ago as 1911, its true significance was not discovered until 1979 when Simo Parpola presented his paper on "The murderer of Sennacherib" to the 26th Rencontre Assyriologique in Copenhagen (Parpola 1980). He showed that this letter to King Esarhaddon of Assyria (680-669 BCE) was a report on the intrigues surrounding the assassination of his father Sennacherib (704-681 BCE), and that it identified one of the assassins as an older son of the king by the name of Arad-Mullissu. From here it is only a relatively small step to the Adramelech of the Bible.

(Beginning lost; restorations not indicated as such)

Our Babylonian brothers ... Shulmu-aḫḫe(?) in the house of ....
When they heard about the conspiracy of ..., one among their number received(?) the royal order. When Nabu-shuma-ishkun[1] and Ṣillaia came, they asked him: "Your royal order — about whom is it?" He replied: "About Arad-Mullissu." They covered his face with his cloak and stationed him before Arad-Mullissu himself, saying: "Read the tablet (and) recite what is in your mouth!" He then said as follows: "Arad-Mullissu your son will kill you!" After they had uncovered his face (and) Arad-mullissu had interrogated him, they killed him and his brothers.[a]

(Rest too fragmentary for translation)

[a] 2 Kgs 19:36f.; Isa 37:37f.

"Letters from gods" represent a canonical sub-genre of correspondence; though never attested in duplicate copies, they sometimes carry a colophon and formed parts of libraries rather than archives. They occur as early as Old Babylonian times; see the survey by Keller 1991 and add Moran 1993. Among the seven or eight Neo-Assyrian examples known (Grayson 1983-4, Livingstone 1989:107-115), the following one has been regarded as referring to the murder of Sennacherib (von Soden 1990).

The great lord, the king of the gods, Ninurta, has sent me.
Speak to the prince, the instrument of my hand,[2]
to the recipient of scepter, throne, and regalia,
to the commander by my own authority;
Thus says Ninurta, the great lord, the son of Enlil:

I am upset, I am wroth, I am angry [in my temple].
I am upset, who will ...?
I am wroth, who will ...?
I am angry in my temple, who will ...?
Surely [he has raised his hand?] against his begettor.
Where is the oath? The replacement for him whom we have killed?

(Remainder of the letter largely or wholly lost)

(The text concludes with a standard colophon of the library of Assurbanipal [668-627 BCE])[3]

[1] Probably to be identified with the son of Merodach-baladan (Marduk-apal-iddina) II and with the Nebosumishkun of the story of Ahiqar; see Dalley 2001:153.
[2] Lit., "the stretching forth of my hand."
[3] See Hunger 1968 No. 319d).

REFERENCES

Text and studies: *ABL* 1091; Parpola 1980; Zawadski 1990; von Soden 1990; Hallo 1991a:162f., 1999:40f.

A LETTER REPORTING MATTERS IN KALAḪ (KALḪU) (3.96) (SAA 1.110)

K. Lawson Younger, Jr.

This letter (NL 16; ND 2765; IM 64159) comes from Kalaḫ (Nimrud) and dates between 720 and 715 BCE during the reign of Sargon II. Therefore its contents cannot refer to the aftermath of the campaign against Ashdod in 712/711 BCE (see note 1). Beside the issues regarding a festival that has recently been celebrated in the city and certain bull colossi that the governor, Marduk-rēmanni, had been placing in their appropriate locations, the letter also records the arrival of emissaries from the southern Levant and Egypt (including one from Judah), all bearing their tribute.

(lines 1-3)
[To the king] my lord, [your servant M]arduk-rēm[anni].[1] [Good health] to the king, my lord.

(lines 4-7)
[The festi]val has been celebra[ted]. The god [x] ⸢came out⸣ (and) returned [in pe]ace. May Nabû and Marduk bless ⸢the king⸣.

(lines 8-15)
As to the bull colossi about which the king, my lord, has written me, I have assigned (them). I have placed (them) at the [gate]s of the ⸢pala⸣ces[2] (and) they are hewing (them). We will place the hewn colossi before the ... house[3]; they will hew the large ones; (and) we will place (them) in front of the middle gate.

(lines 16-19)
As for the ⸢hired men(?)⸣[4] of which I spoke to the ⸢king⸣, my ⸢lord⸣, I will make them responsible (and) return them to (work on) the colossi. We ⸢will place⸣ (them) in front of the middle gate.

(lines 20-24)
Perhaps the king, [my] lord, [will say]: "(It is) hard work [...]" The work [...]; honestly, one cubit [...], bull colossi [...]

(four lines are lost in a break)

(lines 29-r.3)
Let them draw (and) send me a sketch of [ ] [about which] I [spoke] to the ⸢king⸣, my lord; (and) [I will plant] the saplings accordingly.

(lines r.4-14a)
I have received 45 horses of the [pala]ce.[5] The Egyptian, Gazaite, Judahite, Moabite and Ammonite emissaries[6] entered Kalaḫ[a] on the 12th day with their tribute[7] in their hands. The 24 horses of the Gazaite (emissary) were in his hands. The Edomite, [Ashdo]dite, and Ekronite[8] (emissaries)[9] [...]

(lines r.14b-17)
The Quean ⸢emissary⸣ went out [...]; (and) is going [to] the *Bow* [river][10]; the [...] of the commander-in-chief (*turtānu*)[b] is with him.

a Gen 10:11-12

b 2 Kgs 18:17

[1] Postgate (1974:118) states: "A collation of l. 2 indicates that the author of the letter is named [$^{m.}$]^{d}ŠID-*rém*-[(*an*-)*ni*]; a man of this name is attested in 728 BCE as governor of Kalhu, and from the content of this letter it is clear that he was still the governor, the predecessor of Aššur-bani. For this occurrence, see Postgate 1973:135 (#108.6-7): $^{m.d}$ŠID-*rém-ni* $^{(7)}$⸢LU⸣.EN.NAM *šá* ^{uru}*kal-ḫa*. The letter should be dated between about 720 and 715." See the hand copy of Parpola 1987:258 (110.2). However, Saggs (2001:220) states: "but ^{d}MEŠ (sic) does not appear to be a possible reading of the traces. Another possible but uncertain restoration is $^{m.d}$[*n*]*abû*$_3$-*ba*[*l*]-*liṭ*, for which name see ABL 577, obv. 15." For this letter, see SAA 1:70 (#75.15) where this Nabû-balliṭ is one of three possible candidates for appointment as household manager of the Assur temple. It seems unlikely that a household manager of the Assur temple would be the author of this letter reporting the particular contents that it records. A governor of Kalḫu is the more likely the author. In addition, there appears to be space for one or two signs after the LID sign. Thus the reading [$^{m.}$]^{d}MES-*rém*-[(*a*-)*ni*] seems preferable. See *PNA* 2/2:720-721, #5; Postgate and Reade 1976-80:321. Aššur-bani, the governor of Kalhu, was eponym for the year 713 (Millard 1994:47; see also *PNA* 1/1:158-159, #5). Thus the contents of this letter cannot refer to the results of the campaign against Ashdod in 712/711 BCE that some scholars have supposed included a campaign against Judah.

[2] Parpola 1987:92 reads: *ina* UGU ⸢x⸣.MEŠ-*te* $^{(11)}$ *ša* ⸢É!.GA⸣L.MEŠ *ak-ta-ra-ar*. Saggs 2001:219 reads: *ina muḫḫi bā*[*bāti*]?$^{meš.te}$ *ša* ^{amēl}*rabûte*(GAL)^{meš} *ak-ta-ra-ar*. See also *CAD* K 208 s.v. *karāru*.

[3] Parpola 1987:92 reads: *ina* IGI É *la* DU.DU-*ni*. Saggs 2001:219 reads: *ina pān bīti la-ap-du-ni*. Either reading is difficult.

[4] Parpola 1987:92 reads: "As to the ⸢stone bulls⸣ (⸢NA$_4$?.AM!⸣.MEŠ) of which I spoke to the ⸢king⸣, my ⸢lord⸣, they will *modify* them (*ú-pa-ḫu?šú-nu*) and turn them into bull colossi." Saggs 2001:219-221 reads: "Concerning the *hired men* ([L]Ú?.A?.GÀR?.MEŠ) of which I spoke to the king my lord, I will make them responsible (*ú-pa-al-šú-nu*) (and) return them to (work on) the colossi." See also *CAD* A 2:165, #7.

[5] See Parpola 1987:92 and esp. the copy on p. 258 (110:r.4).

[6] ^{lú}MAḪ.MEŠ(*ṣīrāni*). For a discussion of this term, see Machinist 1983:723.

[7] *ma-da-na-t*[*e*]-*šú-nu*. See Cogan 1974:118, n. 5 and Postgate 1974:118.

[8] See Cogan 1974:118, n. 5.

[9] See Millard 1992:36. To the same years may belong a wine list from Nimrud. See Dalley and Postgate 1984 #135.

[10] Parpola (1987:92, n. to r.16) states: "Restore possibly [ÍD].GIŠ.BAN, a river in the vicinity of Guzana, and cf. Tell Halaf 11:6." Postgate (1974:117) reads the entire sentence differently: LÚ.[M]AḪ *aš-du-ud?-a-a* $^{(15)}$ [x x (x) U]RU.*kal-ḫi ú-ṣa-a* $^{(16)}$ [x (x x) UR]U.*ẓab-ban il-la-ka* "The Ashdodite emissary went out of Kalhu and is going to Zabban."

REFERENCES

Text, translations and studies: Saggs 1955:134-135, pl. xxxiii (NL 16); Postgate 1974:117-118 (reverse 4-17); Cogan 1974:118 (reverse 4-15); Parpola 1987:92-93 (#110); Saggs 2001:219-222, pl. xliii.

A LETTER CONCERNING THE GRAIN TAX OF THE SAMARIANS (3.97) (SAA 1.220)

K. Lawson Younger, Jr.

This letter has the horizontally oblong "report" format (Parpola 1987:170).

(lines 1-3)
To Nabû-duru-uṣur, a letter (lit. "tablet") from Arīḫu,[1] good health to my son.

(lines 4-r.3)
As to the grain tax[2] of the Samarians,[3] [a] my ⌈lord⌉ should s⌈end a report⌉ — ⌈whether⌉ it [exists] ⌈or not⌉ — so that we may be content about (it).[4] The men in charge are passive. They do not go to do their work. We cannot give them orders.

(lines r.4-s.1)
Since last year until now I have approached you repeatedly[5] concerning the incoming payments,[6] but we have not brought in any incoming payments. Now send a report whether it exists or not.

a 2 Kgs 17:4-6

[1] *PNA* 1/1:131, #1. "Official in Laqê (reign of Sargon II) ... [m]*a-ri-ḫi* is mentioned in a fragmentary letter to the king as the person to whom the unknown sender of the letter is to be brought SAA 1 261:2′ (not dated)."

[2] For this tax, see Postgate 1974:174-186; *CAD* N 2:351-352, s.v. *nusāḫū*.

[3] KUR.*sa-mir-na-a-a*.

[4] Lit. "so that our heart may be good about (it)."

[5] See *CAD* M 1:67.

[6] Postgate translates "(corn) receipts[?]" and notes that the meaning of *ēribu* here is very uncertain.

REFERENCES

Text, translations and studies: Parpola 1987:170 (#220); (ABL 1201 = BM 81-2-4,51); Postgate 1974:298; Becking 1992:107-108.

A REPORT ON WORK ON DŪR-ŠARRUKIN (3.98) (SAA 15.280 = *ABL* 1065)

K. Lawson Younger, Jr.

(beginning 3-4 lines lost)

(lines 1′-10′)
[Concerning what the king], my lo[rd] wrote to me: "provide the [Sam]arians,[1] [a] [as many as] are [in] your [ha]nds (with work) in Dūr-Šarrukin,"[2] I thereafter [sent (word) to] the sheikhs [say]ing: "gather [all] the carpenters and potters; let them come (and) [direc]t the deportees [who are in D]ūr-Šarrukin." (But) they did not consent to send (them) to me.

(lines 11′-r.4a)
[As verifica]tion, [I have sen]t letters [to] the sheikhs saying: "[if indeed you do not se]nd me craftsmen (and) they do not perform [service for] me, [al]l [the people who are] here [...] upon you, [...] upon [...]," [they would have se]nt forthwith [the craftsmen] (and) [they would have perform]ed the service[3] [for me].

(lines r.4b-7)
Now (however), [following what the king], my lo[rd], sent to me (as instructions), [...] I do not argue at all with any of [the sheikhs].

(lines 8-15)
I have appointed [the carpenters and po]tters [...]. [...] utensils of the house [...] [... the king], my lord, [...] [...] from [...] [...]

(remainder lost)

a 2 Kgs 17:6

[1] The text reads: [LÚ.*Sa-mi*]*r-i-na-a-a*.

[2] The name of the new capital city built by Sargon II (modern Khorsabad), located in the province of Ḫalaḫḫa (biblical Halah of 2 Kgs 17:6).

[3] A Neo-Assyrian letter shows that the inhabitants of Ḫalaḫḫa were obliged to perform *dullu*-duties. These were duties to work for the king. In Ḫalaḫḫa this meant the digging and the upkeep of the canals aiming at better irrigation of the land and the delivery of straw. See Postgate 1974:81, 83, 226-228.

REFERENCES

Text, translations and studies: *ABL* 1065; Fuchs and Parpola 2001 #280; Parpola 1995.

B. CONTRACTS

1. ALALAKH

SALE TRANSACTIONS (3.99)

THE PURCHASE OF BEER (*AT* 33) (3.99A)

Richard S. Hess

Found in 18th century BCE Alalakh Level VII, this text describes the purchase of jars of beer and the exchange of 135 silver shekels. There is a guarantor in the form of the debtors who must make good their provision of beer. They apparently remain bound to this debt for as long as any among them shall live. The concept of debts held for the life of a person is known elsewhere in the biblical world. They form a background for special provisions for general release from debts, whether as the Mesopotamian *andurārum* and *mēšarum* or the biblical Year of Release (Lev 25:39-42; Deut 15).

The payment (lines 1-4, 16)
1 [One] hundred thirty-five silver shekels,
2 according to the standard of Ḫalab (Aleppo),
3 from Ms. Sumunnabi
4 the citizens of Aʾirraše
16 have received:

The sellers (lines 5-12)
5 Šennakka,
6 Niqma-Addu, Neru,
7 Kusan, Muzi,
8 Išmaʿada, Ḫirše,
9 Šerdiya, Akkulena,
10 Arundi, Teššup-bāni,
11 Puttal, Ḫaruḫʾulla,
12 and Kusaḫ-atal,

The product sold (lines 13-15)
15 given
13 in exchange for one hundred thirty-[five jars of royal beer][1]
14 according to the standard of Ḫalab.

Debt repayment (lines 17-20)[2]
17, 19b The survivor among these,
18 as a guarantor,
20 shall pay
19a the debt.

Witnesses (lines 21-26)
21 Ammi-ṭāba citizen of Karše,
22 Uštanila,
23 Zunna,
24 Weruzzi,
25 Sapsi-Addu, a groom,
26 Taḫšunada, a groom.

Date (lines 27-30)
27 In the month of Mešari,[3]
28 the year when Irkabtum became king,
29-30 and the town of Naštarbi rebelled.

[1] This restoration is based on a parallel text in *AT* 34 line 5. See Tsevat 1958:116. One jar of royal beer for one shekel is standard in these texts; see Zeeb 1991:415.

[2] This passage is difficult as it appears to contain legal terms and formula. It would appear that this is a case of corporate liability for the debt incurred. Repayment remains an obligation as long as the debtors live. See Zeeb 1991:418.

[3] [This month name, attested only here, suggests that such debt-release was practiced at Alalakh too; for *andurārum* see *AT* 65 (below, 3.100)] [Ed.].

REFERENCES

Copies: *AT* pl. xi; Zeeb 1991:436. Transliteration: Zeeb 1991:414-415. Translation: *AT* 43; Zeeb 1991:414-415.

SALE OF A TOWN (*AT* 52) (3.99B)

Richard S. Hess

This is one of several texts at Alalakh from Level VII in which towns are bought and sold (see *AT* 53-58). In this case a woman and her son, and therefore the one living heir, sell the town of Iburia to Yarimlim of Alalakh. The sale of towns recalls their use in payment from Solomon to Hiram (1 Kgs 11:11) and as a wedding gift from pharaoh to Solomon (1 Kgs 9:16-17). See also *AT* 1 (*COS* 2.127) and *AT* 456 (*COS* 2.137).

Sales agreement (lines 1-15)
1 As for the town of Iburia
2 in its full extent
3 and its tax exempt status,
4 from Ḫebat-muḫḫirnē
5 and her son Abiadu,
6 Yarim-Lim,
7 leader of Alalakh,
15 has bought
8 for one thousand silver shekels,
9 one thousand *parisu*-measures of barley,
10 one thousand *parisu*-measures of emmer,
11 six po[ts] of wine,
12 ten pots of oil,
13 [together] with their gifts(?)[1]
14 for the full price.

Satisfaction of both parties (lines 16-17)[2] [a]
16 They are satisfied. Their heart
17 is well.

a Gen 1:4, 10, 12, 18, 21, 25, 31; Deut 3:25

Penalty for breaking the agreement (lines 18-21)
18 Whoever overturns (the agreement),
21 shall pay
19 as much silver and gold (as was the purchasae price) to the (temple of the) god Addu,
20 and as much silver and gold (as was the purchase price) to the palace.

Witnesses (lines 21-25)[3]
22 Atri-Addu an administrator,
23 Išmi-Dagan an administrator,
24 Wirikiba a governor,
25 Gi[ ]

Date (lines 26-28)
26 In the month of Kirari, on the fifth day,
27 the year Niqmepuḫ became king,
28 the year of the plague[4] ...

[1] Wiseman leaves untranslated; Kienast (1980a:51 n. 13) derives from *taqānu* and renders, "Geschenk."

[2] In this agreement this clause suggests that there are no further claims or expectations regarding the sale. The use of *ṭa-a-ab* in line 17 may be compared to the wide use of Heb. "*ṭôb*" in biblical contexts related to the covenantal work of God in creation (Gen 1:4, 10, 12, 18, 21, 25, 31) and his covenantal gifts (e.g., Deut 3:25).

[3] In contrast to other sales and witnessed documents from Alalakh, this one names only high officials. No doubt this is a reflection of the important nature of the document.

[4] The same notation occurs later at Emar, perhaps again to justify transactions concluded under stress; cf. e.g. Beckman 1996:184: *i-na mu-ti ša mu-ta-ni*.

REFERENCES

Copy: *AT* pls. xiii-xiv. Transliteration: Kienast 1980a:51. Translation: *AT* 47; Kienast 1980a:51.

MANUMISSIONS

RECEIPT FOR THE PURCHASE OF A DEBT SLAVE (*AT* 65) (3.100)

Richard S. Hess

This level VII tablet records the purchase of a debt slave. Debt slavery was well known in the ancient Near East. The use of the *andarārum* was a special dispensation that allowed all those in debt to be freed of their debts. In order to circumvent this possibility, Sumunnabi had a special clause written into the agreement. Perhaps this type of permanent servitude, with no exclusions, was what Leviticus 25:39-42 addressed. It required release of all those in debt during the Year of Jubilee. See also the usage of the Hebrew cognate, *d^{e}rôr*, in Isaiah 61:1; Jeremiah 34:8, 15, 17; Ezekiel 46:17. See Wright 1990:123-128, 249-258; Hess 1994a:203.

Purchase (lines 1-5)
1 Twenty-three and one third silver shekels
2 are debited against Ugaia.
3 For service in her household
4 Ms. Sumunnabi
5 has purchased (her).

Exclusion clause (lines 6-7)
6 At a general release
7 she may not be released.[1]

Witnesses (lines 8-12)
8 Diniaddu,
9 Zunna,
10 Irkabtum,
11 *šangû*-priest of Ishtar,
12 Irpa-Addu.

Date (lines 13-15)
13 In the year of Irkabtum,
14 in the month of Addanati,
15 on the seventeenth day.

[1] *ina an-da-ra-ri-im ul i-na-an-da-ar.*

REFERENCES

Copy: *AT* pl. xviii. Transliterations: (partial) *AT* 50; Klengel 1963:11; Kienast 1980a:63; (partial) Loretz 1984:138 n 283. Translations: *AT* 50; Klengel 1963:11; Kienast 1980a:63.

MARRIAGE AGREEMENTS

PALACE RECEIPT FOR THE RETURN OF A MARRIAGE GIFT (*AT* 17) (3.101A)

Richard S. Hess

This text comes from the Middle Babylonian level (Level IV). Although Finkelstein (1969:546) describes the document as the "Abrogation of a Marriage Agreement," that is not its focus nor even is it clear that a marriage agreement is ended. Instead, a traitor is executed and the property is confiscated by the king who must return a marriage gift to the traitor's son-in-law. Although the marriage laws of Ḫalab (Aleppo) are not known, the practice of royal confiscation of the property of someone executed for treason has parallels in the Middle Assyrian laws and in 1 Kings 21. See Westbrook 1991:122-124.

1 Seal of Niqmepa:
2 Šatuwa, the son of Suwa and a citizen of Luba,
3 asked[1] [a] Abra for (the hand of) his daughter
4 so that she might become Šatuwa's daughter-in-law.
5 According to the laws of Ḫalab,
6 Šatuwa gave Abra a marriage gift.
7 Abra then
8 turned into a criminal[2] [b]
9 and was executed for his crime.
10 His estate was confiscated by the palace.
11 Šatuwa
12 came and, according to what
13 belonged to him, he reclaimed six talents of copper
14 and two bronze daggers.
15 As of today,
16 Niqmepa has satisfied Šatuwa.
17 In the future, Šatuwa [cannot] claim
18 any m[ore possessions].

Witnesses (lines 19-23)

19 Abu,
20 Kuša-ibri a *š[angû*-priest],
21 Dura son of ...,
22 Ir-Kabtu, Iriḫalpa,
23 Zitia, Šarruwa, the scribe.

Seal

1 [I][drimi,
2 [ser]vant of Addu.

a 2 Chr 11:23
b 1 Kgs 21:1-16

[1] The expression, "to ask for the hand of," in terms of marriage, is also found in Elephantine documents and 2 Chr 11:23. See Loewenstamm 1980:25 n. 51.

[2] *bēl mašikti*. The expression *mašiktu* occurs in the Idrimi inscription (*COS* 1.148, line 4), where it denotes the political troubles that forced Idrimi to leave the country. See Loewenstamm 1980:25-26 who compares 1 Kgs 21:1-16 and the story of Naboth. Naboth was also accused of treason and executed, and the king confiscated his property.

REFERENCES

Copy: *AT* pl. ix. Transliteration: *AT* 40. Translation: *AT* 40; Landsberger 1954:60 n. 129; Finkelstein 1969:546.

MARRIAGE CUSTOMS (*AT* 92) (3.101B)

Richard S. Hess

This is an important Level IV text for understanding marriage customs in Late Bronze Age Alalakh. Unfortunately, it is fragmentary and difficult to interpret due to grammatical anomalies. Apparently this is a "pre-nuptial agreement" that provides for contexts in which the the wife may offend the husband and thereby cause a divorce. The settlement of the divorce is envisioned and different for each case (lines 6′-14′).[1] As in so many other marriage documents from the second millennium BCE (especially from Hurrian cultures such as Nuzi), barrenness was unacceptable for the marriage and resulted in an alternative woman, in this case the wife's niece, being brought into the relationship for purposes of giving birth to an heir. This has parallels with the concern of Abraham for an heir (Gen 12-20) and with

[1] See Malul 1988:111-112; Rowe and van Soldt 1998:133 n. 21.

Sarah's suggestion of Hagar as a substitute mother (Gen 16). Further, this implies that the special inheritance of the first-born son could be legally transferred to someone else (Mendelsohn 1959), as with Abraham's adoption of Eliezer (Gen 15:2-3) and Jacob's choices of Joseph instead of Reuben (Gen 48:14, 22; 49:3-4) and of Ephraim instead of Manasseh (Gen 48:13-14).

Legal creation of a sister (*aḫātu*) (lines 1′-5′)

1′ [Iw]aššura [ ]
2′ [has g]iven. If [ ]
3′ [ ] daughter of Ku[pšer
4′ [If,] regarding his daughter, Kupšer ...
5′ he has given the status of a sister [t]o his daughter.

Divorce for abuse (lines 6′-9′)

6′ If Naidu rej[ect]s(?) Iri-ḫalpa
7′ and drives her away,[2] then the
8′ young woman retains her bride price, (and) whatever
9′ of her father's house is assigned to her. She(!) will leave.

Divorce for insults(?) (lines 10′-14′)

10′ If the bride
11′ pulls at his nose,
12′ she(!) must return the bride price but whatever belongs to her father's house
13′ which she(!) brought and was assigned to her,
14′ she(!) will keep. She will leave.

Barrenness (lines 15′-20′)

15′ If Naidu has not given birth to an heir, then the daughter of her brother,
16′ Iwaššura, shall be given (to Iriḫalpa).
17′ If Tatadu(?)
18′ gives birth first for Iri-ḫalpa, and afterwards
19′ Naidu gives birth, then
20′ the older(?) woman shall not be given anything ... god [ ]

Inheritance (lines 21-24)

21′ If Naidu should die, and she(!) does not have
22′ a son or daughter or bride price,
23′ everything of the [young woman's]
24′ from her father's house ...

[2] For the translation of this line as here, see Speiser 1954:24-25. Speiser notes that there is a confusion of the gender of pronouns throughout this document. He suggests it may reflect the absence of grammatical gender in Hurrian.

REFERENCES

Copy: *AT* pl. xxiii. Transliteration: *AT* 55. Translation: *AT* 54-55.

SEVEN YEARS OF BARRENNESS BEFORE A SECOND WIFE (*AT* 93) (3.101C)

Richard S. Hess

This text, from Level IV, compares with the manner in which Jacob worked seven years for Laban before he was allowed one of his daughters as a wife (Gen 29:15-35). However, there are significant differences because with Jacob the issue was not barrenness but his desire for Rachel.

1 *x x du*
2 From this day, before [Niqmepa the king:]
3 The daughter of Ilimili,
4 Zunzuri, Idat[ti(?)
5 has taken for a wife.
6 Two hundred shekels of silver and thirty shekels of gold
7 he has given as a bride price.
8 [I]f she does not give birth after seven years,
9 he (Idat[ti]) may take a second wife.
10 [ ] his (bridal price?) for the second wife
11 [ ] he shall give it
12 to the palace.

REFERENCES

Copy: *AT* pl. xxiii. Translation: *AT* 55.

LOAN TRANSACTIONS

SECURITY FOR A LOAN (*AT* 18) (3.102A)

Richard S. Hess

AT 18-28 are all Old Babylonian documents from Alalakh level VII. They describe *mazzazzānūtu* or stand-ins, people who function as security deposits until a debt owed to the king is paid. This has been compared to those who dwell in the house of the Lord (similar phrasing) in the Psalms (e.g., Pss 23:6; 27:4). The translation of *AT* 18 follows the readings of Zeeb (1992:452) who incorporates readings from thirteen lines found on the tablet case (AT 39/184, 2+3) but not on the tablet itself.

1 Seal of Ammiaddu.
2 One-third mina and one shekel of silver
3 belonging to king Ammitaku
4 is debited against Ammiaddu, a fowler.
5 Ayašarri and Bendiaddu,
6 the sons of Ammiaddu,
7 his wife and his sons,
8 he gave.
9 In correspondence to this silver
10 for security
12 they are to remain
11 in the house of Ammitaku.[1]
13 They are fowlers of the king.

14 Other than the king at the palace
17 there is no one
15 else
16 who must be supported.[2]

17-18 During his lifetime he will pay the silver.

Witnesses
19 Ewirikiba[3] a royal official,
20 the Ishtar *šangû*-priest,
21 Talmammu,
22 Immeri,

---

23 Ḫirše son of a *šangû*-priest,
24 ⌜A⌝[dai]šlubar.

---

25 In the month of [Att]annatim,
26 during the ye[ar I]arimlim became kin[g].

---

27 The seal of Weri[kiba],
28 the seal of Adaišlubar, the seal of a *šangû*-priest,
29 the seal of Niqmepa, the seal of [ ]

[1] Zeeb (1992:452) translates, "in der Wirtschaftseinheit des Ammitaqum."

[2] Zeeb (1992:452, 454) restores from the case, *ša it-ta*[*-na-šu-ú*]. This is understood to forbid any possible obligation on the part of the debtor to provide a similar debt servitude to anyone else as long as the present obligation is in force. If this is the correct understanding of this text, and if this practice was consistent in Alalakh and in Israelite society, then Zeeb (1995:653-654) may be correct in comparing Amos' attack on Israelite society in Amos 2:6-8 in terms of this sort of debt servitude. Forbidden to sell such "security deposits" into slavery, that is just what the rich Israelites were doing to their fellow citizens. Forbidden to use these people for other than services of debt servitude, the wealthy Israelites turned the women into sex objects.

[3] Ewirikiba, a Hurrian name whose first element, the Hurrian word for "lord," may resemble a form of the first element in the name of the individual from whom David bought the threshing floor and where Solomon built the Temple: Arawanna. The metathesis of the "*r*" and the "*w*" may be a scribal error, further demonstrating that the Heb. scribes were unfamiliar with the name and unclear how to record it. Compare the different spellings of the name in Kings and Chronicles and in the Masoretic Text and the Septuagint.

REFERENCES

Copies: *AT* pl. ix; Zeeb 1992:477. Transliteration: Eichler 1973:66; Zeeb 1992:452. Translation: (summary) *AT* 40; Eichler 1973:67; Zeeb 1992:453. See also Klengel 1963.

TRANSFER OF CREDITORS (AT 28) (3.102B)

Richard S. Hess

This Level VII text describes the debt owed by the fowlers (lines 1-4) and their family. The debt is transferred from one creditor (Kurbišan) to another (Ammitaku).

The debtors (lines 1-5)
1 Ašma-Addu son of Inakabiti,
2 Wikken,
3 Zuḫerasi,
4 (and) Taʾuzen,
5 the fowlers.

The change of creditors (lines 6-12)

6 Regarding the principal investment of thirty silver shekels,
7 Kurbišan son of Niminašu
8 has seized them.
9 Ammitaku
12 then took them
10 for thirty silver shekels
11 from Kurbišan.

Reaffirmation of the debt (lines 13-23)

13 The principal of thirty silver shekels
14 is debited against Ašma-Addu,
15 Yikken,
16 Zuḫerasi,
17 Taʾuze,
18 and against their wives
19 and their sons
20 is the silver of the security.[1]
21, 24 One among them will pay the silver
22 that belongs to Ammitaku, the king
23 of Alalakh.[2]

[1] On *mazzazzānim* compare *AT* 18 above (3.102A), line 10. *AT* 18-28 all describe this surety that is pledged until the debt may be paid.

[2] Wiseman (*AT* 18) and Eichler (1973:72) read these lines on the left edge of the tablet, "He who raises a claim shall have lead poured into his mouth." Zeeb (1993:467) does not read these lines on either the photo or copy used by him. A 13 February 1997 collation of this tablet did not reveal any evidence of writing on the left edge of the tablet. These lines do not exist on this tablet.

REFERENCES

Copies: *AT* pl. x; Zeeb 1993:472. Transliteration: Eichler 1973:71-72; Zeeb 1993:464-465. Translation: *AT* 42; Eichler 1973:72; Zeeb 1993:464-465. The transliteration followed here is that of Zeeb.

---

2. PROPERTY CONVEYANCES FROM UGARIT

Michael Heltzer

There are several hundred property conveyances from Ugarit, dating from the 14th to the beginning of the 12th centuries BCE. This is a representative selection of documents of various aspects of property conveyances, including land sales and purchases, mortgages, land grants, and donations for royal service.

LAND SALES AND PURCHASES

LAND PURCHASE TEXT (3.103)
(*Ugaritica* 5.6 = RS 17.149)

Munaḫimu[1] — the scribe.

From the present day on, before witnesses, Rashap-abu and Pidda, his wife, have purchased 4 *ikû* fields, with olive grove with its slaves, with its (fruit) trees, among the fields of Ṣaʾu[2] from Yarimanu, son of Ḫuzamu, for 400 (shekels) of silver.[3] The fields (and) olive-grove are bound like the sunny day[4] to Rashap-abu and Pidda, his wife, and to their sons forever. If in future Yarimanu and his sons rescind their decision,[5] he is liable for 1 thousand (shekel) of silver. And the fields (belong) to Rashap-abu and Pidda. And if Rashap-abu and his wife rescind their decision, so this land remains for them.[6] Further: formerly these fields were of Izalda, the father of Pidda, and now the fields are returned to Pidda and Rashap-abu.[7]

Witness: Abu, son of Ḫagbanu, Witness: Naʾam-Rashap,[8] son of Guddanu, Witness: Abdi-Milki,

[1] The name Munaḫimu means "The consoler." Common West Semitic name. Cf. Heb. *Mᵉnaḥem* (2 Kgs 15:14-23).

[2] A well-known village of the kingdom of Ugarit. See below, 3.106, n. 2.

[3] The Ug. shekel was ca. 9.5 g.

[4] The phrase, *ṣāmid ina šamši ūmi*, was a legal formula binding the property to its new owner. See *COS* 3.106, n. 5 below.

[5] Lit. "from their heart."

[6] Nougayrol translates: "il en ira de même pour eux."

[7] It seems that the former owner, or his descendent had the right to buy before other buyers. Possibly, Izalda lost his land because of economic reasons and now Pidda, his daughter and her husband, Rashap-abu, are returning it to the family.

[8] The name Naʿam-Rashap means "(the god) Rashap is pleasing." Cf. Abdi-Rashap.

son of Shumu-ramu,[9] Witness: Abdi-Nikal,[10] son of Piʾdaya, Witness: Munahimu, son of Shapidanu.

[9] The name Shumu-ramu means "The name (of the God) is high."
[10] The name Abdi-Nikal means "Servant (slave) of (the goddess) Nikkal." This was an Ug. deity whose name is of Sum. origin.

REFERENCES

Text and studies: Nougayrol, *Ugaritica* 5.6 (RS 17.149); Heltzer 1976:100-101.

LAND PURCHASE TEXT (3.104)[1]
(RS 8.213)

From the present day on, before witnesses, Yashinu, son of Addulanu, freed the *dimtu*[2] which is between the fields of Ḫuppatu[3] with the fields of Shuqalu,[4] its olive-trees with its orchards (and) vineyards for 400 (shekels) of silver[5] from the hands of Aziranu and Abdi-Adati,[6] son of Buranu. Further, if in future Aziranu and Abdi-Adati, son of Buranu, and their sons (and) grandsons change their decision,[7] they shall pay 1 talent of silver[8] to the king.

And if Yashinu and his sons change their mind about the bronze objects[9] — they have to pay 1 talent of silver to the king.[10]

(Names of ten witnesses and the scribe).

[1] Published by Thureau-Dangin 1937. No date is given in the text.
[2] Akk. *dimtu* "tower, watchtower, fortified dwelling" is used here for the entire estate. In this case it included the landed property with all farm buildings.
[3] A well-known village settlement of the kingdom of Ugarit.
[4] Shuqalu was a village in the kingdom of Ugarit.
[5] The Ug. shekel was ca. 9.5 g.
[6] The name Abdi-Adati means "Servant (slave) of the Lady" — *Adatu* — "Lady" in Ug. and Phoen. Here *Adatu* is an epithet of a goddess.
[7] Lit. "from their heart."
[8] The Ug. talent consisted of 3000 shekels or ca. 30 kg.
[9] Lit. "shall return to the bronze objects."
[10] Despite the fact that we see here the redeeming of the lands of Yashinu, which were formerly given over to mortgage, the fee for changing the mind of the parties had to be given to the king. It seems that the equivalent of 400 shekels of silver was paid in bronze vessels.

REFERENCES

Thureau-Dangin 1937; RS 8.213.

FORECLOSURE AND REDISTRIBUTION OF LAND (3.105)
(*Ugaritica* 5.9 = RS 17.61)

From the present day on, before witnesses: the governor,[1] Irib-Ilu[2] of Riqdi,[3] has taken the house, the fields (and) all that belongs to her,[4] from the daughter of Yaknu and the daughter of [...]yabi, the *nayyālu*,[5] and has given it to Abdi-Yaraḫ,[6] son of Kum-U,[7] for 300 (shekels) of silver.[8] The fields are bound. In the future, nobody shall take them from the hands of Abdi-Yaraḫ, and from his sons.

[1] MAŠKIM normally in Akk. *rābiṣu*, but in Akk. at Ugarit *sākinu*, the equivalent of Ug. *skn*.
[2] The name Irib-Ilu means "(the god) Ilu is the guarantor," or "adversary," or "fighter." Cf. the Heb. personal name *Yārīb* (1 Chr 4:24; Ezra 8:16; etc.).
[3] A village of the kingdom of Ugarit.
[4] The person from whom the real estate is being taken is a woman.
[5] *Nayyālu*, a person who did not perform tax or royal service obligations (Heltzer 1982a:19-21). There are other texts about *nayyālū* at Ugarit.
[6] The name Abdi-Yaraḫ means "Servant (slave) of Yaraḫ," the West Semitic moongod. Cf. Heb. *Yārēaḥ* "moon, month" and *Yᵉrîḥô* "Jericho" (named after the Canaanite moongod).
[7] The last sign of this name designates a deity. The reading in Akk. is not clear.
[8] It seems that the governor of one of the largest villages of Ugarit took this action by permission of the king. The silver was given to the governor, but it had to be handed over to the king.

Witness: Tuppiyānu, son of Arsuwanu. Witness: Imidanu, son of Kuzani. Witness: Abdum, son of Abdi-Rashap.[9] Witness: Ili-Rashap,[10] son of Tubanu. Witness: Abdi-Rashap, son of Tubbitenu; Witness: Abdi-Asharti,[11] son of Yanḫammu. The seal of Irib-ilu, Ilu-Milku,[12] the scribe.

[9] The name Abdi-Rashap means "Servant (slave) of Rashap," the West-Semitic deity of war, pestilence and fire. Cf. Ug. *Ršp*. Heb. Rešef (Ps 78:48; Job 5:7; Deut 32:24; etc.).

[10] The name Ili-Rashap means "My God is Rashap." Cf. previous note.

[11] The name Abdi-Asharti means "Servant (slave) of (the goddess) Ashartu." Cf. Ug. *ᵓṯrt*; Heb. *ᵓăšērāh* (2 Kgs 21:7; 23:6, 15; etc.).

[12] The name Ilu-Milku means "(the god) Ilu is the King." Cf. Abdi-Milku and the Heb. personal name ᵓElīmelek (Ruth 1:2; 2:1, 3; etc.).

REFERENCES

Text and studies: Nougayrol, *Ugaritica* 5.9 (RS 17.61); Heltzer 1976:55-57.

LAND SALE (3.106)
(*Ugaritica* 5.159 = RS 17.86)

From the present day on, before witnesses, Iliya, son of Siniya, and Padiya, his brother, and his sons sold 4 (*ikû*)[1] which are among the fields of Ṣaᵓu[2] for 180 (shekels) of silver[3] to Sharelli,[4] the queen. (These) 4 (*ikû*) fields are bound like the sunny day[5] to Sharelli, the queen,[6] forever. Witness: Shipiṭ-Baᵓal.[7] Witness: Shubammu. Witness: Abdi-Milki,[8] son of Yakunu. Witness: Anantenu, son of Binanu. Witness: Matenu, majordomo[9] [a] of the queen. Witness: Abdi-Yaraḫ, the scribe.

a Gen 41:43

[1] *Ikû* = ca. 0.35 hectares.

[2] A well-known village of the kingdom of Ugarit. See above, 3.103, n. 2.

[3] The price of 1 *ikû* was usually 45 shekels of silver, ca. 400 g.

[4] Queen Sharelli was the wife of King Ibiranu (1235-1225 BCE) and the queen mother at the time of Niqmaddu III (1225/1220-1215 BCE); see Singer 1999:291f.

[5] See note 4 to RS 17.149 (above 3.103).

[6] The queen at Ugarit had to conform to all of the formalities like any other person purchasing land.

[7] The name Shipiṭ-Baᵓal means "(the god) Baᶜal is the ruler" or "judge."

[8] The name Abdi-Milki means "Servant (slave) of the King." Milk(u) — one of the epiphets of the god Ilu.

[9] *Abarakku*. The queen Sharelli had her own palace and treasury.

REFERENCES

Text and studies: Nougayrol, *Ugaritica* 5.159 (RS 17.86); Heltzer 1976:94-95.

LAND GRANTS AND DONATIONS

LAND DONATION FOR SERVICE RENDERED (3.107)
(*PRU* VI 30 = RS 18.500)

From the present day on, Ammistamru, son of Niqmepa, king of Ugarit,[1] has taken the houses and fields of Abutenu and given them to Abdi-Ḫagab,[2] son of Shapidanu, and his sons forever. And the *pilku*[3]-service of tradership[4] he has to perform.[5] Next: while Abdi-Ḫagab performs this *pilku*-service

[1] Ammistamru II (ca. 1260-1235 BCE).

[2] The name Abdi-Ḫagab means "Servant (slave) of Ḫagab," one of the minor gods of Ugarit.

[3] The term *pilku* refers to royal service for land donation or to the land allotment itself (Heltzer 1982b; Huehnergard 1987).

[4] The word *tamkāru* ("trader", "merchant") refers in this case to the royal trader (Heltzer 1978:122-123).

[5] The land is given by the king to a royal trader and his descendants on condition of performing tradership (*tamkārūtu*) service.

of tradership, nobody shall take from the hands of Abdi-Ḫagab and from the hands of his sons (and) grandsons (the houses and fields) forever.

The great seal of the king.[6]

Ilu-ramu,[7] the scribe.

[6] The impression of the royal dynastic seal is stamped before the beginning of the text.

[7] The name Ilu-ramu means "God is high."

REFERENCES

Text: *PRU* VI 30 (RS 18.500).

LAND DONATION BY THE KING (3.108)
(*PRU* III 15.Z)

From the present day on, Niqmaddu,[1] son of Ammistamru, king of Ugarit[2] has taken the house of Yatarmu, son of Sharupshu, and the fields of Ṣariru with all that they have, and has given them to Bin-ilu, Yaṣiru, and Abi-irshi,[3] and their sons forever. In future nobody shall take (it) from their hands. It is a grant forever.

The seal of Niqmaddu, son of Ammistamru, king of Ugarit.

First the king gave them and, secondly, 200 (shekels) of silver they shall give to the king.[4]

[1] Ug. *Nqmd*, **Nqm(ʾ)d* "(the god) Addu (Hadad) avenges."

[2] Niqmaddu III reigned ca. 1225/1220-1215 BCE.

[3] The name Abi-irshi means "My Father (i.e. God) will inherit."

[4] It is not clear whether this is a land sale by the king to these three persons, or whether this is a paid land grant that was connected with some kind of service.

REFERENCES

Text: *PRU* III 15.Z.

ROYAL LAND GRANT (3.109)
(*PRU* III 15.136)

From the present day on, before Ammistamru, son of Niqmepa, king of Ugarit,[1] Kalbiya, son of Kabityanu, has released 6 *ikû* fields,[2] around the fields of the city[3] for 520 (shekels) of silver[4] to Kurwanu,[5] son of Baʾal-azki and to his sons. These fields are granted[6] to Kurwanu and to his sons forever. No person shall take away these fields from the hands of Kurwanu, or from the hands of his sons forever. And there is no *pilku*-service from these fields.

The seal of Ammistamru, son of Niqmepa, king of Ugarit.

Yaʾadidu, the scribe.

[1] Ammistamru II reigned ca. 1260-1235 BCE.

[2] Ca. 2.1 hectares.

[3] Possibly, fields which administratively belonged to the capital city, Ugarit.

[4] This is the highest price for land known from Ugarit and possibly from Western Asia in the 2nd millennium BCE: 87.5 (shekels) for 1 *ikû*. Possibly, the high price for the land and the fact of its sale, where the king received at least a part of the sum, indicate that the land was not service-land, and that the land was in the very near vicinity of the capital city of Ugarit. See Heltzer 1978:116.

[5] Kurwanu is a Hurrian name.

[6] *Ṣamid*.

REFERENCES

Text: *PRU* III 15.136.

ROYAL LAND GRANT (3.110)
(*PRU* III 16.153)

From the present day on, Ammistamru, son of Niqmepa, king of Ugarit[1] has given to Yaṣiranu, son of Ḫuṣanu, the village (*ālu*) E[--]ish with everything it has forever, (also) to his sons and grandsons. Its grain, its beer (*šikaru*)[2] of its (the village's) tithe, and the sheep — the pasturing tax (*ma-aq-qa-du*)[3] shall be for Yaṣiranu. The silver of the gifts and silver of the bridegroom's friend and service boys (*sú-sa-pi-in-nu-ti*)[4] shall be for Yaṣiranu.[5]

[1] Ammistamru II reigned ca. 1260-1225 BCE.
[2] *Šikaru*. Akk. "beer" (from barley or dates).
[3] *Ma*ᵓ*aqqadu* was pasturing tax. Cf. Heltzer 1982:18; 1974.
[4] *Susapinnūtu* "friend-of-the-bridegroom service; participating in the ceremony." It was taxed. See *CAD* S 416; Malul 1989.
[5] Yaṣiranu thus received all the service obligation including the tithe from the whole village for himself. On the tithe at Ugarit, see also above 3.82-83.

REFERENCES

Text: *PRU* III 16.153.

---

3. NEO-ASSYRIAN CONTRACTS*

SALE OF THREE SLAVES (3.111)
(SAA 6 #34)

K. Lawson Younger, Jr.

This text is dated by eponym to 709 BCE (Mannu-kī-Aššur-lēᵓi, see Millard 1994:47). It records the sale of three slaves (two men and a woman) to a chariot driver named Šumma-ilāni (known from other texts). Another chariot driver, Nadbi-Yau (*ᴵna-ad-bi-ia-a-ú*), is also mentioned; his name contains the Yahwistic theophoric element. He serves as a witness to the transaction.

(lines 1-2)
Seal of D[agan-milki], the owner of the people being [sold].

(blank seal space)

(lines 3-4)
Immannû,[1] the woman U[n...]ni, and Milki-uri, a total of 3 persons.

(lines 5-9)
Šumma-ilāni, chariot driver of the royal corps,[2] has contracted and taken them from Dagan-milki[3] for 3 minas of silver by the mina of Carchemish.[4]

(lines 10-13a)
The money is paid completely. Those people are purchased and taken. Revocation, lawsuit (or) litigation are void.

(lines 13b-r.5)
Whoever in the future, at any time, lodges a complaint (or) obstructs, whether Dagan-milki, or his brothers or his nephews or any relative of his or

* For discussions of the genre and particular formulae of Neo-Assyrian contracts, see Postgate 1976; 1997; Radner 1997:316-356; 2001:265-288.
[1] See *PNA* 2/1:538.
[2] Written ᴵKA.KÉŠ.LUGAL. The determinative must be a scribal error. Hence simply *kiṣir šarrūti* (the Assyrian "home army") seems to be intended. See Kwasman 1988:201. For the *kiṣir šarrūti*, see Dalley and Postgate 1984:27-47; Mattila 2000:149-157.
[3] *PNA* 1/2:366.
[4] For the mina of Carchemish, see Fales 1996:16-17; Powell 1996; Radner 1999a:130-131. For possible historical contexts for this mina's use, see Müller 1997:120. For the price(s) paid for slaves, see Radner 1997:230-248.

anyone powerful, (and) seeks lawsuit or litigation with Šumma-ilāni, his sons (or) his grandsons, shall pay (Reverse) [x min]as of silver and 1 mina of gold to Ištar of Arbela, and shall return the money tenfold to its owners. He shall contest in his lawsuit, but shall not succeed.

(lines 6-12)

Witness: Addâ,[5] the scribe;
Witness: Aḫi-rāmu,[6] ditto;

a 1 Chr 3:18

Witness: Paqaḫa,[7] village inspector/manager[8];
Witness: Nadbi-Yau,[9] [a] chariot driver;
Witness: Bēl-ēmuranni[10];
Witness: Bin-dikiri[11];
Witness: Ṭab-šar-Issar;
Witness: Tabnî, the keeper of the tablet;

(lines 13-14)

Month of Ab, day 20, eponymy (*limmu*) of Mannu-kī-Aššur-lēʾi.

[5] A scribe from Dūr-Šarrukin (reign of Sargon II). See *PNA* 1/1:43-44; Fales 1991:111.

[6] A scribe from Kalḫu (reign of Sargon II). See *PNA* 1/1:67.

[7] Perhaps the same individual mentioned in TFS 99 i.2. See Dalley and Postgate 1984:171, n. i.2.

[8] For this same office, LÚ.GAL-URU.MEŠ (*rab ālāni*), "village inspector/manager," see Kwasman and Parpola 1991 #61, line 15 (3.113, n. 8).

[9] For this Yahwistic theophoric name, see Zadok 1979; 1997. In the biblical text, cf. *ndbyh* (1 Chr 3:18); for extra-biblical *ndbyhw*, see *HAE* 2/1:75.

[10] See *PNA* 1/2:293-294, #10.

[11] For this name and its origins, see *PNA* 1/2:344-345.

REFERENCES

Text, translations and studies: ARU 523; Kwasman 1988 #355; Kwasman and Parpola 1991:38.

SALE OF A SLAVE WOMAN (3.112)
(BM 103956)

K. Lawson Younger, Jr.

Dating to approximately 642 BCE (see note 8 below), this text (BM 103956) records the sale of a slave woman named Bānât-Esaggil. The person selling the slave woman has a Yahwistic name, Yadiʾ-Yau. This same woman appears to have been sold some years later (see note 6 below).

(lines 1-3)

The seal of Yadiʾ-Yau,[1] the [...] of the chief of public works,[2] owner of the woman being sold.

(Seals, faded)

(lines 4-8a)

Nabû-metu-uballiṭ, the subordinate[3] of Aššur-šarru-uṣur,[4] the supervisor of the women of the crown prince,[5] has contracted and taken the woman Bānât-Esaggil,[6] his (Yadiʾ-Yau's) maidservant, for 34 shekels of silver.[7]

(lines 8b-11a)

The money is paid completely. That woman is purchased and taken. Revocation, lawsuit (or) litigation are void.

(lines 11b-r.4)

Whoever in the future, at any time, lodges a complaint (or) obstructs, whether Yadiʾ-Yau, his sons, his grandsons, his brothers, his relative, or anyone of his, (reverse) (and) seeks lawsuit or litigation with Nabû-metu-uballiṭ, his sons, or his grandsons, will pay 10 minas of silver.

(lines 5-6)

Month of Ululu, day 15, eponymy (*limmu*) of Šarru-mītu-uballiṭ.[8]

(lines 7-12)

Witness: Ilu-iddina,[9] royal bodyguard;
[Witness: x]pamūnu[10]
[Witness: x]ṭubašti[10]

[1] *PNA* 2/1:486.

[2] For the *rab pilkāni*, see Postgate 1974:44, 228.

[3] Reading LÚ.TUR(*ṣeḫru*) instead of LÚ.DUMU.

[4] *PNA* 1/1:218-221, #16.

[5] Reading GAL MÍ.MEŠ *ša* A MAN (following a recent collation of the tablet). See Jursa and Radner 1995-96:95. Fales 1979:243 read: GAL(*rab*) *pi-ir-ra-a-ni* "chief of collections" (for this office, see Postgate 1974:163-166).

[6] About a decade later, Bānât-Esaggil is sold for 35 shekels of silver to a man named Kiṣir-Aššur. See *PNA* 1/2:263, #3.

[7] For the price(s) paid for slaves, see Radner 1997:230-248.

[8] Written ᴵMAN.UŠ.TI. For the date, see Reade 1998:256-257. For the cuneiform writings of the name, see Millard 1994:119. The name's Aramaic spelling is *srm[t]blṭ* in a text from Tell Sheikh Ḥamad (Röllig 1997:373, n. 30). Thus the eponym's name very likely was Šarru-mītu-uballiṭ, not Šamaš-mītu-uballiṭ.

[9] *PNA* 2/1:529, #5.

[10] Fales (1979:245) comments: "Two Egyptian names would seem to be attested here ... and thus easily to be related to the deportation policies

[Witness: x]-Aššur
[Witness: x]-ilu

[Witness: ...]la
(lines 13-16 missing)

of Esarhaddon and Ashurbanipal from Egypt."

REFERENCES

Text, translations and studies: Fales 1979:243-245, 254 (#11).

A SLAVE REDEMPTION (3.113)
(SAA 6 #61)

K. Lawson Younger, Jr.

This tablet dates to the reign of Sennacherib, specifically to the year 700 BCE (eponymy [*limmu*] of Metūnu). While there are only a few conveyances that describe the release of an object from pledge, it is clear that these are phrased in most respects like an ordinary sale text. Thus a pledge redemption text bears the seal impression of the creditor so that it is clear that the object had already become his property. As Postgate (1976:29, 49-50) notes, such pledge redemptions are often characterized by the verb *paṭāru* "to release" (as in this text) or the verb *šēṣuʾu* "to bring out."[1] Furthermore, it was not necessary that the person redeeming the object be the previous owner. For further discussion of this inscription, see Kwasman 1988 #50.

(lines 1-3)
Inst[ead of their seal]s they impressed their fingernails. The fingerna[il of Zak]kur, the finger[nail] of Dukur-il,[2] the owners of the man being sold.

(four fingernail impressions)

(lines 4-7)
Baḫianu has contracted and released[3] Mannu-kī-Arbail, the son of Aḫi-Yau[4] [a] from Zakkur and Dukur-il [for] 30 minas of copper.

(lines 8-10a)
[The money] is paid completely. That man is purchased and taken. Revocation, lawsuit (or) litigation are void.

(lines 10b-12)
Whoever in the future, at any time, lodges a complaint, shall pay out [10 mi]nas of silver to redeem the man.

(lines 13-14)
[(Guaranteed against) seizures] of epilepsy[5] for 100 days (and against) fraud[6] in perpetuity.

(lines 15-r.4)
[Witness Bē]l-dūri,[7] the village manager[8];
[Witness] Dusus‌u[9];
(Reverse)
Witness M[i]lku-il;
Witness Bēl-ēmuranni[10];
Witness Šamaš-šēzib;
[Witness] Attāra[11];
[Witness] I[nūrta]-mušēzib[12];

(lines 5-8)
[Month A]b, day 5 [...] ..., eponymy (*limmu*) of

a 1 Sam 14:3, 18; 1 Kgs 4:3; 11:29; 12:15; 14:2, 4-6, 18; 15:27, 29, 33; 21:22; 2 Kgs 9:9; Neh 10:27; 1 Chr 2:25; 8:7; 11:36; 26:20; 2 Chr 9:29; 10:15

[1] The term *šēṣuʾu* is generally a substitute in Neo-Assyrian for *paṭāru* (primarily a Middle Assyrian term). See Postgate 1997:162, n. 11.

[2] For this individual, see *PNA* 1/2:387. Fales 1991:112, n. 99 proposes to read this name as ^{I}*kin*$_7$*-nat*-DINGIR.

[3] The verb *paṭāru* "to release" indicates that this is a pledge redemption. See Radner 2001:280-284. For slave release, see Hallo 1995.

[4] For the name ^{I}PAP(*aḫi*)*-ia-ú*, see TFS 99:ii.22 (*COS* 3.128); *PNA* 1/1:63; and Fales 1991:112, n. 97. For the Hebrew name *ʾḥyhw*, Aḥiyahu/Aḥiah, see *HAE* 2/1:58; and *CWSSS* 479 s.v. Various individuals bear this name in the biblical text; see scripture note *a*.

[5] On this part of the guarantee clause, see the Laws of Hammurabi (*COS* 2.131, §278). For *bennu* disease, see Stol 1993:133-135. For a discussion of *ṣibtu* "seizures," *bennu* "epilepsy," and *sartu* "fraud," see Radner 1997:174-179.

[6] The term *sartu* presents a difficulty in translation. Postgate (1976:26) suggested: "the purchaser either is indemnified if the slave is taken from him because of some crime he (the slave) has committed, or if the seller was not entitled to sell the slave and was guilty of a criminal deception in so doing." *CAD* (S 188, #3) seems to follow the second possibility but with a slightly different angle, namely that *sartu* connotes "stolen property." Hence the guarantee is that the slave is not stolen property unloaded on the unsuspecting buyer. In many of its contexts, *sartu* denotes a lie, falsehood, or treachery. Hence the translation "fraud" might cover all of those conditions in which the buyer would possibly suffer loss. See also Radner 1997:175-176.

[7] See *PNA* 1/2:291-293, #11.

[8] For this same office, see *COS* 3.111, n. 8.

[9] *PNA* 1/2:392.

[10] *PNA* 1/2:293-294, #14.

[11] *PNA* 1/1:234.

[12] *PNA* 2/1:553.

Metūnu, governor of Isana.

(lines 9-11)
[Witness Na]bû-nadin-aḫḫe, [scribe, keep]er of the conveyance. Two minas of copper for their finger-nail (impressions).

REFERENCES

Text, translations and studies: ARU 469 and 630; Kwasman 1988 #50; Kwasman and Parpola 1991:60-61.

SALE OF A SLAVE (3.114)
(Tel Aḫmar Tablet 13)

K. Lawson Younger, Jr.

Recently a number of inscriptions from Tīl Barsip (Tel Aḫmar) have been published.[1] Most of the Neo-Assyrian cuneiform documents from the site seem to come from a single archive, that of a man named Hanni.

Interestingly, three of the tablets (13, 18 and 20) mention a man named Issār-dūri who is further identified as "the son of Samiraya" ("the Samarian").[2] Two of the other personal names in this tablet are gentilics like Samiraya: Hamataya (lit. "the Hamathite") and Tabalaya (lit. "the Tabalite"). The tablets apparently date to the latter days of the reign of Assurbanipal. In Tablet 13, Issār-dūri appears as a witness, and in Tablet 20 he is the sealer and perhaps therefore also the creditor of a loan of silver. Tablet 18 is a fragmentary administrative list.

Excavated in 1993, this tablet (4.3 x 8.2 x 2.2 cm) is dated to 644 BCE (during the reign of Assurbanipal) (see note 11 below).

(lines 1-2)
The seal of Tabaya, the owner of the man being sold.

(lines 3-6a)
The harem governess has contracted and taken Pān-Sēʾ, his (Tabaya's) slave, for ½ mina and 5 shekels of silver.[3]

(lines 6b-10)
The money is paid completely. That man is purchased and taken. Revocation, lawsuit (or) litigation are void.

(lines 11-16)
Whoever in the future, at any time, transgresses, shall return the money tenfold to his owner. He shall contest in his lawsuit, but shall not succeed.

(lines 17-29)
Witness Idrî,[4] the son of Hamataya[5];
Witness Sime-šarru, the steward;
Witness Aya-ammu,[6] son of Tabalaya[7];
Witness Adda-dalâ,[8] the son of Mallimīni;
Witness Issār-dūri,[9] the son of Samiraya;
Witness Ubru-Iššār;
Witness Nabûʾa;
Witness Adad-ilaya[10];
Witness Zabini.

(lines 30-31)
Month of Ayyar, day 21, eponymy (*limmu*) of Šamaš-da[ʾin]anni(?).[11]

[1] Dalley 1996-97; Hawkins 1996-97; Bordreuil 1996-97. For Tīl Barsip's conquest, see *COS* 2.113A, lines i.29b-36a and notes 2-3. For earlier discoveries, see Hallo 1966.

[2] Written ^{I}15-BÀD DUMU ^{I}*sa-mir-a-a*. See Dalley 1996-97:82-84, Tablet 13.24-25.

[3] 1 mina = 480 grams (g); 1 shekel (*šiqlu*) = 1/60 of a mina, i.e. 8 g; thus 1 1/12 minas or 280 g of silver were paid for Pān-Sēʾ. For the price(s) paid for slaves, see Radner 1997:230-248.

[4] See *PNA* 2/1:506.

[5] See *PNA* 2/1:446.

[6] See *PNA* 1/1:89-90.

[7] This name occurs in another tablet from Til Barsip (Tablet 8, line 24).

[8] Dalley reads the name as ^{I}⸢U$^{?}$⸣-AŠ-A "Adad-nadin-apli(?)" (1996-97:83). However, this is not the normal way that these elements of the name appear; the usual order is: ^{I}10-A-AŠ "Adad-aplu-iddina" (see *PNA* 1/1:22-23). Thus it seems preferable to read the name as ^{I}⸢10$^{?}$⸣-*dàl-a* "Adda-dalâ," since this name is attested among the personal names in this general region (see *PNA* 1/1:45).

[9] The name (^{I}15-BÀD) means "Ištar is my (protective) wall." See *PNA* 2/1:568-571 s.v. Issār-dūri, # 27. Issār-dūri's name demonstrates two things. First, later generations of deportees adopted non-Israelite — specifically Assyrian — names. This reinforces Fales' assertion that a certain "Assyrianization" was at work that is attested along "generational" lines (fathers → sons) which witnesses to an assimilation toward Assyrian (Fales 1991:104-105). Second, some of the deportees could attain reasonably high social positions in their respective communities.

[10] See *PNA* 1/1:26.

[11] I.e. 644 BCE. For this eponymy, see Reade 1998:256-257.

REFERENCES

Text, translation and study: Dalley 1996-97:82-84 + pl. 3.

LAND SALE (3.115)
(Tel Hadid G-117/95)

K. Lawson Younger, Jr.

Dated by eponym to 698 BCE, this recently published Neo-Assyrian land sale tablet was discovered in 1995 during rescue excavations at Tel Hadid (biblical Hadid),[a] located about 4.5 km northeast of Lod. The tablet was found *in situ* on a floor dated to the second half of the eighth century BCE (Brand 1996:3, fig 4). The right side of both the obverse and reverse is damaged with the ends of many lines eroded; but because it seems to follow the typical conveyance formulae, the general content of the transaction can be discerned. All of the personal names mentioned in the inscription are Akkadian, except for one Aramaic name beginning with the theophoric element Attar-; hence none is indigenous. This, along with the fact that the conveyance was written in cuneiform, indicates that both parties belonged to the deportees or their descendants brought to the area by Assyrian monarchs (in this case, given the date on the tablet, most probably Sargon II,[1] though Sennacherib cannot be completely ruled out).

(lines 1-7)
The finger[nail of ...] the son of A[ ] the [[2]];
the fingernail of Urd[u-];
the fingernail of Attar-[ ][3];
the fingernail of Aya-⌜šēb⌝ši [ ].
Total of four men [owners of the field? being sold].

(damaged surface for fingernail marks)

(lines 8-13a)
[ ] ⌜culti⌝vated(?)[4] [ ] [ ] Marduk-[bēlu-uṣur(?)][5] [has contra]cted and [taken] from [these] men for 1 mina of silver (by the mina) of the king.[6]

(lines 13b-r.1)
The mon[ey] has been pa[id] completely. That [field] is purchased (and) [taken]. Revocation, lawsuit (or) (Reverse) litigation are void.

(lines r.2-10)
Whoever in the future, at any time, whether these men or their sons or [relatives] seeks a lawsuit or litigation against Marduk-bēlu-u[ṣur] or his sons (or) his r[elatives] [shall return] the money tenfold [to its owner]. [He shall contest] in his lawsuit, [but shall not succeed].

(lines r.11-19)
Witness: Zazakku,[7] the [ ];
Witness: Šamaš-zēr[u-];
Witness: Šamaš-aḫḫa-[ ];
Witness: Lēšer[u[8]] owner of [ ];
Witness: Nād[inu[9]];
[Witness]: ⌜Ṣil(?)-šarri(?)⌝;
[Witness]: [ ]
[ ]

(End 1)
Month of Araḫ-samni (Marheshvan), day 24, eponymy (*limmu*) of Šulmu-šarri.[10]

a Ezra 2:33; Neh 7:37; 11:34

[1] See Na᾽aman's discussion (Na᾽aman and Zadok 2000:177-183).
[2] Perhaps the individual's profession.
[3] For names starting with the Attar element, see *PNA* 1/1:234-237.
[4] See Zadok's discussion (Na᾽aman and Zadok 2000:162).
[5] This is Zadok's suggested restoration of the name (Na᾽aman and Zadok 2000:160-161). See *PNA* 2/2:714, #7.
[6] See Zadok's collection of citations regarding the royal mina (Na᾽aman and Zadok 2000:168-169). See also Radner 1999a:130-131; Powell 1996; Fales 1996.
[7] See Zadok's remarks (Na᾽aman and Zadok 2000:169).
[8] For this name, see *PNA* 2/2:659-660.
[9] For this name, see *PNA* 2/2:919-921, #7.
[10] See Kwasman and Parpola 1991:118, 121 and Millard 1994:50.

REFERENCES

Text, translation and study: Na᾽aman and Zadok 2000:159-169.

A DEBT NOTE (3.116)
(Tel Hadid G/1696)

K. Lawson Younger, Jr.

This second tablet from Tel Hadid is dated by eponym to 664 BCE. It was discovered *in situ* in rescue excavations in 1997 on a plaster floor of the central unit of a three-room late Iron II building (Brand 1998). The tablet is nearly intact and very readable.

The text is a debt-note with an antichretic pledge[1] — a pledge of a person or persons (usually family members) in lieu of the interest on the principal of a loan. There are no risk or redemption clauses. In this case, the debtor pledges his wife[2] and sister (presumably an unmarried sister under his care). The period of the transaction is about 3 months, since apparently the debtor expected to be able to repay the principal after the harvest of cereals in mid-summer. If he does not repay by the month of Ab, the debt will accrue interest at 33.33% (see lines 8-11 below).[3] During the period of the debt, the pledged persons lived in the house of the creditor and were expected to work for him. Moreover, the debtor was responsible for feeding and clothing the pledged persons while they resided (*kammusu*) in the creditor's home (see note 7 below).

In this text, the names of the debtor's wife and sister are West Semitic (one of them Canaanite, see below). This may imply that the debtor was indigenous. On the other hand, the fact that the first two witnesses' names are Akkadian and the fact that the text is written in cuneiform may indicate that the creditor was not indigenous, but perhaps one from the second generation of Babylonian deportees brought to the northern kingdom after its demise (2 Kgs 17:24). For further discussion of the historical implications, see Naʾaman's treatment (Naʾaman and Zadok 2000:177-183).

(lines 1-3)
1 mina and 6+2+[x] [shekels of silver] belonging to Ki[ ], at the disposal of Ši(?)[ ].

(lines 4-7)
In lieu of the interest for the silver,[4] Ḫammāya[5] his wife[a] and Munaḫimā[6] his sister stay[7] as pledge.[b]

(lines 8-11)
In Ab[8] he will pay the silver. If he does not pay, the silver will accrue interest by one third (of the principal).

(lines 12-16)
Witness: Silimu;
Witness: Ṣilli-Bēl;
[Witness: Š]ašmāyu, the Egyptian;
Witness: Padî.[9]

(lines 17-18)
Month of Iyyar,[8] day 16, the eponymy (*limmu*) of Šarru-lū-dāri.[10]

a Jer 6:12
b Deut 24:10-12; Prov 6:1-5; 11:15; 17:18; 22:26

[1] For a debt-note with an antichretic pledge very similar to this text, see Parker 1954:33 (ND 2078). In that text, in place of the interest for a principal of one mina of silver, the debtor pledges his wife and sister. See also 3.136E-G. For a discussion of debt, see van de Mieroop 2002.
[2] Concerning the pledge of wives, see Zadok's discussion (Naʾaman and Zadok 2000:174). Cf. the link of wives with land in *COS* 3.55.
[3] The more common interest rate was 25% (see Radner 1997:379-380); but cf. Dalley and Postgate 1984: #37.
[4] The phrase *kūm rubê* KÙ.BABBAR confirms that what follows is an antichretic pledge (Nutzpfand). See Postgate 1976:47-48.
[5] See Zadok's discussion of this name (Naʾaman and Zadok 2000:170).
[6] For this name, see Zadok's discussion (Naʾaman and Zadok 2000:170); *PNA* 2/2:768.
[7] *kammusu* "stay, reside" (used in NA as a substitute for *ušābu*). The use of this verb confirms the possessory aspect of the pledge. See Radner 2001:270-271.
[8] For a discussion of the period of the debt note, see Naʾaman and Zadok 2000:175. See further van de Mieroop 1995.
[9] See the Assyrian Aram. barley loan from Guzāna (*COS* 3.58, note 6).
[10] 664 BCE. See Millard 1994:53.

REFERENCES

Text, translation and study: Naʾaman and Zadok 2000:169-177.

SALE OF AN ESTATE (3.117)
(Gezer 1)

K. Lawson Younger, Jr.

Dating to 652 BCE, the tablet was discovered in 1904 by R. A. S. Macalister during excavations at Gezer. The text is a sale contract for an entire estate: land, house, servants, etc. Unfortunately, because of the fragmentary nature of lines 6-9, the particulars (including the sale price) are missing.

The personal names mentioned in the text give an important insight into the mixed population of the city of Gezer during the period of its integration into the Assyrian empire following its conquest by Tiglath-pileser III (see Younger 1998:205). This accords well with the situation described in 2 Kings 17:24 (see Becking 1981-82:78-80; 1992:114-118; Naᵓaman and Zadok 1988:42-46).

(lines 1-4)
Seal of Marduk-erība, son of [...]
Seal of Abu-erība,[1] son of [...]
Total: two men, owners of houses (and) field[s]
the estate of Lū-aḫḫē in [its] entir[ety].

(four seal impressions)

(lines 5-6a)
The slaves Ṭuri-Aya,[2] his two wives, his son;
Three people [ ]

(lines 6b-9 too fragmentary for translation)

(Reverse 1′-3a)
He shall return [the money tenfold to its owners].[3]
[He shall contest in his lawsuit, but] shall not succeed.[4]

(Guaranteed against) seizures of epilepsy[5] for 100 days (and against) fraud[6] in perpetuity.

Month of Simanu (Siwan), day 17, eponymy (*limmu*) after Aššur-dūru-uṣur,[7] the governor of Bar-ḫalsi.

Witness: Zaggî[8];
Witness: Kanūnāyu[9];
Witness: Bēl-aplu-iddina[10];
Witness: Marduk-nāṣir of city [...];
Witness: Ḫur-waṣi,[11] the mayor;
Witness: Qar-rāpiᵓ,[12] the royal trade agent[13] [a];
Witness: Zēru-ukin, son of Kanūnāyu[14];
Witness: ḪI(?)-*ta-din*[15];
Witness: Sēᵓ-[...];
Witness: Mannu-kī-Arbail[16];
Witness: [...]
Witness: Zēr-ūtu.

[a] Nahum 3:16-17

[1] *PNA* 1/1:16, #8.

[2] Written ^{I}*Ṭu-ri-*^{d}A-*a* "(My) rock is Aya." This is an Aram. name containing *ṭwr* "rock" and the divine name Aya (for this element, see Galter 1995 and cf. Gen 36:24; 2 Sam 3:7; 1 Chr 7:28).

[3] With the use of this verb here, it is reasonable to assume the standard legal clause *kas-pu a-na* 10.MEŠ-*te a-na* EN.MEŠ-*šú ú-ta-ra*.

[4] With the preserved *la i-laq-qe*, the standard legal clause can be restored: *ina la de-ni-šú* DUG$_4$.DUG$_4$-*ma la i-laq-qe*.

[5] For *ṣibtu bennu*, see *COS* 3.113, note 5 above.

[6] For the term *sartu*, see *COS* 3.113, note 6 above.

[7] *PNA* 1/1:180, #4. See also Millard 1994:53, 83.

[8] Reading ^{I}*Zag-gi-i*. Becking 1981-82 reads ^{I}*Zak-ki-i*, but see Zadok 1985:568, n. 3. According to Zadok, the sign GI does not have the value *kí* or *ké* in Neo-Assyrian.

[9] ^{I}ITI.AB-*a*-⸢*a*⸣. See *PNA* 2/1:601-604, #47 and Zadok 1985:568; Becking interpreted the name as Ṭebeṭaya "(born) in the month of Ṭebeṭ" (1981-82:84); but there are many different individuals with the name Kanūnāyu written ^{I}ITI.AB-*a-a*.

[10] See *PNA* 1/2:286-287, #15.

[11] The name is Egyptian "Horus is sound" (*PNA* 2/1:481-482, #4). See also Becking 1981-82:84-85; and Giveon 1972.

[12] For the reading ^{I}*qar-ra-pi-i*ᵓ, see Radner 1999b:108; Elat 1998.

[13] LÚ*.DAM.[GÀR] (*tamkāru*) "the royal trade agent." See Radner 1999b:101-109; Elat 1987; Deller 1987. For Nahum 3:16-17 which describes the coming judgment on the Assyrian traders, see Elat 1987:248f.

[14] See note 9 above.

[15] Becking interprets as Ṭabta-uballīṭ.

[16] This name also occurs in 3.113 above where it is the name of a man who is the son of an Israelite (Aḫi-Yau).

REFERENCES

Text, translations and studies: Pinches 1904; Becking 1981-82; 1992:114-117; Zadok 1985:567-570.

LAND SALE (3.118)
(Gezer 2)

K. Lawson Younger, Jr.

Dating to 649 BCE (reign of Assurbanipal), this tablet was discovered by Macalister during excavations in 1905 (a year after the first tablet, Gezer 1, see above). It records the sale of a plot of land by an Israelite named Natan-Yau. Like Gezer 1, this text's personal names demonstrate the mixed population of the city as well as the role that some Israelites continued to play in the economics of the region.

(lines 1-2)
Seal of Natan-Yau[1] owner of the field being sold.

(Three seal impressions)

(lines 3-4)
A (single) lot[2] of [x *su*]*tu* of the field adjacent to that of Sinî.[3] [ ] adjacent to that of Sinî.

(Reverse 1′-4′)
Witness: [ ]
Witness(?): [ ]
Witness: (incomprehensible name)[4];
Witness: Zēru-ukin[5];
Witness: Nergal-šarru-uṣur[6] [a];

(lines 5′-6′)
Month of Shabatu, day 4, the eponymy (*limmu*) of Aḫu-ilāya,[7] governor of Carchemish.

a Jer 39:9

[1] This is the Heb. personal name *ntnyhw* "Natanyahu" (see *HAE* 2/1:77). See Zadok 1985:567-570; *PNA* 2/2:937.
[2] The sign É (*bētu*) probably implies that the area in question is a single lot, and not distributed into separate parcels (Postgate 1976:23).
[3] The owner of the adjacent land. The name is non-Semitic, probably Egyptian.
[4] Becking reads: [I]GÍD.SIG.SUKKAL.GIŠ (1981:87); Zadok (1985:568) gives the suggestion(s): *B/Pu-s/šig/k/q*(or *zik/q* or *b/pik/q*)-*ti*(?)-*is/ṣ/z*.
[5] This name occurs in Gezer 1 (line 11′).
[6] See *PNA* 2/2:954-956. According to 2 Kgs 17:29-30 some of the deportees to Samaria worshipped Nergal. Cf. a Babylonian officer at the time of the siege of Jerusalem with the same name mentioned in Jer 39:9.
[7] *PNA* 1/1:76-77, s.v. Aḫu-ilāʾī #11e; see Millard 1994:54, 80.

REFERENCES

Text, translations and studies: Johns 1905; Galling 1935; Becking 1981-82:86-88.

C. COURTCASES

1. BABYLON

THE SLANDERED BRIDE (3.119)

William W. Hallo

Case law or "conditional law" is often based on actual precedent, and sometimes the provisions of Old Babylonian law, or even biblical law, seem to reflect situations encountered in court cases. A little dossier of three documents dating to the reign of Samsu-iluna (ca. 1749-1712 BCE), illustrates provisions in the Laws of Hammurapi, his father and predecessor, as well as the casuistic legislation of Deuteronomy.[1] In addition to a wedding document and a supplemental agreement regarding dowry, it includes this litigation regarding the consummation of the marriage.

The bronze weapon of the divine Ninurta[2] took its stand in the quarter, and his alderwomen[3] took their stand, and they did not convict Ama-sukkal of speaking insolently against Enlil-issu; they did, however, convict Enlil-issu of slandering and abusing her.[4] [a]

Thereupon Enlil-issu spoke as follows, saying:

[a] Deut 22:13-21

"You may convict me (even) more than now, (still) I will not marry her.[5] Let them imprison me and (then) I will pay money (instead)."

(The reverse contains a list of nine witnesses, the last of them the scribe, and the date; the upper and lower edges contain the seal impressions)

[1] See esp. Finet 1973 and Locher 1986 respectively.

[2] Like the Bible in a modern courtroom, the deity's symbol adds religious sanction to the proceedings. For the role of Ninurta in Sum. court-cases, see below, 3.134A; 3.141:17-21.

[3] Others: "female witnesses"; so e.g. Landsberger 1968:90-92; Dombradi 1996 II 89, n. 395.

[4] I.e., presumably, impugning her virginity. Others: "(that) she had been left a virgin" (Westbrook 1988:43f. and 116) or "not having had intercourse with her" (*CAD* B 128a). On the much debated question of the exact nature of Enlil-issu's offense, see Hallo, *Origins* 249 and n. 28.

[5] I.e., consummate my marriage with her. Presumably the marriage contract was a form of engagement ("inchoate marriage") perhaps even involving an under-age bride.

REFERENCES

Text: BE 6/2:58 = UET 5:256. Studies: Hallo 1964; 1996:247-250; Locher 1986.

---

2. HAZOR

A LAWSUIT FROM HAZOR (3.120)

William W. Hallo

Hazor, "formerly the head of all those kingdoms" (Josh 11:10), was a major citadel in northern Israel, and the terminus of a trade route which led westward from the Euphrates at Mari, where it is sometimes mentioned in the royal correspondence. A smattering of cuneiform tablets, probably from the end of the Middle Bronze Age (ca. 1600 BCE) has so far turned up there (see most recently Horowitz and Shaffer 1992a, b; Horowitz 1997). Among these is a courtcase which helped to clinch the identification of the modern site with the ancient citadel (Yadin 1972:201); for the approximate story of its recovery see Shanks 1976.

Mar-Hanuta[1] [a] and Irpa-Addu[2] and Sum-Hanuta, three(?) servants(?), brought a lawsuit against the woman Sumu-la-ilu, in the matter of the house and orchard in the city Hazor and the orchard in the

[a] Judg 3:31; 5:6

[1] This name may be compared to Ben-ᶜAnat, "son of (the goddess) Anat," which occurs as a name in the Book of Judges (3:31; 5:6), at Taᵓa-nach (*COS* 2.84 and Glock 1971 line 6) and elsewhere. It has also been regarded as a title (Craigie 1972) or as a nickname (Heltzer 1994-95).

[2] The same name can be restored in a newly discovered letter from Hazor; see Horowitz and Shaffer 1992b.

city Giladima.[3] [b] They came before the king for litigation. The king [judged] the case of the woman Sumu-la-ilu. Henceforth,[4] whoever [shall bring] a lawsuit shall pay 200 (shekels?) of silver.[5]

(Witnesses and date formula largely lost)

b Hos 6:8

[3] For the possible comparison with Biblical Gile'ad, cf. the later spelling *Ga-al-ʾa-a-[di]* in an inscription of Tiglath-pileser III (Tadmor 1994:186 *ad* 3 and 297); for Gile'ad as a city, cf. Hos 6:8.

[4] Lit., "today (and to)morrow."

[5] A standard clause in "peripheral" Akk. Cf. esp. a text from Late Bronze Emar (ca. 1200 BCE) which reads: "Henceforth, 'brother' shall no wise bring a lawsuit against 'brother.' Whoever brings a lawsuit about the slaves (and) slave-girls shall pay 200 (shekels) of silver"; see Sigrist 1982.

REFERENCES

Text and study: Hallo and Tadmor 1977.

3. NUZI

THE GORING OX AT NUZI (3.121)

William W. Hallo

The favorite textbook illustration of negligence in the law collections of the ancient Near East is that of the goring ox (Finkelstein 1973, 1981; Jackson 1974). In reality, cases of oxen goring may have been rare; only one such case has been identified in the surviving documentation. It illustrates, to some extent, a provision found in the Laws of Eshnunna (*COS* 2.130 §53) and the Covenant Code (Exod 21:35f.). It happens to come from Nuzi, a site east of the Tigris where, in the 15th to 14th centuries BCE, legal practices are thought to be sometimes reflected in the background of the patriarchal narratives (Eichler 1989; differently Maidman 1995:947).

Tehip-tilla son of Puhi-shenni went to court before the judges against Taia son of Warad-ahi, (saying): "Taia the oxherd of Tehip-tilla — he[1] injured one ox." Said Taia: "his fellow(-ox) injured (this) ox out on the range."[a] But the judges said to Taia: "Bring your witnesses to the effect that his fellow(-ox) injured (him) on the range." Taia said: "My witnesses are not there." The judges said: "(It is) you who injured him. Pay the equivalent of the ox." Tehip-tilla won the lawsuit and (the judges) ordered Taia (to pay) one ox (out) of (his) own herd (or: funds).[2]

Seal of Shakarakti son of Ar-tirwi
Seal of Ninu-atal son of Arip-asherum?
Seal of Tanni-musha son of Imbi-ili
Seal of Ba'i-sheri? son of Qabuta?
Hand of Ith-apihe the scribe.

a Exod 21:35f.

[1] For the resumptive use of *ù* in the Nuzi dialect see Wilhelm 1970:54-60.

[2] For the double meaning of *sukullu* (*sugullu*) and its Hebrew cognate *segullā*, see *Origins* 18.

REFERENCES

Text: Chiera 1934 No. 341. Translations and studies: Hallo 1967:63f.; 1991b:140; Finkelstein 1981:21.

4. NEO-ASSYRIAN

A COURT ORDER FROM SAMARIA (3.122)
(Samaria 1825/Fi 16)

K. Lawson Younger, Jr.

Located today in Istanbul, this blackish tablet (2 x 4.9 x 1.9 cm) was discovered in excavations at Samaria by Harvard University during the early part of the twentieth century, i.e. 1908-10 (see Reisner 1924 1:247; and photo, 2: pl. 56). It was found in the construction trench of the wall of the Hellenistic fort. It belongs to a genre known as "šumma texts" (Jas 1996:76-81).[1] It is quite likely that such tablets were made out for the successful contestant in whose debt the court's decision had placed his opponent.

The recent collation by Donbaz (1998) has greatly clarified the reading and interpretation of the inscription.[2] Rather than dealing with a grain loan (as previously read), the text deals with the repayment of a loan for work animals (donkey and oxen). Unfortunately the tablet is not dated.

The text is evidence of the mixed population in Samaria after the fall of the northern kingdom of Israel described in 2 Kings 17:24, 29-30. The first personal name, Nergal-šallim,[3] is Akkadian, hardly indigenous. The second personal name, normalized here as Aya-aḫḫē, appears to be West Semitic. According to Zadok, it may be potentially Israelite (see note 4 below).

(seal impression)

(lines 1-5)
If on the tenth day of the fifth month (Abu), Nergal-šallim[a] [does not give] the donkey and 9 oxen of Aya-aḫḫē[4] to the village manager,[5] ⌜he shall give⌝ [x+]2 *qa*, 10 oxen, (and) 6 ⌜shekels of silver⌝.

(rest broken off)[6]

a 2 Kgs 17:24, 29-30

[1] Also known as "orders in court" (Postgate 1976:59-60).

[2] For other recent transliterations and translations, see Donbaz 1988:6, n. 13; Radner 1995; and Jas 1996:80-81.

[3] According to 2 Kgs 17:29-30, the deportees to Samaria from Cutha worshipped Nergal.

[4] Written: ¹A-*a*-PAP.MEŠ. See *PNA* 1/1:89, #8. Zadok proposes an alternative interpretation, potentially Israelite (1991:31, 1:5; and Naʾaman and Zadok 2000:176).

[5] See Kwasman and Parpola 1991: #61, note 7.

[6] Usually a date and witnesses follow the operative section.

REFERENCES

Text, translations and studies: Reisner et al., 1924 1:247; 2: pl. 56; Radner 1995; Jas 1996:80-81; Donbaz 1988:6, n. 13; 1998; and Zadok 1991.

5. NEO-BABYLONIAN

A NEO-BABYLONIAN DIALOGUE DOCUMENT (3.123)

David B. Weisberg

A widely used legal formulation, which scholars have entitled the "Dialogue Document," makes its appearance in the Middle and Neo-Babylonian periods of ancient Mesopotamia (late second and first millennia BCE). Many students of these texts (see bibliography) have noticed striking parallels to Genesis 23, which tells of Abraham's purchase of a burial cave for his wife, Sarah. The name "Dialogue Document" derives from the fact that the negotiations between the parties to the transaction are recorded not in an "objective" style (i.e., in the third person) but in a "subjective" formulation in which the participants speak in the first person.

The five components of the Dialogue Document are:

1. Proposal for transaction, formulated in the first person.
2. Agreement of the second party, expressed by the verb *šemû* ("to hear").
3. Weighing out of the silver (including "additional payment").
4. Declaration of the consummation of the transaction.
5. Witnesses.

The Dialogue Document is employed in slave sales, real estate sales and real estate leases as well as in adoptions and marriages.

Below are pointed out examples of the features of the Dialogue Document as recorded in the adoption tablet of a girl from the time of rule of the Elamite king, Hallušu,[1] on a tablet from the collection of the Oriental Institute of the University of Chicago, Museum Number A 33248, as well as the parallel form in Genesis 23. The biblical parallels are: Ephron's proposal (v.15); Abraham's agreement (v. 16); weighing out of the silver (v. 16); declaration of transfer of ownership of property to Abraham, and description of property (v. 17) and witnesses (v. 18).

(1-4) Šamaš-uṣur, descendant of Ṣillā (and) Kidinnīti, his wife, spoke thus to Ninurta-iddin and Lū-bēlti: "Akkaiti,[2] your daughter, give me, let her be my daughter."[a]

(5-9) Afterwards, Ninurta-iddin listened to him (and) gave his daughter, Akkadīti, in adoption, to Šamaš-uṣur.[b] Šamaš-uṣur, of his own free will, gave a TUG$_2$.KUR.RA garment[3] (and) a *šir'am* garment, as additional payment to Ninurta-iddin and Lū-bēlti.[c]

(10) Wherever Akkadīti goes, she is our daughter.

(11-17) [...] ..., at such time as the family of the house of Šamaš-uṣur should come forward with a claim and do not say to Akkaiti as follows: "You are a maidservant, Akkadīti." Akkaiti is a free woman (lit. "a daughter of Nippur"), no one shall have any authority over her, nor ... shall he return [X mi]nas of silver.[d]

(18-19) Whoever ⌈changes⌉ [this] agreement — may Anu, Enlil and Ea, ⌈the great gods,⌉ curse him with an irrevocable curse.

(20) At the sealing of this document (were)[e]
Šumā descendant of [X.X.X]
(21) Kinēnuā descendant of Rīmūt
Ninurta-mukīn-x (line 22) descendant of Ninurta-aḫ-iddin
[X-X-]kidin descendant of Aḫḫēšā
The scribe (was)
(23) Aḫ-lūmur descendant of Bēlšunu
(At the) city of Sumundanaš[4]
(24) (in the) month of Addaru, day 15, (in the) 15th year of Ḫallušu,
(25) King of Elam.

a Gen 23:15
b Gen 23:16
c Gen 23:16
d Gen 23:17
e Gen 23:18

[1] According to "Chronicle I" edited by Grayson 1975, and other sources, Ḫallušu ruled Elam for six years (699-693 BCE). But this is contradicted by the date on this economic document, which assigns him (at least) fifteen years total. Several possible solutions have been proposed by the present author (Weisberg 1984:216), but none of them is conclusive.

[2] The name of the girl is spelled two different ways in the document. The name can mean "a woman of Akkad (=Babylonia)" or perhaps, it may be a shortened form of a name meaning "she who belongs to the goddess of Akkad."

[3] The nature as well as the reading of this garment are unknown.

[4] A southern Elamite city whose precise location is unknown; cf. Weisberg 1984:215 and n. 22.

REFERENCES

Text, translations and studies: Grayson 1975:77-79; Petschow 1965; 1974; Roth 1989; San Nicolò 1925; 1931; Tucker 1966; Weinfeld 1982; Weisberg 1984; in press.

D. ACCOUNTS

1. OLD BABYLONIAN

OFFERINGS TO THE TEMPLE GATES AT UR (3.124)

William W. Hallo

Account texts are extremely numerous and cover many areas of individual and collective activity. Some texts, for example, provide an objective, after-the-fact accounting of the performance of a ritual against the possibility of a future audit of the expenditures incurred. They can therefore be designated as "descriptive rituals." Other examples of this sub-genre are known from Ugaritic (Levine 1963, 1983) and even, in a sense, from the Pentateuch (Levine 1965; Rainey 1970b). When they include verbs at all, these are typically in the past tense; by contrast, "prescriptive rituals" are phrased in the imperfect or imperative, and belong to the canonical category.[1] The following text dates to the reign of Hammurapi. Though disposed in linear form on its tablet, it is presented here in "two-dimensional" or tabular form for greater clarity; other Babylonian account texts of all periods actually employed such a tabular form to begin with.[2]

[1] For a Ug. example, cf. *COS* 1.95; for a biblical example, cf. the description of the building of the tabernacle in the wilderness (Exod 35-40) contrasted with the prescription for its construction (Exod 25-30).

[2] See Hallo, in press.

	(a)	(b)	(c)	(d)	(e)			(f)	
		2				for the libation	temple of Sin at the basin		
				13		for the libation	to/for the "jug"		
	5	30	20			for assorted cups			
			15	15		for the libation and the inner bolt	meal of Ekishnugal, at twilight		
	5	30	20			for assorted cups			
			15	15		for the libation and the inner bolt	meal of the late evening		
Subtotals	10	60	70	43			meal(s) of Ekishnugal		
					30	inner bolt of the upper court			
			40			inner bolt of the principal court and the outside	for the inner bolts		
			10			for the libation	assorted copper statues and other "properties"		
	2					for assorted cups			
			2			for the libation			
					2	for the inner bolt of Dublamah			
(Subtotals)	12	62	122	43	32			271	
its barley-(content)	24	93	122	64½	32			335½	meals of [...]

		10	10			inner bolt of Ekishnugal inner bolt of the upper court	festival of the 15th day		
		10	10			inner bolt of Ekishnugal inner bolt of the upper court	festival of the 7th day		
		10	10			inner bolt of Ekishnugal inner bolt of the upper court	festival of the 15th day		
		6	10			inner bolt of Ekishnugal inner bolt of the upper court	festival of the 25th day		
(Subtotals) its barley-(content)		36 54	40 40					76 94	4 festivals of one month

temple of Nanna, material of one month ... month V, day 1, year Hammurapi 32 (ca. 1761 BCE) (all entries in "liters" = SÌLA)

(a) = 2:1 dark(?) beer (*šikaru dalhu, šinnû*)
(b) = 1 1/2:1 fine beer
(c) = 1:1 beer (*malmalu*)
(d) = 1 1/2:1 "wine-beer" (*kurunnu, karānu*)
(e) = 1:1 emmer beer (*ulušinnu*)
(f) = total ... beer

REFERENCES

Text and studies: UET 5:507; Levine and Hallo 1967; Hallo 1991b:59, 64, 81, 143f., 151f.

2. ALALAKH

LIST OF HAPIRU SOLDIERS (*AT* 180) (3.125)

Richard S. Hess

This is a representative of many lists from Alalakh that record the names of conscripts to serve in various parts of the military of Alalakh. This Level IV text introduces *ḫāpiru*-soldiers. The *ḫāpiru*, although regarded as enemies of society in texts from Amarna and elsewhere in the second millennium BCE, serve in key administrative roles in Level IV of Alalakh. There are diviners (*AT* 182 line 16) and governors (*AT* 182 line 13) who are *ḫāpiru*. In this text, line 20, a priest is one of the *ḫāpiru*. In the Idrimi inscription, Idrimi credits the *ḫāpiru* with providing shelter for him and this may be the origin of the cordial relationship between Alalakh and the *ḫāpiru*. From texts such as *AT* 180, *ḫāpiru* appear as a special section of the army. This list identifies each individual by name followed usually by the name of their place of origin. The place name in the heading may record where they are presently stationed. In a few cases an occupation replaces the place of origin. For discussion of *ḫāpiru* texts and the question of their relationship with biblical Hebrews, see Bottéro 1954; Greenberg 1955; Loretz 1984; Hess 1994a:205-208. For the linguistic distinction between *ḫāpiru* and Hebrews, see Rainey 1989.

1 Troops of *ḫāpiru*-soldiers:
2 from Marmarukum
3 Dagun of Zalḫe,
4 Išur of Sunnadu,
5 Betammu an Ibadkuti(?),
6 Eḫli-Šarra of Matḫia,
7 ... of Durrazu,
8 Aḫu[ ] of Zal[ḫe],
9 Šarni[a] of Zaraḫ[e],
10 Erata a fowler,
11 Beia[ ] of Šimeri,
12 Šepra a charioteer(?),[1]
13 Unapše of Širimazu,
14 Eḫli-Teššub of Kadume,
15 Anani-LUGAL of Indawa,
16 Ḫubita a thief,
17 Luzza of Ulla,
18 Agab-Dagan of Ašt[a-],
19 Ḫubita of Ša[ ],
20 Tulpia a *šangû*-priest of Iš[ḫara],

[1] The reading of the signs for this occupation is not certain. See von Dassow 1997:197, n. 101.

21 Eḫli-Teššub of Ḫutammana,
22 [ ] of Uri
23 Šarnitḫama of Kitgi.

---

24 Troops: twenty commanders of chariots:
25 Erada,
26 Lulule.

---

27 Troops: Eḫli-LUGAL, ZAG-ŠUR,
28 Ḫumia an envoy,
29 Šanitḫama,
30 ᴵTulpi-eḫli, Annari.

---

31 Troops from the "commoners:"
32 Ušt[apša]uri,
33 Mina[aḫ?]ḫu.

---

34 Twenty nine [citizens of ?]
35 *Ḫāpiru*-troops from Šarkuḫe;
36 [ ]tisu of Ebla,
37 [ ]lazuzuan,
38 [ ] of Nupanni,
39 Nam[u] of Nupanni,
40 Kaliza of Šanuka.

REFERENCES

Copy: Wiseman 1954:11. Transliteration: (lines 1, 34-35) Bottéro 1954:34; Greenberg 1955:20-21. Translation: (summary) *AT* 71.

ADMINISTRATIVE RECORD (*AT* 457) (3.126)

Richard S. Hess

This Level IV text contains a list of "citizens" from Taya. More than sixty lines list individuals and their place of origin. The places, where they can be identified, appear to be located in the regions around Alalakh and Aleppo. Several place names recur. One group, Akubia, Mudue and Paḫliš, occur together in AT 457 and two other administrative texts, *AT* 223 and *AT* 343. The personal names can be analyzed according to the languages of the various ancient Near Eastern ethnic groups of the second millennium. There are perhaps twenty-two Hurrian names, eight West Semitic names, four Akkadian names, three Anatolian names and two Indo-Aryan names. See Hess 1994b. This composition is characteristic of Late Bronze Age Alalakh as demonstrated by the remainder of the onomastic and linguistic evidence from the texts of Level IV. Hurrian was the dominant linguistic group represented by the population of Alalakh. West Semitic was second in influence.

1 Citizens of Tay[a:]
2 Utta f[ro]m Tiliše,
3 Šutardu from Nupan[ni],
4 Šakuzzi from Akubia,
5 Šeniše from [-]subite,
6 Muna(?)duina from Mukiš,
7 Azira from Šinurḫen[a],
8 Eḫliga from Akubia,
9 Kunna from Aladu[n],
10 Piḫḫae from Tiliše,
11 Akkulia [fr]om Wilimae,
12 Talma from [ ],
13 Tukla [from] Wilimae,
14 Pu[from] Auš[un],
15-17 [illegible]
18 Puru[š] from Ki[ ],

[rest of obverse (c. 10 lines) illegible]

29 [ ] an[ ]
30 [ ] i [ ]
31 [ ] x [ ]
32 [from] A[ ]
33 [ ]na-[-g]an-[ ]
34 [ ]ḫe fro[m] Mu[ ]
37 [Š]a(!)we from Mudue,
38 Galtari from Paḫliš,
39 Šaru-KI.TA from Mukiš,
40 Susiae from Paḫliš,
41 Takuia, Tabbu[1] from [ ]li(?) [ ]
42 Ḫeni from Suḫaruwe,
43 Ḫammara from Irkili,
44 Pušerra from Irkili,
45 Ḫutia from Irkili,
46 Katinile from [ ]ḫi,
47 Ḫamuiae from Ibiria,
48 Tarkizia from Ibiria,
49 [K]urmae from Ibiria,
50 Araia from Ibiria,
51 Kardue fr[om] Ibiria,
52 Andutta [fro]m Iarka[ni],
53 Ḫuputta from Ṣirimeni,
54 Azira from Ṣirimeni,
55 Umbina from Ṣirimeni,
56 Katuteni from [Ṣi]rimeni,
57 Erata from [ ]tama,
58 Šaška from [Si]rimeni,

[1] This is the only line with two personal names appearing on it. The first one has no place name with it. Perhaps both persons originate from

59 Šadumi from Ḫanie,
60 Išinumue from Aštate,[2]
61 IGI-šeni from[3] Šulaka,
62 Ma-zi-a itizen of Šatae from [ ]
63 Šakue from Šila[pa]zi[ri](?)
64 [ ]anni from Pilla[ ]
65 [-n]ite from Šakue[ ]
66 [ ]biazza from [ ]
67 Ebil-x(?)

(right edge)
68 [...]naḫra.

the broken place name at the end of the line.
[2] Probably the area of Emar (Aštata).
[3] The customary Akk., *i-na* "from," is missing.

REFERENCES

Transliteration and Translation: Wiseman and Hess 1994b:501-503.

3. NEO-ASSYRIAN

AN ASSYRIAN WINE LIST (3.127)
(NWL 8)

K. Lawson Younger, Jr.

Discovered during the 1957-63 excavations of Nimrud (ancient Kalḫu) in an area known as Fort Shalmaneser, this fragmentary tablet (ND 10047) is one of the administrative documents known more specifically as Wine Lists. These Nimrud Wine Lists date from the 8th century BCE (as early as the reign of Adad-nirari III and as late as Tiglath-pileser III as recent collation has shown; see note 3 below). In the light of recent research,[1] it seems that these texts recorded the distribution of wine at an annual ceremonial feast that occurred at the turn of the Assyrian calendar year, which coincided with the vernal equinox, sometime in Addaru, more often in Nisannu (Fales 1994:368-370; Dalley and Postgate 1984:24-25). This annual feast may have been connected with the yearly muster of the army.

(lines 1//8)[2]
Month of Addaru (12th month), day 1, eponym (*limmu*) [ ]-šallimanni[3]

(lines 2-3//9-10)
[x] *sūtu* (seahs), [x *qa* (liters) regular contributions (offerings);
2 *qa* (liters), the augurs.

(lines 4-30//11-38)
5 *qa* (liters), for cups in the morning;
3 *qa* (liters), for cups in the evening;
3 *sūtu* (seahs), the queen (*ša ekalli*)[a];
1 *sūtu* (seah), the chief eunuch (*rab ša-rēši*)[b];
3 *sūtu* (seahs), 1 *qa* (liter), the royal bodyguards;
1 *sūtu* (seah), 5 *qa* (liters), the conscripts of the ⌜chief eunuch (*rab ša-rēši*)⌝;
1 *sūtu* (seah), 5 *qa* (liters), the wine master;
1 *sūtu* (seah), the [eu]nuch[s];
⌜1 *sūtu* (seah)⌝, the domestic personnel;
⌜1 *sūtu* (seah)⌝, Nabû-šarḫu-ilāni[4];
[x] *qa* (liters), the "third men"[c];
[x] *q*]*a* (liters), the chariot-fighters of the gods[5];
[x *q*]*a* (liters), the mule stable personnel;
[x *q*]*a* (liters), the *bēt qiqî* personnel;
[x *q*]*a* (liters), the *ša-dunāni* personnel[6];
[x *qa*] (liters), the [Šam]aš contingent;
[x *qa*] (liters), the *ša muḫḫi qaqqari* personnel[7];
[x *qa*] (liters), the chariot-fighters, shield-bearers;
[x *qa*] (liters), the chariot-drivers of the *mugerru*-chariots[8];
[x *qa*] (liters), (ditto) of the *labbašute*[9];
[5 *qa*] (liters), the [fodder]-master;
[x *qa*] (liters), the palace supervisor;

a Ps 45:10; Neh 2:6
b 2 Kgs 18:17; Jer 39:3, 13
c Exod 14:7; 15:4, etc.

[1] For earlier opinions, see Kinnier Wilson 1972:1-2 and Parpola 1976:165-174.
[2] The obverse is numbered differently in the two editions. The first number here is that of Kinnier Wilson 1972; the second is that of Fales 1994. The numbering of the reverse is the same in both.
[3] Kinnier Wilson (1972:2, 136) restored: [^{I}EN].⌜BA-*šá*⌝-*a-ni*. Through a collation by C. Walker and S. Dalley, the eponym should be read as: [*ša*]*l-lim-a-ni*. Furthermore, taking into consideration all the various connections, the date of 735 BCE is most likely (i.e. the eponym of Aššur-šallimanni, during the reign of Tiglath-pileser III). See Dalley and Postgate 1984:22-23; and Fales 1994:365, 371.
[4] This individual is mentioned in a number of other Wine Lists tablets.
[5] The LÚ.A.SIG [DINGIR.ME]Š-*ni* (*mārē dammaqūte ša ilāni*) is a group attested in a number of wine lists and letters. See Kinnier Wilson 1972:50, 61-62.
[6] Kinnier Wilson (1972:54-55) suggests a meaning of "standard bearers."
[7] For a list of occurrences of this profession, see Fales 1994:373, n. 59.
[8] See Postgate 1990:37.
[9] See Fales 1994:373, n. 61.

2 *qa* (liters), the cupbearer;
½ *qa* (liter), the son of the cupbearer;
2 *qa* (liters), the physicians; 2 *qa* (liters), the diviners;[10]
2 *qa* (liters), the male exorcists; 2 *qa* (liters), the victuallers[11];
⌜2⌝ *qa* (liters), the [ ]; 2 *qa* (liters), ⌜the bakers⌝;
[ ] [ ]

(Reverse) (beginning lost)
(lines 1′-19′)
[x *q*]*a* (liters), [the chari]ot-owners [ ]
[x *qa*] (liters), the chariot-owners [ ]
1 *qa* (liter), (the man) Kuniya; 1 *qa* (liter) [PN];
1 *sūtu* (seah), the palace women;
7 *qa* (liters), the woman of [Ḫar]ran; (the woman) [PN];
6½ *qa* (liters), the Hit[tite] female singers;
5½ *qa* (liters), the Arpa[dite] female singers;
2 *sūtu* (seahs), the Elam[ites];
7½ *qa* (liters), the [ ];
1 *šap*[*pu*-container];
2 [ditto, the *ša-še*]*pi* guard;
1 dit[to], the [ ] men;
[ ] in the [even]ing;
1 left over;
3, the Samarians[d];
3, the Manaeans[12];
2, the Car[chemish]ites;
5 *qa* (liters), the Samʾalians; [ ]

Total: 5 *emāru* (homers), 2 *sūtu* (seahs), 5½ *qa* (liters).[13]

d 2 Kgs 17:6; 18:11

[10] LÚ.ḪAL.MEŠ (*bārû*) "diviners (usually by extispicy)."
[11] LÚ.SUM.NINDA.MEŠ (*karkadinnu/kakardinnu*) "victualler." For this military officer, see Dalley and Postgate 1984:28.
[12] For the Mannaeans, see the Bukān Inscription (3.89).
[13] A total of approximately 525½ liters. For further discussion, see Powell 1992; 1993.

REFERENCES

Text, translations and studies: Kinnier Wilson 1972:136-137; Fales 1994:371-374.

AN ASSYRIAN HORSE LIST (3.128)
(TFS 99)

K. Lawson Younger, Jr.

This tablet (10 x 15 cm), with two columns on the front and two columns on the back, was discovered during the 1957-63 excavations of Nimrud (ancient Kalḫu) in an area at the southeastern corner of the lower city known as Fort Shalmaneser. The text is one of the administrative documents known more specifically as the Horse Lists.[1] Apparently, it was a formal check list either preceding or following the actual muster lists, which were less carefully written. It dates between 710-708 BCE with Sargon II's Babylonian campaigns providing the background against which it should be interpreted (Dalley and Postgate 1984:176).

The tablet is divided into sections, one of which details a Samarian unit.[2] This was a new unit which was allowed to retain its national identity, and was not amalgamated with the unit of the *šaglûte*-deportees. Sargon II added a corps of Israelite chariotry into his army after the 720 BCE campaign according to his Great "Summary" Inscription (*COS* 2.118E) and Nimrud Prisms (*COS* 2.118D).[3]

(Obv. ii.16-23)
§E (16)Ibba-dalâ[4] Dalâ-aḫi[5]
(17)Yaū-gâ[6] Atamru[7 a]
(18)Aḫi-idri[8] Abdi-Milki[9]
(19)Bēl-dūri[10] Narmena

a Exod 6:23; 28:1; 38:21; Lev 10:6, 12, 16; Num 3:2, 4; 4:28, 33; 7:8; 26:60; Ezra 8:2; 1 Chr 5:29 [6:3]; 24:1-6

[1] There are three kinds of Horse List texts from Nimrud. Some of these deal explicitly with horses and mules, while others contain numbers which may be deduced to refer to equids. Finally, some of the texts list only men but join the group by virtue of close prosopographical connection. All the Horse Lists refer to personnel from the cavalry and chariotry of the Assyrian army, and are tablets of military administration used "for organizing the campaign, and checking the horses, mules, chariots, military equipment and enemy booty" (Borger 1956:59).
[2] For a discussion of these names, see Dalley 1985:31-36; Ephʿal 1991:41-42; Fales 1991:104; Becking 1992:74-77; and Zadok 1997.
[3] Naʾaman (2000) has recently argued for the accuracy of the Great "Summary" Inscription over the Nimrud Prisms. See also Younger 2002.
[4] See *PNA* 2/1:499.
[5] See *PNA* 1/2:372.
[6] See *PNA* 2/1:497; Zadok 1988:23.
[7] Biblical "Itamar. See *PNA* 1/1:231; *HALOT* 44.
[8] See *PNA* 1/1:64; Zadok 1997:213.
[9] See *PNA* 1/1:6-7, #1.
[10] See *PNA* 1/2:291-293.

(20)Gabbê[11]	Samâ[12]			(22)Aḫī-Yāu[15]	Total 13, city of Samaria,
(21)Aḫi-idri[13]	Baḫî[14]			(23)	hand of Nabû-bēlu-ukin[16]

[11] See *PNA* 1/2:411-412.

[12] Dalley and Postgate (1984:173, note to ii.20) state: "*Sama* could be the same man as occurs in ARU 59; 186; 201; and 554 (probably all dated 694 and 693 B.C.) ^I^*sa-ma-*ᵓ*a*, whose profession is given as *murabbânu ša mār-šarri/Nergal-zeru-*[*ibni*]. He occurs next to equestrian witnesses in all four texts, which suggests the possibility that *murabbânu* in Neo-Assyrian could mean 'horse breeder/trainer' rather than 'tutor.' Possibly the borrower of silver in BT 101, dated 710 B.C." [The abbreviation BT = Parker 1963.]

Dalley (1985:41) concludes: "From this evidence it is reasonable to suggest that Samaᵓ the Samarian commander of teams who served Sargon as a reliable, professional soldier in the royal army of Assyria, was a close friend of the king and had access to and perhaps influence over members of the royal family. As such he would have had opportunities to become closely acquainted with Sargon's vizier Nabu-belu-ukin who probably acted as the first commander of the Samarian unit. Whether or not Samaᵓ actually played a part in negotiating preferential treatment for Samaria, the evidence for his career is an indication of the important role played by Samarians in Nimrud and Nineveh in the late 8th and early 7th centuries."

[13] See note 8 above.

[14] See *PNA* 1/2:251-252.

[15] ^I^PAP(*aḫi*)*-i-ú* (probably a copyist's error for ^I^PAP-*ia-ú* — written this way in the other texts). Cf. TFS 113:13 and 118:10. For this name and the five individuals known to have held it, see *PNA* 1/1:63-64; Fales 1991:112, n. 97. See also 3.113, n. 4 above.

[16] This man may be the *sukkallu* who wrote several Kouyunik letters and NL 63 and perhaps 42 (S. Parpola, OAC XVII p. 137 chart 3), although he does not have any connection with Samaria in those contexts. See Dalley and Postgate (1984:173, n. to ii.23).

REFERENCES

Text, translations and studies: Dalley and Postgate 1984:167-179, pls. 25-26; Dalley 1985:31-36; Ephᶜal 1991:41-42; Fales 1991:104; Becking 1992:74-77; and Zadok 1997.

E. WILLS

1. ALALAKH

INHERITANCE OF A BROTHER AND A SISTER (*AT* 7) (3.129)

Richard S. Hess

This Old Babylonian text from Alalakh resolves an inheritance dispute before the court of the king. In so doing it is clear that both sister and brother receive shares of the estate. It is thus clear that women could inherit property and take a share of their father's estate, as in the famous case of the daughters of Zelophehad (Num 27:1-11; Josh 17:3-6). In both accounts, however, the decision is made before the leader of the nation and thus the impression is that of an exceptional case. Compare also examples at Nuzi and Emar. See Ben-Barak 1980; Paradise 1980; 1987; Huehnergard 1985; Hess 1992; 1996:258-259. In several ways a comparison can also be drawn with Genesis 13 and the division of the "inheritance" of the land between Abram and Lot, relatives who also resolve a dispute through this decision. Here, however, Abram, whose right of the first part of the inheritance is not disputed, willingly give this privilege to his younger nephew Lot.

Dispute (lines 1-12)

1 Concerning the estate of Ammurabi's wife:
2-3 Abbael has brought a suit against his sister Bittatti,
4 [as foll]ows: "It [is (all) mine.]
5 Bit[ta]tti, you are not reckoned[1] (an heir) in this house."
6 [B]ittatti [replied as follows:]
7 ... in the town of Suḫaruwa,
8 [with] my [m]other I am reckoned (as an heir).
9-10 [W]hy have you taken the extra share (of the estate)?
11-12 Let us divide your father's estate equally.

Petition (lines 13-28)

13-14 They considered the matter before king Niqmepa.
15, 17-18 Abiadu testified before king Niqmepa that Bittatti
16 has a share of the estate.

Decision (lines 19-24)

19 The king replied as follows:
21 Let Abbael choose and take
20 from the estate the property that he wants.
22 The property that he rejects, Bittatti
23 shall take.
24 Thus the king replied.

Enactment (lines 25-41)

25 Gimil-Addu and Niwariadu
26 of the throne
27 were sent to the estate to be divided.
28-29 Abbael chose and took the upper property which was the upper storey.
30-31 He gave the lower property to Bittatti his sister.
32-33 It shall never again be changed.
35, 37 Abbael shall not claim against
34 Bittatti's portion of the estate
36 nor shall Bittatti (claim) against Abbael.

38 Whoever should claim
40 must pay
39 five hundred gold shekels to the palace
41 and forfeit their portion of the estate.

Witnesses (lines 42-46)

42 Ms. Bintikidia,[2] Iliku[papa],
43 Namidagan, Ikumšarrum a governor,
44 Kumidaba, Iatarmalik,
45 Murmeni servant of Ammitaku, Yarimlim,
46 Iriškubi a substitute.

Date (lines 47-49)

47 On the thirteenth day of the month of Izalli,
48 the year when king Niqmepa
49 captured Arazik.

[1] For "reckoned" (*pá-al-la-ti*), see Speiser 1963; 1965. Difficulties with this abstract concept in biblical usages (e.g., Exod 21:22-23) are dicussed by Jackson 1975:79-80.

[2] Note the presence of a woman acting as a witness in this royal inheritance decision.

REFERENCES

Text: Photo: Walker 1987:26. Copy: *AT* pls. v-vi. Transliteration: *AT* 34-36; Ben-Barak 1980:28-29. Translations: *AT* 34-36; Finkelstein 1969:545-546; Loewenstamm 1980:23-24.

AKKADIAN BIBLIOGRAPHY

ADAMTHWAITE, M. R.

1992 "Labaya's Connection with Shechem Reassessed." *Abr-Nahrain* 30:1-19.

ADLER, H.-P.

1976 *Das Akkadische des Königs Tušratta von Mitanni*. AOAT 201. Kevelaer, Neukirchen-Vluyn: Butzon & Bercker.

ALBERTI, A.

1990 "AN.BU = *a-nu-bu*$_x$." *NABU* 1990:102 No. 124.

BAFFI GUARDATA, F., M. BALDACCI and F. POMPONIO.

1989 "Bibliografia Eblaita II." *SEL* 6:145-164.

1993 "Eblaite Bibliography III." *SEL* 10:93-110.

1997 "Eblaite Bibliography IV." *SEL* 14:109-124.

BALDACCI, M., and F. POMPONIO.

1987 "Bibliografia Eblaita." Pp. 429-456 in Cagni 1987.

BECKING, B.

1981-82 "The Two Neo-Assyrian Documents from Gezer in their Historical Context." *JEOL* 27:76-89.

1992 *The Fall of Samaria: An Historical and Archaeological Study* (SHANE, 2; Leiden: E. J. Brill).

BECKMAN, G.

1996 *Texts From the Vicinity of Emar in the Collection of Jonathan Rosen*. HANE 2. Padua: Sargon srl.

BELD, S. G., W. W. HALLO and P. MICHALOWSKI.

1984 *The Tablets of Ebla: Concordance and Bibliography*. Winona Lake, IN: Eisenbrauns.

BEN-BARAK, Z.

1980 "Inheritance by Daughters in the Ancient Near East." *JSS* 25:22-33.

BORDREUIL, P.

1996-97 "The Aramaic Documents from Til Barsib." *Abr-Nahrain* 34:100-107.

BORGER, R.

1956 *Asarh*.

BOTTÉRO, J.

1954 *Le problème des Ḫabiru*. Cahiers de la société asiatique 12. Paris: Imprimerie nationale.

BRAND, E.

1996 *A Rescue Excavation at the Foot of Tel Hadid: Preliminary Report*. Tel Aviv (Hebrew).

1998 *A Rescue Excavation at the Foot of Tel Hadid: Preliminary Report*. Tel Aviv (Hebrew).

CAGNI, L., Editor.

1981 *La Lingua de Ebla*. Naples: Istituto Universitario Orientale.

1987 *Ebla 1975-1985: Dici anni di studi linguistici e filologici*. Naples: Istituto Universitario Orientale.

CHIERA, E.

1934 *Proceedings in Court*. Joint Expedition with the Iraq Museum at Nuzi 4. Philadelphia: University of Pennsylvania.

COGAN, M.

1974 *Imperialism and Religion*. SBLMS 19. Missoula, MT: Scholars Press.

CRAIGIE, P. C.

1972 "A Reconsideration of Shamgar ben Anath (Judg 3:31 and 5:6)." *JBL* 71:239f.

DALLEY, S. M.

1985 "Foreign Chariotry and Cavalry in the Armies of Tiglath-Pileser III and Sargon II." *Iraq* 47:31-48.

1996-97 "Neo-Assyrian Tablets from Til Barsib." *Abr-Nahrain* 34:66-99.

2001 "Assyrian Court Narratives in Aramaic and Egyptian Historical Fiction." *RAI* 45/1:149-161.

DALLEY, S., and J. N. POSTGATE.

1984 *The Tablets from Fort Shalmaneser*. CTN 3. Oxford: British School of Archaeology.

VON DASSOW, E. M.

1997 *Social Stratification of Alalah under the Mittani Empire*. Ph.D. dissertation. New York University. Ann Arbor, MI: UMI.

DELLER, K.

1987 "*Tamkāru*-Kredite in neuassyrischer Zeit." *JESHO* 30:1-29.

DOMBRADI, E.

1996 *Die Darstellung des Rechtsauftrags in den altbabylonischen Prozessurkunden*. 2 vols. FAOS 20/1-2. Stuttgart: Franz Steiner.

DONBAZ, V.

1988 "Some Neo-Assyrian Contracts from Girnavaz and Vicinity." *SAAB* 2:3-30.

1998 "Once Again Fi. 16 (= Samaria 1825)." *NABU* no. 22.

DOSSIN, G.

1957 "Kengen, pays de Canaan." *RSO* 32:35-39.

EDZARD, D. O.

1970 "Die Tontafeln von Kāmid el-Lōz." Pp. 50-62 in *Kāmid el-Lōz — Kumidi: Schriftdokumente aus Kāmid el-Lōz*. Saarbrücker Beiträge zur Altertumskunde 7. Ed. by D. O. Edzard, et al. Bonn: Rudolf Habelt.

1976 "Ein Brief an den 'Grossen' von Kumidi aus Kāmid al-Lōz." *ZA* 66:62-67.

1980 "Ein neues Tontafelfragment (Nr. 7) aus Kāmid al-Lōz." *ZA* 70:52-54.

1981 "Neue Erwägungen zum Brief des Enna-Dagan von Mari (TM.75.G.2367)." *Studi Eblaiti* 4:89-97.

1994 "Ebla ou la grande surprise de l'histoire du Proche-Orient ancien." *Akkadica* 88:18-29.

EICHLER, B. L.

1973 *Indenture at Nuzi: The Personal Tidennūtu Contract and its Mesopotamian Analogues*. Yale Near Eastern Researches 5. New Haven and London: Yale University Press.

1989 "Nuzi and the Bible: a Retrospective." Pp. 107-119 in *Studies Sjöberg*.

ELAT, M.
1987 "Der *tamkāru* im neuassyrischen Reich." *JESHO* 30:233-254.
1998 "*###*." Pp. *##* in *Studies Borger*.
EPHᶜAL, I.
1991 "The Samarian(s) in the Assyrian Sources." Pp. 36-45 in *Studies Tadmor*.
FALES, F. M.
1979 "Studies on Neo-Assyrian Texts II: 'Deeds and Documents' from the British Museum." *ZA* 73:232-254.
1991 "West Semitic Names in the Assyrian Empire: Diffusion and Social Relevance." *SEL* 8:99-117.
1993 "West Semitic Names in the Šeḫ Ḫamad Texts." *SAAB* 7:139-150.
1994 "A Fresh Look at the Nimrud Wine Lists." Pp. 361-380 in *Drinking in Ancient Societies. History and Culture of Drinks in the Ancient Near East. Papers of a Symposium held in Rome, May 17-19 1990*. HANE 6. Ed. by L. Milano. Padova: Sargon.
1996 "Prices in Neo-Assyrian Sources." *SAAB* 10:11-35, charts i-vii.
FALES, F. M., and J. N. POSTGATE.
1995 *Imperial Administrative Records, Part II. Provincial and Military Administration*. SAA 11. Helsinki: Helsinki University Press.
FINET, A.
1973 "Hammu-rapi et l'épouse vertueuse. À propos des §§133 et 142-143 du Code." Pp. 137-143 in *Studies Boehl*.
FINKELSTEIN, J. J.
1952 "The Middle Assyrian *Šulmānu* Texts." *JAOS* 72:77-80.
1969 "Documents from the Practice of Law." *ANET* 542-547.
1973 "The Goring Ox." *Temple Law Quarterly* 46:169-290.
1981 *The Ox That Gored*. TAPhS 7/1-2.
FUCHS, A., and S. PARPOLA.
2001 *The Correspondence of Sargon II*. Part III. *Letters from Babylonia and the Eastern Provinces*. SAA 15. Helsinki: Helsinki University Press.
GALLING, K.
1935 "Assyrische und Persische Präfekten in Geser." *PJB* 31:81-86.
GALTER, H. D.
1995 "Aya." *DDD* cols. 235-238.
GELLER, M. J.
1987 "The Lugal of Mari at Ebla and the Sumerian King List." *Eblaitica* 1:141-145.
GIVEON, R.
1972 "An Egyptian Officer at Gezer?" *IEJ* 22:143-144.
GITIN, S., and M. COGAN.
1999 "A New Type of Dedicatory Inscription from Ekron." *IEJ* 49:193-202.
GLOCK, A. E.
1971 "A New Taᵓannek Tablet." *BASOR* 204:17-30.
GRAYSON, A. K.
1975 "Chronicle I." in *ABC* 77-79.
1983 "Literary Letters from Deities and Diviners: More Fragments." *JAOS* 103:143-148; rep. *Studies Kramer* 2 (1984) 143-148.
GREENBERG, M.
1955 *The Ḫab/piru*. AOS 39. New Haven: American Oriental Society.
HALLO, W. W.
1964 "The Slandered Bride." Pp. 95-105 in *Studies Oppenheim*.
1966 "Til-Barsib." Pp. 584-586 in *The Biblical World: a Dictionary of Biblical Archaeology*. Ed. by C. F. Pfeiffer. Grand Rapids: Baker.
1967 "Review of *RlA* 3/1." *JAOS* 87:62-66.
1971 Collations of WB 1923, 444 (unpubl.; see Vincente 1995).
1991a "The Death of Kings." Pp. 148-165 in *Studies Tadmor*.
1991b *BP*.
1995 "Slave Release in the Biblical World." Pp. 79-93 in *Studies Greenfield*.
1996 *Origins*.
1999 "Jerusalem under Hezekiah: an Assyriological perspective." Pp. 36-50 in *Jerusalem: its Sanctity and Centrality to Judaism, Christianity, and Islam*. Ed. by L.I. Levine. New York: Continuum.
in press "Bookkeeping in the 21st Century BCE." International Scholars Conference on Ancient Near Eastern Economics 3. Ed. M. Hudson and M. Van De Mieroop.
HALLO, W. W., and H. TADMOR.
1977 "A Lawsuit from Hazor." *IEJ* 27:1-11.
HAWKINS, J. D.
1996-97 "A New Luwian Inscription of Hamiyatas, King of Masuwari." *Abr-Nahrain* 34:108-117.
HELTZER, M.
1976 "Mortgage of Land Property and Freeing from it in Ugarit." *JESHO* 19:89-95.
1978 *Goods, Prices and the Organization of Trade in Ugarit*. Wiesbaden: Reichert-Verlag.
1982a *The Internal Organization of the Kingdom of Ugarit*. Wiesbaden: Reichert-Verlag.
1982b "Zum Steuersystem in Ugarit (*pilku-ubdy* und Ähnliches)." *AfO* 19:112-120.
1994-95 "*Ben-ᶜanat we-shamgar ben-ᶜanat*." *ᶜAl Hapereq* 8 (in Hebrew).
HESS, R. S.
1992 "Milcah." *ABD* 4:824-825.
1993a *Amarna Personal Names*. ASORDS 9. Winona Lake, IN: Eisenbrauns.
1993b "Smitten Ant Bites Back: Rhetorical Forms in the Amarna Correspondence from Shechem." Pp. 95-111 in *Verse in Ancient Near Eastern Prose*. AOAT 42. Ed. by J. C. de Moor and W. G. Watson. Kevelaer: Butzon & Bercker; Neukirchen-Vluyn: Neukirchener Verlag.

1994a “Alalakh Studies and the Bible: Obstacle or Contribution?” Pp. 199-215 in *Studies King*.

1994b “Alalakh Text 457.” *UF* 26:501-508.

1996 *Joshua. An Introduction and Commentary*. Tyndale Old Testament Commentaries. Leicester and Downers Grove: IVP.

HOROWITZ, W.

1997 “A Combined Multiplication Tablet on a Prism Fragment from Hazor.” *IEJ* 47:190-197.

HOROWITZ, W., and A. SHAFFER.

1992a “An Administrative Tablet from Hazor: a Preliminary Edition.” *IEJ* 42:21-33, 167.

1992b “A Fragment of a Letter from Hazor.” *IEJ* 42:165-167.

HUEHNERGARD, J.

1985 “Biblical Notes on Some New Akkadian Texts from Emar (Syria).” *CBQ* 47:428-434.

1987 *Ugaritic Vocabulary in Syllabic Transcription*. Atlanta: Scholars Press.

1989 *The Akkadian of Ugarit*. HSS 34. Atlanta: Scholars Press.

1996 “A Byblos Letter, Probably from Kāmid el-Lōz.” *ZA* 86:97-113.

HUEHNERGARD, J., and W. H. VAN SOLDT.

1999 “A Cuneiform Lexical Text from Ashkelon with a Canaanite Column.” *IEJ* 49:184-192.

HUNGER, H.

1968 *Babylonische und assyrische Kolophone*. AOAT 2. Kevelaer: Butzon & Bercker.

JACKSON, B. S.

1974 “The Goring Ox Again.” *JJP* 18:55-93; reprinted in Jackson 1975:108-152.

1975 *Essays in Jewish and Comparative Legal History*. SJLA 10. Leiden: Brill.

JAS, R.

1996 *Neo-Assyrian Judicial Procedures*. SAAS 5. Helsinki: The Neo-Assyrian Text Corpus Project.

JOHNS, C. H. W.

1905 “The New Cuneiform Tablet from Gezer.” *PEFQS* 37:206-210.

JURSA, M., and K. RADNER.

1995-96 “Keilschrifttexte aus Jerusalem.” *AfO* 42-43:89-108.

KELLER, S. R.

1991 “Written Communications between the Human and Divine Spheres in Mesopotamia and Israel.” *SIC* 4:299-313.

KIENAST, B.

1980a “Die altbabylonischen Kaufurkunden aus Alalaḫ.” *WO* 11:35-63.

1980b “Der Feldzugsbericht des Ennadagan in literarischer Sicht.” *OA* 19:247-261.

1984 “Zum Feldzugsbericht des Enna-dagan.” *OA* 23:18-32.

KINNIER WILSON, J. V.

1972 *The Nimrud Wine Lists. A Study of Men and Administration at the Assyrian Capital in the Eighth Century B.C.* CTN 2. London: British School of Archaeology.

KLENGEL, H.

1963 “Zur Sklaverei in Alalaḫ.” *Acta Antiqua* 11:1-15.

KWASMAN, Th.

1988 *Neo-Assyrian Legal Documents in the Kouyunjik Collection of the British Museum*. Studia Pohl, Series maior 14. Rome: Pontificio Istituto Biblico.

KWASMAN, Th., and S. PARPOLA.

1991 *Legal Transactions of the Royal Court of Nineveh*. Part 1: *Tiglath-pileser III through Esarhaddon*. SAA 6. Helsinki: The Neo-Assyrian Text Corpus Project.

LAMBERT, W. G.

1987 “The Treaty of Ebla.” Pp. 353-364 in Cagni 1987.

LANDSBERGER, B.

1954 “Assyrische Königsliste und ‘dunkles Zeitalter’.” *JCS* 8 (1954) 31-45, 47-73, 106-133.

1968 “Jungfräulichkeit: ein Beitrag zum Thema ‘Beilager und Eheschliessung.’” Pp. 41-105 in *Studies David*.

LEVINE, B. A.

1963 “Ugaritic Descriptive Rituals.” *JCS* 17:105-111.

1965 “The Descriptive Ritual Texts of the Pentateuch.” *JAOS* 85:307-318.

1983 “The Descriptive Ritual Texts from Ugarit: Some Formal and Functional Features.” Pp. 467-475 in *Studies Freedman*.

LEVINE, B. A., and W. W. HALLO.

1967 “Offerings to the Temple Gates at Ur.” *HUCA* 38:17-58.

LIVERANI, M.

1998-99 *Le lettere di el-Amarna*. Vol. 1: *Le lettere dei “Piccoli Re”*. Vol. 2: *Le lettere dei “Grand Re”*. Testi del Vicino Oriente antico 3.1-2. Brescia: Paideia Editrice.

LIVINGSTONE, A.

1989 *Court Poetry and Literary Miscellanea*. SAA 3. Helsinki: Helsinki University Press.

LOCHER, C.

1986 *Die Ehre einer Frau in Israel: exegetische und rechtsvergleichende Studien zu Deuteronomium 22, 13-21*. OBO 70. Freiburg/Göttingen: Universitätsverlag/Vandenhoeck & Ruprecht.

LOEWENSTAMM, S. E.

1980 “Notes on the Alalakh Tablets. A Comparison of the Alalakh Tablets with the Ugaritic Documents.” Pp. 17-26 in *Comparative Studies in Biblical and Ancient Oriental Literatures*. AOAT 204. Ed. by S. E. Loewenstamm. Kevelaer: Butzon & Bercker; Neukirchen-Vluyn: Neukirchener. Originally published in *IEJ* 6 (1956) 217-225.

LORETZ, O.

1984 *Habiru-Hebräer*. BZAW 160. Berlin and New York: Walter de Gruyter, 1984.

MACALISTER, R. A. S.

1912 *The Excavations of Gezer, I*. London: Palestine Exploration Fund.

MACHINIST, P.
1983 "Assyria and its Image in the First Isaiah." *JAOS* 103:719-737.
MAIDMAN, M. P.
1995 "Nuzi: Portrait of an Ancient Mesopotamian Provincial Town." Pp. 931-947 in *CANE*.
MALUL, M.
1989 "*Susapinnu*, the Mesopotamian Paranymph and his Rule." *JESHO* 32:241-278.
MATTHIAE, P.
1980 *Ebla: an Empire Rediscovered*. Trans. by Ch. Holme. Garden City, NY: Doubleday.
MATTILA, R.
2000 *The King's Magnates. A Study of the Highest Officials of the Neo-Assyrian Empire*. SAAS 11. Helsinki: The Neo-Assyrian Text Corpus Project.
MENDELSOHN, I.
1959 "On the Preferential Status of the Eldest Son." *BASOR* 156:38-40.
MICHALOWSKI, P.
1993 *Letters from Mesopotamia*. SBLWAW 3. Atlanta: Scholars.
VAN DE MIEROOP, M.
1995 "Old Babylonian Interest Rates: Were They Annual?" Pp. 357-364 in *Studies Lipiński*.
2002 "A History of Near Eastern Debt?" Pp. 59-94 in *Debt and Economic Renewal in the Ancient Near East*. International Scholars Conference on Ancient Near Eastern Economics 3. Ed. by M. Hudson and M. van de Mieroop. Bethesda, MD: CDL.
MILANO, L.
1995 "Ebla: a Third-Millennium City-State in Ancient Syria." *CANE* 2:1219-1230.
MILLARD, A. R.
1992 "Assyrian Involvement in Edom." Pp. 35-39 in *Early Edom and Moab: The Beginning of the Iron Age in Southern Jordan*. Ed. by P. Bienkowski. Sheffield: J. R. Collis.
1994 *The Eponyms of the Assyrian Empire 910-612 BC*. SAAS 2. Helinski: The Neo-Assyrian Text Corpus Project.
MORAN, W.
1963 "The Ancient Near Eastern Background of the Love of God in Deuteronomy." *CBQ* 25:77-87.
1975 "The Syrian Scribe of the Jerusalem Amarna Letters." Pp. 146-166 in *Unity and Diversity*.
1992 *The Amarna Letters*. Baltimore and London: Johns Hopkins University Press.
1993 "An Ancient Prophetic Oracle." Pp. 252-259 in *Studies Lohfink*.
MOSCATI, S.
1959 "Sulla storia del nome Canaan." Pp. 266-269 in *Studia Biblica et Orientalia III: Oriens Antiquus*. AnBib 12. Rome: Pontifical Biblical Institute.
MÜLLER, G.
1997 "Gedanken zur neuassyrischen Geldwirtschaft." Pp. 115-121 in *RAI* 39.
NA᾿AMAN, N.
1986 "Habiru and Hebrews: The transfer of a Social Term to the Literary Sphere." *JNES* 45:271-288.
1995 "Amarna *sakānu* ('to govern') and the West Semitic *sôkēn* ('governor')." *NABU* 1995/2:36 No. 42.
2000 "The Number of Deportees from Samaria in the Nimrud Prisms of Sargon II." *NABU* 2000/1:1 No. 1.
NA᾿AMAN, N., and R. ZADOK.
1988 "Sargon's Deportations to Israel and Philistia." *JCS* 40:36-46.
2000 "Assyrian Deportations to the Province of Samerina in the Light of Two Cuneiform Tablets from Tel Hadid." *Tel Aviv* 27:159-188.
OWEN, D. I.
1981 "An Akkadian Letter from Ugarit at Tel Aphek." *Tel Aviv* 8:1-17 and pls. 1f.
PARADISE, J.
1980 "A Daughter and Her Father's Property at Nuzi." *JCS* 32:189-207.
1987 "Daughters as 'Sons' at Nuzi." Pp. 203-213 in *General Studies and Excavations at Nuzi 9/1*. SCCNH 2. Ed. by D. I. Owen and M. A. Morrison. Winona Lake: Eisenbrauns.
PARKER, B.
1954 "The Nimrud Tablets, 1952 — Business Documents." *Iraq* 16:29-58.
1963 "Economic Tablets from the Temple of Mamu in Balawat." *Iraq* 25:86-103.
PARPOLA, S.
1976 "Review of Kinnier Wilson 1972." *JSS* 21:165-174.
1980 "The Murderer of Sennacherib." Pp. 171-182 in *RAI* 26.
1987 *The Correspondence of Sargon II*. Part I. *Letters from Assyria and the West*. SAA 1. Helsinki: Helsinki University Press.
1995 "The Construction of Dūr-Šarrukin in the Assyrian Royal Correspondence." Pp. 47-77 in *Khorsabad, le palais de Sargon II, roi d'Assyrie. Actes du colloque organisé au musée du Louvre par le Service culturel les 21 et 22 janvier 1994*. Louvre conférences et colloques. Ed. by A. Caubet. Paris: La Documentation Française.
PETSCHOW, H.
1965 "Die neubabylonische Zwiegesprächsurkunde und Genesis 23." *JCS* 19:103-120.
1974 *Mittelbabylonische Rechts- und Wirtschaftsurkunden der Hilprecht-Sammlung Jena*. Abhandlungen der Sächsischen Akademie der Wissenschaften zu Leipzig. Phil-hist. Kl. 64/4. Berlin: Akademie Verlag.
PETTINATO, G.
1980 "Bollettino militare della campagna di Ebla contro la città di Mari." *OA* 19:231-245 + pls. xivf.
1981 *The Archives of Ebla: an Empire Inscribed in Clay*. Garden City, NY: Doubleday.
1995 "'Napoleone' ad Ebla: un generale o un verbo?" *AO* 13:75-106.
PFEIFFER, R.
1935 *State Letters of Assyria*. AOS 6. New Haven: American Oriental Society.
PINCHES, Th. G.
1904 "The fragment of an Assyrian Tablet found at Gezer." *PEFQS* 36:229-236.

POMPONIO, F.
1999-2000 "All'alba della storia siriana, ovvero il trionfo di Sa'umu." *AfO* 46-47:45-49.
POSTGATE, J. N.
1973 *The Governor's Palace Archive*. CTN 2. London: British School of Archaeology.
1974 *Taxation and Conscription in the Assyrian Empire*. Studia Pohl: series maior. Rome: Biblical Institute Press.
1976 *Fifty Neo-Assyrian Legal Documents*. Warminster: Aris & Phillips.
1990 "The Assyrian Porsche." *SAAB* 4:35-45.
1997 "Middle Assyrian to Neo-Assyrian: the Nature of the Shift." Pp. 159-168 in *RAI* 39.
POSTGATE, J. N., and J. E. READE.
1976-80 "Kalḫu." *RlA* 5:303-323.
POWELL, M. A.
1992 "Weights and Measures." *ABD* 6:897-908.
1993 "Masse und Gewichte." *RlA* 7:457-517.
1996 "Money in Mesopotamia." *JESHO* 39:224-242.
RADNER, K.
1995 "Samaria 1825 = Fi. ̹16. Zum Verbleib einer NA Urkunde aus Sāmirīna (Samaria)." *NABU* 1995/4:90 No. 100.
1997 *Die neuassyrischen Privatrechtsurkunden als Quelle für Mensch und Umwelt*. SAAS 6. Helsinki: The Neo-Assyrian Text Corpus Project.
1999a "Money in the Neo-Assyrian Empire." Pp. 127-157 in *Trade and Finance in Ancient Mesopotamia. Proceedings of the First MOS Symposium (Leiden 1997)*. MOS 1. Ed. by J. G. Dercksen. Leiden: Nederlands Historisch-Archaeologisch Instituut te Istanbul.
1999b "Traders in the Neo-Assyrian Period." Pp. 101-126 in *Trade and Finance in Ancient Mesopotamia. Proceedings of the First MOS Symposium (Leiden 1997)*. MOS 1. Ed. by J. G. Dercksen. Leiden: Nederlands Historisch-Archaeologisch Instituut te Istanbul.
2001 "The Neo-Assyrian Period." Pp. 265-288 in *Security For Debt in Ancient Near Eastern Law*. CHANE 9. Ed. by R. Westbrook and R. Jasnow. Leiden: E. J. Brill.
RAINEY, A. F.
1970a *El-Amarna Tablets 359-379*. AOAT 8. Kevelaer, Neukirchen-Vluyn: Butzon & Bercker.
1970b "The Order of Sacrifices in Old Testament Ritual Texts." *Biblica* 51:485-498.
1978 *El-Amarna Tablets 359-379*. 2nd edition, revised. Kevelaer, Neukirchen-Vluyn: Butzon & Bercker.
1989 "Review of W. Moran, *Les lettres d'el-Amarna: Correspondance diplomatique du pharaon*." *Biblica* 70:566-572.
1995-96 "A New English Translation of the Amarna Letters." *AfO* 42-43:109-121.
READE, J. E.
1998 "Assyrian Eponyms, Kings and Pretenders, 648-605 BC." *Or* 67:255-265.
REISNER, G. A., et al.
1924 *Harvard Excavations at Samaria, 1908-1910*. 2 Vols. Cambridge, MA: Harvard University Press.
RÖLLIG, W.
1997 "Aramaica Haburensia II. Zwei datierte aramäische Urkunden aus Tall Šēḫ Ḥamad." *AoF* 24:366-374.
ROTH, M.
1989 *Babylonian Marriage Agreements: 7th-3rd Centuries B.C.* AOAT 222. Kevelaer: Butzon & Bercker; Neukirchen-Vluyn: Neukirchener Verlag.
ROWE, I. M. and W. H. VAN SOLDT.
1998 "The Hurrian Word for 'Brideprice' in an Akkadian Text from Alalaḫ IV." *AO* 16:132-133.
SAGGS, H. W. F.
1955 "The Nimrud Letters, 1952 — Part II." *Iraq* 17:126-154.
2001 *The Nimrud Letters, 1952*. CTN 5. London: British School of Archaeology in Iraq.
SAN NICOLÒ, M.
1925 "Zur Entwicklung der babylonischen Urkundenformen." Pp. 23-35 in *Abhandlungen zur antiken Rechtsgeschichte: Festschrift für Gustav Hanausek zu seinem siebzigsten Geburtstage am 4. September 1925*. Graz: J. Meyerhoff.
1931 "Beiträge zur Rechtsgeschichte im Bereiche der Keilschriftlichen Rechtsquellen." Pp. 152-160 in *Instituttet for sammenlignende kulturforskning: beretning om dets virksomhet inntil sommeren 1931*. Ed. by F. Stang. Oslo: H. Aschehoug & Co.
SHANKS, H.
1976 "American Tourist Returns 'Hazor' Tablet to Israel after 13 Years." *BAR* 2/2:35f., 44.
SIGRIST, M.
1982 "Miscellanea." *JCS* 34:242-252.
SINGER, I.
1999 "A Political History of Ugarit." Pp. 603-733 in *HUS*.
VON SODEN, W.
1981 "Das Nordsemitische in Babylonien und Syrien." Pp. 355-361 in Cagni 1981.
1990 "Gibt es Hinweise auf die Ermordung Sanheribs im Ninurta-Tempel (wohl) in Kalah in Texten aus Assyrien?" *NABU* 1990:16f., No. 22.
VAN SOLDT, W. H.
1996 "Studies in the Topography of Ugarit (I). The Spelling of Ugaritic Toponyms." *UF* 28:653-692.
SOLLBERGER, E.
1980 "The So-called Treaty between Ebla and 'Ashur'." *Studi Eblaiti* 3:129-155.
SPEISER, E. A.
1954 "The Alalakh Tablets." *JAOS* 74:18-25.
1963 "The Stem *pll* in Hebrew." *JBL* 82:301-306.
1965 "Pālil and Congeners: A Sampling of Apotropaic Symbols." Pp. 389-393 in *Studies Landsberger*.
STOL, M.
1993 *Epilepsy in Babylonia*. Cuneiform Monographs 2. Groningen: Styx.

TADMOR, H.
1994 *The Inscriptions of Tiglath-Pileser III King of Assyria*. Jerusalem: The Israel Academy of Sciences and Humanities.
THUREAU-DANGIN, F.
1922 "Nouvelles lettres d'el-Amama." *RA* 19:91-108.
1937 "Trois contrats du Ras-Shamra." *Syria* 18:247-253.
TSEVAT, M.
1958 "Alalakhiana." *HUCA* 29:109-134.
TUCKER, G.
1966 "The Legal Background of Genesis 23." *JBL* 85:77-84.
DE VAUX, R.
1968 "Le Pays de Canaan." Pp. 23-30 in *Studies Speiser*.
VINCENTE, Cl.-A.
1995 "The Tall Leilān Recension of the Sumerian King List." *ZA* 85:231-270.
WALKER, C. B. F.
1987 *Cuneiform*. Reading the Past. London: Trustees of the British Museum.
WATERMAN, L.
1930-36 *Royal Correspondence of the Assyrian Empire*. Humanistic Studies 17-20. Ann Arbor, MI: University of Michigan.
WEINFELD, M.
1982 "Commentary to Genesis 23." P. 147 in *The Encyclopedia of the World of the Bible*. Jerusalem: Revivim (Hebrew).
WEISBERG, D. B.
1984 "The Length of the Reign of Ḫallušu-Inšušinak." *JAOS* (Studies in Islam and the Ancient Near East Dedicated to Franz Rosenthal) 104/1:213-217.
In press *The Neo-Babylonian Texts of the Oriental Institute Collection*. OIP 122.
WESTBROOK, R.
1988 *Old Babylonian Marriage Law*. AfO Beiheft 23.
1991 *Property and the Family in Biblical Law*. JSOTSup 113. Sheffield: Sheffield Academic Press.
WILHELM, G.
1970 *Untersuchungen zum Hurro-Akkadischen von Nuzi*. AOAT 9. Neukirchen-Vluyn: Neukirchener Verlag.
1973 "Ein Brief der Amarna-Zeit aus Kāmid el-Lōz." *ZA* 63:69-75.
WISEMAN, D. J.
1954 "Supplementary Copies of Alalakh Tablets." *JCS* 8:1-30.
WISEMAN, D. J., and R. S. HESS
1994 "AT 457." *UF* 26:501-508.
WRIGHT, C. J. H.
1990 *God's People in God's Land: Family, Law, and Property in the Old Testament*. Grand Rapids: Eerdmans; Carlisle: Paternoster.
YADIN, Y.
1972 *Hazor*. The Schweich Lectures of the British Academy 1970. London: Oxford University Press.
YOUNGER, K. L., Jr.
1998 "The Deportations of the Israelites." *JBL* 117:201-227.
2002 "Recent Study on Sargon II, King of Assyria: Implications for Biblical Studies." Pp. 288-329 in *Mesopotamia and the Bible. Comparative Explorations*. JSOTSup 341. Ed. by M. W. Chavalas and K. L. Younger, Jr. Sheffield: Sheffield Academic Press.
ZACCAGNINI, C.
1997 "On the Juridical Terminology of Neo-Assyrian and Aramaic Contracts." Pp. 203-208 in *RAI* 39.
ZADOK, R.
1985 "Samarian Notes." *BiOr* 42:567-572.
1988 *The Pre-Hellenistic Israelite Anthroponymy and Prosopography*. OLA 28. Leuven: Peeters.
1991 "On the Onomasticon of the Old Aramaic Sources." *BiOr* 48:25-40.
1997 "The Ethnolinguistic Composition of Assyria Proper in the 9th-7th Centuries BC." Pp. 209-215 in *RAI* 39.
ZAWADSKI, S.
1990 "Oriental and Greek Tradition About the Death of Sennacherib." *SAAB* 4:69-72.
ZEEB, F.
1991 "Studien zu den altbabylonischen Texten aus Alalaḫ. I: Schuldscheine." *UF* 23:405-438.
1992 "Studien zu den altbabylonischen Texten aus Alalaḫ. II: Pfandurkunden." *UF* 24:447-480.
1993 "Studien zu den altbabylonischen Texten aus Alalaḫ. III: Schuldabtretungsurkunden." *UF* 25:461-472.
1995 "Alalaḫ VII und das Amosbuch." *UF* 27:641-656.

SUMERIAN ARCHIVAL DOCUMENTS

A. LETTERS

1. A LETTER FROM AN ANGRY HOUSEWIFE (3.130)

William W. Hallo

Following the interpretation of its original editor, this unusual letter seems to involve a woman's defending herself against charges of waste and mismanagement of her husband's estate as dealt with both in §§141-143 of the Laws of Hammurabi (*COS* 2.131) and in a model court-case (below, 3.140). It may thus represent a model letter rather than a "functional" one, using the terminology of Roth (1979:101f.; for a different sense of "functional," see *COS* 2:91, 211, 327, 405.

(1-2) To "the beloved"[1] say:[2]

(3-5) Why on account of the children does he demean my reputation?[3]

(6-7) Have I tied up as much as one flat loaf of bread[4] (or) 20 (liters) of flour in a leather sack?[5]

(8) Whatever barley there is in the house has not been tied up for the woman (of the house).

(9) There is no (cause) for worrying about his storehouse. I have not entered it![6]

(10) (But even if I had,) would I be scattering our possessions which he has acquired?

(11) I took (only) 11 (loaves of) beer-bread which were there out of his house (and) disbursed them to the household.

(12-13) (As for) the barley for the seed-plowing, it was carried off by the personnel. In the house there is no barley (left) at all.

(14) On account of the (seed-plowing of the) field I spoke to Lu-Nanna.

(15) He said to me: "I will provide (the seed-plowing) for you."[7]

(16-17) If he has not given the field into his (Lu-Nanna's) hand I will have to seize a seed-plower for myself somewhere else.

(18) On account of the oxen (for seed-plowing), let him send me an attendant for it!

(19) There isn't any barley in the house with me.

(20) Let him deliver[8] barley to me!

(21) It is urgent![9] Let him bring it to me!

(22) Igidu[10] [a] said to me: "The messenger of the divine Shara has betaken himself to him.

(23) May you not detain (lit. seize) him! Let him come to me.[b]

a Num 24:3, 15

b Prov 31:10-31

[1] Sum. [KI].ÁG, partly restored. This could be a personal name, as commonly at the beginning of letters (and attested as such), or an epithet, here perhaps used sarcastically. Note in this connection that the addressee is spoken of in the third person throughout the letter except in the very last line. Note also the first person plural possessive in line 10.

[2] At this point letters normally continue with "this is what PN (the sender) says." The absence of this formula may indicate the state of agitation she was in, or the high degree of familiarity between the correspondents.

[3] Alternatively: why does he complain against me/sue me, lit., "say (do) my claim"; cf. *CAD* s.vv. *baqāru*, *ragāmu*.

[4] Lit., "one bread smeared (i.e. on the inside of the oven like pita)." Alternatively: 60 (liters) of bread by the *šīqu* measure; see *CAD* Š 3:102, s.v. *šīqu* C.

[5] See *CAD* s.v. *naruqqu*. For KUŠ.A.GÁ.LÁ.KÉŠDA cf. *CAD* s.v. *raksu* and Letter B2:9 in Ali 1964:63.

[6] Alternatively: Not having been born in his/her store-house, I cannot enter it.

[7] Lit., "I will give it to you."

[8] For this sense of ŠU.TAG_4.TAG_4, see Powell 1978:190f.; he reads ŠU-DA_x-DA_x.

[9] Lit., "it is of a flood!" A standard expression at the end of letter-orders.

[10] As in line 1, it is not certain whether this is a personal name or an epithet or professional name, lit. "the one whose eyes are open," which may be a skilled laborer; cf. the antonym, IGI.NU.DU_8, which seems to stand for "unskilled laborer."

REFERENCES

Text and translation: Owen 1980.

2. A LETTER TO THE KING (3.131)

William W. Hallo

The royal correspondence of the dynasties of Ur, Isin and Larsa served as models for epistolary art and therefore entered the scribal curriculum or canon; see *COS* 1.164 and 165 for examples. But they ultimately derived from genuine archival copies in the royal chanceries, as suggested by their many correspondences with details known from contemporaneous sources, and illustrated by this example.

(1) Speak to my king![1]
(2) This is what Irmu your servant says:[2]
(3) Oh my king, your command is the word of Heaven that is not to be altered.
(4) Your destiny like that of a god is granted to you.
(5) The wall whose work my king has entrusted to me is accomplished.
(6) The way[3] to the heartland has been barred to the enemy.
(7-8) They have carried the lofty name of my king from the lower land to the upper land, from sunrise to sunset (and) to the very edges of the entire heartland.
(9) The Amorites have stirred up(?) the whole enemy country.
(10-12) Kunshi-matum they [sent back?] to Shulgi,[4] to the fortress of Igi-hursanga,[5] and Aba-indasa [...][6]
[Break]
(13′) The letter of my king [...]
(14′) Whatever the king commands I will surely do.
(15′) May my king know it!

[1] According to Michalowski (1980-83:52f.), the king in question is Shulgi of Ur, although Irmu only served as a high official under Shulgi's successors, and Shulgi appears in the third person in line 10.

[2] Irmu is the shorter form of the name Ir-Nanna and was borne by one of the highest officials of the Ur III empire who served in numerous capacities and was the virtual viceroy of the realm. See most recently Huber 2000.

[3] Lit., foot.

[4] According to other sources, both archival and monumental, Kunshi-matum, whose name means "submit, oh land!," was the daughter of Shu-Sin of Ur and affianced to a succession of rulers of distant Simanum; Michalowski 1975.

[5] A great wall across the narrowest part of the valley between Tigris and Euphrates that was intended to keep the Amorites at bay.

[6] An official known from two other royal letters.

REFERENCES

Text: PBS 10/4:8. Studies: Wilcke 1969:2f.; Michalowski 1975; 1976:177-182; 1980-83:52f.

3. A LETTER-ORDER (3.132)

William W. Hallo

Functional letters were chiefly of a simpler cast. Most often they were simply orders to furnish the bearer with specified materials out of the state stores on the authority of the letter-writer. Except for the fact that the payment was in kind rather than in cash (silver), they thus served much the same purpose as modern checks or bank-drafts. In the following unique case, the envelope enclosing the letter-order is preserved, and serves as a kind of receipt, sealed by the recipient. For comparable Hebrew "letter-orders," see *COS* 3.42F, 3.43A-H. For a possible Ugaritic parallel, see *COS* 3.45Q and n. 100.

(Tablet)

Say to Hesa that he should give to Shu-Adad 95 bushels of barley in the temple of Shara. Let him not argue!

(Envelope)

Shu-Adad the herdsman received 95 royal bushels of barley from Ilum-bani the temple-administrator, in the temple of Shara.

(Seal impression on envelope)

Shu-Adad, the royal herdsman, son of Gamilum.

REFERENCES

Text and study: Owen 1971-72.

B. CONTRACTS

1. SALE TRANSACTIONS

SLAVE SALE (3.133A)

Piotr Steinkeller

This text comes from Lagaš and dates to the Sargonic period (ca. 2250 BCE).

(lines 1-6)
Gala, Geme-LIŠ (and) her two daughters — they are his wife and children (i.e., of Gala); Lu-TAR (and) Šadu — they are his brothers.

(lines 7-10)
Lugal-ušumgal, the governor of Lagaš, bought them from Šu-ilišu, the judge.

(lines 11-16)
Puzur-Adad, son of Dudu, brother of Šu-ilišu, brought them from Akkade[a] (and) made them "cross over the stick."[1]

[a] Gen 10:10

(lines 17-28)
Šuruš-kin, the policeman, Edenbiše, the scribe, Ilum-bani, the physician, Gudea, Nani, (and) Dada, the captains, Ipqum, son of Nani, the governor, Mesag, brother of Ur-mega, the captain, Dada, the ⌜...⌝, Ur-nigzu, son of [...] (— these are the witnesses).

[1] For this ritual action, symbolizing the transfer of the sold person from the seller to the buyer, see most recently Steinkeller 1989:34-42.

REFERENCES

Text, translations and studies: Thureau-Dangin 1903:44 no. 80; Edzard 1968:94-96 no. 46.

SLAVE SALE (3.133B)

Piotr Steinkeller

This text comes from Nippur and dates to the Ur III period (5th year of Ibbi-Sin, the 10th month, ca 2024 BCE).

(lines 1-7)
One woman — her name being Geme-Ezida; her price being 4 shekels of silver — Ur-Nuska, the NU-ÈŠ(*nešakku*) priest, bought from Zanka, her mother.

(line 8)
Ur-G⌜ula⌝, the merchant, was the one who weighed out the silver.

(lines 9-10)
Lugal-namtare is the guarantor.

(lines 11-12)
They swore by the name of the king not to contest one against the other.

(lines 13-17)
Ur-sukal, Lu-balašaga, Lugal-nesage, (and) Ur-nigingar — these are the witnesses.

(lines 18-20)
Month Ab-è, year that the king's daughter was married to the ruler of Zabšali.

Seal: Zanka, daughter of Ur-dun.

REFERENCES

Text, translations and studies: Owen 1982 pl. 196, no. 903; Steinkeller 1989:225-226, no. 49.

REAL ESTATE TRANSACTION (3.133C)

Piotr Steinkeller

This text comes from Šuruppak and dates to the Fara period (ca. 2400 BCE).

(lines 1-2)
1 mina (i.e. a pound) of copper (is) the price of the field.

(line 3)
1 sar (is the size of) the field.

(lines 4-5)
2 minas of copper (is) the additional payment.

(lines 6-7)
6 minas of copper (is) the gift.

(lines 8-11)
10 loaves of breads, 10 cakes, 2 PAB-measures of soup, (and) 2 PAB-measures of fish chowder (is the food offering).

(lines 12-15)
Ur-ensahara, Urni, (and) Ku(g)-pad, (are) the sellers.[1]

(lines 16-35)
Ur-Sud, the master (house-surveyor), Ur-Gula, the scribe, Ur-Sud, the gate keeper, Anene, the ..., Dugani, the oblate, Šu-abi, Lugal-uma, Muni-eš, the cup-bearer, Ezi, (member of the household) of Gula, Ur-Sud, the bailiff, and Kini-muzu — (these are) the witnesses.

(lines 36-38)
Ur-Enlil, the chief constable, (is) the buyer.[2]

(lines 39-40)
(During) the term of office of Nammah.

(line 41)
(The field is located in) ⌜X⌝.TUR.

[1] Lit., "the ones who ate the price."
[2] Lit., "the one who bought the house."

REFERENCES

Text: Grégoire 1981 pl. 27, no. 86.

REAL ESTATE TRANSACTION (3.133D)

Piotr Steinkeller

This text comes from Umma and dates to the Ur III period (before Šulgi's 33rd year, ca. 2062 BCE).

(lines 1-14)
1⅓ sar of a house — 17 1/6 shekels of silver being the price of the house; 1 mina of wool, 1 headband, (and) 1 liter of oil being the gift for the house — Ur-nigingar, son of Girini, the chief constable, bought (this) house from Gugu, son of Ušmu, (and) Išagani, his wife, from both of them.

(line 15)
He (i.e, Ur-nigingar) completed this transaction.

(lines 16-23)
Hana'a, the mason, Ur-E.MIR.ZA, the mason, Lugal-sig, the scribe, Alla, son of Ur-du, the cattle-fattener, the son-in-law of Gugu, Inimanizi, son of Inna'a, (and) Arad, son of Lugal-TAR — these are the witnesses.

(lines 24-25)
200 table-breads (and) 60 bowls of beer (for) Inim-Šara, the master (house-surveyor).

(line 26)
When Ahu'a was the governor of Umma.

REFERENCES

Text, translations and studies: Steinkeller 1989:275-278, no. 88*, pl. 7.

2. MANUMISSIONS

THE MANUMISSION OF UMANIGAR (3.134A)

Piotr Steinkeller

This text comes from Nippur and dates to the Ur III period (the 6th year of Amar-Sin, ca. 2041 BCE).

(lines 1-5)
In the city-gate of Ninurta (named) "Lofty-city-gate-of-heaven-and earth,"[1] Atu, his father, manumitted[2] Umanigar, the slave of [PN], because of his being the (only) heir.[3] [a]

(lines 6-9)
Lu-kirizal (and) Lu-dingira, brothers of Atu, swore by the name of the king that (in the future) they will not contest (the estate of Atu).

a Gen 15:3

(lines 10-19 + break)
Before Lugal-azida, the (chief) worker-recruiter[4] of Nippur, (before) Ur-Ababa, the chief town-crier, (before) Un-daga, the gendarme, (before) Lugal-apin, (before) Šeš-kala, (before) Lugal-magure, (before) Lu-melam, (before) Lala, (before) Amar-šuba, (before) ⌜Balala?⌝ [(before) X PNs — these are the witnesses].

(line 1′)
Year that king Amar-Sin destroyed Šašru.

[1] Reading [K]Á.GAL-mah-ki-a[n-na] / ^{d}Nin-urta-k[a]. Cf. Steinkeller 1989:73 n. 209.

[2] Lit., "he established his freedom" (ama-ar-gi$_4$-ni ì-gar).

[3] Lit., "for / because of heirship (nam-ì-gi$_4$-la-šè)." This clause suggests the existence of a legal provision (otherwise undocumented) by which debt slaves (as undoubtedly is the case in this transaction) were subject to automatic manumission upon their becoming the only heirs.

[4] UGULA.URU (lit. "chief of the city") is probably to be read ZILULU. See Gelb, Steinkeller, and Whiting 1991:99.

REFERENCES

Text: Owen 1982 pl. 199, no. 920.

THE MANUMISSION OF ŠARAKAM AND UR-GUNA'A (3.134B)

Piotr Steinkeller

This text originates from Umma and dates to the Ur III period (5th year of Amar-Sin, 8th month, ca. 2042 BCE).

(lines 1-8)
Gudaga, their mother, manumitted[1] Šarakam (and) Ur-guna'a, both of them, from Mansum, for ⅓ mina (= 20 shekels) of silver.

(lines 9-11)
Mansum swore by the name of the king that (in the future) he will not raise claims regarding this silver.

(lines 12-17)
Before Lugale-banšag, before Lugal-e, before Dingir-sig, before Ur-gipar, son of X-TUR, before Nigingar-kidug, son of Dagu, before Lu-kinšaga (— these are the witnesses).

(lines 18-19)
Month É-iti-6; year that the EN priest of the great shrine of Inanna of Uruk was installed.

[1] Lit., "she freed/released them" (IN.ŠI.DU$_8$).

REFERENCES

Text: Fish 1932:132 no. 541; Gomi 1982:118 (collations).

3. MARRIAGE AGREEMENTS

THE MARRIAGE OF UR-NANŠE AND ŠAŠUNIGIN (3.135A)

Piotr Steinkeller

The text comes from Lagaš and dates to the Ur III period (6th year of Šu-Sin, ca. 2032 BCE).

(lines 1-4)
A completed judgment: Ur-Nanše, son of Bašišara-gi, married Šašunigin, daughter of Uše-hegin, the cowherd.

(lines 5-6)
They swore by the name of the king before the judges.

(line 7)
Ur-Igalim, son of Lumu, was the bailiff.

(lines 8-11)
Lu-Šara, Ur-Ištaran, (and) Lu-dingira were the judges.

(lines 12-14)
Year that Šu-Sin, king of Ur, set up the great stela for Enlil (and) Ninlil.

REFERENCES

Text, translations and studies: Crawford 1954:46; Falkenstein 1956:1-2 no. 1.

THE MARRIAGE OF PUZUR-HAYA AND UBARTUM (3.135B)

Piotr Steinkeller

This tablet and its envelope originate from Lagaš and date to the Ur III period (4th year of Ibbi-Sin, ca. 2025 BCE).

(lines 1-4)
Puzur-Haya took Ubartum as his wife.

(lines 5-11)
Before Ur-Damu, son of Ur-meme, (before) Ur-Dumuzi, (before) Bulali, (and before) Alduga, son of Ur-Dumuzi, the witnesses, before them, the oath by the name of the king was sworn.

(line 12)
Year that En-amgalana, the high-priest of Inanna, was installed.

REFERENCES

Text, translations and studies: Çiğ, Kizilyay, and Falkenstein 1959:76-78, no. 17. Tablet and envelope.

4. LOAN TRANSACTIONS

A LOAN OF SILVER TO ŠU-AŠLI (3.136A)

Piotr Steinkeller

This tablet and its envelope come from Nippur and date to the Ur III period (5th year of Šu-Sin, 2nd? month, ca. 2033 BCE).

(lines 1-3)
Šu-Ašli received 25 shekels of silver from A-zida (as an interest-free loan).

(lines 4-5)
He is to return the capital of the silver to Nippur till the month Apin-du$_8$-a (= 8th month).

(lines 6-8)
If he does not return (this) silver (as specified), he will measure out 2 kor (= 600 liters) of barley for each (shekel of silver) after the harvest (as a penalty).

(lines 9-11)
Before Turam-ili, before An-daga, before Lugal-ezen (— these are the witnesses).

(lines 12-13)
Month Elunum, [the year] after the Mardu-Wall was built.

Seal: Šu-Ašli, the silver-smith,[1] son of Šarrum-bani.

[1] Written KUG.DÉ (lit. "silver-caster"), replacing the usual KUG.DÍM (lit. "silver-fashioner").

REFERENCES

Text: Owen 1982 pl. 67, no. 266 (tablet and envelope).

A LOAN OF SILVER TO UR-GA (3.136B)

Piotr Steinkeller

This tablet and its envelope originate from Nippur and date to the Ur III period (2nd year of Amar-Sin, 7th month, 20th day, ca. 2045 BCE).

(lines 1-4)
Ur-ga received 10 shekels of silver from Adda'a as a loan; the yearly interest is 1 shekel for each 5 shekels.

(lines 5-6)
He is to restore it (any time) between the 20th day of the month DU_6.KUG (= 7th month) and the (next) month DU_6.KUG.

(lines 7-10)
Before Damu, (before) Puzur-Aššur, (and before) Lala, the scribe — these are the witnesses.

(lines 11-12)
Year that king Amar-Sin destroyed Urbilum.

Seal: Ur-[ga], son of Erra-ur[sag], the shepherd of Nin[urta].

REFERENCES

Text: Owen 1982 pl. 47, no. 168. Tablet and envelope.

A LOAN OF SHEEP FAT (3.136C)

Piotr Steinkeller

This text comes from Nippur. It dates to the Ur III period (9th year of Šu-Sin, 10th month, 23rd day, ca. 2029 BCE).

(lines 1-5)
Adda-kala and Pussa, his wife, received 20 *qû* (liters) of sheep fat from Adda-kala (as an interest-free loan).

(lines 6-7)
They are to return it till the 30th day of the month ZÍZ.$DURU_5$ (= 11th month).

(lines 8-13)
They swore by the name of the king that, if they do not return it (as specified), they will substitute 20 liters of barley for each liter of sheep fat (as a penalty).

Lu-Enlila, A-kala, Lugal-magure, (and) Lugal-apin — these are the witnesses.

Month KUG.SU_x, 23rd day, the year king Šu-Sin built the temple of Šara in Umma.

Seal: Adda-kala, son of Muni-mah.

REFERENCES

Text: Owen 1982 pl. 25, no. 72.

A LOAN OF SILVER TO GINA AND MANI (3.136D)

Piotr Steinkeller

This text was found in Nippur[1] and dates to the Ur III period (3rd year of Ibbi-Sin, 12th month, ca. 2026 BCE).

(lines 1-5)
Gina and Mani, (his mother),[2] received 8 shekels of silver from Adda-kala (as an interest-free loan).

(line 6)
They are to restore it by the month Nesag (= 4th month).

(lines 7-8)
They swore by the name of the king that, if they do not restore it (as specified), they will double it (as a penalty).[3]

(lines 9-10)
Before Ur-Šulpae (and) before Nabašag (— these are the witnesses).

(lines 11-12)
Month Dumu-zi, the year Simurrum was destroyed.

Seal 1: Gina, son of A'addaga. Seal 2: Mani, wife of A'addaga.

[1] As is shown by the fact that the tablet uses Umma month names, the transaction had apparently taken place in Umma.
[2] See the seals.
[3] Cf. Limet 1969.

REFERENCES

Text: Owen 1982 pl. 46, no. 164.

A LOAN OF SILVER TO ŠUNA (3.136E)

Piotr Steinkeller

This tablet and its envelope come from Nippur and date to the Ur III period (1st year of Ibbi-Sin, 6th month, ca. 2028 BCE). The transaction involves an antichretic arrangement, in which the interest on the loan is paid off by the labor of the pledged slave woman (see also the next two loans, 3.136F and 3.136G and above, 3.116).

(lines 1-6)
Šuna received 7 shekels of silver from Šeš-dada (as a loan); in lieu of its interest he placed (for service) Uba'a, [his] slave [woman]).[1]

(lines 7-10)
He swore by the name of the king to measure out 5 liters (of barley) as (her) daily wages, if she stops working.

(lines 11-14)
Lu-šaga, Ur-Tumal, and Lu-Sin — these are the witnesses.

(line 15)
Month Kin-Inanna, the year Ibbi-Sin (became) king.

[1] The reconstruction D[AM-NI], "his wife," is also possible.

REFERENCES

Text: Pohl 1937 pl. 9, no. 32. Tablet and envelope.

A LOAN OF SILVER TO UR-ENLILA (3.136F)

Piotr Steinkeller

The text may originate from Nippur and dates from the Ur III period (1st year of Šu-Sin). This is an antichretic loan transaction, in which the interest on the loan is covered by the produce of the pledged field (see 3.136D above and 3.136G below).

(lines 1-5)
Ur-Enlila, the farmer, received from Ga'akam 9 shekels of silver (as a loan); its interest (is) 2 shekels and 36 grains of silver.[1]

(lines 6-7)
(In lieu of the interest) he (i.e., Ur-Enlila) gave to him 9 IKU of land for cultivation.

(lines 8-9)
He (i.e., Ur-Enlila) promised to give this silver (back) at the threshing floor.[2]

(lines 10-14)
He swore by the name of the king that, if he does not it return it (as specified), he will measure out 1 kor and 120 *qû* (= 420 liters) of barley for each shekel of silver (as a penalty).

(lines 15-18)
Before Ur-Haya, before Ur-Baba, the supervisor of oxen, before Lu-dingira, son of Dudu, and before Lu-dingira, the scribe (— these are the witnesses).

(line 19)
The year Šu-Sin (became) king.

[1] I.e., almost 25%.
[2] I.e., at harvest time.

REFERENCES

Text, translation and studies: Çiğ, Kizilyay and Falkenstein 1959:86-88, no. 24.

A LOAN OF SILVER TO GIRINI (3.136G)

Piotr Steinkeller

This tablet and its envelope originate from Nippur and date to the Ur III period (6th year of Šu-Sin, 5th month, ca. 2032 BCE). It is an antichretic loan transaction. For similar transactions, see 3.136E and 3.136F above).

Girini borrows 6 shekels of silver from Ur-Nanibgal. At the same time, Ur-Nanibgal rents, for 5 years, Girini's house. The yearly rent of the house (⅔ shekel) will be deducted from the yearly interest on the loan ($1^1/5$ shekel).

(lines 1-4)
Girini received 6 shekels of silver from Ur-Nanibgal as a loan; the interest for (each) 5 shekels (is) 1 shekel.[1]

(lines 5-7)
The rent of the house (which Ur-Nanibgal agrees to rent from Girini), being ⅔ shekel, will be deducted from the interest on his silver (loan); he (i.e., Ur-Nanibgal) gave his word (to reside in the house) for 5 years.[2]

(lines 8-14)
Lu-Enlila, Šu-Kubum, Habaluke, Lu-kala, Nibalu'e, Lu-Ninšubur — these are the witnesses.

Month NE.NE-gar, the year the great stela was set up.

Seal: Girini, son of Ur-ga(?)-X-X.

[1] I.e., 20% (per annum), the typical interest for silver loans.
[2] The envelope (read according to Oppenheim's transliteration) has instead: "He (i.e., Ur-Nanibgal) gave his word to live in the house for 5 years. Its rent, being ⅔ shekel of silver, will be deducted from the interest on the silver (loan)."

REFERENCES

Text, translations and studies: Oppenheim 1948:133-134, S 3; Sauren 1978 pl. xci, no. 276. Tablet and envelope.

5. RENTAL AND HIRE TRANSACTIONS

A LEASE OF LAND (3.137A)

Piotr Steinkeller

The text originates from Nippur and dates to the Ur III period (7th year of Šu-Sin, 3rd month, ca. 2031 BCE).

(lines 1-10)
Madake, Ur-gagi'a, Katar, (and) Lu-melam leased out[1] 6 iku of land, (located in) the field Dalbana,[2] to Ur-Sin, son of A-kala, for 3 years, (in exchange) for ⅓ (of its produce).

(line 11)
They (i.e., the lessors) swore by the name of the king (not to contest the agreement).

(lines 12-15)
Lu-Inanna, Šeš-kala, (and) Ur-ganuna — these are the witnesses.

(lines 16-17)
Month Sig$_4$<-ga>, 13th day, the year king Šu-Sin <destroyed> the land of Zabšali.

[1] Lit., "gave."
[2] Lit., "in-between" (*birītu*).

REFERENCES

Text: Fish 1932:126 no. 40; Gomi 1982:95 (collations).

A RECORD OF HIRE (3.137B)

Piotr Steinkeller

The text originates from Nippur and dates to the Ur III period (8th year of Šu-Sin, 12th month, ca. 2030 BCE).

(lines 1-6)
Geme-Nungal and Šu-Durul, her son, received from Lugal-azida 1 shekel of silver, the wages of Ur-Iškur.[1]

(lines 7-14)
Before Ur-Iškur, before <PN>, son of Ur-Sin, before Lu-Iškur, (and) before Tulta, son of Lugal-hegal, they swore by the name of the king to measure out 6 liters of barley (as his daily wages), if he (i.e., Ur-Iškur) stops working.

(lines 15-16)
Month Še-KIN-kud; the year the great barge of Enlil was caulked.

Seal: Šu-Durul, son of Geme-Nungal.

[1] Almost certainly, Ur-Iškur was Geme-Nungal's son. Note that, three years later, the same Lugal-azida hired Geme-Nungal's son Šu-Durul (see 3.137C below), here acting as a co-lessor.

REFERENCES

Text: Pohl 1937 pl. 7 no. 24.

ANOTHER RECORD OF HIRE (3.137C)

Piotr Steinkeller

The text comes from Nippur and dates to the Ur III period (2nd year of Ibbi-Sin, 6th month, ca. 2027 BCE).

(lines 1-6)
Geme-Nungal received from Lugal-azida 3 shekels of silver, the yearly wages of Šu-Durul, (her son).[1]

(lines 7-11)
She swore by the name of the king to measure out 10 liters of barley (as his) daily (wages), if Šu-Durul stops working.

(lines 12-16)
Abinu'a, Lateniš, Lu-Sin, (and) Adda-kala — these are the witnesses.

(lines 17-18)
Month of Kin-[d]Inanna, the year the EN-priest of Inanna of Uruk was selected by an omen.

Seal: Hubatum, son of Bagina.[2]

[1] See 3.137B above.
[2] Hubatum probably was a relative of Geme-Nungal.

REFERENCES

Text: Owen 1982 pl. 31, no. 98.

6. A MODEL CONTRACT (3.138)

William W. Hallo

Model contracts were part of the scribal curriculum, and may have been ultimately derived, like literary letters, from real archival copies, but they typically lack the witness list and date of archival contracts; cf. Veldhuis 1997:60f.; Bodine 2001.

(1-3) In the street(s) of his city, he (the herald) sounded the horn.
(4-6) They ordered his sealed tablet (of manumission) to be fired on his forehead.
(7-9) (Thus the owner) cleared his forehead, he released his foot fetters, (and) he smashed his pot.[1]
(10-11) (Thus) he established his freedom.
(12-13) Moreover he left for him the sealed tablet of the fact that he had cleared him.[a]

[a] Exod 21:2-4; Deut 15:12-15; Jer 34

[1] Three symbols of manumission; with the foot-fetters cf. the handcuffs, likewise made of wood (GIŠ-ŠU).

REFERENCES

Roth 1979:33.

7. A SHIPPING CONTRACT (3.139)

William W. Hallo

Functional contracts typically end with a witness list and a date. In the latter, note that the month name in the standard Babylonian calendar became the basis of the later Hebrew month names, replacing the Canaanite names of pre-exilic times. The present text also features a Persian Gulf seal, crucial for dating the civilization of the Persian Gulf.

(1-3) 4 talents of *haltikku*-wool,[1] 2 bushels of wheat, 2 (bushels) of sesame
(4-7) Hatin-Ibanum son of Apkallum (received) from Luma'a.
(8-10) (At) the safe conclusion of the journey, he will give (an oath of) clearance to Luma'a.
(11) He swore to this in the name of the king.
(12-13) Before Ur-Shula'e the seer (and) before Erishti-ili the foreman of the fishermen.
(14-15) (In) the month Aiaru,[a] the 20th day, of the year (when King Gungunum) brought the two great emblems into the temple of Nanna.[2]

[a] 1 Kgs 6:1

[1] A better type of wool, perhaps that which embraces the neck. Cf. most recently MSL 13 (1971) 230:362.
[2] This is the date formula for the tenth year of Gungumum of Larsa, or ca. 1923 BCE.

REFERENCES

Text and discussion: Hallo 1965. Studies: Buchanan 1965; Porada 1971.

C. COURTCASES

1. MODEL COURTCASES

A TRIAL FOR ADULTERY (3.140)

William W. Hallo

No more than eight examples of Sumerian "model court cases" are known so far. They belong to the scribal school curriculum and are thus, strictly speaking, canonical texts. But they ultimately derive from genuine archival records, particularly of the early Isin I Dynasty, and were preserved because they were thought to illustrate some particularly interesting points of law. See in detail, Hallo in press.

(1-4) Ishtar-ummi the daughter of Ili-asu was taken in marriage by Erra-malik.
(5-6) In the first place she broke into[1] his granary.[a]
(7-10) In the second place she opened his pots of sesame-oil and covered them with cloths.
(11-14) In the third place he caught her on top of a man; he bound her on the body of the man in the bed (and) carried her to the assembly.
(15-18) The assembly, because the man was caught on top of her (sic!),
(19-20) set his (Erra-malik's) divorce-money at [... pounds of silver].
(21) They shaved [half (of her head)] (and the place of) urine, (her) pudenda.
(22-23) They pierced[2] her nose with an arrow.[3]
(24-26) For going around the city she was given over by the king.
(27) It was a case accepted for trial by the king.
(28) Ishme-Dagan-zimu was its bailiff.

[a] Exod 22:2f.

[1] The verb used is the same as that in line 23, making the punishment fit the crime.
[2] See the previous note.
[3] Lit., "a straight nail."

REFERENCES

Van Dijk 1963:70-77; Greengus 1969-70.

INHERITANCE (3.141)

William W. Hallo

(1-2) Ur-Suena son of Enlil-mashsu and Anne-babdu his brother
(3) by mutual agreement divided (their inheritance) by lot.
(4-5) After Ur-Suena died — 10 years having passed —
(6-9) Anne-babdu confronted the assembly of Nippur, appeared (in court) and declared:
(10-12) "One-third pound (20 shekels) of silver, the price of 2 slave-girls, Ur-Suena my older brother in no wise whatever gave to me!"
(13-14) Aabba-kalla son of Ur-Suena appeared (in court) and declared:
(15-16) "His heart was satisfied at that time with that money!"
(17-19) The judges remanded Aabba-kalla to the gate of Ninurta for taking the oath.
(20-21) By the gate of Ninurta each man was made to go towards (accommodate) the other.
(22-26) By mutual agreement Aabba-kalla gave 4(?) shekels of silver to Anne-babdu.
(27-32) 8 rods of orchard within the field of ... in lieu of the respective inheritance shares not yet adjudicated according to the wish (lit. heart) of Mullil-mashsu[1] Aabba-kalla and his two brothers, the heirs of Ur-Suena, gave to Anne-babdu.
(38) Anne-babdu swore in the name of the king that he would henceforth not raise a claim against the heirs of Ur-Suena

[1] The dialectal form of the name Enlil-mashsu.

(33) for the office of anointing priest of Ninlil and its prebend field,
(34) or the office of "elder" or the office of gate-opener(?),
(35) house, field, orchard, slave-girl, male slave,
(36) or any (other) property of the patrimony whatsoever
(37) on the basis of an old document regarding the inheritance share of Aabba-kalla.

REFERENCES

Hallo in press.

2. A FUNCTIONAL COURTCASE (3.142)

William W. Hallo

Functional court cases are well-attested for both Old Sumerian and neo-Sumerian periods. See in detail Edzard 1968 and Falkenstein 1956 respectively.

(1) A completed judgment:
(2-4) Shesh-kalla the son of Ur-Lamma declared here: "I am not the slave of Ur-Sahar-Ba'u."[1]
(5-9) That Ur-Lamma the father of Shesh-kalla was given barley rations and wool rations from the hand of Shu-Alla the scribe in the house of Ur-Sahar-Ba'u the son of Namu in return for (his son's) slave-status
(10-12) and that it was in the place of Ur-Sahar-Ba'u that Shesh-kalla the slave was born to Ur-Lamma[2] [a]
(13-15) Lu-duga (and) Dudumu swore.
(16-17) The slave was confirmed to the heirs of Ur-Sahar-Ba'u.
(18) Ti-Emahta was the bailiff.
(19) Lu-Shara was the judge.
(20) Year that King Shu-Sin erected the great stele(s) of Enlil and Ninlil.[3]

[a] Gen 17:12f., 23, 27; Lev 22:11

[1] Contesting their slave status in court was one of several techniques for securing their freedom that were available to slaves in the ancient Near East; see Falkenstein 1956 2:49-72. For others, see Snell 2001.

[2] He was thus "a slave for life," functionally equivalent to the Akk. *(w)ilid bītim, ilitti bītim* and the Heb. *yᵉlîd bayit*; see Hallo 1995:87f.

[3] I.e. the sixth year of Shu-Sin, ca. 2031 BCE. Note the same stele(s) apparently being manufactured(?) in a text dated the previous year; cf. Sharlach 2000:135 and below, *COS* 3.145, n. 4.

REFERENCES

Falkenstein 1956 2:53f.

D. ACCOUNTS

1. THE DEATH OF SHULGI (3.143)

William W. Hallo

Account texts are probably the single most abundantly attested genre in Sumerian, and certainly in neo-Sumerian. They reflect an economy largely managed by the state. But occasionally they reveal, if only incidentally, details of other aspects of daily life, including ritual belief and practice, as in the following text.

19 slave girls (working) full time (and) 2 slave girls (working) ⅔ time, for seven days,[a] their (total) labor being the equivalent of 142⅓ (wo)man-days, when the divine (king) Shulgi was taken up in(to) heaven as doorkeeper,[1] were withdrawn from the account of Anana. Date: eleventh month of Shulgi's last year.[2]

a Gen 7:4, 10; 50:10; Job 2:13

[1] Probably in the guise of Dumuzi, the deity whom the king represented in the sacred marriage; cf. *COS* 1.173. For other evidence of a seven-day mourning period, cf. Hallo 1991:158f.

[2] Ca. 2047 BCE. By this time the recently deceased king was already receiving funerary offerings according to other texts; cf. Hallo 1991a:180f.

REFERENCES

Text: Watson 1986 No. 132. Studies: Hallo 1991, 1991a.

2. A SUMERIAN AMPHICTYONY

William W. Hallo

In the neo-Sumerian period (21st century BCE), the sacrificial cult at the temples in the religious capital of Nippur were supported by the contributions, mostly in livestock, of the central provinces as forwarded by their governors.[1] Each took a turn (BALA) which was normally a month but could be up to three months for wealthy provinces and as little as ten days for poorer ones. The institution is here illustrated by (a) a calendar text identifying the turns of a given year and (b) a text for that year detailing some of the BALA-contributions for one month.[a]

CALENDAR TEXT (3.144A)
(HTS 138)[2]

(1-3) Month I, month II: turn of the governor of Girsu.[3]
(4-5) Month III: turn of the governor of Adab.
(6-7) Month IV: turn of the governor of Marad.
(8-9) Month V: turn of the governor of Kazallu.
(break)
(10′) [Month XIII:] turn of the governor of Girsu.[4]
(11′) Year that Enmahgal-anna the high priestess of Nanna was installed.[5]

a 1 Kgs 4:7-19

[1] For some details and bibliography see above, Introduction, at nn. 32-36 and 44.

[2] The text was part of the collection of Hartford Theological Seminary (HTS) when first published; it is now part of the collection of the Horn Archaeological Museum of Andrews University, where it bears the accession number AUAM 73.3161; see L. T. Geraty *apud* Sigrist 1984:vi.

[3] The names of the months of the imperial calendar have been converted to Roman numerals in this translation.

[4] The restoration of the last entry (after the break) is reasonably sure since the year in question is known from other sources as a leap year, and the intercalary month normally came at the end of the year.

[5] This is the name of the fourth year of King Amar-Suen of Ur (ca. 2042 BCE).

THE *BALA*-CONTRIBUTIONS FOR ONE MONTH (3.144B)
(AUCT 1:209)

(1-2) 1 fatted ox (for) Ninsun, the evening of the first day of the month,[6]
(3-5) 2 fatted oxen, the evening of the second day of the month, 1 fatted ox, the evening of the third day of the month, (for) Enki-nin-ul-íl,[7]
(6-8) 1 fatted ox, (for) Ulmashitum, 1 fatted ox (for) Annunitum, the evening of the seventeenth day of the month,
(9-10) 1 fatted ox (for) Ninhursag-nubanda, the evening of the twentieth day of the month:
(11-13) turn (BALA) of Nanna-zishagal governor of Girsu, withdrawn from Ur-shugalamma.
(14-15) Month I, year that Enmahgal-anna the high priestess of Nanna was installed.

[6] Lit., "one day had elapsed (from) the month."
[7] A rare manifestation of Enki; his temple is mentioned in another Drehem account text dated two years later; cf. Sauren 1978:333.

REFERENCES

Texts and translations: *COS* 3.144A: Hallo 1960:93, 113; *COS* 3.144B: Sigrist 1984:209.

3. WEIGHTS AND MEASURES (3.145)

William W. Hallo

Babylonian weights and measures find some echo in biblical metrology; cf. Powell 1987-90; 1992.

(1) 3 vessels of one large *kor*[1] [a]
(2) 1 second-quality vessel[2]
(3) 7 one-*seah* vessels[3] [b]
(4) for the stele of Enlil[4]
(5) from Inim-[...]
(6) receipted by Nig-urum
(7) in the month of (Umma's) BALA-obligation.[5]
(8) Year after the year when the wall (against) the Amorites was built.[6]

(Seal impression)
Nig-urum the scribe, son of Lu-Shara.

a 1 Kgs 5:2 etc.
b 2 Kgs 7:1 etc.

[1] For the DUG.GUR.LAGAB$_2$, see Salonen 1966:59, 285f. and cf. Sigrist 1990:243:9(!).
[2] Cf. Salonen 1966:61.
[3] Cf. Salonen 1966:285.
[4] This is the stele for which the next year was named; cf. above, 3.142, n. 3.
[5] Cf. above, 3.144, n. 1.
[6] I.e. the fifth year of Shu-Sin, or ca. 2032 BCE. The wall is probably a remake of Shulgi's wall (above, 3.131, n. 5).

REFERENCES

Sigrist 2000 No. 1562; Sharlach 2000:135.

SUMERIAN BIBLIOGRAPHY

ALI, F. A.
1964 *Sumerian Letters: Two Collections from the Old Babylonian Schools*. Ann Arbor, MI: University Microfilms.

BODINE, W. R.
2001 "A Model Contract of an Exchange/Sale Transaction." Pp. 41-54 in *Historiography in the Cuneiform World*. RAI 45/1. Ed. by T. Abusch et al. Bethesda, MD: CDL Press.

BUCHANAN, B.
1965 "A Dated 'Persian Gulf' Seal and its Implications." Pp. 204-209 + pl. xvi in *Studies Landsberger*.

ÇIĞ, M., H. KIZILYAY and A. FALKENSTEIN.
1959 "Neue Rechts- und Gerichtsurkunden der Ur III-Zeit aus Lagaš aus den Sammlungen der Istanbuler Archäologischen Museen." *ZA* 53:51-92.

CRAWFORD, V. A.
1954 "Texts and Fragments." *JCS* 8:46.

VAN DIJK, J.
1963 "Neusumerische Gerichtsurkunden in Bagdad." *ZA* 55:70-90.

EDZARD, D. O.
1968 *Sumerische Rechtsurkunden des III. Jahrtausends aus der Zeit vor der III. Dynastie von Ur*. ABAW Phil.-hist. Kl. Abhandlungen n.F. 67. Munich: Bayerische Akademie der Wissenschaften.

FALKENSTEIN, A.
1956 *Die neusumerischen Gerichtsurkunden*. 3 vols. ABAW Phil.-hist. Kl. Abhandlungen n.F. 40. Munich: Bayerische Akademie der Wissenschaften.

FISH, T.
1932 *Catalogue of Sumerian Tablets in the John Rylands Library*. Manchester: Manchester University Press.

GELB, I. J., P. STEINKELLER, and R. M. WHITING.
1991 *Earliest Land Tenure Systems in the Near East: Ancient Kudurrus*. OIP 104. Chicago: Oriental Institute, University of Chicago.

GOMI, T.
1982 *Wirtschaftstexte der Ur III-Zeit aus dem British Museum*. Materiali per il Vocabolario Neosumerico 12. Rome: Multigrafica Editrice.

GREENGUS, S.
1969-70 "A Textbook Case of Adultery in Ancient Mesopotamia." *HUCA* 40-41:33-44.

GRÉGOIRE, J.-P.
1981 *Inscriptions et archives administratives cunéiformes*. Materiali per il Vocabolario Neosumerico 10. Rome: Multigrafica Editrice.

HALLO, W. W.
1960 "A Sumerian Amphictyony." *JCS* 14:88-114.
1965 "A Mercantile Agreement from the Reign of Gungunum of Larsa." Pp. 199-203 in *Studies Landsberger*.
1991 "The Death of Kings." Pp. 148-165 in *Studies Tadmor*.
1991a "Information from Before the Flood: Antediluvian Notes from Babylonian and Israel." *Maarav* 7:173-181.
1995 "Slave Release in the Biblical World in Light of a New Text." Pp. 79-93 in *Studies Greenfield*.
In press "A Model Court Case Concerning Inheritance." Pp. 139-152 in *Studies Jacobsen 2*.

HUBER, F.
2000 "Au sujet de nom du chancellier d'Ur III, Ir-Nanna ou Ir-mu." *NABU* 2000/1:10 No.6.

LIMET, H.
1959 "La clause du double en droit néo-sumérien." *Or* 38:520-532.

MICHALOWSKI, P.
1975 "The Bride of Simanum." *JAOS* 95:716-719.
1976 *The Royal Correspondence of Ur*. Ph.D. dissertation. Yale University.
1980-83 "Königsbriefe." *RLA* 6:51-59.

OPPENHEIM, A. L.
1948 *Catalogue of the Cuneiform Tablets of the Wilberforce Eames Collection in the New York Public Library*. AOS 32. New Haven: American Oriental Society.

OWEN, D. I.
1971-72 "A Unique Ur III Letter-Order in the University of North Carolina." *JCS* 24:133f.
1980 "A Sumerian Letter from an Angry Housewife (?)." Pp. 189-202 in *Studies Gordon 2*.
1982 *Neo-Sumerian Archival Texts Primarily from Nippur*. Winona Lake: Eisenbrauns.

POHL, A.
1937 *Rechts- und Verwaltungsurkunden der III. Dynastie von Ur*. TMH n.F. 1/2. Leipzig: J. C. Hinrichs.

PORADA, E.
1971 "Remarks on Seals found in the Gulf States." *Artibus Asiae* 33:331-337 and pls. ix-x.

POWELL, M. A.
1978 "Ukubi to Mother ... The Situation is Desperate." *ZA* 68:163-195.
1987-90 "Masse und Gewichte. *RLA* 7:457-517.
1992 "Weights and Measures." *ABD* 6:897-908.

ROTH, M. T.
1979 *Scholastic Tradition and Mesopotamian Law: a Study of FLP 1287, a Prism in the Free Library of Philadelphia*. Ph.D. Dissertation. University of Pennsylvania.

SALONEN, A.
1966 *Die Hausgeräte der alten Mesopotamier ... Teil II: Gefässe*. AASF B 144.

SAUREN, H.
1978 *Les tablettes cunéiformes de l'époque d'Ur des collections de la New York Public Library*. Publications de l'Institut Orientaliste de Louvain 19. Louvain-la-Neuve: Institut Orientaliste, Université Catholique de Louvain.
SHARLACH, T.
2001 Review of Sigrist 2000. *JCS* 52:131-137.
SIGRIST, M.
1984 *Neo-Sumerian Account Texts in the Horn Archaeological Museum*. AUCT 1.
1990 *Tablettes du Princeton Theological Seminary: Époque d'Ur III*. Occasional Publications of the Samuel Noah Kramer Fund 10. Philadelphia: University Museum.
2000 *Texts from the Yale Babylonian Collections*. 2 vols. Sumerian Archival Texts 2-3. Bethesdada, MD: CDL Press.
SNELL, D. C.
2001 *Flight and Freedom in the Ancient Near East*. CHANE 8. Leiden: Brill.
STEINKELLER, P.
1989 *Sale Documents of the Ur III Period*. FAOS 17. Stuttgart: Franz Steiner.
THUREAU-DANGIN, F.
1903 *Recueil de tablettes chaldéennes*. Paris: Ernest Leroux.
VELDHUIS, N.
1997 *Elementary Education at Nippur: the Lists of Trees and Wooden Objects*. Ph.D. Dissertation, University of Groningen.
WATSON, P. J.
1986 *Neo-Sumerian Texts from Drehem*. Warminster: Aris & Phillips.
WILCKE, C.
1969 "Zur Geschichte der Amurriter in der Ur-III-Zeit." *WO* 1-31.

ADDENDA

1. THE DISPUTE BETWEEN A MAN AND HIS *BA* (3.146)

Nili Shupak

This work was probably written in either the First Intermediate Period or at the beginning of the Middle Kingdom. The surviving papyrus — Berlin 3024 — dates to the Middle Kingdom. The beginning of the manuscript — which probably contained a narrative frame in prose similar to those appearing in other compositions belonging to the genre of speculative wisdom literature[1] — is lost. The existing text suffers from some lacunae and at times contains obscure passages. This difficult work has given rise to controversy in research, and various translations and interpretations have been given.[2]

The text is usually taken to be an account of a discussion between an individual and his *ba* (soul) weighing up the value of life against the merits of death. According to this view, one of the disputants, either the man or the *ba*, favors death over life.[3] But this interpretation forces one to assume serious inconsistencies and contradictions in the text.[4] Hence a preferable assumption would be that of a monologue reflecting the internal struggle of a despairing man.[5] The man, weary of life as a result of private misfortune, wrestles with two opposing perspectives of life versus death. This being the inner psychological situation of the man, one should not look for systematic thought or a rational plot in the composition.

One of the important topics in the monologue is the futility of practices designed to bring about immortality. Another subject which occupies center stage is the relation of the *ba* to the body. The traditional belief that the dead man might not achieve resurrection unless his *ba* rejoins him in the world beyond, finds here its expression.[6]

"The Dispute" is composed in three main styles: prose, symmetrically structured speech, and lyric poetry.[7] The climax of the whole composition lies in the poetical section which contains four poems presented by the man.[8]

The juxtaposition of the sufferings of our hero and the replies of his *ba* call to mind the figure of the tortured righteous man and the dispute between him and his friends in the Book of Job. The doubt about immortality and the summons to enjoy life while it lasts is reminiscent of the doctrine of Ecclesiastes as well as the reflections expressed in the Egyptian Harpers' Songs.

There is also a resemblance in form and content between this work and the following Mesopotamian wisdom texts: "Man and his God," "The Poem of the Righteous Sufferer," "The Babylonian Theodicy," and "The Dialogue between Master and Servant," as well as "The Epic of Gilgamesh."[9]

The First Speech of the Ba (1-3)[10]

[...] (1)[...] their tongue is not partial [...] payment their tongue is not partial.[11]

The First Speech of the Man (3-30)

I opened my mouth to my *ba* that I might answer[a]
what it had said:[12]

(5) This is too much for me today,
My *ba* does not talk with me.
It is too great for exaggeration,
It is like ignoring me.

[a] Pss 103:1, 2, 22; 104:1, 35; Lam 3:24; Eccl 1:16; 2:1, 15; 3:17-18

[1] Cf. "The Eloquent Peasant," "The Complaints of Khakheperre-sonb," and "The Prophecies of Neferti." See *COS* 1.43-45.

[2] For a summary of the variety of interpretations see Williams 1962:49-52; Barta 1969:101-116; and lately Tobin 1991:341-343.

[3] E.g. Wilson 1955:405; Erman 1966:86; Goedicke 1970 passim; Faulkner 1972:201; Lichtheim 1973:163; Griffith 1992:110.

[4] See Faulkner 1956:31 n.11.

[5] Žabkar 1968:122; Tobin 1991:341-363; Renaud 1991:52-53.

[6] Herrmann 1957:69-71, 78-79; Žabkar 1968:122-123.

[7] Cf. Lichtheim 1973:163; Renaud 1991:18-19.

[8] The poems usually consist of three verses of uniform theme and structure: The first verse of every stanza belonging to the same poem is identical. This usage of identical opening formulas is common also in "The Admonitions" (*COS* 1.42) n. 2; and "The Eloquent Peasant" (*COS* 1.43); see Shupak 1989-1990:38-39, Table II.

[9] See Beyerlin 1978:133-142. Cf. esp. "Man and his God" (*COS* 1.179) l. 35ff; and "The Poem of the Righteous Sufferer" (*COS* 1.153) Table I, ll. 48ff, 85-92 with "The Dispute" 103-104, 114-115, 117-118; "The Poem of the Righteous Sufferer" (*COS* 1.153) Table I, l. 53 with "The Dispute" 86ff.

[10] *ba* "soul, personality."

[11] This passage probably concerns an appeal to the gods to intervene in the dispute and to pass judgement between the two litigants.

[12] For the usage and the meaning of the literary pattern of man speaking to his soul or to his heart in Eg. and Heb. speculative wisdom literature see "The Prophecies of Neferti" (*COS* 1.45) n. 9 and "The Complaints of Khakheperre-sonb" (*COS* 1.44) n. 13.

My *ba* shall not go,[13]
It shall attend to me in this [...]
[...] in my body like a net of cord.[14]
(10) It will not succeed in fleeing on the day of pain!
Behold, my *ba* misleads me (but) I do not listen (12) to it;
It drags me towards death, before I come to it,[15]
And casts [me] on the fire until I am burned.
... (15) It shall approach me on the day of pain,
And it shall stand on that side as does Neḥepu.[16]
It is that which goes out and brings itself.[17]
My *ba* is too ignorant to subdue suffering in life,
Leading[18] me towards death before I come to it,
Sweeten (20) the West for me! Is it difficult?
Life is a transitory state: The trees they fall.[b]
Trample on evil, put down my misery!
May Thoth[19] who appeases the gods, judge[20] me[c];
May Khons (25) who writes truly, defend me;
May Re who calms the sun-bark, hear my complaint;[21]
May Isdes[22] defend me in the Holy Chamber ...[23]
Because my suffering is too heavy a burden ...[24]
It will be pleasant that the gods defend the secrets of my body.

The Second Speech of the Ba (30-33)

What my *ba* said to me:[25]
"Are you not a man? Are you not alive?
What do you gain when you worry about life like a possessor of wealth?"

The Second Speech of the Man (33-55)

I said:
I did not go (even though) that is on the ground.[26]
Surely, if you run away, nobody will (35) take care of you.[27]
Every criminal says: "I shall seize you."
Although you are dead, your name lives;
That place[28] of rest, the heart's goal,
The West is a dwelling place, a voyage [...]
(40) If my *ba* listens to me without malice,
And its heart is in accord with me, it will be fortunate.
I shall cause it to reach the West like him who is in his pyramid,
Whose burial a survivor attends.
I shall make a shelter (?)[29] over your corpse,
So that you make envious another *ba* (45) which is weary.
I shall make a shelter (?),[29] then it will not be cold,
So that you will make envious another *ba* which is hot.
I shall drink water at the pond, where I shall raise up a shade,
So that you will make envious another *ba* which is hungry.
If you lead (50) me towards[30] death in this manner,
You will not find a place to rest in the West.
Be tolerant, my *ba*, my brother,
Until my heir comes, one who will make offerings,
Who will stand at the tomb on the day of burial,
And prepare (?) a bier (55) for the necropolis.

The Third Speech of the Ba (55-85)

My *ba* opened its mouth to me (56) that it might answer what I said:
If you think of a burial it is a broken heart. It is a bringing of tears by saddening a man. It is

b Job 14:1-2, 5
c Job 31:6

[13] It seems that the passage refers to the *ba*'s threat to desert the man, thus bringing an end to his existence.

[14] Obscure sentence. For the possibility that it may refer to the release of the *ba* and its departure from the body, see Williams 1962:53.

[15] Here and in ll. 18, 49 the *ba* is described as "dragging" (*sṯᵓ*) and "leading" *(ihm)* the man to death. It is even accused of being ready to take part in his death by fire. This negative behavior of the *ba* stands in contrast to the manner of the ideal *ba* as described in "The Instruction Addressed to Merikare" (*COS* 1.35) 51-53.

[16] The man urges the *ba* to stay with him after his death "on that side," on the world beyond. *Nḥpw* is an obscure word which according to some scholars should be connected with *nḥp*, potter's wheel, i.e. a creator god who recreates the deceased in the world beyond. See Barta 1969:31, n. 17.

[17] An obscure sentence which may describe the visits of the *ba* to the corpse after death.

[18] Eg. *ihm*. The interpretation of this word, which recurs in l. 49, is crucial for understanding the text. The rendering "lead toward," "urge on," "drive" should be preferred to "hold back," "restrain" since *sṯᵓ* "drag" used in l. 12 supports it.

[19] The man appeals to the gods to judge and defend him. Cf. n. 11 above and "The Instruction Addressed to Merikare" (*COS* 1.35) 53-57. The mention of Thoth, the god of writing, and Re, the sun god, in this context is obvious: Thoth plays the role of a secretary in the Judgement of the Dead while Re is the creator of justice (*mᵓᶜt*); cf. "The Eloquent Peasant" (*COS* 1.43) B1 268-269 and ibid. n. 48.

[20] Eg. *wḏᶜ*; see "The Eloquent Peasant" (*COS* 1.43) n. 43.

[21] Eg. *mdw* (*mdt*); see ibid., n. 38.

[22] A deity connected with funerary matters.

[23] The celestial Hall of Judgement.

[24] Cf. ll. 127-128 below and "The Eloquent Peasant" (*COS* 1.43) B1 275.

[25] In the following passage the *ba* urges the man to enjoy life and to forget worry.

[26] The man argues that although he has lost all his wealth (which is "on the ground") he has not died.

[27] In the following lines the unfortunate state of the *ba* which deserts its owner is contrasted with the advantages gained by the *ba* which is loyal to its owner and adheres to him.

[28] I.e. the world beyond.

[29] Eg. *niᵓi* is obscure. For various explanations, see Goedicke 1970:117.

[30] See n. 18 above.

taking a man from his house, casting him on high ground.[31] You will never go out to see (60) the sun![32] [d]

They who built in blocks of granite, and constructed halls (?) in nice pyramids of fine work; the builders become gods,[33] yet their offering stones are destroyed, like the weary ones,[33] who are dead on the riverbank without a survivor (65). The flood takes its toll, and the sun likewise. The fishes of the water's banks talk to them.

Listen to me! Behold, it is good for people to listen.[34] [e] Follow the happy day and forget worry![35] [f]

A commoner[36] plowed his plot. He loaded his harvest (70) into a boat. He towed the sail. When his feast day approached he saw coming the darkness of the north, for he was watching in the boat. As the sun set, he came out with his wife and children but they perished, on a lake infested (75) with crocodiles at night. When at last he sat down, he broke out saying: "I do not weep for that mother, for whom there is no return from the West for another (term) on earth. I grieve for her children broken in the egg, who have seen the face of the crocodile[37] (80) before they have lived."

A commoner asked for a meal and his wife said to him: "It is for supper." He went out to complain (?) for a while. When he came back to his house he was like another person. His wife reasoned with him and he did not listen to her ....

The Third Speech of the Man (85-147)

I opened my mouth to my *ba* that I might answer what it said:

First Poem (86-103)[38]

Behold, my name is detested,[39] [g]
Behold, more than the smell of vultures,
On summer days when the sky is hot.

Behold, my name is detested,
Behold, [more than the smell of] a catch of fish,
(90) On a fishing[40] day when the sky is hot.

Behold, my name is detested,
Behold, more than the smell of ducks,
More than a reed-covert full of waterfowl.

Behold, my name is detested,
Behold, more than the smell of fishermen,
More than the (95) marsh-pools where they had fished.

Behold, my name is detested,
More than a smell of crocodiles,
More than sitting by banks full of crocodiles.

Behold, my name is detested,
More than a woman
About whom lies are told to a man.

Behold, my name is detested (100)
More than a sturdy child,
About whom it is said "He belongs to his (father's) hated one."[41]

Behold, my name is detested,
[More than] a monarch's (?) town,
That plots rebellion behind his back.[42]

Second Poem (103-130)

To whom shall I speak today?[43]

d Job 10:21-22; 17:13; 18:18

e 1 Sam 15:22; Prov 1:8; 4:1, 10, 20; 5:7; 7:24; etc; Eccl 4:17

f Eccl 2:24; 3:12, 22; 5:17; 8:15; 9:7-9; 11:7-8

g Ps 31:12; Job 19:17

---

[31] For a similar description to that appearing in the following lines, i.e. corpses abondoned on the ground or thrown into the river without a burial, see "The Admonitions" (*COS* 1.42) 2.6-2.7; 4.3-4.4 (‖ 5.6-5.7 [not translated]); 6.13.

[32] The image of the world beyond, as a dark place without light from where there is no return brings to mind the description of Sheol (the netherworld) in the Bible; see Scripture References *d*.

[33] The appellations "gods" and "weary ones" relate to the dead. The *ba* argues that the end of kings who build for themselves pyramids and expansive tombs is not better than the poor men whose corpses are scattered on the dyke and are damaged by the water and the sun.

[34] A citation of a wisdom saying, also appearing in "The Tale of Shipwrecked Sailor" (*COS* 1.39) 182. The demand to hear and to listen to the words of the parent-sage-teacher is common in Eg. and other ancient Near Eastern wisdom literature. Cf., e.g. "The Instruction of Ptahhotep" 534-562 (esp. 541); "The Instruction of Amenemope (*COS* 1.47) 3.9ff.; "The Story of Aḥiqar" 57 and Scripture References *e*. For more examples and further discussion, see Shupak 1993:51-57.

[35] The phrase "follow the happy day" meaning "make holiday" reflects ideology that regards a life of pleasure as essential and is the motto of the Harpers' Songs from the Middle and New Kingdom. These songs, which were sung at funeral banquets, contain as well a similar denial of the efficiency of the burial preparations. Cf. Lichtheim 1973:193-197. The declaration that pleasures are the very essence of living also appears in Ecclesiastes and in the Babylonian "Epic of Gilgamesh;" see Scripture References *f* and *ANET* 90; cf. also "The Admonitions" (*COS* 1.42) 8.5-7.

[36] The significance of the two following parables is debated. It seems that they are meant to convey to the man that there are misfortunes greater than his. Cf. Faulkner 1972:204 n.19. For different explanations see Hermann 1939:349 and Goedicke 1970:45-48, 130. For a summary of the various interpretations, see Barta 1969:116-121.

[37] See "The Eloquent Peasant" (*COS* 1.43) n. 24.

[38] The final argument of the man consists of four poems: The first poem concerns the man's private misfortune; the second poem contains a general social admonition; the third one is an eulogy of death while the last one describes the fortunate state of those who live in the world beyond.

[39] I.e. to have a bad reputation. Cf. "The Instruction of Ani" (*COS* 1.46) 3.17: "... lest your name stinks;" cf. also ibid., 5.15 and the Akkadian wisdom text "The Poem of the Righteous Sufferer" (*COS* 1.153) Table I l. 53 (= Beyerlin 1978:138). For a similar description in the Bible, of a sufferer who becomes distasteful to his fellow-men, see Scripture References *g*.

[40] Lit. "catching".

[41] I.e., the child is the offspring of his father's rival.

[42] Lit. "While his back is seen."

[43] The content of the second poem calls to mind similar social admontions appearing in other works belonging to the speculative wisdom

Brothers are evil,[h]
The friends of today do not love.

To whom shall I speak today?
Hearts are greedy,
Everyone robs his friend's property.[i]

[To whom shall I speak today?]
Kindness has perished,
Violence has come to all men.[i]

To whom shall I speak today?
One is contented with evil,
Goodness is cast to the ground everywhere.

To whom shall I speak (110) today?
He who should enrage a man with his evil deeds,
He makes everyone laugh at his evildoing.

To whom shall I speak today?
Men plunder,
Everyone robs his friend.[i]

To whom shall I speak today?[44]
The wrongdoer is as an intimate friend,
The brother with whom one used to collaborate has become (115) an enemy.[j]

To whom shall I speak today?
Yesterday is not remembered,
No one at this time acts for him who has acted.[45]

To whom shall I speak today?
Brothers are evil,[j]
One goes to strangers for affection.

To whom shall I speak today?
Faces are blank,
Everyone turns his face from (120) his brothers.

To whom shall I speak today?
Hearts are greedy,
There is no man's heart in which one can trust.

To whom shall I speak today?
There are no righteous ones,
The land is left to wrongdoers.[46] [k]

To whom shall I speak today?
There is no intimate friend,
One brings an unknown man (125) to complain to him.

h Ps 55:12-13; Job 19:13-14, 19

i Job 24:2-4, 13-17

j Ps 55:12-13; Job 19:13-14, 19

k Eccl 3:16; 5:7

l Job 3:11-13, 20-22; 10:18-19; 13:15; 14:13; 17:13-14

To whom shall I speak today?
There is no contented man,
He with whom one walked is no more.

To whom shall I speak today?
I am burdened with grief,[47]
For lack of an intimate friend.

To whom shall I speak today?
Sin roams the land,
(130) There is no end to it.

Third Poem (130-142)
Death is before me today,[48] [l]
[Like] a sick man's recovery,
Like going out-doors after detention.

Death is before me today,
Like the smell of myrrh,
Like sitting under a sail on a windy day.

Death is before me today,
(135) Like the smell of lotuses,
Like sitting on the shore of drunkenness.

Death is before me today,
Like a trodden way,
Like a man coming home from a campaign.

Death is before me today,
Like the clearing of the sky,
As when a man discovers (?) (140) what he knew not.

Death is before me today,
Like a man who desires to see his home,
After he has spent many years in captivity.

Fourth Poem (142-147)
Truly, he who is there will be a living god,[49]
Punishing the evildoer's crime.

Truly, he who is there will stand in the bark of the sun,
Causing choice things to be given (145) therefrom to the temples.

Truly, he who is there will be a sage,
Who will not be prevented from appealing to Re when he speaks.

---

literature: Cf. ll. 103-104, 114-117 to "The Prophecies of Neferti" (*COS* 1.45) 44-45; 105-106 to ibid., 47; 107-108 to "The Admonitions" (*COS* 1.42) 5.10; 114-115 to ibid., 1.5, 5.10; 115-116 to ibid., 2.2 (not translated), 5.12-5.13.

[44] The stylistic pattern of series of contrasts used in the following lines is characteristic to the speculative wisdom literature see: "The Eloquent Peasant" (*COS* 1.43) n. 32; "The Admonitions" (*COS* 1.42) n. 11; "The Prophecies of Neferti" (*COS* 1.45) n. 29; "The Complaints of Khakheperre-sonb (*COS* 1.44) n. 16.

[45] I.e. kindness is not repaid in the present.

[46] The adjectives $m^{\supset c}tyw$ (righteous ones) and *irw isft* (wrongdoers) derive from the antonyms $m^{\supset c}t$ "justice" and *isft* "wrong" which are signficant to the wisdom ideology; see: "The Eloquent Peasant" (*COS* 1.43) n. 27; "The Prophecies of Neferti" (*COS* 1.45) n. 39; "The Admonitions" (*COS* 1.42) n. 20; "The Complaints of Khakheperre-sonb" (*COS* 1.44) n. 16.

[47] See n. 24 above.

[48] The following eulogy to death calls to mind Job's longing for death; cf. Scripture References *k*. Similar utterances also appear in "The Admonitions" (*COS* 1.42) 4.2-4.3; cf. ibid. n. 16.

[49] The dead will share in the privileges of the gods in the world beyond.

The Fourth Speech of the Ba (147-154)
What my *ba* said to me:
"Throw complaints on the peg,[50] my comrade, my brother. Make offering on the brazier,[51] (150) and cleave to life, as you have said; love me here, when you set aside the West. But when it is wished that you attain the West, that your body goes to earth, I shall alight after you have become and then we shall dwell together.

Colophon (154-155)
It is finished (155) from the beginning till the end as it was found in writing.

[50] Eg. *ẖ*ˀˀ. The meaning of the word is unknown but the determinative indicates a wooden object.

[51] The *ba* urges the man to make offerings to the gods and go on with normal life, promising him to stay with him till his natural death and dwell with him in the hereafter. Cf. Faulkner 1956:39 n. 113. For another opinion which assumes that the reference to offerings suggests funerary ceremonies and therefore the *ba* demands that the man choose between life and death, see e.g. Williams 1962:55-56; cf. also Brunner-Traut 1967:10.

REFERENCES

Text, translations and studies: Barta 1969; Beyerlin 1979; Brunner-Traut 1967; Erman 1966:86-92; Faulkner 1956; 1972:201-209; Goedicke 1970; Griffith 1992; Hermann 1939; Herrmann 1957:62-79; Lichtheim 1973; Renaud 1991; Shupak 1989-90; 1993; Tobin 1991; Williams 1962; Wilson 1955; Žabkar 1968.

BIBLIOGRAPHY

BARTA, W.
1969 *Das Gespräch eines Mannes mit seinem BA*. Berlin.

BEYERLIN, W.
1979 *Near Eastern Religious Texts Relating to the Old Testament*. London.

BRUNNER-TRAUT, E.
1967 "Der Lebensmüde und sein *BA*." *ZÄS* 94:6-15.

ERMAN, A.
1927/66 *The Literature of the Ancient Egyptians*. Trans. by A. M. Blackman. London: Methuen & Co. Reprint New York, 1966 as *The Ancient Egyptians; A Sourcebook of Their Writings*. Original: *Die Literatur der Aegypter*. Leipzig, 1923.

FAULKNER, R. O.
1956 "The Man Who Was Tired of Life." *JEA* 42:21-40.
1972 "The Man Who Was Tired of Life." Pp. 201-209 in *The Literature of Ancient Egypt*. Ed. by W. K. Simpson. New Haven and London: Yale University Press.

GOEDICKE, H.
1970 *The Report about the Dispute of a Man with His Ba*. Baltimore: John Hopkins University Press.

GRIFFITH, J. G.
1992 "The Impress of Egyptian Religion on the Mediaeval 'Dialogue of the Soul and Body'" Pp. 103-118 in *Studies Brunner-Traut*.

HERMANN, A.
1939 "Das Gespräch eines Lebensmüden mit seiner Seele." *OLZ* 42:345-352.

HERRMANN, S.
1957 *Untersuchungen zur Überlieferungsgestalt mittelägyptischer Literaturwerke*. Berlin.

LICHTHEIM, M.
1973 *AEL* 1:163-169.

RENAUD, O.
1991 *Le Dialogue du Désespéré avec son âme. Une interprétation littéraire*. Genève.

SHUPAK, N.
1989-90 "Egyptian 'Prophecy' and Biblical Prophecy: Did the Phenomenom of Prophecy, in the Biblical Sense, Exist in Ancient Egypt?" *JEOL* 31:1-40.
1993 *Where Can Wisdom Be Found? The Sage's Language in the Bible and in Ancient Egyptian Literature*. OBO 130. Freibourg: Universitätsverlag.

TOBIN, V. A.
1991 "A Re-assessment of the *Lebensmüde*." *BiOr* 48:341-363

WILLIAMS, R. J.
1962 "Reflections on the *Lebensmüde*." *JEA* 48:49-56.

WILSON, J. A.
1955 *ANET*, 405-407.

ŽABKAR, L. V.
1968 *A Study of the Ba Concept in Ancient Egyptian Texts*. SAOC 34. Chicago: University of Chicago Press.

THE AKKADIAN ANZU STORY (3.147)

Marianna Vogelzang

The Akkadian Anzu story, known from its incipit as *bin shar dadme*, is an epic or at least narrative poem which describes how the monstrous and legendary bird Anzu steals the Tablet of Destinies from the supreme god Enlil, and in doing so misappropriates the sovereignty over the universe. The terrified gods meet in a formal assembly under the presidency of the god Anu, in order to select and nominate a champion who will have to defeat Anzu, kill him, retrieve the Tablet of Destinies and thus avert disaster. Their appeals to the gods Adad, Girra and Shara are in vain. The young hero Ninurta however, beseeched by his mother Belet-ili, accepts the order. With the tactical help of Ea, the god of wisdom, he defeats Anzu and thus earns for himself great fame and universal worship.[1]

The most fully preserved version of the Anzu story is the Standard Babylonian (SB) one. It was apparently produced during the last half or quarter of the second millennium BCE and became the canonical version.[2] It differs from the Old Babylonian version in certain aspects, but the differences do not affect the story's basic plot or format. And despite revision of wording, the SB text and the OB text from Susa[3] correspond to each other so closely that there may have been a genetic relationship, although this cannot be stated with certainty.[4]

STANDARD BABYLONIAN VERSION

(Tablet I)

Prologue (lines 1-14)

Of the son of the king of habitations, the illustrious, the beloved of Mami,
The Mighty One, I will ever chant, the divine child of Enlil.
Ninurta, the illustrious, the beloved of Mami,
The Mighty One, I will praise, the divine child of Enlil.
The offspring of the Ekur, foremost among the Anunnaki, the Eninnu's hope,
Who brings water to the fold, arbor, *slough* , country and town.
The floodwave of battles, the dancer with the sash, (so) brave.
Whose attack the tireless raging demons fear.
Hear the praise of his power, of the mighty one,
Who in his fierceness conquered, captured the Mountain of Stones,
Who mastered winged Anzu with his weapon,
Who killed Kusarikku[5] in the midst of the sea.
The strong one, a killer with his weapon,
The mighty one, the fleet one, who knows how to handle battle and fight.

The Introduction of Anzu (lines 15-64)

Up till that time among the Igigi no daises had been built,
And the Igigi were gathered for the supremacy over them.
Fashioned were the rivers, the Tigris and the Euphrates,
But the [sourc]es were not sending [their] waters to the land.
And the seas [ ]
The clouds were absent from the horizon [ ].
The [Igig]i, being gathered from all parts,
To Enlil, their father, the war[rior]
His children bring [the news]:
"He[ed you well] the happy word!
On Mount Hihi a tree [ ]
In her bosom the Anu[nnaki]
Anz[u] has been born.
A saw [his be]ak [ ]

[six fragmentary lines]

At [his] scre[ech]
The southwind [ ]
The mighty [ ]

[1] So it appears that the story contains the following main oppositions of persons: a. Anzu versus Enlil (demon :: supreme god); b. Ninurta versus Anzu (hero :: demon); c. Ninurta versus Enlil (son :: father). These three oppositions form the basis of the three major divisions of the story, and thus of the different actions: the theft of the Tablet of Destines, the battle of the hero and the rebellious son. For those who are interested in universal literary themes and motives, see Thompson 1977.

[2] The SB mss. of the text span a period from Middle Assyrian till Neo-Assyrian and Neo-Babylonian times; at the latest then, the editing and rewriting that produced the Standard version occurred about 1200 BCE. But the copying of the OB text did not necessarily cease, as the mss. from Susa may show, nor did the copying of other traditional stories about Ninurta and Anzu.

[3] Susa was the capital of Elam, situated on the Ulai river.

[4] For a somewhat different opinion, see Reiner 1985:63-66; Bottero 1976.

[5] Bison or bull-man; cf. Ellis 1989.

The mass [ ]
Duststorms [ ]
They gathered together a[nd]
The four-fold wind A[nzu?]
The fa[ther of the gods] saw him,
And thou[ght] of what th[ey] had said.
He studied Anzu closely [ ]
Deliberated wi[th Ea?]
"Who bore [ ]
Why this [ ]?"
[Ea] answered the query of his heart,
Ninshiku[6] [addresses a word] to Enlil:
"Of course the waters of the flo[od?]
The pure waters of the A[psu?]-gods [ ]
And the wide earth conceived him.
It is he who [was born?] in the mountain-rocks.
It is Anzu you have seen [ ]
Let him enter your service, don't let hi[m fly away from you!]
In the sanctuary, to the cella-seat, let him ever bar the entrance!

[three fragmentary lines]

To the ad[vice] he spoke to him the gods con[sented].
The shrine he took for evermore [ ]
And the assignments he gave to all the gods.
He repeated the decree and Anzu took [his place].
With the entrance of the cella, which he had brought to completion, Enlil (had) charged him.

The Theft of the Tablet of Destinies (lines 65-87)

He often bathed before him in the pure waters.
His eyes often watched the tokens of the supremacy:
His crown of sovereignty, his robe of divinity,
The Tablet of Destinies which he controlled did Anzu often watch.
He often watched the father of the gods, the god (of) Duranki[7]
And in his mind imagined removing the supremacy.
Anzu often watched the father of the gods, the god (of) Duranki,
And in his heart imagined removing the supremacy:
"I myself will take the gods' Tablet of Destinies
And gather the assignments of all the gods.
I will win the throne, be the master of the offices!
I will give command to all the Igigi!"
Thus his heart plotted rebellion,
And at the entrance to the cella, where he used to gaze, he awaited the break of day.
When Enlil was bathing in the pure waters,
Naked, while his crown lay on the throne,
To the Tablet of Destinies his hands reached out.
The supremacy he took — suspended are the offices!
Anzu flew off and to his mountain [made his way].
Numbness spread about; si[lence] prevailed.
The father, their counsellor Enlil, was speechless.
The cella shed its awesome sheen!
[In the up]perworld they milled about at the news.

The assembly of the gods and the selection of the hero (lines 88-209; Tablet II, lines 1-27)

Anu opened his mouth to speak,
Said to the gods, his children:
"Who shall slay Anzu and
Thereby exalt his name in all habitations"?
[The Canal-Inspec]tor they summoned, the son of Anu.
Explaining to him the news, he addresses him.
Adad, the Canal-Inspector they summoned, the son of Anu.
Explaining to him the news, he addresses him:
"Mighty Adad, ferocious Adad! Your attack must not turn back!
Strike Anzu down with your weapon!
Your name will be great in the assembly of the great gods.
[Among the go]ds, your brothers, you shall have no rival.
Daises there shall be and be built.
Place your shrines across the world.
Your shrines shall reach into the Ekur.[8]
Distinguish yourself before the gods and Mighty One shall be your name!"
Adad answered the charge,
Addresses the word to Anu, his father:
["My father], who would hasten off to the unaccessible [mountain]?
[Who] can Anzu's [conquer]or be among the gods, your children?
To the [Tablet of Destini]es his hands reached out.
[The supremac]y he took, suspended are the offices.
[Anzu] flew off and to his mountain made his way.
[The utterance] of his mouth [has become] like that of the god, the god (of) Duranki.
[If he speaks, the one he curs]es shall turn to clay!"
[At the utterance of hi]s [mouth], the gods [were dispirited].
[He turned away, refused to go].
[Girra they called, the son of Annunitu].
[Explaining to him the news, he addresses him]:

(Identical request and refusal; lines 117-125)

[Shara they cal]led, the son of Ishtar.
[Explaining to him the ne]ws, he addresses him:

(Identical request and refusal; lines 128-156)

[6] A manifestation of Enki/Ea.
[7] A temple at Nippur; hence a name of Nippur as "bond of heaven and earth."
[8] The temple of Enlil at Nippur.

The gods grew silent, abandoned counsel;
The Igigi, where they sat, were gloomy, in troubled mood.
****
[But] the lord of wisdom, who dwells in the Apsu, the sagacious one,
With the cunning of his mind, formed a plan.
The wise Ea formed (it) in his heart.
Whatever he had thought of in his mind, to Anu he tells:
"Let me speak and seek out a god,
And designate the conqueror of Anzu in the assembly!
Let me alone seek out a god,
And designate the conqueror of Anzu in the assembly!"
When the Igigi heard this word of his,
The Igigi, of burden free, ran to kiss his feet.
Ninshiku opened his mouth to speak,
Telling the plan to Anu and Dagan:
"Let them summon Belet-ili,[9] the sister of the gods,
The sagacious one, the coun[sellor of] the gods, [her] brothers.
Her supreme dignity let them proclaim in the as[sembly].
The gods must honor [her] in their assembly.
The plan that is in my heart, [I will tell] her!"
They called Belet-ili, the sister of [the gods],
The sagacious one, the counsellor of the gods, [her brothers].
Her supreme dignity they proclaimed [in the assembly].
The gods, in their assembly, hon[ored her].
With the cunning of his mind Ea revealed the plan.
"Previously [we would address you as] Mami,
Now Mistress of al[l the gods shall be your name]!
Give (us) the Mighty One, the illustrious, [your beloved],
The Broad of Chest, who knows how to hand[le battle and combat!]
Give (us) the Mighty One, the illustrious, your beloved,
The Broad of Chest, who knows how to handle battle and combat!
Lord in the assembly of the gods [ ]
Most glorious he shall be in [ ]
In al[l the dwellings he shall exalt his name?]
A shrine [ ]
Lord [ ]
[ ]
In [ ]."
[When she heard this speech of his],
[The most exalted Mistress of the gods agreed to it].
[After she had spoken, the Igigi rejoiced],
[From burden free, they ran to kiss her feet].
[From the assembly of the gods she summoned her son],
The beloved of her heart; instructing him she said to [him]:
"I[n the presence of Anu and Dagan]
The st[ate of their offices they have discussed in the assembly].
[It is to all] the Igigi [that I gave birth].
I formed al[l of them, each and everyone].
I formed the totality of the gre[at Anunnaki].
The supremacy [to my brother],
To Anu the kingsh[ip of heaven I assigned].
The Tablet of Destinies, which in the assembly [ ] [ ]
He took away from Enlil, [he has spurned your] fat[her].
The offices he has stolen, [gather]ed all of th[em]".

(Tablet II)

"Bar [the road], put an end to it!
For the gods whom I have created bring forth brightness!
Mobilize your entire battle-array!
Let your seven evil winds go against him!
Defeat the winged Anzu!
Calm the earth I created, disturb his abode!
Let terror thunder over him!
Let him tremble at your furious battle!
Let the entire whirlwind hem him in!
Draw the bow, let the arrows carry poison!
Like a demon's let your countenance become!
Send out a fog, so that it discloses not your appearance!
Let your radiance go against him!
May your onslaught be majestic, an awesome glow be yours!
May the sun not shine above (him),
May the bright day turn into (the deepest) darkness for him!
Slit his throat, defeat Anzu!
Let the winds carry his wings as (good) tidings
To your father Enlil's house, the Ekur.
Surge through the midst of the mountains, hurry and
Cut the throat of evil Anzu!
Let kingship (re-)enter the Ekur,
Let the offices return to the father who begot you!
Daises there shall be and shall be built!
Place your shrines across the world!
Your [shrines] shall reach into the Ekur!
Distinguish yourself before the gods and Mighty One shall be your name!"

Ninurta goes to battle, but fails (lines 28-69)

When the hero heard the speech of his mother,
He braced himself, trembled and went to his mountain.
My lord harnessed the Seven-of-Battle.

[9] "Mistress of the gods," a name of the mother goddess.

The hero harnessed the seven evil winds,
Seven whirlwinds which stir up the dust.
He mobilized raging battle, initiated combat.
They rush into combat at his side.
On the mountain-side Anzu and Ninurta saw one another
And when he saw him, Anzu, he raged at him.
He gnashed his teeth like an Umu-demon, his awe-inspiring glow covered the mountains.
He roared like a lion, seized with anger!
In the ire of his heart, he called to [the he]ro:
"I have carried off every single office,
And the assignments of all the gods I direct!
Who are you to come to fight with me? Reveal your intention!"
He rushed against him and forth to him went the word of his mouth;
The hero Ninurta [answered] Anzu:
"I [am Ninurta, the ho]pe(?) of the god (of) Duranki!
He who prese[rves the foundation of] the wide earth, Ea, king of destinies,
According to his [destiny (for me)] I have come to fight with you, to crush you!"
When Anzu heard the word of his mouth,
He raged and let loose in the midst of the mountain his shriek.
It became dark, the face of the mountain was covered.
Shamash, the light of the gods, became quite dark.
With Anzu's scream, the attack roared forth.
In the midst of the strife, the battle drew near, the turmoil thickened.
The front of the armor is drenched with blood.
The clouds of death sent rain, arrowheads flashed.
It whizzed between them, the battle roared!
The Mighty One, the illustrious, the son of Mami,
The hope of Anu and Dagan, the beloved of Ninshiku,
[Be]nt, nocked[10] the bow with a reed-arrow.
From the breast of the bow he loosened the reed-arrow at him,
But it did not approach Anzu: the reed-arrow turned back!
For Anzu called to it:
"O reed-arrow that has come to me, return to your canebrake!
Frame of [the bow], to your forests!
String, to the back of the sheep! Feathers, return to the birds!"
As he raised the Tablet of Destinies of the gods with his hands,
The darts, carried by the bowstring, could not approach his body.
The battle stilled, the combat ceased.
The weapons ceased functioning in the midst of the mountain; they did not vanquish Anzu!

Ninurta asks for help (lines 70-99)

He called Adad, addressing the word to him:
"Report to him, to Ea-Ninshiku, the event you have seen.
'O lord, thus Ninurta: Anzu was encircled.
Ninurta, covered with the dust of warfare,
[Bent], nocked the bow with a reed-arrow;
Drew the bow and loosened the reed-arrow at him.
But it did not approach Anzu, the reed-arrow turned back!"
For Anzu called to it:
"O reed-arrow that has come to me, return to your canebrake!
Frame of the bow, to your forest!
String, to the back of the sheep! Feathers, return to the birds!"
As he raised the Tablet of Destinies of the gods with his hands,
The darts, carried by the bowstring, could not approach his body.
The battle stilled, the combat ceased.
The weapons ceased functioning in the midst of the mountain;
they did not vanquish Anzu!'"
(Prince) Adad bowed down, took the message.
The news of the fight he brought to Ea-Ninshiku.
Whatever the lord had said to him, he repeated to Ea:

(follows the identical message; lines 87-100)

The advice of Ea-Ninshiku (lines 101-144)

When [Ninshi]ku heard the word of his son,
He called [Adad], addressing the word to him:
"Report to your lord the burden of my message.
Whatever I say, transmit safely to him:
'Let battle not abate, prove your strength!
Wear him out; at the onslaught of the stormwind
make him droop his wings.
Take the sword after (shooting?) your arrow.
Cut off his wings, scatter (them) to the right and the left!
Let him see his wings; this will rob him of speech.
"Wings to wings!" he will cry; fear him no (longer)!
Bend your bow and from its breast let loose the reed-arrows like lightning!
Let wings and pinions dance like bloody things!
Slit his throat, defeat Anzu!
Let the winds carry his wings as (good) tidings
To your father Enlil's house, the Ekur.
Surge through the midst of the mountains, hurry, and
Cut the throat of evil Anzu!
Let kingship (re-)enter the Ekur.
Let the offices return to the father who begot

[10] Lit. "filled"; cf. *CAD* M/1:185 j.

you.
Daises there shall be and shall be built.
Place your shrines across the world.
Your shrines shall reach into the Ekur.
Distinguish yourself before the gods, and Mighty
One shall be your name!'"
Adad bowed down, took the message,
Brought the news of the fight to Ninurta.
Whatever Ea had said, he repeated to him:

(The identical message follows; lines 127-145)

When the lord [heard this speech] of Ea-Ninshiku,
He braced himself, trembled and went to his mountain.
[My] lord harnessed the Seven of Battle,
The hero harnessed the seven evil winds,
Whirlwinds which stir up the dust of warfare!

Tablet III

Ninurta's second and final battle

[two lines fragmentary]
Armor [ ]
Constantly striking one another [ ]
The blaze, its glow [ ]
To the four winds the stormwind [ ]
The weapons — in dread protection — he struck and struck.
Both were bathed in the sweat of battle.
Anzu grew tired — at the onslaught of the storm wind he drooped his wings.
The Lord took his arrows *towards the bottom*.
He cut off his pinions, scattered them both right and left.
When he (Anzu) saw his wings, they took away *the formula* of his mouth.
When he cried "Wings to wings" — the arrow flew against him.
The shaft passed through the *casing* of his heart,
He made the dart pierce through pinion and wing.
The shaft pierced through his heart and lungs.
He flooded, brought violent action to the midst of the mountains.
Flooded in his fury the wide world.
Flooded the midst of the mountains, killed evil Anzu!
The hero Ninurta took control of the Tablet of Destinies of the gods.
As a sign of his good tidings
The wind bore Anzu's wings.
When he saw his sign, Dagan rejoiced.
He summoned all the gods, saying to them in joy:
"The Mighty One has *outroared* Anzu in his mountain.
"He has regained control of Anu and Dagan's weapons.
"Go to him, that he may come to us.
"Let him rejoice, let him dance, let him make music,
"Let him stand with the gods, his brothers,
that he may hear the secrets,
"[ ] the secrets of the gods.
"[ ] with the gods, his brothers, let [ ] bestow on him the offices."
[Ea?] opened his mouth and spoke,
Saying [to] Dagan these words:
"[ ] he took the skin.
When he killed evil Anzu in the mountains,
The hero Ninurta regained the Tablet of Destinies of the gods.
Send to him, let him come to you,
Let him place the Tablet of Destinies in your lap!"
Enlil opened his mouth and spoke,
Saying to Nusku, his vizier, these words:
"Nusku, go outside,
"Bring Birdu before me!"
Nusku went outside,
Brought Birdu into Enlil's presence.
Enlil opened his mouth and spoke,
Saying to Birdu these words:
"Birdu, I will send you [ ]

[gap of a few lines]

Ninurta's rebellion

Ninurta [opened] his mouth [and spoke,]
[Saying these words] to Birdu:
"Birdu, why did you come here so aggressively?"
Birdu op[ened his mouth and spoke,]
[Saying these words] to Ninurta, his lord:
"My lord [ ] to you.
"Your father Enlil sent me,
"To say: 'The gods have heard
'That [you killed] evil Anzu in the midst of the mountain.'
"They were happy, glad and [ ].
"Before you [ ]
"Go to him [ ]
"Let him be hap[py]

[three lines fragmentary]

Ninurta [opened his mouth and spoke, saying to Birdu:]
"Why [surrender] the para[phernalia of the supremacy!]
"Like the coun[sellor of the gods has become the utterance of my mouth!]
"The Tablet of Destinies I will not g[ive back !"]

[fragmentary lines, then breaks off]

Speech to Ninurta (lines 113-160)

"Let [ ] not be built,
"[ ] Anzu in the Ekur.
"[ ] the sign of the hero.
"Let him look upon evil Anzu [in] the greatness of his might.
"Hero, in your might you could slay mountains.
"You captured Anzu, you could slay his might.
"You could slay the might of winged Anzu.
"Because you were so brave and slew the

mountains.
"You have made all enemies submit before your father Enlil.
"O Ninurta, because you were so brave and slew the mountains!
You have made all enemies submit before your father Enlil!
"You have gained lordship, each and every divine authority,
"Who was ever created like you, divine authority of the mountain!
"Greatness has been given you at the daises of the gods of destinies.
"Nisaba they called your purification rites.
They called your name in the furrow Ningirsu.
"They assigned to you the entire shepherdship of the people.
"Your name Guardian of the Throne they have given (the exercise of) kingship.
"In Elam they gave (you) the name Hurabtil.
"In Susa they speak of you as Inshushinak.
"In Ibbi-Anum they gave you the name Lord of Mystery.
"[ ] among the gods your brothers.
"[ ] you father.
"[ ] who marches in front (?).
"They gave [(you) your name Pabilsag] in Egal-mah.
"They [cal]led [your name] in Ur.
"They gave [(you) your name] Ninazu in Ekur-mah (?).
"[ ] you your birth(place?) Duranki.
"[In Der?] they speak of you as Ishtaran.
"[In] Zababa.
"[ ] they call (as) his name.
"Your heroism [ ] Enlil over all the gods.
"[ ] to make surpassing your divinity.
"[ ] I praise you!
"In NI.SUR they gave[(you) your name] Lugal-banda.
"In E-igi-kalama (?) they gave [(you) your name] Lugalmarada.
"In E-sikilla they gave [(you) your name] Hero Tishpak.
"[ ] in Bube in Enimma-anku [ ].
"In Kullab they called (you) by your name Hero of Uruk.
"[ ] Belet-ili your mother.
"[ ] Lord of the boundary.
"[ ] Panigingarra.
"[ ] they called.
"[ ] Papsukkal who marches in front.
"[ ] lord, your names are surpassing great among the gods.
"[Lord] of understanding, capable, awesome one.
"Your [counsellor?] Ninshiku, your father Anu.
"[ ] battle and conflict.

[rest fragmentary]

THE OLD BABYLONIAN VERSION

(Tablet II)

After the theft of the Tablet of Destinies: the assembly of the gods and the selection of the hero (lines 1-72)

The supremacy he took away; suspended are the offices.
The father, their counsellor Enlil, was speechless.
<Numbness> was spread about, silence prevailed.
Confused were the Igigi, each and every one of them.
The cella shed its awesome sheen!
The gods of the land came together at the news.
Anu opened his mouth,
Said to the gods his children:
"Gods, who wants to kill Anzu?
I will make his name great everywhere!"
The Canal-Inspector they summoned, the son of Anu;
explaining to him the news, he addresses him:
["O Adad] your attack, strike Anzu down with your weapon!
[Your name will be great] among the great gods.
[Among the gods, your brothers], you shall have no rival!
[Distinguish yourself before] the gods; Mighty One shall be your name!"
[The Canal-Inspector addr]es[ses the word to Anu, his father]:
["My father, who would hasten off to the inaccessible mountain!]
[Who can An]zu['s conqueror be] among [your] children.
[To the Tablet of Destinies he reached out his hands]; he took of the god [his] su[premacy].
[He flew off] to his mountain, has raised his head.
His command [has become] like that of the god (of) Duranki.
[If he speaks, the one he curs]es shall turn to clay!"
[When they heard] his [ans]wer, the gods became upset.
[He turned away], refused to go.
[Gibil they called, the son of Annunitum.
[Explaining to him the ne]ws, he spoke to him.
[Shara they called], the son of Ishtar.
[Explaining] to him the news, he spoke to him.
The gods grew silent, abandoned counsel.

The Igigi, together, we[re gloomy], in troubled mood.
Then the lord of wis[dom, who dwells in the Apsu], the sagacious [Ea],
Told the word of his heart [to Anu], his [father]:
"Let me make a spe[ech and] designate [the conqueror] of Anzu in the assembly!"
When the go[ds of the land] heard [this] word of his,
Of burden free, they ran [to kiss] his feet.
And [he called] Dingirmah, the mi[stress of the de]crees; he pronounced her supreme dignity in the assembly.
"[Give (us)] the Mighty One, the illustrious, your beloved,
The Broad of Chest, who knows how to handle the Seven of Battle.
Ningirsu, the Mighty One, [the illustrious], your beloved.
The Broad of Chest, who knows how to handle the Seven of Battle."
When [she heard] this word of his, the most exalted Dingirmah agreed to it.
After she had spoken, the gods of the lands rejoiced and from burden free ran to kiss her feet.
From the assembly of the gods she summoned
Her son, the beloved of her heart; instructing him, she said to him:
"Before the authority of Anu and Dagan,
The state of their offices they have discussed in the assembly.
It is to all the [Igig]i that I gave birth.
[I formed] the assembly of the gods, I Mami!
I assigned [the supremacy t]o my brother and to Anu the kingship of heaven.
[He has confused the king]ship I assigned.
He took away [the supremacy], he has spurned your father.
[Bar the road], set a time limit!
[For the gods whom] I have created bring forth brightness!
Mobilize your [entire] battle-array!
[Let your seven evil winds] go up to the mountain!
Catch the [winged] Anzu!
[Calm the earth I have cre]ated, disturb his abode!"
[let him] tremble [ ].

[three lines fragmentary]

[Dr]aw the b[ow], let [the arrows] carry poison!
May the curse you shout cast gl[oom] on him!
May he move through darkness, become confused, his vision fail!
Let him not fly away from you; in confrontation may his wings fall.
Like a demon's let your face become; send out a fog so that it discloses not your appearance!
May the E[ver-ris]ing not rise up high; may the bright day become gloomy for him!
Slit his throat, defeat Anzu!
Let the winds carry the wings as (good) tidings
Towards the Ekur, to your father.
Let the winds carry the wings as (good) tidings!"

Ninurta goes to battle (lines 73-80; Tablet III)

When the hero heard the speech of his mother,
The valiant in battle felt strong, [went] to his mountain.
The hitched-up seven [evil winds],
Seven whirlwinds which stir up the dust.
[ ] the hitched-up seven *gululu*'s.
[ ] his battle.
[The seven] evil winds went up to the mountain.
[On the si]de of Anzu's mountain the god met (him).
And when he sa[w him], Anzu, he raged at him.
He gnashed his teeth like an Umu-demon, his awe-inspiring glow wreathed the mountain.

(Tablet III)[11]

[And when he saw him, Anz]u, he raged at him.
[He gnashed his teeth like an Um]u-demon, his awe-inspiring glow wreathed the mountain.
[He roared] like a lion, seized [with] anger.
[In the ire] of his heart, he called to the hero:
["I have carried off] every single office!
You are coming [to fight] with me? [Rev]eal your intention!"
At his words, the hero N[ingirsu] answered Anzu:
[" Duran]ki, who established Duranki, who fixes the decrees,
I have come [to fight with you], as your crusher!"
[ ] [wh]irlwind as armor.
[When he heard] him, he cried out in the midst of the mountains his fu[riou]s shriek.
[ ] bathed in blood.
[ ] the battle roared.
[The son of M]ami, the hope of Anu and Dagan, the beloved of Ninshiku,
He loosed [a reed-arrow] at him, but it did not approach Anzu!
[For he called t]o it: "O arrow that has come to me, re[turn to your canebrake!]
[ ] reed-arrow that has come to me, r[eturn to your canebrake!"]

[Gap of about forty lines]

["] ri[ght and left].
[the w]ord of [his] mouth [ ].
[ ] do [not] fear him!
[the ro]ad!
[ ] his wings may dance!
Surge through [the midst of the mountain], hurry
And do [not] spare [Anzu's] life!

[11] What follows is largely from a ms. based on the so-called Mosul-fragment as published by Saggs 1986; also on the work of Foster 1993:481-485, and Moran 1988:24-28.

[ ] the Ekur, let the offices return to the father who begot you!
(70) [ ] your daises shall be built!
Place your shrines across the [world!"]
[When the hero heard] the speech of his father,
The valiant in battle felt strong, returned to [the mountain].
[in the mi]dst of the battle the fourfold winds there.
[ ] the earth shook, filled [ ].
[The s]un [darkened], the skies were overcast, [his eyes] were ob[scured].
[Anz]u, at the onslaught of the stormwind, [drooped his] wings.

[Tablet ends, continuation lost]

REFERENCES

Text and studies: Labat 1970; Hruška 1975; Bottéro 1976; Hallo and Moran 1979; Saggs 1986; Vogelzang 1988; Dalley 1989; Foster 1993; Cavigneaux 2000; Annus 2001.

BIBLIOGRAPHY

ANNUS, A.
2001 *The Standard Babylonian Epic of Anzu*. SAACT 3. Helsinki: University of Helsinki.
BOTTÉRO, J.
1976 "L'epopée de la Creation." Pp. 77-126 in *Annuaire de la IVe section de l'école des hautes études* 1975-1976, (republished as Ch.IV in J. Bottero, *Mythes et rites de Babylone*. Paris: Libr. H. Champion, 1985) 113-162.
CAVIGNEAUX, A.
2000 "Anzu dans la rue." *NABU* 2000/1:20, no. 19.
DALLEY, S.
1989 *Myths from Mesopotamia*. Oxford: Oxford University Press. 203-227.
ELLIS, M. de Jong
1989 "An Old Babylonian *kusarikku*." Pp. 121-135 in *Studies Sjöberg*.
FOSTER, B. R.
1993 *BM* 1: 481-485.
HALLO, W. W., and W. L. MORAN.
1979 "The First Tablet of the SB Anzu Myth." *JCS* 31:65-115.
HRUŠKA, B.
1975 *Der Mythenadler Anzu in Literatur und Vorstellung des alten Mesopotamien*. Assyriologia 2. Budapest: Eötvös-Loránd-Universität.
LABAT, R., et al.
1970 "Les grands textes de la pensée babylonienne." Pp. 15-349 in *Les Religions du Proche-Orient asiatique*. Paris: Fayard/Denoël.
MORAN, W. L.
1988 "Notes on Anzu." *AfO* 35:24-29.
REINER, E.
1985 *Your Thwarts in Pieces, Your Mooring Rope Cut*. Michigan Studies in the Humanities 5. Ann Arbor: University of Michigan.
SAGGS, H. W. F.
1986 "Additions to Anzu (Mosul-fragment)." *AfO* 33:1-29.
THOMPSON, S.
1977 *The Folktale*. 1st ed. 1946. Berkeley: University of California Press.
VOGELZANG, M. E.
1986 "Kill Anzu! On a point of Literary Evolution." Pp. 61-70 in *RAI* 32.
1988 *Bin Shar Dadme*. Edition and Analysis of the Akkadian Anzu poem. (unpubl. diss.); Groningen: Styx Publications.

INDICES

SCRIPTURE INDEX

GENERAL INDEX

The index aims to include all proper names and to identify their referents as follows:

CN	=	composition name
DN	=	divine name
DNf	=	divine name — feminine
EN	=	ethnic name, language name
GN	=	geographical name
GNm	=	geographical name — modern
MN	=	month name
PN	=	personal name
PNf	=	personal name — feminine
RN	=	royal name
RNf	=	royal name — feminine
TN	=	temple name

No attempt has been made to standardize transcriptions from all the languages represented, as follows:

Akk.	=	Akkadian
Aram.	=	Aramaic
Eg.	=	Egyptian
Heb.	=	Hebrew
Hitt.	=	Hittite
Sum.	=	Sumerian
Ug.	=	Ugaritic
WS	=	West Semitic

Diacritics are entered to the extent feasible. Vowel length is not marked, nor are h, ḥ and ḫ distinguished. Aspirated sibilants are indicated indifferently by sh or š.

REGISTER OF CONTRIBUTORS

Allen, James P.	1.1-17; 3.1-5
Alster, Bendt	1.174-177
Aufrecht, Walter E.	2.24-26; 3.84-85
Averbeck, Richard E.	2.155
Beal, Richard H.	1.79; 2.16
Beaulieu, Paul-Alain	2.121-2.123
Beckman, Gary	1.55-57; 1.60; 1.78; 1.80-82; 2.15
Cogan, Mordechai	2.119; 2.124
Cohen, Chaim	1.106
Collins, Billie Jean	1.61-70
Dalley, Stephanie	1.108-110; 1.113; 1.131-132
Demsky, Aaron	1.107
Edzard, D. O.	1.121
Farber, Gertrud	1.157; 1.161
Fitzmyer, Joseph A.	2.82
Fleming, Daniel	1.96; 1.122-126
Foster, Benjamin R.	1.111; 1.114-117; 1.129-130; 1.133; 1.151-154
Fox, Michael V.	1.29; 1.49-52
Frayne, Douglas	2.92-112; 2.138-2.141
Gragg, Gene B.	1.178
Guinan, Ann K.	1.120
Hallo, William W.	1.112; 1.118-119; 1.160; 1.163-165; 1.167-168; 2.120; 2.125; 2.134; 2.142-145; 2.152-154; 3.90; 3.93-95; 3.119-121; 3.124; 3.130-132; 3.138-145
Hamilton, Gordon	2.84
Hawkins, J. D.	2.20-2.22
Healey, J. F.	2.43-46; 2.67-69
Heimpel, Wolfgang	1.162
Heltzer, Michael	2.79-80; 3.82-83; 3.103-110
Hess, Richard S.	2.127-129; 2.136-137; 3.91; 3.99-102; 3.125-126; 3.129
Hoffmeier, James K.	1.37; 2.1-2.3; 2.6
Hoffner, Harry A. Jr.	1.58-59; 1.71-75; 2.18-19; 3.13-40
van den Hout, Th. P. J.	1.76-77
Hurowitz, Victor	1.127; 1.139; 2.135
Jacobsen, Thorkild	1.158; 1.170; 1.173
Katz, Dina	1.171
Kienast, Burkhart	2.89-91
Kitchen, K. A.	2.4-5
Klein, Jacob	1.159; 1.166; 1.172; 1.179
Levine, Baruch A.	1.89; 1.95; 1.105; 2.27; 3.88
Lichtheim, Miriam	1.24; 1.26-28; 1.30-31; 1.35-36; 1.38-41; 1.46-48; 1.53-54; 2.7
Livingstone, Alasdair	1.128; 1.140-146; 1.155-156
Longman, Tremper III	1.147-150
McCarter, P. Kyle	2.47; 2.49; 2.52-59; 2.83; 2.85-88

McMahon, Gregory	1.83-85
Millard, Alan	1.134-138; 2.34-35; 2.39-40; 2.70I-V; 2.81
Moran, William	3.92
Pardee, Dennis	1.86-88; 1.90-94; 1.97-98; 1.100; 1.102-103; 3.41-45
Pitard, Wayne T.	2.33
Porten, Bezalel	2.41; 2.51; 2.60-66; 3.46-54; 3.59-81; 3.87
Powell, Marvin A.	2.126; 2.146-151
Ritner, Robert K.	1.18-23; 1.25; 1.32-34; 2.8-14; 3.6-12
Roth, Martha	2.130-133
Sefati, Yitschak	1.169
Segert, Stanislav	2.29; 2.32
Shupak, Nili	1.42-45; 3.146
Singer, Itamar	2.17
Smelik, K. A. D.	2.23
Steiner, Richard C.	1.99; 1.101
Steinkeller, Piotr	3.133-137
Tigay, Jeffrey H.	2.70A-H; 2.71-78
Vanstiphout, H. L. J.	1.180-186
Vogelzang, Marianna	3.147
Weisberg, David	3.123
Younger, K. Lawson Jr.	1.104; 2.28; 2.30-31; 2.36-38; 2.42; 2.48; 2.50; 2.113-2.118; 3.55-58; 3.86; 3.89; 3.96-98; 3.111-118; 3.122; 3.127-128